"COME WHAT MAY, ALL BAD FORTUNE IS TO BE CONQUERED BY ENDURANCE."

– VIRGIL

Virgil has always been a guide to the lost. A real person, he was the poet who created the Aeneid, an epic and beautiful poem showing the journey and destiny of a hero whose destiny is to establish Rome itself. His wisdom and impact were so great, that Virgil appears as a character – again – a guide, perhaps the guide, in The Divine Comedy, Dante's epic tale of a journey through Hell and Purgatory. And as Halo stalwarts know, his namesake, Vergil, was the AI guide in *Halo 3: ODST*, leading the character Sadie to safety through the chaos and destruction of a Covenant invasion.

Virgil's words, both real and fictionalized, have always acted like a trail of breadcrumbs for the lost. But guides have become more than that. This work will show you how to complete the game in pretty conventional (and occasionally unconventional) way. It will give you advice and tactics that will stand you in great stead. It will map and describe problems and locations you'll conquer and traverse, and it will even give you a glimpse of ways to improve your competitive skills.

But it's also a kind of artifact. Aside from the obvious utility of maps and assistance, guides have in recent times, become more and more a kind of extension of the game experience and content, capturing not only strategy, but art and universe too.

Incredible attention to detail goes into crafting and curating the look and feel of the book, not simply to make it easy to read and understand, but to make it a kind of small object of desire, a glossy, glittering encapsulation of the characters, concepts and creatures that comprise the experience.

We make art books. Coffee table tomes, creakingly full of every painting, model and matte that went into the game, but this strategy guide is also a kind of art book, like an illuminated manuscript of yore, with the words and wisdom set out to instruct and inform, but always with the idea that the words themselves should be beautiful, and contextualized in a way that is collectible as well as recollectable.

So this guide will serve as your guide, your Virgil. We're not suggesting hell and purgatory lie ahead, but there will be choices and challenges, complexities and calamities, and sometimes a calm voice is just what you need to lead you through the darkness and doubt. And so here is that voice, that vision, that Virgil.

– Frank O'Connor
Franchise Development Director, 343 Industries

 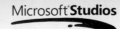 

> CONTENTS

WELCOME TO HALO 4

Halo 4 is the product of years of development by 343 Industries, a continuation of an epic franchise and the start of an entirely new story within the *Halo* universe. The Master Chief captured the hearts and minds of gamers back in 2001 with *Halo: Combat Evolved* launching on the Xbox. The series has gone on to influence the entire first-person shooter genre with entertaining experiences, lively weapons, intimidating enemies, and an incredibly popular multiplayer mode. Halo is a standard that has thrived in the gaming industry to such a level that it's spilled over to a pop culture phenomenon. This guide is another drop of influence and expertise from a rich and extending franchise.

We organized this guide in such as way that you should feel well prepared and eager to play as the Master Chief as he battles a new enemy class or as a Spartan-IV in one of many War Games or Spartan Ops environments. You're about to launch into an amazing adventure and we want you to be prepared for whatever lies ahead. Reference any of the chapters for reputable strategy from our seasoned authors and Major League Gaming (MLG) professionals.

Master Chief is back...We hope you're ready!

GUIDE OVERVIEW

The *Halo 4 Official Strategy Guide* is divided into multiple sections designed to help maximize your enjoyment of the game in both the Campaign and the extensive online multiplayer universe.

> BASIC TRAINING

The Basic Training section of this book will help reinforce the easy stuff, like movement, aiming, shooting, and surviving. We break down the heads-up display, and go into beginner combat tactics, providing fundamentals that will help you stay in one piece.

> CAMPAIGN WALKTHROUGH

The Campaign Walkthrough provides a breakdown of the four difficulty settings available for *Halo 4*. This includes information about the Skull modifiers that change various aspects of the game. As with every preceding title in the series, *Halo 4* is meant to be played on Heroic difficulty, which is the basis for the Campaign Walkthrough. Every major battle is covered in detail, including alternate approaches when appropriate, and specialized tactics for Legendary difficulty. Maps are designed to help players navigate the battlefield and locate important weapons caches that will keep them armed and ready for anything the enemy throws their way. Additionally, the seven Domain Terminals hidden throughout the game are revealed in both the walkthrough and on the relevant maps.

> INTEL

Every weapon, armor ability, vehicle and enemy type, including their variants are detailed in this section. This is for players interested in learning more about the tools of the trade, how to use them, and how best to apply them against the enemy.

> INFINITY MULTIPLAYER

This section covers War Games multiplayer, the co-operative missions found in Spartan Ops, and discusses the new features found in the Forge map editor. For tips on how to be a better player on all of the new maps in *Halo 4*, we turned to Major League Gaming's upper ranks of professional players. Marcus "Elumnite" Lovejoy, Michael "Strongside" Cavanaugh, Michael "Flamesword" Chaves, and Brett "Naded" Leonard have brought their unique perspective on what it takes to be a better player. After weeks of intense play, our team from MLG have produced tips that will help you be a better player, from how to hold your controller, to what your mindset should be. We also have put together strategies for the five Spartan Ops missions that will be available on day one.

The Infinity Multiplayer section includes a primer for how to handle the features specific to War Games and Spartan Ops, and also contains breakdowns of all the rewards and unlocks players can look forward to as they increase in rank. The MLG pros include their own breakdowns of every weapon, vehicle, armor ability, Support Upgrades, and Tactical Packages, and even provide their preferred loadouts that they felt were most effective during their time at 343 Industries. Before you even enter the competition, there's enough information here to help elevate your game.

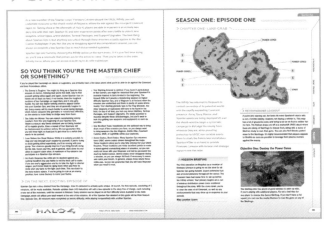

Longtime Halo fans know that playing the Campaign is one thing, but it isn't enough to prepare you for competitive multiplayer. Tapping into the talents of four highly rated Major League Gaming players, the War Games section breaks down the competitive side of *Halo 4*. Having spent weeks dissecting the various maps and weapons that will be available on day one, MLG pros will teach those willing to learn about how to be a better player. Read this section and learn the maps, the tactics, and how to dominate using all of the weapons, vehicles, and armor abilities. The pros also explain the XP system, and recommend weapons and custom loadouts.

In the wake of the events in the Campaign, the UNSC has deployed Spartan-IV soldiers onto a strange Forerunner world. Their mission is to secure its technological riches from the threat of the Covenant. Acting as a continuation of the *Halo 4* story, Spartan Ops allows up to four players to take their customized Spartan-IVs into battle against vast numbers of enemies across multiple environments. Each mission plays a part in a larger story that will unfold weekly via free content updates from 343 Industries. Each of the five missions from Episode 1 are covered in this section, with future mission walkthroughs provided in your complimentary eGuide on the Prima Games website.

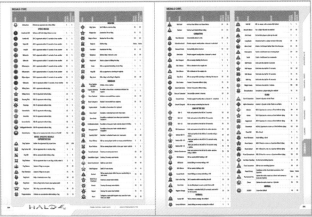

Weapon and Enemy stats, Achievements, Commendations, Medals, Specializations, Emblems, Challenges, Skulls, and Terminals can all be found here. This content can found throughout the guide, but this chapter was created for easy reference. This chapter will prove to be very useful and contains some of the most valuable information.

A BRIEF HISTORY OF THE HUMAN-COVENANT WAR

In the year 2525 on the human colony world of Harvest, a twenty-eight-year conflict between humanity and the alien collective known as the Covenant began. It was the most devastating conflict humans had ever been involved in. In the end, more than twenty billion human lives were lost during the war. Colonies were destroyed, worlds were rendered uninhabitable, and yet, because of one Spartan, humanity endured, survived, and ultimately won.

> HALO: REACH

Released: September 14, 2010 for Xbox 360

July 24, 2552. The Human-Covenant War reached toward its climax. The Covenant secretly invaded the planet Reach, the most important world to the United Nations Space Command, its nerve center. The Spartans of Noble Team were sent to investigate a silenced communications relay, only to discover the Covenant presence on the planet, which was hidden by means of sophisticated stealth technology. Over the next month, Noble Team fought valiantly, but was cut down one-by-one in the face of overwhelming odds. Eventually, only Noble Six, the newest member of the team, stood alone in the face of the impending glassing of the world. Before joining the rest of Noble Team in death, the Spartan was able to deliver the AI Cortana to the UNSC cruiser *Pillar of Autumn* and the waiting Master Chief. The vessel made its escape from the slaughter, with a Covenant fleet in pursuit.

> HALO: COMBAT EVOLVED

Released: November 15, 2001 for Xbox

Rereleased as *Halo: Combat Evolved Anniversary* on November 15, 2011

The *Pillar of Autumn* was unable to escape the Covenant despite performing a blind slipspace jump. As they returned to normal space, they found a gas giant planet called Threshold. Orbiting it was Halo: an impossibly massive ring structure, built by the Forerunners more than 100,000 years ago. The Covenant had beaten the *Pillar of Autum* to the Halo, and the ship was forced to deploy its Marines and the Master Chief to the ringworld and execute a crash landing. The Covenant engaged the humans in battle throughout the ring, and the Master Chief played an instrumental role in the fighting.

Eventually, he and the AI Cortana discovered that the Halo was part of an array of similar installations placed throughout the galaxy. The Halo Array itself was a weapon of last resort against a virulent parasite known as the Flood, which was sealed on the ringworld for study by the Forerunners. If fired, the Halos could wipe out all life in the galaxy. The Covenant unwittingly unleashed the parasite across the ring, and both they and the humans incurred heavy casualties as a result. In a desperate bid to destroy the Flood and escape the Halo, the Master Chief returned to the crashed *Pillar of Autumn* and set it to self-destruct. This shattered the ring and seemingly ended the Flood threat. The Master Chief made a narrow escape with Cortana.

INTRODUCTION

BASIC TRAINING

INTEL

CAMPAIGN

INFINITY

APPENDIX

> HALO 2

Released: November 9, 2004 for Xbox

October 20, 2552. The Master Chief returned to Earth and was decorated as a hero. Meanwhile, the Covenant Elite who led their forces in battle upon the Halo was deemed a heretic by the Covenant leadership. The Covenant Prophet of Regret, on a mission to discover new Forerunner artifacts, stumbled across the planet Earth and, despite being outnumbered assaulted the human homeworld and managed to occupy the African city of New Mombasa. The Master Chief led a successful counterattack that drove the Prophet of Regret off-world and brought the Earth a moment's reprieve. The Master Chief, along with the UNSC fleet, pursued the Prophet of Regret.

The Prophet of Regret discovered a new Halo, also known as Installation 05. During these events, the disgraced Elite commander was named an Arbiter, a representative of the will of the Prophets, and was unleashed against the Covenant heretical rebels who wished to be free of the Prophets. The Arbiter, betrayed by Tartarus, the leader of another Covenant species known as the Brutes, eventually joined forces with the Master Chief after many battles and more shocking revelations. *Halo 2* also contained the Flood parasite, but it was no longer merely hordes of mindless souls absorbed into the collective. Rather, this Flood had central mind, a Gravemind. Worse yet, the Covenant, now led by the Brutes, intended to fire the Halo Array to initiate the Great Journey, as their religion demanded. They were now at open war with a significant Separatist movement, led by the Elites. Ultimately, the Master Chief and the Arbiter prevented the firing of the Array, killing Tartarus in process. Unfortunately, Cortana was left behind on the Covenant mobile homeworld of High Charity, where the Flood Gravemind resided and was beginning to expand its already countless army.

Returning to Earth aboard a Forerunner Dreadnought controlled by Covenant loyal to the Prophet of Regret, the Master Chief prepared to finish the fight.

> HALO: ODST

Released: September 22, 2009 for Xbox 360

During the Prophet of Regret's invasion and subsequent retreat from New Mombasa on Earth, the UNSC deployed its elite Orbital Drop Shock Troopers into the war zone. One team was in mid-drop just as the Prophet's assault carrier executed a slipspace jump in the Earth's atmosphere. The Rookie of this team, separated from his comrades, fought his way through New Mombasa alone for several hours before reuniting with his squad and encountering a member of another Covenant species, the Huragok. The new alien signaled its willingness to work alongside its UNSC captors out of hatred for its Brute oppressors.

Meanwhile, the Covenant occupation of the Earth continued, and the excavation of New Mombasa revealed an enormous Forerunner installation that had been dormant for millennia.

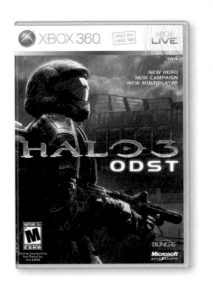

> HALO 3

Released: September 25, 2007 for Xbox 360

November 17, 2552. The Master Chief returned to Earth and joined up with UNSC survivors and the Arbiter, who leads the Elites, which have now fully turned against the Covenant. After a series of battles, the combined forces struck at the Forerunner artifact found buried underneath the city of New Mombasa, where the Prophet of Regret had landed the Forerunner Dreadnought. The artifact produced a massive slipspace portal through which the Covenant retreated. Simultaneously, a Covenant cruiser filled with the infectious Flood crashed into the African city of Voi.

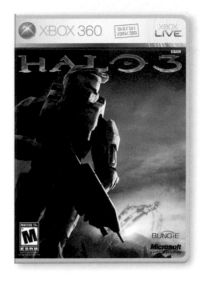

After the immediate Flood threat to Earth was contained, Master Chief learned that Cortana left a message aboard the crashed ship. She described a solution to the Flood that did not involve firing the Halo Array: Beyond this portal was the Ark, a massive Forerunner facility located outside our galaxy. A combined UNSC-Elite task force, including the Master Chief and the Arbiter, left Earth through the portal to pursue the Prophet of Regret to the Ark, thereby beginning a desperate fight to prevent the Array from being fired.

After many battles, the Arbiter ultimately had his vengeance against Truth. Meanwhile, the Flood crashed the mobile homeworld High Charity into the Ark, and threatened to overwhelm the forces gathered there. It was discovered that the Ark facility manufactured Halo rings that later dispersed themselves to key points within the galaxy, and that it was currently crafting the replacement for the destroyed Installation 04. The Master Chief saw this as an opportunity to destroy the Gravemind. To fire the replacement Halo, he first had to retrieve Cortana from the Gravemind's clutches. Fighting their way to the Halo's control room, Cortana used the Activation Index retrieved from the first Halo to fire the weapon.

The Master Chief and the Arbiter raced to the UNSC frigate *Forward Unto Dawn* in an attempt to escape the Halo's firing and the destruction of the Ark. Unfortunately, the slipspace portal collapsed mid-jump, sundering the frigate in half. The forward half, containing the Arbiter, made it back to Earth. The aft of the vessel, containing Master Chief and Cortana, was left stranded in an unknown part of the galaxy.

With rescue unlikely to be any time soon, the Chief prepared to enter cryosleep, knowing that he might drift for years. Cortana activated a beacon, advising him that it might be awhile before anyone responded, to which he replied, "Wake me, when you need me."

On Earth, the Arbiter, his Elites, and the surviving UNSC forces mourned the apparent loss of humanity's greatest hero.

> HALO 4

Four years have passed since the Master Chief and Cortana went missing in action. Fans who finished *Halo 3* on the Legendary difficulty discovered that the story was far from over, as the ruined portion of the *Forward Unto Dawn* drifted toward a mysterious planet during a bonus cinematic. The Master Chief and Cortana now face a new threat that has been building throughout the entire series on data terminals hidden throughout the games, and in books written by numerous authors. Some questions may be answered, but more will undoubtedly replace them. The Forerunner world of Requiem awaits.

INTRODUCTION

BASIC TRAINING

INTEL

CAMPAIGN

INFINITY

APPENDIX

CHARACTERS

> THE MASTER CHIEF

Official Designation:

Master Chief Petty Officer John-117

Abducted at age six for the SPARTAN-II program, John was subjected to harsh training and extensive physical enhancements as he grew. He survived the harsh regimen, and would be fitted for the Mjolnir combat armor system. As a Spartan, John's physical abilities far exceed that of any normal human: He was a new kind of man for a new kind of war. His exploits against the Covenant eventually propelled him to the rank of Master Chief Petty Officer. In 2552, the Master Chief and his AI partner Cortana discovered the first Halo installation, the Flood, and ultimately unlocked the means to humanity's salvation.

All Spartans are known for their ability as combatants, but the Master Chief is known also for his considerable luck, as he has survived some of the bloodiest and most costly battles of the Human-Covenant War. After sleeping four years adrift in space, his luck will be sorely tested on Requiem.

INTRODUCTION

BASIC TRAINING

INTEL

CAMPAIGN

INFINITY

APPENDIX

Official Designation:
CTN 0452-9

A "smart" Artificial Intelligence, Cortana was born via the scanning of a flash cloned brain of Dr. Catherine Halsey. One of the most important figures of the Human-Covenant War, Cortana was paired with the Master Chief. The Spartan acted as her protector and partner throughout the initial Halo incident, and the two formed a close bond through combat, though it was strained when she was left behind on the Flood-infested High Charity and interrogated by the Gravemind. Ultimately, the two were reunited, and using the knowledge gleaned from the first Halo, destroyed the Ark, the Flood, and ended the war between humanity and the Covenant. She has maintained a vigil over the sleeping Master Chief for the last four years.

As a "smart" AI, Cortana has an effective lifespan of seven years before degrading into rampancy. Cortana has been in active service for eight years.

INTRODUCTION

BASIC TRAINING

INTEL

CAMPAIGN

INFINITY

APPENDIX

> CAPTAIN ANDREW DEL RIO

A 30-year veteran of the UNSC Navy, Captain Del Rio garnered a reputation for bringing his ships home during a war where whole fleets were nearly annihilated by superior Covenant numbers and technology. This made him a prime candidate for command of the newest vessel in the UNSC fleet, the *Infinity*. Having come across the Forerunner world of Requiem, Captain Del Rio's reputation and his command will face their greatest challenges yet.

HALO 4

> COMMANDER THOMAS LASKY

A career soldier who almost wasn't, Lasky became dedicated to service in 2526 during the Covenant offensive against the Outer Colonies. His lengthy career as a pilot and naval officer was distinguished enough to land him a post aboard the *Infinity* as its Executive Officer.

BASIC TRAINING

INTEL

CAMPAIGN

INFINITY

APPENDIX

> COMMANDER SARAH PALMER

One of the earliest recruits to the new Spartan-IV program, Palmer served twelve tours of duty during the Human-Covenant War as a UNSC Marine. Her combat skills and natural leadership ability were a natural fit for the role of Commander of all Spartans assigned to *Infinity*.

> DR. CATHERINE HALSEY

The "mother" of Cortana and the key brain behind the Spartan-II and MJOLNIR programs. Halsey is considered to be one of the most valuable assets to the UNSC, and is in no small part responsible for humanity's victory over the Covenant. Despite this, her achievements have been clouded by her questionable ethics. In the aftermath of the war, Halsey continued her research into Forerunner artifacts before being transferred to a new posting at the behest of ONI (Office of Naval Intelligence). The Master Chief believes he can save his AI companion so long as he is able to find Halsey because she is Cortana's creator.

> DR. SANDRA K. TILLSON

Dr. Tillson is a lead researcher assigned to Ivanoff Station, near Gamma Halo (Installation 03). She is one of the many scientists that the UNSC has tasked with learning about the Forerunners' massive ringworlds, as well as any artifacts discovered within. The discoveries Tillson and her associates have made are revealing the locations of other Forerunner remnants throughout the galaxy.

INTRODUCTION

BASIC TRAINING

INTEL

CAMPAIGN

INFINITY

APPENDIX

BASIC TRAINING

BASIC TRAINING

Halo 4's game controls are the product of years of refinement. You will appreciate the simplicity and responsiveness of the controls while threading your Spartan through dangerous situations. If they aren't to your liking, *Halo 4* comes with a wide variety of options to cater to your tastes. In addition to the alternate control layouts, you can also customize things like look sensitivity, autolook centering, crouch behavior, clench protection and flight inversion.. We'll go over the control basics based on the standard configuration.

Half of any battle is about controlling and understanding the information you're given, and then acting on it. The heads-up display should also be familiar to fans, but for players who may be new to the franchise, we dissect the HUD (Heads Up Display) and explain its various features and functions.

Once you know how to control your Spartan and understand the data on your HUD, you can start getting into combat strategy. General advice regarding how to fight and survive, on foot or behind the wheel, can be found here.

Let's begin your basic training. "You have been called upon to serve."

CONTROLS

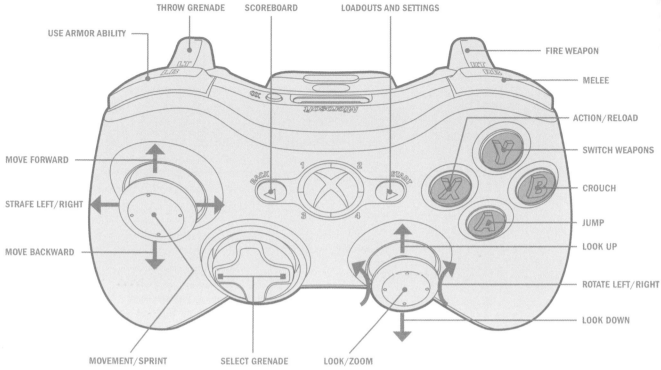

THROW GRENADE
SCOREBOARD
LOADOUTS AND SETTINGS
USE ARMOR ABILITY
FIRE WEAPON
MELEE
ACTION/RELOAD
SWITCH WEAPONS
MOVE FORWARD
STRAFE LEFT/RIGHT
CROUCH
MOVE BACKWARD
JUMP
LOOK UP
ROTATE LEFT/RIGHT
LOOK DOWN
MOVEMENT/SPRINT
SELECT GRENADE
LOOK/ZOOM

INTRODUCTION

BASIC TRAINING

INTEL

CAMPAIGN

INFINITY

APPENDIX

DEFAULT CONTROLS: Many players enjoy the standard control setup, so we'll give you a quick rundown of this control method here. Vehicles are controlled differently than a Spartan, but across multiple vehicles the controls are oftentimes shared.

> ON FOOT

Left Analog Stick

Default Function— Movement: One of the most important things you will ever do in combat, besides shoot, is move. The analog stick can control how fast you move depending on how far you tilt the stick in a given direction. This is a very important aspect of movement in multiplayer games. If you move too fast, you show up on the motion sensors of everyone next to you. Effective movement combines using the left analog stick and your activity to sprint and jump, can be augmented by very specific armor abilities.

Right Analog Stick

Default Function—Looking/Aiming: You're a dead Spartan walking if you're not paying attention to your immediate surroundings. This isn't just a saying, it's the truth. As with basic movement, the speed at which you scan the environment varies depending on how much you tilt the right analog stick. You can further customize your look sensitivity in the options menus. Some players want the sensitivity high, even maxed out, which lets them aim to get quick shots off. Other players prefer the sensitivity be lowered to help them aim accurately. Try practicing with different settings to see what you feel most comfortable with.

L3 (Click Left Analog Stick)

Default Function—Sprint: This is one of the biggest additions to the Halo gameplay formula. Sprinting was originally an armor ability when it first appeared. Now you can sprint without having a special item equipped, although you will sacrifice some maneuverability as well as the ability to fire while sprinting. The problem here is that if you suddenly need to shoot at an enemy, you must stop sprinting, and that short delay while you ready your weapon can prove fatal. Sprint if you must, and always with purpose.

R3 (Click Right Analog Stick)

Default Function—Aim/Zoom In: For weapons that have a scope, or are linked to the Spartan's helmet, aiming allows you to zoom in on a target for more accurate fire. There are some drawbacks: aiming at enemies makes you move slower, and you can't sprint while aiming. There's also a loss of situational awareness, as you lose much of your peripheral vision and your motion sensor. If you are equipped with a weapon that does not have a scope, the helmet visor acts as a set of binoculars, but you can't shoot while using this feature, it automatically disengages.

Left Trigger

Default Function—Throw Grenades: Grenades are an important part of your toolkit as a Spartan. There are 3 different types of grenades available, all of which serve a distinct purpose. You can only carry two of each type, so make each of your grenades count.

Right Trigger

Default Function—Shoot: Aim at the target, squeeze the trigger, make the shot. Shooting isn't hard, but shooting well takes some practice. Don't get discouraged if you're having trouble tracking the enemy while trying to line up a shot. Don't pull the trigger recklessly and make sure your aim is true before you fire.

Left Bumper

Default Function—Armor Ability: Armor abilities can be found in the field during the main Campaign or Spartan Ops. In War Games multiplayer, players can make custom loadouts that include preferred armor abilities. These abilities allow you some additional tactical flexibility in the field. They have limited use before they require time to recharge, so use your armor abilities wisely.

Right Bumper

Default Function—Melee Strike: If the enemy gets close, or if you get close to the enemy, and you want to make a statement, use your melee attack. A good punch in the face is enough to give most enemies a moment's pause, and any regular melee attack to the back of most enemies (and all players in War Games) will be an instant kill. If you manage to get behind an enemy and hold down the Melee Attack button, you can perform a special assassination animation, the perfect way to humiliate the inattentive. Just don't attempt an assassination when the victim has friends, otherwise you could be joining them in short order.

Default Function—Detach Turret: If you have taken up position on a mounted weapon, such as a Plasma Cannon or a Gun Turret, you can tear the weapon free of its mount and roam around the battlefield with it. Enjoy the benefits of such powerful heavy weapons without being confined to a single spot! However, you move considerably slower while carrying a heavy weapon.

A Button

Default Function—Jump: Jumping allows you to reach elevated positions, and can sometimes help you find ways to bypass enemy defenses. However, once you jump, you have limited control over where you're going. You can still shoot, aim, throw grenades, and even use melee attacks while jumping, but you're quite vulnerable and are moving slower than you would if you just chose to sprint. Still, jumping is an effective way to throw off your enemy's aim or evade explosive ordnance. Be careful about where you choose to jump—a long fall can cost you a chunk of your shielding, or possibly kill you.

B Button

Default Function—Crouch: If you are in a situation where you need to get behind low cover, crouching can help reduce your profile on the battlefield. It cuts down your speed, but it can help you move without making your presence known by motion sensors.

X Button

Default Function—Action: At times, you will be required to activate a control panel or press a switch. You can also use this button to pick up weapons off the field, or take control of mounted heavy weapons.

Default Function—Reload: Most weapons you find in the field have limited magazines or energy cells that must be reloaded periodically. Reloading is not just something you do when you run out of bullets, it's a tactical option that must be exercised carefully. While you are reloading your weapon, you cannot shoot. If an enemy rushes you while you are in the middle of reloading, you're in trouble. Before any engagement, know how much ammo is in your weapons, and reload if necessary. There's nothing worse than running dry just before you score a kill. It's worth noting that you shouldn't necessarily ignore picking up a weapon you are already holding. Sometimes it's worth picking up to see if it contains more ammo than the one you have.

Default Function—Board/Exit Vehicle: Boarding a vehicle is simple. Stand next to it and press the action button. Some vehicles have multiple seating options, and you can choose one by standing close to that seat before pushing the action button. You can exit a vehicle in the same way. Vehicles that have been flipped over can be turned back by pressing this button.

Y Button

Default Function—Switch Weapon/Drop Heavy Weapon: Spartans can only carry two primary firearms. This limitation can be worked around by choosing weapons that compliment each other. Switching weapons can sometimes be faster than simply reloading, but it depends on the guns you're switching between. The smaller the gun, the faster the animations.

Directional Pad

Default Function—Switch Grenade Types: There are three types of grenades in *Halo 4*. Pressing left or right on the directional pad can allow you switch between them. When possible, be sure to use the right grenade for every situation.

Default Function—Call Down Ordnance/Switch to Special Weapon: During the campaign, pressing down on the directional pad allows you to switch to a Target designator after it has been recovered in mission 5. For certain multiplayer game types, players who score enough kills can call down special ordnance pods containing new weapons to enhance their arsenal.

> **Note**
> Be sure to check the Start Menu for more controller options. The Southpaw configuration often works well for left-handed players.

> IN A LAND VEHICLE

Left Analog Stick

Acceleration/Deceleration: Warthog, Scorpion, Wraith, Ghost, Mantis, Mongoose

Right Analog Stick

Looking/Steering: Warthog (Driver), Ghost (Driver), Mongoose (Driver)

Aiming Weapon: Warthog (Gunner, Passenger), Scorpion (Driver, Gunner, Passenger), Wraith (Driver, Gunner), Mantis, Mongoose (Passenger), Shade Turret

Right Trigger

Brakes: Warthog, Mongoose

Fire Weapon 1: Warthog (Gunner), Scorpion, Wraith, Ghost, Mantis

Left Trigger

Powerslide: Warthog, Mongoose

Boost: Ghost, Wraith

Fire Weapon 2: Mantis

Right Bumper

Melee Stomp: Mantis

Y Button

Crouch: Mantis

Switch Weapons: Warthog passenger

> IN AN AIR VEHICLE

Left Analog Stick

Acceleration/Deceleration: Banshee, Broadsword

Be aware that decelerating too much with a Banshee will cause you to lose altitude rapidly. Make sure you're not about to fall into a hazardous situation.

Roll Left/Right: Banshee, Broadsword

Right Analog Stick

Change Pitch/Heading: Banshee/Broadsword

Right Trigger

Fire Weapon: Banshee, Broadsword

Left Bumper +Left Analog Stick

Evasive Maneuvers: Banshee

This unique ability is limited to the Banshee alone, and is highly effective at throwing off anti-aircraft defenses and other hostile fliers. Simply pressing the Left Bumper allows for a quick vertical loop. By tilting the Left Analog Stick left or right while pressing Left Bumper, you can roll the Banshee in those directions.

Left Trigger

Boost: Banshee, Broadsword

Y Button

Switch Weapons: Banshee, Broadsword

INTRODUCTION

BASIC TRAINING

INTEL

CAMPAIGN

INFINITY

APPENDIX

THE HUD

The heads-up display, or HUD, is a enhancement to your vision that tells you everything you need to know about your current situation. It is easy to read, and does not get in the way when you are trying to make sense of a firefight. So long as you pay attention to what it's displaying, you can effectively plan for, and react to, anything the enemy throws at you.

1 Shot Indicator—When you get shot, a portion of the screen flares up. Use this as a secondary radar, so to speak. If the lower-right corner of the screen flares up, the enemy is behind you and to the right.

2 Target Reticle—The target reticle changes depending on which weapon you have equipped, but it serves the same purpose for all firearms. The reticle allows you to maintain relative accuracy while firing a weapon "from the hip." Certain precision weapons, like the Sniper Rifle, retain their deadly accuracy even when fired without using the scope. Others lose accuracy, and this is often reflected by the reticle becoming larger. When enemies are within optimal range of your equipped weapon, the reticle turns red. For allies, it turns green. One of the most valuable features about the target reticle is that it can indicate headshots. When a headshot-capable weapon is aimed at a target's head, a smaller dot will appear at the center of the reticle. This can act as a cue for you to shoot. Lastly, special hit markers will flash around the reticle to indicate whether or not you are hitting a target. This is especially useful if you're fighting enemies using Active Camouflage.

3 Grenade Indicator—Inevitably, the enemy will be lobbing explosives at you. The grenade indicator lets you know that you are in dangerous proximity to a grenade. You can use this information to get to safety. No grenade indicator, no immediate danger. Now, if only there were a "This Object Will Explode And Kill You" indicator.

4 Shield Meter—The Shield Meter can also be called your life meter, and it's one of the most crucial things displayed on the HUD. Each attack you sustain drains this meter precipitously. Once it falls below half, a pinging alarm begins to sound, warning you to take cover. When the meter is empty, the pinging becomes louder and the HUD will begin to flash red. Your shields have been broken! If you take further damage in this state, you will die. It's possible to survive minor injuries, but don't count on your luck to last very long unless you find cover quickly.

5 Weapon and Ammo Indicator—Ammo management during a firefight can mean the difference between life and death. The weapon and ammo indicator shows you what weapon is currently active, how much ammo remains in the current magazine, and how much you have left in reserve. This is a redundant system, some weapons have ammo indicators build into their frames, but it is still a valuable piece of information to have on hand.

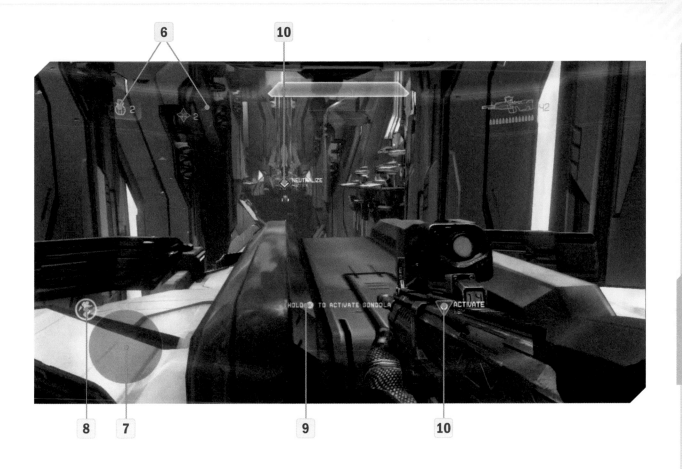

INTRODUCTION

BASIC TRAINING

INTEL

CAMPAIGN

INFINITY

APPENDIX

6 Grenade Count—You can carry two of all three types of grenades, which are displayed in the upper-left corner of the screen. As you switch between grenades, the grenade count indicator will prominently mark the active grenade in your inventory, so you know what you're about to throw with a quick glance.

7 Motion Sensor—Tracking moving and shooting targets up to 30 meters away from you, the motion sensor is invaluable for determining enemy numbers, movements, and safe routes for flanking. Red dots on the tracker are hostile, yellow dots are allies. Not only does the tracker show enemies on the same level as you, it also can track and mark enemies at higher and lower elevations, adding up or down arrows to their tracker contacts accordingly.

8 Armor Ability—The currently equipped armor ability is displayed by this icon, as well as how much power remains in this armor ability before it requires time to recharge.

9 Action Prompt—Whenever you draw close to any object you can interact with, such as any gun you can pick up or any vehicle you can drive, or are suddenly out of ammo and need a new gun, you will see an action prompt appear in the lower center of the HUD.

10 Waypoint—Mission objectives often are marked on the HUD by a waypoint marker, although sometimes waypoints also indicate new weapons caches or specific hostiles.

COMBAT

The controls are setup just right and you're properly acquainted with the HUD. That's good! However, actually applying this knowledge during combat is a whole different ball game. Take the advice here to heart, and you'll be on the road to becoming a proper Spartan.

> SITUATIONAL AWARENESS

This can be boiled down to "keeping your eyes peeled," but it's a bit more complex than that. It's not just about what you can see directly in front of you, but also about watching for the telltale glow of a charged plasma pistol off to the side, tracking a sniper's position by following the tracer of his Beam Rifle, noticing the subtle distortion of Active Camouflage being used, or using your knowledge of the area to be able to flank them.

Vision isn't the only important factor. *Halo 4* has an impressive sound design that can tell you everything you need to know about what is going on around you. You can tell what weapons are being used, what types of enemies are around the corner, and how close they, just by listening carefully. This is especially important for multiplayer games where the motion sensor might be disabled as part of the game type.

> MOVING WELL

The importance of effective movement is commonly overlooked by new players, who just run to where the action is, only to die time and again. You should have a basic understanding of where you are in order to move effectively while under fire. Knowing your environment lets you avoid getting stuck on terrain as you move, and more importantly, lets you find cover when you need it. You should know when to move slowly, when to run, and when to sprint. When you start getting shot at, things get tougher. Generally, you don't want to be out in the open if you can help it. If you're in a safe spot, you should hold onto it, and only move to a new position when you can safely do so.

When you sustain damage, you temporarily slow down. Your first instinct may be to jump, which you should try to avoid. On lower difficulties or against less skilled players, that might be good enough to throw them off. On the higher difficulties, or against a pro, you're still just another target, but now you're moving in a predictable fashion from the moment you jump all the way until you land. Instead, "juke" your opponents and force them to constantly correct their aim. You might even get a skilled sniper to miss a perfect shot.

Most importantly, when you choose to move while under fire, stay moving! Many deaths happen simply because the player hesitates while out in the middle of the open, then promptly eats a sniper shot to the face. Don't be that guy.

> ON THE OFFENSE

Offense can be broken down to several requirements: Being equipped with and using the right weapons, knowing where the enemy is, and attacking when it's advantageous. You can apply this mind-set to both the Campaign and multiplayer.

Equipping and using the right weapons is quite simple. The biggest problem is that you can only carry two weapons at a time, and only two of each of the three types of grenades. You can't have everything you want all at once, and you can't cover every weakness for every enemy in the game. The right weapon setup depends entirely on your circumstances. For example, with an energy weapon like the Plasma Pistol, you can take out the shields of an Elite quickly, while the Magnum can instantly kill the unshielded elite with a single headshot. Against a Hunter, this loadout might not be the best, so fall back and find a weapon that can be more effective, like a Rocket Launcher. Remember that every enemy in the game has weaknesses that can be exploited by multiple weapons in the *Halo 4* arsenal.

Sometimes, guns aren't enough, and you're forced to resort to melee attacks. This isn't a disadvantage! Melee combat is something Spartans excel at; it's an excellent way to finish off enemies who survive an assault just as your weapon runs dry. Running across an open field at a Shade Turret to try to punch the gunner in the face might sound cool if you play some dramatic or sad music in the background, but you're probably just going to die.

Grenades are some of the most useful tools in your arsenal, and you have three different types to exploit. You can effectively shut down groups of enemies with one properly thrown Frag Grenade. In multiplayer, sticking an enemy with a Plasma or Pulse Grenade moments before your own death ensures that you will not die alone.

Knowing where the enemies are before you attack goes right back to situational awareness. Pay attention to the world around you during combat, pay attention to your HUD, and you can start forming a plan. When you go on the offensive, be prepared to react to what the enemy is going to do and exploit any mistakes they make. Take advantage of them being distracted by other events going on around them. Attack from the side or from behind. Crouch and hold your fire until the last moment to hide from motion sensors. Use grenades to flush enemies out of hiding, or toss them around corners to weaken anyone on the other side before charging in.

Make sure you finish off your targets. Elites and multiplayer Spartans can recharge their shields if given a few moments. Be careful, sometimes enemies may turn this second chance against you. Do what you can to deny them that opportunity.

Lastly, always go for headshots. Learn to aim for the head of all enemies throughout the Campaign, and especially in War Games. If you're going to survive against long odds, the best course of action is headshots. Remember this mantra: strip the shields, shoot the head.

For more information about all of the weapons in the game, go to the Intel chapter.

> ON THE DEFENSE

You are going to get shot. This is fact. Statistically, 100% percent of *Halo 4* players will get hit by enemy fire at some point, and a staggering number will eventually die. What is important about getting shot is how you react to it. If you run headlong into a wall, throwing grenades blindly, you probably deserve what's coming to you.

There are two things about defense that are absolutely important. One goes all the way back to movement, that is, doing it well. The second is shield management. When you take damage, determine the source and general location it came from as soon as possible. Take note of how much shielding you just lost. If you're below half, you should probably take, or make yourself a difficult target. Depending on the situation, you also might be able to fight back and even kill your attacker, but if they got the drop on you, this can be very difficult. If you realize you can't win and you have no choice but to retreat, use grenades to cover your escape and run. Unless the enemy is so close that turning your back is essentially suicide, facing the direction you are retreating is faster than running backward through an area. You can at least sprint this way.

Advanced players who know the terrain well may be able to retreat while moving backward successfully, but even the best know when to cash in their chips and get out of town. Always remember: so long as you have a few seconds where you aren't taking damage, you can start regenerating your shields.

This is where shield management comes into play. You will take damage during battle; you have to be willing to soak up some hits to dole out some of your own. This is a skill the best players have mastered. They know how many shots it takes for a given weapon to bring them from full shields to death, and they can plan around that. You can do the same in the campaign, either when playing alone or with friends. How much shielding you have should determine how aggressive or defensive you're going to be.

If your shields are broken, you're not out of the game, but these moments should act as a wake up call. You can either press your luck and go for that kill, and maybe die in the process, or fall back to safety and regenerate to fight again.

> WHEN TO DRIVE

Knowing when to use a vehicle, when you should ditch one, and when or how to fight one is very important for both the Campaign and War Games. There are many different types of vehicles. Some are lightly armed and fast, others are well armed and armored. Vehicles change the dynamic of any battle, so it's important to understand and respect their capabilities when operating one or defending yourself against one.

Just having a vehicle does not make you invincible. Even the mighty Scorpion tank can be taken down by a lone Spartan with a Plasma Pistol and a well-aimed rocket to the driver's compartment. The odds may actually be worse against a coordinated group of enemies. At the same time the Scorpion can rain utter hell all over the enemy before they even have a chance to fight back.

Information about all the vehicles and their strength and weaknesses can be found in the Intel chapter.

> ARMOR ABILITIES

Longtime Halo fans know how the introduction of armor abilities and special equipment changed the nature of the game, in the campaigns and in multiplayer. They return in *Halo 4*, having been streamlined since their first appearance.

Armor abilities are introduced incrementally throughout the Campaign, and you get a taste of how effective they truly are throughout the various engagements you're thrown into. In War

Games, you unlock armor abilities to place in your loadouts. As with any weapon in your arsenal, knowing how and when to use these enhancements marks the difference between winning and losing.

All information about the various armor abilities and how to make the best use of them can be found in the Intel chapter.

INTRODUCTION

BASIC TRAINING

INTEL

CAMPAIGN

INFINITY

APPENDIX

INTEL

WEAPONS
31

ENEMIES
51

VEHICLES
58

INTEL

Fast reflexes, sharp aim, and good instincts are all important aspects of surviving a firefight. However, if you're going to survive Requiem, you need every advantage you can muster. You need intel. Knowing the tools at your disposal, how to apply them, and what you'll be up against is an enormous advantage that shouldn't be taken lightly.

WEAPONS

Halo 4 offers 32 equipable weapons from three different factions. It would not be a stretch to say that for every situation you ever encounter in this game, there exists a weapon best suited for making it go away. You can only equip two weapons, not including grenades. At first, beginners may feel overwhelmed, but there are a few basic rules that you can follow to help you stay armed and ready.

> **Use the right weapons for the job:** Put simply, some guns work better in certain situations. The vast majority of the UNSC arsenal, for example, fires solid ammunition. Against flesh, they are quite effective. Energy shields that mask Elites and Promethean Knights, severely reduce the power of bullets. However, weapons like the Plasma Pistol or the Storm Rifle all fire plasma bolts that chew through energy shielding swiftly, but struggle to finish the job once the enemy's skin is exposed. Try to base your arsenal around this dynamic: One weapon to defeat the enemy's protection, the other to finish them off. Note that some weapons buck this trend somewhat. For example, the LightRifle is an excellent general-purpose weapon that allows for some additional flexibility in your second slot.

> **Be flexible:** You're not always going to have your favorite weapons available during the Campaign. Switch out weapons if they are low on ammo, or if you're finding that they are not suited to your current predicament.

> **Headshots are the best shots:** *Halo* has always distinguished weapons in a variety of ways, the obvious being factors such as the rate of fire, whether or not a weapon fires solid ammunition or plasma, or how much damage they cause. The biggest of these is whether or not a weapon is capable of killing an enemy with a single headshot. On Easy or Normal, this may not matter much. On Heroic and Legendary, survival depends on eliminating enemies quickly, and headshots are the fastest way to do this. You should always try to keep at least one headshot-capable weapon on hand at all times.

> **Balance your loadout:** Although it may sound cool to carry an Incineration Cannon and a Binary Rifle, just because you can doesn't necessarily mean you should. If you want to carry a power weapon, compliment it with something that can be more general-purpose. Another bad example would be to carry a Sniper Rifle and a Beam Rifle. Both are exceptional weapons, but both suffer from limited ammunition, and both are primarily geared for long-range shooting. A lot of your fighting will be done at shorter ranges, and these weapons are limited in such circumstances.

> UNSC WEAPONS

ASSAULT RIFLE

Designation: MA5D Individual Combat Weapon System

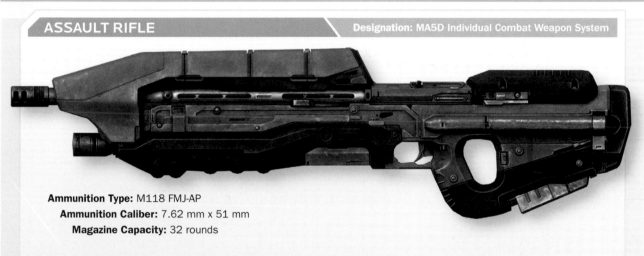

Ammunition Type: M118 FMJ-AP
Ammunition Caliber: 7.62 mm x 51 mm
Magazine Capacity: 32 rounds

The workhorse weapon of the UNSC. Leverages a high rate of fire in order to overwhelm defensive shielding and armor, though players are encouraged to fire in short, controlled bursts to conserve ammunition per magazine. Most effective at short- and mid-ranged combat.

> "Short, controlled bursts" isn't just a neat catchphrase. If you're engaging the enemy outside of close- or mid-range and want your bullets to actually hit the target consistently, don't hold down the trigger. Used correctly, the Assault Rifle can even be effective against Elites on Heroic difficulty.

> Best complimented by weapons like the Plasma Pistol, DMR, Magnum, or even the Storm Rifle. Once the shielding on Elites or Knights are down, the AR can kill them very quickly at close- to mid-range.

> On Legendary you will want to find another gun. The Assault Rifle loses a lot of its effectiveness due to increased enemy health and shield pools. Even enemies like the Promethean Crawlers can absorb a distressing amount of ammunition, and the 32-round magazine of the AR will feel entirely too small to threaten Elites and Knights without having something else to soften them up first. While the AR can still score kills on Legendary, there are usually better options available.

BATTLE RIFLE

Designation: BR85 Heavy-Barrel Service Rifle

Ammunition Type: M634 X-HP-SAP
Ammunition Caliber: 9.5 mm x 40 mm
Magazine Capacity: 36 rounds

Stressing accuracy over a high rate of fire, the Battle Rifle is an effective weapon at nearly any range, provided the operator is skilled enough to use it. Recoil is minimal and easily controlled. Veteran users of the weapon are actually capable of using the recoil to take advantage of enemy vulnerabilities.

> Hands down one of the most effective weapons in the game. Even by itself, on any difficulty level from Easy to Heroic, the Battle Rifle is a solution to most problems.

> The burst fire is extremely useful against Elites. Each bullet in a burst counts as a hit, so it's possible for a burst to break the Elite's shields and score a headshot.

> The overall lower rate of fire of the Battle Rifle is actually a luxury, not a curse; it allows users to stay on target easier.

> Works extremely well alongside Covenant plasma weaponry, specifically the Plasma Pistol. Break Elite shields with a charged Plasma Pistol shot, then use one burst of the Battle Rifle to finish them off.

> The Battle Rifle remains an exceptional weapon on Legendary if paired with the Plasma Pistol, but is somewhat less effective by itself due to increased health and shielding pools.

DMR

Designation: M395 Designated Marksman Rifle

Ammunition Type: M118 FMJ-AP
Ammunition Caliber: 7.62 mm x 51 mm
Magazine Capacity: 14 rounds

A rifle that brings near-sniper rifle accuracy and power in a compact package. The DMR fills much the same role on the battlefield that a Battle Rifle does, and shares the same ease of control and maneuverability under similar circumstances. However, the DMR is primarily favored for longer ranged engagements.

> As with the Battle Rifle, the DMR is arguably one of the best UNSC weapons available. Laser-like accuracy makes this weapon the bane of any non-shielded infantry, short of a Hunter.

> Can be somewhat difficult to use at close range for less skilled players. Every missed DMR shot is more costly than with other weapons due to its slow rate of fire. Unlike the Battle Rifle, the DMR can't kill an Elite with the same shot that defeats its shielding.

> Paired with a Plasma Pistol or Storm Rifle, you should fear no Elite, and even Knights and their armored face plating are not safe from the armor-piercing capabilities of the DMR

> One of the better UNSC weapons for Legendary, it's only held back by its relatively low ammunition pool and lower rate of fire. Always know where adequate replacement weapons are available if you're taking a DMR into a big firefight.

MAGNUM

Ammunition Type: M225 SAP-HE
Ammunition Caliber: 12.7 mm x 40 mm
Magazine Capacity: 8 rounds

The Magnum has been the premier personal sidearm among UNSC personnel since its inception—and for good reason. The stopping power of a raging bull is contained within the weapon's compact frame, and its helmet-linked 2x scope allows users to counter-snipe marksmen from surprisingly long ranges.

> The Magnum is amazing for a pistol, and like the DMR and Battle Rifle, is a headshot-capable weapon. If it had a larger ammunition pool (only 40 rounds total can be carried), it would be overpowered. You are never at a serious disadvantage with this weapon on hand.

> Works extremely well with shield-breaking weapons. Some may actually prefer the Magnum to fill in the role normally reserved for the Battle Rifle and the DMR, while carrying a Storm Rifle to defeat shielding.

> As with any weapon on Legendary, some effectiveness is lost due to increased enemy health totals, but its headshot capability still keeps it in the fight. Just keep an eye firmly on your ammo count.

SNIPER RIFLE

Ammunition Type: M232 APFSDS
Ammunition Caliber: 14.5 mm x 114 mm
Magazine Capacity: 4 rounds

One of the most demoralizing weapons to face, the Sniper Rifle combines extreme accuracy, range, and killing power. Its armor-piercing rounds are capable of breaking through shielding while maintaining their full momentum for potentially lethal shots. The rifle is exceptionally balanced for its size, and the recoil stabilizers allow a marksman to fire all four rounds per magazine at a high rate with little detriment to accuracy.

> An uncommon weapon, but generally most welcome whenever it's available. Particularly prominent during Campaign Mission 5.

> Surprising amount of accuracy even when not using the scope. For situations when an Elite surprises you while you are sniping distant targets, the Sniper Rifle can be rapidly hip-fired at said Elite for a kill.

> The scope has two levels of zoom. The second level should not be maintained for anything beyond extreme long-range shooting, as it removes nearly all of your situational awareness.

> Sniper Rifle rounds can bounce off hard surfaces if the angle is shallow enough. This can result in some unfortunate mishaps.

> Sniper Rifle shots will penetrate almost all enemy infantry. Only heavy armor found on vehicles and on Hunters can withstand these rounds.

> Many enemies that fall to single Sniper Rifle shots to the body on Heroic can possibly survive two or even three rounds before falling on Legendary. Headshots are essential. Elites and Knights in particular are more frustrating to deal with. Once they know they have been targeted by a sniper, they will make it difficult to score the multiple shots necessary to break their shields and bring them down. Couple that with the general lack of ammunition and it makes the Sniper Rifle a less attractive option.

INTRODUCTION

BASIC TRAINING

INTEL

CAMPAIGN

INFINITY

APPENDIX

RAILGUN

Ammunition Type: M645 FTP-HE
Ammunition Caliber: 16 mm x 65 mm
Magazine Capacity: 1 HE Round

Firing high-explosive armor-piercing shells via a linear acceleration system, the Railgun for short, can defeat infantry and light armored vehicles with ease. Fully charged, a single shell can blow through multiple targets at once before detonation. The delay before firing a shell at full power requires a certain amount of nerve in users of the weapon.

> Utterly brutal and powerful. Can one-shot most any infantry it is deployed against on any difficulty up to Legendary, even the most dangerous variants of Elites and Knights.

> Limited ammo requires that the weapon be employed judiciously. Take a primary weapon such as a LightRifle or Battle Rifle for the smaller fry, and break out the Railgun when the real nasties show their faces.

> There is no form of scope for the Railgun—its other major deficiency. The weapon is still accurate, but suffers at long-range shooting. Because of this, it is actually better to think of the Railgun as a mid-range weapon.

> The Railgun will automatically fire its shot once it has accumulated a full charge. This does not affect how much damage the shot does. However, if you let go of the trigger too soon, you will not fire. You can use the charge-up time to fine tune your aim at the last moment.

> Knights of all varieties can survive a fully charged Railgun shot on Legendary, which is a serious blow to its overall effectiveness. It is still one of the fastest ways to destroy their shielding and expose them to follow-up shots from other weapons.

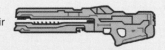

SAW

Ammunition Type: M118 FMJ-AP
Ammunition Caliber: 7.62 mm x 51 mm
Magazine Capacity: 72 rounds

The SAW is a light machine gun that overwhelms armor and energy shielding by raining a high volume of lead on a target. Few other weapons possess the same combination of raw power and suppressive capability. Even Spartans have difficulty managing the intense recoil of the weapon on full-auto.

> If you ever have a choice between a SAW and an Assault Rifle, take the SAW every time. The SAW is more powerful per shot, and if you control its recoil can be more accurate in short to mid-range encounters. The weapon has a tendency to "walk" upward while firing at full-auto, but this is easy to compensate for. Controlled bursts are still the way to go.

> Remarkably effective against Elites and Knights alike, as their shield systems are unable to handle so much hitting them at once.

> The 72-round magazine suffers from taking too much time to reload. As a general rule, if your current magazine is near a quarter capacity, consider finding a safe spot to fall back and reload before you continue to press the attack.

> The SAW is still a capable weapon on Legendary, but as with any other weapon not capable of headshots, it struggles more to chew through the enemy's increased health and shields. The weapon remains an excellent choice for non-shielded opponents.

STICKY DETONATOR

Ammunition Type: M9030 HEI/RD
Ammunition Caliber: 12 cm
Magazine Capacity: 1 grenade

The weapon is a simple design; it fires a single grenade over a distance to a target surface or infantryman. What the Sticky Detonator fires is complex. The sticky grenade is a time-delayed explosive that can be manually triggered by the gun, even in mid-flight. A motion sensor built into the launcher and the grenades allows users to wait for the optimal moment before detonation. The grenade contains enough explosive power to destroy grouped squads.

〉 Appearing only in Mission 7, this is one of the rarest weapons in the game. It's a shame, as the Sticky Detonator is easily one of the most amusing weapons available.

〉 Amazing killing power. A single properly placed grenade can kill almost a dozen Covenant light infantry, and still take out the shields of any Elites that stray into the blast radius.

〉 Very effective weapon to use against Hunters, requiring finesse and good reflexes to use. Get behind them and stick a grenade directly to their exposed flesh to cause serious damage.

〉 Can stick to any enemy and almost any surface. Most enemies stuck by the mine should be considered dead aliens walking. One possible use of the weapon is to stick a Grunt, who in their ensuing panic may run toward their friends. Watch the motion sensor display on the gun to detonate the grenade at the right moment.

〉 High-ranking Elites can survive being stuck on Legendary, but their shields will not. Compliment the Sticky Detonator with a DMR or Magnum to handle situations like this.

SHOTGUN

Ammunition Type: M296 TS
Ammunition Caliber: 8 Gauge
Magazine Capacity: 6 shells

One of the most effective close-quarters weapons in the UNSC arsenal, the Shotgun has enough stopping power to make even Elite Zealots stagger from the 8-gauge blasts striking their shields. One blast is usually enough to overwhelm personal shielding, and few species can stand up to multiple shots. Brave Marines and Spartans have used this weapon successfully against the mighty Hunters.

〉 Intense killing power limited to very short range. Don't expect to snipe anyone with this weapon. Popping the defensive shielding on an Elite or Knight requires that you get close before firing.

〉 High-risk weapon. If you're in effective range to use the Shotgun, you are definitely in range of the enemy. Against Elites, Hunters, and Knights, this is not at all a safe choice to make due to their melee capabilities.

〉 The Shotgun retains much of its power on Legendary, but due to increased enemy resilience, Elites, Knights, and Hunters may not stagger even from point-blank shots to their respective weak spots, which can result in your taking a fatal melee strike from these enemies.

INTRODUCTION

BASIC TRAINING

INTEL

CAMPAIGN

INFINITY

APPENDIX

ROCKET LAUNCHER

Designation: M41 SSR Medium Anti-Vehicle/Assault Weapon

Ammunition Type: M19 SSM
Ammunition Caliber: 102 mm Rocket
Magazine Capacity: 2 rockets

A classic anti-tank rocket system, the "SPNKR" saw increasing use as an antipersonnel weapon as the Covenant War raged on. The unique design of the launcher allows for two rockets to be fired in rapid succession at a target. The weapon can also lock onto aerial targets, and the rockets will guide themselves to the victim, making it a solid choices for bringing down Banshees.

> Nearly all Covenant infantry, save for the Hunter, will fall to a single rocket. Most Elites won't even survive a near miss, and those that do will always be staggered by the blast and therefore defenseless.

> The lock-on system for the Rocket Launcher does not always perform as well as advertised. Banshees can evade rockets with alarming frequency, which forces you to wait until the Banshee commits to an attack and is in fairly close range before firing to guarantee a kill.

> Limited ammunition means that each use should be carefully considered.

> The Rocket Launcher is still a powerful weapon on Legendary, but enemy reactions are heightened on this difficulty, so they are more likely to evade direct hits from the rockets. Counter this by firing at their feet, using the blast radius to score kills.

SPARTAN LASER

Designation: Weapon/Anti-Vehicle M6 Grindell/Galileian Nonlinear Rifle

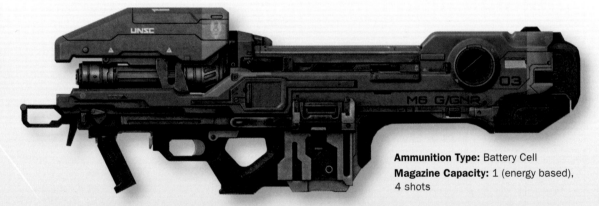

Ammunition Type: Battery Cell
Magazine Capacity: 1 (energy based), 4 shots

The iconic Spartan Laser continues to shine its crimson light across whole battlefields, destroying armor and infantry alike with disturbing ease. Little can stand up to a single shot, let alone multiple shots. Unlike traditional anti-armor weapons, the Spartan Laser reaches its target almost instantaneously upon discharge, but requires a lengthy charge up just before firing.

> Another extremely rare weapon, found primarily in Mission 7 of the Campaign, and only near the very end of the mission.

> A guaranteed kill against most infantry. Hunters will probably survive all four shots a Spartan Laser can manage unless it is hit in its weak points.

> The charge delay before firing requires that users keep their intended target sighted nearly at all times. This can tempt users into taking up unsafe positions while trying to line up a shot.

> There honestly isn't much call for this weapon on any difficulty. The vaunted power this weapons system possesses is unfortunately overshadowed by the readily available Mantis combat mech. However, during Co-op gameplay, the player with the Spartan Laser can still contribute to the final battle of Mission 7 on foot. Spartan Ops players may see this weapon appear in ordnance drops for larger battles.

TARGET DESIGNATOR

Designation: H-165 Forward Observer Module

Artillery is only at its best when guided in by those who can actually see the target. If satellite surveillance can't do it, the boots on the ground have to. The Target Designator allows infantry to guide weapons mounted on larger platforms such as the UNSC *Infinity*, or the Mammoth.

> Not necessarily a weapon on its own, the Target Designator fires a guidance laser that paints a target for destruction. It appears only in Mission 5 of the Campaign.

> Outside of destroying the Mission 5 objectives, the Designator can be used to help the Mammoth blot Phantom dropships out of the sky.

MACHINE GUN

Designation: M247 Heavy Machine Gun

Ammunition Type: M340 HVE
Ammunition Caliber: 12.7 mm x 99 mm
Magazine Capacity: 255 rounds (detached)

One of a number of machine gun emplacements deployed in the field, the M247 is the weapon used by UNSC to lock a defensive position. Powerful, yet very heavy, the weapon is typically locked to a tripod mount. However, Spartans are able to rip the weapon free of the mount and carry it into direct contact with the enemy.

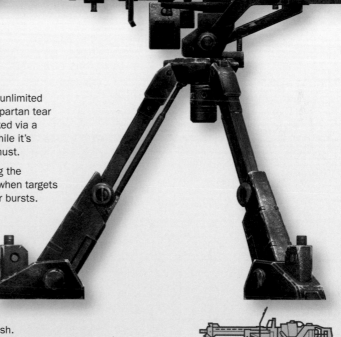

> When mounted to its tripod, the Machine Gun has unlimited ammunition and a limited range of fire. Should a Spartan tear it free, it loses the unlimited supply. Ammo is tracked via a percentage meter. If you're manning the weapon while it's mounted, don't tear it free unless you absolutely must.

> Overheating issues make it necessary to stop firing the weapon to allow it to cool. Avoid this by firing only when targets are available, and then occasionally cutting off your bursts.

> Takes a second or two to spin up to full firing speed.

> Spartans are strong, but not strong enough to sprint around carrying this weapon. The lack of mobility makes this a very dangerous weapon to take into battle, particularly on Legendary. As powerful as the Machine Gun is, taking it into a head-on encounter with tough and fast enemies like Elites or Knights is almost a death wish.

INTRODUCTION

BASIC TRAINING

INTEL

CAMPAIGN

INFINITY

APPENDIX

FRAG GRENADE

Designation: M9 High Explosive Dual-Purpose Grenade

Filler Type: ComL
Filler Volume: 6.7 oz (190 g)

The traditional Frag Grenade follows concepts refined over the course of centuries. A high explosive distributes metal fragments in a radius around the grenade, killing or wounding enemy personnel.

> Powerful, but has limited range. Attentive enemies, particularly on Legendary, will easily get out of the lethal blast radius.

> Grenade will not detonate until it strikes a hard surface, and then only after a short delay. You can use this to your advantage by skipping a grenade off a surface directly at an enemy. This is a good way to catch Elites off guard, or kill clusters of light infantry.

> Not a particularly effective weapon against Knights and Elites on Legendary. They will shrug off one or two Frags unless they are practically on top of the grenades when they detonate.

> COVENANT WEAPONS

PLASMA PISTOL

Designation: T-25 Directed Energy Pistol

Ammunition Type: Superheated Plasma
Magazine Capacity: 50 shots, 5 charged shots

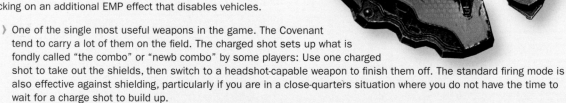

The Plasma Pistol is the Covenant equivalent to the Magnum, acting as a personal sidearm for most Covenant infantry. Its standard firing mode is somewhat weak, but its secondary function is where the weapon truly shines. Sacrificing much of its internal plasma reserves, the pistol can fire a charged shot that destroys most personal shielding in a single blow, tacking on an additional EMP effect that disables vehicles.

> One of the single most useful weapons in the game. The Covenant tend to carry a lot of them on the field. The charged shot sets up what is fondly called "the combo" or "newb combo" by some players: Use one charged shot to take out the shields, then switch to a headshot-capable weapon to finish them off. The standard firing mode is also effective against shielding, particularly if you are in a close-quarters situation where you do not have the time to wait for a charge shot to build up.

> The EMP effect can cripple even the Scorpion tank and the Mantis combat mech, the latter of which suffers from the longest EMP recovery time in the entire game.

> Charged shots can be locked onto infantry and vehicles. Wait for the target reticle to turn red and display three additional red triangles, signifying a lock, before firing.

> The weapon can overheat after rapid fire or after a charged shot, and cannot be fired again until it cools.

> Absolutely essential for Legendary or any speed run. Enemies with shields can be taken out quickly with good use of the combo, and Legendary requires that you have this concept mastered.

NEEDLER

Ammunition Type: Crystalline Shards
Magazine Capacity: 22 needles

Through means the UNSC has yet to fully grasp, the Needler fires crystalline shards that home in on targets from a significant distance. The shards themselves are not powerful individually, but should a target be hit by enough shards, an energy reaction is triggered that is on par with a small-scale Frag Grenade, almost assuredly killing the victim.

> The subject of nerfs and buffs throughout the franchise, the Needler is back in fine form. Its homing ability can guarantee hits even at mid-range.

> The "supercombine" that occurs after a target receives enough needles can trigger the detonation of nearby grenades. Remember this while firing.

> Needler shots do not home in around corners. Use this knowledge to your advantage if you're on the receiving end of the weapon.

> While it remains quite lethal even on Legendary, certain Elite variants can survive a supercombine, and Knights can survive multiple supercombine blasts. There are simply more efficient ways to kill the enemy than a Needler on Legendary.

STORM RIFLE

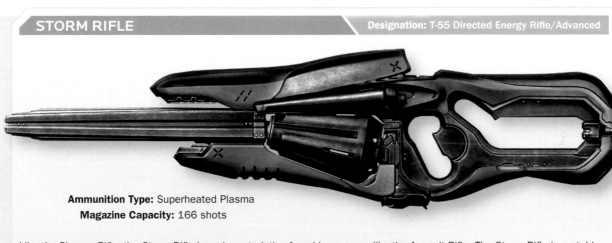

Ammunition Type: Superheated Plasma
Magazine Capacity: 166 shots

Like the Plasma Rifle, the Storm Rifle has characteristics found in weapons like the Assault Rifle. The Storm Rifle is a stable firing platform, and has an impressive rate of fire while maintaining similar accuracy found in the Assault Rifle.

> The Storm Rifle is an effective general-purpose weapon, but leans more toward anti-shield duty. It's much more powerful per shot than the standard Plasma Pistol shot.

> High rate of fire easily destroys personal shielding, but the weapon tends to overheat quickly.

> On Legendary, this weapon is solid if there is no Plasma Pistol available. Generally you will want to switch to something more powerful once the enemy defenses are down.

INTRODUCTION

BASIC TRAINING

INTEL

CAMPAIGN

INFINITY

APPENDIX

COVENANT CARBINE

Ammunition Type: Caseless Radioactive Round
Ammunition Caliber: 8.7 mm x 60 mm
Magazine Capacity: 18 rounds

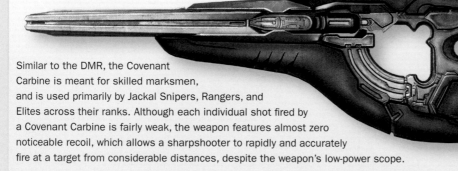

Similar to the DMR, the Covenant
Carbine is meant for skilled marksmen,
and is used primarily by Jackal Snipers, Rangers, and
Elites across their ranks. Although each individual shot fired by
a Covenant Carbine is fairly weak, the weapon features almost zero
noticeable recoil, which allows a sharpshooter to rapidly and accurately
fire at a target from considerable distances, despite the weapon's low-power scope.

> Despite the lack of stopping power, the Covenant Carbine is one of the best headshot-capable weapons in the game, so it is a prime candidate for use in conjunction with the Plasma Pistol or Storm Rifle. Amazingly accurate with or without its integrated scope, it is the bane of all unshielded hostiles in the game.

> Note that unshielded Knights require two headshots to kill with the Covenant Carbine: one to blast off the armor in front of their weak point, and another to finish off the Knight.

> Features more ammunition than the DMR (and the Battle Rifle, in practical terms), and a rate of fire that is more dependent on how fast you can pull the trigger.

> Retains its usefulness on Legendary. Despite its lack of power, you can still score headshots, and that's what you need most on Legendary. Always use it alongside something that can really break down enemy shielding, and the Covenant Carbine should be more or less as effective on Legendary as it is on easier difficulty settings.

BEAM RIFLE

Ammunition Type: Ionized Particles
Magazine Capacity: 10 shots

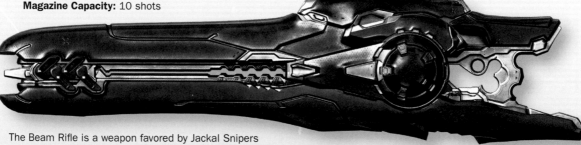

The Beam Rifle is a weapon favored by Jackal Snipers
and Rangers. It's able to overload most defensive shielding in
a single shot, and the lack of recoil allows for a fatal follow-up shot moments later. The shots are powerful, yet have been observed to skip or bounce off hard surfaces, while still resulting in kills. Possessing a powerful dual-range scope, the Beam Rifle is exceptionally accurate. Overheating and limited battery life remain a concern for operators of the Beam Rifle.

> Equivalent to the Sniper Rifle in many ways, the Beam Rifle has two distinct advantages. One, as an energy weapon, it is better suited to tearing apart defensive shielding, which makes it dangerous even to the Mantis mech. Two, it does not have to be reloaded after four shots. Players using the weapon to score kills on follow-up shots don't have to stop to reload and thereby give the target a chance to escape.

> It takes a Beam Rifle a long time to recover from overheating, so do not fire the weapon too rapidly.

> Arguably the best pure sniping weapon in the game for all practical purposes. Only the Binary Rifle is more powerful, and it suffers the reloading issue that the Sniper Rifle does, and is nowhere near as accurate as the Beam Rifle when fired from the hip.

> Sniping on Legendary is hard for reasons that have already been mentioned, but the Beam Rifle's nature makes a player keen to take rapid shots on targets, which usually leads to the weapon overheating. So long as you stay calm, you can still use the Beam Rifle effectively on Legendary.

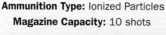

SHADE TURRET

Ammunition Type: Superheated Plasma

A powerful defensive turret that is typically turned on infantry, yet is quite capable at destroying light armor or aircraft if given the chance. The gunner is unfortunately exposed to incoming fire, and the Shade Turret's immobile nature makes it a prime target for Rocket Launchers and Sniper Rifles alike.

> The Shade Turret is encountered throughout the campaign, but honestly, there is little call to man it. If you do, you're completely exposed to enemy fire, you're immobile, and mounting or dismounting from the weapon takes time that you may not have in emergencies. On Legendary, it's best if you destroy them to prevent other Grunts or Elites from trying to take the controls.

CONCUSSION RIFLE

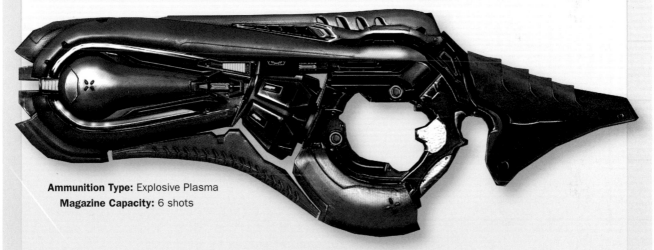

Ammunition Type: Explosive Plasma
Magazine Capacity: 6 shots

Firing bursts of explosive plasma, the Concussion Rifle is a weapon designed to suppress and disorient enemy infantry while still causing significant damage to equipment and personnel. Light vehicles can be upended by repeated concussive blasts.

> On Easy and Normal, you can get away with using the Concussion Rifle whenever it appears. The concussion shots can set off grenades lying on the ground, which can lead to some hilarious moments.

> Although they are surprisingly long-ranged, the shots travel so slowly that the enemy can easily evade them, unless you're up close or you're playing on easier difficulties and enemies just stand there and take the hits.

> Direct hits or hits on the ground near the enemy will knock them a short distance away. This can be useful at suppression duty, but there are plenty of weapons that can suppress and kill the enemy faster than the Concussion Rifle does.

> Don't use the weapon on Legendary. Even Grunt Heavies have been observed to survive up to three direct hits by this weapon. Pass it up any time you see it.

INTRODUCTION

BASIC TRAINING

INTEL

CAMPAIGN

INFINITY

APPENDIX

FUEL ROD CANNON

Designation: T-33 Light Anti-Armor Weapon

Ammunition Type: Fuel Rod
Ammunition Caliber: 38 mm
Magazine Capacity: 5 fuel rods

The Fuel Rod Cannon is primarily used for anti-armor purposes, but is also effective in anti-infantry roles. Often carried by Grunt Heavies and high-ranking Elites, the weapon can be devastating in the right hands. Light vehicles are especially vulnerable, but even heavy armor, such as that of the Scorpion tank, are prime targets for fuel rods.

> The weapon is highly effective against infantry and armor alike. Only the relatively slow speed of the projectiles holds the Fuel Rod Cannon back.

> Five rods per magazine, along with a larger ammo pool, allows it to be a powerful general-purpose weapon in your hands for longer than the Rocket Launcher or Railgun's ammo would allow.

> There is a delay before the fuel rod activates after contact with the air, which can be used to bounce fuel rods around corners. This can also cause accidental misses in close-range fighting.

> A dangerous life-taker even on Legendary, but especially when you are on the receiving end. Direct hits are harder to manage but remain lethal against most unprotected infantry, and even the toughest Elites fall after a few direct hits.

ENERGY SWORD

Designation: T-1 Energy Weapon/Sword

Ammunition Type: Shaped Plasma

The Energy Sword is a traditional dueling weapon that is seen both as a symbol of honor, and a last resort for cornered Elites. Used primarily by Elite Zealots, the Energy Sword has been seen to defeat all known forms of personal defensive shielding. Blows from the Energy Sword are almost always instantly fatal; the rare survivors are those lacking a limb or two.

> As with weapons like the Shotgun or Scattershot, the Energy Sword is a high-risk, high-reward weapon. Manage to get close to the enemy, and they will suffer greatly for letting you near.

> The Energy Sword retains its lock-on lunge strike from previous Halo appearances. There are two attack buttons with an Energy Sword: the Right Trigger, and the Right Bumper. Both attacks are capable of lunging you towards the enemy, however the Right Trigger strike has the best range.

> Avoid the weapon on Legendary. As it does with Elites, having an Energy Sword seems to inspire players into making suicidal charges at large groups of enemies in the hopes of scoring one more kill. Of course, if you pull it off, you'll look like a big boss at close-quarters combat. The other, more tangible problem is that some high-ranking Elites can survive a full-on lunge strike if it isn't from behind.

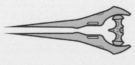

GRAVITY HAMMER

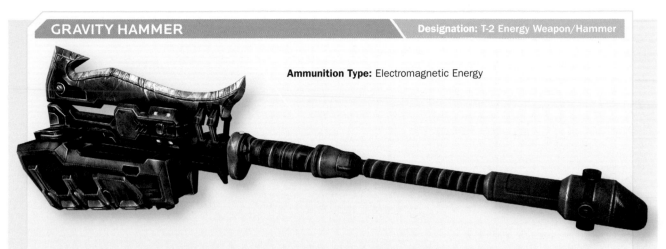

Ammunition Type: Electromagnetic Energy

Once the symbol of a Brute Chieftain's authority, this melee weapon has not been seen in the field since the Brutes virtually disappeared in the aftermath of the Covenant's defeat. Emitting powerful gravity waves, each swing of a Gravity Hammer crushes enemies with many times more force than what seems possible.

❭ Behold the rarest weapon in the game, which is presented to you in the very last mission—just in time to use it against enemies that excel at ranged combat and will cut short any reckless charges against them. As much love as we have for this weapon based on previous showings, its appearance in the Campaign is too little, too late. On Easy and Normal, you might find it useful and fun to mash Crawlers and Knights, but on Heroic and Legendary, this is a weapon that screams "Please kill the person holding onto me, they asked for it." The Prometheans are more than eager to oblige.

PLASMA CANNON

Ammunition Type: Superheated Plasma
Magazine Capacity: 255 shots
(detached)

The Covenant equivalent to the UNSC M247 Heavy Machine Gun, the Plasma Cannon (and its many variations) can be found on all manner of Covenant vehicles, and has been used to hold key positions in concert with infantry. These heavy weapons have been seen torn free of their mounts and carried into battle by Spartans.

❭ Take what you know about the Machine Gun, take away some of its effectiveness against flesh, and then add some more effectiveness against shielding, and you'll have the Plasma Cannon. It, too, contains unlimited ammunition until ripped free of its mount. The Plasma Cannon does overheat a little faster than the Machine Gun.

INTRODUCTION

BASIC TRAINING

INTEL

CAMPAIGN

INFINITY

APPENDIX

PLASMA GRENADE

Designation: T-1 Antipersonnel Grenade

Filler Type: Latent Plasma
Filler Volume: 9.3 oz (263.7 g)

The Plasma Grenade is a cruel and effective weapon. When the latent plasma filler ignites, the grenade can then "bond" with organic material or most surfaces, once it is thrown, allowing victims a brief moment of abject terror before the grenade detonates.

› The iconic Plasma Grenade is one of the best tools to have in your kit, provided you've got a good eye and a good arm. Sticking most Covenant infantry results in a kill, unless it's a high-ranking Elite or a Hunter, or unless you are playing on Legendary.

› Prometheans Crawlers and Watchers tend to evade most Plasma Grenade tosses (and in the case of the latter, tend to throw them back at you), but Knights can be de-shielded on Heroic and Legendary with a good toss.

› The Plasma Grenade has a weaker area of effect blast than the Frag Grenade, and can take longer to detonate. As such, it isn't the best weapon for scoring mass kills on lower difficulties, though stuck Grunts might panic and flee into the arms of their comrades.

> FORERUNNER WEAPONS

BOLTSHOT

Designation: Z-110 Directed Energy Pistol/Exotic

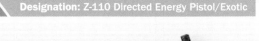

Ammunition Type: Ionized Particles
Magazine Capacity: 10 shots, 2 charged shots

This Forerunner sidearm shoots charged particles at targets accurately and as quickly as the user is willing to pull the trigger. The secondary function of the Boltshot allows the user to charge five shots at once, unleashing them as a short-range shotgun-style burst that can destroy personal shielding.

› Accurate and headshot-capable in its standard firing mode, yet deceptively powerful up close with its secondary mode, the Boltshot is an effective secondary weapon to have on hand.

› Unlike the Magnum, the Boltshot does not come with a scope. This can make longer ranged engagements with the Boltshot more difficult.

› The secondary fire mode uses up to five shots in the magazine, and can be used even if less than five shots are available. However, the charge shot only fires after a full charge has been collected. This delay makes it dangerous to use in close quarters unless you anticipate enemy movements in advance. You can't rely on it as a defensive reaction, especially on Legendary.

› You can still use the Boltshot on Legendary, but as with all other difficulties, the Boltshot typically appears alongside of the LightRifle, which ultimately is a better weapon for most of the fighting you'll be doing. That said, it doesn't make a bad secondary weapon, and being headshot-capable makes it great for clearing out Grunts, Jackals, and Crawlers.

SUPPRESSOR

Ammunition Type: Light Mass
Magazine Capacity: 48 bolts

The Suppressor could be considered the equivalent to a UNSC Submachine Gun; it features a high rate of fire and peppers targets with light bolts, devastating organic material. While not particularly accurate, the Suppressor appears to be made to cover a wide area.

⟩ The Suppressor is effective against defensive shielding and organic material. Like the Boltshot, its bolts are a little slower than the shots fired by most UNSC and Covenant weapons, which limits it to close range for maximum effectiveness.

⟩ The magazine feels bottomless, but mostly because it has to. Even at short ranges, the accuracy of the weapon makes it ill-suited for smaller targets, with many shots potentially going wild.

⟩ While it can be useful, on Legendary you're better off looking for weapons that can kill fast.
The Suppressor is not one of those weapons.

SCATTERSHOT

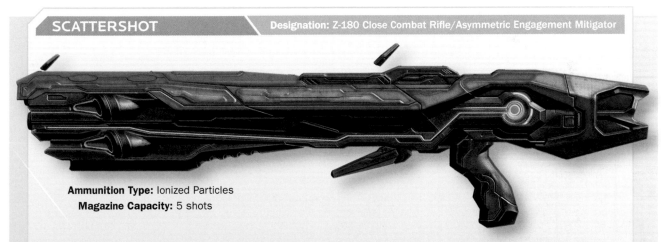

Ammunition Type: Ionized Particles
Magazine Capacity: 5 shots

A powerful Forerunner shotgun that was designed for maximum firepower. The Scattershot can be fired incredibly fast, and like the charged shot from a Boltshot, it devastates personnel up close. It appears to be a further evolution of weaponry specifically designed to destroy organic material in such a way that nothing remains. Victims hit by this weapon at point-blank range have been observed to completely disintegrate.

⟩ While limited to close-range, the Scattershot is unmatched in its class. Even the Shotgun doesn't wreck faces quite like the Scattershot.

⟩ The individual bolts fired by a Scattershot can be deflected off hard surfaces, turning any small corridor into a potential kill zone.

⟩ As it is such a specialized weapon, it is hard to recommend for Legendary. Getting up close to the enemy is already a dangerous proposition, and the Scattershot can have only five shots chambered before it needs reloading. This might be fine against a lone Elite or Knight, but you will find that they are rarely alone. Still, the Scattershot is an excellent weapon to compliment other Forerunner weapons, like the LightRifle or Boltshot.

INTRODUCTION

BASIC TRAINING

INTEL

CAMPAIGN

INFINITY

APPENDIX

LIGHTRIFLE

Designation: Z-250 Directed Energy Engagement Weapon

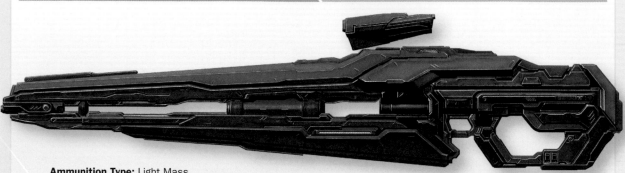

Ammunition Type: Light Mass
Magazine Capacity: 36 shots, 12 (scoped)

A unique weapon, the LightRifle fires hardlight bolts in groups of three, similar to how the Battle Rifle is normally set to fire. When scoped in, the weapon switches to a different firing mode, combine three bolts into one for devastating effectiveness on targets. The LightRifle is a precision weapon, easily as accurate as its UNSC and Covenant equivalents.

> This is possibly the best gun in the game. Combining the three-shot burst of the Battle Rifle, and the single-shot power of the DMR, the LightRifle is capable of outmatching either weapon.

> Capable of headshots in either firing mode, the LightRifle is best paired with weapons better designed for anti-shield duty.

> One of the best weapons to have on hand for Legendary, particularly for some of the later missions, where ammo for it is plentiful. Can fill any role in combat, at any range. The only caveat against it is that, like any precision weapon, using it well while under fire can be somewhat demanding, but if you're playing on Legendary you are probably used to that by now.

BINARY RIFLE

Designation: Z-750 Special Application Sniper Rifle

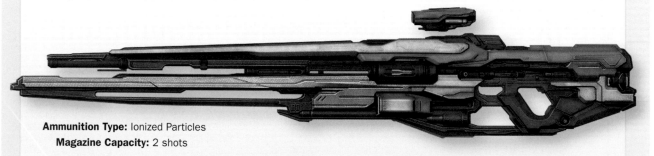

Ammunition Type: Ionized Particles
Magazine Capacity: 2 shots

A further evolution of the scoped rifle in single-shot firing mode found on the LightRifle, the Binary Rifle fires a powerful stream of ionized particles that can destroy organic matter entirely in a single shot. No other weapon in any arsenal combines such extreme precision and power into one package.

> If it weren't limited to two shots per magazine, this would be the best, purest sniping weapon in the game. However players who are great shots might argue that it already is the best, and the limited magazine is just ta balancing factor. As with the other sniper rifles, the Binary Rifle has a scope with two zoom modes.

> Can kill weaker Elites on Legendary in a single headshot, while higher ranking Elites and Promethean Knights will require two headshots: One for their shields, one for their faces.

> A weapon this specialized is not a good call to waste on small fry, though you may be tempted at times to destroy Watchers with single shots from a Binary Rifle.

> Highly inaccurate when hip fired. If you're ever in a situation where this is necessary, switch to something else. If you have nothing else, well, you can always get lucky or try the battle again.

> In a way, this weapon is better in the hands of an allied Marine or Spartan. Trade it to them and enjoy their benefits of having unlimited ammo to snipe the enemy with.

INCINERATION CANNON

Designation: Weapon/Anti-Material Z-390 High-Explosive Munitions Rifle

Ammunition Type: Ionized Particles
Magazine Capacity: 1 shot

The ultimate particle weapon found in the hands of Promethean Knight Commanders throughout the game, the Incineration cannon destroys targets it directly hits with a bundle of explosive ionized particles. After impact, the particle bundle scatters, further saturating the target area with the weapon's damaging effects. Very little can survive a direct hit from this weapon.

⟩ There isn't a more powerful infantry weapon in the game. On any difficulty, the Incineration Cannon is a guaranteed kill on a direct hit on any Covenant or Promethean short of a Phantom dropship, a Wraith, or a Hunter.

⟩ Accurate and possessing a zoom function, the Incineration Cannon is capable of scoring kills at ranges usually reserved for sniper rifles. The shot travels a bit slow, so it's best to use it at mid range for guaranteed kills.

⟩ This weapon can make certain portions of Mission 6 and Mission 8 significantly easier on Legendary, and so we highly recommend it as a staple weapon in your arsenal.

PULSE GRENADE

Designation: Z-040 Attenuation Field Generator/Localized

Ammunition Type: Electromagnetic Energy

A small-scale attenuation field generator that can be used to drive hostiles out of prepared positions. The spherical field generated lasts for nearly four seconds. Afterward, the generator explodes, obliterating nearby organic material still caught within the blast radius.

⟩ The Pulse Grenade is not as immediately lethal as the Frag or Plasma Grenades, but it does have some special uses. It does not bounce. Where it impacts after it is thrown is where the pulse field is generated. You can use this to seriously damage Elites and Knights by throwing it at their feet.

⟩ It is an excellent area-denial weapon. You can drive enemies out of cover by throwing the Pulse Grenade at them, and also prevent them from returning to it right away.

⟩ The field generated by the Pulse Grenade is especially effective against opponents with little room to maneuver as well as large targets in general. However, to get the full effects on Knights and Elites, you will have to display a certain amount of finesse to throw it accurately while also taking into account their evasive ability.

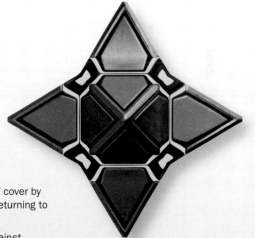

INTRODUCTION

BASIC TRAINING

INTEL

CAMPAIGN

INFINITY

APPENDIX

ARMOR ABILITIES

Armor abilities allow players to change their play style in ways that may allow for feats not normally possible, or improve survivability under fire. During the Campaign, you're typically introduced to new abilities with every mission from the second onward. While we may suggest specific armor abilities, as they were what worked best for us, it's up to you to decide which abilities you want to use, and how you want to use them.

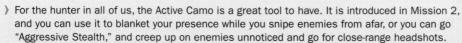

ACTIVE CAMOUFLAGE   Designation: T-3 Refraction Dissonance Modifier/Camouflage

The Active Camouflage system, acquired during the early years of the Covenant War, is a refraction dissonance modifier that effectively bends light around the surface of an object, masking its presence through advanced pattern realignment. Although pervasive among specific Sangheili units, it has seen some use among Spartans of all classes.

> For the hunter in all of us, the Active Camo is a great tool to have. It is introduced in Mission 2, and you can use it to blanket your presence while you snipe enemies from afar, or you can go "Aggressive Stealth," and creep up on enemies unnoticed and go for close-range headshots.

> Active Camo is not perfect invisibility. It degrades as you move, and turns off entirely if you sprint. Even when standing stock still, you can be noticed by attentive enemies, especially on higher difficulties.

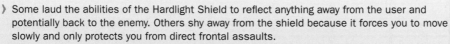

HARDLIGHT SHIELD   Designation: Z-90 Photonic Coalescence Emitter/Aegis

The Hardlight Shield appears to be a photon emitter that can fuse particles of light into a rigid, dissipative barrier. For Spartans who choose to integrate it, the technology functions as a full-size, aegis-class antipersonnel defensive shield.

> Some laud the abilities of the Hardlight Shield to reflect anything away from the user and potentially back to the enemy. Others shy away from the shield because it forces you to move slowly and only protects you from direct frontal assaults.

> The Hardlight Shield is hard for enemies to break. It can be used to help assist retreats behind other, more solid cover, giving you a chance to regenerate your shielding.

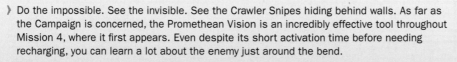

PROMETHEAN VISION   Designation: Z-5080 Short-Range Spectrum Augmenter/Vision

This armor ability is a short-range, full-spectrum enhancement package that enables users to detect shapes and movement through solid barriers. Coupled with the VISR 4.0 tech suite, this software is one of the most formidable abilities leveraged by GEN2 armor systems.

> Do the impossible. See the invisible. See the Crawler Snipes hiding behind walls. As far as the Campaign is concerned, the Promethean Vision is an incredibly effective tool throughout Mission 4, where it first appears. Even despite its short activation time before needing recharging, you can learn a lot about the enemy just around the bend.

> Use Promethean Vision in bursts, if possible. When Knights use this tech, notice how they appear on your Motion Sensor, accompanied by a red pulse emanating from their position? That's what you look like to them on their trackers.

HOLOGRAM

Designation: T-27 Responsive Holographic Form Emulator

The Hologram is a responsive emulator that generates an extremely realistic copy of the user's physical form and movement. This copy is used as a decoy in the field to trick enemy infantry and armored vehicles into revealing their position, thereby placing them at a disadvantage.

> You might laugh at the idea of a decoy of the Master Chief running ahead and distracting the enemy while you shoot them in the back. In proper practice, this is exactly what the Hologram can do. So long as they don't see you deploy it, they will focus their efforts on the hologram until it fizzles out.

> The Hologram is *not* solid. Don't be the guy who runs out behind it at a Knight Lancer armed with a Binary Rifle. It might just snipe you and the decoy in one shot for your insolence.

AUTOSENTRY

Designation: Z-2500 Automated Protection Drone

The Autosentry is an intriguing combat-capable drone unit now typically deployed in a supporting role during enemy engagements. The full measure of its original use is unknown. Other human-originating APD units similar to this Forerunner sentry have been used by the UNSC for years, but none with this level of mobility, functionality, and sustained power.

> It's easy to discount the small puffs of light the Autosentry spits out as being useless. Say that to the Knights it one-shot or two-shots when their shields are down. Autosentries make excellent decoys or assistants in holding a defensive position. Coordinating your fire with an Autosentry can score kills much sooner.

> You can self-destruct a deployed Autosentry, harming anything near the blast, including yourself. Remember this if you want to redeploy the gun elsewhere: you can always do this early and start the armor ability recharge process while you're on the move.

> Unfortunately, on Legendary, the Autosentry is reduced to a decoy, but it's still a good decoy that can shoot back. Just make sure that during the gun's setup you're not vulnerable to incoming fire or flanking maneuvers.

> The turret takes a couple of seconds to set up, and during that time you are forced to sit still and watch the turret be constructed. Try to avoid doing this while you're getting shot at.

JET PACK

Designation: Series 12 Single Operator Lift Apparatus

The Jet Pack is a gravity mitigation device latched to the back of infantry BDU, allowing personnel to traverse vertically challenging terrain and generally be more mobile in the battlefield. The Jet Pack was designed with Spartan-IV assets in mind, though it can be used more broadly.

> The Jet Pack is essentially mandatory for the Master Chief in Mission 5, but it's also the best demonstration as to why the ability is so awesome. You can often ignore any low-lying cover the enemy uses simply by flying over it.

> Mission 6 also can be made much easier with careful Jet Pack use. In general, any area that has ledges only the Jet Pack can easily reach is likely going to be a solid sniping position.

> Surviving long falls with the Jet Pack is easy, but don't expect it to save you from falling into an abyss. The limited charge on the pack can do only so much.

INTRODUCTION

BASIC TRAINING

INTEL

CAMPAIGN

INFINITY

APPENDIX

REGENERATION FIELD

Designation: M2705 Regenerative Kinetic Dispersal Field

The Regeneration Field package is a kinetic dispersal system that has two primary operations: The first is a burst of shunting energy that forces friend-or-foe-designated enemies away from the user, the second is a Mjolnir component-stabilizing system which recharges the local allies' combat viability through the short-term of reappropriation of specific power systems.

》 Limited entirely to War Games multiplayer, the Regeneration Field can turn the tide of battle by providing a safe zone for you and any allies you might have, as it constant restores their shields.

》 This ability is excellent for locking down key positions or supporting flag carriers on foot. If the enemy isn't bringing power weapons or vehicles to the fight, they will never stop a good, coordinated team that uses multiple fields in succession.

THRUSTER PACK

Designation: M805X Forward Acceleration System—Fulcrum Mitigating

The Thruster Pack, not terribly different from other extra-vehicular activity-intended thrust modules, is a forward acceleration system that mitigates the need for a fulcrum or pivoting articulation by the user. This ability allows the user to move quickly and aggressively through the field of combat for a limited duration.

》 The Thruster Pack has a very specific primary function: last-second dodges. You are first introduced to this during Mission 7 when you fight a pair of Hunters in an enclosed space. You get one burst from the pack before it needs to recharge, so make every use count!

》 You can use the Thruster Pack in mid-jump, so it's perfect for throwing off snipers you know are targeting you. It alters your otherwise easily tracked direction and speed.

》 In a way, this ability is a bit too specific in nature. To be perfectly honest, unless you're playing on lower difficulties in the Campaign, enemy fire and snipers in general are a bit too sophisticated for the Thruster Pack to help you dodge at the last moment. Chances are, you'll be hit. Much of the fighting in Mission 7 takes places at shorter ranges, and the Thruster Pack's long recovery time leaves you vulnerable to incoming fire anyway.

> **Note**
> Information for Support Upgrades and Tactical Packages can be found in the Infinity Multiplayer chapter.

ENEMIES

INTRODUCTION

BASIC TRAINING

INTEL

CAMPAIGN

INFINITY

APPENDIX

> COVENANT

GRUNTS

Formal Name: Unggoy

Species: *Monachus frigus*
Homeworld: Bahalo

Average Height: 4 ft 6.5 in–5 ft 7 in (138.4 cm–167 cm)
Average Weight: 248.3 lbs–260.1 lbs (112.6 kg–118 kg)

A popular saying among Grunts: "When in doubt, flee!" It is a maxim that has kept their species alive on the terribly inhospitable homeworld, through the most miserable battles and conditions imposed upon them by the Covenant. Despite their earlier alliance with the Brutes, many Grunts have aligned with Elites in recent years, mostly out of fear, but also out of a growing (and begrudged) respect between the two races.

Grunts alone are a cowardly lot, but with strong leadership that is often provided by the Elites, a squad of Grunts can become a pack of vicious killers, until their leaders are dead. Despite this, the Grunts are, for better or worse, the true backbone of the Covenant. They provide the numbers, they fight where they are told, and hope to live long enough to see another day.

> Grunts have two general states in combat: aggressively attacking the enemy, and running in fear from the enemy. What determines their behavior is whether there's leadership they can look to. This is usually provided by an Elite, although later in the Campaign you will see Knights giving orders.

> You can break the will of the Grunts in a general area by killing a leader. This causes one of two things to happen: The Grunts scatter like leaves in the wind, screaming in terror, or they pull out two Plasma Grenades and decide that nobody gets to be a winner today, and then start running at you. Sometimes, whole squads of Grunts go suicidal, and while this may seem mindless, it isn't. Suicide Grunts hold onto their Plasma Grenades until they are killed or until they get close to a target, which is going to be you 99 percent of the time.

> You can hear distinct hissing of Plasma Grenades and shouted chatter from Suicide Grunts. If you suspect they are close, check your motion sensor. If they get close enough that your grenade indicator is lighting up, it might already be too late.

> Grunt squads that aren't lead by an Elite or a Knight can still be broken if you kill large numbers of them quickly enough.

> Headshots are the preferred method for dealing with Grunts. Since they are among the most common enemies in the game, you should always try to have a weapon on hand that can deal out that sort of swift justice.

> The four Grunt types have different color variants, but color does not appear to affect their resilience to damage as is the case with the color variants of the Elites.

> On Legendary, all Grunts receive a significant boost in their damage-soaking potential, further emphasizing the importance of headshots. Also, Grunt Heavies with Fuel Rod Cannons become increasingly more common. There's nothing like rounding a corner and eating six fuel rods to the face.

STORM GRUNT

Armament: Plasma Pistol, Needler

IMPERIAL GRUNT

Armament: Plasma Pistol, Needler

GRUNT RANGER

Armament: Plasma Pistol, Needler

GRUNT HEAVY

Armament: Fuel Rod Cannon

JACKALS

Formal Name: Kig-Yar

Species: *Perosus latrunculus*
Homeworld: Eayn
Average Height: 6 ft 2 in–6 ft 8 in (190 cm–203 cm)
Average Weight: 195 lbs–206.1 lbs (88 kg–93 kg)

The other backbone of the Covenant, the Jackals, are an important client race. Braver than the Grunts, Jackals continue to fight even if the leaders of the fight have fallen. Early feuding between their classes has led to lasting tension between the Jackals and the Grunts.

Jackals specialize in two types of warfare: close combat, and sniping. Some of the most lethal snipers throughout the Human-Covenant War were Jackals, and their Jackal infantry's distinct Point-Defense Gauntlets have long heralded the advance of a Covenant vanguard.

Jackals are a physically frail species, though they make up for this by being one of the swiftest of all Covenant races. Their excellent senses allow them to detect possible threats for the rest of their squads, or make the initial sniper shot that surprises would-be ambushers with the loss of one of their own.

STORM JACKAL

Armament: Plasma Pistol, Point-Defense Gauntlet

> Jackals with Beam Rifles can be incredibly frustrating, but remember that the weapon literally draws a line back to their position. Stay calm, recharge your shields if necessary, and let them reveal themselves before you attempt to counter-snipe.

> You can divide the Jackal presence on Requiem into two specific roles: marksmen (Jackal Rangers, Jackal Snipers) and Jackal infantry (Storm Jackals, Jackal Heavies).

> The Jackal infantry is tenacious and resilient despite their physically frail nature. Their Point-Defense Gauntlets being a chief reason. These gauntlets can deflect or absorb almost absurd amounts of punishment before finally failing. Even a charged shot from a Plasma Pistol isn't enough to overload a gauntlet.

> Jackal infantry often come equipped with Needlers or Plasma Pistols, both of which are very dangerous, particularly on Legendary.

> All Jackal infantry, regardless of their rank or color, can be killed with a single headshot. However, their Point-Defense Gauntlets may be protecting their head. You can shoot any exposed limbs to get the Jackal to stagger, and then score the headshot when the head is exposed.

> Jackal Rangers and Snipers provide the ranged combat capability for the Covenant. While on low difficulties they are a nuisance, Legendary Jackal marksmen will put two in your head before you know what hit you, and they are exceptional at keeping you locked down behind cover.

> Both Jackal marksman types tend to lock into place when they finally engage you, only moving if you haven't been seen in some time. You can use this bloodthirstiness against them by moving undetected to new position and sniping them from there.

JACKAL RANGER

Armament: Covenant Carbine

JACKAL SNIPER

Armament: Beam Rifle, Covenant Carbine

JACKAL HEAVY

Armament: Needler, Point-Defense Gauntlet

HALO 4

HUNTERS

Species: *Ophis congregation*
Homeworld: Te

Average Height: 12 ft 1 in–12 ft 3 in (368.7 cm–373.4 cm)
Average Weight: 10,500 lbs (4,800 kg)

A Hunter is not actually an individual entity, but is actually a collective of wormlike beings known as Lekgolo. When Lekgolo join in sufficient numbers, they become Mgalekgolo and can fit into a variety of carapaces derived from heavy armor plating. Armed with Assault Cannons and protected by their heavy shielding, Hunters are rightfully called living tanks by those on the receiving end of their weapons.

Deployed in pairs, the Hunters are some of the most violent and dangerous Covenant troops in combat. Able to take repeated strikes from anti-tank munitions, Hunters can be as immovable as a mountain one moment, then swiftly springing into action when enemies draw close, using their shields as lethal melee weapons.

> Fighting Hunters from afar is a losing proposition without the right weapons. Their Assault Cannons spew fuel rods at distant targets, and they hunker down with their shields if necessary. So long as you try to attack a Hunter head-on, they will always survive more punishment than you have to deal out.

> Taking the fight up close to a Hunter is very dangerous, but it is the best way to get access to their weak points: the gaps in their armor that reveal the Lekgolo within. When you draw close, the Hunters immediately attempt to attack you with melee strikes from their shields or their cannon. You can use these wide swings to flank the Hunter and then fire on their exposed worms. Any weapon can do damage to these weak points, but Shotguns, Scattershots, Fuel Rod Cannons, and Rocket Launchers are especially effective. Plasma Grenades and Sticky Detonator grenades are also great weapons to use.

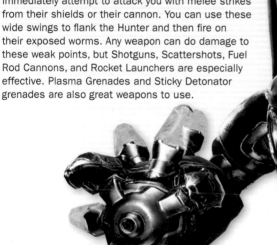

> It is possible to knock Hunters' shields aside with a powerful blast and expose their "stomachs" for a brief moment. Whether or not you are in position to exploit this is a different matter.

> Hunters are always deployed in pairs, and this makes combatting them individually a difficult prospect. They always cover each other, so concentrating on one is to receive a fuel rod from the other. In all actuality, you'll probably end up spending a lot of ammo trying to kill the first Hunter in order to make it easier to fight off the second.

> Hunters rarely beat tanks by themselves, but they are capable of doing so if you let them. Their Assault Cannons can devastate heavy vehicles on higher difficulties. If you're engaging Hunters in a Scorpion, stay on the move.

HUNTER

Armament: Assault Cannon, Heavy Shield

INTRODUCTION

BASIC TRAINING

INTEL

CAMPAIGN

INFINITY

APPENDIX

ELITES

Species: *Macto cognatus*
Homeworld: Sanghelios

Average Height: 7 ft 4 in–8 ft 6 in (223 cm–259 cm)
Average Weight: 307 lbs–393 lbs (139 kg–178 kg)

The Elites were once another Covenant race, in prime leadership position, before being betrayed by the Prophets. The Elites staged a successful rebellion that broke the old Covenant in the twilight of the Human-Covenant War. Previously, they struggled in a civil war on their homeworld to determine the direction of their species. One side favored reconciliation with the humans, the other did not. The leaders of the newly formed Covenant appear to be part of a fringe, fanatical sect, not clearly aligned with either side.

Elites are considered the overall best fighting soldiers the Covenant has to offer. They are stronger, faster, and better than the average human in combat, and are driven by their devout religious beliefs. Their archaic honor systems that have at times cost them good soldiers in suicide charges by their violent desire to bring an end to the human species.

Elites are the closest thing the Covenant has to an equal to a Spartan. They are aggressive and smart battlefield commanders with excellent tactical and strategic foresight, with a good record of leading inferior numbers of troops against long odds and still achieving victory. They give no quarter and expect none in return. They should rightfully be respected as equals in the field of battle.

> Elites are some of the most dangerous enemies you'll face in traditional combat, being your equal right down to the energy shielding they have for protection. However, for all their bluster and power, they fall to one good headshot. To that end, on any difficulty but especially on Legendary, you should always have the means to break their shields quickly. This means carrying Plasma Pistols and, to a lesser extent, Storm Rifles.

> Elites are leaders. Their presence in battle stabilizes other Covenant troops, particularly the Grunts. Should they die, panic will strike the ranks. Some say that Grunts make better early targets due to the threat of their suicide charges, but we believe this just makes them easier to mop up once the threat of the Elites is dealt with.

> Elite Zealots and Warriors are among the most dangerous Elites you'll face. Warriors carry the Fuel Rod Cannon, but Zealots favor the Energy Sword, and have the physical constitution to push through a charged shot from a Plasma Pistol and still try for a kill. Zealots also use the Active Camo armor ability, so do not lose contact with them, lest you get ambushed from behind minutes later.

STORM ELITE

Armament: Storm Rifle, Covenant Carbine

ELITE RANGER

Armament: Covenant Carbine

ELITE COMMANDER

Armament: Concussion Rifle, Covenant Carbine

ELITE WARRIOR

Armament: Fuel Rod Cannon

ELITE ZEALOT

Armament: Energy Sword, Active Camouflage

CRAWLERS

Homeworld: Requiem

Average Height: 4 ft 11 in (149.9 cm)
Average Weight: 371 lbs (168.3 kg)

Crawlers are Forerunner constructs that exhibit tendencies like wolf packs. These machines are surprisingly well armed, and are able to crawl on most vertical terrain, hence their name. Crawlers specialize in massed combat tactics, such as attempting to encircle and bombard targets from all sides, and they use their claws and mandibles to slice into armor should their enemy draw close.

Despite their aggressiveness, Crawlers know when to fall back and give ground. They try to lure enemies into ambushes and counterattacks, and take advantage of sniping positions only they can reach. Despite their short stature, Crawlers cannot be ignored, as they are the vanguard of the Promethean forces on Requiem.

> Crawlers are some of the fastest enemies you'll face in battle. Flanking maneuvers are common tactics, so do not put yourself in a position where you can be quickly surrounded.

> Of all Crawler variants, the Snipe is the gravest threat. Armed with a Binary Rifle, the Snipe can destroy your shields in a single blast on any difficulty save for Legendary, where they kill you outright with a single shot regardless of your shield levels. Know where the little buggers are, and kill them first.

> All Crawlers are vulnerable to headshots, and have no additional shield protection unless it is provided by a Watcher. A precision headshot weapon is a must.

> Never chase down large groups of Crawlers that are retreating. This is almost always a setup. They can quickly turn around and counterattack while you are exposed.

CRAWLER

Armament: Boltshot

CRAWLER SNIPE

Armament: Binary Rifle

ALPHA CRAWLER

Armament: Suppressor

INTRODUCTION

BASIC TRAINING

INTEL

CAMPAIGN

INFINITY

APPENDIX

WATCHER

Average Height: 4 ft 2 in (127 cm)
Average Weight: 318 lbs (144.2 kg)

The Watcher is a Forerunner construct deployed by Promethean Knights. Providing battlefield support to their allies, Watchers emit Hardlight Shields that protect their chosen ally from incoming fire. Using a gravity beam, they can pick up thrown grenades, suspend their fuses, and throw them back at the enemy. More troubling, a Watcher is able to revive fallen Crawlers or Knights or even construct Beam Turrets to combat their enemies.

❯ Always kill the Watchers first. In any encounter they must die immediately. You do not want to kill a Knight only to see it revived moments later, staring at you from behind. We recommend expending even Binary Rifle or Beam Rifle shots to ensure the Watchers are dead. Whatever it takes, if they are dead, you have effectively limited the Promethean onslaught in that battle.

PROMETHEAN WATCHER

Armament: Boltshot

KNIGHTS

Average Height: 9 ft 11 in (302.3 cm)
Average Weight: 934 lbs (423.7 kg)

The imposing figure that stands as the leaders of the Forerunner forces is the Promethean Knight. Because they use sophisticated weapons and are armored better than any soldiers in the Covenant or UNSC, once Knights appear at any battle, you can expect the challenge to increase significantly. They are able to deploy Watchers in battle for support, and are capable leaders in their own right. Skilled at ranged and close combat, and able to use teleportation to flank and confuse their enemies, the Knight is one of the most dangerous threats found on Requiem.

KNIGHT

Armament: Suppressor, LightRifle

❭ Knights have the fastest regenerating shields in the game. It is not uncommon to see their shields wholly restored after a single teleporting retreat, which makes combat with them an exercise in frustration at times.

❭ All Knight variants can teleport rapidly at their enemies for a powerful melee attack that can flatten the toughest opponents. On Legendary, getting hit by this attack is immediately fatal.

❭ It could be argued that any of the variants of the Knight, the Commander, Lancer, and Battlewagon, are the most dangerous. Commanders wield the Incineration Cannon, one of the most dangerous weapons in the game. The Battlewagon is one of the toughest to kill of all the Knight variants, and the Scattershot it favors is one of the most powerful close-quarters weapons available. However, it's our opinion that the Knight Lancer, armed with a Binary Rifle, is the most annoying and infuriating enemy in the entire game.

❭ When their shields are broken, Knights can be killed quickly by two headshots: one to expose their skull, and the other to destroy it. These skulls are heavily armored across all variants, but only the standard Knight will willingly expose it after their shields are downed in a display of anger or intimidation.

❭ The armored carapace behind the head of a Knight is almost impenetrable to weapons fire. This is also where Watchers are deployed from.

❭ Knights are extremely dangerous in melee combat. Their forearm blade gives them an impressive reach, so it is a bad idea to stay close.

❭ Knight Commanders take their melee combat to a different level by emitting a shock wave that damages the shielding of nearby enemies and knocks them back a fair distance.

❭ When a Knight dies, it releases a glowing essence that can destroy the weapon it held. This function can cost you access to weapons like the Incineration Cannon, so move quickly to retrieve the weapon.

❭ Unlike their carapace and their skulls, the rest of a Knight is not so well armored. One valid tactic is to break their shields with a charged Plasma Pistol shot, then pour on fire from any rapid-fire weapon you have on hand, aiming for their torso or even their limbs. The moment they take enough damage, they will immediately dissolve.

❭ The Sniper Rifle, Beam Rifle, and Binary Rifle can destroy a Knight in two headshots on Heroic difficulty. On Legendary, it takes the Sniper Rifle and the Beam Rifle three shots.

KNIGHT LANCER

Armament: LightRifle, Binary Rifle, Autosentry

KNIGHT COMMANDER

Armament: Incineration Cannon, Autosentry

KNIGHT BATTLEWAGON

Armament: Scattershot, Promethean Vision

INTRODUCTION

BASIC TRAINING

INTEL

CAMPAIGN

INFINITY

APPENDIX

VEHICLES

> UNSC VEHICLES

WARTHOG
Designation: M12 Force Application Vehicle

Crew Capacity: 1 driver, 1 passenger, 1 gunner
Primary Armament: Machine Gun Turret, Gauss Cannon, Rocket Launcher

The Warthog is the symbolic ground transport for the UNSC, which remains in use to this day. Versatile and quick, the Warthog continues its proud service and tradition of being tough as hell. Three variants of the Warthog are available in *Halo 4*.

> When playing alone, allow a Marine or Spartan to take up the mounted gun on any Warthog you commandeer. They are incredibly accurate with these weapons. Gunners on a Warthog also enjoy some added resistance to gunfire, which is also a big plus.

> Don't sit still for long. The Warthog is built for speedy transport and maneuverability in warfare, so use it right. So long as you have a gunner, you can concentrate on defensive driving while they do all the killing.

MONGOOSE
Designation: M247 Ultra-Light All Terrain Vehicle

Crew Capacity: 1 driver, 1 passenger

If recon needs to get somewhere quickly, they can take a Mongoose. One of the fastest UNSC land vehicles, the Mongoose can take a pair of soldiers over the same terrain a Warthog can, and is a harder target to hit.

> The Mongoose appears available during the Campaign on Mission 4. It is far more prominent in multiplayer as a flag capture vehicle or small transport. A driver gets a runner to the enemy base, the runner gets the flag, gets back on the Mongoose, and then they ride off to victory. That's how it works in theory. In practice, both driver and passenger are exposed to fire from all sides. You will have to put your driving skills to the test if you want to survive such a brazen strategy.

SCORPION
Designation: M808 Main Battle Tank

Crew Capacity: 1 operator, 1 gunner, 4 passengers
Primary Armament: Primary Cannon
Secondary Armament: Machine Gun

The Scorpion is another UNSC mainstay, having proved its worth on hundreds of battlefields across the galaxy in the fight against the Covenant. A popular Marine saying is "Tank beats everything!" You would be hard-pressed to disprove it.

> With a gunner on the machine gun, and some infantry riding aboard the tank, getting close to a Scorpion is a hazardous activity at best. The main gun on a Scorpion outranges just about any vehicle in the game. A properly driven and supported Scorpion will never be in danger.

PELICAN DROPSHIP

Designation: Dropship 79 Heavy Troop Carrier

Crew Capacity: 3 crew, 10–14 passengers
Primary Armament: Autocannon

The standard UNSC dropship has seen refinements over the years, but has remained the same craft throughout its service. Despite its size, the Pelican is surprisingly agile and quick, allowing it to place troops into hostile or otherwise tight landing zones. The unique profile of the Pelican signals relief and reinforcements for troops on the field.

PELICAN GUNSHIP

Designation: Gunship 79 Heavy Troop Carrier/Mobile Armory

Crew Capacity: 3 crew, 10–14 passengers, 2 gunners
Primary Armament: Autocannon
Secondary Armament: Laser Cannon
Tertiary Armament: Heavy Cannon
Quarternary Armament: Machine Gun x 2, Heavy Cannon

A variant on the standard Pelican dropship, this gunship meant for more than just battlefield transport. Armed to the teeth with an Autocannon, Laser Cannon, Heavy Cannon, and two Machine Guns, the Pelican Gunship is the deadliest transport fielded by the UNSC.

〉 Sadly, you only have one opportunity to fly a Pelican Gunship, and that is in Mission 6 of the Campaign. If you're playing on Co-Op mode, all of the gun stations can be manned by players, making it one of the most powerful fliers in the game.

MANTIS

Designation: HRUNTING/YGGDRASIL Mark IX Armor Defense System

Crew Capacity: 1 operator
Primary Armament: Machine Gun
Secondary Armament: Missile Launcher

The Mantis combat mech towers over the battlefield, ruling it through size and firepower of its heavy machine gun and its guided missile launcher. Should enemies draw close, the Mantis can execute a lethal stomp maneuver to clear its surroundings. Unlike most other UNSC land vehicles, the Mantis possesses energy shielding technology, allowing it to weather firepower intended to take down full-sized tanks.

〉 The newest addition to the UNSC arsenal possess awesome killing power, but suffers from a fairly low movement speed. It also takes the longest of all vehicles in the game to recover from the EMP effects of a charged Plasma Pistol shot. Do not let the enemy get the chance to stun your Mantis or you can expect a swift death.

INTRODUCTION

BASIC TRAINING

INTEL

CAMPAIGN

INFINITY

APPENDIX

BROADSWORD

Designation: F-41 Exoatmospheric Multirole Strike Fighter

Crew Capacity: 1 operator
Primary Armament: Autocannon x 2
Secondary Armament: Missile Launcher x 2

A newer UNSC space fighter, the Broadsword contains defensive shielding to withstand the trip into the anti-fighter defenses found on hostile capital ships. Broadswords are capable of carrying Havoc-grade nuclear payloads to ensure enemy capital ship destruction.

❯ Only piloted during the final mission.

MAMMOTH

Designation: Mobile Anti-Aircraft Weapons Platform M510 Siegework/Ultra-Heavy

Crew Capacity: 3 crew, 20–30 passengers
Primary Armament: Magnetic Acceleration Cannon (MAC)
Secondary Armament: Rocket Turret x 2

One of the largest UNSC land vehicle in existence, the Mammoth comes armed with multiple anti-armor/anti-infantry systems, and carries a sizable contingent of ground troops. The most dangerous weapon on a Mammoth is the Magnetic Acceleration Cannon (MAC). Firing a slug at a fraction of the speed of light, the MAC gives the Mammoth the ability to support the destruction of larger vessels.

❯ Appears in Mission 4. Cannot be driven, sadly, but one can dream. You can direct the MAC to fire on air targets, like Phantoms and Banshees using the Target Designator.

GHOST

Designation: T-32 Rapid Attack Vehicle

Crew Capacity: 1 operator
Primary Armament: Plasma Cannon x 2

Ghosts provide rapid transport and close ground combat support for Covenant troops. Ghosts are surprisingly durable for their size, and their overall profile protects drivers from frontal assaults.

❯ The Ghost is a fantastic land vehicle to commandeer. The boost system can help you evade most common land warfare threats while returning fire withe the dual Plasma Cannons.

❯ Can be hijacked from its driver. It's best to disable it with a Plasma Pistol first. Trying to run down a Ghost is futile if they know you're coming.

WRAITH

Designation: T-26 Assault Gun Carriage

Crew Capacity: 1 driver, 1 gunner
Primary Armament: Heavy Plasma Mortar
Secondary Armament: Plasma Cannon

The sight of Wraith's Plasma Mortars falling gracefully onto UNSC positions has become a recurring nightmare for many war veterans. The Wraith is a prime example of Covenant technology, emphasizing extreme firepower in a purple, curved, and armored package. The mounted Plasma Cannon makes approaching from the front difficult. The Wraith's antigravity drive gives the vehicle incredible speed and maneuverability that a Scorpion could only dream about.

❯ Always engage a Wraith from long range if you're in a Scorpion. The Wraith's Plasma Mortar is brutally powerful, particularly on Legendary, where it can one-shot your tank.

❯ If you're in a Warthog, stay on the move. The Wraith's boost system can propel the tank through your Warthog, if its Plasma Cannon hasn't already gutted you, or if a near miss from a Plasma Mortar hasn't already flipped you end over end.

❯ If you are on foot, use a Plasma Pistol to disable the Wraith. You also can get close to the machine, board it, and destroy it with a grenade. If you have no grenades, you can literally punch it to death once you've boarded it. Do not board a Wraith from the front unless the gunner is dead. Otherwise he will just kill you for being a so careless.

INTRODUCTION

BASIC TRAINING

INTEL

CAMPAIGN

INFINITY

APPENDIX

BANSHEE

Designation: T-26 Ground Support Aircraft

Crew Capacity: 1 operator
Primary Armament: Plasma Cannon x 2
Secondary Armament: Fuel Rod Cannon

The unique wailing sound of a Banshee in the air is a warning to take cover. The pilots of these fighters are skilled enough to pick off infantry with the fighter's mounted Plasma Cannons or Fuel Rod Cannon. Although its aerial grace has cost the Banshee armor, shielding, and survivability, the fighter is typically deployed in such numbers that these amenities are not a concern for their commanders.

> Banshees are extremely light on armor. While you're piloting one, you can survive a pounding on Easy and Normal, but on difficulties higher than that it feels like you're flying a paper airplane against flamethrowers.

> The Banshee is capable of special flight maneuvers designed to throw off enemy gunners and fighters. In practice, this works better against the player than it does against the AI. The Covenant pilots have a sixth sense to avoid homing missiles and incoming gunfire, and they can do this while lining up a fuel rod shot or preparing for a Plasma Cannon strafing run.

> If you're trying to bring a Banshee down on foot, the Plasma Pistol is one of the best weapons for the job, if you can lure the craft close. The Rocket Launcher can lock on and kill it in one hit, but the Banshee can easily evade any rockets with one of its special maneuvers. The Plasma Pistol method is preferred, since a disabled Banshee can be hijacked!

PHANTOM

Designation: T-44 Troop Carrier

Crew Capacity: 1 pilot, 1 weapons officer, 20–30 passengers
Primary Armament: Plasma Autocannon
Secondary Armament: Plasma Cannon x 2

A heavily armed and armored dropship that can perform operations on complex terrain, and boarding actions capital ships in and out of atmospheric conditions, Phantom quickly became a feared symbol of Covenant onslaught. For a time, it was the best armed troop transport fielded by the alien collective.

> Phantoms are tough, but not invincible. A Scorpion or a Wraith are equally capable of bringing down a Phantom in short order. A Mantis is also capable of single-handedly bringing down a Phantom, but it has to work harder for it.

> The guns mounted to a Phantom can all be destroyed. If you're in a Scorpion or a Mantis this is a good idea to try, as these vehicles have the hardest time evading the Phantom's attacks.

LICH

Crew Capacity: 1 pilot, 1 weapons officer, 30–40 passengers
Primary Armament: Plasma Autocannon
Secondary Armament: Plasma Cannon x 4

Rarely seen throughout the Human-Covenant War, the Lich is the largest troop transport seen in the Covenant arsenal. Armed with multiple Plasma Cannons and a beam weapon powerful enough to sunder the armor of a Mammoth, the Lich brings an impressive compliment of ground troops to the field.

❯ The only Lich you face in combat is met in Chapter 5, and it's a costly battle to fight. No known weapons can bring the Lich down from the outside. It can only be destroyed from the inside. Boarding the vessel, killing your way through its crew, and then destroying the reactor is no easy task.

INTRODUCTION

BASIC TRAINING

INTEL

CAMPAIGN

INFINITY

APPENDIX

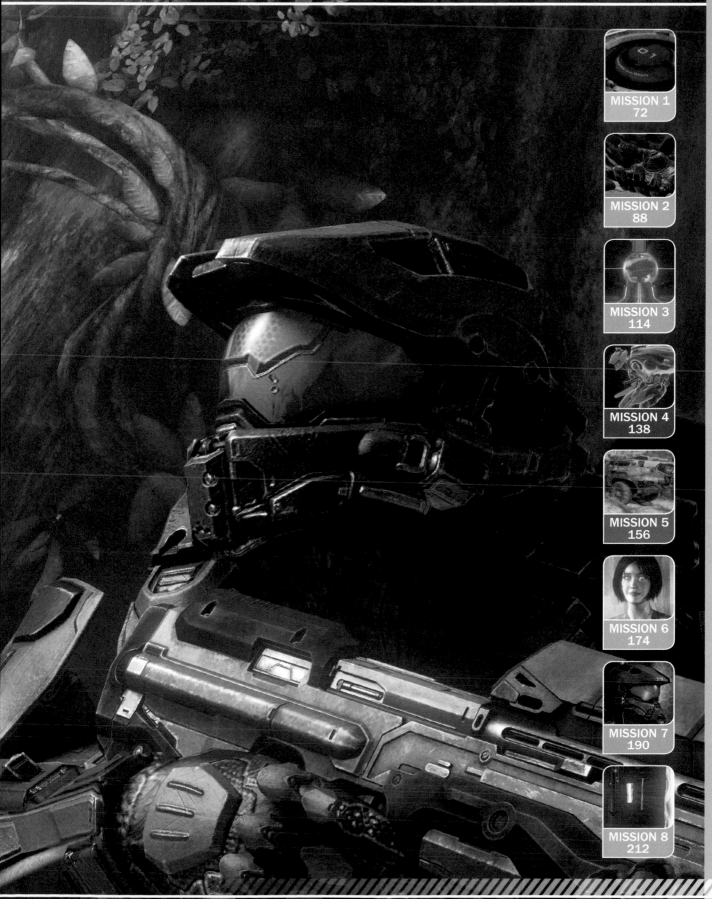

CAMPAIGN

CAMPAIGN

THE CAMPAIGN

Halo 4's Campaign mode consists of eight missions of increasing length, complexity, and challenge. Whether you are a seasoned *Halo* veteran, or rookie making your first foray into this first-person shooter (FPS) franchise, *Halo 4* will provide you with a variety of tactical challenges for all skill levels. As the Master Chief, you will be expected to fight on land and in the sky, fielding any weapon or vehicle you can get your hands on. You will certainly be outnumbered, and definitely outgunned. If you're going to survive, you'll need to know how and when to pick a fight, and how to handle yourself when the fight inevitably comes to you.

When you first begin *Halo 4*, you are able to select from four distinct difficulty settings, allowing you to determine how much of a challenge you want out of the game, or at least to show off how much confidence you have in your abilities. Whether or not that confidence is warranted, the game will determine, with torrential rains of plasma fire and possibly repeated views of the swirling camera angle of death.

Changing the difficulty affects attributes like enemy reactions to immediate danger, the speed in which they decide to act, their overall accuracy, the power of their weapons, the speed their projectiles travel in, how much damage enemies can sustain, and how much they can dish out. There is a marked difference in the overall speed of the game between Easy and Legendary.

Easy

A difficulty suited to players new to the genre or for those with general inexperience with video games, Easy is set up to field the weakest of all enemy types, and the most challenging foe is often only a few steps up the food chain. The Master Chief is more resilient to damage, allowing his shields to absorb enormous levels of punishment before failing, and his own personal vitality is greater than that found on other difficulties. This is a great setting for learning the levels and enemy locations, or for those more interested in the story than in a test of skill.

Normal

You're no longer the sharpest proverbial hot knife cutting through Covenant flesh. Fights against many enemy types have become more tactically demanding, and you can expect to see a greater variety of ranks among them. The enemy becomes tougher, more accurate, and lethal. In particular, enemy snipers become a much greater concern. You'll start to see the benefits of becoming skilled with more weapons than just your favorites. If the difficulty levels stopped at Heroic, this would be a great middle ground for the average FPS player. You're still able to run and gun, but you'll have to dial it back somewhat.

Heroic

The difficulty described across the entire franchise as the way the games are meant to be played, and the setting this guide sets much of its focus upon. Heroic mode is where the gloves have not just come off, they've already been slapped across your face several times. Expect the highest-ranking foes to show up sooner and more often, and expect the lethality of every enemy to have greatly increased. Don't be surprised when a sniper takes you out from beyond your visual range, or when a Ghost runs you down faster than you can react. The enemy will leverage superior numbers and positioning against you to great effectiveness. Make no mistake: Heroic is *hard*, but it is still *fair*. Your mistakes will have amplified consequences, but your deaths here will still definitely be your fault. On easier difficulties, you may have felt comfortable wading into the thick of battle, running head-on into tough foes and putting your fists firmly into faces. This tends only to get you killed faster here. Aggression is still rewarded, but only in measured amounts when correctly and precisely applied.

Legendary

If you're a first-time *Halo* player, we really recommend that you don't start off with Legendary. Even veterans are encouraged to start with Heroic, if only to become better acquainted with the areas you fight through and the locations of all major enemy encounters. Legendary difficulty rewards cautious, methodical players who have learned the lessons taught in other difficulties, and are able to apply them even when the world is crashing down around them. Legendary is not harder because it throws more enemies at you; it's harder because every individual foe provides greater challenge, with the most devious and aggressive tactical mind-set when it comes to dealing with you and any friends you might have with you. This is *Halo 4* at its hardest and fastest. You're going to die, but if you're lucky, it might seem glorious.

Legendary could be confused for some sort of misplaced vendetta the developers have against you, your friends, your family, your controllers, and anything you might throw them into. Your margin for error is incredibly narrow, and you will definitely find yourself relying on some of that luck our Spartan is supposedly blessed with. The hardest enemy ranks come out to play even earlier and more often than they did in Heroic, and they tend to kill you with alarming speed and frequency. Hiding behind cover will become a reflex, and you'll spend a good amount of time doing this in every firefight while waiting for your brief chance to shoot back. You'll be switching guns often, and your emphasis here is definitely not on what you think is cool, but on what is most effective for your current situation.

INTRODUCTION

BASIC TRAINING

INTEL

CAMPAIGN

INFINITY

APPENDIX

> CO-OP CAMPAIGN

A longtime staple of *Halo*, the Campaign can be played with up to four players on the team, working as a precision strike force that can flank the enemy, advance while providing cover fire, and call out to each other trouble spots or surprise enemy attacks. Or they could run at the enemy as a uncoordinated mob, "spot" snipers by letting their friends run out into the open first to get picked off, or "accidentally" stick Plasma Grenades to each other while on the attack. Whichever works.

Co-op in *Halo 4*'s Campaign does not change the story outcome, but it can make certain trouble spots much easier to deal with when you can set up attacks from multiple angles. You can turn up the challenge by activating Skulls, so if Legendary with four players just isn't getting your blood (or rage) pumping, there's options for rock stars like yourself.

> SKULLS

Halo 4 difficulty is comfortably layered into four specific settings, but this is not the only way that players can customize their gameplay experience. Skulls are special difficulty modifiers that provide different effects, typically making the game much harder.

Iron

The Iron Skull disables all forms of quick respawning in the Campaign. In single-player, what this means is that death sends you back to the very beginning of the level. As you might imagine, this Skull can be very frustrating to deal with. In Co-op Campaign, this sends your group *only* to the last checkpoint—nowhere near as crippling as it is in single-player, but this can still be incredibly demoralizing, especially if you're "that guy" who happens to get stuck with a Plasma Grenade just moments before a firefight draws to a successful close. Activating this Skull while playing on Legendary is not for the faint of heart. Don't say we didn't warn you.

Black Eye

As Skulls go, this one isn't the worst, but it still provides a special brand of pain. Black Eye disables the natural shield regeneration of your armor. The only way to recharge your shields is to melee an enemy. Not exactly the friendliest Skull to activate during Heroic or Legendary difficulty, as you'll be having a hard enough time during ranged combat that rushing the enemy to melee them is tantamount to suicide.

Tough Luck

The sixth sense of every enemy receives a healthy boost with this Skull active, ensuring that all enemies will do their best to avoid damage and death. In particular, the Tough Luck Skull vastly reduces the effectiveness of all manner of grenades, as enemies tend to run or dive out of range before the grenade even lands at its intended point. You may get lucky with chain reaction detonations of grenades, or the enemy may dive off a cliff, but don't expect miracles.

Catch

This is the Skull by which you are more likely to catch all manner of grenades (especially Plasma Grenades) with your face. The enemy is certainly not lacking in their chosen favorite explosive, which can turn all firefights into a lethal pyrotechnic display within seconds of contact. Safety no longer is about finding a good spot to hole up, but is now about moving frantically to avoid the blasts from the massive barrage of grenades.

Cloud

Losing your motion sensor is one of the more crippling disadvantages to suffer, and this is exactly what this Skull does. You'll have to keep scanning the area around you all the time if you want to survive, and the enemy is always eager to flank you and any friends you've got with you.

Famine

Weapons dropped both by allies and by enemies fallen in combat contain much less ammunition. Suddenly, every shot counts that much more, as resupplying is more difficult during combat. Careful management of weapon caches, the only source of fully loaded weapons, becomes paramount.

Thunderstorm

Enemies in *Halo 4* come in many types, and there are multiple ranks in each type. The Thunderstorm Skull gives all enemies many promotions. On Legendary, this can lead to whole battlefields filled with the best of the best of every species arrayed against you, armed with even heavier firepower.

Tilt

An interesting Skull that essentially forces players to make the best use of each type of weapon to cause very specific types of damage. With Tilt active, weapons like the Assault Rifle and the DMR become practically useless against shielding of any type. Weapons such as the Storm Rifle and Plasma Pistol become invaluable resources that can strip away these defenses, but lose their utility against actual flesh and metal. This can be mitigated during Co-Op games very easily if you always make sure at least one player has the heaviest energy weapons available to help tear down shielding.

Mythic

In the event the game just wasn't hard enough with other Skulls activated, you can always toggle the Mythic Skull and give all enemies double their standard health. Marvel as Jackals survive multiple Sniper Rifle shots, and Hunters, already known for their ability to soak up damage, eat full loads of grenades and entire magazines of ammo before going down. Sticking Elites with Plasma Grenades no longer guarantees a kill, and you'll even see enemies survive multiple Needler-induced explosions.

> SECONDARY SKULLS

These Skulls provide additional effects that add a little extra flavor to a firefight. Two of these Skulls are definitely more for amusement, while the other two can really up the challenge.

Cowbell

The Cowbell Skull makes all explosions have three times their usual force. A well placed grenade could send a victim flying literally hundreds of feet. As you might imagine, this is very funny to watch. Less amusing is that this applies to any moveable object on the field. Guns can be sent flying out of reach, crates can be launched at lethal velocities through enemies and allies alike. Light vehicles, like the Warthog and the Ghost, become many times less safe to use. Combine this with the Catch Skull, then find a good place to hide.

IWHBYD

This Skull makes all uncommon dialogue more common, while common dialogue becomes rarely heard. You might be surprised at some of the things Marines say in battle!

Blind

Blind takes away all of your HUD elements, and hides your character's arms and the weapon they are holding. This is a very tough Skull to play under, since you can't tell what weapon you have out, or how much ammo you have left. You can somewhat cheat the system by hitting the Back button on your Xbox 360 Controller to see which weapon is equipped, but you still can't determine your ammo levels.

Grunt Birthday Party

The best birthday present for a Grunt is to have them automatically explode like grenades if they are killed without a headshot. This can be averted by scoring a headshot, which causes them to explode into confetti. This Skull is obviously quite amusing, but it can add some danger to any firefight. Suicide Grunts become much more dangerous to deal with if they are in close range and you are not armed with a headshot capable weapon. This is very exploitable to use among large groups of enemies, particularly if the Cowbell Skull is active!

INTRODUCTION

BASIC TRAINING

INTEL

CAMPAIGN

INFINITY

APPENDIX

Across any difficulty, these basics can make the difference between winning a fierce battle, or looking at another panoramic sweep of the area surrounding your virtual corpse. With these hints, you should have a few good ideas on how to approach the war looming over the horizon.

» KEY COMBAT TIPS

Trigger Control: The most important skill is making certain that every time you're pulling the trigger, you're hitting the enemy. Firing wildly isn't just a waste of ammo, it's also not intimidating anyone and doesn't do anything to slow down the enemy. At most, you might get them to dodge behind cover, but you've still wasted ammo. Even the lowliest Grunt on the Heroic difficulty can absorb a decent amount of punishment if you're not making calculated headshots. Remember that simply because a weapon has a high rate of fire doesn't mean it's a good idea to hold down the trigger and cut loose. Even the standard Assault Rifle gets more mileage per magazine if you fire it in controlled bursts.

Conserve Ammunition and Grenades: This is an extension of the previous bit of advice, but it is worth keeping as its own separate hint. Even if you come into a firefight with the weapons you find most effective for the enemies you encounter and a full load of grenades, you still don't carry enough ammo to be totally reckless. Don't throw grenades carelessly if you know they aren't going to be effective, you can carry only two of all three types.

Use the Right Weapons: Part of conserving ammo is also about using the right weapons for the right situation, and on higher difficulties, this becomes ever more important. It's not necessarily as lopsided as when playing with the Tilt Skull activated, but the mind-set that Skull encourages applies to regular gameplay. As a general rule, energy weapons, like the Plasma Pistol, do a better job at stripping away the additional shielding layer that many of your toughest opponents come equipped with. For example: Rather than burning ten shots from a DMR to destroy an Elite's shielding so that you can score that critical headshot, use a charged Plasma Pistol shot to take out the shields and stun the Elite. Then switch to the DMR and land the headshot.

Balance Your Loadout: You can equip whatever you find effective, but a good rule of thumb to follow is to not take two weapons that accomplish more or less the same task. The Storm Rifle shouldn't be paired with the Assault Rifle. Try to have a long-ranged weapon and something else that can perform well at short- to mid-range. At the same time, be willing and prepared to pick up whatever you need off the ground to adjust to new battlefield conditions. As you get farther in the game, you will find that your loadout will become far more fluid as you deal with increasing varieties of hostiles.

Prioritize Your Targets: Combat situations in *Halo 4*, especially on Heroic and Legendary difficulties, bear no small resemblance to a puzzle of sorts—a puzzle that tries to make you explode every five seconds. Try to reduce the number of guns shooting at you as quickly as possible before focusing on hardened targets. For example, when fighting the Covenant, take out Grunts and Jackals early in any firefight. They tend to be the fastest to die when you start to pay attention to them. Elites, while always dangerous, take time to kill, and while you're doing that, the smaller enemies might flank you.

At the same time, recognize opportunities when you see them. Covenant Elites provide leadership to Grunts, and if you kill an Elite near a group of Grunts, this can send them temporarily into a panic, a weakness you can exploit.

Of course, when snipers enter the equation, you want to prioritize and eliminate them as early as you can. Your priorities once again shift around when vehicles come into play, and you'll want to make sure enemies vehicles are destroyed first, or at least made inoperable.

Focus Fire: This tip is definitely geared around Co-Op, but a specific armor ability lets you use it in single-player. As you'll likely discover for yourself when playing alone, having many guns focused on one of you tends to kill you very fast. When you're working with allies, you can turn this on your enemies to take them out quicker. If you're playing by yourself, and you receive the Autosentry armor ability. Its firepower can augment your own, letting you take down hardened targets sooner.

Destroy All Snipers: It cannot be stressed enough: Unless you're safely inside a vehicle where the enemy can't directly hit you, snipers are arguably the greatest threat to your survival while on foot. On Legendary, the Binary Rifle sported by Knight Lancers can put you down in a single shot, and typically they are positioned with a good angle to attempt this. Taking out snipers should be one of your highest priorities while fighting on foot.

Intelligent Assassination: It's tempting to hold down the melee button and start up a lengthy assassination animation on the enemy whenever you're lucky enough to sneak up on one. However, you can get shot and killed while doing this. If you know a lot of enemies are on the field, consider using just a couple of standard melee strikes to your victim's back to minimize the risk you take by getting close. Later on in the game, you may encounter foes for whom a couple love taps to the back will not suffice.

Pick Up Your Visual Scanning: The motion sensor is an invaluable tool when determining your position in relation to the enemy. It has a few drawbacks though. The range is limited to a circle 30 meters around the player. Threats beyond that range must be located with the eyes, and incoming fire tracked back to the source. Enemies that aren't moving or shooting do not appear on the motion sensor. Because of this, you absolutely must keep your head on a swivel. Relying on the tracker alone will just get you killed. Consequently, if the tracker tips you off to an enemy flanking maneuver, adjust your position accordingly and pay attention to what is coming around that corner.

It's not just enemies you need to be on the lookout for. Be aware of any environmental hazards that you can use against the enemy, or that could be used against you. If you're sitting near a pile of grenades, you might want to consider moving away from them until you can pick them up, as a stray blast can set them all off and end you, if you're too close. Explosions from vehicles and canisters also tend to be highly hazardous to your health.

Stay Calm: It's easy to say this, but in practice it can be tough to do. *Halo 4* is a very challenging game on the Heroic and Legendary difficulties. There are many battles later in the game that will feel entirely unfair at first. If you're getting really frustrated or dying repeatedly, take a moment to think about what is going wrong and consult this guide before you try the mission again.

The Campaign Walkthrough divides each mission of the game into specific sections, based on the major checkpoints or areas of the levels. The opening pages of the walkthrough include an overall map of the level, with callouts that show you where hidden data terminals and major firefights are located. A mission briefing provides essential intelligence for the situation you're entering, and what you can expect throughout the mission.

When a level walkthrough begins, the full level map precedes actual walkthrough text. Important points and battle locations are marked to be referenced in the text.

Major Firefight

Map

Mission Briefing

INTRODUCTION

BASIC TRAINING

INTEL

CAMPAIGN

INFINITY

APPENDIX

General combat tips are provided as part of the walkthrough, but when you reach major firefights, the guide goes into more detail. A major firefight is broken down into multiple subsections. We go over the types of enemies to expect at these points, and we discuss which enemies are particularly troublesome and explain why they are priority targets. We'll also recommend a loadout that is effective during that firefight. After you're briefed, we walk you through a general approach to the battle, with special data boxes that suggest alternative actions or threats to focus on as you progress through the fight.

On top of this, we include special tactical advice for Legendary difficulty at each of these major firefights.

» KEY COMBAT TIP

Resist the urge to pick up the Energy Sword! It might be a safer bet on Normal or Easy, but on Heroic and Legendary, the mad rush you must make to get into melee range to use the weapon usually ends with your being stuck by Plasma Grenades or riddled by enemy fire.

General Combat Tips

> RECOMMENDED LOADOUT

A Covenant Carbine and Plasma Pistol are safe and effective weapons to rely on for this fight, though a well-timed super-combine from a Needler barrage can be effective at wiping out groups of enemies, and can set off grenades dropped by the fallen. Just be sure you're not too close to the enemy when setting up the big bang.

Major Firefight Recommended Loadout

Legendary Strategy

This battle might be the first serious wall players face during a Legendary run. Because of the ramped-up health totals, it becomes imperative that you eliminate the Grunts and Jackals as quickly as possible with headshots from a Magnum. This, of course, is much easier to say than to execute, as every enemy on Legendary is more prone to evasive action, and also hits you that much harder. You absolutely need to avoid the possibility of being flanked while dealing with the Elites later, so make sure you've dealt with the small fry entirely first.

Major Firefight Legendary Difficulty

CAMPAIGN

MISSION 1: DAWN

"Wake up, Chief. I need you."

Four years have passed since the Master Chief saved the galaxy from the imminent threat of the Flood and the firing of the ancient Halo Array, a devastating Forerunner weapon that was intended to cleanse the galaxy of all sentient life. His escape from the final battle did not go as planned, and only half of the UNSC frigate *Forward Unto Dawn* made it through slipspace to Earth. The other half, his half, now drifts listlessly through space. His AI companion, Cortana, has stood a lonesome vigil over the war hero as he has slept in cyrogenic stasis, but his well-deserved rest is about to be interrupted.

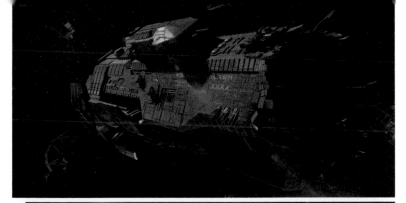

⋀ MISSION BRIEFING

You're given a little time to acclimate yourself to basic movement before being thrust into combat with the Covenant infantry who have boarded the drifting wreck. Your first objective will be to reach the Observation Deck, where you discover the extent of the Covenant presence on and around the *Dawn*. From that point forward, your primary objective is to reach the manual missile launch controls located on the outer hull of the ship. Expect extensive resistance throughout the corridors leading to the outer hull. Dozens of troops, deployed by Phantom dropships, arrive in waves on the outer hull itself. After dealing with the immediate capital ship threat, exit from the *Dawn* as quickly as possible.

ENEMIES ENCOUNTERED:

Elites   Grunts   Jackals

VEHICLES ENCOUNTERED:

Phantom Dropships

WEAPONS ACQUIRED //////////////////
Assault Rifle
Battle Rifle
Magnum
Storm Rifle
Plasma Pistol
Needler
Covenant Carbine
Concussion Rifle
Beam Rifle

INTRODUCTION

BASIC TRAINING

INTEL

CAMPAIGN

INFINITY

APPENDIX

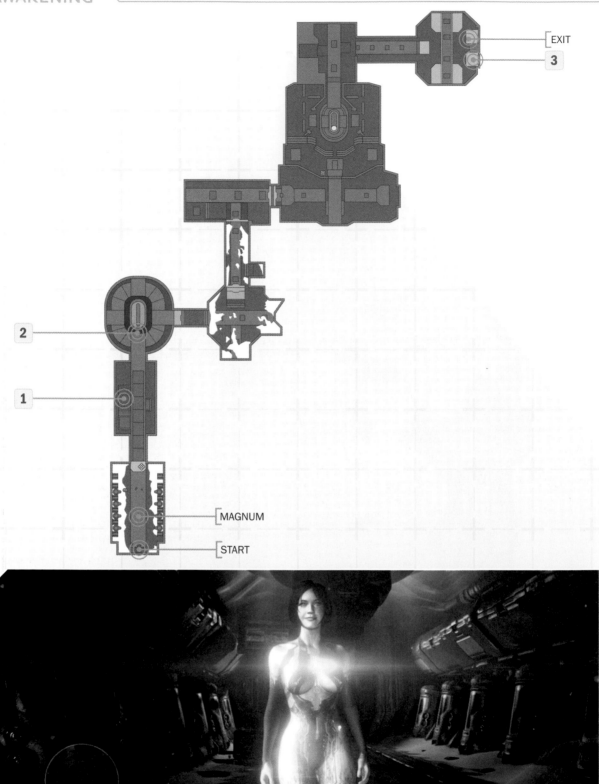

EXIT

3

2

1

MAGNUM

START

Cortana's voice is filled with a hint of fear or possibly desperation when she awakens the Master Chief. Follow her instructions: Look up to the top of your cryo chamber and press the X button to yank on the emergency release and leave the chamber. The Master Chief automatically walks over to Cortana's AI plinth and places her storage chip back inside his helmet. The pair are properly reunited once more. Your current mission is to get to the Observation Deck to investigate intruder alerts being triggered throughout the *Dawn*. As you leave, don't miss picking up the Magnum pistol from the floor near the cryotube.

HALO 4

WEAPON ACQUISITION

ASSAULT RIFLE

A staple weapon of the UNSC and the one the Master Chief starts with. The Assault Rifle boasts a 32-round magazine and a fire rate that can empty it in seconds. While the weapon is capable of fully automatic fire, the Assault Rifle performs better at longer ranges when fired in controlled bursts. A workhorse weapon, the Assault Rifle can be used adequately against shielded or unshielded targets, should they stay still long enough for a magazine to be dumped into them.

MAGNUM

The Magnum is a powerful pistol that comes with a 2x scope linked directly to the Master Chief's helmet. It's your first sniping weapon, and has plenty of stopping power to fulfill that role. A headshot from this pistol can instantly kill enemies like Grunts or unshielded Elites. Skilled operators can score a kill with each shot in the magazine. Used in conjunction with the Plasma Pistol to break the shielding of any enemy, the Magnum can be a devastating weapon to keep handy.

1 There are some interesting information panels you can inspect on the way to the Observation Deck. The first is located just outside of the cryo chamber. You'll see a set of stairs leading down to a small room with a computer console. Using the console lets you listen to a very abridged version of the Master Chief's accomplishments throughout the Halo series. **2** Back up on the main floor, you will find a computer generated hologram of what remains of the *Forward Unto Dawn*. A control panel lets you inspect the ship's systems. The *Dawn* is in very bad shape.

You'll pass a holographic navigation map as you proceed, showing the *Dawn* being pulled toward a planet of some kind. At the same time, a powerful light phases through the whole ship. Something is scanning the vessel, but you can't even begin to get some answers until you reach Observation.

FORWARD UNTO DAWN

A UNSC frigate assigned to Commander Miranda Keyes. In the closing days of the Human-Covenant War, the *Dawn* played a critical role in ferrying the Master Chief to the Ark to prevent the full Halo Array from firing and put an end to the Flood threat. The Master Chief and his AI partner Cortana are the only remaining crew members aboard the ruined vessel.

3 Past the navigation map, you reach a sealed elevator door and are prompted to pull it open. The portion of the ship beyond it has been depressurized, sucking air and debris out into space and nearly taking the Master Chief with it. Follow the prompts to pull the Master Chief up the walls toward safety. When he turns his head to the left or right, that is your cue to move the analogue stick in that direction to avoid falling debris.

You reach relative safety at the top of the shaft, only to be accosted by an Elite armed with a Energy Sword. Follow the melee prompt to end the Elite's life. After killing the ambusher, the Master Chief pulls himself up into a corridor that faces the Observation Deck.

ENEMY ENCOUNTER

ELITES

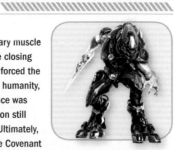

Although they were once the military muscle of the Covenant, events during the closing days of the Human-Covenant War forced the Sangheili to seek an alliance with humanity, betraying the Covenant. The alliance was formed out of necessity, and tension still remained between both species. Ultimately, the alliance managed to break the Covenant Empire after costly battles. The surprise attack on the Master Chief suggests that much has changed in the four years that followed the end of the war.

This is your first real fight against a Covenant force. After you overwhelm the group found on the deck, reinforcements soon crash their way into Observation from two separate Phantom dropships. A bad position can have you planted firmly in the center of a pincer attack, which on Heroic and Legendary is a good way to earn a quick dirt nap.

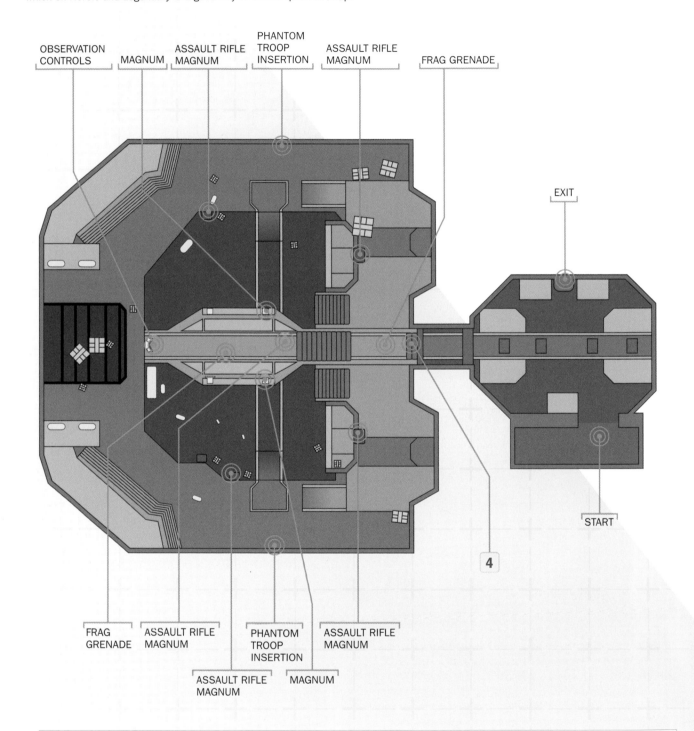

OBSERVATION CONTROLS

MAGNUM

ASSAULT RIFLE MAGNUM

PHANTOM TROOP INSERTION

ASSAULT RIFLE MAGNUM

FRAG GRENADE

EXIT

START

4

FRAG GRENADE

ASSAULT RIFLE MAGNUM

ASSAULT RIFLE MAGNUM

PHANTOM TROOP INSERTION

MAGNUM

ASSAULT RIFLE MAGNUM

> RECOMMENDED LOADOUT

Unless you love blue LED displays with ammo counters, you should replace your Assault Rifle immediately with a Plasma Pistol and use it in conjunction with a Magnum. Charged Plasma Pistol shots destroy Elite shields instantly, and while the Elites stagger, you can switch to the Magnum and score a lethal headshot. You can find Magnum pistols on racks mounted below the platform where the first Elite stands; there's plenty of ammo to keep the weapon restocked, if needed.

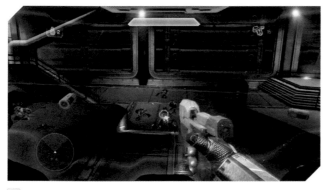

4 You enter the Observation Deck facing a set of stairs leading up to the controls that open the protective shields so that you can look outside. At the top of the stairs, near the controls, an Elite stands with his back turned to you. A squad of Grunts patrols the lower area. Crouch to avoid detection and sneak up on the Elite. Hold down the Melee Attack button to perform an assassination and instantly kill him. His death will not go unnoticed, and the Grunts on the lower level then attack you with Plasma Pistols. Drop down and eliminate them.

Alternate Approach

You can take out the Grunts by sitting on the upper level and shooting them with your Assault Rifle, Magnum, or the Storm Rifle dropped by the Elite. There are also Frag Grenades on the upper level, which can be used to great effect on the Grunts, but you may want to save these for the next wave.

WEAPON ACQUISITION

FRAG GRENADES

Pull the pin, toss, wait a few seconds, listen to the boom. The standard issue Frag Grenade has proven its worth against the Covenant across multiple battlefields, and it still is an effective weapon now.

The powerful detonation of a Frag Grenade can kill or seriously wound most unshielded foes. Elites and other shielded targets are spared the worst damage from a grenade until their shields are down.

STORM RIFLE

Successor to the old Plasma Rifle, the Storm Rifle is the Covenant response to the MA5 series of UNSC assault rifles. It boasts a high rate of plasma

fire that shreds shielding quickly. Unfortunately, it also suffers the same accuracy issues the Assault Rifle does when fired at full auto, with its other disadvantage of being subject to overheating, which forces you to stop firing for a moment while the weapon cools. The other problem is that the Storm Rifle, like other plasma-based Covenant weapons, cannot be reloaded. Once a Storm Rifle is out of power, you need to find a replacement weapon.

PLASMA PISTOL

A classic Covenant weapon, the Plasma Pistol offers a rate of fire that is almost as fast as one can pull the trigger, and it is devastating to shielding systems. But the real draw of this weapon is the ability to

charge and fire a shot that can home in on a target, immediately destroying the shields of opponents like the Elites. As an added bonus, the charged shot provides an EMP effect that temporarily disables vehicles struck by it.

INTRODUCTION

BASIC TRAINING

INTEL

CAMPAIGN

INFINITY

APPENDIX

You have time to resupply when the room is cleared, so take a look around and scavenge what you think will be useful. After you're armed up, go to the controls to open up the Observation Deck, discover a stunning and possibly demoralizing sight, and get ready for the next wave of enemies.

Two Phantom dropships float into view just outside of the Observation Deck, before moving to flank the room. After breaking the glass to insert docking tubes, two squads of Grunts leap onto the deck, each led by an Elite. Try to take out the Elites first to incite panic among the Grunts. Focus on one group first. Ideally, you will have weakened or killed off one of the squads entirely before the second squad has a chance to spread out behind you. By the time you deal with the first team, the second will be spreading out across the deck, which means the other Elite that dropped could be quite close. Seek him out and remove him from the picture, then finish off the Grunts. Once the room is clear, Cortana chimes in with more bad news. A Covenant cruiser is en route, and the only defenses the *Dawn* has left are Hyperion missiles that must be fired from a control station on the outer hull.

Alternate Approach

After the dropships insert their docking tubes into the Observation Deck, if you post yourself right next to one of them with your back to the tube entrance, the Covenant tend to jump down right in front of you. This can be used to set up a quick assassination of one of the Elites. Be careful, as the panic incited by killing the Elite right away may cause one or more of the Grunts accompanying him to attempt a suicide grenade rush against you, and they are all in close proximity if you use this approach.

GRUNTS

Short, squat, brave when sufficiently inspired, and suicidal when the chips are down, Grunts make up the bulk of the Covenant's armies. Despite their short stature and required methane supply, they can be surprisingly durable. Grunts are versatile and can pilot certain Covenant vehicles or man gun emplacements in an effort to stop you. Grunts can and will attempt suicidal charges if they are sufficiently wounded, terrified, or just plain driven, arming a pair of Plasma Grenades and running straight at potential victims.

Legendary Strategy

You'll probably follow similar tactics to what you used on Heroic, but this time your enemies will be considerably more resilient and harder hitting. Start off by assassinating the first Elite, then go to work on the Grunts below. The second wave is where things get a little hairy.

Don't forget about the Frag Grenades you can procure throughout the room. When the Phantoms deploy their docking tubes through the glass, it's still a good idea to saturate the areas troops are being deployed at with grenades. Strongly consider using a Plasma Pistol and Magnum combo to break their shields, followed by a swift headshot. The Magnum gets a lot of mileage simply because it's so effective at popping heads quickly. Always remember, head shots are the key to Legendary.

TO NEXT
SECTION

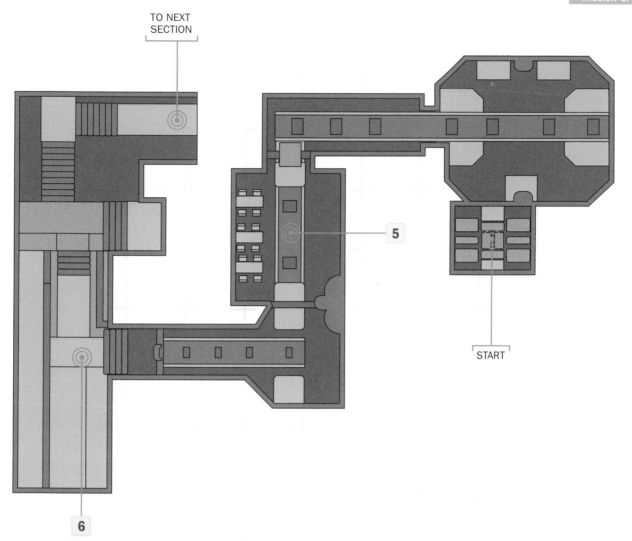

5

START

6

INTRODUCTION

BASIC TRAINING

INTEL

CAMPAIGN

INFINITY

APPENDIX

5 Just past this door, you encounter a pair of Grunts with their backs turned to you, with an Elite at the other end of the hall looking right at you. You can use a Frag Grenade to try to take out the Grunts, but the Elite is more likely to evade a frag. You might luck out and find some Plasma Grenades among the corpses of this group, as well as some Needlers. Past this group of enemies is another corridor with a sealed door that opens when you approach.

WEAPON ACQUISITION //////////////////////////////

PLASMA GRENADES

The Plasma Grenade is an especially devious explosive. The latent plasma charge produces a blue glow when armed. After it's thrown, a Plasma Grenade can bond with targets, giving victims a moment to consider just how doomed they are before detonation.

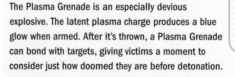

NEEDLER

The Needler is a unique Covenant weapon that fires energized crystals that can home in on designated targets. The needles bounce off most surfaces and easily burrow into flesh, detonating after a short delay. A Needler's true effectiveness can be seen after a target has been struck by enough needles, which results in a much larger and more lethal explosion.

6 Another Elite and a squad of Grunts awaits on the other side. Try to take out this Elite quickly, as it will try to retreat farther into the ship and join up with another Covenant squad. A Needler can help you cut down the Elite quickly on Heroic or Legendary. The Grunts, living or dead, may act as his shields against the needles, so be careful.

7 Another Elite at the end of this corridor is the leader of a Grunt team. You can use the large shipping container **8** in the corridor as cover, but be aware that large explosions can shift this container around. The Covenant are also experts at throwing Plasma Grenades over the container to try to stick you. After killing the Elite, execute any surviving Grunts.

After dealing with the enemy at point **8** , you enter a room that has a rack filled with Assault Rifles and Magnums, along with some  Frag Grenades. **9** This last group of Grunts lead by an Elite is joined by a pair of shield-equipped Jackals. This is an especially dangerous encounter if you stick too close to the enemy, and often they refuse to chase you deeper into the ship, electing instead to hold this position. Some of the Covenant here come armed with Needlers, which makes cover absolutely essential. After this firefight, a checkpoint will be activated.

Legendary Strategy

9 The final squad in this chain can be very tough if you're unprepared on Legendary difficulty. It's close quarters with fairly little room to maneuver, which can lead to quick deaths if you're unlucky. Try to enter this battle with an Magnum and a Plasma Pistol, if only to wipe out the Elite immediately. If there are still Needlers available from previous battles, consider going back and snagging those in exchange for the Plasma Pistol. The super-combine explosions from a Needler barrage can take out multiple Grunts. When the Jackals make their appearance, remember that the Magnum can put them down in two shots: one to the exposed hand that's holding their weapon, which causes them to move their shield, and another to their head as they stagger from the first shot.

ENEMY ENCOUNTER /////////////////////////

JACKALS

A client race of the Covenant, Jackals are skilled and crafty fighters in their own right. They provide a mix of long-ranged combat expertise and tenacious frontline support to their fellow Covenant. The energy shields wielded by many Jackals provide sturdy protection to incoming weapons fire, and are even capable of resisting grenade blasts  before giving out. Jackal Rangers and Jackal Snipers are notorious for their accurate shooting, and can be the source of major headaches on high Campaign difficulties.

> MAJOR FIREFIGHT: BEFORE THE AIR LOCK

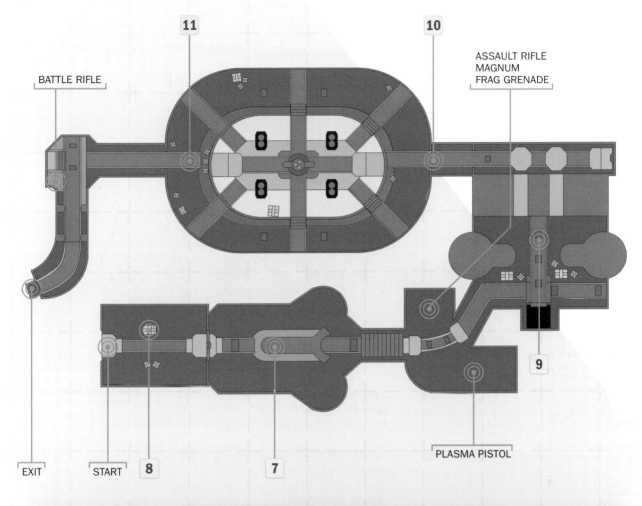

BATTLE RIFLE

11

10

ASSAULT RIFLE
MAGNUM
FRAG GRENADE

9

PLASMA PISTOL

EXIT

START

8

7

INTRODUCTION

BASIC TRAINING

INTEL

CAMPAIGN

INFINITY

APPENDIX

HOLD Ⓧ TO PICK UP ASSAULT RIFLE

10 The large room just before you reach the air lock to the outer hull is divided into two sections: a room within an outer ring. There are four points of access between the outer ring and inner room. Cover dots both sections, but the inner room is not a safe place to try to hole up, due to the fact that enemies can use the outer ring to flank you from multiple directions simultaneously.

A large squad of Grunts start off patrolling the central area, with shield-equipped Jackals in the outer ring. The real threat holds position near the air locks you need to pass through—a trio of Elites. Fortunately, if you play your cards right, you can avoid engaging them until you've cleared out the vast majority of the other enemies.

Because of the large numbers of threats you'll be facing in relatively close proximity, you'll want to have a quick and efficient way to cut them down, and the Magnum pistol is perfect for wiping out the Grunts and Jackals. When dealing with the Elites, you'll be drawing them out one by one ideally, so a Plasma Pistol is a good secondary weapon to deal with their shielding.

Start the party by engaging the Grunts in the central area. If you move fast when starting this encounter, you might catch the Jackals there as well. Avoid charging into the central area until you've ensured that you have sufficiently cleared it of threats.

11 The three Elites steadfastly try to stay near the exit to the air lock you need to pass through. It is possible to draw them off one at a time. It's best if you can avoid getting them to join up with the other Covenant in the room, so don't pursue any retreating stragglers toward them. One of the Elites may be armed with a Concussion Rifle. If that's the case, make sure you know your surroundings well enough that you're able to retreat while facing him. Trying to stand your ground against that level of firepower is not a good call.

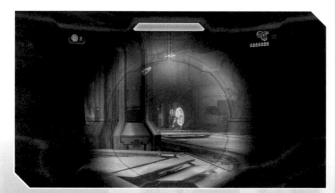

The Jackals have a tendency to retreat to the outer ring. If they start to fall back toward **11**, don't pursue them recklessly, as that is where the Elites are holding court.

WEAPON ACQUISITION

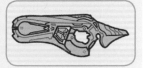

CONCUSSION RIFLE

The Concussion Rifle fires explosive bolts that can send victims flying a fair distance away, and is also capable of setting off grenades that have been dropped on the ground. While not a particularly common weapon to see among the Covenant, when these weapons are on the field, take notice. The Master Chief's shields can withstand a few near impacts, but direct hits are ruinous to them. The push-back effect of the concussion shots can also completely halt your forward movement, temporarily stunning you and leaving you vulnerable to follow-up shots.

Legendary Strategy

This battle might be the first serious wall players face during a Legendary run. Because of the ramped-up health totals, it becomes imperative that you eliminate the Grunts and Jackals as quickly as possible with headshots from a Magnum. This, of course, is much easier to say than to execute, as every enemy on Legendary is more prone to evasive action, and also hits you that much harder. You absolutely need to avoid the possibility of being flanked while dealing with the Elites later, so make sure you've dealt with the small fry entirely first.

In the aftermath of this fight, proceed toward the air lock, but don't miss out on the Battle Rifles that appear on wall mounts. If you've kept your Magnum this whole time, now's the time to part with it. You're going to need the Battle Rifle's superior ranged capability as soon as you exit the air lock.

WEAPON ACQUISITION

BATTLE RIFLE

A prominent UNSC weapon that saw heavy use when the Human-Covenant War finally reached Earth, the Battle Rifle is a weapon that excels in the hands of a skilled operator at nearly any range. The three shot burst from a Battle Rifle can deliver lethal headshots on all manner of Covenant foes. Against shielded Elites, the Battle Rifle loses a bit of its punch, but it can make dealing with them that much easier at range. The recoil from each burst can let you "walk" the weapon up the length of an Elite to score a headshot.

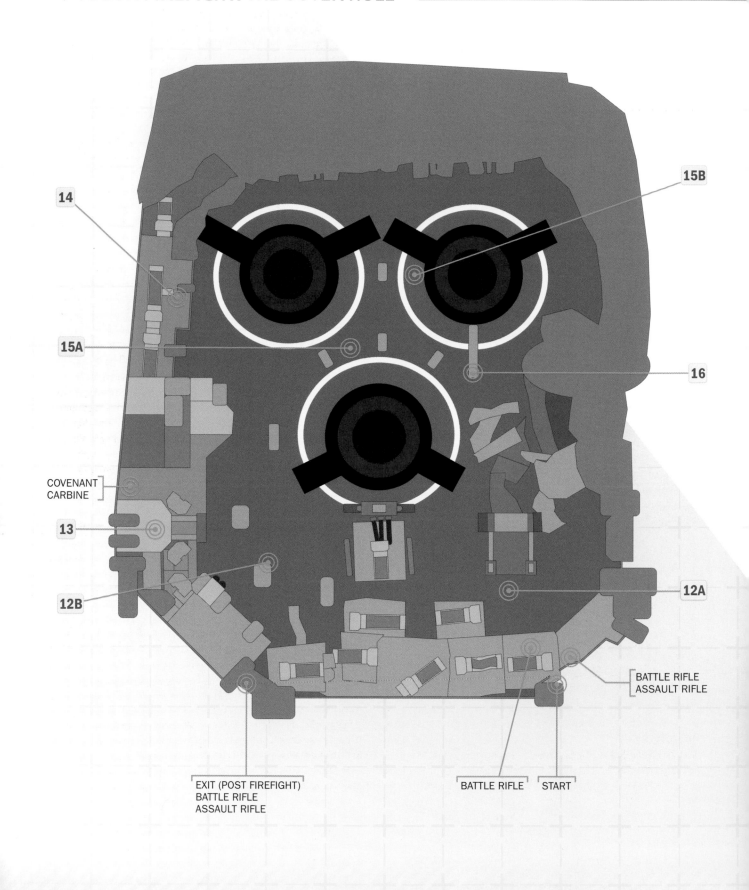

14

15B

15A

16

COVENANT
CARBINE

13

12B

12A

BATTLE RIFLE
ASSAULT RIFLE

EXIT (POST FIREFIGHT)
BATTLE RIFLE
ASSAULT RIFLE

BATTLE RIFLE   START

12A **13** **14** **15A** **15B** **16** Soak in the sight of the ruined hull, the enormous planet in the distance, and the Covenant fleet hovering ominously nearby, then get ready to go to work. The climactic battle that leads to the firing the Hyperion missile is divided into two phases. As you step out from the air lock, a pair of Phantoms drop off Covenant troops on the lower section of the hull, while Jackal Rangers snipe from the walkways on the other side of the hull from where you enter. After you fight your way to the launch controls and fire the weapon, more Phantoms drop off Covenant reinforcements near the missile tube, and they're intent on stopping you from completing your mission. Be aware that the outer hull is a low-gravity environment, which makes your jumps much floatier than usual. Dead enemies will float away from the hull, and so will their weapons, which makes rearming with Covie weapons a bit tougher than usual.

> RECOMMENDED LOADOUT

The Battle Rifle will serve you well throughout this firefight, and there are racks that contain more ammo for the weapon, so you can stay well stocked for the duration of the fighting. Jackal Snipers are carrying the Covenant Carbine, which can make a good weapon to switch the Battle Rifle out for if the ammo runs low. The long ranges can potentially make the Plasma Pistol less reliable for dealing with Elites, but it should still be considered if you come across an Elite in close range. A Storm Rifle is also a good compromise.

The battle starts as soon as you set foot onto the outer hull. Phantom dropships begin off-loading troops at points marked **12A** and **12B** on the map, while Jackals snipe from position marked **13** .

ENEMY ENCOUNTER \\\

PHANTOM

The iconic dropship that became the symbol for the terror the Covenant visited upon countless battlefields. Special attention must be paid to Phantoms every time they appear in a battle. Their nose-mounted cannon and side-mounted plasma turrets can put a swift end to careless soldiers who are not aware of the Phantom's position. Most Phantom pilots loiter over the battlefield long enough to provide some fire support to the troops they've just deposited upon the enemy doorstep, which makes for a lethal combined arms assault.

The dropship closest to where you start leaves behind Grunts and shield-equipped Jackals, while the far ship drops off the same, along with a pair of Elites. More Elites can be found along the walkway where the snipers are positioned, and that walkway happens to be where you need to go to reach the missile controls.

You must find some way to deal with the Jackal Rangers before engaging anyone else, and there's a couple of ways to do that. You can stick near the air lock you came from, using the nearby walls on the walkway for cover. Once you spot the snipers, the Battle Rifle can snipe them, even if the target reticle doesn't turn red to indicate a valid target. With the snipers down, you can more safely take on the dropship team at **12A** .

It's also possible just to rush the first dropship team, sticking them with Plasma Grenades if you've got them, and hosing the rest down with the Battle Rifle. This has the obvious drawback of exposing you to their guns, and the Phantom, if it's still nearby, may join in with its own firepower. The snipers may also have a line of sight, but there are structures scattered throughout the hull that may interfere. You can use this to your advantage while clearing out the hostiles at **12B** , but beware the Elites that join the fun here.

Another option is to stick to the upper walkway and try to work your way along this perimeter toward the snipers, using the elevated position to cut down the Covenant stalking the lower hull. You'll still want to wipe out the snipers early on, along with any shield-equipped Jackals that join them on the walkway, but this keeps you relatively safe from the dropship troops.

INTRODUCTION

BASIC TRAINING

INTEL

CAMPAIGN

INFINITY

APPENDIX

COVENANT CARBINE

The Covenant Carbine is the Covenant answer to the Battle Rifle, and it fills the same role as the Battle Rifle. The weapon enjoys slightly greater effectiveness per round against shielding, but requires a bit more skill to get the most out of it. The three-shot burst from a Battle Rifle ultimately does more damage, and makes it easier to get results against moving opponents, while the Covenant Carbine is a proper semi-automatic weapon that fires one shot per trigger pull.

The controls at 14 , as well as the walkway leading to them, will have more Jackals and an Elite guarding it. Once they've been dealt with, fire the Hyperion missile!

It would be just too easy if there weren't complications. The missile is stuck in the launch tube, and you need to go over to the tube and force the launch doors open completely. Around this time, more Phantoms show up, intent on deploying troops at 15A and 15B . The hostiles closest to the missile silo 16 will include Elites. It's possible to flank them using the walkway to take a long walk around the perimeter, and get closer to the missile safely, sniping as you go with the Battle Rifle. Trying to fight straight through them is possible, but quite risky should you get outmaneuvered.

Alternate Approach

If you're fast, and start making your way to the missile the moment you trigger it to fire, you might be able to reach the stuck release clamp just before the enemy reinforcements arrive. However, you must sprint as much as possible over to the clamp, otherwise the Phantoms will not only be dropping off troops, they'll also likely have spotted you and will turn their cannons on you.

Legendary Strategy

Caution is the order of the day. Having so many enemies spread out over such ranges can be nightmarish to deal with, particularly the snipers. The big difference here is that the Jackal Rangers may come equipped with powerful Beam Rifles. Because of the danger presented by those rifles, you want to use the Battle Rifle to take out the snipers as early as possible. Sticking to the upper walkway, near where you first cross onto the outer hull, is a safe way to reduce the effectiveness of the snipers while dealing with the troops on the lower hull. Above all else, proceed methodically to ensure that you haven't left any potential threats to flank you. Don't forget the low-g nature of the environment, and avoid making careless jumps out in the open, lest you get cut to pieces by anyone who can draw a bead on you.

To speed things up after attempting to fire the missile, you can still rush quickly over to the missile tube to trigger the final launch sequence. This isn't as easy as it may have been on easier difficulties, as the Phantoms have much longer detection ranges. They'll start peppering you vicinity with plasma quickly, and if you get stuck on any terrain, they will zero in on you. The troops they deploy also react to you much sooner when they get their feet onto the deck.

After manually triggering the missile launch, watch as the missile travels on target to the Covenant cruiser. However, you merely exchange one problem for another, as a bright light issues forth from the planet in the distance, scanning across the Master Chief. Moments later, the planet appears to open up and starts sucking in Covenant vessels, the *Dawn*, and anything else not tied down

into the widening maw. You need to get back inside your ship and find an escape pod, now! Watch out for debris flying off the hull of the ship toward the planet; it can seriously harm or kill you. Once you get back to the designated air lock, it takes a moment to cycle before letting you proceed forward.

A blast has taken out a portion of the deck here. You'll need to sprint to be able to make the jump across the gap. There's a wounded Elite and some Grunts in the corridor just beyond the gap. Use melee attacks to quickly shove your way past the Covies and get to the vehicles bay, where the escape pods await.

As you run back through the *Dawn*, you'll enter this chamber with a quartet of Grunts trying to make their own escape. A portion of the roof collapses in on them, sending them to the lower levels. Try to stay on the upper level once the explosions subside. If you take the upper route, you'll enter the next chamber that is filled with more Covenant, all of whom are conveniently dealt with as the ship continues to implode all around you. If you fall to the lower deck, proceed with caution to avoid getting crushed when the upper decks inevitably fail.

Unfortunately for the Master Chief and Cortana, their great escape doesn't go exactly as planned.

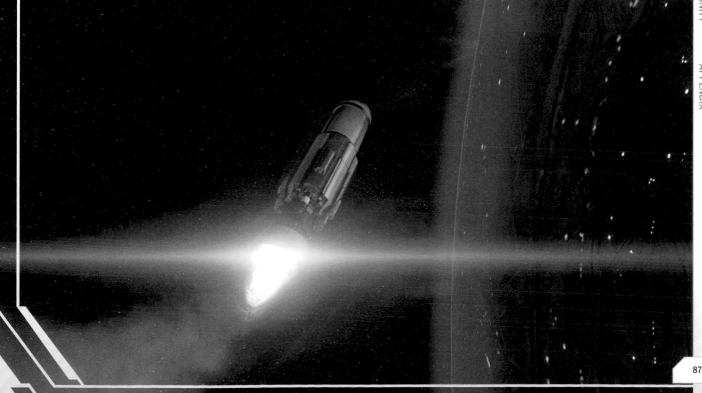

CAMPAIGN

MISSION 2: REQUIEM

"I was put into service eight years ago. AIs deteriorate after seven, Chief."

Against all odds, the Master Chief survived entering the planet's atmosphere and the ensuing tumble through the sky down to the ground, accompanied by the remains of the *Dawn* and a massive portion of the Covenant fleet. Waking inside of the new graveyard of ships and souls, the Master Chief and Cortana are stranded in a new environment, without any support. It soon becomes apparent that Covenant forces have survived the unexpected disaster in great numbers, but this new challenge only signifies an opportunity to the pair; the Covenant presence means that there may be plenty of ships to hijack for a trip back to Earth. They must hurry, for Cortana is falling toward a condition known as rampancy, and only her creator may be able to save her now.

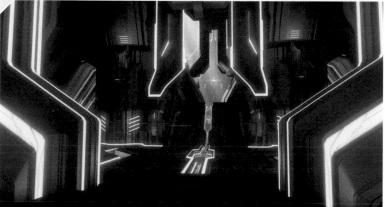

⌃ MISSION BRIEFING

After escaping the initial crash site, acquire a means of transport and prepare to perform some aggressive reconnaissance. The Covenant have moved quickly to take advantage of the opening in the planet's outer surface, deploying infantry throughout the canyons leading away from your starting location. After you push through the enemy defenses to reach a Forerunner facility, the Cartographer found within reveals that a UNSC ship, the *Infinity*, may already be on this planet. You'll cross over a bridge linking the Cartographer facility to a terminus that contains a transport system that will hopefully lead to a way off the planet.

ENEMIES ENCOUNTERED:

| Elites | Grunts | Jackals | Hunters |

VEHICLES ENCOUNTERED:

| Shade Turrets | Ghosts | Banshees |

Phantom Dropships

WEAPONS ACQUIRED
Assault Rifle
Battle Rifle
Magnum
Storm Rifle
Plasma Pistol
Needler
Covenant Carbine
Concussion Rifle
Fuel Rod Cannon
Beam Rifle
SAW
Sniper Rifle
Rocket Launcher

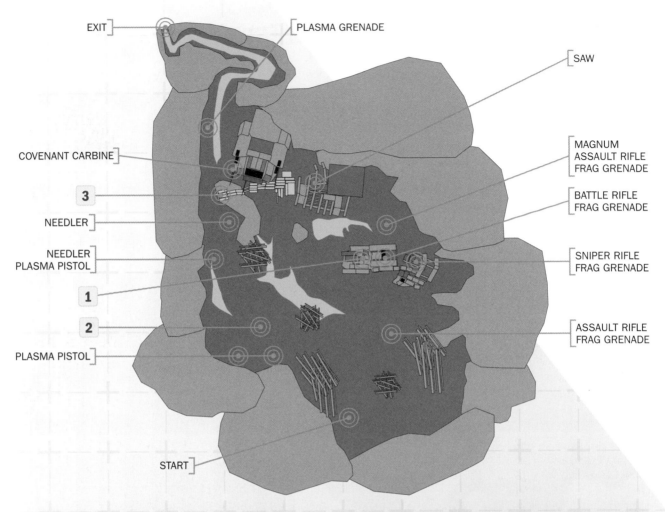

EXIT

PLASMA GRENADE

SAW

COVENANT CARBINE

MAGNUM
ASSAULT RIFLE
FRAG GRENADE

3

BATTLE RIFLE
FRAG GRENADE

NEEDLER

NEEDLER
PLASMA PISTOL

SNIPER RIFLE
FRAG GRENADE

1

2

ASSAULT RIFLE
FRAG GRENADE

PLASMA PISTOL

START

The Master Chief starts off with an Assault Rifle and a Magnum. Fortunately, the shattered vessels that crashed down all around him came with an arsenal of weapons, both human and Covenant. While exploring the destruction, there are three data terminals 1 2 3 you can reach, and each provides some new information about your current situation. Cortana's translations of Covenant transmissions reveal that their fleet hovered outside of the planet's shell for *three years* before the incident that occurred minutes ago gave them access. It seems patience and misguided piety go hand in hand.

You can find a variety of weapons among the wreckage. Terminal **1** is found inside a portion of the *Dawn* that you can climb onto, revealing weapons like the Sniper Rifle and the Battle Rifle. Next to terminal **3** a set of Covenant Carbines can be found, an excellent complement to the smattering of Storm Rifles and Plasma Pistols in the area. You can even find a Fuel Rod Cannon among the Grunt corpses in the area. If you follow the makeshift bridge from this terminal into another portion of the wrecked *Dawn,* you can find a SAW with a full load of ammo. If you're interested in a direct upgrade to your Assault Rifle, this is more than acceptable. Just be aware that you're not going to find a whole lot of spare ammo for this weapon. As you explore the wrecks, you might encounter Covenant survivors of the crash. These guys are hardly in condition to fight, much less even be standing.

WEAPON ACQUISITION

SAW

Combining a high rate of fire and a high capacity magazine, the SAW (Squad Automatic Weapon) can shred most infantry defenses because of the sheer volume of lead it spews. Unfortunately, caches containing spare ammunition for the SAW are somewhat rare. If the UNSC had an established presence on this world, perhaps it could remain a reliable addition to your arsenal.

WEAPON ACQUISITION

SNIPER RIFLE

Firing fin-stabilized, high-caliber rounds designed to penetrate light armor and most known forms of infantry protection, the Sniper Rifle has enough power to penetrate the protective shielding on an Elite or a Spartan to score a hard kill in a single shot. Each box magazine holds four shots, and the rifle can be fired rapidly with minimal recoil even by standard human infantry, which makes it a very dangerous weapon to be on the wrong side of.

To leave the ship graveyard, you'll need to follow a tunnel in the direction the Master Chief faces at the start, through a winding canyon.

INTRODUCTION

BASIC TRAINING

INTEL

CAMPAIGN

INFINITY

APPENDIX

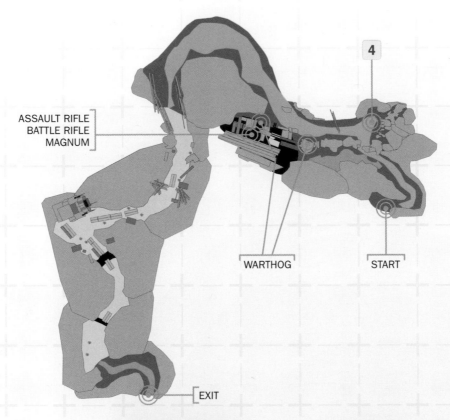

ASSAULT RIFLE
BATTLE RIFLE
MAGNUM

4

WARTHOG

START

EXIT

4 Take in the staggering vista, then proceed along the cliff edge to reach another part of the fallen *Dawn*. The Warthogs here will definitely come in handy, and there are enough to carry four players in a full Co-op session. The path winds through more remains of your ship but is more or less a simple and safe drive— safe, at least until you reach a box canyon filled with rocky side paths and a trio of Covenant outposts with Covenant watchtowers.

VEHICLE ENCOUNTER

WARTHOG

A lightly armored troop transport best known as a dependable and adaptable combat vehicle. The Warthog saw service on the front lines of every important battle in the Human-Covenant War, consistently meeting the demands thrust upon it. These Warthogs come equipped with heavy Machine Gun turrets, but other variants of the Warthog exist, armed with Gauss Cannons or Rocket Launchers.

> MAJOR FIREFIGHT: THE OUTPOST CANYON

INTRODUCTION

BASIC TRAINING

INTEL

CAMPAIGN

INFINITY

APPENDIX

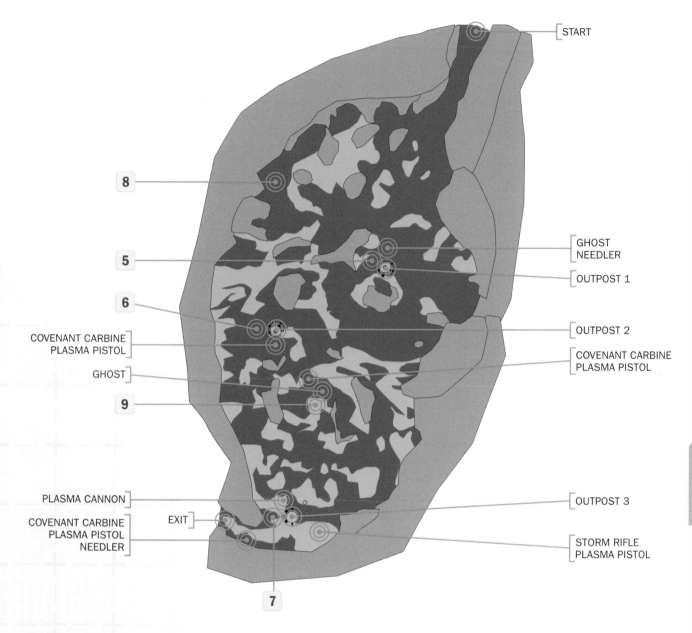

START

8

GHOST
NEEDLER

5

OUTPOST 1

6

OUTPOST 2

COVENANT CARBINE
PLASMA PISTOL

COVENANT CARBINE
PLASMA PISTOL

GHOST

9

PLASMA CANNON

OUTPOST 3

COVENANT CARBINE
PLASMA PISTOL
NEEDLER

EXIT

STORM RIFLE
PLASMA PISTOL

7

The Covenant have wasted no time establishing an extensive presence throughout this world. Three Covenant watchtowers dot the canyon at locations 5 , 6 , and 7 , where the enemy will be most concentrated. You'll likely have arrived just in time to see Phantoms dropping off Covenant troops across the entire area, Elites of various ranks in command of a wide assortment of Grunts and Jackals. This firefight introduces the Ghost as a new factor to consider in combat. You're significantly outnumbered, as always, but fortunately you've got a lot of say on how you can approach this situation. It's even possible to ignore two of the outposts altogether if you move quickly enough.

> RECOMMENDED LOADOUT

The Covenant Carbine you should have picked up at the ship graveyard will serve you incredibly well here, but if you skipped it, you can find a cache of these weapons at next to the guard platform at outpost 6 . The Covenant Carbine will be your weapon of choice to cull the unshielded herd of Covenant. The Elites that drop in throughout the canyon tend to play a ranged game, but you'll still want to try to get close enough to make a Plasma Pistol's charged shots home in.

Alternatively, it is possible to steal the Ghost from outpost 5 , or locate another parked at point 9 and guarded by a number of Grunts. Its twin Plasma Cannons and speed boost ability can carry you through every single fight in this canyon, so long as you don't allow yourself to take too much incoming fire. Co-op players may wish to keep the Warthogs to use their blistering firepower. Even solo players can position the Warthog in such a way that you are safe from most sniping attempts while using the mounted gun.

GHOST

The Ghost flies over terrain that would stop or slow down traditional wheeled or tracked vehicles through the use of antigravity units. The relatively lightweight machine features an open cockpit that leaves the rider vulnerable to small arms fire, but the maneuverability and speed of a Ghost can allow a skilled driver to thread a needle through any defense, or just run over any infantry too slow to react to its speed boost-powered charges. The Ghost's twin Plasma Cannons are surprisingly accurate at range and while on the move.

FUEL ROD CANNON

There's a chance that one or more of the Grunts in this area could be packing a Fuel Rod Cannon. This devastating explosive weapon can fire five fuel rods in fairly rapid succession, cauterizing an area in cleansing green flame. Be careful how close you are to targets when firing this weapon; the blast can hurt you as well.

Outpost 5 is the closest to where you enter the box canyon, and it is also where the first Ghost can be located. As with all of the outposts in the canyon, the hovering guard platform provides enemies with an elevated position from which to shoot at you. You can sit with a Warthog atop the hill overlooking this outpost and use the mounted gun to destroy the platform, as well as hose down any Covenant who dropped from the Phantom. As a rule, you generally want to make sure nobody gets a chance to ride the parked Ghost, unless you're the one doing the riding.

Alternate Approach

Rather than sitting back and giving the enemy time to get set up, it's possible on both Heroic **and** Legendary to drive the Warthog at top speed into the outpost and steal the Ghost for yourself. This has the obvious drawback of putting you into close range of the enemy as they drop from the Phantom, not to mention the mounted turrets on the Phantom itself.

Another option is to ignore outpost 5 and drive along the side path 8 on the right from where you enter the canyon toward outpost 6 . This elevated position provides good cover and sniping positions against 5 , but the enemy is more likely to turn the Ghost on you. It's also possible to more or less ignore outpost 5 altogether.

Outpost 6 overlooks a small path on the canyon floor. Part of the elevated area acts as a stone ramp that can help you flank 7 . If you're in a hurry you can also fly though this area, but we recommend that you take out the guard platform at the very least.

The path this outpost watches over is protected by Grunts, and on Heroic or Legendary, there's a good chance you'll find them armed with Fuel Rod Cannons. Don't take the little guys lightly, particularly if you're intending to charge through them to reach the Ghost at 9 .

The real challenge will be centered around outpost 7 , and this place might possibly be the scene of several deaths. In addition to the raised

platform held by Jackals, the Covenant have set a mounted gun that covers almost every approach from the first two outposts. Should Grunts man the gun, they can be easily sniped, but if one of the Elites at this outpost takes the gun, he can prove to be a real problem to dislodge.

The camp itself is filled with Grunts and Jackals that will be taking your attention away from the Elites. Taking a Ghost to this position can make clearing the kill zone in front of the mounted gun much easier, and also help you handle any poor shmuck who tries to take up the weapon.

Unfortunately, you aren't meant to leave this canyon with a vehicle and you'll have to climb up to a ledge that leads you through another tight pass to the next area (though with perseverance it is possible to force a Ghost or even a Warthog up the ledge and through the pass). An Elite, usually armed with a Concussion Rifle, tends to stick to this slightly elevated position near a weapon cache. If you're gutsy, after you clear out the rest of the camp you can dance between his shots with a Ghost while returning fire. Restock at the cache once you're clear.

Watch out for the squad of Grunts in the narrow pass leading to the next section. One of them might be packing a Fuel Rod Cannon, and in these tight quarters you don't have a lot of time to react to these weapons.

Legendary Strategy

This canyon can be brutal on Legendary. Any brash tactics you might have tried before tend to just get you in trouble here. You can still open up the battle by driving straight to the Ghost parked at `5`, but if your timing and luck are off, you can just get blasted by the Phantom and any ground troops it has deployed. Taking up the Warthog gun near the canyon entrance looking toward `5` is very unsafe, as the Phantoms tend to pick you up at greater ranges, and their turrets are deadly accurate. It's almost a better idea to let the Phantoms depart before you mount your assault. If you can't take the Ghost at `5`, make sure the enemy doesn't get to either. The Elites dropped at this location tend to try to meet up with their allies at `6`, so keep that in mind while taking the paths to that outpost.

Outpost `6` isn't so rough if you're patient and don't give the Jackals on the platform good sniping chances. The real craziness is going to go down at `7`. The sheer number of hostiles here, combined with the fact that the Covenant occupies some of the best cover inside the outpost, makes going on the offensive a real pain.

Try to flank this outpost from your left to deny the mounted Plasma Cannon opportunities to lay into you. From there, methodically pick your way through the Grunts and Jackals with a Covenant Carbine. A Plasma Pistol is absolutely essential here: the Elites can and will likely rush your position, save for the one guarding the canyon exit. The charged shot/headshot combo can save you a lot of grief during those moments.

Be particularly aware of Grunt positions as you work through the canyon. Armed with either Plasma Pistols or Fuel Rod Cannons, they can quickly disable and destroy any vehicle you choose to take into the fight.

INTRODUCTION

BASIC TRAINING

INTEL

CAMPAIGN

INFINITY

APPENDIX

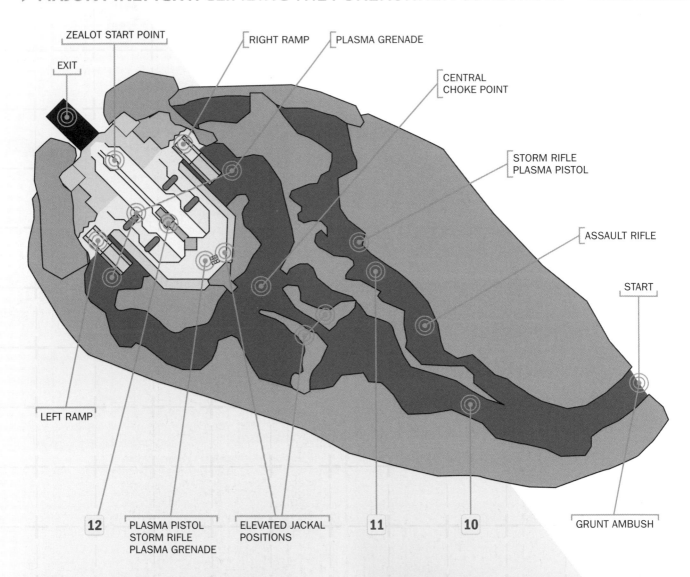

ZEALOT START POINT

EXIT

RIGHT RAMP

PLASMA GRENADE

CENTRAL CHOKE POINT

STORM RIFLE PLASMA PISTOL

ASSAULT RIFLE

START

LEFT RAMP

12

PLASMA PISTOL STORM RIFLE PLASMA GRENADE

ELEVATED JACKAL POSITIONS

11

10

GRUNT AMBUSH

There's not much time to catch a break after fighting your way out of the box canyon. You encounter a massive Forerunner structure built into the stone, with ramps leading up to the top. Entry into the construct will require you to fight your way past another army of Covenant, and make a choice to assault up the tower from the left or right set of ramps. At the top of the tower, an Elite Zealot commands the forces centered around the entrance, and he's got his hands on some vital equipment that will help you guide the Master Chief and Cortana through the rest of this mission.

> RECOMMENDED LOADOUT

A Covenant Carbine and Plasma Pistol are safe and effective weapons to rely on for this fight, though a well-timed super-combine from a Needler barrage can be effective at wiping out groups of enemies, and can set off grenades dropped by the fallen. Just be sure you're not too close to the enemy when setting up the big bang.

10 Start this fight by eliminating or driving off the Jackals taking potshots at you from the nearby raised ledges and from the tower itself. (Although the tower sniper may not actually have an angle on you, which means you will not have an angle on him.) An Elite leading a patrol of Grunts and shield-equipped Jackals will be approaching you from a path directly ahead of you as you enter this arena, so be prepared to greet him with a charged shot/headshot combo. The panic you instill in the Grunts may encourage them to attempt a suicide charge with Plasma Grenades, so keep your eyes open for that.

After beating back the initial attack, the enemy will congregate near the base of the construct. Expect more Elites on the other end of the path the first group marched through. It's possible to tackle them head on, but you'd be restricting your maneuverability. Instead, consider flanking that pathway to the right **11**, using the elevated position to continue picking off Jackals and Grunts. You can find a cache of human and Covenant weapons here to restock with. If you weren't able to take out the sniper in on the second level of the construct, be especially on guard here. Elites may try to rush your little camping spot, or lob grenades up toward you, but you should be able to remain relatively safe so long as you stay mobile and alert. Once you clear out the area at the front of the tower, you have a choice to make: the left ramps, or the right ramps.

The middle level of the construct contains the ramp leading up the final defensive line set up by the Covenant. Grunts and Jackals will be guarding this level, and they'll make use of a passage beneath the central ramp that connects the left and right halves of the tower. Watch your motion sensor to detect flanking attempts early.

There is a third option here. Using the rocks, you can climb up the wall at the foot of the construct. This lets you bypass the enemy forces guarding the ramps to the flanks, but a few enemies may try to pursue you. Be prepared for that!

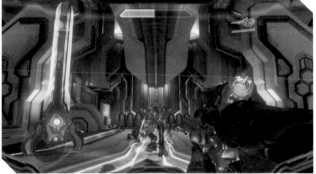

12 The final group of Grunts and Jackals here are led by an Elite Zealot that is armed with a Energy Sword and Active Camouflage. The Zealot can snuff out your life in a single swipe of his blade and he's more than willing to charge head-on at you to make his attempt count. Draw him out by hugging the ramp and picking off his soldiers. Once he rushes out to stop you, pop his shields, switch to your Covenant Carbine (assuming you have ammo for it), and drill one between his eyes. Clear out his remaining troops, then pick up the Active Camouflage he dropped. This is your first armor ability, and you are going to be very best friends with it for the duration of this chapter!

In terms of the forces encountered on either side, you'll face a more or less even distribution of Grunts and Jackals. The right path is lit up by the sun, which can help you spot enemies easier. The left path rests in the shadow of the Forerunner construction. Whichever you choose, be thorough when clearing your flanks as you make your way toward the ramps.

INTRODUCTION

BASIC TRAINING

INTEL

CAMPAIGN

INFINITY

APPENDIX

ARMOR ABILITY ACQUISITION

ACTIVE CAMOUFLAGE

Allowing for near-perfect invisibility while standing still, Active Camouflage is a patient Spartan's dream. The effect diminishes slightly while crouch-walking, but skilled users can use this armor ability to escape between kills, while the built- in motion sensor jammer fills motion sensors, yours included, with false contacts, inciting confusion and panic among the enemy.

WEAPON ACQUISITION

ENERGY SWORD

The preferred weapon of Elite Zealots, the Energy Sword's distinct shape and sound has haunted survivors of Covenant ambushes for years. A high-risk, high-reward weapon, the shaped plasma passes through most shielding tech with ease, and the flesh behind such protection just as effortlessly. Even the armor of a Spartan can't withstand full-on contact with a Energy Sword for very long.

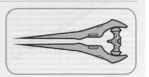

≫ KEY COMBAT TIP

Resist the urge to pick up the Energy Sword! It might be a safer bet on Normal or Easy, but on Heroic and Legendary, the mad rush you must make to get into melee range to use the weapon usually ends with your being stuck by Plasma Grenades or riddled by enemy fire.

Legendary Strategy

You'll more or less be able to apply much of the same strategies you put to use in the Heroic difficulty, but you'll have to be much quicker to react to enemy fire. This is made difficult by the fact that the fighting ranges here are relatively short. Be methodical. After clearing out the initial assault, don't even think about rushing the base of the tower until you are certain you have cleared out the Elites. Also be aware that the Jackal Sniper on the middle level of the tower may be armed with a Beam Rifle, a powerful Covenant weapon likely not yet seen on a Heroic playthrough. Beam Rifles can take out your shields in a single shot, even if they aren't fully charged, and the follow-up shot will almost certainly be fatal.

The Elite Zealot at the top of the tower moves even faster, so it's imperative that you save a Plasma Pistol and at least some ammo for a Covenant Carbine to deal with him. Everything else in the area can be killed adequately with any other weapon, but the Elite Zealot **must** be dropped quickly, or he'll one-shot you back to the start of this battle.

› THE CARTOGRAPHER

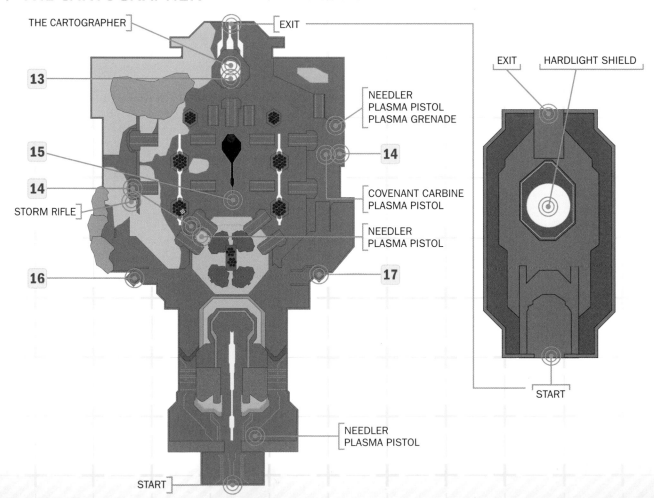

INTRODUCTION

BASIC TRAINING

INTEL

CAMPAIGN

INFINITY

APPENDIX

You're greeted by Sentinels just as you enter the Forerunner construct. Fortunately, the Sentinels are not hostile, and only vanish through portals if they are attacked. They ignore the Master Chief and fly toward the back of the symmetrical hall, as though attempting to guide you toward something. Platforms will rise from the ground, allowing you to jump your way across the center of the room toward a control panel, which is guarded by the corpses of unlucky Covenant troops. However, don't be too hasty to activate the console **13** that you're led to. Numerous weapons racks **14** are placed throughout the room, and also there are the weapons next to the fallen Covenant soldiers, so make sure you are fully stocked with your weapons of choice.

FORERUNNER ARTIFACT

15 Underneath the central dividing platform in this room lies a hidden Forerunner artifact. When you inspect it, Cortana is able to translate a message from the artifact regarding a creed: the Mantle of Responsibility.

CARTOGRAPHER

First encountered on Halo Installation 04, the Cartographer was a computer system that contained a map of the Forerunner installation. Cartographers have been found on nearly every Forerunner installation yet encountered by the UNSC. As they are connected to many other systems on a Forerunner installation, locating a Cartographer can give UNSC AIs such as Cortana the run of an entire installation.

SENTINELS

The Forerunners left Sentinels to protect and maintain their various hidden installations around the whole galaxy, and the shield world of Requiem is no exception. Unless otherwise commanded by their central AI construct, Sentinels have no interest in the actions of organics, unless they threaten the Sentinels or the Installation they are assigned to guard, or unless they are the Flood. The dead Covenant troops near the Cartographer are most likely the work of the Sentinels.

After activating the terminal marked by Cortana, you discover that this shield world is known as Requiem, and the Cartographer of this facility is able to provide some data to help the duo better understand their situation. However, before Cortana is able to pull more information from the ancient network, her access is stripped from her and the Cartographer shuts down. Reactivating it will require you to trigger a pair of control panels **16 17** to provide power to the system. You can trigger them in any order. Just be ready for the inevitable Covenant ambush that ensues when you activate one of the switches.

The Covenant arrive in two waves, one wave for each activated switch. Elites, Jackals, and Grunts—nothing you haven't seen before. There's no correct order for the switches, but one will be recommended simply to make the second wave a little less troublesome to manage. This battle is made significantly easier by virtue of having the Active Camouflage armor ability equipped. The Master Chief and Cortana have been hunted almost since the moment he awoke aboard the *Dawn*. It's time to return the favor.

> RECOMMENDED LOADOUT

You can acquire a Covenant Carbine and a fresh Plasma Pistol from one of the weapon racks **14** found throughout the room. However, a Needler still makes a good impression against clusters of Grunts, and can even be effective against the Elites.

16 From the Cartographer and facing the direction from which you entered the room, the switch on the right is an ideal starting point. You

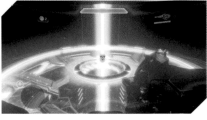

can find a Covenant Carbine on the ground near the weapon's cache close to the switch chamber. As you approach this switch, a flight of Sentinels hovers from the chasm and flies past the Master Chief. This first switch activates a light bridge that allows you to cross the pit and activate a second switch. The column of energy behind the second switch flares up briefly, completely draining your shields. Don't panic, you're not under attack—yet.

The platform where you hit the second switch lowers down to a floor below, and a new light bridge eventually allows you to cross back over the pit and reach the part of the main chamber where the platforms originally raised to allow you to reach the Cartographer. Grunts now patrol this area, with Jackals guarding the ramp that will take you over to the second set of switches that must be activated to restart the Cartographer. Use your Active Camouflage to help with wiping out these hostiles. You can fire while cloaked, and as long as you remain crouched while moving, you can stay hidden.

» KEY COMBAT TIP

Just because you can cloak doesn't make you perfectly invisible. Get close enough to any enemy, and they'll notice the distortion of the Active Camo, no matter how still you stand. Also, if stray fire hits you while cloaked, the flare up of your shielding gives your enemies something to track you by.

Behind the Jackals at the top of the ramp, more Grunts and an Elite will probably be moving to investigate the death cries of their comrades, while a second Elite stalks the next set of ramps that lead to the switches at 17 . After killing them, make your way to the next switches.

Alternate Approaches

It's entirely possible to stealth your way around the vast majority of the enemies here with careful movement and use of the Active Camo, or simply by taking the long way around. This isn't advisable simply because the second wave will enter the room as soon as both sets of switches have been hit, and the combined force will be that much harder to deal with.

You can also attack these switches in opposite order. The enemies that arrive after the first switch has been activated are the same regardless of which switch you press first. The author's preference is to hit 16 first mostly because lighting conditions on the 17 side of the room make it easier to pick up targets visually. Also, one of the weapon racks on that side of the room contains a supply of Covenant Carbines, and being closer to them at the start of the second wave is much more beneficial.

Switches Activated

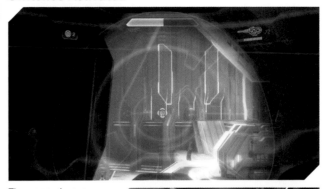

The second wave of enemies arrives as you ride the platform down to the lower level from the second switch, and it's a much larger force compared to the first group. Expect well over a dozen Grunts patrolling the ground levels and central platform near the artifact, accompanied by some Jackals. Jackal Snipers also guard the side routes to the Cartographer, where a small team of Elites now waits for you. Knock out the Rangers and Snipers, then go to work thinning out the rest of the foot soldiers, leaving the Elites close to your objective for last.

The Cartographer's Elite guards have the advantage of terrain to hide behind, but the Active Camouflage will let you set up charged shots to pop their shielding with near impunity. You should have more than enough Covenant Carbine ammo to take on the whole chamber, thanks to the weapon rack closest to 17 . After the room is clear, reactivate the Cartographer.

Legendary Strategy

As with the Heroic tactics, you'll want to make extensive use of your Active Camouflage to help with cutting down the resistance. Whichever switch you hit first, consider making an extra sweep of the room to make sure you haven't missed any stragglers before triggering the second switch and the reinforcements that come with it. The fewer hostiles you have to deal with at once, the better.

Be especially careful about the Elites close to the Cartographer. On Legendary every enemy has upgrades and rank promotions. The area around the Cartographer is prime territory for Elites with Concussion Rifles or Fuel Rod Cannons to make your life really miserable if you're unlucky with the splash damage. If you're feeling uncertain about your remaining Active Camouflage time, don't press your luck, and fall back to let it recharge. So long as you're standing still or are crouched, the enemy will not pursue you unless they know for certain where you are.

INTRODUCTION · BASIC TRAINING · INTEL · CAMPAIGN · INFINITY · APPENDIX

With the enemy no longer a threat, reinsert Cortana back inside the Cartographer. She discovers the source of the garbled transmissions being heard throughout the mission are the UNSC *Infinity*. The shield world appears to be interfering with Cortana's ability to triangulate its location. It also appears that the shield world consists of multiple layers. Fortunately, Cortana has been able to locate potential means for signalling the *Infinity*.

The next room contains a new armor ability for you on top of a pedestal, at the cost of giving up your Active Camo. Once you've made your choice, step through the next door to come across an elevator that overlooks a bridge that leads to where you want to go. The Covenant are one step ahead of you, and Phantoms begin disgorging troops across the whole bridge, joining a group of Jackals and Grunts at the base of the elevator. The Covenant knows you're coming, and that you need to cross this bridge to get to the tower that Cortana says may contain the means to travel quickly around Requiem.

ARMOR ABILITY ACQUISITION

HARDLIGHT SHIELD

This armor ability allows the Master Chief to activate a temporary Hardlight Shield in front of himself, at the cost of mobility and being able to fight back. The shield lasts for a short amount of time, though sustained enemy fire can shorten its effective time. It's possible to bounce back thrown grenades with well-timed activation of the shield.

» KEY COMBAT TIP

While there are some really neat things you can do with the Hardlight Shield, on Heroic and Legendary the shield just doesn't last long enough under fire to outweigh being mostly invisible. For now, we recommend you pass up the Hardlight Shield and stick with Active Camo.

> MAJOR FIREFIGHT: THE BRIDGE

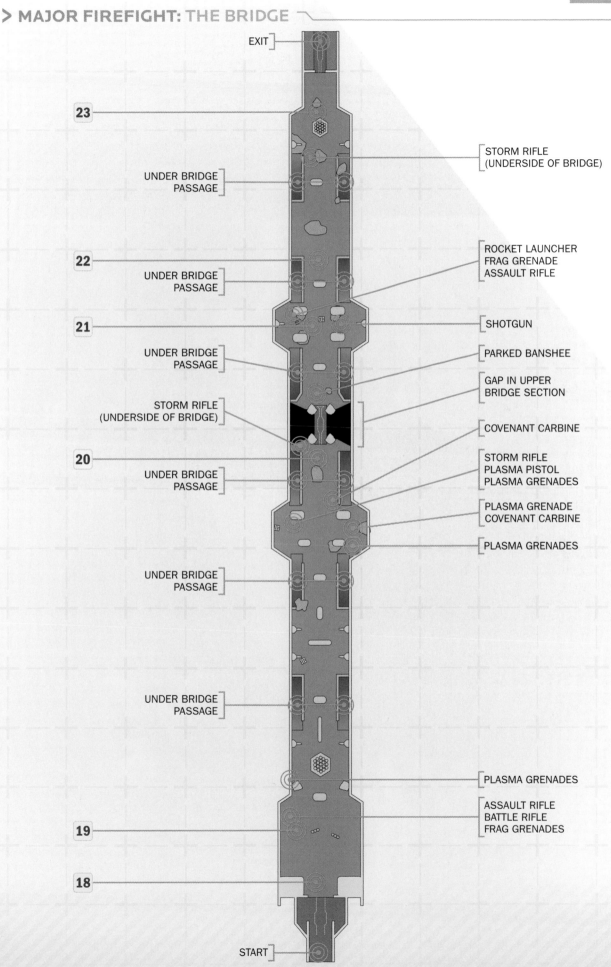

EXIT

23

UNDER BRIDGE
PASSAGE

STORM RIFLE
(UNDERSIDE OF BRIDGE)

22

UNDER BRIDGE
PASSAGE

ROCKET LAUNCHER
FRAG GRENADE
ASSAULT RIFLE

21

SHOTGUN

UNDER BRIDGE
PASSAGE

PARKED BANSHEE

GAP IN UPPER
BRIDGE SECTION

STORM RIFLE
(UNDERSIDE OF BRIDGE)

COVENANT CARBINE

20

STORM RIFLE
PLASMA PISTOL
PLASMA GRENADES

UNDER BRIDGE
PASSAGE

PLASMA GRENADE
COVENANT CARBINE

PLASMA GRENADES

UNDER BRIDGE
PASSAGE

UNDER BRIDGE
PASSAGE

PLASMA GRENADES

ASSAULT RIFLE
BATTLE RIFLE
FRAG GRENADES

19

18

START

INTRODUCTION

BASIC TRAINING

INTEL

CAMPAIGN

INFINITY

APPENDIX

103

Welcome to one of the harder battles in the entire game, if you're unlucky. Covenant Grunts, Jackals, and Elites populate much of this narrow span, with Phantoms dropping in more reinforcements the farther you advance. Complicating things are the presence of Banshees, the standard Covenant fighter, patrolling the skies above and sometimes below the bridge. The enemy presence here is substantial, to say the least.

> RECOMMENDED LOADOUT

The staples of a Covenant Carbine and a Plasma Pistol always will serve you well here, but you can find a UNSC weapons cache that comes with the Battle Rifle very close to where the elevator lowers at the start of the bridge. Ideally you'll have kept the Active Camo. The real coup to aim for here is to hijack one of the Banshees. If you can pull that off (and then survive long enough to climb out of range of enemy fire, you can repeatedly bombard the enemy with Fuel Rod Cannon shots or the twin Plasma Cannons. Just make sure you don't commit yourself to a bombing run where the enemy can focus too much fire on you, or that first you have eliminated any other hostile Banshees in the air.

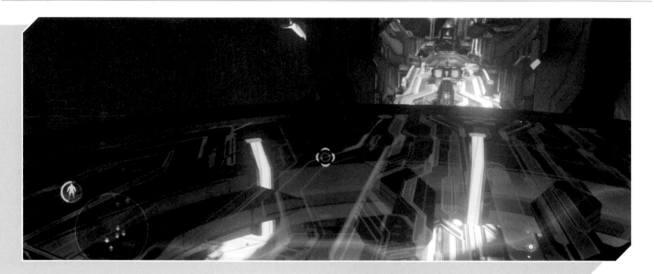

18 As you walk onto the elevator, you'll see the Phantoms in the distance beginning their deployments. The one closest to you may take some potshots with its mounted guns, so use your Active Camouflage and go into a crouch while the elevator drops down to the bridge. Eliminate the Grunts and Jackals that are swarming nearby. The UNSC weapons cache **19** contains Battle Rifles and Assault Rifles. Don't take both at once. If you still have Covenant Carbine ammo, use it up entirely in conjunction with a Plasma Pistol, then fall back and replace the Covenant Carbine with the Battle Rifle. This weapons cache also includes Frag Grenades, and they are perfect for bouncing off the ground and beyond any cover the Covenant uses.

You can work your way forward, ignoring the side ramps that take you to the lower bridge level, but you may have to contend with the Phantoms' turrets supporting the ground troops, and Banshees join the effort on the latter half of the bridge, providing close-air support. Give them a couple of seconds and they can melt careless players into puddles of goo with their Plasma Cannons. This is what your Plasma Pistol is for, specifically to swat these fliers out of the sky before you can get access to the Rocket Launcher at **21**. A short distance from the launcher, a Banshee is parked at the center of the bridge.

There are two major methods for dealing with The Bridge: By land, or by air.

Crossing On Foot

Sticking to the bridge results in a grueling cover-to-cover slog through a stiff layered defense. You'll still need to deal with those Banshees, so you'll want to keep Plasma Pistols handy whenever you're on the upper bridge level. Elites pose a serious threat throughout the fighting here, as you've got limited room to maneuver. The bridge is filled with lots of small pieces of cover that can easily conceal enemy movement or give Elites a chance to recover their shields. The Active Camouflage can give you a chance to set up quick kills on Elites, so don't be shy about using it.

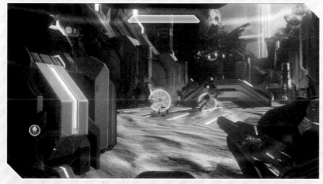

Shield-equipped Jackals are a major nuisance throughout the entire bridge, and this is why weapons like the Battle Rifle or the Covenant Carbine are so useful here. A good shot at their arm to stagger, followed by a head shot.

20 At this point you can't progress across the top of the bridge and must drop down to the connecting light bridge on the lower level. Don't just jump down here! There are many Grunts and Jackals here, including an Elite. Before crossing the light bridge, make sure you've eliminated the threat. This is an especially dangerous crossing to make, as a stray grenade can easily knock you into the abyss. If you did switch to the Hardlight Shield, you could potentially reflect the grenades back at the Covenant, but this isn't a very reliable tactic.

Take note of the Banshee parked across this gap.

21 When you reach this Rocket Launcher, this is your chance to finally swat those Banshees out of the sky decisively. Typically, there are two of these fighters in the general area. Beware of the Grunts that are among the troops dropped from a Phantom that swoops in just as you arrive. They try to rush this position when you finally reach it. On the other side of the bridge next to the Rocket Launcher, you can find a Shotgun to handle any short-range surprises. Do NOT use rockets on the Phantom! You can't hope to take it down with the limited ammo you have, and ideally you'll save them for Banshees or the Elites as you progress closer to the bridge exit.

WEAPON ACQUISITION

ROCKET LAUNCHER

The Rocket Launcher is an effective weapon that fires a powerful shaped charge. The blast has devastating effects on all known battlefield armor and infantry deployed by the Covenant. The relatively low speed of the rocket is negated by a lock-on system that ensures it will strike most vehicles with great accuracy. The Rocket Launcher can also be fielded against aircraft like the Banshee.

SHOTGUN

Handy for close encounters, the Shotgun is a devastating weapon to use at point-blank range, and it's capable of defeating Elites in two quick blasts: one to the shields, and one to the body. Unfortunately, the wide spread from each shot makes the Shotgun a poor weapon to use outside of close range, and it requires you to get within arm's reach of your targets to maximize the weapon's potential.

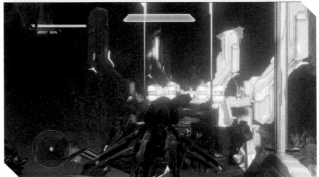

22 After dealing with the immediate Banshee threat, advance forward cautiously. Consider using any remaining rockets you have on clusters of light infantry, or on Elites, but remember that you may still have another Banshee or two to contend with. Scarier still, there is another section under the bridge where many Grunts and Jackals hide. Killing Elites may inspire them to flank you from behind with suicide charges, so watch your motion sensor.

» KEY COMBAT TIP

It cannot be stressed enough how useful Active Camouflage is for this final bridge section. Engaging enemies at range, and then vanishing from their sight can save you from the worst of their return fire while still allowing you to pick them off with relatively ease.

It's not particularly safe, but it is possible to capture a Banshee for yourself by taking the one parked near **20**, on the opposite side of the gap on the upper level of the bridge that forces you down to the lower area.

23 A final group of Grunts and Jackals, lead by higher ranking Elites, stands as your final obstacle before exiting this kill zone, while another Banshees menaces you from above. If you get past them on your first try, go get yourself a soda. Pet a dog. Take a walk—something, anything—you've earned it.

If you do this, your major threats are other Banshees, Phantoms, and the small arms fire from Covenant infantry. In particular, the Covenant will try to use charged Plasma Pistol shots on you as well, so be alert. Banshees are quite fragile; they succumb to sustained fire in just a few seconds. Make sure you're being proactive at eliminating enemy Banshees, and don't test your luck hunting Phantoms. They have too much armor for you to reliably take one out, and their mounted guns are quite accurate.

If a Banshee gets the jump on you, you're already in serious danger. You can use the melee button to trigger some special stunts, but this doesn't do a whole lot to get them off your tail, and neither does hitting the boost and flying straight. Turn as fast as you can on the enemy fighter and try to drive it off with plasma fire or a fuel rod shot. Always make sure you confirm the kill so you don't get surprised by the Banshee again.

Taking the Banshee

VEHICLE ENCOUNTER //////////////////////

BANSHEE

The standard Covenant fighter craft whose wailing engine signature lives up to its name, the Banshee is an effective and adaptable fighter, capable of serving in atmospheric or vacuum conditions, while retaining extreme maneuverability. Its twin Plasma Cannons are accurate and powerful, able to cut down even fully shielded Spartans in seconds, while their Fuel Rod Cannons provide powerful anti-armor capability.

When clearing out infantry, try to stick to the Fuel Rod Cannon. It's murderous on Grunts and Jackals alike, and while Elites can evade each shot, you can still score hits and kills through splash damage. Getting close enough to them to use the Plasma Cannons only exposes you to return fire that your ship can't sustain for long.

Lastly, remember that you don't need to kill absolutely everything to get through this section! If you're only just trying to make it through, you can bypass much of the enemy's ground units and concentrate your efforts on other Banshees and the final group of infantry closest to the exit.

Whichever method you choose, once you break through this Covenant position, Cortana chimes in with some disappointing news. The Covenant have ordered all of their troops to defend the tower, and they are converging there as you leave bridge behind. It's not over yet.

Legendary Strategy

The Banshee strategy is still an effective and easier method for completing the crossing, but on this difficulty the Banshees seem even more vulnerable to incoming fire when you're behind the wheel (despite being tougher for you to take down when you're shooting them). You can still make it work, but you're in for a relatively slow grind as you constantly dance out of the extended enemy ranges. Hostile Banshees can destroy you even faster than on Heroic difficulty, so you'll have to constantly scan the skies for them and ignore everything else until you know you're safe.

The Active Camouflage is life on this bridge if you take the ground route. You absolutely must control the pace of combat and make certain you don't bite off more than you can chew. Use it to score quick stealth melee kills (do not trigger the assassination animation!) on Elites if the opportunity presents itself. The Rocket Launcher at 21 will most likely be limited entirely to anti-Banshee duty, but if you're lucky, you can use it on ground troops.

Make certain you leave this bridge with a healthy amount of Battle Rifle or Covenant Carbine ammo, as well as a Plasma Pistol!

INTRODUCTION

BASIC TRAINING

INTEL

CAMPAIGN

INFINITY

APPENDIX

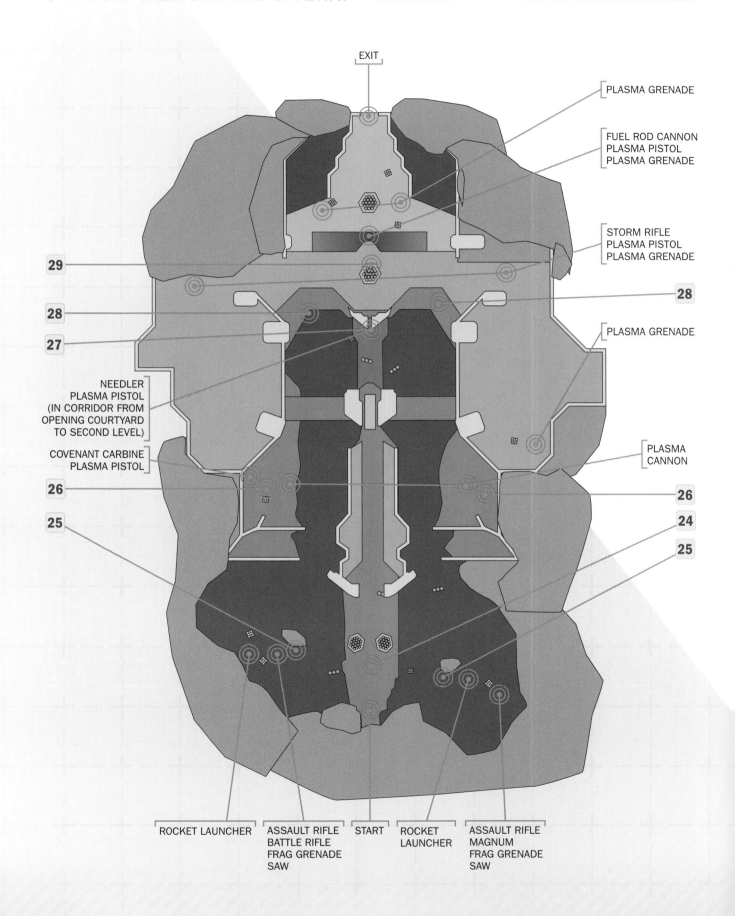

EXIT

PLASMA GRENADE

FUEL ROD CANNON
PLASMA PISTOL
PLASMA GRENADE

STORM RIFLE
PLASMA PISTOL
PLASMA GRENADE

29

28

28

27

28

PLASMA GRENADE

NEEDLER
PLASMA PISTOL
(IN CORRIDOR FROM
OPENING COURTYARD
TO SECOND LEVEL)

COVENANT CARBINE
PLASMA PISTOL

PLASMA
CANNON

26

25

26

24

25

ROCKET LAUNCHER

ASSAULT RIFLE
BATTLE RIFLE
FRAG GRENADE
SAW

START

ROCKET
LAUNCHER

ASSAULT RIFLE
MAGNUM
FRAG GRENADE
SAW

The passage leading from the bridge takes you to a field that sits before a massive Forerunner facility connected to the tower destination. The Covenant are already here, and the field is being patrolled by Grunts freshly deployed from a Phantom, with snipers and Shade Turrets on either side of the symmetrical fortification. Ghosts deploy as soon as your presence is detected, and the minimal cover in the field makes you vulnerable to sniping. The center of the field is dominated by a raised walkway, where more Covenant have gathered.

The starting ground level is just a taste of things to come, it only gets worse the farther you climb up toward the facility entrance. The second level starts with a Grunt and Elite Zealot sandwich, and then you pick between two routes to climb up to the third and fourth levels, where you encounter your most dangerous Covenant foes yet.

> RECOMMENDED LOADOUT

You'll want a good headshot-capable Covenant Carbine or Battle Rifle for the opening gambit, which means taking out the Grunts closest to where this battle begins and dealing with the snipers and Shade Turret gunners. A Plasma Pistol is good medicine for handling the Ghosts, and you might want to hijack one to make clearing out the first area easier.

The pair of UNSC weapons caches near the point you enter from **25** both contain a Rocket Launcher, an effective weapon against the Ghosts and the Shade Turrets.

Opening Gambit

24 Hopefully, you kept your Active Camouflage armor ability. The ability to vanish from sight makes handling ranged threats easier. Activate it as soon as you enter this field. To your left and right are two raised balconies, each guarded by a Shade Turret on the ground level. Above them, Jackal Snipers are on patrol. They all have potential line of sight on you as soon as you enter this arena.

In front of you, being dropped off by a Phantom, are Grunts. Deal with them quickly, and take cover near one of the small barriers.

By now, Phantoms have thrown Ghosts into the mix, but if you were quick at getting to cover and killing the first group of Grunts, you might have a chance to counter-snipe one or both snipers. If you're even luckier, you can try for the Shade Turret gunners. If you don't have a sniping weapon, you're kind of in a tough spot, but it's still workable.

When the first Ghost attacks, and it will attack, quickly disable it with a charged Plasma Pistol shot, then take it for yourself. If you haven't wiped out the Shade Turret gunners or Jackal Snipers yet, now's the time! A second Ghost will make an appearance shortly after you encounter the first, so time is of the essence. Don't forget that Ghosts leave you exposed to incoming fire, so drive defensively to avoid taking hits.

WEAPON ACQUISITION

SHADE TURRET

The Shade Turret chops through infantry formations as a sword would air, which makes them priority targets for marksmen on the receiving end. Though they lack protection for their operators against small arms fire, a Shade Turret can still be extremely dangerous should an Elite hop aboard.

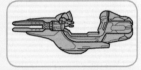

» KEY COMBAT TIP

Just because you eliminate the gunners does not mean a Shade Turret is no longer a threat. Considering using the Rocket Launchers or a Ghost to completely destroy them, if only to prevent brave Grunts or Elites from retaking the guns and turning them against you.

With a Ghost, the rest of this opening battle is a simple matter of cleanup. Wipe out the stragglers, including the Elite, at the central structure, then proceed closer to the main building and finish off another Elite/Grunt team. You'll have to part ways with the Ghost for now, sadly. Before you follow the ramps up to the next level, check out the balconies that the Jackal Snipers and Shade Turrets guarded **26**, and make sure you pick up a Covenant Carbine and a fresh Plasma Pistol.

Legendary Strategy

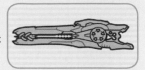

This opening section on Legendary can go badly once the enemy is on to your position. Because of the lethality of Jackal Snipers, and the possibility that one or both snipers may be carrying Beam Rifles, taking them out becomes one of your top priorities. Be especially aware of the Ghosts in the area as you make your way to one of the weapons caches near the start of this firefight. If you're caught out in the open, they will cut you down almost as fast as the Jackal Snipers can. You might be tempted to destroy them with a Rocket Launcher, but it would be wasteful to destroy them both. Having a Ghost available makes the fighting after the Shade Turrets and snipers are down much easier. Deal with the nearest Shade Turret gunner, then take out the sniper as soon as you get an angle. Then rip up the Grunts near your starting point and work your way in relative safety back toward the other side of the field to kill off the sniper and Shade Turret pair. Remember to move and fire while cloaked by Active Camo, if possible, until you've dealt with the all of the snipers and Shade Turret gunners!

Level Two

27 As you head toward the ramps leading up to the second level, Cortana warns of more enemy reinforcements along the way. Four Grunts

and an Elite Zealot stand guard here. Use grenades to wipe out the Grunts while drawing out the Elite, and used a charged shot/headshot combo on him. Alternatively, you can burn a rocket to take him out, but a miss could lead to a Energy Sword-assisted restart of the battle.

28 You've now got a choice to go to the left or right. Both sides are more or less identical in design and enemy composition. Expect shield-equipped

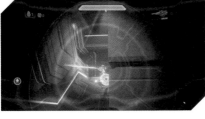

Jackals and a few Grunts lead by an Elite. When you reach the ramps, there typically is a trio of Jackals, one of whom could be a Jackal Sniper with a Beam Rifle. Atop the ramps on either side of the base are more Covenant weapons caches that include Covenant Carbines, Storm Rifles, and Plasma Pistols.

WEAPON ACQUISITION \\\\\\\\\\\\\\\\\\\\\\

BEAM RIFLE

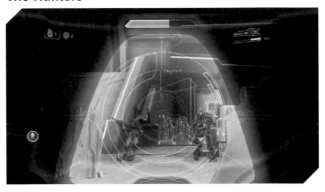

The Beam Rifle fires a highly focused energy beam that punctures through most infantry shielding at extreme ranges. At shallow angles, this beamshot has been known to bounce off surfaces while still producing a hard kill. As with all Covenant weapons, the Beam Rifle has the advantage of not requiring reloading, but once the battery is drained, the weapon is rendered useless until recharged. Also, users must be aware that rapidly firing shots may cause the weapon to become too hot to hold until the cooling system lowers the weapon's temperature.

The Hunters

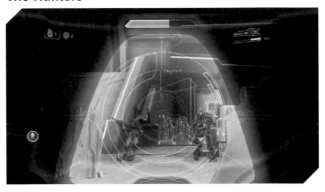

29 The last section of this firefight starts with a Phantom dropping off a pair of Elites that are ordered to guard the ramps that lead to the entrance of the Forerunner facility. It is driven off by a concentrated assault by Sentinels, who are fighting the Covenant alongside you. Meanwhile, the courtyard in front of the door is occupied by a pair of massive Hunters, who are taking on a swarm of Sentinels and are winning quite easily. Ensure that the Elites are no longer a problem, then pick up a Fuel Rod Cannon from the cache at the base of the ramps leading up to the Hunters, and prepare to go to work.

ENEMY ENCOUNTER \\

HUNTERS

Often described as living tanks, Hunters are the largest and most resilient infantry fielded by the Covenant, and arguably the most dangerous. Their very presence changes the dynamics of any battle. Almost always deployed in pairs, the Hunters wield enormous Fuel Rod Cannons that are grafted to their armor. In addition to being crack shots with their weapon, Hunters are savage in melee combat, able to crush the life out of a Spartan in a single strike.

Once a Hunter goes down, you can fight its partner a little more safely. Stay mobile, and keep circling around it. There's a sweet spot, about one and a half Hunter-lengths away, where you're not too close that you'll get punched to death, but still not likely to get a fuel rod in your skull. It will just keep trying to spin and punch at you. If you want to play it safer, retreat using Active Camo, and then circle around behind it after it stops pursuing you. If you keep landing shots onto its weak point, the second Hunter will eventually succumb. The path into the facility is clear. Do your preferred victory dance; that's the last battle of the chapter!

Hunters are always a problem when they show up, but they can be especially frustrating here. They often refuse to chase you down the ramp to where the pair of Elites are assigned, and the area they command has little in the way of solid cover you can use to avoid getting pasted by fuel rods. Focusing on only one will often get you blind-sided by the other, and they are not afraid to shoot fuel rods at one another if it means they can kill you.

Concentrate on one Hunter at a time. If you're lucky and hit the exposed orange flesh with a full load of fuel rods, that should end it. If it survives, try to stick it with a Plasma Grenade or four, if you can. If it looks like the Hunters getting too close, retreat from the platform and use Active Camouflage to break free, then close in once again and attempt to flank them. You want to get shots on their flesh, and any weapon you can scrounge up can potentially do the job.

Legendary Strategy

Hunters are jerks on this difficulty: faster to attack, faster to react, and as always incredibly resilient. You will be disappointed to see Hunters surviving far more rockets or fuel rods than they would on Heroic. The same basic strategy can be employed, but you'll have to be smarter about your firepower and not waste your chances. If you're lucky, you can still eliminate or severely weaken one Hunter before they both turn on you. If you run short on ammo, you must play the most dangerous game, that is, getting close enough to the Hunter to bait it into melee combat before slipping behind it and striking the exposed flesh on its back. If you're quick about this, you might also be able to distract the Hunters for any surviving Sentinels to fire their cleansing lasers directly into their weak spots as they lumber after you.

INTRODUCTION

BASIC TRAINING

INTEL

CAMPAIGN

INFINITY

APPENDIX

111

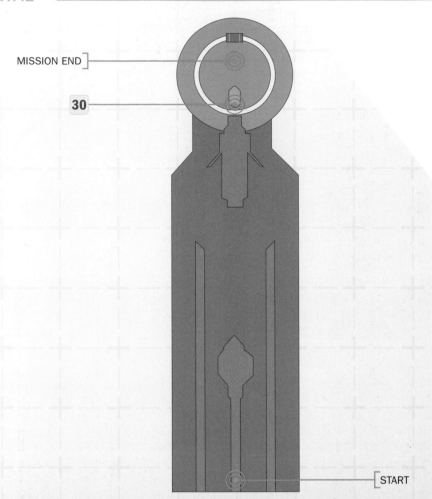

MISSION END

30

START

After crossing through the door to enter the facility, an elevator takes you into the depths of the tower. You see a massive hall with constantly shifty geometry hanging from above. Head toward the elevator at the central platform dead ahead.

DOMAIN TERMINAL

30 But don't climb that ramp just yet. Check underneath the ramp to find a Domain Terminal, and inspect it to unlock special information on *Halo Waypoint*.

After taking the elevator up, the Master Chief and Cortana arrive in another massive hall surrounded by pillars. The Master Chief inserts Cortana into the system as she attempts to pinpoint the *Infinity*'s location, in the hopes of using shield world's portal system to get aboard the vessel. Unfortunately, she is unable to determine the *Infinity*'s whereabouts. Things take a turn for the worse when the pillars behind the Master Chief light up, revealing new aliens never encountered before—but it is obvious that they are not friendly. Activating the portal grid, Cortana urges the Spartan to hurry and get them both out of there before they learn just how unfriendly these aliens can be.

INTRODUCTION

BASIC TRAINING

INTEL

CAMPAIGN

INFINITY

APPENDIX

CAMPAIGN

MISSION 3: FORERUNNER

"Hope you don't mind hoofin' it a little."

The strange armored constructs that suddenly surrounded the Master Chief and Cortana only moments before their narrow escape appear to be related to the Sentinels, but unlike the typically docile drones, the new arrivals appear intent on hostilities. The Master Chief has no choice but to keep moving forward, in hopes of finding the means to pinpoint the *Infinity*'s location and get him and Cortana off the shield world.

PRIMA OFFICIAL GAME GUIDE / WWW.PRIMAGAMES.COM

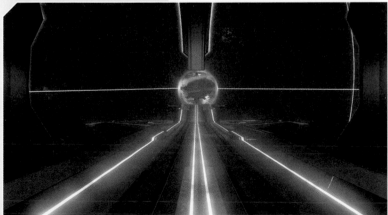

⌃ MISSION BRIEFING

To locate the *Infinity*, you've got your work cut out for you. Cortana reveals that the central satellite producing the interference preventing communications with the ship is protected by a shield. That shield is being projected by two large emitter towers. Unfortunately, to reach each tower, you will have to fight your way through rough terrain guarded by the new Forerunner constructs that appeared at the end of the previous mission. After disabling the first tower, Covenant forces once again make themselves a problem by attacking the second tower. This opens up a three-way battle between the Covenant, the Forerunner warriors, and the Master Chief. The final objective has you tearing through battles being waged by Covenant forces and the Forerunner machines on the central satellite, as you attempt to make contact with the *Infinity*.

ENEMIES ENCOUNTERED:

Elites   Grunts   Jackals

Crawlers   Knights   Watchers

VEHICLES ENCOUNTERED:

Phantom Dropships   Ghosts   Banshees

WEAPONS ACQUIRED
Assault Rifle
Magnum
Storm Rifle
Plasma Pistol
Needler
Covenant Carbine
Concussion Rifle
Fuel Rod Cannon
Beam Rifle
Boltshot
Suppressor
LightRifle
Binary Rifle
Scattershot

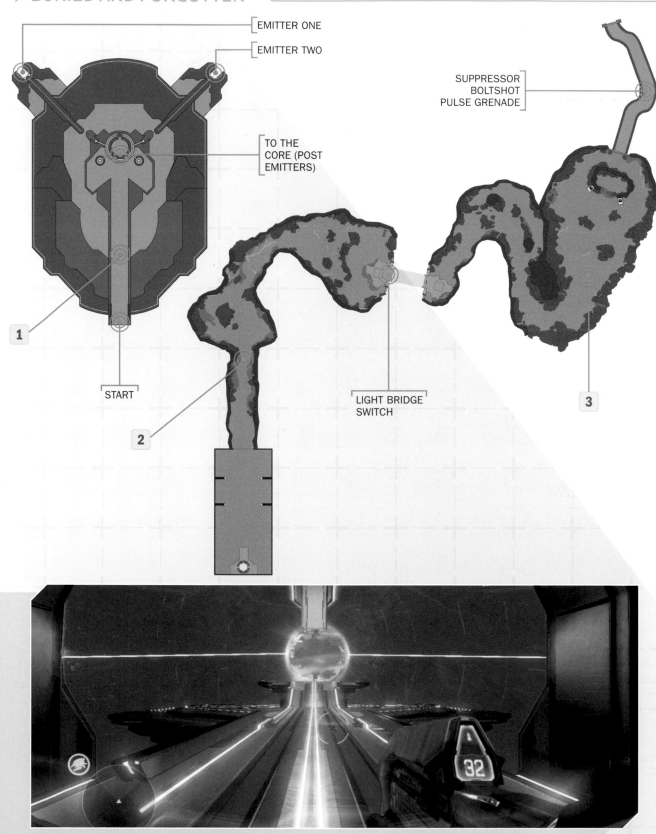

EMITTER ONE

EMITTER TWO

SUPPRESSOR
BOLTSHOT
PULSE GRENADE

TO THE
CORE (POST
EMITTERS)

1

START

2

LIGHT BRIDGE
SWITCH

3

1 Shortly after passing through the portal to escape the new threat, you arrive in a small chamber—lacking the ever-so-useful Active Camouflage armor ability from the previous mission. It has been replaced by a Hardlight Shield armor ability. In the very chamber you start in, you can find an Autosentry armor ability, and we highly recommend it over the Hardlight Shield. You also begin with an Assault Rifle and a Magnum, with modest ammunition for both.

ARMOR ABILITY ACQUISITION

AUTOSENTRY

This armor ability is Forerunner in origin, yet Cortana is able to immediately devise a means to allow the Master Chief to use it. The hovering Autosentry fires at targets that fall within visual range, but it suffers from a lack of decisive killing power. Fortunately, the Autosentry provides a helpful distraction that gives the you a chance to flank enemies.

Leaving the starting position, you enter a massive hall with a control panel that Cortana asks to be plugged into. She gives you the basic tactical and strategic rundown: The UNSC *Infinity* is not on Requiem. A satellite in the visible distance is scrambling the signal, making it impossible to pinpoint. Two power stations are beaming energy toward the satellite, and Cortana believes that by shutting it down she will be able to finally contact their potential saviors. She then opens a portal that leads to the first power station.

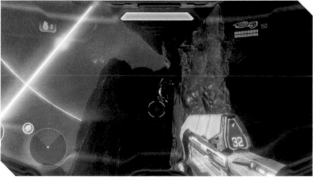

2 Or at least within (lengthy) walking distance of the station. Just as you exit the portal room, you encounter strange, wolflike creatures crawling all along the stone walls surrounding the Master Chief. They chatter and observe him for a moment before scattering and running away.

ENEMY ENCOUNTER

CRAWLERS

The basic soldier unit of the Forerunner constructs running wild across Requiem, Crawlers exhibit wolf-pack traits, such as working in groups as often as possible. They tend to restrict their actions to set territories, and aggressively assault any hostiles who enter these areas. Once the enemy retreats out of these areas, Crawlers tend to hang back and pepper their foes from afar with a collection of Forerunner armaments, but when challenged to close range combat, Crawlers are capable of surprisingly vicious melee attacks.

Following the Crawlers around the bend, you find that they haven't retreated, but have instead regrouped for a combined assault. When combatting Crawlers of any variety, weapons capable of headshots are best, such as the Magnum you start the mission with, or a Battle Rifle. Crawlers move quickly while on land, but when clinging to walls, they are much slower and can be easy targets to score headshots. Use your Magnum to pop as many Crawlers as possible, then switch to the Assault Rifle. Short bursts from the AR can land many shots on their vulnerable heads, putting them down fairly quickly. Once they are finished, you should seriously consider picking up the two new Forerunner weapons that they left behind, the Boltshot, and the Suppressor. Afterward, proceed to the marked waypoint to activate a light bridge to the next section.

Legendary Strategy

While this isn't a major firefight, it's worth mentioning that on Legendary, Crawlers are far more difficult to deal with due to the increased speed and accuracy of their projectiles and the overall increase in their aggression. Headshots are still excellent solutions, but the Assault Rifle loses a great deal of its effectiveness. Avoid pursuing retreating Crawlers too far, they are excellent at setting up lethal ambushes.

WEAPON ACQUISITION

BOLTSHOT

A headshot-capable Forerunner pistol that fires highly ionized particles, the Boltshot is quite accurate even at fairly long ranges. Boltshots also have the ability to overcharge and expend one half of an energy pack in a powerful close-range energy burst.

SUPPRESSOR

A Forerunner weapon with an extremely high rate of fire, the Suppressor is specifically designed to throw as much firepower downrange as possible in the shortest amount of time possible. The recoil on the weapon forces even the Master Chief to fight to keep it under control. While not blessed with the stopping power of other weapons, the particle shots fired by a Suppressor devastate shielding and flesh alike by sheer volume.

INTRODUCTION

BASIC TRAINING

INTEL

CAMPAIGN

INFINITY

APPENDIX

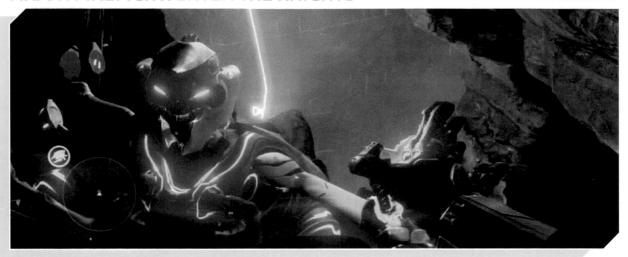

3 After crossing the bridge, you are attacked without warning by one of the constructs seen at the end of the previous mission. The meeting is short, and almost fatal for the Master Chief, but the Knight suddenly teleports away after the close encounter. You're not nearly done with it yet. After a short walk, with more of the creatures phasing in and out of existence on the cliffs in the distance, you reach a wall where one of the Knights stands on a ledge, roaring a challenge. Crawlers stream over the walls to your left. This marks your first battle with the Knights and the floating constructs that their kind are capable of deploying: the Watchers.

> RECOMMENDED LOADOUT

If you were able to keep a hold of a good supply of Magnum ammo, you probably want to use that alongside the Suppressor or the Assault Rifle. The Magnum is capable of taking out the Crawlers and Watchers quickly, while also providing the needed punch to finish off a Knight once its shields are down. The Boltshot can earn its keep here as well.

ENEMY ENCOUNTER

KNIGHTS

Bipedal Forerunner warriors, Knights are designed purely for fast-paced offensive combat. Though they look mechanical, there is evidence that suggests they have emotions, and they can be observed roaring in apparent anger when any of their number are defeated, or if their powerful personal shielding is broken. Knights of all varieties are capable of handling Forerunner weapons with great skill. For their size, they are deceptively fast and dangerous melee opponents with their built-in forearm blades. Their armored carapace and face shields are nearly impenetrable even after their energy shields have been disabled. Effective kill shots to their heads are difficult to achieve, and when sufficiently enraged or pressed, Knights are capable of rapidly teleporting toward their enemies to deliver a powerful melee slash.

WATCHERS

Confounding floating constructs that primarily operate in support of the Knights that deploy them, and of any designated allies in the area, Watchers flit over a battlefield, casting defensive Hardlight Shields in front of endangered allies, or flinging back grenades at the enemies who threw them. Watchers are capable of ranged combat using Boltshots. The most dangerous function of a Watcher is one of repair and reconstruction. The energy residue left behind by fallen Forerunner units can be reconstituted back into their original, fully active state, which makes Watchers priority targets in any battle.

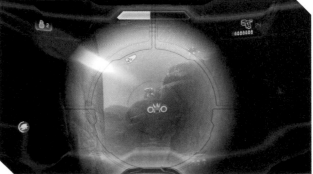

The Knight will attempt to deploy a Watcher after it leaps down to confront you. This can be prevented with well placed Frag Grenades, which also can break its shields and allow for quick headshots. The Knight is likely to be armed with a LightRifle or a Suppressor. If it's the former, it will hang back and bombard you with accurate fire, which makes staying out in the open a mistake. A Suppressor-equipped Knight will try to take the fight to you.

Of course, there is fairly limited cover in this field, and what exists is easily flankable by the Knight and the Crawlers. Despite the obvious threat of the Knight, focus first on bringing down the Crawlers to get as many hostile guns off the field as possible, then take on the Knight.

When fighting a Knight, know that they are rarely dissuaded from their attacks unless they are hit with sufficiently powerful weapons, or if their shields are broken. Based on your loadout, Knights can be tough to defeat. A good method that baits a Knight into standing still longer is to use an Assault Rifle or Suppressor and fire in rapid bursts. They tend to soak up these barrages for as long as their shields hold out, only sidestepping occasionally.

When their shields are down, Knights will either teleport to safety behind nearby cover, or they will teleport at you to melee attack. They also may stand in place and roar, exposing their skull at the Master Chief, though certain Knight variants, such as the Knight Commander and the Knight Battlewagon, do not reveal this weak spot. This is a prime opportunity to drill one or two in between the glowing eye-sockets with a Magnum. A Boltshot's charged shot is also capable of staggering or outright killing an unshielded Knight, allowing bolder players to fight these hostiles in close quarters. It's also possible to continue to open fire on their now exposed torso and limbs with the Suppressor or Assault Rifle to bring them down.

Be mindful of their grenades. While not as immediately lethal as the Frag or the Plasma Grenade, the Knight's Pulse Grenades rapidly damages anything in its area of effect. After several seconds, the Pulse Grenade detonates, destroying unprotected targets.

Alternate Approach

If you took the Autosentry, it's possible to distract a Knight with this armor ability, and sprint behind it to attempt an Assassination melee attack. It's a risky tactic for risky players to be sure, but beware that all Knights have amazing peripheral awareness and will often detect you sprinting at them from angles up to 90 degrees to the left or right!

Legendary Strategy

Your first Legendary encounter with a Knight can be almost heartbreaking at first if you struggled with them on Heroic. Their tendency to teleport away just as their shields fail gives them enough time to completely restore their defenses while you frantically search for them. The order of engagement should remain similar to how it was on Heroic, but the Knight should be treated with much more respect, as even this standard Knight can put you down in one swift strike. Additionally, Knights on Legendary are much more willing to throw Pulse Grenades as though they were handing out candy—explosive candy that dissolves unlucky players in seconds.

WEAPON ACQUISITION

LIGHTRIFLE

The Forerunner equivalent to the Covenant Carbine, or the DMR, a LightRifle combines the accuracy of those weapons with the material penetration and power of a more specialized sniper system. Knights armed with a LightRifle should be considered extremely dangerous and be prioritized accordingly. Similar to the Battle Rifle when fired from the hip, a LightRifle fires three bolts in rapid succession. When the weapon's scope is in use, the three shots are condensed into a single, powerful shot. Because of this, the LightRifle is equally capable of filling the roles of the Battle Rifle and the Covenant Carbine.

PULSE GRENADE

The Pulse Grenade is a powerful anti-infantry weapon that upon detonation creates a spherical energy field damaging any targets within its area of effect. Once the field reaches critical mass, it violently collapses disintegrating any target unfortunate enough to be within range.

After this first Knight battle, the wall that the Forerunner machines protected reveals a passage that contains a weapons cache. Fill up on Suppressor and Boltshot ammo.

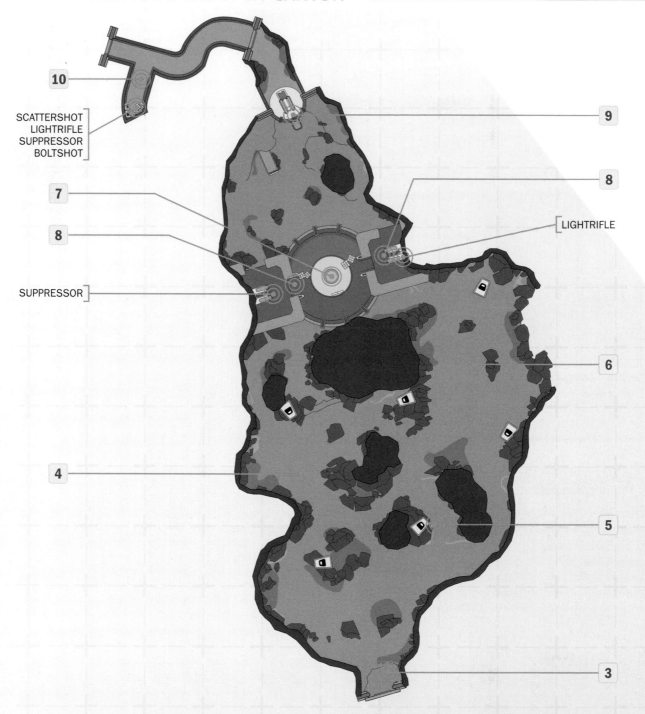

10

SCATTERSHOT
LIGHTRIFLE
SUPPRESSOR
BOLTSHOT

9

7

8

8

LIGHTRIFLE

SUPPRESSOR

6

4

5

3

3 This next series of battles can be frustrating because the Checkpoints in between each section can set you back quite a bit if you die, as they are spread quite thin. The canyon is split into two major paths that eventually intersect atop a Forerunner Structure, where further progress is challenged by a Knight Battlewagon. The whole time, you will run into increasingly larger packs of Crawlers.

> **RECOMMENDED LOADOUT**

If the first Knight of this section carries a LightRifle, and you passed it up after your first Knight encounter, consider picking it up now. The LightRifle can easily replace the Boltshot as your ranged headshot machine because it's perfect for culling herds of Crawlers, and useful at putting down Knights stripped of shields. Keep a Suppressor handy for closer Knight encounters. While a fully charged Boltshot can wreck their shielding, the weapon also puts you in range of their blades. LightRifles are also very good at scoring headshots on Knights after their shields fail. In fact, if the shot that breaks their shielding hits directly on the face of a standard Knight, it can result in an immediate kill.

At the end of the passage, the door opens to a canyon with a path straight ahead and another path that branches off to the right. A pair of Knights warp into view and split off to guard each path. You can take this pair down, one at a time, and it's even possible to ignore the Knight that teleports to the right path. If you've obtained the Autosentry, it's possible to use the small stone just in front of the passage door to cover your flanking attempt by setting the Autosentry right at the door. The Knight usually tries to shoot the turret down, and if you're fast, you can assassinate it. From this position, you can choose your route.

Going Straight

4 Going straight is the quickest way to reach the next major firefight. A Knight will appear on the rocks just beyond the first Knight. Then it will retreat further into the canyon to join a pack of Crawlers to try to hold you off from point **7**, where another major encounter awaits.

To the Right

5 The second Knight, if given time alone, will begin patrolling the right path, which means there is a good amount of time where its back will be turned. If you are fast, it's possible to take advantage of the Knight's slow movement and assassinate it. If it notices you, it will try to teleport down the hill further to the right, into a more open section of the canyon **6**, where another set of Crawlers, another Knight, and Watchers are on patrol. You can avoiding fight two Knights at once here, by falling back and letting the first Knight come back up the hill toward you. The roaming Crawlers may try to intervene on the first Knight's behalf, but careful Boltshot or LightRifle action can deal with them.

With the first Knight down, you can take on the second group **6**. Make sure the two Watchers go down first!

INTRODUCTION

BASIC TRAINING

INTEL

CAMPAIGN

INFINITY

APPENDIX

The Knight Battlewagon and the Watcher

7 This platform is flanked by a pair of ramps with weapon caches atop the balconies **8** . The field you must travel through to continue beyond this point is where a Knight Battlewagon stands guard, protected by a Watcher it deploys. Meanwhile, two Crawler packs infest the cliff sides to the left and right of the Knight, while another smaller pack roams the grounds near it. With so much convenient LightRifle ammunition available in the racks, wiping out the Crawlers should be a first priority. Should the Watcher move to protect a Crawler, ignore that one and move on to another target. So long as you don't rush the Knight, it will most likely stand back and fire ineffectually at you with its Scattershot from afar.

Once the Crawlers no longer present a significant threat, take out the Watcher, then go to work on the Knight Battlewagon. Its Scattershot is incredibly dangerous, and once the Watcher is dead, this will inspire the Knight to come forward and deliver hot death up close and personal. Do not let it get close, and make sure that you keep it distracted with an Autosentry if you need to retreat quickly.

Alternatively, you can shoot at the Watcher once, which will cause it to clam up and not help any of its allies while it tries to regenerate. The Knight will still hang back a safer distance away. If you're on point, keeping the Watcher suppressed with the occasional LightRifle shot while putting in the work on the Battlewagon, this last fight can go slower, but much safer.

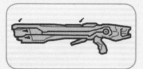
Legendary Strategy

You'll can generally follow the tactics used on Heroic, but anything that involves you closing in on a Knight is generally not encouraged. They'll just cut you to ribbons while you struggle to bring down their shields. You absolutely must do your best to keep the Knights from working in tandem. For the final battle, the alternate suggestion for Heroic difficulty becomes the most recommended for Legendary. Drive the Watcher off, but don't kill it! The Knight Battlewagon will try to charge you if you kill the Watcher. The Scattershot held by a it will be almost certain death for players at close range, and the Knight is keen to leap directly on the platform at **7** to do just that.

DOMAIN TERMINAL

9 After killing off the last group of Prometheans near **7** , don't miss this Domain Terminal sitting underneath the balcony that leads to the next section.

10 Another corridor will take you past this weapons cache. You should consider keeping a LightRifle for this next section, but a Scattershot is not a bad idea if you're interested in more aggressive play against Knights.

> MAJOR FIREFIGHT: THE FIRST SHIELD EMITTER

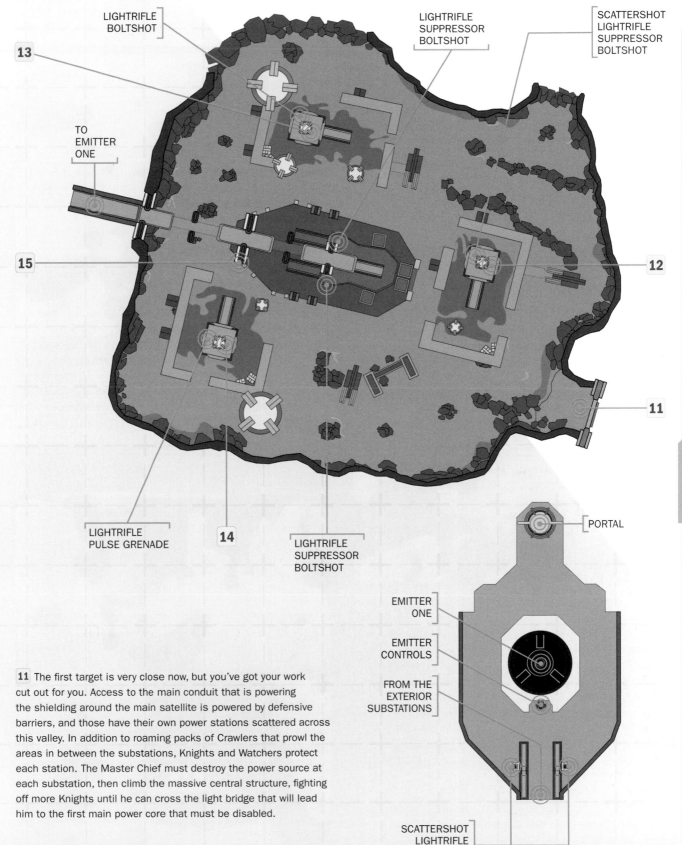

LIGHTRIFLE
BOLTSHOT

13

LIGHTRIFLE
SUPPRESSOR
BOLTSHOT

SCATTERSHOT
LIGHTRIFLE
SUPPRESSOR
BOLTSHOT

TO
EMITTER
ONE

15

12

11

LIGHTRIFLE
PULSE GRENADE

14

LIGHTRIFLE
SUPPRESSOR
BOLTSHOT

PORTAL

EMITTER
ONE

EMITTER
CONTROLS

FROM THE
EXTERIOR
SUBSTATIONS

SCATTERSHOT
LIGHTRIFLE
SUPPRESSOR
BOLTSHOT

INTRODUCTION
BASIC TRAINING
INTEL
CAMPAIGN
INFINITY
APPENDIX

11 The first target is very close now, but you've got your work cut out for you. Access to the main conduit that is powering the shielding around the main satellite is powered by defensive barriers, and those have their own power stations scattered across this valley. In addition to roaming packs of Crawlers that prowl the areas in between the substations, Knights and Watchers protect each station. The Master Chief must destroy the power source at each substation, then climb the massive central structure, fighting off more Knights until he can cross the light bridge that will lead him to the first main power core that must be disabled.

The LightRifle should be your primary weapon throughout this section, as the infestation of Crawlers is best solved by this weapon, and any Watchers in the air will hardly have the time to be the nuisance they are designed to be. While the Scattershot is clearly a risky weapon, it is powerful enough to break a Knight's shielding at close range (even on Legendary), and can stagger most Knight variants long enough to allow a follow-up kill shot.

Ideally, Pulse Grenades can devastate Knights and Crawlers, but in practice most of the time the enemy tends to dive right out of its area of effect. You have to lure or force enemies into a Pulse Grenade's energy field to get the most out of the weapons.

Crawler Cleanup

11 The moment you pass through the door to enter this valley, you can see the first substation **12** to your right on the ground below your perch. You'll most likely see a Knight patrolling atop the substation, deploying a Watcher. Meanwhile, along the ground at the foot of the cliff, you can spot the Crawler packs already converging upon your position. You need to take out the Crawlers as quickly as possible, preferably before the Knight and its Watcher decide to join the fun and pepper you with LightRifle shots.

» KEY COMBAT TIP

As a general rule, regardless of the difficulty, hunting down any Crawlers near the substations and the area surrounding the central tower is a good way to balance the odds in your favor, but this is especially true on Legendary. It is the height of frustration to work through the shields of a Knight, only to see it warp away to a position where it has a lot of Crawlers to protect it, or when your attack is interrupted by a fatal Crawler flanking maneuver.

Substation One

Once you've eliminated enough Crawlers that you have a good amount of open space, drop down and get to one of the protective walls surrounding the first substation **12** and finish off the stragglers. Now you can take on the Knight and Watcher team in relative safety. If you're willing to take the risk, the Scattershot can kill a Knight in two close-range shots. Once you're clear, enter the substation and attack the glowing orb inside with a melee attack to disable the station. Two more to go!

Substation Two

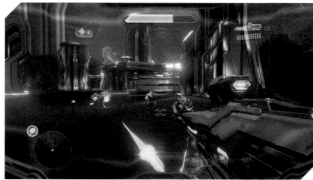

13 At each substation, you can expect at least one Knight who will deploy a Watcher upon noticing you, and Crawler packs in the general vicinity.

Substation Three

14 This particular substation presents a greater challenge than the others. There are more Crawler packs prowling the area close to it, and you'll want to deal with them before you disable the last of the substations.

Alternate Approach

Some players may actually want to take out substations two and three first, and there is a benefit to doing so: When all three substations are taken out, multiple Knights spawn near the entrance ramp to the tower **15**, close to the last two objectives, and they can be tough to fight from those locations after they spawn relatively close to you.

Tower Climb

15 With all of the substations disabled, you now need to climb the tower. Your first obstacle spawns right near the foot of the ramp you need to take to get to the mid level: two Knights. At the same time, a Knight Battlewagon spawns on the balcony overlooking substation **14**. Even at that range, the Scattershot it has can be very dangerous in combination with the two Knights on the ground. As always, you can expect at least one Watcher to be deployed.

The Knight Battlewagon has the advantage in speed, strength, and defense. Getting close to you is its goal. Bust out the LightRifle and lead it on a chase around the platform. Shoot it in the face a lot, and it can't hurt you nearly as bad as it can with its Scattershot. Once you finish it off, the way to the first main power generator is clear!

Legendary Strategy

It's possible to pull off the Scattershot gambit against Knights on Legendary, but you have much less room for error, and because you're often not able to separate paired Knights from each other, charging at one just exposes you to fire from multiple sources. Just save yourself the wailing and gnashing of teeth, and focus on smart and relatively safe ranged tactics. You can tackle the substations in any order you please, but the key thing to remember is to be thorough when clearing out a substation. You trigger a quicksave for each one you disable, so you can take some solace in that. It cannot be stated enough: Kill those Crawlers! With them out of the picture, you can handle the Knight guardians of the substations in battles you can more easily control.

When it's time to climb the tower, your first challenge is to get past the two Knights that warp in right in front of the tower's ramp entrance. Set up an Autosentry to add to your own fire and to provide a momentary distraction while you try to land hits. Once inside the tower, be especially wary of the Knight Battlewagon that is carrying a Scattershot. In any close-range duel, it has a distinct advantage. It's possible to lead it through a Pulse Grenade field, which will help you bring it down that much faster.

INTRODUCTION

BASIC TRAINING

INTEL

CAMPAIGN

INFINITY

APPENDIX

125

Enter the elevator on the other side of the light bridge to reach the beam control and disable the device. Cortana learns that *Infinity* is actually now in orbit outside the shield world, and is now in danger of being drawn in just like the Covenant and the Master Chief were. Before taking out the generator and leaving this room, check the weapons caches on either side of the elevator to stock up on Forerunner weapons. Cortana will open a portal that takes you back to the very first portal room, where she opens another portal that drops you close to the second power station. As you soon see, the Covenant apparently have the same idea as the Master Chief, and are racing toward the same destination.

> THE ROAD TO STATION TWO

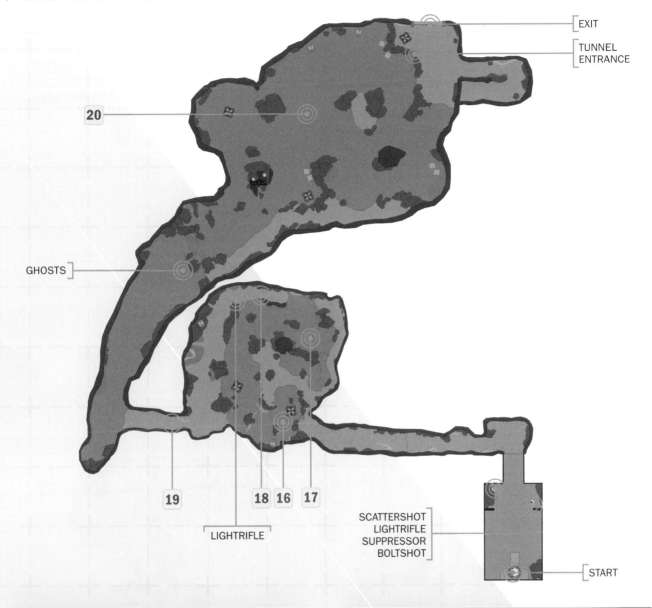

EXIT

TUNNEL
ENTRANCE

20

GHOSTS

19   18 16 17

LIGHTRIFLE

SCATTERSHOT
LIGHTRIFLE
SUPPRESSOR
BOLTSHOT

START

INTRODUCTION

BASIC TRAINING

INTEL

CAMPAIGN

INFINITY

APPENDIX

16 Fortunately, the Prometheans do not appear to discriminate. Covenant drop pods land throughout this canyon and are immediately beset by a vicious Knight counterattack. You're under no obligation to help one side over the other, but as you may have learned in previous encounters, the Knights are made of annoyingly resilient stuff. The first battle here, however, almost always goes poorly for the Covenant, no matter how much you try to "help."

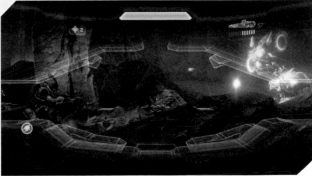

17 This fight, however is much more even, but it still tips somewhat in favor of the Knight Battlewagon. Higher ranking Elites are having trouble breaking down the defenses provided by a pair of Watchers. If you take the Watchers out, you can force the Battlewagon to get more aggressive, which will lead to Elite casualties eventually, particularly if you take out a few for yourself.

18 After clearing the initial kill zone in the valley, you can climb along this cliff-side path, where you encounter an Elite getting utterly dominated by a Knight. If you sprint quickly along this path and are armed with a Scattershot, you can possibly interrupt the Knight and prevent the initial escape. If not, it will pull back toward the next part of the route. A pair of Watchers will teleport into the area **19** . The Watchers are priority targets! They will both try to craft new threats for you to face. The Watcher trying to craft on the path itself will make a Knight, while the Watcher at the top of the cliffs will summon a powerful Forerunner anti-infantry turret.

⟫ KEY COMBAT TIP

Fair warning, on Legendary the Forerunner anti-infantry turret will cut you down in seconds, so if you're forced to choose which thing to prevent from happening, the Forerunner anti-infantry turret should go. It can control almost the entire path, which really restricts your movement when fighting the Knights.

20 Another Covenant-Promethean battle goes very poorly for the Covenant here, but you're able to make things go badly for everyone. The Ghost gives you a lot of flexibility to flank and otherwise harry both sides of the conflict. If you're in a hurry, you can actually blitz past most of the hostiles here by heading straight for the tunnels.

19 As you leave the cliff-side path and pass through the gap in the wall, a pair of Elites on Ghosts suffer Knight-induced road rash and are relieved of life and vehicles. The Knight will teleport next to the Ghosts, as though to guard your new rides. Eliminate the Knight, and take one of the Ghosts for yourself.

21 After breaking through another small battle featuring Grunts and Jackals against Crawlers, you enter this tunnel, which is another chance to rearm and prepare for the next power facility. You can pick through multiple weapons caches here, and can find another Ghost at **22** , if your current means of transport is looking a little roasted by plasma.

› MAJOR FIREFIGHT: THE SECOND SHIELD EMITTER

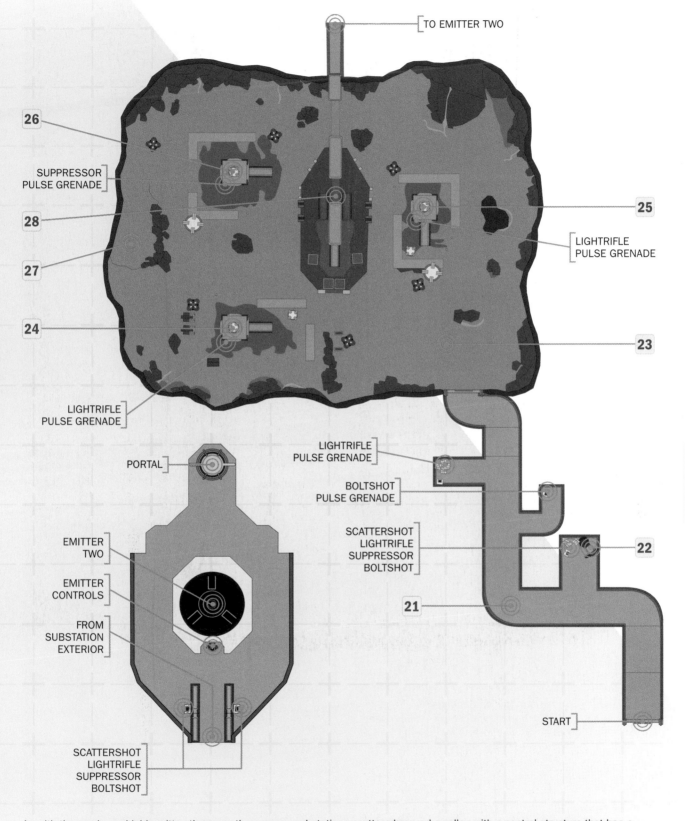

TO EMITTER TWO

26

SUPPRESSOR
PULSE GRENADE

28

27

24

25

LIGHTRIFLE
PULSE GRENADE

23

LIGHTRIFLE
PULSE GRENADE

PORTAL

LIGHTRIFLE
PULSE GRENADE

BOLTSHOT
PULSE GRENADE

EMITTER
TWO

SCATTERSHOT
LIGHTRIFLE
SUPPRESSOR
BOLTSHOT

22

EMITTER
CONTROLS

FROM
SUBSTATION
EXTERIOR

21

START

SCATTERSHOT
LIGHTRIFLE
SUPPRESSOR
BOLTSHOT

INTRODUCTION

BASIC TRAINING

INTEL

CAMPAIGN

INFINITY

APPENDIX

As with the previous shield emitter, there are three power substations scattered around a valley, with a central structure that has a connecting light bridge leading to the emitter controls. These facilities are currently being occupied by an extensive Covenant presence, including a small squadron of Banshees providing air cover. Fortunately, there are plenty approaches that enterprising Spartans can take to quickly run roughshod over the defenders.

> RECOMMENDED LOADOUT

It's possible to beat this assault with a LightRifle and Plasma Pistol combo, and there are plenty of Covenant packing the Plasma Pistols, so you can keep rearming on the run. The Covenant vehicles in the area can be easily disabled with charged shots, which allows for hijacking. If you have arrived on a Ghost, then aside from strafing runs from Banshees, the defenders around the substations will be hard-pressed to deal with a skilled driver. There is, of course, always the option to steal a Banshee of your own.

One Banshee Down, A Good Start

23 As soon as you enter the valley, an Elite near the door will start to fall back toward a parked Banshee. There is no reason to let him make it to the flier. With him out of the picture, you have a number of options. You can take the abandoned Banshee immediately, but by this time a hostile Banshee will likely already be closing in from above. Stick with the Ghost to evade the first strafing run, and then proceed with your chosen plan.

》 KEY COMBAT TIP

As with the previous power substations, the three in this zone are deactivated in the same way, and all three contain weapon racks that can be used to restock if necessary.

Option One: The Ghost

To reach the three substations 24 25 26 the quickest, the Ghost is a solid option. Your greatest vulnerability will be from above, either from Elites and other Covenant in the central structure sniping down at you, or from the Banshees in the air. Both of these are relatively easy to negate. For the former, you can use the terrain and other Forerunner constructions to deny snipers clean shots. Taking a Ghost up against a Banshee isn't a safe option. The Banshee Plasma Cannons can melt your ride very quickly, and their pilots are deadly accurate, preferring to attack your Ghost from angles from which you can't shoot back. Speed and movement are life if you're insisting on the ground game.

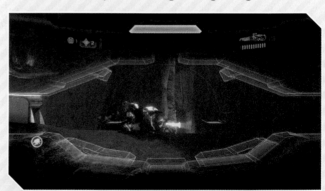

Multiple hostile Ghosts are patrolling the substations, and they can be problematic if they flank you. Elites can hijack you if you let them get near, so be sure that you gun them down from afar, and if you have to get close, it should be because you hit them while holding down the speed boost for your own Ghost. The last problem with the Ghost is that you don't have the means to easily take out all the Covenant protecting the central building, so you're forced to hoof it.

Option BYOB: Bring Your Own Banshee

23 **27** There are two Banshees you can get quick access to. The first is obviously the one you prevent from being manned as soon as you enter the area. The second is on the other side of the valley from where you begin. On a Ghost, you can quickly make your way to it, but doing so early on is asking for trouble, as there are hostile Banshees in the air, not to mention the numerous Covenant infantry on the ground defending the two substations near it.

Banshees are incredibly fragile to incoming fire, and if you steal the first Banshee you find, you're in a tight spot because multiple Banshees are in  the air close by, ready to shoot you down. Get some altitude immediately to get out of range of Covenant infantry, and then make hunting down all the hostile fliers your top priority. The hardest part of this option is literally right at the moment you take off, when you're in range of many angry Covenant firing from almost every direction.

With air superiority yours, you can bomb every single defender next to the substations into submission. Just make sure that when you land your 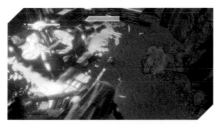 Banshee, there aren't any Elites loitering close by to turn your ride against you. Avoid loitering at low altitudes when battling infantry from above, Grunts are savants when it comes to using charged Plasma Pistol shots to bring down hostile fliers. Whatever option you pick, as soon as you disable all three substations, get to the top of the central structure and make your way to the second shield emitter to shut it down.

›› KEY COMBAT TIP

It is possible to fight your way to each substation on foot, but it can be rather time consuming, in addition to being difficult to handle constant strafing runs from the Banshees.

Alternate Approach

One thing you can try on any difficulty is to use a Banshee's Fuel Rod Cannon to destroy the substations from above. It's not easy to thread a shot to hit each generator, but if you do, you can avoid a lot of hassle once they are destroyed and just land your Banshee atop the tower and flee across the light bridge to safety.

The Central Structure

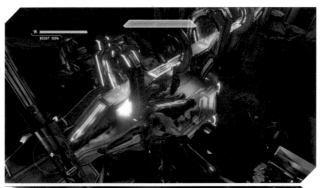

28 Multiple Elites control all of the central ramps that lead up to the light bridge. You can bypass or destroy much of this resistance by using a Banshee, but if you're stuck taking them on while on foot, you can't beat the LightRifle and Plasma Pistol combo for sheer efficiency.

Legendary Tactics

A major problem with your starting position is that you're essentially surrounded by enemies, and you can't ignore the fact that there's a Banshee you can prevent from taking to the sky and joining ones that may already bearing down upon you. However, trying to take the Banshee for yourself stands a good chance of ending within seconds of your boarding it. Ghosts aren't much safer, but they are faster and smaller targets, which can give you a chance to keep the first Banshee grounded while evading the others. Do what you can to clear the skies directly over the starting point **23** from the ground. From there, you have to make sure that you deal with the hostile Ghosts protecting the two closest substations. If you take out the troops from substation **24**, you've given yourself a good window to take to the skies in some measure of safety.

INTRODUCTION · BASIC TRAINING · INTEL · CAMPAIGN · INFINITY · APPENDIX

As you reach the final emitter and shut it down, the worst-case scenario happens in spite of your efforts. The *Infinity* begins its descent to the planet's core, where it will inevitably be trapped by Requiem's gravity well. Restock at the nearby weapons caches, then travel through the new portals Cortana opens. You reach the central satellite just as the Covenant begin their assault. You have to choose which path you want to fight through to reach the controls.

> **MAJOR FIREFIGHT: THE CORE**

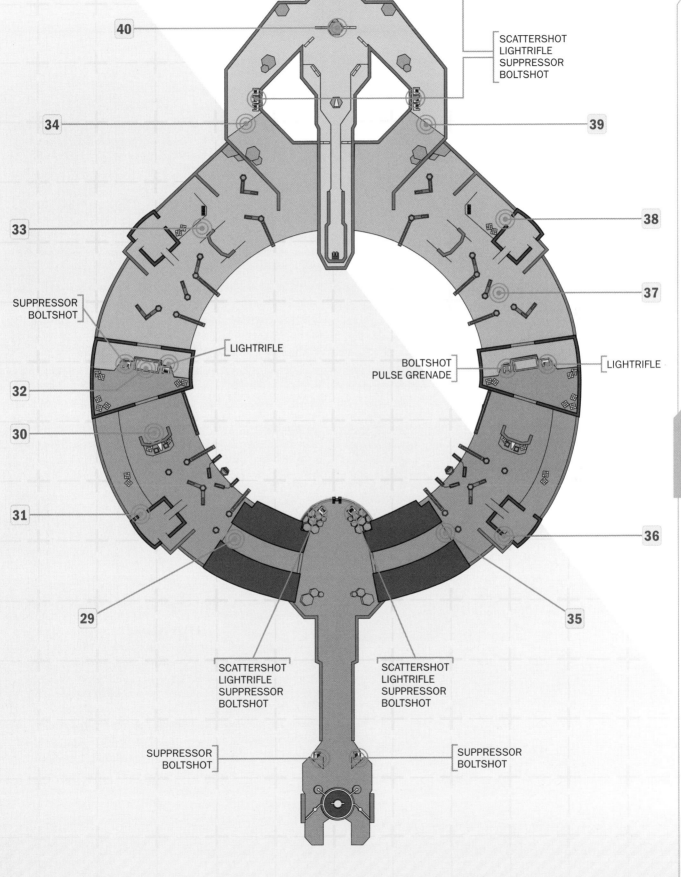

40

SCATTERSHOT
LIGHTRIFLE
SUPPRESSOR
BOLTSHOT

34

39

33

38

37

SUPPRESSOR
BOLTSHOT

LIGHTRIFLE

BOLTSHOT
PULSE GRENADE

LIGHTRIFLE

32

30

31

36

29

35

SCATTERSHOT
LIGHTRIFLE
SUPPRESSOR
BOLTSHOT

SCATTERSHOT
LIGHTRIFLE
SUPPRESSOR
BOLTSHOT

SUPPRESSOR
BOLTSHOT

SUPPRESSOR
BOLTSHOT

INTRODUCTION

BASIC TRAINING

INTEL

CAMPAIGN

INFINITY

APPENDIX

This is the last chance to warn off the *Infinity*, and the odds of making it in time to a system that will let you contact the ship are not good. There are two paths to the controls on the opposite side of the satellite: The path to the left **29** sets you up against a large Knight contingent that is holding out well against a Covenant assault. The right path **35** has you taking on the Covenant as they finish off the last of the Prometheans. Whichever you choose, you are in for the hardest fight of the mission by far.

> RECOMMENDED LOADOUT

Hopefully you've kept your Autosentry. Having the extra firepower and distraction is going to be crucial. You can always rely on the Plasma Pistol to break through shielding quickly, and on either route you'll have the opportunity find replacements for this gun to keep loaded. LightRifles compliment the Plasma Pistol well, and you'll eventually encounter the incredibly useful Binary Rifle, the most powerful sniping weapons available. A Scattershot is also useful for putting down Knights and Elites alike.

To the Left: Knight Lancers, Forerunner Turrets, Dying Covenant

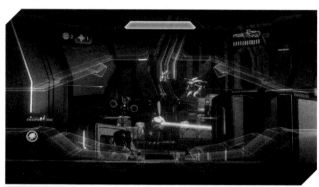

29 As you crest the ramp leading to this room, your first sight may be an Elite getting disintegrated by a single shot from a Binary Rifle, which is wielded in the distance by a Knight Lancer that is protected by a Watcher. More Knights flank the Knight Lancer, charging into the Covenant and fighting to take back the balcony to the left, while a Forerunner anti-infantry turret tries to lock down the lower level in conjunction with the Knight Lancer. There are a couple of ways to handle the threat from the Knight Lancer. One is to use the Covenant in the area as a moving, living shield while you move from cover to cover to get close enough to it to put it down. The Grunts and Jackals will not last long against the Knight Lancer, but they aren't meant to. Use them to help take out the Watcher and Forerunner anti-infantry turret first. If you're lucky, you can scrounge up Plasma Grenades to try to stick the Knight Lancer.

WEAPON ACQUISITION

BINARY RIFLE

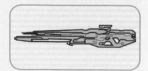

This is a powerful sniper rifle that is capable of puncturing some of the strongest personal shielding available and scoring kill shots. The only thing holding back the Binary Rifle from being a sniper's dream weapon is the limited ammunition per energy cell: only two shots. Even if you manage to acquire the weapon from a Knight, you need to be extremely precise to take advantage of the few uses you'll have.

30 The Knight Lancer's Binary Rifle can pop your shields in a single shot, and the lethal follow-up is almost always within seconds. Do *not* stand out in the open! Destroying the Forerunner containers can clear out the turret and nearby enemies.

31 The other is to use your Autosentry as a distraction to try to close in on the Knight Lancer via the balcony. Assuming it hasn't been sniped, there will likely be an Elite along with a couple of Grunts taking on a Knight. By taking the balcony you get a chance to take on the Knight Lancer from an elevated position.

» KEY COMBAT TIP

Take the Knight Lancer's Binary Rifle. You still have another room filled with Knights (including another Knight Lancer) and Watchers to contend with. Having the power of a Binary Rifle can really help thin out the Prometheans, which will give the Covenant a chance to distract the Knight Lancer for longer.

Legendary Strategy

The biggest change to this battle on Legendary—aside from the usual increased speed and accuracy of enemy fire, the increased health of all enemies, and the improved shielding on enemies that have shields—is that the Binary Rifle is a one-shot kill regardless of your shield levels. As you might imagine, this ... complicates matters. If standing in the open was a bad idea before, it's a guaranteed death sentence now. While it's possible to advance forward using the Covenant as a distraction, they will not last even half as long as they did on Heroic, and that Knight Lancer has such a lockdown on the lower level that even if you manage to get close, you'll have next to no support, and you still have to contend with the Knights guarding the ramps that lead up to the Knight Lancer's perch. Its split-second reaction times at close range will probably grant you a trip back to the last checkpoint, where you get to fight your way back to it all over again. You should still start this battle by eliminating the Watchers and the Forerunner anti-infantry turret. If you're lucky, the Covenant might be able to hurt the Knight Lancer, giving you an opening to finish the job.

The balcony route is "safer." You need to "rescue" the Elite from the Knight on that level. It, combined with an Autosentry, can provide a reasonable enough distraction that you can try to stick the Knight Lancer with Plasma Grenades, assuming you have any. If you don't, you can still shoot it out with the Knight Lancer. It tends to try to stick to its post. You'll just have to be extremely careful.

Whatever you do, take the Binary Rifle from this dead Knight Lancer if possible. It is incredibly useful for the next section.

32 The room that the Knights were protecting contains weapons caches that feature Suppressors and LightRifles. It's recommended that you take a LightRifle to compliment the Binary Rifle we hope you have acquired. Once you ride the short elevator up to the door, you can't come back for the weapons stored here.

Room Two

33 A similarly designed arena to the previous battle, the same problems apply here. The Knights hold the far end of the room, with a Knight Lancer on a central platform. Unlike the previous room, they have a place to fall back to: the ramp leading up to the core. Ideally, you should not let them retreat that far, as the ground between their previous position and their new one has less cover for you to use. With the LightRifle, you should be able to take out the Watchers, as well as any Covenant who turn their guns on you. You especially want the Watchers dead to prevent them from rebuilding a Knight. Save the Binary Rifle for the Knights, particularly that Knight Lancer, which should be your first target after eliminating the Watchers. Two consecutive Binary headshots can bring down a Knight Lancer quickly, the trick is to land those shots.

To make things a little easier, you can stick to the door near the elevator. So long as you don't actually cross into the arena, you have a good safe spot to snipe from. Once the area is clear, proceed up the ramp toward the top of the satellite core. You have the opportunity to stock up at weapons caches located on the ramp **34** .

If you should push the Knight Lancer back toward the ramp leading out of the area, you're now somewhat in a bind because it can get good angles on you regardless of how you approach. You'll have to go from cover to cover to get into position to disable its shields, most likely with a Plasma Pistol or LightRifle. Body shots are still lethal for an unprotected Knight.

Legendary Strategy

Another Knight Lancer and its Binary Rifle dominate the center of this area. Unlike the previous Knight Lancer, this one has a lot of room to fall back and recover its shields, and can even retreat to higher ground to maintain a positional advantage. It is still the priority target after you've eliminated the Watchers. You have a very limited window of opportunity to take out the Knight Lancer, as the Covenant that are bravely sacrificing themselves will not provide a distraction for long. After the Knight Lancer is out of the picture, the rest of this battle can more or less fall into a predictable, though still dangerous, pattern of exploiting the surviving Covenant to help bring down the Knights.

To the Right: Fallen Prometheans, a Resurgent Covenant

35 The right route mirrors the left route in terms of appearance. The only changes are in enemy composition. After a Phantom crashes into the last vestiges of serious Promethean resistance, the first room falls under the command of a squad of Elites, with shield-equipped Jackals and Grunts patrolling the area. The Covenant knows you're coming. Gather up a Plasma Pistol, as well as any headshot-capable weapon, and go to work. The Elites here are all high ranking, so expect to contend with Fuel Rod Cannons and Concussion Rifles.

INTRODUCTION BASIC TRAINING INTEL CAMPAIGN INFINITY APPENDIX

36 The balcony is not necessarily a safe spot. The Covenant tend to charge aggressively into the balcony to try to dislodge you, and the close-quarters fighting against the Elites is always a dangerous prospect. If you post yourself up there, watch your Motion Sensor for flanking maneuvers. As soon as you eliminate all resistance, travel through the locked doors to the elevator room. As with the left route elevator, you have a set of weapons caches to rearm yourself. Make sure to take a LightRifle.

37 You actually have a major advantage entering this room. Covenant on the ground level are concentrating on the remaining Prometheans at the central platform. Take out the Elite leading the ground level team to incite panic or suicidal rage among the Grunts, and punish them accordingly. Jackals will likely fall back to take up positions on the central platform, while the balcony **38** will possibly have more Grunts and Jackals to deal with.

» KEY COMBAT TIP

The central platform may have a Binary Rifle. Save it for the final push to the control station, particularly if you're playing on Legendary.

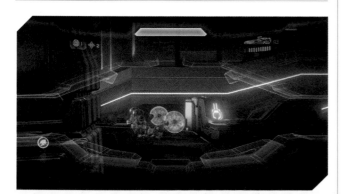

Mop up the Covenant that are guarding the rear of this room, then take the ramp up to the top of the satellite and be ready for a final brawl. Rearm at the weapon caches along the way **39**.

Legendary Strategy

You've fought the Covenant enough by now to know what to expect from the Elites, and in a sense the right path is a test of your ability to manage larger numbers of Elites while still suppressing other types of Covenant infantry. While you always want to focus on reducing enemy numbers quickly at the start of any battle, keep an eye out for any Elites carrying heavy weapons like the Fuel Rod Cannon. If they get gutsy and charge you, be ready with a charge shot combo to take them down. On Legendary, you have a poor chance of survival if they get the first shot.

A LightRifle, if you have one available, is the best all-around weapon for these rooms, providing a good mix of range, damage, and safety. If you ever are unable to use the Plasma Pistol to take out Elite shields, you can still put them down relatively fast with the LightRifle alone. While it might be tempting to turn a Fuel Rod Cannon against the enemy, they tend to be too evasive for the weapon to achieve its full potential.

The Last Line

40 A squad of Elites takes on a determined defensive line consisting of Knights, Knight Battlewagons, and a Knight Lancer, and it appears to be at a temporary stalemate. The Elites here are all high ranking and are able to survive most of what the Knights can dish out. Use this to your advantage, and take out a Knight or two to encourage them to push forward. This can distract the Knight Lancer and give you the opportunity to eliminate it before it becomes a problem. If you're too proactive at killing Knights and leave the Elites alive, they in turn will take up positions to try to block your advance on the communications controls. Share the love equally amongst your enemies!

Alternate Approach

It is entirely possible to reach the target control pillars by taking out the Knights and Elites on the side of the arena you enter from, then making a mad dash toward it. On Legendary this tactic is much less likely to work due to the increased perception of all enemies.

> NEXT STOP, CERTAIN DEATH

INTRODUCTION

BASIC TRAINING

INTEL

CAMPAIGN

INFINITY

APPENDIX

You have been deceived. Disabling the shielding around the core and trying to use it as a communications interface has only unleashed something—someone—ancient, and utterly furious at his apparent betrayal and imprisonment. Declaring that the Forerunners have returned, he easily brushes aside the Master Chief, while the Prometheans and surviving Covenant all kneel to this being's professed authority.

After barely escaping, the Master Chief comes to as a gravity well begins drawing everything toward the satellite core. There is no time to discuss the issue further. Calling the new enemy the Didact, Cortana urges you to get on a Ghost and make a run for a portal.

Fortunately, there are no special side routes, and no special items to locate along the way, you would have maybe seconds to try to collect any of it as is. The best advice would be to avoid the walls by laying off the boost to regain sharper turning, and to take every major jump at full speed and as close to straight on as you can manage, what with the ground in upheaval all around you as you race through the narrow canyons.

Because you're in a hurry, Cortana shifts your shield generator to power the boost function on the Ghost. This gives you unlimited boost, but serious crashes can easily kill you. Dawdling will also kill you, so you have to take the risk and ride as hard and fast as you possibly can. It's possible to get turned around after a bad crash, but if you are ever lost, just pay attention to which way the Grunts are running.

You eventually reach a portal and fly through it, which takes you to the planet at the center of the shield world. The UNSC *Infinity* streaks overhead toward the horizon. The Didact's satellite flies after it in hot pursuit. The Master Chief orders Cortana to plot a route to the *Infinity*; the survivors will need their assistance.

CAMPAIGN

MISSION 4: INFINITY

"It's not all right. Nothing about it is all right."

The *Infinity* has crashed onto Requiem and is being assaulted by Covenant. Meanwhile, the Master Chief and Cortana make their way on foot through a perilous jungle. Scouts from *Infinity* have tried to establish forward bases to recon the area around the ship, but they are being overwhelmed by the vicious Knights and their Crawler packs.

⌃ MISSION BRIEFING

The first section of this mission does not contain the massive battles that you've probably come to expect, but this does not make the enemy any less dangerous than usual. The Prometheans and the Marines are scattered throughout the jungle, with the former hunting the latter. Once contact with the enemy has been made, expect to come across squads of Prometheans in regular succession. Things heat up quickly after joining up with a combined Marine-Spartan force led by Commander Lasky as you lead a push through Promethean territory to reach a Landing Zone to evacuate casualties. Afterward, you lead an armored assault at the besieged *Infinity*, into and through it, ultimately reaching the ship's outer hull, where you make a final stand against the combined forces of the Didact and the Covenant.

ENEMIES ENCOUNTERED:

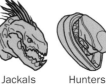

Elites   Grunts   Jackals   Hunters

Crawlers   Knights   Watchers

VEHICLES ENCOUNTERED:

Phantom Dropships   Ghosts   Banshees

Wraiths

WEAPONS ACQUIRED

Assault Rifle
Magnum
DMR
Battle Rifle
Storm Rifle
Plasma Pistol
Needler
Covenant Carbine
Concussion Rifle
Fuel Rod Cannon
Beam Rifle
Boltshot
Suppressor
LightRifle
Binary Rifle
Scattershot
Railgun
Rocket Launcher

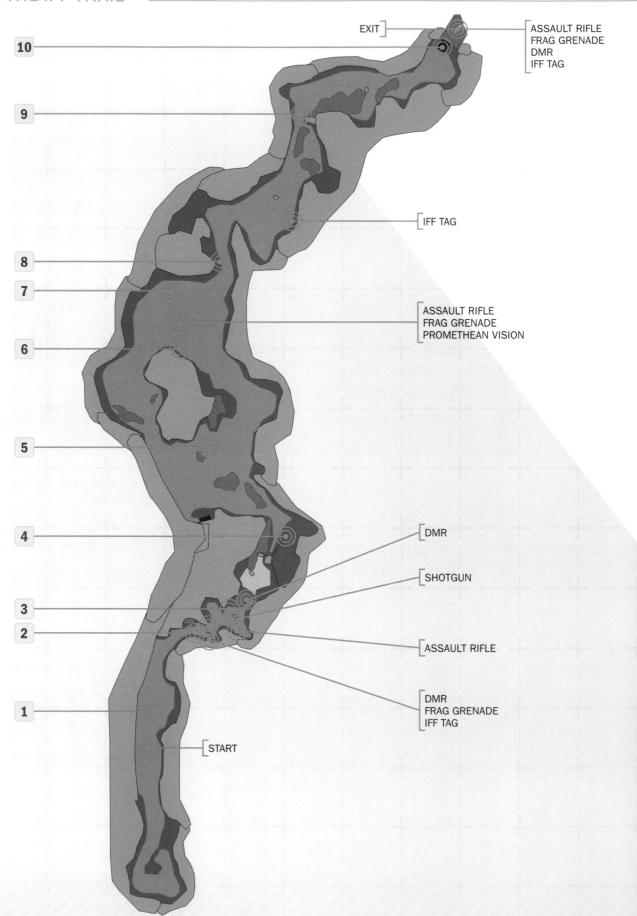

EXIT

ASSAULT RIFLE
FRAG GRENADE
DMR
IFF TAG

10

9

IFF TAG

8

7

ASSAULT RIFLE
FRAG GRENADE
PROMETHEAN VISION

6

5

4

DMR

SHOTGUN

3

2

ASSAULT RIFLE

DMR
FRAG GRENADE
IFF TAG

1

START

INTRODUCTION

BASIC TRAINING

INTEL

CAMPAIGN

INFINITY

APPENDIX

1 When you regain control of the Master Chief, the *Infinity* is in dire straights. Covenant ships roar overhead to join their brothers in the assault on the vessel, and in the distance, the Didact's satellite flits across the sky, scanning the *Infinity*, searching for something. Over the open UNSC network, beleaguered Marines are requesting assistance. Cortana marks the nearest Friend/Foe Tag (IFF Tag). Run into the jungle to assist!

2 Unfortunately, you're already too late to save at least some of the Marines. The Knights responsible for killing this squad teleport away just as you arrive. Pick up the IFF tag to listen to the Marines' final words, then scour the area for weapons. Most importantly, each Marine in this squad carried a DMR. Take the weapon and all the ammo you can carry, these Marines don't need it any longer.

WEAPON ACQUISITION

DMR

Filling the need for a mid- to long-range counter-sniper system, the DMR is an accurate rifle capable of bringing high-powered armor piercing capability to a Marine in a relatively compact package. The DMR is especially popular in concert with weapons like the Plasma Pistol, and is able to exploit defeated shielding systems with a single precise shot between the eyes of the target.

3 A pack of Crawlers rushes forward to ambush you here. With a Magnum or a DMR, they are at best nuisances. Even pulsed fire from an Assault Rifle can be effective.

4 Now for some real resistance. A Knight deploys a Watcher here, and is joined by more packs of Crawlers. If you can take out the Watcher immediately, do so. Otherwise fall back a short distance and pick off the Crawlers that give chase. When an opening presents itself, take out the Watcher, then go to work on the Knight. To the left of where the Knight is encountered, the jungle path is guarded by more Crawlers.

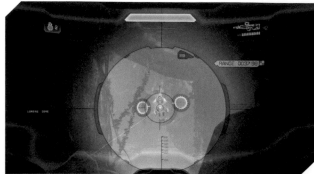

5 A Watcher hovers into view here, attempting to construct reinforcements from the remains of fallen Crawlers. If it's put down quickly enough, you can prevent the resurrection, but this isn't the only threat here. More Crawlers leap down from the trees, and farther down this path is the most dangerous of all Crawler variants: the Crawler Snipe. Armed with Binary Rifles, these Crawlers are priority targets. Their heads have a telltale halo effect that signifies their readiness to fire. Farther down this section **6**, a Knight and a Marine kill each other in final acts of defiance. The Knight drops something that Cortana wants you to pick up. Check out the surrounding area to restock on Frag Grenades and Assault Rifle or Magnum ammo.

⟫ KEY COMBAT TIP

Crawler Snipes are the bane of your existence on Legendary. Any time you encounter them on Heroic should be cause for concern, but on Legendary, their positions should not only be remembered, but your DMR should be pointed at their position through every twist in the jungle to ensure their quick execution. Their Binary Rifles will kill you in one shot on Legendary, so they are targets of the highest priority.

ARMOR ABILITY ACQUISITION \\

PROMETHEAN VISION

Used by certain Knight variants to reveal the locations of targets before hunting them down, this vision modification tracks in-motion objects accurately through most terrain. It is powerful enough even to portray the shape of the objects and highlight them for easy identification. Unfortunately, the activation of this modification creates an audible sound that can clue in hostiles of the user's location, and also causes the user to appear on motion sensors.

> INTO THE FOG

INTRODUCTION

BASIC TRAINING

INTEL

CAMPAIGN

INFINITY

APPENDIX

7 With the Promethean Vision now in your possession, you have the perfect opportunity to use it against the enemy in the portion of jungle below. You do not want to jump blindly down there, however. Crawler Snipes hang in the trees, while another pack of Crawlers as well as a Knight hold the ground. Before even approaching the ledge that overlooks this area, use the Promethean Vision to locate the Crawler Snipes and put them down immediately. Once you're certain it's clear, maintain your superior position and gun down the Crawlers below before focusing on the Knight.

You may remember that there were Crawlers just before you got to this overlook, and at least one was a Crawler Snipe. Consider taking its Binary Rifle with you if you can locate it, as it can make short work of any Knights you encounter, and you can stock up on ammo for it from the Crawler Snipes that you've killed.

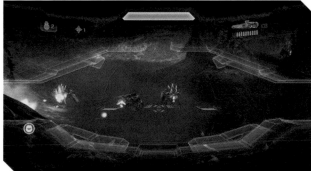

8 Another Knight and pack of Crawlers ambush you here. After working your way past them, keep moving forward until Cortana marks another IFF tag to inspect. Beyond the tag **9**, yet another Knight and Watcher pair in command of a large pack of Crawlers (including some Snipes) await you. Do yourself a favor and activate Promethean Vision before rounding the corner to spot the Crawlers in the trees: The Crawler Snipes tend to favor higher ground, and picking them off early is the key to success.

10 Cortana correctly describes this path filled with winding tree roots as a chokepoint. Crawlers infest the trees, making the path more perilous. Frequently toggle Promethean Vision to avoid the unpleasant surprise of a Crawler dropping from the tree branches and delivering a melee strike to the back of your head. Eventually, you reach a locked facility door, with the IFF tag belonging to another Marine. If you're interested in switching over to a DMR, you can find one next to an Assault Rifle and a UNSC crate full of Frag Grenades. Once you make your picks, inspect the IFF tag.

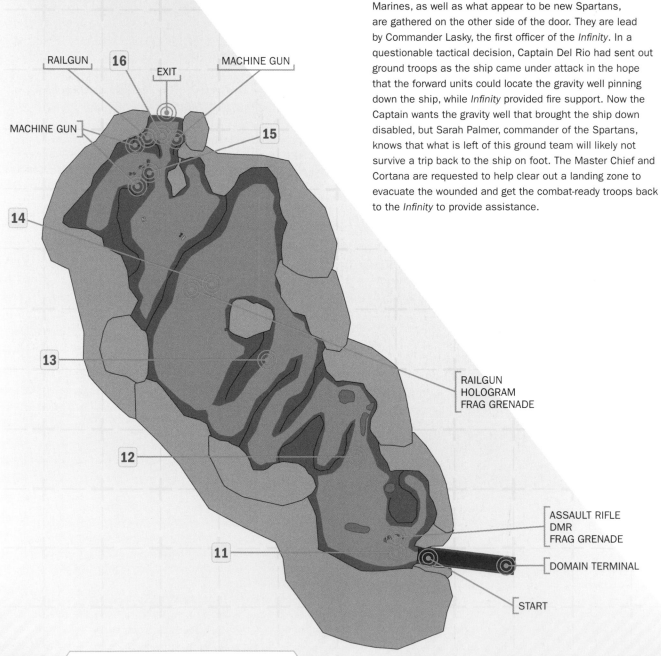

RAILGUN   16   EXIT   MACHINE GUN

MACHINE GUN

15

14

13

12

11

RAILGUN
HOLOGRAM
FRAG GRENADE

ASSAULT RIFLE
DMR
FRAG GRENADE

DOMAIN TERMINAL

START

Marines, as well as what appear to be new Spartans, are gathered on the other side of the door. They are lead by Commander Lasky, the first officer of the *Infinity*. In a questionable tactical decision, Captain Del Rio had sent out ground troops as the ship came under attack in the hope that the forward units could locate the gravity well pinning down the ship, while *Infinity* provided fire support. Now the Captain wants the gravity well that brought the ship down disabled, but Sarah Palmer, commander of the Spartans, knows that what is left of this ground team will likely not survive a trip back to the ship on foot. The Master Chief and Cortana are requested to help clear out a landing zone to evacuate the wounded and get the combat-ready troops back to the *Infinity* to provide assistance.

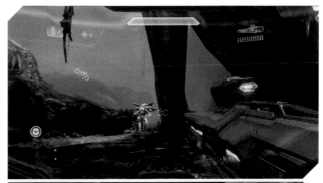

11 With Marines in tow, the Master Chief exits the makeshift triage to begin the push to the designated landing zone. Another Knight just outside deploys a Watcher and calls in a pack of Crawlers to stymie your advance. Sandbags have been set up near the ramp leading back into the facility, which contains additional weapons and ammunition. Because of the canopy of tree roots, it's not a bad idea to use a Binary Rifle shot to eliminate a Watcher quickly, just to prevent it from fleeing and using the environment to hide and regenerate.

» KEY COMBAT TIP

Marines, as well as any allies you get in the future, can trade weapons with players as long as there is at least one round of ammunition in the weapon being offered. If you've got a LightRifle or Binary Rifle, consider giving it to a Marine. It will not necessarily make them tougher to kill, but they do enjoy unlimited ammo and surprising accuracy, which will make that Marine more useful to you. Don't feel *too* bad if they don't survive the Promethean onslaught. For all the training they may have endured, the standard-issue human body does not react well to weapons that disintegrate flesh and bone.

DOMAIN TERMINAL

This terminal is amazingly easy to miss. Right after you regain control of the Master Chief and before the firefight begins, turn around to find it sitting right behind you.

12 Another Knight deploys a Watcher a little farther away from the first attackers at **11**, but they tend to stay out of direct contact unless you or their allies draw close to their position. A little farther up the path **13**, a Knight attempts to warp in behind you and any Marines with you, while a small pack of Crawlers charges in from the front.

INTRODUCTION

BASIC TRAINING

INTEL

CAMPAIGN

INFINITY

APPENDIX

14 Commander Lasky radios in with some bad news: Another Marine squad up ahead is in dire straights and is about to be overrun by a large force of Knights and Crawlers. Originally these Marines were set up to guard the door that lead to the emergency LZ, but they were driven back to this point. If you hurry, you can save some of these Marines, work with them to retake their positions by the door, and, while Cortana works the lock, help them defend against the inevitable counterattack.

> RECOMMENDED LOADOUT

The LightRifle and DMR are both solid choices for wiping out Crawlers and Watchers that any Knights spawn. As soon as you reach the Marines, you can get your hands on a Railgun, one of the most powerful weapons in the UNSC arsenal. You'll want to save all of the ammo for this weapon to bring down Knights quickly. If you manage to arrive to this battle with a Binary Rifle, you will find that there are a number of Crawler Snipes you can kill to resupply it, and while it doesn't have the same sort of power that the Railgun has, its shots reach a target faster and more accurately.

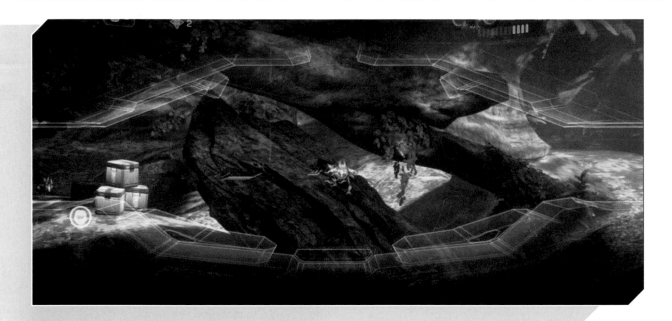

14 To put it succinctly, these Marines are screwed. More specifically, while the Knight and Watcher combo is always dangerous, the Crawler pack includes a number of Crawler Snipes among them. If your allies have any hope for seeing the end of the day, much less the rest of this battle, the Crawler Snipes must go as soon as you take out or drive off the Watcher. You'll probably still lose Marines while hunting down these snipers, but you can track the tracers from the Binary Rifles back to the source. Once you are certain that the snipers are gone, get rid of that Knight. Before you begin the charge up the next hill, collect the Railgun, and the Hologram armor ability, if you wish. Things are about to get bad.

WEAPON ACQUISITION

RAILGUN

Launching a high-explosive shell via a linear accelerator, the Railgun is designed to decisively kill hardened infantry and light armor in a single shot. The weapon

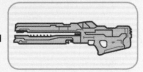

will fire where it's pointed with almost unerring accuracy, however the current model deployed on Requiem has no built-in scope, and to fire the weapon requires it to first build up a charge, which forces the operator to keep the weapon trained directed at the enemy before firing. Skilled users can build a charge and aim the weapon at the last instant, but this is a dangerous practice that can result in wasted ammunition, serious injury, or death.

ARMOR ABILITY ACQUISITION

HOLOGRAM

Holographic projections have long been used by Covenant Elites to deceive their enemies moments before the fatal strike. The usefulness of this armor ability cannot be underestimated. The lifelike projection can fool even the Knights, giving friendly soldiers a chance to bring down the enemy while they are distracted.

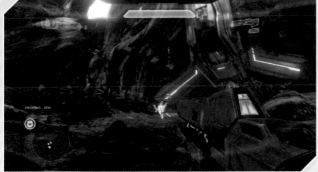

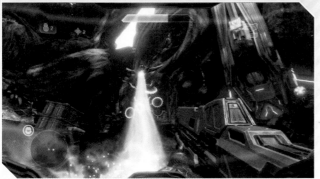

15 Two Watchers flank Knights that warp in just in front of the barricade the Marines originally held. The Watchers immediately begin attempting to construct a pair of Forerunner anti-infantry turrets, and then attempt to summon additional Crawlers to join the group that charges down the hill from the sealed door. If you're lucky, any surviving Marines may actually pitch in and try to shoot the Watchers down. Chances are you will not be so lucky. If you manage to down the Watchers, this fight gets much easier.

If the Watchers get the turrets up, they have got to go first, as they close down many viable flanking routes and can slaughter any Marines you've got left. Punish the Watchers, then get rid of the Crawlers. Don't feel pressured to stay at the top of the hill, fighting tooth and nail. Fall back if you feel you're about to get overrun. When you get the opportunity, make the Knights eat Railgun shot. With the barricade retaken, get Cortana to the marked door lock, and then man the sandbags and mounted machine guns with any allies you have left. The counterattack will be vicious, so be ready.

Perishable Knights

16 Cortana places the new objective "Defend the Hilltop" at the top of your HUD, signaling the attack of *seven* Knights, supported by a Crawler pack and the ever-present Watchers, all coming from the hill you just fought your way up. You can describe a fight as being "hard" only in so many ways, but it is what it is. Your best bet is to shut down the Knights before they can get close.

If you have any Marines with you and they take up the mounted machine guns, force one of them off and take the gun for yourself. You will be more effective than the Marines, who tend to fire in short bursts that are barely a threat to the Knights. Hose the Knights down as they reveal themselves. Don't forget, you can tear the Machine Guns off of their tripods and carry them into battle with the enemy.

The Watchers try to revive any fallen allies, which gives you a chance to kill them (or the Knights they are supposed to protect) with some ease. Don't feel as though you need to stick to the machine guns. Break free if you are about to get flanked. Cortana calls for you to retrieve her from the AI plinth once the area is clear. The cave beyond the door is where the landing zone is located. Gather up any Railgun ammo you can find, but if you have too few shots, consider taking up a Binary Rifle to replace it.

Alternate Approach

It's also possible to play a more mobile game against this attack. There's a good supply of Railgun ammunition to use against the Knights. A single shot is almost a guaranteed kill. Combined with proper use of a Hologram, the Railgun will let you get many free shots at enemy backs. Also, rather than abandoning a machine gun when the enemy draws near, you can detach the gun from its mount and fall back while firing. This costs you the unlimited ammo a mounted gun enjoys, but it can save your life.

Legendary Strategy

Don't get attached to the Marines at **14**. If the snipers don't get them, the other Crawlers don't overrun their meager defenses, or the Knights don't kill them outright, they still have the rest of the fight to try to survive and the odds are against them. For the first section, the Crawler Snipes can prove to be the most frustrating threats. Don't be surprised to fall more than a few times at this juncture.

Before even considering pushing forward to **15**, crush any and all resistance from every last Promethean you can find. Winning the next portion of the battle is all about minimizing your risks, so try to avoid having stragglers join up with the reinforcements. The second phase of this fight plays out in similar fashion to Heroic difficulty, with the usual Legendary twist—all the enemies are much tougher.

For the last stand, manning the guns in a stationary position is nearly suicidal. You simply can't kill the enemies fast enough to avoid getting overrun. If you take up a gun, use it from its tripod for as long as you can safely manage. If the enemy appears to be flanking you or just getting too close, rip the gun free of its mount and try to make use of the terrain to funnel the enemy into your kill zone while minimizing your exposure to incoming fire. Better still, stick with a LightRifle to put down the Crawlers and Watchers, and lean on the Railgun or Binary Rifle to kill the Knights quickly. Even at this difficulty, a fully charged Railgun can still flatten a Knight, or at least weaken it so that a follow-up LightRifle shot can finish the job.

INTRODUCTION

BASIC TRAINING

INTEL

CAMPAIGN

INFINITY

APPENDIX

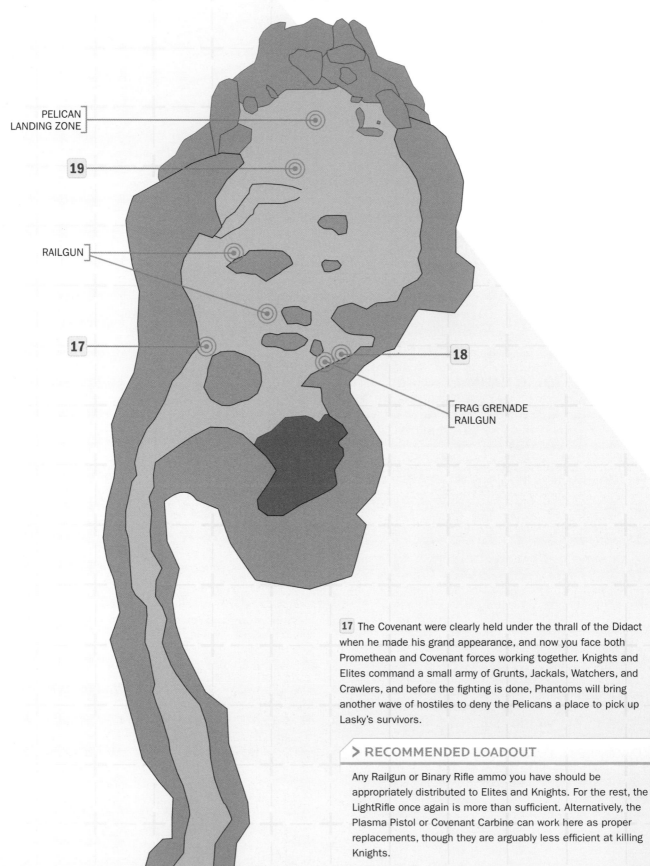

PELICAN
LANDING ZONE

19

RAILGUN

17

18

FRAG GRENADE
RAILGUN

START

17 The Covenant were clearly held under the thrall of the Didact when he made his grand appearance, and now you face both Promethean and Covenant forces working together. Knights and Elites command a small army of Grunts, Jackals, Watchers, and Crawlers, and before the fighting is done, Phantoms will bring another wave of hostiles to deny the Pelicans a place to pick up Lasky's survivors.

> **RECOMMENDED LOADOUT**

Any Railgun or Binary Rifle ammo you have should be appropriately distributed to Elites and Knights. For the rest, the LightRifle once again is more than sufficient. Alternatively, the Plasma Pistol or Covenant Carbine can work here as proper replacements, though they are arguably less efficient at killing Knights.

INTRODUCTION

BASIC TRAINING

INTEL

CAMPAIGN

INFINITY

APPENDIX

17 Initial contact with Grunts and Jackals starts here. A Knight is attempting to direct them to attack you. Killing it outright causes panic among the Covenant enemies, so be prepared for potential Grunt suicide charges. You'll find more Covenant scattered throughout the cave as you go deeper. **18** You can try to use this side path, which is guarded by a Jackal Sniper, for cover and flanking maneuvers, and another cache of Railgun ammunition can be found here.

19 After eliminating the first group, the Knight and Watcher pair in the back of the cave receive a Phantom's worth of reinforcements, which brings Elites into the fray, along with more Jackals and Grunts. Elites are smaller and more maneuverable than Knights, which means they are tougher targets for the Railgun. Because there's so much spare ammo available for the weapon, you can afford a few misses, but you should use that surplus to make certain that any Watchers in the air are taken care of. Watchers have a tendency to sit still when protecting their allies. As a bonus, any enemies near the Railgun shot's blast will also sustain some damage. The most dangerous enemy, a Knight Battlewagon, is a part of this group. So long as you keep it at a distance, its Scattershot will not be a serious threat. Remember, Battlewagons are far more resilient than the basic Knight; they are able to survive at least one fully charged Railgun shot.

A Pelican Dropship arrives once the area is clear. *Infinity*'s forces are losing ground against a determined assault, and any able troops under Lasky and Palmer's command, along with the Master Chief, are needed for the fight.

Legendary Strategy

The Railgun's lack of a scope makes it tough to do, but you can reliably snipe if you have some patience. While the opening sections are relatively easy, things get complicated when the Phantom arrives. The Knight Battlewagon, once its Watcher support is destroyed, becomes very aggressive and tries to chase you down. You can retreat back toward the cave entrance, if necessary, in order to try another approach. A well-placed Hologram is also effective at drawing enemy attention on any difficulty, and so long as they don't notice you deploying it, this can make a tricky fight easier.

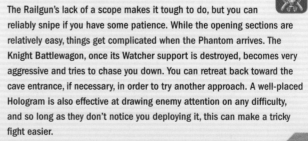

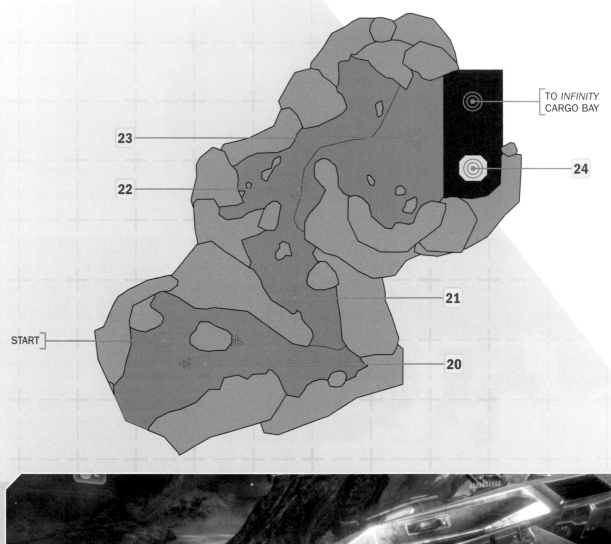

TO *INFINITY* CARGO BAY

23

22

24

21

START

20

20 The Pelican drops you off in the middle of an intense firefight. Marines and Spartan-IVs are under fire from Ghosts supported by infantry and a Phantom. Fortunately, the Marines have more than just a Warthog at their disposal. A Scorpion tank is parked near the LZ, and you are offered to take the controls. Use the tank to annihilate the Covenant troops, but watch your fire and avoid hitting the friendlies in the Warthog. No need to ditch your support/distraction just yet. Any surviving allies who aren't on the Warthog climb aboard the Scorpion to provide additional fire support.

» KEY COMBAT TIP

You should clear out some of the closest Covenant infantry before you board the Scorpion. Charged Plasma Pistol shots can freeze your tank in place, leaving you vulnerable to incoming fire and unable to fight back unless an ally jumps into the turret.

VEHICLE ENCOUNTER

SCORPION

The Scorpion is effective and a symbol of the UNSC's resilience in ground warfare. Armed with a 90 mm smoothbore auto-loaded main gun, and a machine gun turret for anti-infantry/light armor duty, this tank is more than capable of beating the best that the Covenant has to offer in combat, despite the relatively primitive design.

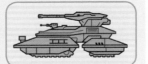

Legendary Strategy

There is a major difference to the start of this engagement on Legendary, and that is the presence of a Wraith directly ahead of where the tank is parked. Don't charge at the tank just yet. Work on clearing the immediate area of Covenant troops while you're on foot, letting the Wraith fire plasma mortar shots at you while you remain on the move. The reason for this is to avoid getting killed before you even climb into the cockpit, as well as to prevent Covenant from stunning your vehicle using charged Plasma Pistol shots.

Small outposts encountered along the path forward should be obliterated to prevent any nasty surprises from behind when you come across real

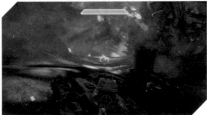

resistance, such as Wraiths 21. Their plasma mortars can ruin the Scorpion. Use the superior accuracy and range of your main gun to safely deal with the Wraiths.

VEHICLE ENCOUNTER

WRAITH

The sight of the Wraith's plasma mortars will likely haunt the nightmares of Covenant War veterans for years to come. Wraiths hover over terrain that would slow or stop most human-made ground vehicles, and their mortar, while slow compared to the ballistic weapons employed by a Scorpion, is still incredibly dangerous. Like the Scorpion, a Wraith is also equipped with a turret to deal with infantry and light vehicles. Wraiths can supercharge their engines to ram enemies at high speed, which makes approaching one even more difficult if the crew is alert.

» KEY COMBAT TIP

The Wraiths are utterly brutal on Legendary. A single direct hit from the plasma mortar will send you back to the previous checkpoint in small flaming pieces. Combined with the propensity of Covenant ground troops to attempt to disable the Scorpion, the relatively simple shoot 'n' scoot through the area is a serious challenge.

22 Another Phantom drops off a Wraith to help defend the series of Covenant outposts in this area. Be especially careful of the floating guard platforms here, as there may be hostiles wielding Fuel Rod Cannons perched among them. Being thorough equals being safe!

23 The last of the Covenant ground forces, including another Wraith, is throwing itself against a meager defense line set up by the Marines trying to prevent any more hostiles from entering the Infinity's vehicles bay. Once the enemies are clear, follow the path to the cargo elevator that takes the tank up into the ship to help repel the boarders.

24 Inside the cargo bay, a stalwart few Marines are breaking under the Covenant assault lead by Elites and a pair of Hunters. Now that you've brought a tank into the equation, the battle should turn in the favor of the UNSC. Prioritize the Hunters as targets to knock their Fuel Rod Cannons out of the mix, then deliver high-explosive justice to anything else not human. Captain Del Rio radios in, saying that the ship is currently disabled and helpless against the Covenant assault. He wants you to get to the ship's outer hull to help repel the enemy, and he's got the perfect ride for you to use in a nearby dock.

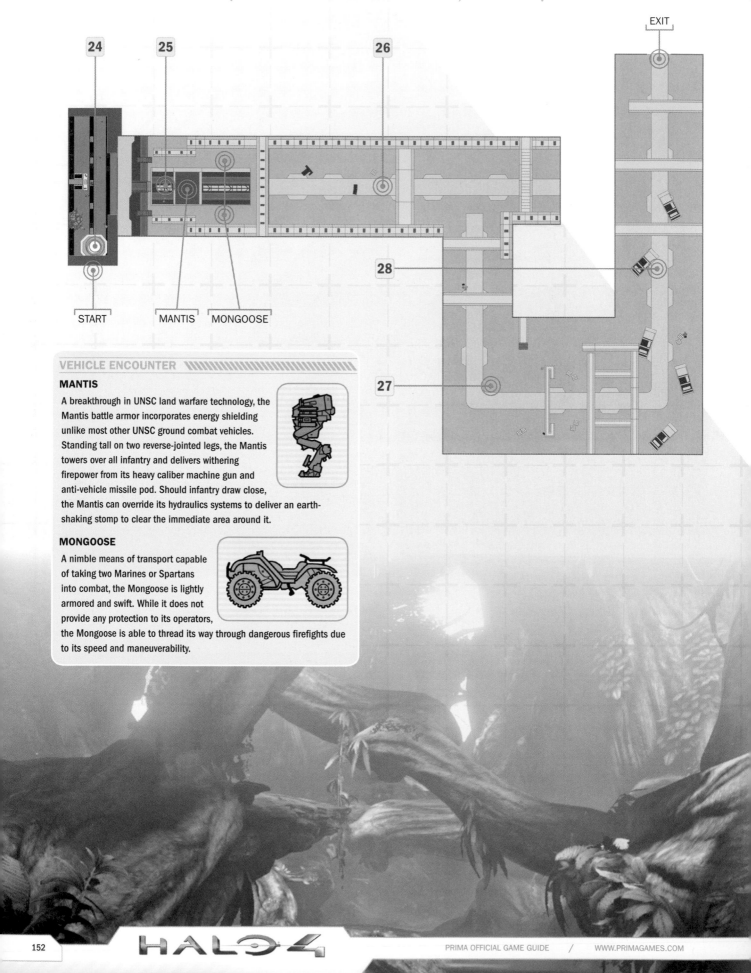

VEHICLE ENCOUNTER

MANTIS

A breakthrough in UNSC land warfare technology, the Mantis battle armor incorporates energy shielding unlike most other UNSC ground combat vehicles. Standing tall on two reverse-jointed legs, the Mantis towers over all infantry and delivers withering firepower from its heavy caliber machine gun and anti-vehicle missile pod. Should infantry draw close, the Mantis can override its hydraulics systems to deliver an earth-shaking stomp to clear the immediate area around it.

MONGOOSE

A nimble means of transport capable of taking two Marines or Spartans into combat, the Mongoose is lightly armored and swift. While it does not provide any protection to its operators, the Mongoose is able to thread its way through dangerous firefights due to its speed and maneuverability.

25 After you activate the designated control console, the Mantis dock unseals, revealing the massive combat mech. Climb aboard and get acquainted with the controls and weapon systems. You'll have to shoot your way through the doors that lead to the rest of the ship.

26 You have spent the majority of this adventure so far outnumbered, outgunned, and possibly out of your mind from trying to survive. The Scorpion was nice, but the Mantis is a monster in combat, and it's the perfect stress relief after everything you've been through. This section of the cargo holds is a lengthy, winding corridor. All manner of Covenant troops and Prometheans attempt to stop you. And yet, you'd have to *try to lose* for them to stand a chance. Even the dangerous Fuel Rod Cannons held by Grunts, Hunters, or Elites can pose a threat only if you give them a chance to fire, and the Mantis's weapons can easily outrange them all.

» KEY COMBAT TIP

Confidence in the Mantis is still warranted even on Legendary, but the usual caveats of caution apply. When the mech's shielding fails, the Mantis cannot absorb nearly as much damage as it can on Heroic. One of your greatest threats is, believe it or not, the humble Plasma Pistol. The Mantis takes the longest of any vehicle in the game to recover from the EMP effects of a charged shot, and during the time that it's disabled, the Covenant are quick to pile on the punishment. Co-Op players may be disheartened by the fact that there is only only one Mantis to commandeer at this time. Fortunately, there are a number of Mongoose vehicles for the other players to take. Bear in mind that the firepower of a Mantis makes driving a Mongoose in front of one almost as hazardous as it is to drive in front of the enemy.

If you're playing the Campaign alone, it might be prudent to exit the Mantis whenever it is clear to pick up a Fuel Rod Cannon and all the ammo you can carry. You can recover this weapon from many of the Grunts encountered throughout this section.

Forerunner turrets are more dangerous. The constant damage they can dish out can quickly overload the Mantis's shields. Any time you see Watchers attempting to build, it's most likely going to be a Forerunner anti-infantry turret. The turrets are often placed atop destroyable platforms or walkways.

Speaking of walkways, destroy every last one you see. Grunts with Fuel Rod Cannons like to use them to try to get the drop on your Mantis. A little collateral damage can be explained away when it's done in the line of duty.

27 This ramp area is the site of a series of defenses marked by Forerunner anti-infantry turrets, Grunts, Jackals, and Knights. Be careful not to charge too quickly up the hill without ensuring that you have eliminated anything that could potentially flank you. Charged Plasma Pistols can completely disable the Mantis.

28 This section is actually quite dangerous. The narrow passage is fiercely guarded by Grunts, Knights, and Forerunner anti-infantry turrets. You have little room to maneuver, so keep your guns trained and firing on the enemy as you maneuver around obstacles to prevent them from getting off any free shots. The last door between you and the cargo elevator to the deck of the *Infinity* opens to reveal a squad of Grunts ready to make a final suicide charge on your Mantis. Don't get blindsided by this.

> MAJOR FIREFIGHT: EVICTION PROCEEDINGS

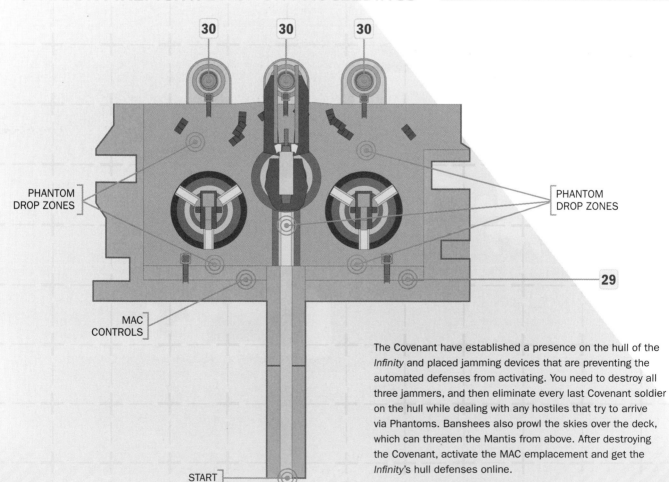

30　30　30

PHANTOM DROP ZONES

PHANTOM DROP ZONES

29

MAC CONTROLS

START

The Covenant have established a presence on the hull of the *Infinity* and placed jamming devices that are preventing the automated defenses from activating. You need to destroy all three jammers, and then eliminate every last Covenant soldier on the hull while dealing with any hostiles that try to arrive via Phantoms. Banshees also prowl the skies over the deck, which can threaten the Mantis from above. After destroying the Covenant, activate the MAC emplacement and get the *Infinity*'s hull defenses online.

> RECOMMENDED LOADOUT

The Mantis solves all manner of problems, and even if it doesn't work and your mech is about to go up in flames, there's always a second Mantis on the deck **29**. If you're stuck on foot, grab a Fuel Rod Cannon to use on clusters of enemy infantry, though on Legendary you might want to just stick with the Plasma Pistol and any headshot-capable weapon.

The three jammers **30** on the hull can be taken down in any order. There's honestly very little that the Covenant ground troops can do to stop the Mantis from dominating them, despite their combined efforts to take it down with charged plasma bolts. Elites may try to surprise you with Fuel Rod Cannons, but their shields can not stand up to your firepower.

With the jammers pounded to dust, the Covenant get desperate and start sending in waves of Phantoms to drop more troops in the hope of overwhelming you. The *Infinity*'s defenses help to soften up the Phantoms, and it's possible to shoot them down. The real threat comes from Banshees. They may try to fly over the firing arcs of the point defense guns to dive-bomb you. Always take a moment to scan for these surprises while stomping your way over to the next Phantom drop site. Eventually, Captain Del Rio radios in to let you know that, as usual, the solution to his ship's defensive network woes requires your direct intervention via a control panel. Cortana marks the spot near the doors where you entered the deck. With the main guns online, the *Infinity* quickly drives off the Didact, and Del Rio orders the ship to stand down.

Legendary Strategy

Things are a bit different on Legendary. While dealing with the jammers is still pretty easy, the Phantoms are a much more credible threat and are tougher to shoot down. Your best bet is to take out the guns on the Phantoms, particularly the nose-mounted concussion cannons, but also the side-mounted plasma turrets, which can do a real number on your shields and should not be ignored. You can also use the various obstacles on the deck as defensive cover from any of the Phantoms.

Banshees are very dangerous, as always, and they can actually attack from such an angle that you cannot bring the Mantis's weapons to bear on them. Keep scanning the skies for Banshees to catch them in advance.

Surprisingly, what you should fear most is not the larger threats, but the little Grunts armed with Plasma Pistols that blend in among their comrades. The Mantis takes longer than any other vehicle in the game to recover from the EMP effects of a charged shot, a recovery time that swiftly proves fatal around a determined Covenant foe.

> AFTERMATH

Despite the rough landing, the *Infinity* is still flight-and-fight-capable, and is more than ready to take it to the Covenant and the Didact.

Or it could flee back to Earth without doing a thing to stop the Didact, which is what Captain Del Rio insists on doing. It's clear that there is some disagreement among the officers gathered on the ship's bridge, but the Captain's orders are absolute, despite being against the suggestions of the Master Chief. The Captain wants the gravity well that is holding down the *Infinity* disabled so that they can retreat. Orders are orders, so the Spartan must prepare for his new mission.

INTRODUCTION

BASIC TRAINING

INTEL

CAMPAIGN

INFINITY

APPENDIX

CAMPAIGN

MISSION 5: RECLAIMER

> "I don't know about you, but I usually like a
> little bit more intel with my intel."

Requiem's gravity well currently denies the *Infinity* the ability to escape through the planetary shell, and a series of massive Particle Cannons are locking the ship into a kind of corridor from which there is no safe escape, as its shields are down. Captain Del Rio is sending the Master Chief, the Spartans from Gypsy Company, and a compliment of Marines led by Commander Lasky, into a direct ground assault on the cannon positions. Del Rio is clearly desperate to escape, so much that he's neglected to send in Force Recon to gather intel on what lays ahead of the ground units, an omission that Cortana is not shy to criticize. The mission will have to succeed, regardless.

HALO 4

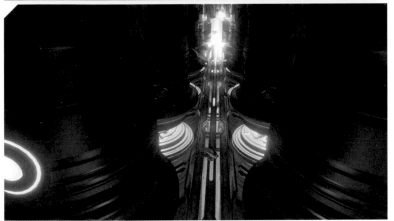

⌃ MISSION BRIEFING

Captain Del Rio's "Blowthrough Op" is a disaster almost from the start. The lack of intel sends you through a series of ambushes. Fortunately, you have heavy armored support to rely on in the form of a Mammoth, but even the largest land vehicle in the UNSC arsenal is not safe from the sheer numbers the Covenant will be throwing at you. After you clear out a portion of the beam cannon network, you will have to enter the Forerunner control facility to bring down the remaining cannons. Afterward this, a UNSC ground team is on station, with Scorpion support, to clear out a canyon filled with Covenant defenders blocking the best observation point overlooking Requiem's gravity well generator.

ENEMIES ENCOUNTERED:

Elites   Grunts   Jackals   Hunters

Crawlers   Knights   Watchers

VEHICLES ENCOUNTERED:

Ghosts   Banshees   Wraiths

Phantom Dropships   Lich

Mammoth

WEAPONS ACQUIRED	
Assault Rifle	Concussion Rifle
Magnum	Fuel Rod Cannon
DMR	Beam Rifle
Battle Rifle	Boltshot
Sniper Rifle	Suppressor
Storm Rifle	LightRifle
Plasma Pistol	Binary Rifle
Needler	Scattershot
Covenant Carbine	Rocket Launcher
	Target Designator

INTRODUCTION

BASIC TRAINING

INTEL

CAMPAIGN

INFINITY

APPENDIX

After the Pelican drops the Master Chief off near the Mammoth, follow the rest of the squad aboard. The Spartans use Jet Packs to reach the top of the Mammoth. You'll have to make your way up to the top deck via the stairs to speak with Commander Lasky. The enormous siege engine is well stocked with Assault Rifles, Battle Rifles, Sniper Rifles, Magnums, and Rocket Turrets, so you'll be able to custom tailor your loadout with great ease.

After talking to Lasky, Spartan Palmer will radio in to remind the Chief that there are Jet Packs available for use. Once you've retrieved the pack, Del Rio says the mission is a go, and the Mammoth trundles toward its first objective.

VEHICLE ENCOUNTER

MAMMOTH

Less of a vehicle and closer to a mobile fortress, the Mammoth easily lives up to its name. Armed with a powerful Magnetic Accelerator Cannon, the Mammoth is capable of destroying a wide variety of aerial targets with disturbing precision and power. The MAC can be slaved to Target Designators carried by infantry, giving them a fighting chance even against major sub-orbital threats, such as a Covenant cruiser or the Forerunner Particle Cannon network. Arguably, the most dangerous weapon of the Mammoth is not the MAC, but rather its compliment of Spartans and Marines. A Mammoth is also capable of carrying Warthogs to help troops get to the front quicker.

ARMOR ABILITY ACQUISITION

JET PACK

The Jet Pack allows the user to bypass obstacles and take up elevated positions to engage the enemy at a moment's notice. Skilled snipers equipped with a Jet Pack are especially feared, as they can suddenly negate any hard cover and shoot over it.

Atop the Mammoth are two Rocket Turrets that can be manned. Take up the one mounted on the left side of the vehicle. Keep your view pointed toward the front of the Mammoth to scan for hostiles, and also to witness the flight of Pelicans get shot down by one of the massive Particle Cannons that hover over the nearby lake. Now you know why the *Infinity* is not keen to get into firing range with it's own MAC guns: That shot was fired by only one gun among an entire battery of them. Unfortunately, *Infinity* cannot fire on the gravity well without eliminating these particle cannons first. The only reason your Mammoth hasn't been glassed along with the entire area is that these cannons do not seem to be willing to damage the planet—much.

At any rate, one of the Pelicans got lucky and survived the shot, crashing into enemy-held territory. Familiarize yourself with how the Rocket Turret works, and then prepare to repel Covenant forces on the left of the Mammoth **1**. They try to use the cliffs and rocky terrain for cover. Jackal Snipers try to shoot you specifically, so look out for their distinct weapon tracers and red glowing helmets. Shade Turrets are set up throughout this area, and the Covenant forces are dangerous not just to the Master Chief, but to the Rocket Turrets also. If these Rocket Turrets are destroyed, they are gone for the rest of the mission, and you'll have lost an offensive and defensive option.

» KEY COMBAT TIP

It is worth noting that on Legendary, manning these Rocket Turrets is quite close to a death sentence. If you're not quick at taking out Covenant before they get in range, they'll either kill you or destroy the turret in short order.

> MAJOR FIREFIGHT: RETRIEVE THE TARGET DESIGNATOR

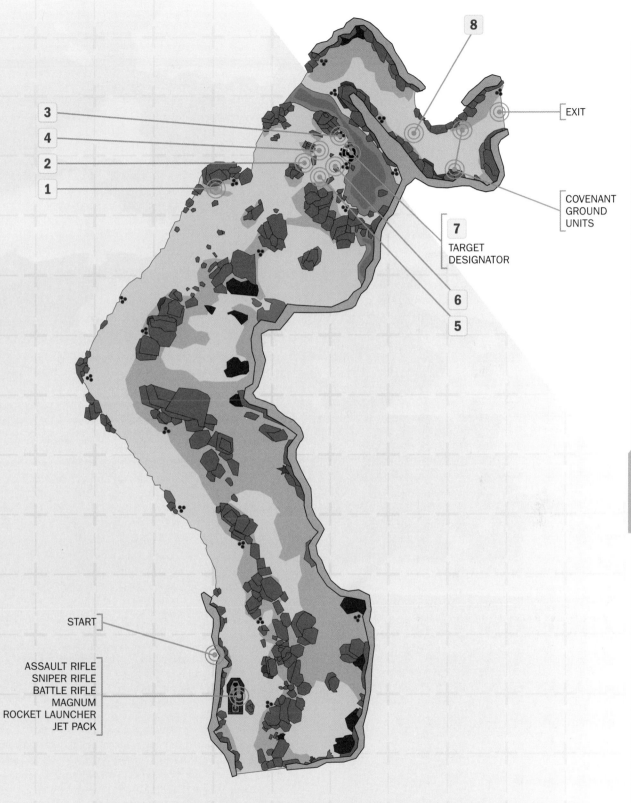

8

3
4
2
1

EXIT

COVENANT
GROUND
UNITS

7

TARGET
DESIGNATOR

6

5

START

ASSAULT RIFLE
SNIPER RIFLE
BATTLE RIFLE
MAGNUM
ROCKET LAUNCHER
JET PACK

INTRODUCTION

BASIC TRAINING

INTEL

CAMPAIGN

INFINITY

APPENDIX

The surviving Pelican crashed behind an outpost to the right of the first ambush 2. The Covenant send ground troops and Phantoms to reinforce the position against the Mammoth's firepower and soldiers. While the men at the Pelican may not survive the next minutes, it is imperative that you cross the terrain between them and the Phantom and retrieve the Target Designator, which will allow you to personally direct the MAC on the Mammoth against aerial targets. This position is apparently important to the Covenant. Expect Phantoms to bring in multiple waves of reinforcements, which will include multiple Wraiths and Ghosts mixed in with the infantry.

This fight can be quite frustrating, but there are many weapon options available. Some players may prefer to use up the Sniper Rifle ammo on the Mammoth, in combination with the Rocket Turrets, to take out as many troops as possible before venturing away from the massive vehicle. More aggressive players may take to the ground immediately, using the Battle Rifle and Plasma Pistol combo to deal with the Elites in the area while also counter-sniping Jackals. Other players still may take one of the two Warthogs in the Mammoth's bay, with their guns manned by Spartans or Marines. The Covenant Ghosts that are parked at 3 and manned during the battle are also solid choices, if you can get them away from their riders.

Starting from the Mammoth

2 The outpost to the right of where the Mammoth halts its advance must be dealt with quickly. The Covenant troops here can reinforce others throughout the area. The fastest way to eliminate the outpost is to bombard it with the Rocket Turret. Unfortunately, this exposes you to vicious counterfire, which may shorten how much time you spend on the battery. Make sure you take out the hovering guard platform at least, which will hopefully eliminate the closest snipers.

A single shot from the Rocket Launcher or Rocket Turret can let you accomplish the same task more safely. You can also snipe safely from the upper decks, and then retreat when enemy fire becomes too intense.

Phantoms introduce pairs of Ghosts among the reinforcement waves, and they have a tendency to use the small stone pillars behind the outpost 4 as cover from your weapons. You can attempt to thin them out somewhat before taking to the ground, but this can take time.

Going All In

The Warthogs in the Mammoth are excellent vehicles to take into this fight. The Marine or Spartan on the gun is very accurate, which means you can concentrate entirely on defensive driving. You'll need to concentrate, as you will likely end up driving around or through the middle of a very hot kill zone to reach the Target Designator: Elites guard parked Ghosts at 3 , a smaller contingent of Covenant with mounted Plasma Cannons is at 5 , and another group of Elites and other Covenant waits at 6 . The center of this circle of death is not where you want to be for long, not without first doing some work to thin the odds. Most troublesome is that eventually the Phantoms drop multiple Wraiths at the very center of this circle, all of which can easily destroy a Warthog with one plasma mortar shot or simply by using their boost to ram the vehicle at high speed. Their Plasma Turrets are also very dangerous, and the gunners manning them can cover the entire frontal arc in front of a Wraith.

» KEY COMBAT TIP

Don't forget, you can trade weapons to your allies. Give your Warthog passenger a Rocket Launcher, and enjoy the fireworks.

You can avoid dealing with the Wraiths if you make a run directly for the Target Designator and take out the Phantom harassing the crash survivors as soon as you get access to the Warthogs. This isn't particularly easy or safe, as there are numerous Covenant infantry and Ghosts already in the area. If you're lucky, the other Warthog carried by the Mammoth will be blessed by a good driver who can provide the necessary distraction for you to get the job done. The upside to this is that once you take out the target Phantom, you can then fall back to the relative safety of the Mammoth, wait for it to finish reloading its MAC gun, and then kill the Particle Cannon to move on.

3 If you lose your Warthogs, a Ghost makes a good replacement for anti-infantry work, but you'll lose much of your effectiveness against the Wraiths. The Elites you face during this firefight are all very tough customers of high rank; they are highly resilient. If they are manning a Ghost, they are an even greater threat, so you have to stay on the move regardless of your vehicle choice.

7 The Pelican crash site, when you manage to reach it, is likely to already be suffering bombardment by a Phantom, so your approach to the Target Designator is problematic. Once you do retrieve the Target Designator, you can put down the Phantom that is bombarding the area from the nearby water by targeting it with the device. The Mammoth turns the big MAC on the unsuspecting dropship and blots it out of the sky with all the subtlety of a sledgehammer on a glass sculpture. Cortana then marks the Particle Cannon for you to target, and once it is destroyed, it's time to move on.

WEAPON ACQUISITION

TARGET DESIGNATOR

Laser-designated armaments have been a staple element in human militaries since the twentieth century, and continued to see service in the UNSC throughout the Human-Covenant War. The Target Designator is meant to paint targets for the Mammoth's MAC system.

Legendary Strategy

The Rocket Turret should not be relied upon for long, as you will likely not be able to kill the enemy at **2** quickly enough to prevent lethal counterfire. No vehicle you can man will last all that long under the sort of firepower you will be surrounded by if you charge straight in. It's possible to skirt around most of the enemy by taking a side path that takes you behind **5** , but if Ghosts are present, they are likely to give chase. It is still possible that if you duck into the Mammoth as soon as it comes to a halt and pick up a Warthog, you can then try blitzing past the Covenant at **3** for a straighter shot at the Target Designator. This is even harder to pull off now, however, as the enemy reinforcements arrive much sooner, in addition to every enemy being that much more lethal on Legendary.

Don't commit your Warthogs to the center of the circle. Your gunner is still pretty deadly on Legendary, but they aren't very likely to survive if you perform the same crazy antics you could get away with on Heroic. When the Wraiths get involved, you need to do everything in your power to not be anywhere inside their frontal arc. Their Plasma Cannon is almost as lethal to Warthogs as their plasma mortars, and unlike those, the turret can easily track a Warthog even when it's moving at full speed. Taking your time to eliminate the reinforcements is somewhat safer than rushing for the Target Designator, but the caution you must exercise during the process will make this battle take longer.

A river prevents you from moving to the next target on a Warthog, so the Mammoth opens its bay to allow you to pass through. You can follow the suggestion and lead the way for the Mammoth on a Warthog, or you can park inside and climb to the top deck, which will get the Mammoth moving. More Covenant try to attack from both sides of the machine as it moves through the canyon, and Phantoms, escorted by Banshees, try to drop reinforcements ahead of it **8** . You can target one of the Phantoms with the Target Designator if the MAC has reloaded.

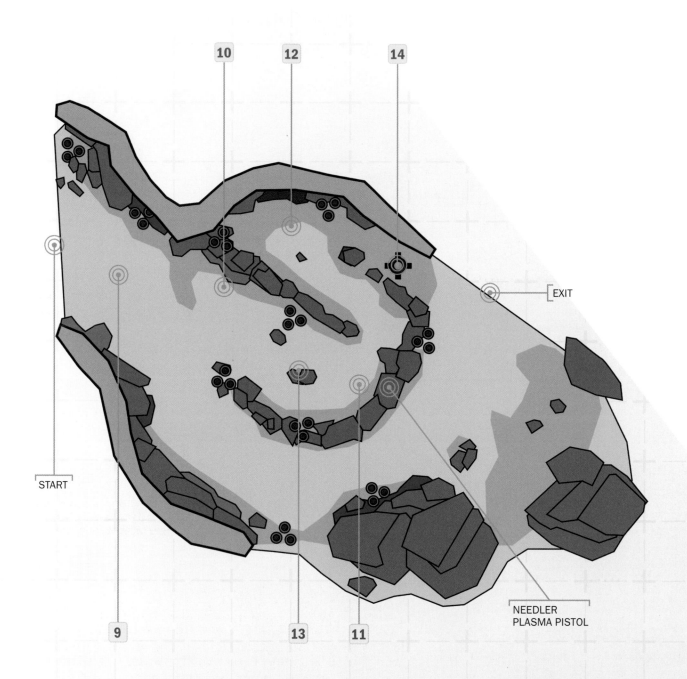

START

EXIT

NEEDLER
PLASMA PISTOL

9 The Mammoth rolls to a halt, spotting numerous obstacles in its path that must be dealt with. A massive energy shield blocks the only viable route for the Mammoth and it needs to be removed. Cortana has detected three generators protected by shielding, which requires you to get up close and personal to destroy them. The Covenant have deployed a substantial force to protect them, and are willing to throw even more forces into the fray to halt your advance.

> RECOMMENDED LOADOUT

If you're in a situation where you no longer have Warthogs available, the Sniper Rifle and Battle Rifle are a great way to take out gunners manning the various Plasma Cannons mounted throughout the zone, while a Plasma Pistol gives you a chance to disable Covenant vehicles to set up hijackings or to destroy them. If you're willing to keep hoofing it back to the Mammoth, you can also bring out the Rocket Launcher when a Wraith becomes a factor. Do not forget the Target Designator to help take out Phantoms before they unload their cargo.

INTRODUCTION

BASIC TRAINING

INTEL

CAMPAIGN

INFINITY

APPENDIX

10 **11** **12** The three generators are spread out in this part of the canyon, which can make hoofing it time-consuming and difficult. In addition to the Covenant squads, led by Elites, standing guard at each generator, Ghosts patrol the ground between the generators, which makes a Plasma Pistol almost too useful to pass up. The shields protecting each generator act as a double-edged sword. Anything inside them is protected from outside threats, but anything inside can't interact with anything outside.

The real challenge starts after you take out one of the generators. Phantoms start bringing in reinforcements, including new Ghosts, Grunts, Jackals, and Elites. Try to use the Target Designator on them. If you're stuck on foot, your best bet is to fight a retreating action toward the Mammoth, which moves farther up the road with each destroyed generator. A vehicle really makes this easier, so if you've preserved a Warthog or can steal a Ghost, use it.

It's also possible to make use of the Mammoth's left-side Rocket Turret, if it has survived the fighting to this point. It can't pierce the shields of the generators, but it can make wiping out the enemy troops in the area simpler. Just remember that the Wraith can and will lob a plasma mortar directly at your Rocket Turret if given the chance.

13 This Shade Turret provides overwatch for generators **10** and **11** . Taking it out should be an early goal.

12 This is most likely the last generator you engage, and it's also the hardest to get to. A Wraith guards the area near this generator, combined

with any additional troops in the area, and you can expect to see the death camera a few times. Adding to the good news is a guard platform **14** that overlooks the area surrounding this generator. The plasma turrets on the platform can reach out and touch you accurately from as far away as the generator. When you finally take out the three generators, return to the Mammoth and get ready to move forward.

» KEY COMBAT TIP

The Wraith has an annoying habit of moving close enough to start lobbing mortars into the area surrounding the two lower generators, and its plasma cannon gunner is as accurate as any Marine or Spartan behind a Warthog gun.

Legendary Strategy

The cautious approach will have you enjoying the accuracy of a gunner in a Warthog while you work your way toward the generators, but only after extensive sniping. If you don't have a Warthog, you still want to have a proper go at sniping. Put a rocket into the Shade Turret **13** if possible, just to ensure that it can never be a problem, and do the same for the guard platform **14** . It might be nice on Heroic to use the Target Designator on Phantoms here, but on Legendary, it's essential. It can mean the difference between success and failure. After taking out a generator, scan the skies for a Phantom, and hope the Mammoth is ready to take the shot.

As you might expect, the Wraith demands special attention and respect. If you notice it making a move to close in on you while on foot, and you don't have the means for a quick kill or a Plasma Pistol to go for the disable, you're probably already dead.

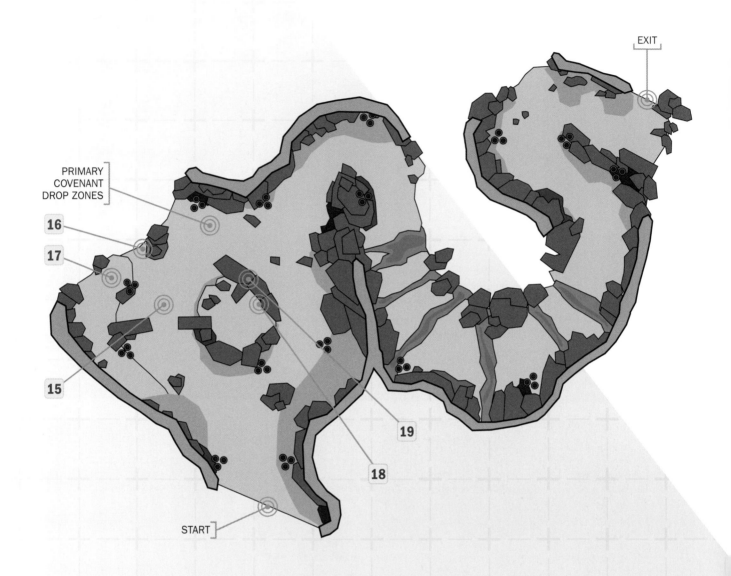

EXIT

PRIMARY
COVENANT
DROP ZONES

16

17

15

19

18

START

15 There's not a lot of time for rest after the last big firefight. The Mammoth eventually rolls into range of the second Particle Cannon. Mark it with the designator and enjoy the fireworks. Before you can move on, a new type of Covenant ship flies into view and opens fire on the Mammoth, disabling the MAC gun . In the ensuing chaos, Phantoms begin to drop troops, Ghosts, and multiple Wraiths into the area. The new ship, a Lich, takes position over a hill to the right of the Mammoth **18** . Lasky needs you and the rest of Gypsy Company to somehow board the Lich and take it out from within.

> **RECOMMENDED LOADOUT**

This is a battle divided into three distinct phases, and there are weapons that can make all three phases much easier. To deal with the initial Ghost and Wraith rush, Cortana marks a Gauss Warthog. It's possible to take this Warthog into the next section, which involves your rushing the hill where the Lich is disgorging troops. When you finally manage to clear the hill, you want weapons that are solid for close-range combat on board the Lich. Plasma Pistol headshot combos are always a solid choice for the Elites on board, but consider also the power of Needlers and their super-combine ability. In close quarters and combined with grenades, you can score multiple kills in rapid succession.

INTRODUCTION

BASIC TRAINING

INTEL

CAMPAIGN

INFINITY

APPENDIX

Phase One: Ghosts and Wraiths

Phase Two: Taking the Hill

15 The initial rush is harsh. Ghosts are dropped into the area in pairs by Phantoms, who also add their own firepower to the fray for the brief moments they are overhead. Cortana quickly calls out the Gauss Warthog, marking it on your HUD **16**. Get down there to drive the Marine gunner around the area, giving him clean shots on the Ghosts. Eventually, Wraiths join the assault; one is dropped on the hill to the left of the Mammoth **17**. It takes, on average, three Gauss shots to destroy a Wraith, which gives it plenty of time to fire multiple mortars at you. Make sure you give the Marine good lines of sight on the enemy armor and stay on the move.

Alternate Approach

If you still have rocket turrets on the Mammoth, you can use them to try to soften the initial enemy assault, but the moment Wraiths get involved you should break free from the gun. This option poses the risk that the Gauss Warthog gets destroyed while waiting for you to get to it. This is a better Co-op strategy, where a player on the rocket turrets can support the allies in the 'Hog.

18 After pacifying the enemy vehicles with copious amounts of Gauss Cannon shots, they eventually stop coming, which leaves the Spartans and Marines of Gypsy Company free to push up the hill and take the fight to the Lich. If you have a Marine or Spartan gunner aboard the Gauss Warthog, they may abandon the gun to join the assault on foot. Feel free to curse this recklessness. The Covenant troops try to stream down the hill in an effort to keep your allies from breaching the barricades and taking the path up to the hilltop. It's possible to annihilate this counterattack simply by placing the Warthog a short distance away from the barricades and manning the gun yourself if necessary, but that runs its own risks of counter-fire. The Covenant are remarkably accurate at throwing Plasma Grenades long distances at unmoving targets.

With the path leading up to the hill secure, you can either join the rest of the troops on foot, or try to force the Warthog up the hill and leverage the Gauss Cannon against the enemy. If you still have a gunner, the latter option is absolutely preferred. Expect plenty of Covenant at the hilltop itself, but after a single wave of reinforcements, the Covenant will cede the hill to the UNSC, leaving the Lich hovering ominously over the battlefield.

Phase Three: Wrath of the Lich

19 The Lich can be considered a super dropship. It has already dropped onto the hill a large number of now-deceased Covenant, but rest assured that there are many more still aboard the vessel. You have two methods of boarding it: The gravity lift underneath the ship can be used, or you can board by flying up to one of the gun platforms on the side of the ship by using your Jet Pack to climb up the nearby rocks, and then flying up to the Lich from there. Both have their drawbacks. The first method potentially places you in the middle of a large number of Covenant, possibly Elites. The second method has you flying into view of mounted Plasma Cannons, and you'll want to take out those gunners to survive the landing.

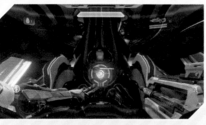

Once aboard, you must get to the upper deck of the ship to gain access to the reactor and destroy it, thereby eliminating the Lich threat. You can try to rush onto the upper deck without clearing the lower one of hostiles, but to fly up there too quickly may expose you to fire from above and below. The upper deck itself is extremely dangerous due to the high number of Elites there, including a Zealot at the main control station at the bridge. Take note: Once the reactor has been destroyed, you must escape from the ship. At this point, ignore any remaining Covenant and leap to safety. Just make sure you pulse the Jet Pack to slow your descent to the ground and survive the landing.

Alternate Approach

It is entirely possible to throw a Frag Grenade to the upper deck from the lower one and destroy the reactor with it. Of course, this isn't easy, but Cortana does mark its location on the HUD, so you do have a point of reference to work with. There also a chance that the Covenant, in their zeal to kill you, will accidentally blow the reactor themselves!

Legendary Strategy

The first phase of the battle is arguably the hardest, simply because of how hard the Ghosts and Wraith Plasma Cannons can hit. The Gauss Warthog can be turned to scrap very fast, and sadly there's no quick way to take out the Covenant vehicles that doesn't involve putting yourself into serious danger. Even if you place yourself at the top of the ramp near **17** and try to force the enemy to come up to you, you still must be able and willing to move to avoid being strafed by the Phantoms or getting mortared by Wraiths.

You should still attempt to get the Warthog atop the hill for the second phase if you manage to keep a gunner. If not, you might be forced to join your fellow Marines and Spartans on foot, using them as distractions while you pick off the gravest threats. Your allies will not last very long without your direct intervention, so work quickly.

The fight aboard the Lich is hard, even if you make use of the charged plasma combo to eliminate the Elites swiftly. With so many enemies in close proximity, it should be no surprise that you have very little room for error. If the Mammoth still has Rocket Turrets available, it's not a bad idea to take one with you as you board the Lich, to help deal with crowds and the Elites. Just watch your proximity to the enemy if you do this.

The Mammoth recovers from its battle damage, and you're to board the Mammoth for the rest of the trip through another canyon filled with dangerous rivers, until it eventually reaches a dead end. A Forerunner facility lies at the very end of the canyon, but as you might expect, the Covenant are ready to throw their lives away to defend it.

> MAJOR FIREFIGHT: APPROACHING THE FACILITY

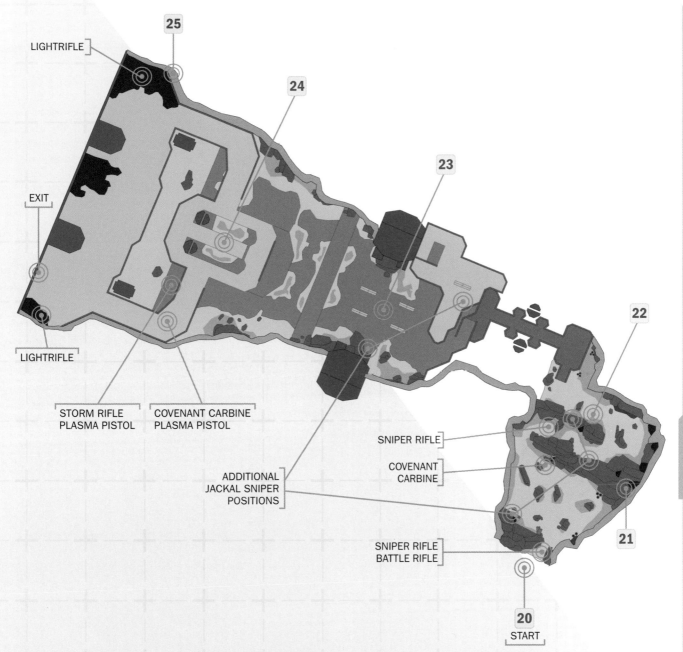

LIGHTRIFLE

25

24

23

EXIT

LIGHTRIFLE

STORM RIFLE
PLASMA PISTOL

COVENANT CARBINE
PLASMA PISTOL

ADDITIONAL
JACKAL SNIPER
POSITIONS

22

SNIPER RIFLE

COVENANT
CARBINE

SNIPER RIFLE
BATTLE RIFLE

21

20

START

INTRODUCTION · BASIC TRAINING · INTEL · CAMPAIGN · INFINITY · APPENDIX

20 The Mammoth cannot progress beyond this point, and the Master Chief elects to press on by himself while Gypsy Company tries to locate another route. You should already get a good idea as to what lies ahead when the first deployed ordnance pod you come across contains a Sniper Rifle and a full load of ammunition. The area before you even cross the bridge leading into the Forerunner structure is infested with Jackal Snipers. Once they've been taken out, you still must contend with a combined Covenant-Promethean force, with a heavy Knight presence making itself known the closer you get to the base entrance.

> RECOMMENDED LOADOUT

Early on, the Sniper Rifle and its ammunition is readily available among the ordnance drops, and it's recommended that you use it for counter-sniping as well as anti-Knight duty. When Sniper Rifle ammo runs low, you might be able to scavenge a Beam Rifle from fallen Jackal Snipers. You might consider taking on a Battle Rifle or Covenant Carbine to help put down close to mid-range threats so you don't waste Sniper Rifle shots. When Knights become a serious factor in the latter portion of the battle, you can also try out a Plasma Pistol to strip them of their shielding.

Counter-Sniping

20 The Jackal Snipers are not limited to long-range positions and Beam Rifles. Some of the snipers are mixed in at the ground level among the Grunts and shield-equipped Jackals. This first area has three snipers covering it. The range is short enough that the Battle Rifle or Covenant Carbine is still quite effective on these guys.

As you follow the hill leading farther into the sniper alley **21**, another pair of Jackal Snipers shows up on the mountain in the distance, and more join up with

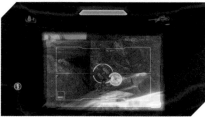

the Grunts and shield-equipped Jackals charging down the hill. Be careful about how you take on this section. While in cover, you want to take out the ground threats if it appears that they are going to get to you before you can outshoot the mountainside snipers.

22 Making the left just as you reach the top of this hill puts you face to face with another Jackal Sniper leading a small squad. In the distance, across the bridge and positioned throughout the opening ramps and walkways of the facility, are five more snipers, all of whom potentially have clean lines of sight over the bridge. You absolutely want these snipers dead before you even consider the idea of crossing the bridge. After they are down, you can cross the bridge, but exercise caution, as the Grunts here may come equipped with heavy weapons like the Fuel Rod Cannon. It is safer to snipe at the remaining enemies before crossing.

Promethean Intervention

23 A Knight and a small group of Crawlers make their appearance here, and as you go farther up toward the ramps that lead to higher levels of the facility, you'll encounter more Crawlers mixed in with Grunts and Jackals. Keep an eye out for any hostiles using charged Plasma Pistols. If you're in close combat with Crawlers, a charged shot can quickly lead to you getting beaten to death.

Watch your surroundings as you crest any ramp in this area because any enemies in this area have a distinct advantage over you. If you're too hasty, you'll just run into the middle of an enemy squad and get cut down.

Legendary Strategy

Snipers armed with Beam Rifles are awful jerks who deserve no sympathy or mercy, but unfortunately their sheer killing power on Legendary forces you to play a cautious game. The opening section is frustrating if you're not good at watching your flanks while also dealing with the snipers.

It's helpful to save up Sniper Rifle ammo or Beam Rifles to deal with the Knights. Whenever you're about to enter an area where you know a Knight is present, it's best to locate a Plasma Pistol and go for a charged combo on them. After their shields are down, a Sniper Rifle doesn't need to score a perfect headshot for a kill. Getting rid of Knights quickly will make the final run to the facility entrance much easier.

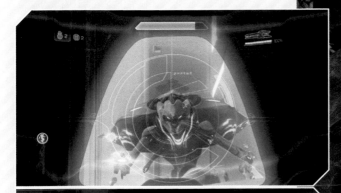

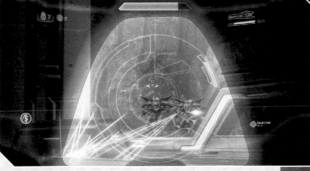

24 The upper level of the facility is a perfect example of why ramps are unsafe: Knights and Crawlers have great sight lines on these narrow points of entry, and the walkways near these ramps are also populated by Grunts. If the Grunts panic and elect a to execute a final suicide rush, you will not have much room to maneuver and may be forced to retreat to the lower levels if they get too close. If you've kept your Jet Pack, you can use it to help avoid suicidal Grunts while lining up headshots on them.

25 As you work your way across the upper walkway, watch out for this Jackal Sniper. He's in a prime position to be missed if you're moving quickly and are not paying attention to the ledges on the cliff face to the far right of the last walkway. He can actually be taken out from the lower levels with clever positioning. Two Knights and a final Crawler pack make up the final line of defense before you finally breach the facility.

INTRODUCTION

BASIC TRAINING

INTEL

CAMPAIGN

INFINITY

APPENDIX

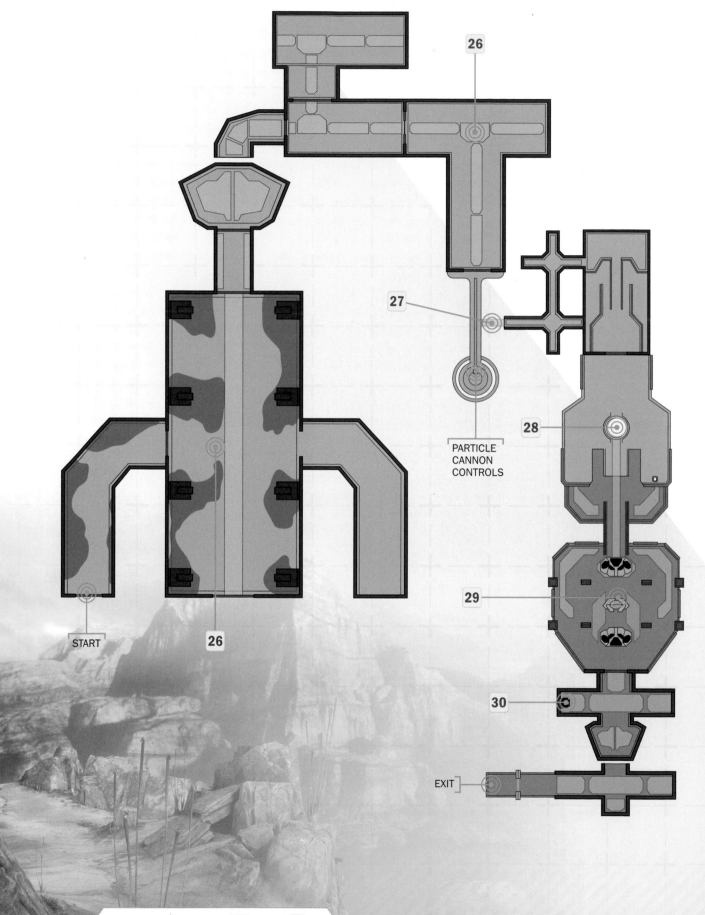

26

27

PARTICLE
CANNON
CONTROLS

28

29

30

START

26

EXIT

HALO 4

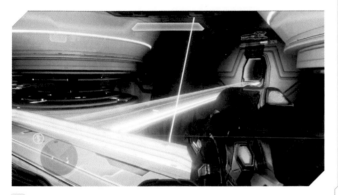

26 This facility is protected by docile Sentinels who lock doors you are not meant to pass through, while opening others for you. For the next few minutes, you have no real concerns other than to follow the path set before you. An elevator drops down deeper into the structure, and after a series of peaceful corridors, you reach the controls to disable the particle cannon network. Cortana easily accomplishes the task, but is suddenly "taken" away from the AI plinth. A new light bridge **27** takes you through the Sentinel passages to a new area. Keep following the path until you encounter a column of light with the faint image of Cortana inside it **28**.

It is here that the Master Chief meets an imprint of the Librarian, an ancient Forerunner with ties to the Didact. She reveals more about the past of her people and the galaxy, and give more information about the Didact and his ultimate goal: to retrieve a device known as the Composer. The Spartan is forced to make a decision just as the Didact enters the picture.

29 After your conversation with the Librarian, retrieve Cortana from the marked console, then get ready to fend off a Crawler pack and a Knight duo. Stick to the higher ground, force the Crawlers to come to you until they've been whittled down enough to start hanging back, then press the attack. Make sure you don't move in so quickly that you find yourself flanked by the Knights.

DOMAIN TERMINAL

This Domain Terminal can be found just after you retrieve Cortana. After defeating the enemy ambush at **29** you can enter a corridor that leads directly to another elevator. Go to the right of the elevator in this small passage to find the terminal **30**.

After locating the Domain Terminal, take the elevator down to the next level, where another teleporter awaits you.

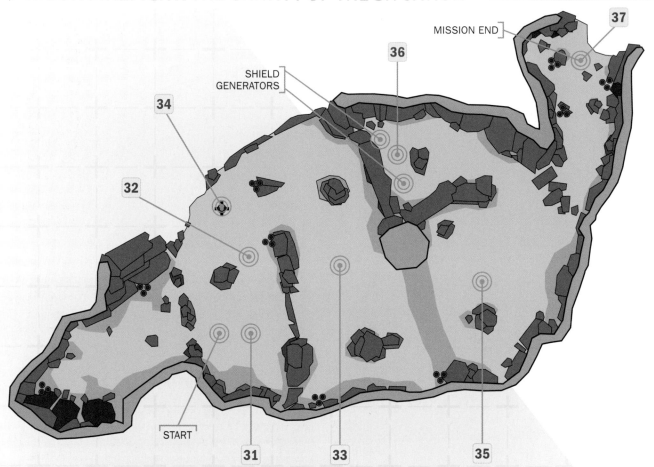

MISSION END

37

36

SHIELD
GENERATORS

34

32

START

31   **33**   **35**

31 The teleporter drops you right in the middle of a large-scale ground battle, and the odds aren't looking good for the UNSC troops. Fortunately, one of them knows what's good, and parks his Scorpion tank right next to the Master Chief. You need to blast your way through an extensive Covenant armored ground force that consists of Ghosts and Wraiths, reinforced by Phantoms with replacement armor and infantry.

The best thing about tank battles like this is it exemplifies just how hard a tank can beat, well, just about anything, given enough high explosives and some decent backup.

32 Ghosts fill the area just in front of where the tank is dropped off, and a pair of Wraiths is on the raised area to the right **33**. Take out the Wraiths first, if terrain permits. Then maul the Ghosts, taking care to avoid any allies, and move up to where the Wraiths were. Watch out for the guard platform **34**, as there may be Grunts and Elites wielding Fuel Rod Cannons on and around it.

35 Another shield prevents you from moving on toward your objective, and this small valley is being held down by a squad of Wraiths. This is the most dangerous part of the battle yet, as a single well-placed mortar can ruin your Scorpion to the point where you can't even fire its main gun! Stay mobile and at range to avoid getting glassed, and be sure to prioritize any Wraiths that attempt to rush in close for a point-blank mortar strike.

36 After you manage to destroy the Wraiths and reinforcements stop entering the valley, climb up the hill to the left of the shield to reach another trio of power generators. It's tempting to try to enter the protective shields with the tank to take a point-blank cannon shot, but you can accidentally kill yourself in the process. Instead, take them out on foot, then fall back to the location where the shield once stood.

37 The tank can't proceed any farther, but you've reached the final destination. Cross through the canyon on foot to reach another Target Designator, and then paint the gravity well generator in the distance. The *Infinity* receives the targeting data and launches a missile that you must guide in manually.

Legendary Strategy

The hardest part of the battle is dealing with the Wraiths. There are so many more of them than there are UNSC tanks, and they are all much more accurate with their mortars on Legendary. In fact, the opening section can start off really badly if a mortar falls on the Scorpion just as you're boarding it!

You need to stay on the move as much as possible, but you can't afford to get too close to the Wraiths, much less leave any infantry at your flanks. A single plasma mortar will kill a Scorpion on Legendary, no questions asked. Don't feel bad if you just sit back during the big brawl in front of the energy shield and constantly retreat to avoid getting killed, this is the safest way to guarantee that you won't be overwhelmed by the number of Wraiths being thrown at you. Survive this, and the ride to the generators is a cakewalk by comparison.

> STRATEGIC COWARDICE

Captain Del Rio has had enough of Requiem and wants to leave now. The Master Chief insists that they must stay to finish off the Didact, as he is vulnerable. Del Rio isn't having it, and Cortana, with her rampancy worsening, doesn't appreciate his attitude. Del Rio commands Lasky and Palmer to restrain the Spartan and to take Cortana's control chip, but nobody moves to follow the order. The Master Chief knows what his responsibilities are, and he stalks off the bridge with Cortana's control chip to continue his mission.

CAMPAIGN

MISSION 6: SHUTDOWN

"Come on, Chief. Take a girl for a ride."

With Cortana's rampancy consuming her by the minute, both she and the Master Chief have elected to stay behind on Requiem even as the *Infinity* and the sniveling Captain Del Rio prepare to make a retreat. Lasky has been ordered by the captain to prevent the Master Chief from leaving the ship at any cost, but he doesn't intend to stop him. Taking control of a Pelican Dropship armed for combat, the Master Chief must brave the skies of Requiem, shut down the Didact's defenses, and take the fight against the Forerunner personally, all without backup from the UNSC.

HALO 4

⌃ MISSION BRIEFING

Without the support of the *Infinity*, your life just got a whole lot more difficult. You need to get access to the Didact's ship, but to do so requires that you penetrate the air defenses near two spires that are controlling his shielding. Once inside the spires, you will have to fight your way past the most fanatical defensive effort put forth by the combined Covenant and Forerunner forces. Even after the shields are down, the defense ships around the Didact will make approaching him impossible. A third spire, with the means to restrain the Didact, will then need to be infiltrated, and with luck, you can manage all of this before Cortana's rampancy gets the best of her.

ENEMIES ENCOUNTERED:

Elites	Grunts	Jackals	Hunters

Crawlers	Knights	Watchers

VEHICLES ENCOUNTERED:

Phantom Dropships   Banshees

WEAPONS ACQUIRED
Assault Rifle
Magnum
DMR
Battle Rifle
Storm Rifle
Plasma Pistol
Needler
Covenant Carbine
Concussion Rifle
Fuel Rod Cannon
Beam Rifle
Boltshot
Suppressor
LightRifle
Binary Rifle
Scattershot
Incineration Cannon
SAW
Railgun

INTRODUCTION

BASIC TRAINING

INTEL

CAMPAIGN

INFINITY

APPENDIX

After Lasky leaves you to your own devices, you can head straight to the Pelican and continue your one-man assault on the combined Forerunner and Covenant forces. Inspect the hangar carefully, as every single Marine and Spartan in the hangar has weapons you can trade for. Combined with the two weapons racks on the Pelican itself, you will not be left wanting for UNSC firearms.

THE MARINES IN THE CORNER

While not vital to the mission, you can find two Marines standing guard near some containers filled with equipment, on the lower level of the flight deck in front of the Pelican. Try chatting them up for a laugh.

Getting airborne is simple. The Pelican is lowered into a launch tube. From there, command prompts appear on screen to help initiate the launch.

With the *Infinity* left behind, take some time to get used to the Pelican's controls and its arsenal. You're going to need its arsenal in the next few minutes.

VEHICLE ENCOUNTER

PELICAN GUNSHIP

To bolster the Chief's chances against the Didact, Lasky has given him a customized Pelican Gunship. It is heavily armed for air combat, and with three additional 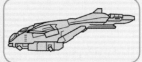 gun stations it is perfect for co-op play. This Pelican is armed with an autocannon and an anti-material laser cannon, as well as two side-mounted turrets and a topside heavy cannon. When properly utilized, this vehicle is an incredibly powerful UNSC asset, easily capable of going head-to-head with the Covenant's Phantom.

» KEY COMBAT TIP

As the pilot, you'll have control over only the nose gun and the laser. However, if you're playing with three other friends, the Pelican becomes a ridiculously overpowered death machine with all the weapon stations manned. Get lost, Phantoms!

Approaching the Didact's satellite is suicide. In addition to active defense systems, a powerful energy shield blocks access to it. Cortana suggests that it may be possible for you to disable the barrier, but you'll have to enter a pair of the floating tower structures to get access to the necessary systems Cortana has targeted for you, essentially flanking the Didact's satellite. You can tackle them in the order you wish, but you will have to fight your way into the towers, and through them, if you're to reach your objective. We do feel that the order the towers are presented here is the ideal order, however, as it allows you to make the best use of resources presented to you.

Both towers are guarded by squadrons of Phantoms. Quite frankly, these poor guys are in the wrong sky at the wrong time. Even flying solo, you've got more than enough firepower to turn these dropships into scrap metal fragments, and if you are flying with some company along for the ride, you're even better off. Just avoid giving them a easy target by staying mobile, and don't let the Pelican get surrounded. Once the skies are clear around a tower, set down on the marked landing pad and go inside.

> MAJOR FIREFIGHT: THE LEFT TOWER

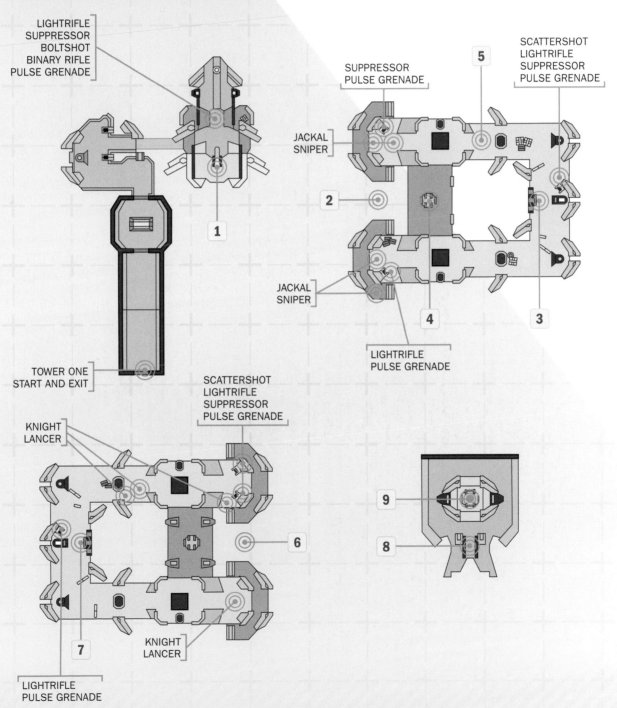

LIGHTRIFLE
SUPPRESSOR
BOLTSHOT
BINARY RIFLE
PULSE GRENADE

1

SUPPRESSOR
PULSE GRENADE

SCATTERSHOT
LIGHTRIFLE
SUPPRESSOR
PULSE GRENADE

5

JACKAL
SNIPER

2

JACKAL
SNIPER

4

3

LIGHTRIFLE
PULSE GRENADE

TOWER ONE
START AND EXIT

SCATTERSHOT
LIGHTRIFLE
SUPPRESSOR
PULSE GRENADE

KNIGHT
LANCER

6

9

8

7

KNIGHT
LANCER

LIGHTRIFLE
PULSE GRENADE

INTRODUCTION

BASIC TRAINING

INTEL

CAMPAIGN

INFINITY

APPENDIX

177

The left tower initially seems completely abandoned and without any form of defense, but this is only the calm before the storm. You need to cross a massive gap to reach the target point by means of a gondola, of sorts. However, the Covenant and the Prometheans have two special stops they will force the gondola to make before you can reach the carrier wave generator.

> RECOMMENDED LOADOUT

You have a good variety of UNSC hardware to pick from on the Pelican. A DMR can be extremely effective at the first stop, though you may want to quickly replace it with a LightRifle found on one of the weapon racks on the gondola. The two platforms the gondola is forced to stop at can also favor close-range weapons like the Boltshot, Scattershot, or the SAW found on the Pelican. The gondola also contains a Binary Rifle, but you probably will want to save it for hard targets like Knights or Elites, as the ammo for it is limited. You can also bring a Railgun from the Pelican, but again, you'll have limited ammunition to work with. You can make up for the limitation with a LightRifle as your primary weapon. Make certain you have a Jet Pack; the vertical mobility will come in handy.

First Stop: Snipers, Grunts, Elites, and Prometheans

After climbing aboard the gondola and sorting out your weapons, hit the switch **1** and make sure you find some form of cover from assaults to your right. Within a minute, the gondola approaches its first stop **2**, and before the ride comes to a halt, four Jackal Snipers take up positions at the station and open fire with Beam Rifles. Counter-snipe with a DMR or LightRifle, and try to eliminate these enemies before the gondola stops. At the stop, the gondola extends a light bridge for you to cross, but consider waiting until you take out any visible hostiles at the station. Focus on easy picks like the Grunts or Jackals, as their numbers can be troublesome in close quarters.

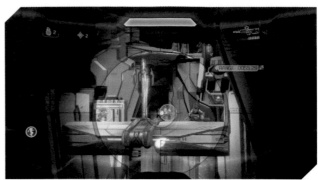

The station consists of two short ramp towers connected by a central bridge at their lowest level, each providing access to the platform where the gondola's override is located **3**. The ramp towers are crawling with Grunts and Jackals and are actually quite dangerous. Their construction makes it difficult to rely on your motion sensor's readings on enemy positions, and there are lots of blind corners. Be especially mindful of suicide Grunts trying to creep up on you via the ramps.

» KEY COMBAT TIP

Watch your footing! The Forerunners did not build this area to any sort of safety standards, meaning there is no guardrail preventing you from stepping off the platforms to your death. Your Jet Pack can do only so much to save you from a fall.

The lower connecting bridge **4** is frequented by an Elite that is stalking the lower levels of both ramp towers. Once you find him, take him out quickly. Losing track of him might mean he gets the drop on you.

The battle around the switch includes multiple Elites. By now you should have plenty of Plasma Pistols to pick up to deal with them. With the Plasma Pistol combined with a LightRifle, you'll find they're relatively easy to kill. Once you've cleared out a path to the override switch, hit it, and get ready for round two.

Alternate Approach

It is possible to ignore many of the goons on the lower levels of this section by using the Jet Pack to fly to the upper platforms. Just be sure that you've taken out the Jackal Snipers before you take flight. This tactic can help expedite your mission, but it can make the next bit a little tougher, especially if the enemies you ignored start climbing up the ramps to get to you.

Knights begin teleporting into the station after the override is activated, taking up positions near the override itself **5** , the gondola, and at the second stop itself. If you brought the Railgun from the Pelican, these are excellent targets for it. But the Promethean attack doesn't end here. A Knight Battlewagon has also teleported onto the gondola itself, and Crawlers now stalk its walkways and the wall opposite to the tower it is connected to. After clearing out the gondola, hit the marked switch to restart it. Two more Knights appear at the front of the gondola halfway to the second stop. Try to put them down quickly; you're getting in range of the next ambush.

Legendary Strategy

Welcome to the hardest chapter in the game on Legendary. This first ambush can be a harsh roadblock before you actually step off the gondola. Jackal Snipers are accurate enough on Heroic, but on Legendary, they're even more dangerous. Grazing hits can be followed up by a lethal shot within a second, so anticipate their appearance and locations (the same as on Heroic) and snipe them first.

On Heroic, you could have charged off the gondola as soon as it came to a stop to engage the enemy up close, if you wanted, but this isn't encouraged here. With relatively little room to move on the towers, and considering how grenade happy the Covenant are, you could find yourself pretty dead, pretty quick. We recommend the LightRifle as your primary weapon for this whole encounter, with the Railgun specially set aside to help take out Elites and later, the Knights. The Plasma Pistol makes a good substitute in place of the Railgun. But on this difficulty the enemy is more apt to dodge charged shots, though they might also throw themselves into the abyss if they're too zealous about their evasive moves. Elites and most Knights are actually able to survive a direct hit from a Railgun on Legendary, so bear that in mind should you take the weapon with you. Lastly, if you are able to, take a Plasma Pistol with a decent remaining charge with you when you return to the gondola. You will want to have access to its charged shot for the next stop.

Second Stop: Knights and Binary Rifles

To the gondola's left, near the carrier wave generator platform, is another structure that shares its design with the previous ambush point. As

the gondola hovers closer to this second stop **6** , Knight Lancers, armed with Binary Rifles, begin to bracket your position. Hopefully you've conserved the Binary Rifle on the gondola weapons caches because it's the best response available. Watchers and Crawlers also fill the various walkways and connecting bridges. If you can take out the Knight Lancers before a Watcher starts to provide shield protection to them, do so. If a Watcher positions itself close to a Knight Lancer, shoot it out of the air with your LightRifle. Once you take out the Knight Lancers, you can take the light bridge onto the platforms to reach the newly marked override switch, or continue to snipe Crawlers and Watchers.

The switch itself 7 is protected by another Knight Battlewagon, a Crawler pack, and possibly another Watcher or two. Remember that eliminating Watchers can spur the Battlewagon to take the fight up close, where its Scattershot can and will destroy you in a single point-blank burst and you'll also contend with its deadly melee attacks. Hit the switch to push the gondola close to your ultimate goal.

It's far from over. As the gondola connects to the platform with the generator, more Knights, including a Knight Commander armed with an Incineration Cannon,

flash into place 8 . This Commander is not fooling around. The shot fired by an Incineration Cannon can disintegrate a player as fast as a Binary Rifle shot, and it has a wider area of effect to make up for the slower shot. If your Binary Rifle still has a few rounds, put them through the Commander.

» KEY COMBAT TIP

Try to take the Incineration Cannon, and hold onto it for as much time as possible. The LightRifle is a great all-purpose weapon to cover the deficiencies of the Incineration Cannon and can effectively deal with just about everything thrown at you in the mission. Having the Incineration Cannon on hand makes Knights or Elites of all varieties much easier to deal with if you're willing to be aggressive and make direct hits with the weapon.

Legendary Strategy

Now things get brutal. There are relatively fewer enemies to deal with at the second stop, but Knights are always problematic on Legendary, particularly Binary-equipped Knight Lancers. This is easily one of the most frustrating battles in the Legendary campaign. The platforms' design gives the numerous Watchers plenty of places to hide from your wrath, which means that they can sneak around and reconstruct fallen Knights the moment your attention is pulled elsewhere. Of course, the Binary Rifles carried by the multiple Knight Lancers in the area are all capable of one-hit kills, which further complicates matters.

You may be tempted to counterattack with your own Binary Rifle, but we actually recommend using the six shots you get with the weapon to guarantee that the Watchers are killed. With the Watchers dead, you can concentrate on eliminating the Knight Lancer threat from afar with careful counter-sniping with a LightRifle. Or, if you took a Plasma Pistol with you, try to get close enough to blast them with a charged shot, then finish them off with unscoped LightRifle shots. Both methods run the risk of your being destroyed by a single Binary Rifle shot (even from a random ricochet), so it's really a matter of whether you prefer to die at the feet of your enemies or at a distance. Regardless of your approach, the Crawler infestation at the second platform should be whittled down as much as possible before you try to reach the override switch.

The Incineration Cannon-wielding Commander near the carrier wave generator is also significantly more threatening. The shot the Incineration Cannon fires is blisteringly fast compared to on Heroic mode, so treat it with greater respect, even from a fair distance.

The Carrier Wave Generator

Even with the ambushes beaten, the danger is far from over. Stand in the carrier wave generator beam 9 to to use your shields in an EMP blast, and then immediately take cover! Your shields are taken down, and a swarm of Watchers rises from beneath the gondola. Their Boltshots are not particularly threatening, normally, but in these numbers and with your shields temporarily offline from the EMP, slow reactions can prove fatal. Let your shields recharge a bit, then go out and knock the Watchers out of the air. Afterward, restart the gondola to make a peaceful, if not quiet, trip back to the Pelican.

> MAJOR FIREFIGHT: THE RIGHT TOWER

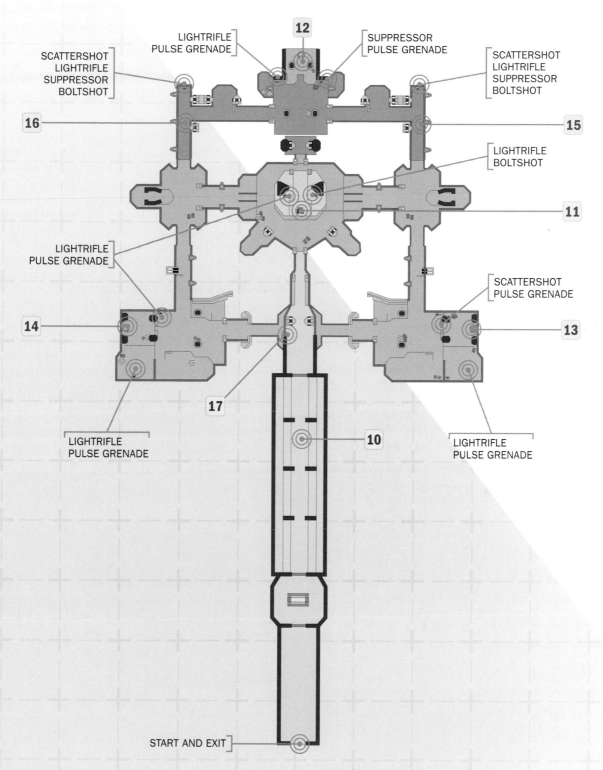

LIGHTRIFLE
PULSE GRENADE

12

SUPPRESSOR
PULSE GRENADE

SCATTERSHOT
LIGHTRIFLE
SUPPRESSOR
BOLTSHOT

SCATTERSHOT
LIGHTRIFLE
SUPPRESSOR
BOLTSHOT

16

15

LIGHTRIFLE
BOLTSHOT

LIGHTRIFLE
PULSE GRENADE

11

14

SCATTERSHOT
PULSE GRENADE

13

17

10

LIGHTRIFLE
PULSE GRENADE

LIGHTRIFLE
PULSE GRENADE

START AND EXIT

There are no gondola rides in this tower, just a lot of interconnected platforms filled with Prometheans protecting the target attenuator that must be destroyed to further interrupt communications between the Didact and his servants. Disabling this tower, however, will require a bit more effort than standing inside an incandescent beam of light.

> RECOMMENDED LOADOUT

The LightRifle once again is your best friend. If you hit the left tower first, you could possibly have an Incineration Cannon, which trivializes the normally intimidating presence of Knights. The LightRifle can easily dispatch any other foes, while the Incineration Cannon can be used on harder targets. If you lack that weapon, you can always pick up a Railgun from the Pelican's weapons caches.

INTRODUCTION

BASIC TRAINING

INTEL

CAMPAIGN

INFINITY

APPENDIX

Revealing the Attenuator

10 Entering the tower takes you to a hallway dotted with pillars. It is guarded by a Crawler pack and a Watcher that tries to add more Crawlers into the mix. As you exit this hall, more Watchers buzz overhead, which heralds the fun that lies ahead. Cortana initially believes the tower attenuator is singular in nature, but when you hit the switch she marks for you **11** she reveals that there are three targets scattered throughout the platforms **12** **13** **14** .

》 KEY COMBAT TIP

One way to make life a little easier as you fight across all the platforms to reach the attenuators is to snipe the all Watchers and Crawlers throughout the area from the central platform. You've got great angles on many hostiles from here, and eliminating them now makes dealing with the Knights that appear once you get closer to the attenuators simpler.

Expect Crawler and Watcher presence at every major walkway and platform between the attenuators. In particular, the lower platform between **14** and **15** can be tricky, as they've got a good chunk of cover in addition to Knight backup.

Attenuator One

12 The closest attenuator to the central switch can be reached easily by dropping down to the lower platforms opposite where you

first entered this chamber. Don't be so quick to make the leap. A Knight phases into existence when you approach, along with two Watchers and a smattering of Crawlers. Pick off the Watchers, then put down the Knight with an Incineration Cannon, if you have it. As a bonus, you might also take out nearby Crawlers with this shot.

If you lack an Incineration Cannon or a Railgun to take out the Knight quickly, you can still take it out with a LightRifle or with the Scattershot found in one of the weapons caches near the center switch. In this case, you'll want to thin out the lesser foes first to allow you to focus on the Knight exclusively. With the Knight down, the attenuator reveals itself from behind its shielding, and you can take out the energy satellite in a single melee strike. From here you have two routes to follow to reach the remaining attenuators. Both mirror each other in appearance and general opposition.

》 KEY COMBAT TIP

With a Jet Pack, you have amazing control over how you start the encounter here, and there are plenty of high ledges you can reach to maintain a positional advantage. One such spot is the platform just above the attenuator itself!

Attenuator Two

15 Facing the central platform from attenuator one and following the path to the left, you will encounter multiple Knights along the walkways, along with any Crawlers or Watchers that you didn't snipe from the central platform. The narrow paths can make Knight encounters more dangerous, so hopefully you still have Railgun, Incineration Cannon, or Scattershot ammo to deal with them quickly before they get too close.

13 The second attenuator's Knight appears in front of it as you draw closer. The L-shaped platform can make fighting it tricky, thanks to the pillars it can use for cover. Before approaching the device and triggering the Knight, eliminate any local Watchers at least before you make your move.

Attenuator Three

If you approach this attenuator from the first target, you'll find this path **16** is a mirror of the one you can take to attenuator two, right down to the sort of resistance you face on the route. It even includes weapons caches in the same locations. If you're traveling over from attenuator two, you'll have to cut across a platform below the entrance **17** to the whole chamber, if you're taking the direct approach. A Watcher tries to construct a Forerunner anti-infantry turret on the platform itself, while another Knight guards the ramp that connects to the platform.

14 Similar to the second attenuator, the third is found on an L-shaped platform that can complicate the fight against the Knight guardian. Any surviving Crawlers and Watchers on the platform also attempt to block your path.

Getting Out

As there is no correct order to taking out the attenuators, your exit strategy will depend on which generator you tackled last. A Knight, Watcher, and Crawler pack typically appears on the connecting walkways that take you to the central platform. From there, get to the bridge that takes you back to the entry hallway.

Your way back to the Pelican is be blocked by Crawlers and a Knight Commander wielding an Incineration Cannon. This fight can be surprisingly annoying, as the Commander's shots can find plenty of places to hit that kill via splash damage. Without a Railgun or Incineration Cannon of your own, you're forced to play a dangerous game of chicken while you try to make the kill with whatever else you have available. Collect his Incineration Cannon, it will be invaluable in the coming battles.

Legendary Strategy

The biggest problem with the trek between attenuators is the amount of open space that you must travel through while vulnerable to incoming fire. To mitigate these dangers, it's crucial to take advantage of the elevated central platform and the bridge connecting it to the entrance of the spire and kill as many Crawlers and Watchers as possible from that position. It's not the bravest plan, but it is more likely to keep you alive. Direct combat against the Knights on these narrow walkways is generally a bad idea, as they are able to quickly close the distance and kill you with their melee attacks. Even Crawler packs are more dangerous if you are not able to quickly defeat them with headshots.

Hopefully, you have managed to horde Incineration Cannon ammo for yourself to deal with the knights near the attenuators faster, but try to make sure you leave at least one shot for the final Knight Commander. If that's not an option, you'll have to use the pillars in the entrance hall and run from cover to cover until you get close enough to make the Knight Commander refuse to fire his weapon, but not so close that he charges in to beat you down. To that end, a Scattershot, if you've managed to locate one, is not a bad option. You can quickly fire three or four shots into its face once you get in close range, which is enough to cut through shields and nail its skull before it can do anything about it.

With both towers disrupted, Cortana marks a third tower for you to infiltrate. If she can gain access to the systems in the tower, she may be able to prevent the Didact from leaving Requiem. It's a long shot, and unfortunately Cortana's conditioning is worsening. Time is running out to stop the Didact—either Cortana fully degrades, or the Didact's own armies will put a stop to the Master Chief. Inside the tower, you enter an antigravity lift that takes you to the first level of the tower.

> MAJOR FIREFIGHT: TOWER THREE, LEVEL ONE

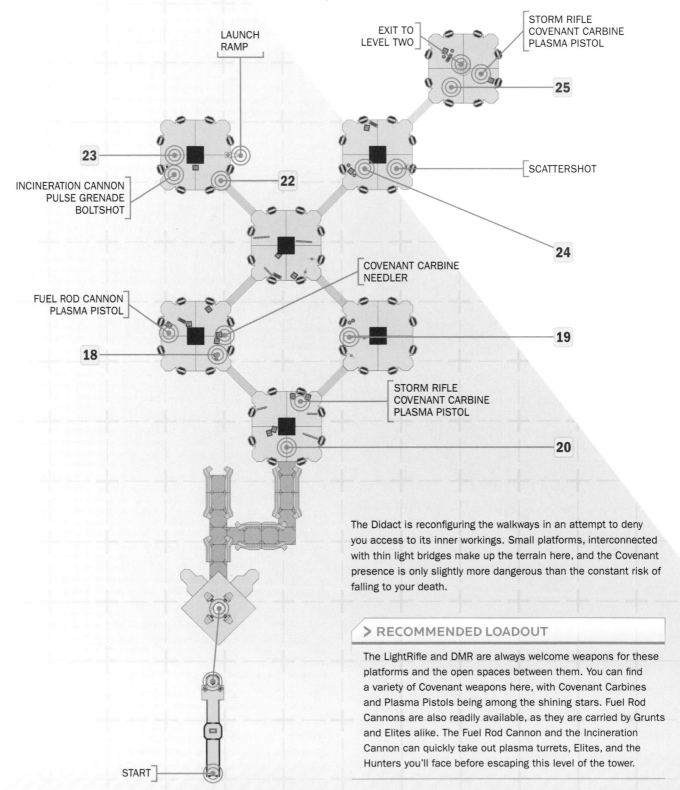

The Didact is reconfiguring the walkways in an attempt to deny you access to its inner workings. Small platforms, interconnected with thin light bridges make up the terrain here, and the Covenant presence is only slightly more dangerous than the constant risk of falling to your death.

> RECOMMENDED LOADOUT

The LightRifle and DMR are always welcome weapons for these platforms and the open spaces between them. You can find a variety of Covenant weapons here, with Covenant Carbines and Plasma Pistols being among the shining stars. Fuel Rod Cannons are also readily available, as they are carried by Grunts and Elites alike. The Fuel Rod Cannon and the Incineration Cannon can quickly take out plasma turrets, Elites, and the Hunters you'll face before escaping this level of the tower.

Your ultimate goal is to reach the designated antigravity lift at other end of the chamber. Expect extensive resistance along the way—the common mix of Grunts and Jackals, with Elites among the crowd.

The bridges that lead to the first platform **20** begin to collapse into the chasm below, and you must make it to the first solid platform quickly or fall to your death. Grunts occupy this first platform while mounted Plasma Cannons **18** **19** try to bombard you from adjacent platforms. The central pillar can be used for cover while you work on killing the gunners.

Near the mounted Plasma Cannon marked **19**, you encounter a number of Grunts supporting the gunner. After taking them down, you can find a cache of Covenant Carbines next to the mounted gun, which can be a useful replacement for the LightRifle or DMR, if you're running low on ammo for these weapons. You can then cross a light bridge to the next platform, where an Elite leads a squad of Grunts and Jackals. This platform lets you go to platform **21**, progress farther toward the exit **24**, or take a very important detour **22**.

DOMAIN TERMINAL

23 This platform contains an important weapons cache: an Incineration Cannon with a full ammo load. Additionally, you can find the Domain Terminal for the chapter hidden against the central pillar here.

24 Things get a little hairy here, with a high-ranking Elite rushing to the light bridge in the hope of taking you out as you cross. There's a good chance he is armed with a Fuel Rod Cannon, which makes crossing the bridge a tough prospect until he's out of the picture. If you picked up that Incineration Cannon from the other platform **23** you should be able to put him and any other Covenant near him out of your misery.

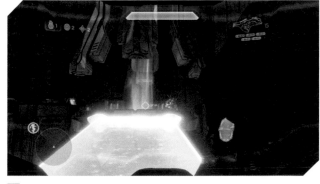

25 The antigravity lift is your destination, but a pair of Hunters make an entrance and drop down from the upper level. With the Incineration Cannon, you can easily put one down, even by means of a frontal assault, and then concentrate on flanking the other. If you're quick, you can convince the Hunters to expose their vulnerable flesh, and a well-placed Incineration Cannon shot destroys them easily. When they are out of the picture, consider going back to the Domain Terminal platform to recover any remaining ammo for the Incineration Cannon, then take the lift up to the next level. A Fuel Rod Cannon can also work well, in a pinch.

≫ KEY COMBAT TIP

If you're not interested completely clearing the enemies in this zone, it's possible to skip two of the platforms and make a straight shot at the lift. By the end, if you lure the Hunters away from the lift, you can leap right in and escape without battling them. There's always the chance that they might paste you with fuel rods before the lift takes you safely away, though.

Legendary Strategy

This is another battle where you have a serious risk of falling to your death, which also translates to a lack of hard cover against shooters positioned on adjacent platforms. The opening part of the fight can be rather tough, as you have to deal with two Plasma Cannon gunners who will take you down in seconds if allowed, and headshots are not at all easy to score. It's not a bad idea to take a Railgun into the tower for this first battle, if only to take out decisively any mounted guns. As always, Elites become a more serious problem, but you can always resort to the charged shot combo. Stick to this to conserve the Incineration Cannon or Fuel Rod Cannon for more specific use against the Hunters, assuming you stick around for the brawl.

> MAJOR FIREFIGHT: TOWER THREE, LEVEL TWO

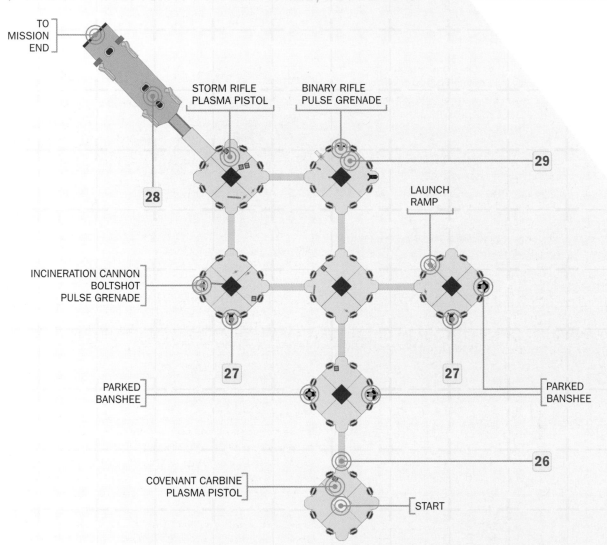

An even larger group of connected floating platforms fills this chamber, and the defenses have increased to match. Banshees now patrol the local airspace, and the Covenant have placed a number of Shade Turrets around many of the platforms, in addition to the usual infantry patrols. The control station lies at the end of the platforms, preceded by a long bridge that is protected by a final defensive line of more Shade Turrets and troops led by high ranking Elites.

> RECOMMENDED LOADOUT

Grinding your way from platform to platform is neither easy nor quick. Elites are more numerous, so you'll want to address them with charged combos or power weapons like the Incineration Cannon or Fuel Rod Cannon, if they're available. Banshees are a big threat and you don't have a Rocket Launcher available to take them down. You can used a charged Plasma Pistol on them, but you have an even better option: Take a Banshee for yourself. Several platforms have Banshees parked and waiting for a pilot.

26 As soon as you leave the lift, you can find a weapons cache with Covenant Carbines and Plasma Pistols. The platform connected to it is guarded by an Elite who may see you arrive; he's guarding a pair of parked Banshees. Take him out, then weigh your options.

By Air

Don't kid yourself, taking a Banshee may sound like the easy way out, but you are still in serious danger if you do. Shade Turrets are the ground threats to your craft, but also plenty of hostile Banshees are in the air and ready for a dogfight. It's almost inevitable that you'll take some damage over the course of the fighting, so know where any spare Banshees are.

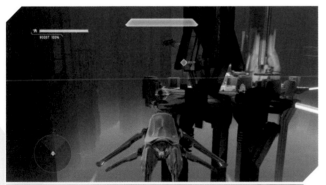

Shade Turrets are easy to take out with the Banshee's fuel rods, but you're forced to dive at them, and the Shade Turret will likely get in a few shots before you destroy it. Plus, you contend with the weapons carried by other ground troops. Check their positions on the map, as they are especially dangerous to fly around. Two Shade Turrets **27** are pointed at the platform where the Banshees are parked, so watch your takeoff.

Dealing with the hostile Banshees requires bit of finesse and strategy. They will try to drag you into areas where the ground troops can add their two cents to the fight, but turning your back on them to fly away from those danger zones isn't much better—they'll just turn around to shoot you in the back. Track enemy fire back toward the sources and award them a fuel rod for the trouble before you turn your attention back to the flier. Above all else, do not let yourself be put in a situation where it's multiple Banshees against you.

» KEY COMBAT TIP

You can fly underneath the platforms to defend against both Shade Turrets and Banshees. Of course, you'll have to fly above the final platform bridge to reach the exit, but this is a good way to avoid the worst of the antiaircraft defenses. Be aware that dropping too far below the platforms will cause your Banshee to self-destruct.

28 The final defense line bridge is guarded by three Shade Turrets and a smattering of Jackals, Grunts, and a high-ranking Elite. It is possible to completely bypass these foes as well, but the approach to the bridge will not be easy. Getting past this last group of Covenant grants you access to the control station Cortana needs to access.

On Foot

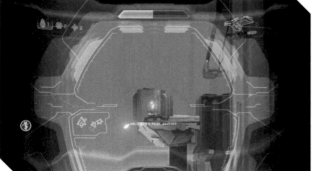

If you're the type of player who *really* likes a challenge, the only choice for you is to be the ultimate foot-slogger the Master Chief was born to be.

Look for weapons caches to locate firepower you can use to take out the Banshees and any Shade Turret gunners, any light bridge crossings should be made only if you've ensured you're not about to get dive-bombed, or blasted by the Shade Turrets or by hostiles just on the other side of the bridge. Charged Plasma Pistols can disable the fliers, but they can also stun Shade Turrets, giving you a chance to take out the gunners while not getting shot at. You can find a Binary Rifle one of the platforms **29**; it goes a long way toward dealing with Shade Turret gunners from afar. Binary Rifles aren't quite as effective at handling Banshees.

Legendary Strategy

The air option is much harder on Legendary, as the Banshee you pilot isn't as durable as the ones the Covenant are flying. This makes taking on the ground forces more dangerous. When you take your first Banshee, kill the closest Shade Turrets. Next, fly high and concentrate on wiping out the enemy aces, then you can work on eliminating the remaining Shade Turrets in the area. Do yourself a favor and don't mess around with low strafing runs against infantry. Fly in, hit your target with a fuel rod, and immediately pull away. On Legendary, enemies armed with Plasma Pistols are prone to use the charged shot more often, and they are incredibly accurate with their shots. If your disabled fighter doesn't fall on a island, you'll most likely die before you can recover from the attack. If you proceed on foot, the usual warning about Covenant foot soldiers on this difficulty applies. Frankly you're only making things harder on yourself, not to mention more time-consuming by trying to fight your way to the control room this way, but it's not impossible.

Keep a Plasma Pistol handy at all times to knock the Banshees out of the sky, and do not proceed to another platform until you're certain you have eliminated the welcoming committee at your destination, and that you do not have a Banshee or two setting up strafing runs on your position. You will have to be the paragon of headshot efficiency with the Covenant Carbine if you want to take this fight on foot, as you can't afford to be fooling around with infantry if the Banshees are still in the air.

If you're not at all interested in killing every last Covenant in the area, you can cut the time spent here by simply taking out the hostile Banshees, then eliminating the Shade Turrets and infantry closest to the exit. Once you've cleared the bridge near the exit, there's no need for you to pick fights with the other Covenant in the area.

> DESPERATE MEASURES

Cortana swiftly assumes control over most of the automated defenses once you place her within the control console, manipulating towers to try to halt the Didact's escape. But her rampancy is growing more and more overwhelming, and she's unable to complete her task. When you tear her free from the system, the Master Chief devises a desperate plan: Cross over the top of a formation of Liches traveling near the third spire, in the hope of following the Didact's ship to its next destination. As soon as the room lowers enough to allow you access to the landing pad, sprint out and leap off the marked ledge.

The Master Chief manages to cling to one of the Liches just as the Didact's new ride begins to blast away from Requiem into a massive slipspace rupture, with the Covenant fleet following closely. The fight to keep the Forerunner away from the Composer is entering the final stages.

INTRODUCTION

BASIC TRAINING

INTEL

CAMPAIGN

INFINITY

APPENDIX

CAMPAIGN

MISSION 7: COMPOSER

"Cortana, it's not over. Not yet."

Having managed to survive the slipspace jump, the Master Chief looks on as the combined enemy fleet emerges in real space next to a Halo—Installation 03, according to Cortana. In the asteroid field near the ring, Ivanoff Station is currently under Covenant assault, and will fall very soon. The Composer is apparently aboard this station. Taking over the Lich, Master Chief signals to the station his intention to assist in its defense, but Cortana's personality continues to slip further into rampancy, and she crashes the Lich into the station.

⌃ MISSION BRIEFING

Ivanoff Station never had the defenses to stop a Covenant incursion of this magnitude, but it can at least slow them down somewhat. Your goal is to locate Dr. Sandra Tillson and begin coordinating a defense against the Covenant. You will fight your way through the station to prevent the Covenant from landing more troops in the unsecured bays and and airlocks throughout the facility. Next, reactivate the MAC defenses to assist evacuation efforts. The Didact is seeking the Composer, and he must be prevented from seeing it at all costs. However, should it be impossible to prevent him finding the artifact, the best solution will be to destroy it, and everything related to it. Expect heavy resistance from the Covenant: They know how close their goal is.

ENEMIES ENCOUNTERED:

| Elites | Grunts | Jackals | Hunters |

VEHICLES ENCOUNTERED:

Phantom Dropships   Ghosts

Banshees   Wraiths

WEAPONS ACQUIRED

Assault Rifle

Magnum

DMR

Battle Rifle

Sniper Rifle

Storm Rifle

Plasma Pistol

Needler

Covenant Carbine

Concussion Rifle

Fuel Rod Cannon

Beam Rifle

Sticky Detonator

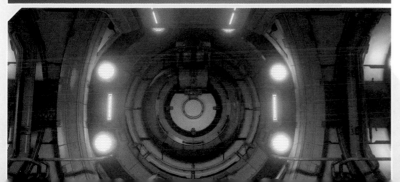

INTRODUCTION

BASIC TRAINING

INTEL

CAMPAIGN

INFINITY

APPENDIX

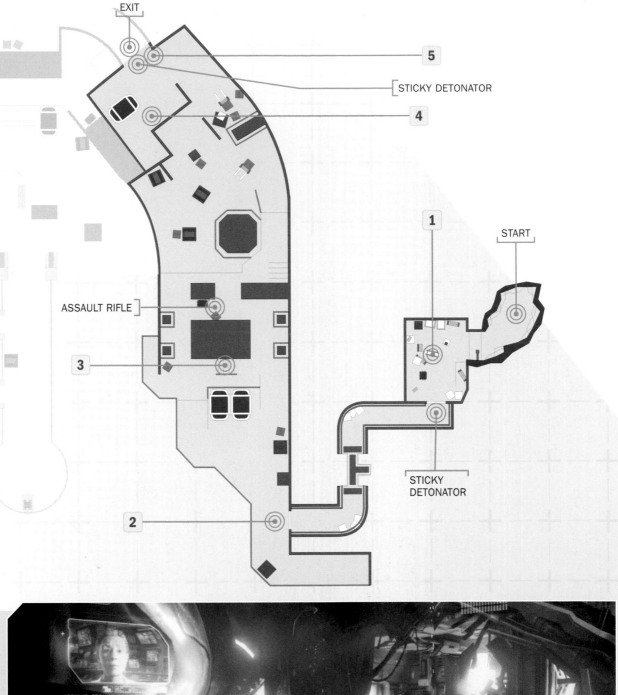

EXIT

5

STICKY DETONATOR

4

START

1

ASSAULT RIFLE

3

STICKY
DETONATOR

2

Recovering from the crash, the Master Chief immediately contacts Dr. Sandra Tillson to urge her to get all UNSC personnel off the station. Unfortunately, the Covenant have already taken over the landing bays, the primary way off Ivanoff at present.

1 You may notice this odd ring with energy pulsing brightly at its center. Jump through it if you enjoy losing a good chunk of your shields. Stand inside it if you enjoy losing everything else. Beyond the nearby door, a Marine scores a final kill against the Covenant invaders before dying himself, leaving behind an invaluable weapon. We recommend that you ditch the Assault Rifle for now and replace it with this new toy, then move through the next corridor to show it off to the next group of Covenant you encounter.

WEAPON ACQUISITION

STICKY DETONATOR

This single-shot weapon fires a small magnetic explosive at a relatively high velocity, enough to cause a full-grown Elite to stagger from the impact. Difficult to remove once it attatches to a target, the explosion occurs after a lengthy delay, but also can be triggered early by the weapon's user. Entire Covenant squads have been devastated by a single, well-placed Sticky Detonator shot.

» KEY COMBAT TIP

There are a lot of nice things to say about the Sticky Detonator, but one of the best is the fact that the weapon contains a motion sensor that tracks if any targets are close to the grenade after it is deployed. You can stick an opponent, then wait until you know his friends are close by before triggering the explosion.

2 You don't have to wait long. The door art the end of the corridor reveals a pair of scientists retreating away from a Marine just as a Jackal leaps at him

to make the kill. If you're a Magnum ace, you can actually save this Marine's life, which gives you an extra body to help you with the ensuing scuffle.

3 Jackals and a variety of Grunts occupy the raised platform and the two short passageways leading under it, with an Elite standing guard within the passages. Shoot down a few hostiles, especially the Jackal Rangers, using your Magnum, as you may want their Covenant Carbines for later. This tends to draw the Elite out, and gives you a perfect opportunity to demonstrate just how powerful the Sticky Detonator truly is. A good tactic is to stick the Elite specifically with the explosive. He might charge at you, or he may hesitate among a number of his fellow Covenant, scoring you a juicy multikill.

4 Jackals snipe from catwalks across the way from the raised platform. If you still have Magnum ammo or have switched to the Covenant Carbine, kill these guys first, preferably from atop the platform **3**. The ground level between your position at the Jackals has a small team of Grunts lead by another Elite. If you've still got Sticky Detonator on hand, the Elite should be a quick kill.

Legendary Strategy

While this battle isn't necessarily big enough to count as a Major Firefight, it deserves some particular attention for Legendary difficulty. To start with, don't commit yourself to running out and saving the Marine. You can still pop the Jackal mauling him from the relative safety of the corridor, and even if you fail it rescue him, his life for the rest of this skirmish is typically measured in seconds .

Once you do step out of the corridor, concentrate on Grunt and Jackal headshots while hugging the crate to the right of the door. The ranges here are relatively short, so the already-fast Covenant plasma is going to seem a lot faster. Normally we'd suggest conserving Sticky Detonator ammo, but they're just too useful to hold back on Legendary. Sticking a Grunt may cause him to panic and run into other allies. However you decide use this weapon, save at least one shot to help put down the Elite quickly. Go for upper torso or head sticks with the Sticky Detonator because Elite shields and health increase enough on Legendary to help them survive at least one Sticky Detonator grenade, but it will deplete their shields and leave them vulnerable to a Magnum headshot.

The Jackals at 4 are pretty mean, and they match their shots well enough that they can drain your shields entirely in the time it takes for you to set your sights on one or both of them. Throwing a grenade in their direction may get them to split up and stop shooting at you, or you can hug the stairs leading up to the top of the raised platform 3 to snipe them one at a time. Whatever you do, do not let the Jackal pair team up against you, especially if they happen to be armed with Beam Rifles.

 5 Stick to the ground level here to locate more Sticky Detonator ammo. There's good call for it in the next section.

> MAJOR FIREFIGHT: SEAL THE HANGAR BAY

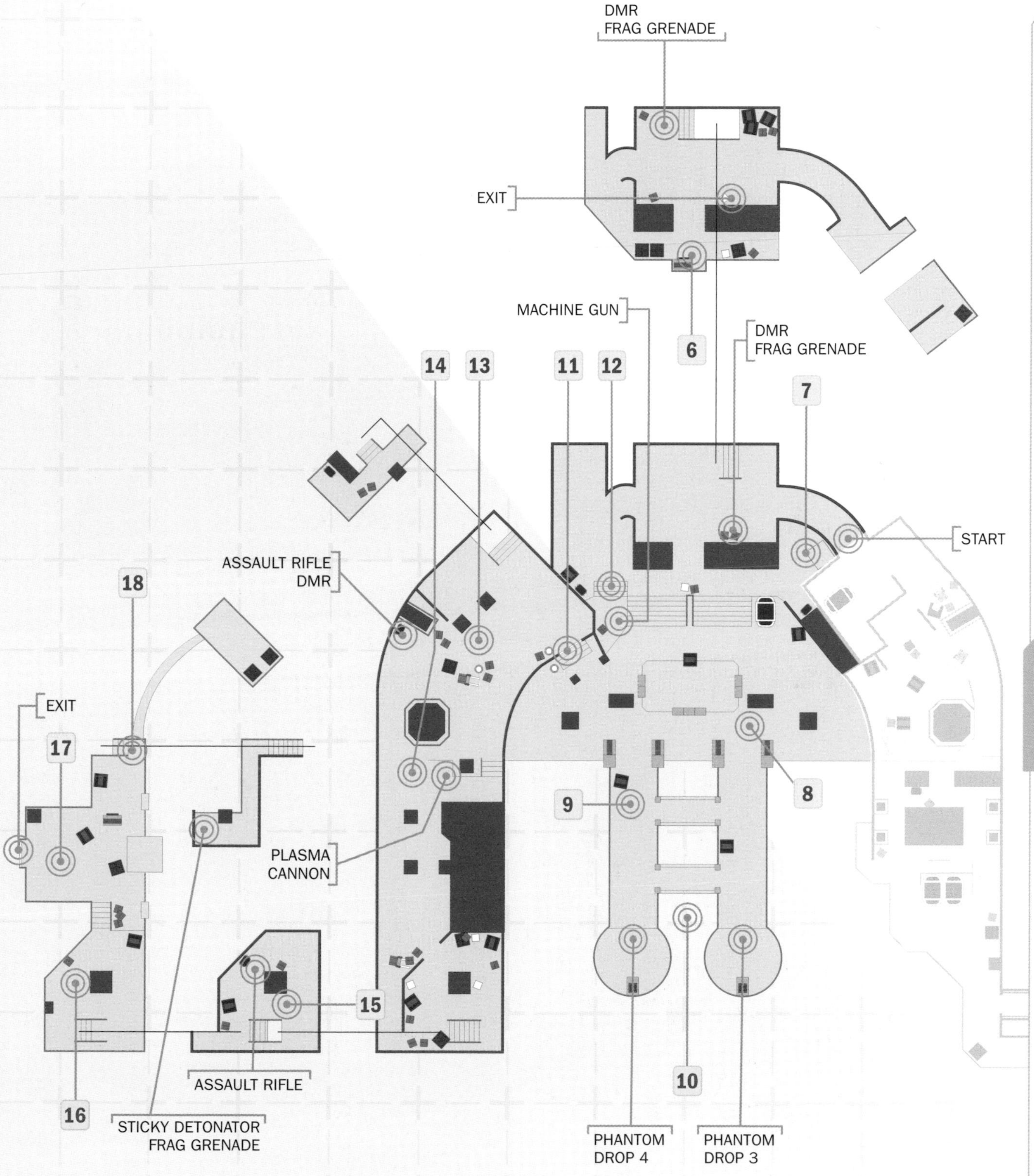

INTRODUCTION

BASIC TRAINING

INTEL

CAMPAIGN

INFINITY

APPENDIX

DMR
FRAG GRENADE

EXIT

MACHINE GUN

6

DMR
FRAG GRENADE

14 **13** **11** **12** **7**

START

18

ASSAULT RIFLE
DMR

17

9

8

16

PLASMA
CANNON

15

ASSAULT RIFLE

STICKY DETONATOR
FRAG GRENADE

10

PHANTOM
DROP 4

PHANTOM
DROP 3

Ivanoff's biggest problem right now is that the Covenant control the hangars, an easy access point to dump hundreds of angry troops directly into the belly of the station. You arrive at this point in between waves of hostiles, with a new batch of enemy troops arriving via Phantom as a dwindling squad of UNSC Marines tries to take position on the catwalks to engage the enemy. You need to get to the hangar controls to activate the shields and prevent any additional landings.

The Sticky Detonator can do some real good work on the squads dropped off by the Phantoms, so it should be in your arsenal. The small holdout where you first meet with the Marines and scientists trapped near the hangar contains some DMRs, with another one found against the railing overlooking the entire hangar. The DMR is a solid solution even for dealing with shielded Elites if you've got a lot of ground between you and them. If you expend your Sticky Detonator completely, switch it out for a Plasma Pistol or a Storm Rifle specifically for handling Elites.

6 Start by getting to the second-floor walkways overlooking the hangar itself. On a ledges to the left **7**, a Jackal Sniper is having a shootout it out with the Marines, take him out before he becomes a problem.

8 The first Phantom drops off troops in front of the left-side docking platform: Jackals and Grunts first, with an Elite dropping in last. Watch out for

the Phantom's guns that try to engage you (sniping one of the side gunners with a DMR or Covenant Carbine isn't a bad idea here) and be ready to move. When you see the first troops drop out of the Phantom, put a Sticky Detonator grenade right at their feet, but do not detonate it until the Phantom drops a pair of Elites. Throw in your favorite grenade if you'd like, then trigger the mine. You'll almost certainly kill anything near the mine that isn't the Elites, and as a bonus, you might even strip his shields for a follow-up headshot. Juicy.

Alternate Approach

If you're lacking the Sticky Detonator, things can get really bad if you're slow to wipe out the first group before the second comes calling. Hopefully you've managed to pick up a Plasma Pistol to help bring down the Elite quickly. The ensuing panic will give you a chance to establish some dominance over the battlefield and claim more kills with the DMR.

Alternatively, there is a mounted machine gun with a firing arc that covers the first two landing sites perfectly **12**. It's a death sentence to keep to yourself tied to the gun while the Phantoms are in the area, though. Even if you tear it free from its mount, you're simply too slow with the heavy weapon in hand, which makes you a perfect target if you trying to push forward towards the enemy. Find a good piece of solid cover, however, and most enemies will crumble before they can get too close.

9 The second Phantom tries to drop its cargo only a few meters to the right of where the first Phantom tried its luck, atop the docking platform that leads directly to the switch you need to hit. This should go about as smoothly for this group of Covenant as it did for Phantom one's unlucky schmucks. There are more Elites in this group than the first, so you may not be able to take this squad as quickly if you misplace the explosive. Use another grenade if available to compound the damage further. Make the Elites priority. Even if the explosives don't kill them, you might break their shields and leave them vulnerable to headshots.

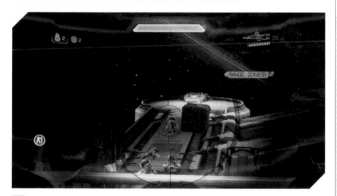

10 With two Phantom's worth of troops dead at your feet, check the bay entrance to see if a third Phantom is close to arriving. If not, run—don't walk—to the control console marked for you at the end of the right-side docking bridge. Activating it will prevent any further reinforcements from joining up, and open the way to the next section. However, if you're slow getting to the switch, the third dropshop will arrive and deploy another Covenant squad adjacent to the pad containing the landing bay controls, and among this group is an Energy Sword-equipped Elite! Keep the bay unsealed after that, and a fourth squad filled with even more hostiles will be deployed right next to the control console itself. The Sticky Detonator will likely be very low on ammo by this point, so make your remaining shots count.

Besides Elites, the other major threat brought in by the Phantoms are Jackal Snipers. If they come equipped with Beam Rifles, you'll have to prioritize them above other enemies. Beam Rifles are too dangerous to ignore.

Alternate Approach

It's tough, but you can put an end to this battle really fast by making a beeline for the bay shield controls as soon as you meet with the Marines. You must kill the Jackal Sniper to prevent his shooting from slowing you down, then sprint for the controls, turning around to take out the Plasma Cannon gunner on the first Phantom. From there, you can finish the run to the console relatively unbothered. The first dropship will still unload any survivors, and you'll have to deal with more Covenant coming in from a previously sealed side door **11**.

11 After sealing the bay, this door is opened, allowing an Elite and several Grunts and Jackals to stream though. One last Sticky Detonator grenade if you've got it, should seal this deal decisively. Otherwise, get yourself close to some cover, take out the Elite first if the opportunity knocks, and deal with the rest accordingly.

Legendary Strategy

The same basic plan from Heroic can still work here, your biggest threat comes from the Elites, all of whom are more resilient. You also may have less Sticky Detonator ammo to work with. Generally, you have to be spot-on with your mine placement to maximize your kills. Don't be too surprised if you take a few dirt naps early on, the Phantom gunners are especially vicious on this difficulty.

If you want to hit the switch early, wait until you've killed off the first Phantom's drop of troops to avoid getting overwhelmed. It's still not a very safe plan no matter how you slice it, but it may be just as unsafe as waiting for all four dropships to make their appearance. The last dropship deploys five Elites, a tough battle under any circumstance made harder by the fact that you have somewhat limited room to maneuver.

Since you know that after you seal the hangar, a group of Covenant will attempt to storm through a previously locked door **11**, this is probably the easiest part of this battle. If you're still blessed with Sticky Detonator grenades, the solution is quite simple. Alternatively, if you managed to dislodge one of Plasma Cannons from a Phantom, or if you took the mounted machine gun **12** from its perch, you can flood the narrow doorway with hot death, and that may be enough to finish off this final push.

13 On the other side of the door, a squad of Marines is collapsing under the assault of another Covenant force consisting of a pair of Jackal Rangers, some Grunts (one is manning a mounted Plasma Cannon), and an Elite shouting orders from a walkway behind all of his men. Below that Elite's perch, just past a ramp leading below him, another squad of Grunts and another Elite await. Typically, they do not join the fray immediately, which should give you time to eliminate the first group. One neat trick is to take out the plasma gunner, which will lure the Elite to take the gun himself. You can then nail him with a Sticky Detonator or a Plasma Grenade. Any surviving Marines join you for the next skirmishes. Be sure you take a good look at their makeshift last-stand barricade to reload on weapons like the DMR or the Sticky Detonator.

» KEY COMBAT TIP

One of the Jackal Rangers may have carried a Beam Rifle. It isn't a bad idea to take it with you, especially if the Sticky Detonator isn't an option.

16 At the top of the stairs, you encounter a group of Jackals and Grunts. Across a short walkway to another section of the upper decks, two Elites surround themselves with more allies **17** . Despite the number of enemies accosting you here, this isn't a particularly difficult battle to win. The Elites typically stay on their side of deck, while their Jackal and Grunt allies make the crossing to support their brothers near your staircase. Use it as cover against enemy fire, and duck below to a lower level if things get too fierce and you need a breather. If you picked up a Beam Rifle earlier, the Elites make for obliging targets. When this top deck is clear, you can move through the indicated door.

14 If you run to the walkways that the first Elite once guarded, you can actually ambush the second group from above. Consider taking the plasma

turret with you to do this, and if it's got any juice left after the slaughter, keep it with you when you encounter the quartet of Grunts coming down the stairs **15** from the upper levels of the hangar.

18 But don't leave so quickly that you pass up on the opportunity to go down the stairs behind where the Elites once stood to locate a Sticky Detonator.

> ELEPHANTS IN THE ROOM

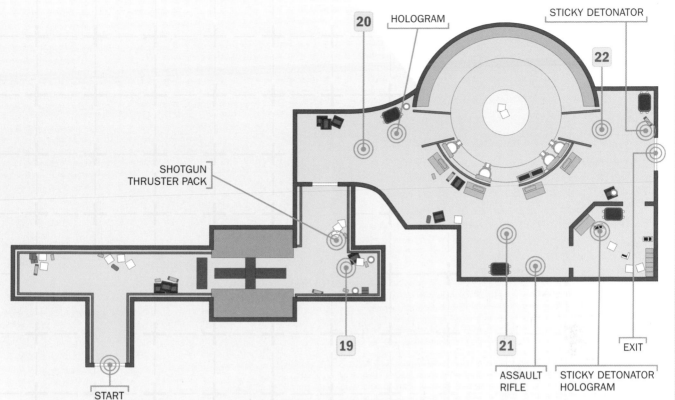

INTRODUCTION

BASIC TRAINING

INTEL

CAMPAIGN

INFINITY

APPENDIX

19 After a short corridor, you encounter a distraught scientist who begs you to help her colleagues a little farther ahead. She offers a Thruster Pack armor ability to assist in dealing with the Hunters laying siege to the next room. We really recommend you pick this up. A Shotgun can also be found next to the Thruster Pack, which can be very effective in the right hands.

ARMOR ABILITY ACQUISITION

THRUSTER PACK

A modified EVA pack designed specifically for Spartan use, the Thruster Pack module allows the user to quickly shift position to evade enemy fire, assault a position, or both simultaneously. A skilled Spartan can run circles around opponents in melee combat situations with judicious use of this system.

20 Two Hunters in an enclosed space sounds like a nightmare, and it can be if you don't have a plan. Fortunately, you do have some advantages. The scientists in the room aren't entirely helpless: They are all packing Magnums and are supported by some Marines with Assault Rifles. Aside from providing a distraction, they're all surprisingly good shots. If you turn the Hunters' backs to them, they will score hits on the Hunters' exposed vitals.

The Hunters are separated. One starts a bit closer to the scientists **21**, while the other is a bit farther back in the room **22**. You ought to have the Sticky Detonator; there's a refill for it in the small office in the corner of this room (along with a data pad with an interesting entry from Dr. Catherine Halsey). The Shotgun is also excellent for dealing with Hunters, especially when combined with the Thruster Pack.

We recommend going after the Hunter that is closest you in the room. You can easily slip past it with the Thruster Pack to reach the small lab behind it, where you can locate more Sticky Detonator ammunition. To reach the one further into the room, you would have to charge through the circular display area filled with artifacts (that you can investigate after there are two dead Hunters) to reach it.

When you get close enough to any Hunter, it almost always try for melee strikes. Use your Thruster Pack to evade around their mighty swings, and put some ammo into the exposed flesh on their backs. A few solid Shotgun blasts or a couple of Sticky Detonator grenades, or even some Plasma Grenades, and that will be that. Wouldn't it be nice to always have a Thruster Pack handy for every encounter with a Hunter pair? Once the Hunters are dead, proceed through the door that Cortana marks on your HUD.

Alternate Approach

You are also able to use the Hologram armor ability to distract the Hunters. This can keep their attention long enough for you to flank them. It's not effective once contact has been made, however. If they see you deploying it, they'll ignore it and go after you most of the time.

> THE COMPOSER

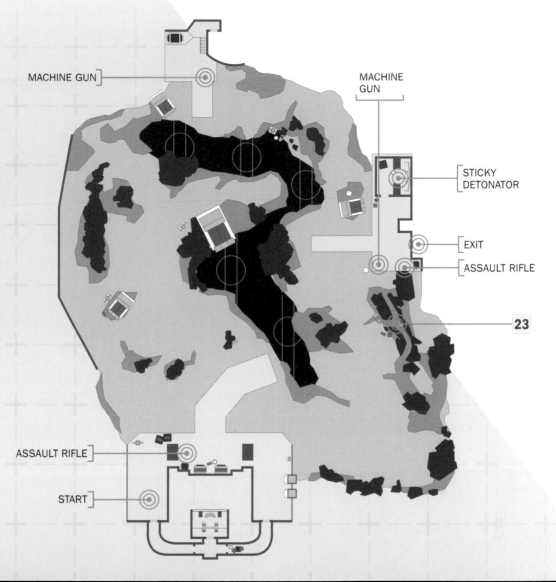

MACHINE GUN

MACHINE GUN

STICKY DETONATOR

EXIT

ASSAULT RIFLE

23

ASSAULT RIFLE

START

INTRODUCTION

BASIC TRAINING

INTEL

CAMPAIGN

INFINITY

APPENDIX

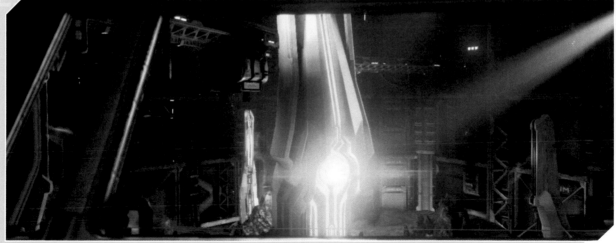

The Master Chief meets with Dr. Tillson, who explains that the Forerunner artifact, the Composer, is much too large to move from the station in the time the Master Chief needs it to be moved and with the resources that are available. His new solution is simpler, but no less effective: Destroy it and the whole station with nuclear weapons. Tillson is less that pleased by this, but relents in the face of reality. The Spartan must now buy time for the station staff to evacuate, while she oversees the preparations for the nukes to be armed and moved into position.

The chamber that holds the Composer is massive. Dozens of Marines dot the field around the device, while others still patrol the perimeter in Mantis mechs. There are a number of information terminals you can locate throughout area to learn more about the Composer, as well as its strange effects on the scientists who were assigned to investigate it.

DOMAIN TERMINAL

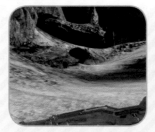
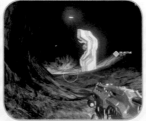

23 The sixth Domain Terminal can be found within a small cave a little ways to the east of the Composer. It's incredibly easy to miss if you're in a hurry, and while you will have a chance later to activate it, the circumstances may not be as accommodating to casual investigation.

Once you've found the Domain Terminal, there's little else to be concerned with in this chamber. If you kept a Shotgun, consider finding a Marine with a DMR or even a Magnum to trade with, then head to the indicated door. In the small office near the exit, you can find more Sticky Detonator ammo.

On the other side of the door, a wounded Marine offers to let you back into the compromised parts of the station. Once you go through the door, there is no turning back, so make sure you are comfortable with your loadout.

24 As the Didact taunts you, power failures grip the station, causing the doors in this corridor to seal themselves. You can take a lighted service tunnel to bypass the doors and flank the unlucky Jackals on the other side. Defending the door **25** that you need to pass through to reach the air locks taken by Covenant troops is an Elite protecting a Plasma Cannon, with more Jackals and Grunts. The door they guarded opens once they have fallen.

> MAJOR FIREFIGHT: THE AIR LOCKS

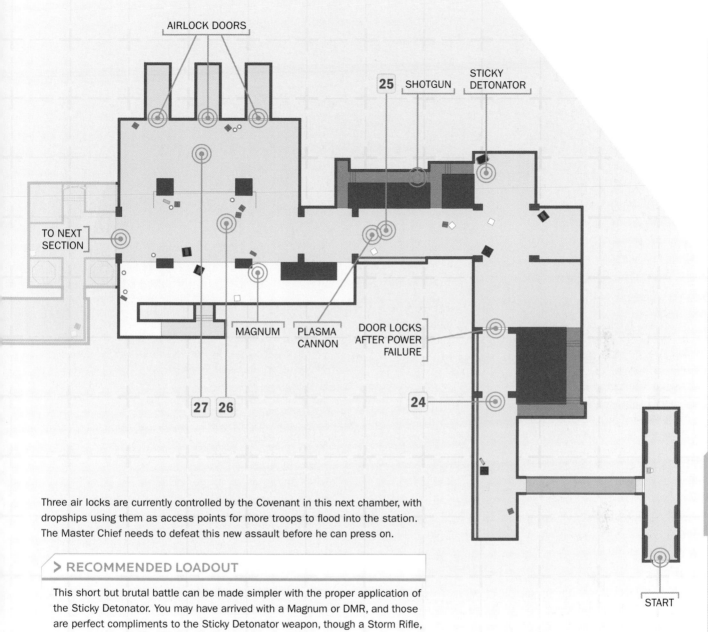

AIRLOCK DOORS

25   SHOTGUN   STICKY DETONATOR

TO NEXT SECTION

MAGNUM   PLASMA CANNON

DOOR LOCKS AFTER POWER FAILURE

27   26

24

START

Three air locks are currently controlled by the Covenant in this next chamber, with dropships using them as access points for more troops to flood into the station. The Master Chief needs to defeat this new assault before he can press on.

> RECOMMENDED LOADOUT

This short but brutal battle can be made simpler with the proper application of the Sticky Detonator. You may have arrived with a Magnum or DMR, and those are perfect compliments to the Sticky Detonator weapon, though a Storm Rifle, Needler, or Covenant Carbine also help in a pinch.

INTRODUCTION

BASIC TRAINING

INTEL

CAMPAIGN

INFINITY

APPENDIX

26 Almost as soon as you open the door to this room, you are confronted by an Elite accompanied by his Grunts and Jackals. One Sticky Detonator grenade is good enough to wipe him out and incite panic among his subordinates. Mop them up as best you can, but immediately move to the air locks.

27 You may see hostiles already gathering inside the air locks, attempting to gain access into the station. You can deal with this by pressing the switch on the door itself, cycling the air lock and jettisoning them into space. If you're unable to get to the doors before they allow hostiles into the room, set a Sticky Detonator grenade at the foot of the door and let the enemy walk onto it before triggering the blast. This method can be quite dangerous, as you're only able to mine one door at a time. If the enemy comes through multiple air locks, you could find yourself quickly overwhelmed by multiple Elites and their cronies.

Whichever solution you choose, keep killing Covenant until you get the all clear from Cortana, who opens a door for you to pass through.

Legendary Strategy

Considering how fast you can shut down the Covenant at the air locks on Heroic, this fight might seem easy here, but Legendary is always ready to kick over your sand castle at any moment. The initial battle as you enter the room will most likely take longer to manage if you fail to eliminate the first Elite right away. Should this be the case, you could already be facing down the reinforcements coming through one of the air locks while you're still trying to finish off the first squad. This isn't to say that it's impossible to use the air lock doors against the Covenant, you'll just have to work much faster than you did before.

Fortunately, you do have a safe option. There is a service tunnel you can use for protection and as a means to funnel Grunts and Jackals to you while you silence them with headshots. This still leaves the Elites, who tend not to venture into the confined space, but you can take the service tunnel to the upper levels and fire Sticky Detonator grenades at them. If you did keep the Hologram from earlier in the mission, this can be a useful tool of distraction to use from the service tunnel or the upper level.

28 A Marine and a group of scientists are making a last stand against an squad of Covenant in the corridor just beyond the air lock. Taking out this group summons another Elite-led squad farther down the corridor. Eliminating them while keeping the UNSC personnel alive will have one of these survivors open a side room that contains more Sticky Detonator ammo, as well as the Autosentry armor ability. You may want to consider picking it up for this next firefight.

29 At the top of this ramp, Grunts try to ambush you.

INTRODUCTION

BASIC TRAINING

INTEL

CAMPAIGN

INFINITY

APPENDIX

> MAJOR FIREFIGHT: AIR LOCK ROOM REDUX

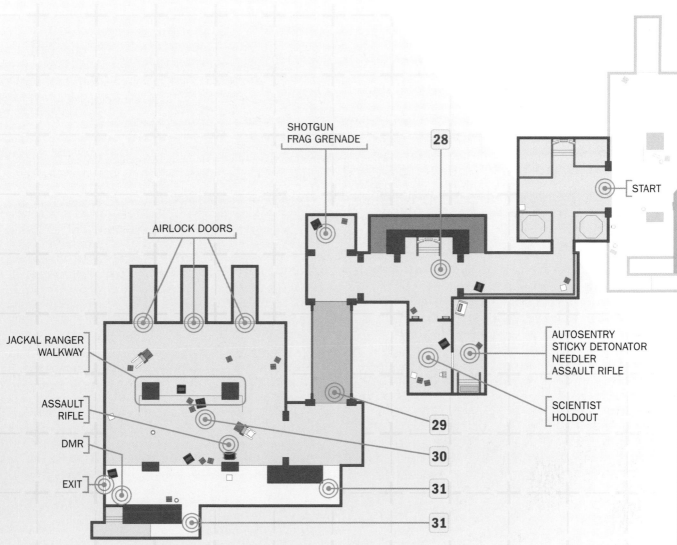

SHOTGUN
FRAG GRENADE

28

START

AIRLOCK DOORS

JACKAL RANGER
WALKWAY

ASSAULT
RIFLE

DMR

EXIT

AUTOSENTRY
STICKY DETONATOR
NEEDLER
ASSAULT RIFLE

SCIENTIST
HOLDOUT

29

30

31

31

30 Another set of three air locks are being used by the Covenant to bring reinforcements into Ivanoff, but this time they are more prepared to hold onto them: Jackals and Grunts occupy the upper levels and have excellent sight lines throughout the entire room, and the service tunnels are now more likely to be used against you.

> RECOMMENDED LOADOUT

Hopefully you still have that Sticky Detonator, but if that isn't an option, you can also use a Plasma Pistol to help whittle down the shields of Elites. Beyond that, weapons capable of headshots are preferred.

Aside from additional obstacles to use as cover, this chamber's design is almost identical to the previous air lock room, and similar solutions to the air lock reinforcements problem apply. However, the Covenant have definitely stepped up their game: Jackal Rangers are on the upper level girders sniping at you with Covenant Carbines (or potentially Beam Rifles). You still want to make sure the first Elite goes down quickly, then switch to a headshot-capable weapon and go to work on his allies. If you manage this quickly, you can then deal with the enemy reinforcements as you desire.

The reinforcements from the air locks are also tougher customers. You can expect higher ranking Elites, including cloaked Zealots, to try to pass through the air locks. This "simple" fight can become seriously chaotic if you lose control of the air lock doors and aren't acting like a hammer in an extraordinarily violent game of whack-a-mole. Once you've caused enough casualties, Cortana opens a door on the upper level that leads to the control room for the station's defenses.

31 Be mindful of the various service tunnel access points in the room. If you stick to the air lock room entrance while dealing with the first Elite, there's a good chance the Grunts in the upper level will suicide-rush down the service tunnels and into your flanks.

Legendary Strategy

While this room's design is similar to the previous air lock chamber, your mind-set will have to adjust for the Legendary difficulty. To start with, a frontal, aggressive approach to air lock management may be out of the question entirely. There are simply too many enemies on the upper level that must be dealt with to avoid getting flanked while you hold down the air locks. And because you might take longer dealing with the initial forces on Legendary, you will have to deal with some reinforcements.

We recommend getting to the upper level via the service tunnels as quick as you can, as soon as the first Elite is down. It's simply more reliable early on than trying to force your way to the air locks to begin cycling Covenant into the vacuum. It's still possible to camp at the air locks, but you'd have to be a crack shot to eliminate any Jackal Snipers that could threaten you while you do the deed at each door.

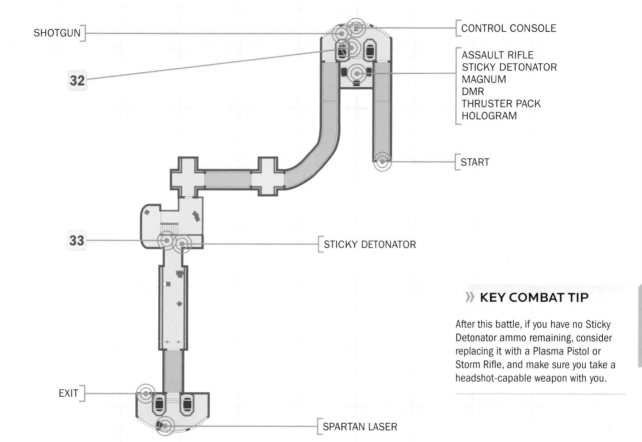

SHOTGUN

32

CONTROL CONSOLE

ASSAULT RIFLE
STICKY DETONATOR
MAGNUM
DMR
THRUSTER PACK
HOLOGRAM

START

33

STICKY DETONATOR

EXIT

SPARTAN LASER

» KEY COMBAT TIP

After this battle, if you have no Sticky Detonator ammo remaining, consider replacing it with a Plasma Pistol or Storm Rifle, and make sure you take a headshot-capable weapon with you.

INTRODUCTION

BASIC TRAINING

INTEL

CAMPAIGN

INFINITY

APPENDIX

32 The control room appears empty when you arrive, but that is far from the truth. Two cloaked Elites are within, one of whom is at the controls you need to access. The other stalks close by. You can use explosives or the Sticky Detonator to help reveal them, or use a plasma-based weapon to strip their shields for a headshot from a Covenant Carbine or DMR. When they are out of the picture, insert Cortana into the control console.

Don't miss the weapons cache in the control room. You can find a full rack of Sticky Detonators waiting for you, along with a variety of UNSC weapons and armor abilities. Most important, though, you want those Sticky Detonators.

Cortana activates the station defenses, and begins to drive back a portion of the invading force. Pull her from the console when she is ready, then continue to the newly opened door to meet up with Dr. Tillson. Some Grunts and Jackals put up a token resistance along the way.

But only if you aren't packing a Sticky Detonator. One or two shots, along with any grenades you might have, will be more than enough to purge the corridor of most hostiles. Be sure you target the Elites first!

33 Grunts and Jackals hold down the ramp leading up to a long, straight corridor where two Elites lead a another contingent of Grunts in a final bid to prevent you from reaching the Composer and aiding in its defense. This has all the makings of a serious firefight.

FREE HALO 4 eGuide with updates!

Visit www.primagames.com and enter the voucher code below to get:

- **Spartan Ops episodic campaign strategies, screenshots, and gameplay videos to complete all missions.**
- **Maps for War Games and the Campaign.**
- **MLG pro strategy for War Games with gameplay highlights.**
- **Legendary tips and gameplay video to help survive the onslaught of enemies.**
- **Access to strategy anywhere you have an internet connection.**

1. Go to www.primagames.com. Select "Redeem Code" located at the top of the page.

Log in | Register   Redeem Code   Shopping cart
0 items $0.00

Platforms: PS3 | Xbox 360 | Wii | PC | DS | PSP | iPhone | 3D

GAMES   LATEST NEWS   DISCUSSION   BLOG   SHOP   CONTACT

2. Enter the voucher code in the text field and click the "Submit" button.

PRIMA GAMES - REDEEM CODE

CODE FORMAT: XXXX-XXXX-XXXX-XXXX

STEP ONE: ENTER CODE

SUBMIT

3. You will be redirected to your content now.

STRATEGY WHERE, WHEN AND HOW YOU WANT IT

HOME

HALO 4

GAME | OFFICIAL EGUIDES | COMMUNITY | GAME NEWS | C

You are here: Games > The Sims 3 Pets > Official Guides > HALO 4 eGuide

INTRODUCTION   ESSENTIALS   WALKTHROUGH   MAPS   INTERACTIVE

VOUCHER CODE

mghs-bpx7-dgsm-n87s

4422

 Follow us on Twitter

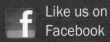 Like us on Facebook

> MAJOR FIREFIGHT: ALL THINGS LOST AND FOUND

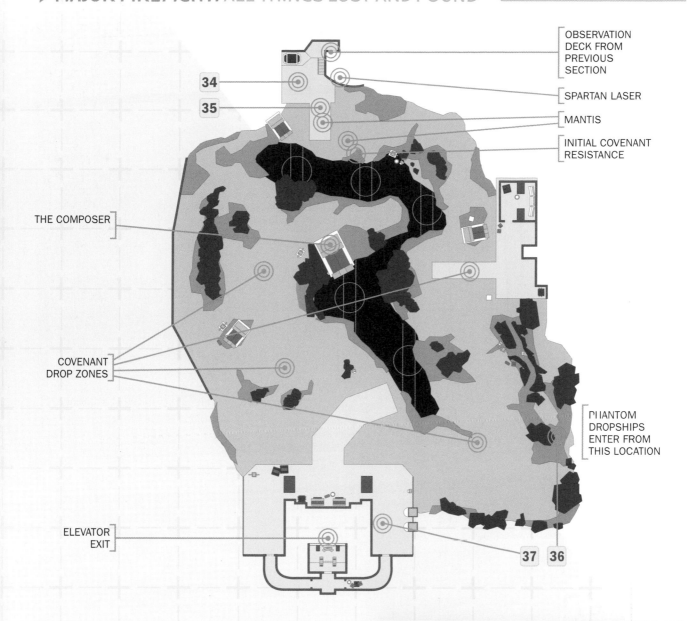

OBSERVATION DECK FROM PREVIOUS SECTION

34

35

SPARTAN LASER

MANTIS

INITIAL COVENANT RESISTANCE

THE COMPOSER

COVENANT DROP ZONES

PHANTOM DROPSHIPS ENTER FROM THIS LOCATION

ELEVATOR EXIT

37 **36**

INTRODUCTION

BASIC TRAINING

INTEL

CAMPAIGN

INFINITY

APPENDIX

34 The Covenant have finally broken the defenders of the Composer and are now celebrating finding the device for the Didact. Unfortunately for them, there are a number of unoccupied Mantis mechs in the area. They brought an army to Ivanoff Station to take the Composer. Now's the time to show them they needed something bigger than an army.

> RECOMMENDED LOADOUT

Mantis CRUSH puny Covenant. It's true that you can also get your hands on a Spartan Laser to try to fight the overwhelming rush of Covenant vehicles and infantry on foot, along with any other weapons you can scrounge up, but the Mantis is really the best way to dispense indiscriminate justice.

In the observation room where you discover that the Covenant have secured the Composer, you can find a Spartan Laser weapon. Take it as backup, in the event you are somehow stuck on foot. Having portable vehicle-stopping power is never a bad idea.

SPARTAN LASER

A heavy anti-vehicle laser, the Spartan Laser is as powerful as any traditional anti-armor weapon, but has the benefit of traveling to its target at a significantly higher speed than any projectile weapon. The weaknesses of this weapon system are the limited uses per battery charge, and that it must be charged up prior to each firing. The long seconds leading up to discharge require that the user keep the target lit by a laser scope to ensure target damage or destruction.

35 The real star of the show, however, is the Mantis. Once you climb into this machine, the Covenant celebration is little more than target practice. They aren't entirely helpless, however, and once they recover from your initial strike, the flood of reinforcements begins. Expect Grunts to be packing Fuel Rod Cannons, which are devastating to your shields, and Jackals with Beam Rifles are also incredibly dangerous if ignored. Constantly scan your surroundings for targets and be on the lookout for the telltale green glow of a charged Plasma Pistol. A Mantis takes the longest of any vehicle to recover from the EMP effects of a charged shot, and that time you spend standing stock-still is a death sentence.

36 Pay attention to this massive gap in the perimeter walls here. This is where all of the Covenant Phantoms bearing reinforcements will push into the area, and things can get rather crazy if you don't make an effort to stem the flow of dropships. You will not be able to destroy them all, but you can at least track their movements and find yourself some cover when they inevitably turn their guns against you.

» KEY COMBAT TIP

It's not as satisfying as killing them outright, but taking out the guns on the Phantoms as they swoop in is a good way to defang the dropships without spending the time and effort on destroying them. In this way, you can shift between multiple targets faster.

Wraiths are also dropped into the battlefield by Phantoms. Their plasma mortars can put a Mantis into a critical state with a single direct  hit. Ghosts are also fielded, and their Plasma Cannons drain your shields quickly if given a chance to focus on you.

When Cortana calls out "Banshees!" you hopefully have cleared out the majority of any ground vehicles in the area and can focus on these fliers. A wave of six begins to bear down on you from the perimeter gap. Like the Ghosts, their Plasma Cannons drain your shields rapidly, but the real danger is getting smacked down by their Fuel Rod Cannons. Stay mobile, and try to catch them with homing missiles as they fly into the arena.

After the initial wave of Banshees is shot down, things get desperate. The Covenant throw another swarm of Phantoms, too many for you to even hope to shoot down, along with another wave of Banshees. Your goal now is simple: to survive until you're informed you need to rendezvous with Dr. Tillson and Cortana places a new waypoint on the HUD. Clean out any stragglers, then make your way over to the waypoint 37 . Remaining Covenant fliers bug out, which makes this easier.

Legendary Strategy

The Mantis is still quite powerful on Legendary, but it is also significantly more fragile. Getting into close range with the Phantoms, much less any vehicle, is not a good idea, but there are so many to deal with that it is practically inevitable. Use the Composer as a shield of sorts to block incoming fire. It's more important than ever to stay mobile at all times.

Missiles are your best friend here. The Ghosts and Wraiths have almost no chance to present a credible threat if you are constantly engaging them at the extreme range of your missiles. Banshees are tougher to deal with due to their speed and propensity to come in at angles that the Mantis cannot defend. Use the hilly terrain around the Composer to give you better sight lines and angles.

The final rush is just plain hard, and there's no way around that. You can mitigate the difficulty somewhat by standing as far back from the perimeter gap as you can, which gives you the most time to lay down fire at the enemy before they can even fight back.

> LOSING YOUR COMPOSER

The marked waypoint leads you to an elevator, presumably where Dr. Tillson will have the nukes ready and the rest of her staff prepared to evacuate. Get the elevator moving. Unfortunately, the Didact has other plans.

Ivanoff Station is all but lost, but the Master Chief and Cortana are still alive, and they still have a chance at stopping the Didact. Cortana prepares a Broadsword fighter in one of the hangar bays. The margin for error is slim, as it has always been, but the Spartan's luck hasn't faltered entirely just yet. He needs only one last shot.

CAMPAIGN

MISSION 8: MIDNIGHT

"I've got to do something you're not going to like."

The Didact's ship is en route to Earth. Having survived the events at Ivanoff Station, the Master Chief takes control of a Broadsword fighter and pursues the Forerunner vessel in a desperate bid to destroy it from within. The fighter is armed with a Havok nuclear weapon, and the Spartan knows that the best chance to destroy the enemy ship is to get as deep inside as possible before triggering the device. He'll need a little help from his friends and the badly ailing Cortana to stand any chance.

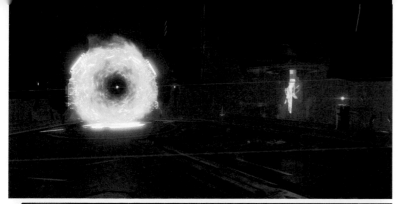

⌃ MISSION BRIEFING

This is your last chance to put an end to the Didact's plans. You know what he is capable of now that he has the Composer. You must fly your way to the core of the Forerunner vessel, evading anti-aircraft defenses as best you can, all while ensuring that you stay within its shielding to avoid being exposed to slipspace. The Didact's destination becomes obvious very quickly, as the ship enters real space in front of Earth. You'll be unable to get the Broadsword into the core of the Forerunner ship, but the UNSC fleet will provide assistance. Your ultimate goal is to get the Havok warhead as deep into the Forerunner vessel as possible, and you will have to fight your way through waves of Knights, Watchers, and Crawlers.

ENEMIES ENCOUNTERED:

Crawlers   Knights   Watchers

WEAPONS ACQUIRED //////////////////

Assault Rifle
SAW
DMR
Battle Rifle
Covenant Carbine
Boltshot
Suppressor
LightRifle
Binary Rifle
Scattershot
Incineration Cannon
Gravity Hammer

VEHICLE ENCOUNTER //////////////////

BROADSWORD

One of the best fighters in the human arsenal, the Broadsword was a direct response to the  speed and maneuverability found in so many Covenant strike craft. Armed with linked twin Autocannons and Missile Pods, this particular Broadsword is a match for nearly any Covenant equivalent in existence. Broadswords are also capable of carrying Havok-grade payloads for anti-capital ship duty.

INTRODUCTION

BASIC TRAINING

INTEL

CAMPAIGN

INFINITY

APPENDIX

Take some time to properly acclimate to the controls of the Broadsword, and get a feel for how sharp it can turn with and without rolling to one side or the other. You're about to get a literal crash course on how to handle a proper trench run. Defensive turrets are positioned throughout the ship. Unless you're flying straight at the incoming fire, you generally can just fly past it all without violent maneuvering using the fighter's afterburners.

Try not to get distracted by the radio chatter from the UNSC fleet. When the Forerunner vessel emerges over Earth, that's not your cue to hold down the boosters on the Broadsword. You're not going to get there faster if you're smashed against the moving walls of the ship.

Your gravest threat will come in the way of energy barriers and the moving parts of the Didact's ship. A head-on collision is almost certainly fatal. Occasionally, you'll come across doors that look as though they're about to block the entire corridor, but they almost always have some sort of gap to fly through. As a general rule, using the afterburner in restricted areas is not the best call. Concentrate on maneuvering as opposed to raw speed, unless you know you can get away with it.

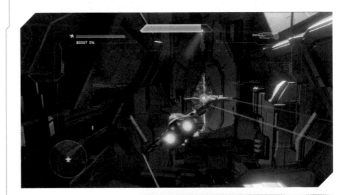

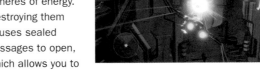

Your primary targets as you pass through the trench are these spheres of energy. Destroying them causes sealed passages to open, which allows you to continue deeper into the ship.

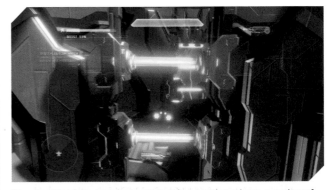

The danger picks up when you reach a section where a series of energy beams fill the trench as it narrows. It's easy to be driven farther down toward the hull when trying to avoid the beams, but do your best to maintain some height to set up your entry into the next section.

Beyond the beam barriers, turrets line the walls of another short trench section that leads to narrow forks in the flight path. These passages are filled with obstacles that can end your trip, so decelerate and concentrate on your maneuvering here.

This fork is followed by another split in the trench, but the choices now are to take an upper or lower path. These sections start off narrow, but the upper route eventually opens up significantly. You're nearly out of the trench at this point, one last spiralling corridor remains, and then you arrive at your target.

> FROM THE CRADLE ...

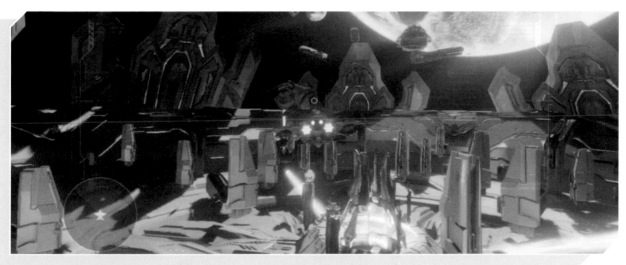

You burst free from the trench to discover a massive space battle taking place directly over the swiftly sealing Cradle that leads to the deeper portions of the Forerunner vessel. Forerunner particle cannons, similar to those found on Requiem, line the cradle and are busy turning UNSC vessels into short-lived flashes of flame. The *Infinity*, having returned to Earth in advance of the Master Chief, is now on station to provide some assistance, but you have to get those particle cannons offline or she'll never have the chance to blast open a path for the Spartan to take.

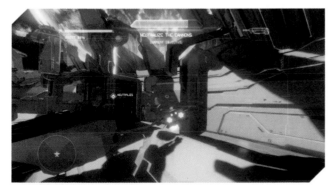

The particle cannons are powered by energy sources that look exactly like the ones you thrashed throughout the trench run, but to gain access to them, you must destroy the central power source. It's not an easy shot to make and it's guarded by multiple turrets. Use missiles to take it out, then move on.

There are four particle cannons to neutralize. You'll have to approach them from their opened sides to get clean shots. Anti-aircraft guns protect both entrances to each energy source, so you'll have to be careful on your approach to and exit from each target. The Autocannon takes longer to kill each energy source, so we recommend that you switch to missiles for quicker target destruction.

INTRODUCTION

BASIC TRAINING

INTEL

CAMPAIGN

INFINITY

APPENDIX

Once all four Particle Cannons are disabled, the *Infinity* blasts open a hole in the Forerunner vessel's armor during the ensuing cinematic, and the Master Chief flies into the gap just as the ship begins resealing itself, almost as though it were alive. The Chief and Cortana narrowly make it into the vessel, just prior to it sealing up. Now they're in the belly of the beast.

> ... TO THE GRAVE

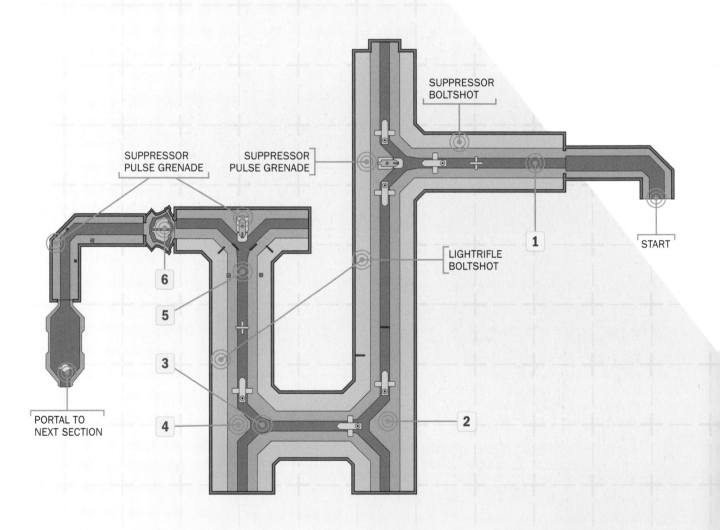

SUPPRESSOR
BOLTSHOT

SUPPRESSOR
PULSE GRENADE

SUPPRESSOR
PULSE GRENADE

LIGHTRIFLE
BOLTSHOT

1

START

6

5

3

4

2

PORTAL TO
NEXT SECTION

DOMAIN TERMINAL

4 The seventh and final Domain Terminal is found at the center of the T-junction room. It blends in somewhat with the rest of the odd geometry in the area and can be easy to miss.

HALO 4

INTRODUCTION

BASIC TRAINING

INTEL

CAMPAIGN

INFINITY

APPENDIX

The Broadsword is no longer a option for the Havok warhead, so the Master Chief takes it upon himself to deliver it directly to the Didact.

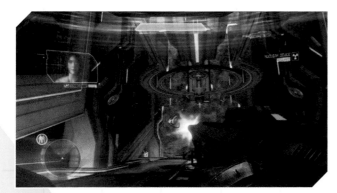

1 You start this portion of the mission with a Battle Rifle and a SAW, excellent weapons for the time being, and a Hologram armor ability. You're nowhere near any UNSC weapons caches at this point, so once your guns run dry, you'll have to replace them with Forerunner weapons. Your first encounter in the starting corridor is a group of four Watchers. They try to build Forerunner anti-infantry turrets, but the process of doing so makes them sitting ducks for your Battle Rifle. Try to conserve the SAW for the moment. You can pick up a LightRifle from a weapons rack if you want to lose the Battle Rifle early.

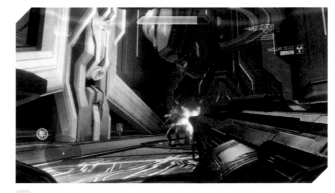

2 A lone Knight Battlewagon controls this next corridor section. As soon as it detects you, it tries to deploy a Watcher. You might be able to stop it with Frag or Pulse Grenades. Failing that, down the Watcher, then hose down the Knight with the SAW. Keep a safe enough distance to avoid getting killed by its Scattershot. Another Knight enters the room from a newly unlocked doorway.

⟩⟩ KEY COMBAT TIP

The Scattershot makes an excellent replacement to the SAW for players who are interested in getting up close and personal with the Knights. Others may prefer a Suppressor to fill roughly the same role of the SAW.

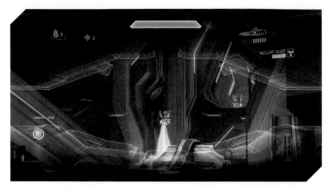

3 Two more Watchers occupy this T-intersection. They can summon Crawlers, so kill them fast to prevent this.

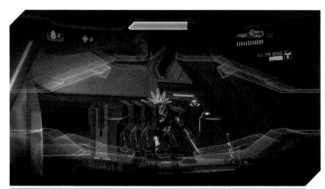

5 Another Knight Battlewagon, along with two standard Knights, are the protectors of this room. This can be a rough skirmish if you lose track of any of the Knights. Focus on taking down the Knight Battlewagon first. It tends to stick closest to the door, while its two cohorts sit farther back in the room, tossing Pulse Grenades and plinking away with LightRifles. If you're lucky, you can get them to inadvertently help you kill off the Battlewagon. After it is out of the picture, this engagement is a simple matter of shooting it out with the remaining Knights, easily accomplished with a LightRifle. If you can convince them to come to you, a Scattershot can utterly ruin them. The Hologram is also quite useful here, allowing you to set up kill shots with a Scattershot, or assassinations while the enemy is distracted.

» KEY COMBAT TIP

If you're playing on Legendary, we highly recommend that you keep the Hologram handy for the entire mission. You'll really need the decoy ability it provides.

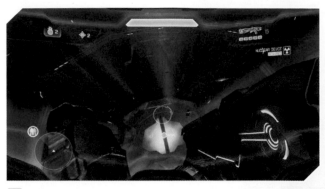

6 After dealing with the enemy, head through the door to the left from where you enter the Knight ambush to find a long drop awaiting you. An antigravity lift slows you down before you hit the ground far below.

On the lower level, the corridor contains a weapons cache with more LightRifle ammo, if you're hurting for some. The door leading out of this corridor takes you to a small platform that overlooks another larger chamber with seemingly nowhere else to go. The only other visible platforms have no apparent way to reach them. Cortana asks to be put inside a nearby console to try to find a way to teleport you closer to your goal. The first portal activates after Cortana struggles with the system for control.

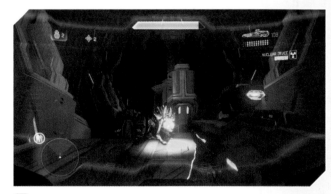

7 On the other side of the portal, you emerge inside a much smaller chamber with a small pack of Crawlers. Once they are eliminated, proceed through the new portal.

> MAJOR FIREFIGHT: RAMPS AND KNIGHTS

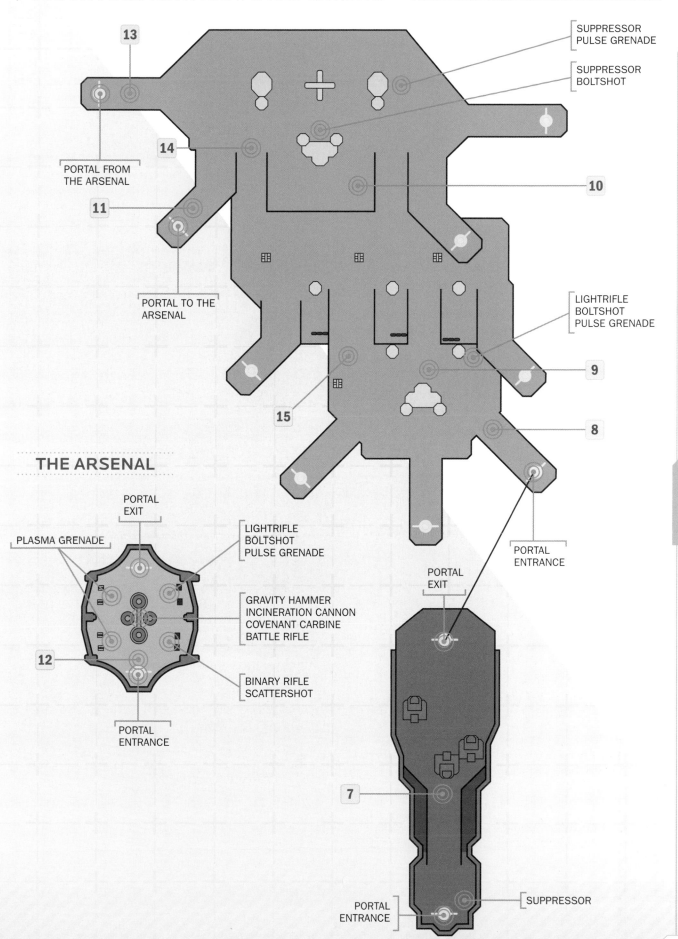

13

SUPPRESSOR
PULSE GRENADE

SUPPRESSOR
BOLTSHOT

14

PORTAL FROM
THE ARSENAL

11

10

PORTAL TO THE
ARSENAL

LIGHTRIFLE
BOLTSHOT
PULSE GRENADE

9

15

8

THE ARSENAL

PORTAL
EXIT

PLASMA GRENADE

LIGHTRIFLE
BOLTSHOT
PULSE GRENADE

GRAVITY HAMMER
INCINERATION CANNON
COVENANT CARBINE
BATTLE RIFLE

12

BINARY RIFLE
SCATTERSHOT

PORTAL
ENTRANCE

PORTAL
ENTRANCE

PORTAL
EXIT

7

SUPPRESSOR

PORTAL
ENTRANCE

INTRODUCTION

BASIC TRAINING

INTEL

CAMPAIGN

INFINITY

APPENDIX

219

8 The portal from the smaller chamber takes you to the larger platform you saw in the distance when you first inserted Cortana into the system—and right into the waiting arms of a Knight-led ambush. Every variety of Knight is represented, including a dreaded Knight Lancer armed with a Binary Rifle. The enemy controls the ramps leading up to each successive level of this section, so they have a positional advantage on top of their numbers. Your portal destination will require you to defeat every last Promethean in the area before it opens.

> ❯ RECOMMENDED LOADOUT

The LightRifle gives you the best all around success against most of the Knights, but the Knight Lancer and its Binary Rifle is still a major problem. You need to distract it with a Hologram, if that is an option. Or, you may have recovered a Autosentry ability from earlier battles, which can provide a temporary decoy. A Hardlight Shield can also help deflect shots for a short time. A Scattershot also makes a convincing argument for close encounters, so long as it's not up against a Battlewagon with one of its own.

From where you begin this firefight, two Knights man the ramps leading up to the next level, paired up with Watchers. The Knight farthest from you is likely a Battlewagon, so avoid running headlong into it. If you rush the ramp closest to you **9**, you might be able to catch the basic Knight as it summons its Watcher. If you're carrying a Scattershot, one double tap is all you'll need for it. If the second Knight is a Battlewagon, drive away its Watcher, then empty a scoped LightRifle magazine into its face. With the two Knights dead, restock the LightRifle at any of the nearby caches.

10 This is where things get scary. A Knight Commander (with Incineration Cannon) and a Knight Lancer (with Binary Rifle) control the upper level, with Watcher support. The Commander tends to stick near the portal as its main defender, while the Knight Lancer camps close to the ramps. It is entirely possible to bull-rush the Knight Lancer if you're armed with a Scattershot, but it helps to have a Hologram handy to distract it. Without a Hologram, you're likely to get sniped before you even get close to it. Pick up the Binary Rifle to take out the Knight Commander.

Alternate Approach

Another trick that can help is simply to plug away with a LightRifle, and make sure you reload just as the Knight Lancer's shields begin to flare blue. When the shields finally break, the Knight Lancer will stagger. Having a fuller magazine in your weapon can help finish it off before it recovers. Just keep an eye on its skull, if the red halo glows bright, it's about to fire and you had better not be visible.

The Commander presents a unique problem: One Incineration Cannon shot is enough to end your life. Fortunately, you've got a lot of cover on the upper level to duck behind and thereby evade direct hit. The Commander isn't dumb, and will try to aim shots near your feet, so keep moving once a shot is in the air, preferably to the next safe spot. It is possible to get close enough to the Commander that it will not use the Incineration Cannon, but this also puts you within melee range. When the Commander dies, the portal to the next section opens **11**.

Legendary Strategy

Well, the good news is that you can still probably kill the first two Knights with relative ease. The real problem is the Knight Lancer. With the enhanced perception of all enemies on Legendary, coupled with the Knight Lancer's Promethean Vision that can spot you through terrain, there's a possibility you could be taking shots from its Binary Rifle throughout the opening scuffle once it finds you. Stick to the lower level when destroying the first two Knights, then make certain you know if the Knight Lancer is pointed toward you before you decide to push up to the second level. Repeatedly use the Hologram armor ability if you still have it to turn the Knight Lancer's attention away from you.

The Commander is a more serious threat because of how fast Incineration Cannon shots travel on Legendary. They are difficult to evade. Stick to ranged combat when dealing with the Commander.

The Arsenal

12 The portal takes you to a small room filled with weapons from the UNSC, Covenant, and Forerunner arsenals, including a rare melee weapon that makes its first and only appearance in *Halo 4*'s campaign.. Once you feel properly stocked, take the new portal that activates.

WEAPON ACQUISITION

GRAVITY HAMMER

A melee weapon that symbolized the authority of its Brute wielder, Gravity Hammers became a more common sight on the Human-Covenant battlefield. In the wake of the original Halo incident, Brutes gained prominence in the Covenant after their rivals, the Elites, were disgraced. The heavy instrument has its crushing power enhanced by a gravity drive that fires off an intense shockwave on impact.

» KEY COMBAT TIP

As awesome as the Gravity Hammer is, resist the urge to go hammer on the Forerunners and leave it behind for now. Instead, take an Incineration Cannon or Binary Rifle and all of the ammo you can carry for them, and supplement your choice with a LightRifle.

In Reverse, Knights, and Ramps

13 The portal places you behind a Knight that is completely oblivious to your presence. Assassinate it.

14 Crawlers begin to rush up the ramps to the upper level, while two Knights hold position on the middle level. Using a LightRifle, execute the Crawlers with headshots until they retreat back toward the Knights. Before taking them on, destroy any nearby Watchers. Try to conserve your Incineration Cannon shots; the LightRifle should suffice for this first pair.

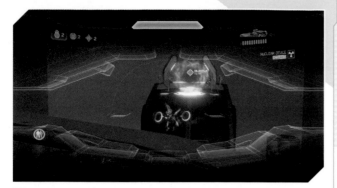

Legendary Strategy

While this isn't a particularly section if you're properly equipped, some things are worth mentioning. Watchers are much more aggressive at placing Hardlight Shields in front of their allies. These barriers can deflect even the Incineration Cannon or Binary Rifle. Save yourself an embarrassing restart and knock out the Watchers first so you can incinerate things in relative safety.

15 The lower level is patrolled by a standard Knight and a Knight Commander, accompanied by more Crawlers and Watchers. Snipe the Watchers, then annihilate the Knights with your Incineration Cannon. Recover any ammo for this weapon from the remains of the Commander, then move through the portal.

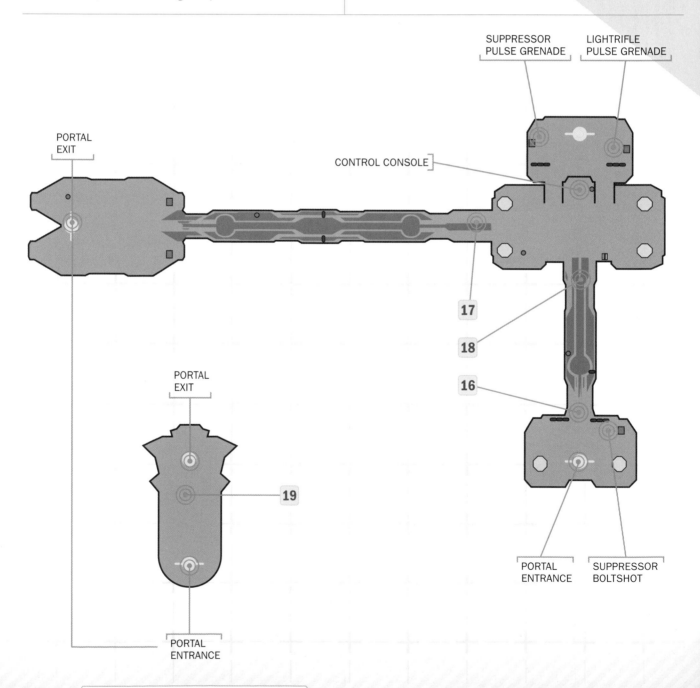

PORTAL EXIT

PORTAL EXIT

SUPPRESSOR PULSE GRENADE

LIGHTRIFLE PULSE GRENADE

CONTROL CONSOLE

17

18

16

19

PORTAL ENTRANCE

PORTAL ENTRANCE

SUPPRESSOR BOLTSHOT

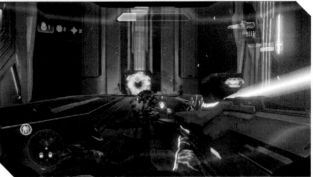

16 The portal sends you to a new chamber. Explosive energy cores line the walkway that leads to a pillar in the distance with Crawlers climbing around it. As you approach, a Knight Lancer teleports in front of the pillar. Greet it with an Incineration Cannon shot, then finish off any surviving Prometheans. A small control console teleports in front of the pillar; it contains Cortana, who is still trying to pinpoint the Composer's new location. Take note of the long bridge that stretches into the distance to the left of the control console.

Eventually, Cortana succeeds in her task, and needs you to pull her free from the console. You have to fight your way down the long bridge through an army of Crawlers to reach the portal that will take you ever closer to the Composer.

This marks the start of a defensive battle against waves of Crawlers. The LightRifle is more than a match for them, and there's a weapons cache near the central pillar containing additional ammo for the weapon. The Crawlers come in waves, first from the long bridge **17** , then from the pillars that flank the path you arrived from **18** . As you continue to fight off the Crawlers, Cortana activates Forerunner anti-infantry turrets to help with the defense. So long as you are consistent with your headshots, holding your ground here isn't particularly difficult.

INTRODUCTION

BASIC TRAINING

INTEL

CAMPAIGN

INFINITY

APPENDIX

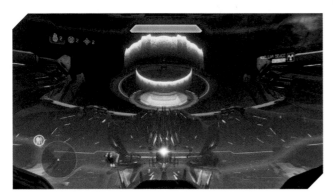

19 The portal takes you to an antigravity lift that pushes you back toward another platform somewhere deep inside the ship's Cradle. Run toward the massive chasm in front of you to be launched across the gap toward the Composer. The roof to the Cradle suddenly opens, revealing that the Composer is now aimed directly at the Earth, and the device gives off an ominous glow as you draw close. Time is running out.

20 At the next computer terminal, Cortana does something "you're not going to like" in order to try lowering the shielding around the Didact and the Composer to make them vulnerable to the nuke. With that done, two objective markers appear on the HUD. Cortana needs to access the Forerunner systems from two more consoles located on floating islands flanking the Composer. They can be reached by taking the indicated antigravity lifts that launch you across the chasm. You can choose left or right. Ultimately you will be taken on a loop around the Composer. The islands containing the consoles are nearly identical in design. For the sake of simplifying things, the guide assumes you choose the left island first.

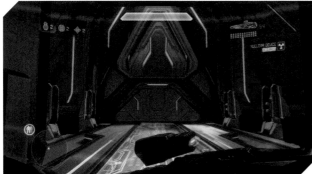

Arriving at the center of the Cradle, you find another large weapons cache. Every type of Forerunner weapon, save for the Incineration Cannon, is represented here. If you're still packing some Incineration Cannon ammo, keep it handy. If not, consider taking a LightRifle and Binary Rifle loadout for the battles to come.

> MAJOR FIREFIGHT: ISLAND HOPPING

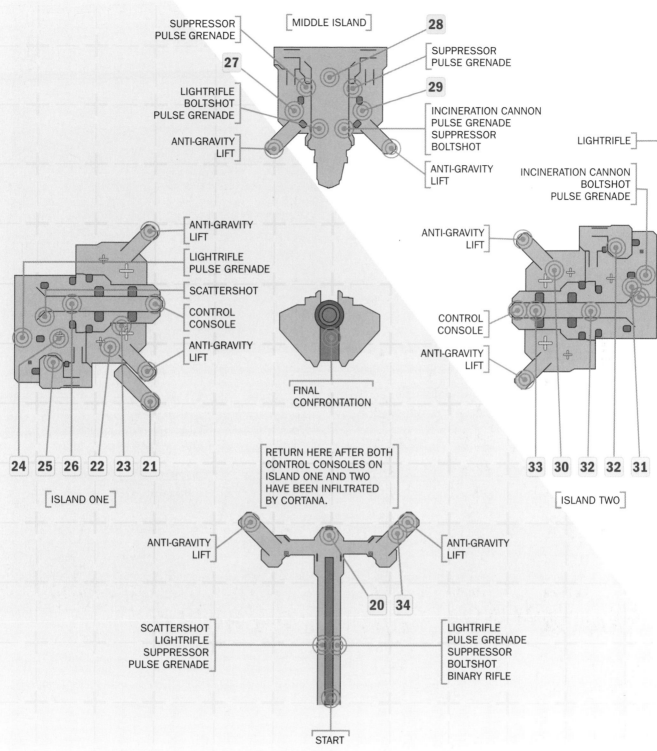

[MIDDLE ISLAND]

SUPPRESSOR
PULSE GRENADE

28

27

SUPPRESSOR
PULSE GRENADE

29

LIGHTRIFLE
BOLTSHOT
PULSE GRENADE

INCINERATION CANNON
PULSE GRENADE
SUPPRESSOR
BOLTSHOT

ANTI-GRAVITY
LIFT

ANTI-GRAVITY
LIFT

LIGHTRIFLE

INCINERATION CANNON
BOLTSHOT
PULSE GRENADE

ANTI-GRAVITY
LIFT

LIGHTRIFLE
PULSE GRENADE

SCATTERSHOT

CONTROL
CONSOLE

ANTI-GRAVITY
LIFT

ANTI-GRAVITY
LIFT

CONTROL
CONSOLE

ANTI-GRAVITY
LIFT

FINAL
CONFRONTATION

24 25 26 22 23 21

[ISLAND ONE]

RETURN HERE AFTER BOTH
CONTROL CONSOLES ON
ISLAND ONE AND TWO
HAVE BEEN INFILTRATED
BY CORTANA.

33 30 32 32 31

[ISLAND TWO]

ANTI-GRAVITY
LIFT

ANTI-GRAVITY
LIFT

20 34

SCATTERSHOT
LIGHTRIFLE
SUPPRESSOR
PULSE GRENADE

LIGHTRIFLE
PULSE GRENADE
SUPPRESSOR
BOLTSHOT
BINARY RIFLE

[START]

21 Taking the left antigravity pad to the first island, you are immediately confronted by Knights, Crawlers, and Watchers. You must fight your way up to the island's top level to get Cortana access to the control systems. It's nothing you haven't seen before, but that doesn't make it any less dangerous. After injecting Cortana into the first console, you travel to a smaller island between you and the second large island, which is where you'll have to fight to the top level to make use of the second control console.

> RECOMMENDED LOADOUT

The LightRifle once again is your staple weapon for cleanup duty against Crawlers and Watchers. If you've managed to preserve some Incineration Cannon ammo, you can make early parts of this battle much easier. The Binary Rifle is a good secondary weapon as well: Two shots are a guaranteed Knight kill if the second shot hits the head. Clever use of the Hologram can give you plenty of point-blank Scattershot opportunities also.

Island One

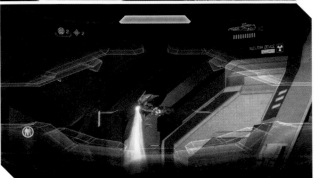

As soon as you arrive on the island **22**, the Prometheans teleport in to start the brawl. A Knight appears almost directly in front of where you land. Another Knight and some Crawlers appear under the central arch next to the ramp leading up to the second level **23**, while more Prometheans appear on a ledge overlooking the landing site. Put down the first Knight, then immediately take cover against the wall behind it to get out of the line of sight of the hostiles on the second level. The Crawlers on the lower level are most likely intervening at this point. Once they are dealt with, finish off the second Knight and climb up the ramp.

More Crawlers infest the ramp leading up to the middle level.

24 A Knight and Knight Battlewagon control the middle level. Scattershots can be found in a side room, but this fight is won most easily at range due to the sheer lethality of the Battlewagon at close-range. With the Knights out of the way, climb the next ramp to reach a switch **25** that will activate a light bridge to the final section where the control console is located.

As soon as the light bridge is activated, Knights teleport to the platform it connects to. One of them tries to cross the bridge to engage you up close. A Scattershot makes a good answer to this sort of boldness. The other Knight hangs back on the other side of the bridge, making a good target for your LightRifle.

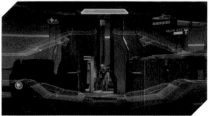

In addition to the first two Knights, three others appear on the central platform **26**, using the pillars as cover and concealment. This can be one of the hardest fights in the whole game—one worthy of all the Incineration Cannon ammo you might have left. As you whittle down this group, a Knight Battlewagon teleports in at the end of the platform, where the control console is. After you've cleared the area, let Cortana work her magic, and follow the HUD to reach another antigravity lift to the next section.

Legendary Strategy

On Legendary, you should be coming into this fight with as much ammo for an Incineration Cannon as possible, specifically for the final encounter near the control console. The lower and middle levels are manageable with just a LightRifle, but things take a turn for the crazy as soon as you reach the light bridge and activate it. With so many Knights in such close proximity, the amount of firepower headed your way can melt you in seconds. Make each shot with the Incineration Cannon count and go for direct hits to guarantee kills. But should the Knights manage to survive, switch quickly to the LightRifle to finish them off.

The Isle in Between

27 This smaller island floats is your stop between the two large islands. You're immediately accosted by another Knight and a Crawler pack as you come in for a landing.

28 More Crawlers and a Watcher cover the top level, along with a Forerunner anti-infantry turret. The weapons racks guarded by the turret hold another Incineration Cannon, so restock if necessary!

29 The antigravity lift to Island Two is guarded by another Knight and Crawler pack.

INTRODUCTION

BASIC TRAINING

INTEL

CAMPAIGN

INFINITY

APPENDIX

Island Two

30 A mirror image of the first island, your primary threats on the first two levels are the Crawler packs, all of which are supported by Watchers.

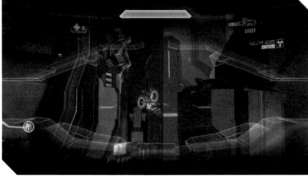

The middle level does throw a bit of a curve ball at you in the form of Crawler Snipes mixed in among other Crawlers. Check the walls carefully to ensure that you don't get blindsided by their Binary Rifle shots.

31 As with the first island, a similar side armory is on the middle level, where you can locate more Incineration Cannon ammo.

» KEY COMBAT TIP

Something to note: There is a dearth of LightRifle ammo to scrounge up on this island. You may be forced to use a Boltshot or Suppressor at some point. We actually highly recommend the Boltshot if it becomes necessary to switch to a new weapon, as it is still capable of headshots and therefore is a good option against the Crawlers. Its secondary function can bring down a Watcher with one good hit, but you'll have to get close to ensure that the hit lands.

32 The fight to the switch on the upper level starts off the same: by activating a light bridge to reach the platform. You're attacked by a large group of Crawlers with Watchers on support. You can slaughter them en masse with an Incineration Cannon, but save at least two shots for the final opponent near the control console.

33 A Knight Commander with its own Incineration Cannon appears as you cut down the Crawler horde. Introduce it to your own brand of incineration, then mop up any surviving resistance. Do not miss out on collecting the Incineration Cannon dropped by the Commander! Then insert Cortana into the control console.

Legendary Strategy

While it is not nearly as rough as the first big island, having so many Crawlers on the field means being out in the open is a bad idea. Recklessness is suicide. Concentrate on solid headshots with a LightRifle, and if an ammo shortage demands it, a Boltshot. The final battle near the control console can be surprisingly frustrating if you lack patience, so hang back and practice your accuracy. Save yourself some trouble by putting an Incineration Cannon round into the Knight Commander the moment you see it teleporting onto the upper platform. Then you're all but home free.

> "IT'S ALL RIGHT. BUT YOU MUST HURRY ..."

INTRODUCTION

BASIC TRAINING

INTEL

CAMPAIGN

INFINITY

APPENDIX

34 After the Cortana successfully shuts down the shields, you are prompted to hurry back to the indicated antigravity lift to return to the island where all of this hopping started. Three more Knight Commanders stand between you and the final indicated lift. Fortunately, you probably still have an Incineration Cannon to fall back upon. Use everything you can to get past this last line of defense. You've come too far to fail now!

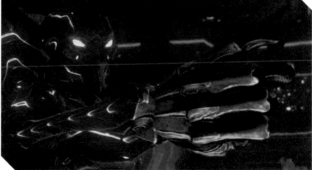

Nothing more stands between you, the Didact, and destroying the Composer.

We'll be as vague as possible to avoid spoiling nature of the last duel: Although the enemy may seem to overpower you, follow the prompts on screen to put an end to the Forerunner's plans for "containment," and witness the dramatic ending to *Halo 4*. You've certainly earned it.

Congratulations for having made it all the way—nothing less could be expected of a Spartan! Now, do it all over again on Legendary with all the Skulls activated.

INFINITY

MULTIPLAYER

Ready for war? Then learn about the many menu decisions here.

> **Note**
>
> If you're a longtime *Halo* aficionado, you'll notice the lack of "Matchmaking" or "Custom Game" options in the game's Main menu. But fear not—you'll still find these options under the Infinity menu!

UNSC *Infinity*

The newest and most powerful vessel in the UNSC fleet, the *Infinity* was originally intended to be fielded against the Covenant. After the war came to its official conclusion, the *Infinity* was re-commissioned for more peaceful space exploration, but it retained much of its military potential, clearly necessary in the wake of the vessel's forced landing on the Forerunner shield world of Requiem. In addition to a sizeable compliment of UNSC Marines, the *Infinity* is also home to a large contingent of Spartans, the newest branch in the UNSC military structure.

This encompasses all of *Halo 4*'s Infinity game modes, including War Games, Spartan Ops, and Forge.

War Games

War Games allows Spartan-IV's to improve their skills in a player-versus-player (PvP) combat experience. Recreating a variety of compellingly life-like locations which generate intense, frenetic combat scenarios, War Games participants are able to hone their skills for any environment they may potentially face in their military service. Special tactics, teamwork, leadership ability, and survival skills are tested in a variety of game types across a full spectrum of simulated environments, and the score-based competitive nature of the games has inspired friendly and not-so-friendly rivalries among the *Infinity*'s Spartan population.

Group up or go it alone in Matchmaking as you take on other players from around the globe in a multitude of game types. Almost all of your favorites have returned for *Halo 4*, including Slayer, Capture The Flag, Oddball, and more, but there's also quite a few new game types to try out and hone your talents on. We explore these game types later into this chapter during the full walkthrough of War Games on page 280.

Spartan Ops Intro

The aftermath of the *Infinity*'s landing on Requiem left thousands of UNSC and Covenant casualties in its wake. Further complicating matters, the Covenant troops that were encountered on Requiem initially made hostile contact with a new threat in the form of the Prometheans, constructs of Forerunner origin that served as the military might the ancients brought to bear against the Flood. The Covenant and the Prometheans now stand united between the UNSC and the secrets of the shield world. The *Infinity* has returned to Requiem replenished with Marines, Spartans, and scientists, all seeking to secure the Forerunner world and its secrets.

Season One of Spartan Ops will contain ten episodes total, and will be free for download on Xbox LIVE. This is an extra twelve hours of new combat scenarios you can play with your buddies!

Playing as a member of Fireteam Crimson, players are able to take their customized Spartan-IV into a series of dangerous missions that follow a unique storyline taking place after the events of the Campaign. In the following five weeks after *Halo 4* releases, 343 Industries will release a new episode each week, containing five new missions to challenge. Each mission in an episode is designed to last close to fifteen minutes. The remainder of Season 1 will arrive early in 2013 after a short hiatus, releasing the remaining episodes in Season One.

As with War Games, playing Spartan Ops online requires an Xbox LIVE Gold membership.

Forge

For those favoring creating over carnage, Forge is back with numerous improvements. The already-robust object editor has been further optimized, including the addition of features like magnets to help line up multiple map elements, and the ability to create special zones that change the gravity of specific areas in a map. Forge has seen an array of visual improvements, and now includes three Forge specific maps to work within. With the combined creative ability of Halo's massive community of fans and the ability to download and share creations, you'll never run out of new maps to enjoy. We've got a breakdown of the new features in Forge on page 314.

Theater

Are you worried that your greatest War Games moments will go undocumented? Well, 343 Industries have made sure that the next time you hear the mantra "Pics, or it didn't happen," you'll be prepared with that and more. Theater comes fully equipped with several enticing features that will please even the most hardcore video-capture fiends. Read more about it on page 313.

> SPARTAN HUB

Grow in stature and rank up at the Spartan Hub.

Create your own Spartan-IV on the UNSC *Infinity* and build your identity, reputation, and customization options through combat in either War Games or Spartan Ops. Add to your prowess by accomplishing Challenges, unlocking Specializations, and customizing your controls and other settings. Additional information about customizing your Spartan and rank progression can be found on Halo Waypoint.

Career

Challenges: Looking to level up your Spartan even quicker? Glance through the "Challenges" section and work on completing these as soon as possible The added XP helps you quickly rank up, which in turn means more Spartan Points and a larger arsenal. There are four categories in which you can accomplish Challenges: Campaign, War Games, Spartan Ops, and Waypoint.

Challenges are a mix of simple and difficult objectives to accomplish, and they can change daily, weekly, and monthly. Challenges are not limited to War Games Player Versus Player. You can earn additional XP for completing Challenges in the Campaign and Spartan Ops modes. If you're interested in seeing how far along you are in a given Challenge, go to the Career screen, and check Challenges within the Start menu.

In addition to the regularly scheduled shifting of Challenges, Halo Waypoint can offer additional Challenges outside of these regular changes. Check in often to see what new opportunities are available!

> **Note**

Consult the Appendix (page 393) for the following:

Ranks and Unlocks: detailed breakdown of how to level up your Spartan.

Skulls: all available Skulls and how to unlock them.

Achievements: all Achievements and how to complete each of them.

Commendations: detailed breakdown of how to obtain every Commendation.

Medals are awarded for scoring points in any number of ways. You can get medals for kills, kill streaks, or kills made in specific ways. Some medal types are awarded specifically for accomplishing game type specific tasks, like capturing a flag, or contesting a designated territory. Medals not only represent point values, but they also add to your ordnance meter in War Games. The greater the ordnance point value, the more the meter fills, and the sooner you will be able to call down ordnance.

KILL MEDALS

ICON	NAME	EVENT	MEDAL POINTS	ORDNANCE POINTS
	Kill	Generic Kill	10	10
	Grenade Kill	Kill an opponent with a grenade explosion	10	10
	Plasma Kill	Kill an opponent with a Plasma Grenade.	10	10
	Headshot	Kill an opponent with a headshot	10	10
	Melee	Hit and kill an opponent with a melee attack	10	10
	Beat Down	Hit and kill an opponent with a melee attack from behind	10	10
	Splatter	Hit and kill an opponent with your vehicle	10	10
	Assasination	Kill an opponent by performing an assassination	15	20
	Airsassination	Kill an opponent by performing a mid-air assassination	25	25
	Supercombine	Kill an opponent with a needle supercombination	10	10
	Sword Kill	Kill an opponent with an Energy Sword	10	10
	Hammer Kill	Kill an opponent with a Gravity Hammer	10	10
	Vehicle Kill	Kill an opponent using a vehicle weapon	10	10
	Rocket Kill	Kill an opponent with a Rocket Launcher	10	10
	Fuel Rod Cannon Kill	Kill an opponent with a Fuel Rod Cannon	10	10
	Sniper Rifle Kill	Kill an opponent with a Sniper Rifle	10	10
	Binary Rifle Kill	Kill an opponent with a Binary Rifle	10	10
	Beam Rifle Kill	Kill an opponent with a Beam Rifle	10	10
	Railgun Kill	Kill an opponent with a Railgun	10	10
	Splaser Kill	Kill an opponent with a Spartan Laser	10	10

BONUS/STYLE MEDALS

ICON	NAME	EVENT	MEDAL POINTS	ORDNANCE POINTS
	Protector	Save a teammate by killing his attacker	5	5
	Killjoy	End an opponents killing spree	5	5
	Hijack	Board a land-based vehicle by forcibly removing the opponent in it	5	5
	Revenge	Kill the opponent responsible for your last death	5	5
	Kill from the Grave	Kill an opponent after you die	5	5
	Ordnance Earned	Earn personal ordnance rewarded from the Infinity	5	5
	Close Call	Kill an opponent while your health is low and survive	5	5
	Avenger	Kill an opponent who recently killed your teammate	5	5
	Reload This	Kill an opponent who is reloading	5	5
	First Strike	Earn the first kill of the match	5	5
	Last Strike	Earn the final Kill Cam	5	5
	Headcase	Kill a sprinting opponent with a headshot	5	5
	Retribution	Assassinate the opponent responsible for your last death	10	5
	Hail Mary	Get a long-range grenade kill	10	5
	Snapshot	Kill an opponent with a sniper rifle while not zoomed in	10	5
	Vehicle Destroyed	Destroy an opponents vehicle, killing the driver	10	10
	Skyjack	Board an aircraft by forcibly removing the opponent in it	10	10
	Vengeance	Kill an opponent that stole your ordnance	15	15
	Showstopper	Stop an assassination by killing the assassinating opponent	15	15
	Busted	Kill an opponent attempting to hijack or skyjack a vehicle	15	15
	Bulltrue	Kill an opponent who is lunging with a Sword	15	15

ASSIST/SUPPORT MEDALS

ICON	NAME	EVENT	MEDAL POINTS	ORDNANCE POINTS
	Assist	Assist a player in achieving a kill	5	5
	Vehicle Destroy Assist	Assist a player in destroying a vehicle	5	5
	Bodyguard	Get a spree of 3 Savior, Protector, or Guardian Angel Medals	5	5
	Wheelman	Drive a vehicle and have a passenger kill an opponent	5	5
	Guardian Angel	Save a teammate's life from a long distance	5	5
	Road Trip	Load up a Warthog or Mongoose with teammates and splatter an enemy player	5	5
	Flyin' High	Achieve a massive jump with a passenger in the Mongoose or Warthog	5	5
	Wingman	Get a spree of any 5 assist types	5	5
	EMP Assist	EMP someone and have a teammate kill them	5	5
	Distraction	Distract an opponent who is then killed	5	5

SPREE MEDALS

ICON	NAME	EVENT	MEDAL POINTS	ORDNANCE POINTS
	Comeback Kill	Achieve a kill after dying 3 times in a row	5	5
	Double Kill	Kill 2 opponents within 4 5 seconds of one another	5	5
	Triple Kill	Kill 3 opponents within 4 5 seconds of one another	5	5
	Overkill	Kill 4 opponents within 4 5 seconds of one another	10	5
	Killtacular	Kill 5 opponents within 4 5 seconds of one another	10	5
	Killtrocity	Kill 6 opponents within 4 5 seconds of one another	10	5
	Killamanjaro	Kill 7 opponents within 4 5 seconds of one another	15	5
	Killtastrophe	Kill 8 opponents within 4 5 seconds of one another	15	5
	Killpocalypse	Kill 9 opponents within 4 5 seconds of one another	25	5
	Killionaire	Kill 10 opponents within 4 5 seconds of one another	50	5
	Killing Spree	Kill 5 opponents without dying	5	5
	Killing Frenzy	Kill 10 opponents without dying	10	5
	Running Riot	Kill 15 opponents without dying	10	5
	Rampage	Kill 20 opponents without dying	15	5
	Untouchable	Kill 25 opponents without dying	15	5

SPREE MEDALS CONT.

ICON	NAME	EVENT	MEDAL POINTS	ORDNANCE POINTS
	Invincible	Kill 30 opponents without dying	25	5
	Inconceivable	Kill 35 opponents without dying	25	5
	Unfriggenbelievable	Kill 40 opponents without dying	50	5
	Extermination	Wipe out an enemy team with at least an Overkill	50	25

MODE SPECIFIC MEDALS

CAPTURE THE FLAG

ICON	NAME	EVENT	MEDAL POINTS	ORDNANCE POINTS
	Flag Capture	Deliver the opponents flag to your base	100	100
	Flag Carrier Kill	Kill an opponent who is carrying a flag	5	5
	Flag Kill	Kill an opponent while holding a flag	5	5
	Flag Defense	Kill an opponent close to your flag, or help return it	5	5
	Flag Runner	Capture 2 flags in one game	15	15
	Flag Champion	Capture 3 flags in one game	25	25
	Flag Assist	Help a teammate score a flag	10	10
	Flag Driver	Drive a Flag Carrier close to your capture point	5	5
	Flag Joust	Kill a flag carrier while holding a flag	15	25
	Flagsassination	Perform an assassination while holding a flag	15	15

REGICIDE

ICON	NAME	EVENT	MEDAL POINTS	ORDNANCE POINTS
	King Spree	Get 5 kills in a row as King	15	10
	Kingtacular	Survive for 30s as King	25	25
	Reign of Terror	Survive for 90s as King	50	50
	Regicide	Kill the King	Varies	Varies
	Execution	Assasinate the King	15	15
	Kingslayer	Kill the King 3 times in a row	15	10
	King Assist	Assist a player in killing the King	5	5
	Savior	Kill an opponent shooting at your King	5	5
	King Kill	Kill an opponent as the king in regicide	5	5
	King Joust	Kill a King as the king in Regicide	10	10

INTRODUCTION

BASIC TRAINING

INTEL

CAMPAIGN

INFINITY

APPENDIX

MEDALS CONT.

ICON	NAME	EVENT	MEDAL POINTS	ORDNANCE POINTS
	DOMINION			
	Base Capture Initiated	Initiate a base capture	5	5
	Capture initiation Assist	Be within a base when a teammate initiates the capture	5	5
	Base Captured	Initiate a successful base capture	10	10
	Base Conqueror	Initiate 5 successful base captures	15	15
	Capture Assist	Be within a base when it is captured	5	5
	Base Saved	Reclaim a contested base your team owns	5	5
	Base Assist	Be within a contested base when your teammate reclams it	5	5
	Fortification Assist	Be within a base your team controls when it fortifies	5	5
	Resupply Assist	Be within a base your team controls when it resupplies	5	5
	Security Chief	Reclaim 5 contested bases your team owns	10	10
	Base Offense	Kill an enemy player inside an enemy controlled base	5	5
	Base Defense	Kill an enemy player inside a base your team controls	5	5
	Turret Destroyed	Destroy an enemy auto-turret	10	10
	Demolition Expert	Destroy 10 enemy auto-turrets	15	15
	Turret Constructed	Build an auto-turret	10	10
	Chief Engineer	Build 10 auto-turrets	15	15
	Gotcha!	Kill an enemy player while they are constructing an auto-turret	15	15
	Shield Door Destroyed	Destroy 5 enemy team shields	5	5
	Breach	Destroy 10 enemy team shields	10	10
	Sapper	Destroy 15 enemy team shields	15	15
	Hero!	Instigate a successful capture that saves the team from Last Stand	25	25
	Kill Shot!	Get the Final Kill in Last Stand Mode	25	25
	Survivor	Survive Last Stand without dying	15	15

ICON	NAME	EVENT	MEDAL POINTS	ORDNANCE POINTS
	EXTRACTION			
	Site Extracted	Successfully extract a site	25	25
	Extraction Assist	Provide support nearby when a beacon is extracted	5	5
	Beacon Armed	Successfully plant a beacon	10	10
	Arm Assist	Provide support nearby when a beacon is armed	5	5
	Arm Stopped	Kill an enemy planting the beacon	5	5
	Site Defense	Kill an attacker in the supply site	5	5
	Site Offense	Kill a defender in the supply site	5	5
	Stay Back	Kill an enemy while planting or defusing the beacon	15	15
	Site Saviour	Convert 3 beacons without dying	15	15
	Expert Extraction	Extract 3 beacons without dying	25	25
	Beacon Converted	Successfully convert a beacon	10	10
	Convert Assist	Provide support nearby when a beacon is converted	5	5
	Convert Stopped	Kill an enemy converting the beacon	5	5
	KING OF THE HILL			
	Hill +5	Hold and survive in the hill for 5 seconds	10	10
	Hill +10	Hold and survive in the hill for 15 seconds	15	15
	Hill +15	Hold and survive in the hill for 30 seconds	25	25
	Hill Dominance	Hold and survive in the hill for its entire duration	25	25
	Vehicle Hill +5	Hold and survive in the hill for 5 seconds using a vehicle	10	10
	Vehicle Hill +10	Hold and survive in the hill for 15 seconds using a vehicle	15	15
	Vehicle Hill +15	Hold and survive in the hill for 30 seconds using a vehicle	25	25
	Vehicle Dominance	Hold and survive in the hill for its entire duration using a vehicle	25	25
	Hill Defense	Kill an enemy while holding a hill	5	5

ICON	NAME	EVENT	MEDAL POINTS	ORDNANCE POINTS
	Hill Assist	Assist killing an enemy taking a hill	5	5
	Hill Offense	Kill an enemy holding a hill	5	5
	Assault Assist	Assist killing an enemy defending a hill	5	5
	Hail to the King	Kill 5 enemies while controlling the hill	25	25
	First Point	Be the first player to earn a point from a hill	5	5
	Regime Change	Overtake a controlled hill (10 seconds) and hold it for 10 seconds	10	10
ODDBALL				
	Carrier Kill	Kill an enemy carrying the oddball	5	5
	Carrier Kill Assist	Assist killing an enemy carrying the oddball	5	5
	Ball Kill	Kill an enemy with a melee Ball attack	5	5
	Smooth Moves	Get a Triple Kill with the oddball	15	15
	First Touch	Be the first player to pick up the ball	5	5
	Long Bomb	Throw the ball to a player at least 15m away	15	15
	Nice Catch!	Catch a ball thrown farther than 15m from you	15	15
	Interception	Catch a ball thrown by an enemy player	10	10
	Catch	Catch a ball thrown by a teammate	5	5
	Ball Holder	Hold onto the ball for 5 seconds	5	5
	Ball Keeper	Hold onto the ball for 15 seconds	10	10
	Ball Master	Hold onto the ball for 30 seconds	15	15
	Ball Hog	Hold onto the ball for 45 seconds	25	25
	Magic Hands	Hold onto the ball for 1 minute	50	50
	Balsassination	Assasinate a player using the oddball	15	15

ICON	NAME	EVENT	MEDAL POINTS	ORDNANCE POINTS
FLOOD				
	Flood Conversion	Convert a Spartan to the Flood	5	5
	Alpha Conversion	Convert a Spartan to the Flood as an Alpha	5	5
	Infector	Kill 2 Spartans in a row as a Flood without dying	10	10
	Carrier	Kill 3 Spartans in a row as a Flood without dying	15	15
	Juggernaut	Kill 4 Spartans in a row as a Flood without dying	25	25
	Gravemind	Kill ALL Spartans in a row as a Flood without dying	50	50
	Flood Kill	Kill a Flood	5	5
	Flood Kill Assist	Assist killing a flood	5	5
	Flood Hunter	Kill 4 Flood in a row as a Spartan without dying	15	15
	Flood Surivor	Kill 6 Flood in a row as a Spartan without dying	25	25
	Flood Exterminator	Kill 10 Flood in a row as a Spartan without dying	50	50
	Last Man Standing	Be the last surviving Spartan	15	15
	Final Conversion	Kill the last remaining Spartan	10	10
	Flood Victory	Contribute to the Flood total conversion of all Spartans	Varies	Varies
	The Ancient One	Survive the entire round as a Flood and convert at least one Spartan	50	50
	Clever	Survive the entire round as a Spartan	50	50
GRIFBALL				
	SCORE!	Score the Grifball	10	10

INTRODUCTION
BASIC TRAINING
INTEL
CAMPAIGN
INFINITY
APPENDIX

Throughout the course of playing *Halo 4*, players are rewarded as they accomplish various tasks in the game such as the effective use of a particular weapon or the neutralization of a specific enemy type. These awards accumulate as they are accomplished, eventually rewarding the player with a Commendation. The type of Commendations available to players may vary, but a player's current progress can be observed under Career > Commendations within the Start menu.

> ❂ **Tip**
>
> In your loadout, turn on "Fast Track" in the Tactical Package to advance more quickly, ranking up faster and therefore unlocking new helmets and armor as quickly as possible. The large number of unlockable armor still takes time to reveal, but Fast Track enables you to choose them sooner than your friends or rivals.

COMMENDATION NAME	DESC.	REQ.	LV1 XP	REQ.	LV2 XP	REQ.	LV3 XP	REQ.	LV4 XP	REQ.	LV5 XP	REQ.	LV6 XP	REQ.	LV7 XP	MASTERY REWARD
WEAPONS																
Assault Rifle	Kill an enemy Spartan with the Assault Rifle	10	250	25	500	50	750	100	1000	250	2500	500	5000	1000	10000	
Magnum	Kill an enemy Spartan with the Pistol	5	250	10	500	25	750	50	1000	100	2500	250	5000	500	7500	
Battle Rifle	Kill an enemy Spartan with the Battle Rifle	10	250	25	500	50	750	100	1000	250	2500	500	5000	1000	10000	
DMR	Kill an enemy Spartan with the DMR	10	250	25	500	50	750	100	1000	250	2500	500	5000	1000	10000	
Sniper Rifle	Kill an enemy Spartan with the Sniper Rifle	5	250	10	500	25	750	75	1000	250	2000					
SAW	Kill an enemy Spartan with the SAW	5	250	10	500	25	750	75	1000	250	2000					
Shotgun	Kill an enemy Spartan with the Shotgun	5	250	10	500	25	750	75	1000	250	2000					
Railgun	Kill an enemy Spartan with the Rail Gun	5	250	10	500	25	750	75	1000	250	2000					
Sticky Detonator	Kill an enemy Spartan with the Sticky Detonator	5	250	10	500	25	750	75	1000	250	2000					
Rocket Launcher	Kill an enemy Spartan with the Rocket Launcher	5	250	10	500	25	750	75	1000	250	2000					
Spartan Laser	Kill an enemy Spartan with the Spartan Laser	5	250	10	500	25	750	75	1000	250	2000					
UNSC Loudout Weapon Mastery	Master all UNSC Loudout weapons	1	12500													Stance (Breach)
UNSC Ordnance Weapon Mastery	Master all UNSC Ordnance weapons	1	12500													Stance (Standoff)
Energy Sword	Kill an enemy Spartan with the Energy Sword	5	250	10	500	25	750	75	1000	250	2000					
Gravity Hammer	Kill an enemy Spartan with the Gravity Hammer	5	250	10	500	25	750	75	1000	250	2000					
Needler	Kill an enemy Spartan with the Needler	5	250	10	500	25	750	75	1000	250	2000					

COMMENDATION CONT.

COMMENDATION NAME	DESC.	REQ.	LV1 XP	REQ.	LV2 XP	REQ.	LV3 XP	REQ.	LV4 XP	REQ.	LV5 XP	REQ.	LV6 XP	REQ.	LV7 XP	MASTERY REWARD
Storm Rifle	Kill an enemy Spartan with the Storm Rifle	10	250	25	500	50	750	100	1000	250	2500	500	5000	1000	10000	
Covenant Carbine	Kill an enemy Spartan with the Covenant Carbine	10	250	25	500	50	750	100	1000	250	2500	500	5000	1000	10000	
Plasma Pistol	Kill an enemy Spartan with the Plasma Pistol	5	250	10	500	25	750	50	1000	100	2500	250	5000	500	7500	
Fuel Rod Cannon	Kill an enemy Spartan with the Fuel Rod	5	250	10	500	25	750	75	1000	250	2000					
Beam Rifle	Kill an enemy Spartan with the Beam Rifle	5	250	10	500	25	750	75	1000	250	2000					
Concussion Rifle	Kill an enemy Spartan with the Concussion Rifle	5	250	10	500	25	750	75	1000	250	2000					
Covenant Loadout Weapon Mastery	Master all Covenant Loadout weapons	1	10000													Emblem - Energy Armor Skin - Recon Surge SURG
Covenant Ordnance Weapon Mastery	Master all Covenant Ordnance weapons	1	10000													Stance - Standoff
Boltshot	Kill an enemy Spartan with the Boltshot	5	250	10	500	25	750	50	1000	100	2500	250	5000	500	7500	
Scattershot	Kill an enemy Spartan with the Scattershot	5	250	10	500	25	750	75	1000	250	2000					
Suppressor	Kill an enemy Spartan with the Suppressor	10	250	25	500	50	750	100	1000	250	2500	500	5000	1000	10000	
LightRifle	Kill an enemy Spartan with the LightRifle	10	250	25	500	50	750	100	1000	250	2500	500	5000	1000	10000	
Binary Rifle	Kill an enemy Spartan with the Binary Rifle	5	250	10	500	25	750	75	1000	250	2000					
Incineration Cannon	Kill an enemy Spartan with the Incineration Cannon	5	250	10	500	25	750	75	1000	250	2000					
Forerunner Loadout Weapon Mastery	Master all Forerunner Loadout weapons	1	7500													Emblem (Hardlight), Armor Skin (Warrior MTRX)
Forerunner Ordnance Weapon Mastery	Master all Forerunner Ordnance weapons	1	7500													Stance (Believe)
Turret	Kill an enemy Spartan with any turret	5	250	10	500	25	750	75	1000	250	2500					Armor Skin (Enforcer TRBL)
Frag Grenade	Kill an enemy Spartan with the Frag Grenade	5	250	10	500	25	750	75	1000	250	2500					
Plasma Grenade	Kill an enemy Spartan with the Plasma Grenade	5	250	10	500	25	750	75	1000	250	2500					
Pulse Grenade	Kill an enemy Spartan with the Pulse Grenade	5	250	10	500	25	750	75	1000	250	2500					
Weapon Mastery	Master all weapon commendations	1	15000													Armor Skin (Protector DRFT)

INTRODUCTION

BASIC TRAINING

INTEL

CAMPAIGN

INFINITY

APPENDIX

COMMENDATION NAME	DESC.	REQ.	LV1 XP	REQ.	LV2 XP	REQ.	LV3 XP	REQ.	LV4 XP	REQ.	LV5 XP	REQ.	LV6 XP	REQ.	LV7 XP	MASTERY REWARD
ENEMIES																	
Grunt Slayer	Kill Grunt Infantry	125	250	250	500	500	750	750	1000	1000	2500	2500	5000			
Grunt Imperial Slayer	Kill Grunt Imperials and Space Grunts	75	250	150	500	300	750	450	1000	600	2500	900	5000			
Grunt Ultra Slayer	Kill Grunt Ultras	25	250	50	500	100	750	150	1000	250	2500	350	5000			
Jackal Slayer	Kill Jackal Infantry	75	250	150	500	300	750	450	1000	600	2500	900	5000			
Jackal Major Slayer	Kill Jackal Majors	25	250	50	500	75	750	125	1000	250	2500	500	5000			
Jackal Ranger Slayer	Kill Jackal Rangers	10	250	25	500	50	750	75	1000	150	2500	300	5000			
Elite Slayer	Kill Elite Infantry	25	250	50	500	75	750	125	1000	250	2500	500	5000			
Elite Zealot Slayer	Kill Elite Zealots and Rangers	10	250	25	500	50	750	75	1000	150	2500	300	5000			
Elite Officer Slayer	Kill Elite Officers	5	250	15	500	30	750	60	1000	90	2500	180	5000			
Elite Hero Slayer	Kill Elite Generals	3	250	7	500	21	750	42	1000	63	2500	84	5000			
Hunter Slayer	Kill Hunters	5	250	10	500	25	750	50	1000	100	2500	250	5000			
Covenant Destroyer	Master all Covenant Kill commendations	1	10000													Emblem (Covenant), Armor Skin (Orbital AEON)
Crawler Slayer	Kill Crawler Infantry	125	250	250	500	500	750	750	1000	1000	2500	2500	5000			
Crawler Specialist Slayer	Kill Crawler Snipers	75	250	150	500	300	750	450	1000	600	2500	900	5000			
Crawler Leader Slayer	Kill Crawler Primes	25	250	50	500	75	750	125	1000	250	2500	500	5000			
Knight Slayer	Kill Knights	25	250	50	500	75	750	125	1000	250	2500	500	5000			
Knight Battlewagon Slayer	Kill Knight Battlewagons and Rangers	10	250	25	500	50	750	75	1000	150	2500	300	5000			
Knight Hero Slayer	Kill Knight Commanders	5	250	15	500	30	750	60	1000	90	2500	180	5000			
Watcher Slayer	Kill Watchers	75	250	150	500	300	750	450	1000	600	2500	900	5000			
Forerunner Destroyer	Master all Forerunner kill commendations	1	10000													Emblem (Promethean), Armor (Vanguard)
VEHICLE																	
Splatter	Splatter an enemy Spartan with a vehicle	5	250	10	500	25	750	50	1000	75	2000						Emblem (Splatter), Visor (Verdant)
Mongoose Destroyer	Destroy enemy occupied Mongooses	5	250	10	500	25	750	50	1000	75	2000						
Warthog Destroyer	Destroy enemy occupied Warthogs	5	250	10	500	25	750	50	1000	75	2000						
Mantis Destroyer	Destroy enemy occupied Mantises	3	250	6	500	9	750	27	1000	75	2000						
Scorpion Desrtroyer	Destroy enemy occupied Scorpions	3	250	6	500	9	750	27	1000	75	2000						
Ghost Destroyer	Destroy enemy occupied Ghosts	10	250	20	500	40	750	80	1000	160	2000						
Banshee Destroyer	Destroy enemy occupied Banshees	5	250	10	500	25	750	50	1000	75	2000						
Destroy Wraith	Destroy enemy occupied Wraiths	5	250	10	500	25	750	50	1000	75	2000						
Wheelman	Earn Vehicle Skill medals	10	250	25	500	50	750	250	1250	250	2500						Armor Skin (Aviator BOND)
Vehicle Mastery	Master all Vehicle commendations	1	10000													Emblem (Vehicular), Armor Skin (Air Assault VERG)

COMMENDATION CONT.

COMMENDATION NAME	DESC.	REQ.	LV1 XP	REQ.	LV2 XP	REQ.	LV3 XP	REQ.	LV4 XP	REQ.	LV5 XP	REQ.	LV6 XP	REQ.	LV7 XP	MASTERY REWARD
PLAYER																
Hail of Death	Call in Personal Ordnance	5	250	10	500	20	750	40	1000	60	2000					Emblem (Ordnance), Armor Skin (EVA BRCH)
Dawn	Complete Campaign Mission 1 on Legendary difficulty	1	0													
Requiem	Complete Campaign Mission 2 on Legendary difficulty	1	0													
Forerunner	Complete Campaign Mission 3 on Legendary difficulty	1	0													
Infinity	Complete Campaign Mission 4 on Legendary difficulty	1	0													
Reclaimer	Complete Campaign Mission 5 on Legendary difficulty	1	0													
Shutdown	Complete Campaign Mission 6 on Legendary difficulty	1	0													
Composer	Complete Campaign Mission 7 on Legendary difficulty	1	0													
Midnight	Complete Campaign Mission 8 on Legendary difficulty	1	0													
Legend	Complete all Campaign Missions on Legendary difficulty	1	0													Emblem (117), Armor (Mark VI), Arms (Mark VI), Legs (Mark VI), Visor (Legendary)
Spartan Slayer	Take out enemy Spartans	25	250	50	500	150	750	300	1000	600	2500	1200	5000	2400	10000	Armor (C.I.O.), Emblem (Extracted)
Bullet in the Brain	Take out enemy Spartans with headshots	15	250	50	500	100	750	200	1000	400	2500	800	5000	1600	10000	Armor Skin (Defender CTRL)
First Strike	Get the first kill in a match	5	250	10	500	25	750	50	1000	50	2000					Stance (Assault)
Multikill	Quickly kill multiple enemy Spartans	5	250	10	500	25	750	50	1000	100	2500	250	5000	500	10000	Armor Skin (Infiltrator TRAC)
Backstab	Assassinate Covenant and Forerunner enemies	10	250	25	500	50	750	100	1000	100	2000					Armor Skin (Venator RPTR)
Assassin	Assassinate enemy Spartans	5	250	10	500	25	750	50	1000	50	2000					Armor (Venator)
Spartan Spree	Kill multiple enemy Spartans without dying	5	250	10	500	25	750	50	1000	100	2500	200	5000	400	10000	Armor Skin (Soldier ZNTH)
Assistant	Earn any Assist medal	25	250	50	500	250	750	500	1000	1000	2500					Visor (Sunspot)
Close Quarters	Earn any CQC medal	25	250	50	500	250	750	500	1000	1000	2500					Arms Skin (Twin-plated AEON)

COMMENDATION CONT.

Commendation Name	Desc.	REQ.	LV1 XP	REQ.	LV2 XP	REQ.	LV3 XP	REQ.	LV4 XP	REQ.	LV5 XP	REQ.	LV6 XP	REQ.	LV7 XP	Mastery Reward
Combat Opportunity	Earn any Combat Skill medal	10	250	25	500	50	750	250	1000	500	2500					Armor (Ranger)
Payback	Kill the enemy Spartan that just killed you	25	250	50	500	250	750	500	1000	500	2000					Legs Skin (Contoured CHVR)
Protector	Protect a teammate	10	250	25	500	50	750	100	1000	250	2000					Armor Skin (Ranger STRK)
Avenger	Kill an enemy Spartan that just killed a teammate	15	250	30	500	90	750	180	1000	360	2000					Visor (Blindside)
From the Brink	Kill an enemy Spartan while close to death	15	250	30	500	60	750	90	1000	180	2000					Visor (Cyan)
Perfection	Complete a match without dying and get at least 15 kills	1	1000	2	2000	3	3000	4	4000	5	5000					Arms Skin (Contoured CHVR)
Exterminator	Killed every enemy Spartan that finished the match	3	1000	5	2000	7	3000	9	4000	18	5000					Legs Skin (Recruit TIGR)

GAME TYPES

Commendation Name	Desc.	REQ.	LV1 XP	REQ.	LV2 XP	REQ.	LV3 XP	REQ.	LV4 XP	REQ.	LV5 XP	REQ.	LV6 XP	REQ.	LV7 XP	Mastery Reward
Slayer Victory	Win a match in any Slayer gametype in matchmaking	10	250	25	500	50	750	150	1000	300	2500					Armor (Gungnir)
Slayer High Score	Finish in the Top 3 Players in any Slayer gametype in mathchmaking	3	250	5	500	15	750	30	1000	50	2000					
Slayer Mastery	Master all Slayer commendations	1	7500													Emblem (The Slayer)
Hail to the King	Win a match in any Regicide gametype in matchmaking	5	250	10	500	25	750	50	1000	150	2500					Armor Skin (EOD SHDW)
Kingslayer	Kill the King in any Regicide gametype in matchmaking	10	250	20	500	40	750	60	1000	80	2000					
Executioner	Assassinate the King in any Regicide gametype in matchmaking	2	250	5	500	15	750	50	1000	50	2000					
Regicide Mastery	Master all Regicide commendations	1	7500													Emblem (Kingslayer)
Flag Victory	Win a match in any Capture the Flag gametype in matchmaking	5	250	10	500	25	750	50	1000	150	2500					Armor Skin (Vanguard CNVG)
Deadly Flag	Kill enemy Spartans while carrying the Flag in any Capture the Flag gametype in matchmaking	3	250	5	500	7	750	15	1000	30	2000					
Carrier Takedown	Kill an enemy flag carrier in any Capture the Flag gametype in matchmaking	10	250	25	500	50	750	75	1000	100	2000					
Defender of the Flag	Protect your team's flag in any Capture the Flag gametype in matchmaking	10	250	25	500	50	750	100	1000	250	2000					
Flag Mastery	Master all Capture the Flag commendations	1	7500													Emblem (Flag)

COMMENDATION CONT.

COMMENDATION NAME	DESC.	REQ.	LV1 XP	REQ.	LV2 XP	REQ.	LV3 XP	REQ.	LV4 XP	REQ.	LV5 XP	REQ.	LV6 XP	REQ.	LV7 XP	MASTERY REWARD
Dominion Victory	Win a match in any Dominion gametype in matchmaking	5	250	10	500	25	750	50	1000	150	2500					Armor (Commando)
Captured	Initiate a base capture in any Dominion gametype in matchmaking	5	250	10	500	20	750	40	1000	60	2000					
Base Defense	Earn Dominion defense medals in any Dominion gametype in matchmaking	10	250	25	500	50	750	75	1000	150	2000					
Dominion Mastery	Master all Dominion commendations	1	7500													Emblem (Dominated)
Hill Victory	Win a match in any King of the Hill gametype in matchmaking	5	250	10	500	25	750	50	1000	150	2500					Armor (War Master)
Top of the Hill	Earn hill hold medals in any King of the Hill gametype in matchmaking	5	250	10	500	25	750	50	1000	75	2000					
Hill Defense	Earn hill defense medals in any King of the Hill gametype in matchmaking	10	250	25	500	50	750	75	1000	150	2000					
Hill Mastery	Master all King of the Hill commendations	1	7500													Emblem (The Hill)
Oddball Victory	Win a match in any Oddball gametype in matchmaking	5	250	10	500	25	750	50	1000	150	2500					Armor Skin (Scout APEX)
Carry the Oddball	Earn Oddball carry medals in any Oddball gametype in matchmaking	5	250	10	500	25	750	50	1000	75	2000					
Oddball Beatdown	Kill an enemy Spartan with the Oddball in any Oddball gametype in matchmaking	5	250	10	500	25	750	50	1000	100	2000					
Drop that Ball!	Kill an enemy Spartan who is carrying the Oddball in any Oddball gametype in matchmaking	10	250	25	500	50	750	100	1000	100	2000					
Oddball Mastery	Earn Max Level in all Oddball Commendations	1	7500													Emblem (Baller)
Flood Victory	Win a match in any Flood gametype	5	250	10	500	25	750	50	1000	150	2500					Armor Skin (Commando FRCT)
The Parasite	Earn Flood medals in any Flood gametype in matchmaking	10	250	25	500	50	750	75	1000	150	2000					
Gravemind	Master all Flood commendations	1	7500													Emblem (Infected)

INTRODUCTION

BASIC TRAINING

INTEL

CAMPAIGN

INFINITY

APPENDIX

Specializations: These allow you to take your Spartan to the next level in terms of mastering specific skill sets. After reaching Level 50, you'll be allowed to choose a Specialization. Players who purchased the Standard Edition of *Halo 4* will have access to two Specializations initially, while the remaining six will become available at a later date. For those who purchase the Limited Edition, all eight Specializations are available to earn at any time. These feature 10 additional ranks and will allow you to earn new pieces of armor as well as Tactical Packages and Support Upgrades for your loadouts.

SPECIALIZATION 0 : SPARTAN-IV

RANK	RANK NAME	SPARTAN POINTS	LOADOUT ITEMS AWARDED	LOADOUT ITEMS UNLOCKED FOR PURCHASE	UNLOCKED APPEARANCE ITEMS
1	SR-1	0	Loadout 1: Weapon - Assault Rifle, Plasma Pistol / Grenade - Frag Grenade / Armor Ability - None / Support Upgrades - None / Tactical Packages - None		Armor (Recruit), Arms (Recruit), Legs (Recruit), Emblem (Recruit), Visor (Recruit), Stance (Recruit)
2	SR-2	1		Weapons: Battle Rifle / DMR	
3	SR-3	1	Armor ability slot in all Loadouts	Armor ability: Thruster Pack / Promethean Vision	
4	SR-4	1			Foreground Emblems (Set 1)
5	SR-5	1		Weapons: Storm Rifle / Covenant Carbine	
6	SR-6	1	Loadout 2	Armor ability: Jet Pack / Hologram	
7	SR-7	1		Tactical Pkgs: Mobility / Shielding	
8	SR-8	1		Weapons: Plasma Grenade / Plasma Pistol	Armor - Warrior
9	SR-9	1			Arms - Twin-Plated
10	SR-10	1		Armor ability: Hardlight Shield / Active Camo	Legs - RG-63 Counter
11	SR-11	1			Armor - Air Assault
12	SR-12	1		Support Upgrades: Dexterity / Ammo	armor ability - Jet Pack
13	SR-13	1			Stance - Heroic
14	SR-14	1	Loadout 3	Tactical Pkgs: Resupply / AA Efficiency	
15	SR-15	1			Armor - Soldier
16	SR-16	1		Armor ability: Autosentry / Regen. Field	
17	SR-17	1			Armor - Aviator
18	SR-18	1		Weapons: Pulse Grenade / Boltshot	
19	SR-19	1			Foreground Emblems (Set 2)
20	SR-20	1		Support Upgrades: Awareness / Sensor	Visor - Solar
21	SR-21	1			Background Emblems (Set 1)
22	SR-22	1		Weapons: LightRifle / Suppressor	Arms - GC-09 Locking
23	SR-23	1			Legs - LG-50 Bulk
24	SR-24	1		Tactical Pkgs: Grenadier / Firepower	Armor - Utility
25	SR-25	1			
26	SR-26	1	Loadout 4	Support Upgrades: Explosives / Ordnance Priority	Armor - Recon
27	SR-27	1			Armor - EVA
28	SR-28	1			Foreground Emblems (Set 3)
29	SR-29	1			Visor - Frost
30	SR-30	2			Arms - Inner-Plated
31	SR-31	1			Legs - Outer-Plated
32	SR-32	1			Stance - Assassin
33	SR-33	1			Background Emblems (Set 2)
34	SR-34	1			Arms - Outer-plated
35	SR-35	1			Legs - XG-89 Narrow
36	SR-36	1			Foreground Emblems (Set 4)
37	SR-37	1			Armor - War Master
38	SR-38	1			Armor - Scout
39	SR-39	1			Arms - Contoured
40	SR-40	2			Legs - Contoured
41	SR-41	1	Loadout 5		Armor - Orbital
42	SR-42	1			Armor - Infiltrator
43	SR-43	1			Armor - Hazop
44	SR-44	1			Background Emblems (Set 3)
45	SR-45	1			Armor - EOD
46	SR-46	1			Visor - Midnight
47	SR-47	1			Armor - Oceanic
48	SR-48	1			Arms - XV-27 Shifting
49	SR-49	1			Legs - Overlocking
50	SR-50	2			Stance (Last Stand), Armor (Enforcer), Foreground Emblem (Rank Up) & Background Emblem (Moving Up)

SPECIALIZATION 1 : WETWORK

RANK	RANK NAME	LOADOUT ITEMS FREEBIES	UNLOCKED APPEARANCE ITEMS
1	WK-1		Foreground Emblems (Wetwork 1-4)
2	WK-2		Chest - Wetwork
3	WK-3		Shoulders - Wetwork
4	WK-4		Helmet - Wetwork
5	WK-5	DMR skin - Noble NBL	Background Emblem (Doused)
6	WK-6		Wetwork Visor
7	WK-7		Chest - Wetwork Skin - Shard - SHRD
8	WK-8		Shoulders - Wetwork Skin - Shard - SHRD
9	WK-9		Helmet - Wetwork Skin - Shard - SHRD
10	WK-10	Mod - Stealth	

SPECIALIZATION 2 : OPERATOR

RANK	RANK NAME	LOADOUT ITEMS FREEBIES	UNLOCKED APPEARANCE ITEMS
1	OP-1		Foreground Emblems (Operator 1-4)
2	OP-2		Chest - Operator
3	OP-3		Shoulders - Operator
4	OP-4		Helmet - Operator
5	OP-5	Magnum skin - Static STC	Background Emblem (Operated)
6	OP-6		Operator Visor
7	OP-7		Chest - Operator Skin - Surface - SRFC
8	OP-8		Shoulders - Operator Skin - Surface - SRFC
9	OP-9		Helmet - Operator Skin - Surface - SRFC
10	OP-10	Mod - Wheelman	

SPECIALIZATION 3 : PIONEER

RANK	RANK NAME	LOADOUT ITEMS FREEBIES	UNLOCKED APPEARANCE ITEMS
1	PR-1		Foreground Emblems (Pioneer 1-4)
2	PR-2		Chest - Pioneer
3	PR-3		Shoulders - Pioneer
4	PR-4		Helmet - Pioneer
5	PR-5	Plasma Pistol skin - Fracture FCT	Background Emblem (Pie Is Near)
6	PR-6		Pioneer Visor
7	PR-7		Chest - Pioneer Skin - Adept - ADPT
8	PR-8		Shoulders - Pioneer Skin - Adept - ADPT
9	PR-9		Helmet - Pioneer Skin - Adept - ADPT
10	PR-10	Mod - Fast Track	

SPECIALIZATION 4 : PATHFINDER

RANK	RANK NAME	LOADOUT ITEMS FREEBIES	UNLOCKED APPEARANCE ITEMS
1	PT-1		Foreground Emblems (Pathfinder 1-4)
2	PT-2		Chest - Pathfinder
3	PT-3		Shoulders - Pathfinder
4	PT-4		Helmet - Pathfinder
5	PT-5	Assault Rifle skin - Predator - PRD	Background Emblem (A*)
6	PT-6		Pathfinder Visor
7	PT-7		Chest - Pathfinder Skin - Core - CORE
8	PT-8		Shoulders - Pathfinder Skin - Core - CORE
9	PT-9		Helmet - Pathfinder Skin - Core - CORE
10	PT-10	Mod - Gunner	

SPECIALIZATION 5 : ENGINEER

RANK	RANK NAME	LOADOUT ITEMS FREEBIES	UNLOCKED APPEARANCE ITEMS
1	EN-1		Foreground Emblems (Engineer 1-4)
2	EN-2		Chest - Engineer
3	EN-3		Shoulders - Engineer
4	EN-4		Helmet - Engineer
5	EN-5	Suppressor skin - Shatter - SHA	Background Emblem (Stalking You)
6	EN-6		Engineer Visor
7	EN-7		Chest - Engineer Skin - Edge - EDGE
8	EN-8		Shoulders - Engineer Skin - Edge - EDGE
9	EN-9		Helmet - Engineer Skin - Edge - EDGE
10	EN-10	Mod - Drop Recon	

SPECIALIZATION 6 : STALKER

RANK	RANK NAME	LOADOUT ITEMS FREEBIES	UNLOCKED APPEARANCE ITEMS
1	SK-1		Foreground Emblems (Stalker 1-4)
2	SK-2		Chest - Stalker
3	SK-3		Shoulders - Stalker
4	SK-4		Helmet - Stalker
5	SK-5	Battle Rifle skin - Dunes - DNE	Emblem 5 - BG
6	SK-6		Stalker Visor
7	SK-7		Chest - Stalker Skin - Crush - CRSH
8	SK-8		Shoulders - Stalker Skin - Crush - CRSH
9	SK-9		Helmet - Stalker Skin - Crush - CRSH
10	SK-10	Mod - Nemesis	

SPECIALIZATION 7 : ROGUE

RANK	RANK NAME	LOADOUT ITEMS FREEBIES	UNLOCKED APPEARANCE ITEMS
1	RG-1		Foreground Emblems (Rogue 1-4)
2	RG-2		Chest - Rogue
3	RG-3		Shoulders - Rogue
4	RG-4		Helmet - Rogue
5	RG-5	Covenant Carbine skin - Reign - RGN	Background Emblem (Going Rogue)
6	RG-6		Rogue Visor
7	RG-7		Chest - Rogue Skin - Focus - FCUS
8	RG-8		Shoulders - Rogue Skin - Focus - FCUS
9	RG-9		Helmet - Rogue Skin - Focus - FCUS
10	RG-10	Mod - Stability	

SPECIALIZATION 8 : TRACKER

RANK	RANK NAME	LOADOUT ITEMS FREEBIES	UNLOCKED APPEARANCE ITEMS
1	TK-1		Foreground Emblems (Tracker 1-4)
2	TK-2		Chest - Tracker
3	TK-3		Shoulders - Tracker
4	TK-4		Helmet - Tracker
5	TK-5	Boltshot skin - Piston - PST	Background Emblem (Found You)
6	TK-6		Tracker Visor
7	TK-7		Chest - Tracker Skin - Adroit - ADRT
8	TK-8		Shoulders - Tracker Skin - Adroit - ADRT
9	TK-9		Helmet - Tracker Skin - Adroit - ADRT
10	TK-10	Mod - Requisition	

SPARTAN POINT COSTS

NAME	SP COST	NAME	SP COST	NAME	SP COST	NAME	SP COST
Assault Rifle (AR)	0	Plasma Pistol	1	Autosentry	3	Resourceful	1
Designated Marksman Rifle (DMR)	2	Boltshot	2	Hardlight Shield	3	AA Efficiency	1
		Frag Grenade	0	Promethean Vision	3	Ordnance Priority	1
Battle Rifle (BR)	1	Plasma Grenade	2	Regeneration Field	3	Explosives	1
Covenant Carbine	2	Pulse Grenade	2	Mobility	1	Firepower	1
Storm Rifle	2	Active Camouflage	3	Shielding	1	Sensor	1
Suppressor	2	Thruster Pack	3	Awareness	1	Ammo	1
LightRifle	2	Hologram	3	Dexterity	1		54
Magnum	0	Jet Pack	3	Grenadier	1		

Service Record: For a brief overview of your Spartan's stats and history, check out the Service Record within *Halo 4*. For more detailed stats, you can go to Halo Waypoint. There are four categories in which you can receive Service Record information: Spartan, Campaign, Spartan Ops, and War Games.

Customize

Your Spartan's loadout options grow as you gain experience. Customize to rule your matches!

Loadouts: These allow you numerous options for choosing the arms and equipment you wish to utilize during a game. By leveling up your Spartan, you can eventually customize up to five loadouts and title them to have a more organized feel for each game type or map. For example, you can title a loadout "BTB" and choose items you've specifically tailored to the Big Team Battle.

When customizing a loadout, you can select the primary weapon, secondary weapon, grenade, armor ability, Tactical Package, and Support Upgrade with which you want to spawn. You can also modify and change your loadout in the middle of a game

if you want to change what you spawn with. This is usually done to surprise the other team or when you want something that's more optimal for a certain situation.

When you begin *Halo 4*, not all options for loadouts are available until you play and earn Spartan Points by progressing through the ranks; then you can unlock more options. Loadouts allow you to play different roles on your team, depending on what you choose: There are several excellent combinations to use for loadouts on all game types and maps; finding your favorite ones allows you to have your own style of play during each game.

> EMBLEMS

Personnel identity in the field is a key component of communication during combat. *Infinity*'s Spartans can personally customize their identity's emblem, selecting from both longstanding and new options. Through increasing one's rank as well as completing Commendations and Challenges conducted by Waypoint, Spartans can gain access to an even wider variety of exclusive emblems.

EMBLEM ICONS FOREGROUND

NAME	UNLOCKED BY
Recruit	SR-1
Tomcat	SR-4
Triad	SR-4
Bear Claw	SR-4
Wasp	SR-4
Campfire	SR-4
Cup of Death	SR-4
Active Rooster	SR-4
Bulltrue	SR-4
Leo	SR-4
Drone	SR-4
Atomic	SR-19
Grunt	SR-19
Dog Tags	SR-19
Yin Yang	SR-19
No Camping	SR-19
Radioactive	SR-19
Crosshairs	SR-19
Anchor	SR-19
Runes	SR-19
Cone'd	SR-19
Flaming Ninja	SR-28
Stuck	SR-28
Halt	SR-28
Black Widow	SR-28
Flaming Horns	SR-28
Wolf	SR-28
Valkyrie	SR-28

NAME	UNLOCKED BY
Spartan Helmet	SR-28
Pirate	SR-28
Snake	SR-28
Headshot	SR-36
Skull King	SR-36
Spartan Swords	SR-36
Horse	SR-36
Crossed Swords	SR-36
Helmet	SR-36
Jolly Roger	SR-36
Spartan League	SR-36
Rank Up	SR-50
Wetworks	WK-1
Stealth	WK-1
Arrow On Target	WK-1
Killer Bee	WK-1
Operator	OP-1
Winged	OP-1
Anchored	OP-1
Hog Tire	OP-1
Pioneer	PR-1
Arrowhead	PR-1
Compass	PR-1
Missile	PR-1
Pathfinder	PT-1
Lens	PT-1
Grid	PT-1
Recon Bot	PT-1

NAME	UNLOCKED BY
Engineer	EN-1
Screw	EN-1
Wrench	EN-1
Network	EN-1
Rogue	RG-1
Muzzled	RG-1
Patch	RG-1
Avian	RG-1
Stalker	SK-1
Foxed	SK-1
Evil Stare	SK-1
The Eye	SK-1
Tracker	TK-1
Planetary	TK-1
The Trail	TK-1
Celestial	TK-1
Mastery	SR-130 - Base + all Specializations
Projectile	Commendation : UNSC Loadout Weapon Mastery
Energy	Commendation : Covenant Loadout Weapon Mastery
Hardlight	Commendation : Forerunner Loadout Weapon Mastery
Splatter	Commendation : Splatter
Covenant	Commendation : Covenant Destroyer
Promethean	Commendation : Forerunner Destroyer
Vehicular	Commendation : Vehicle Mastery
117	Commendation : Legend
Ordnance	Commendation : Hail of Death
The Slayer	Commendation :Slayer Mastery
Kingslayer	Commendation : Regicide Mastery

EMBLEMS CONT.

NAME	UNLOCKED BY		NAME	UNLOCKED BY		NAME	UNLOCKED BY
Flag	Commendation : Flag Mastery		Infected	Commendation : Gravemind		Raider Distort	Waypoint
Extracted	Commendation : Spartan Slayer		Dominated	Commendation : Dominion Mastery		Wiseguy	Waypoint
The Hill	Commendation : Hill Mastery		On Your Shield	Waypoint		1k Club	Waypoint
Baller	Commendation : Oddball Mastery		Raider	Waypoint		LASO	Waypoint

EMBLEM ICONS BACKGROUND

NAME	UNLOCKED BY		NAME	UNLOCKED BY		NAME	UNLOCKED BY
Circle	SR-21		Hexagon	SR-33		Asterisk	SR-44
Diamond	SR-21		Chalice	SR-33		Shield	SR-44
Plus	SR-21		Cog	SR-33		Ball o' Fire	SR-44
Square	SR-21		Octagon	SR-33		Moving Up	SR-50
Triangle	SR-21		Crown	SR-33		Doused	WK-5
Vertical Stripe	SR-21		Cancel	SR-33		Operated	OP-5
Horizontal Stripe	SR-21		Horizontal Stripes	SR-44		Pie is Near	PR-5
Cleft	SR-21		Gradient	SR-44		A*	PT-5
Criss Cross	SR-21		Horizontal Gradient	SR-44		Engineered	EN-5
Buzz Saw	SR-21		Oval	SR-44		Going Rogue	RG-5
Star	SR-33		Vertical Oval	SR-44		Found You	TK-5
Cowboy Hat	SR-33		Blunt Diamond	SR-44		Stalking You	SK-5
4 Diamonds	SR-33		Blunt Diamond 2	SR-44		Maximum	SR-130 - Base + all Specializations
Sun	SR-33						

HALO 4

> ARMOR

Armor: You can make additional (and increasingly specific) changes to the overall look of your Spartan by choosing your own helmet, torso, shoulders, forearms, legs, and visor type. Create the Spartan in the image you wish to convey to your fellow players and rivals.

Your armor choices can reflect your personal play style or preferred appearance. These visual changes do not affect game play. Some players are keen to choose a female look for a perceived "smaller target" or go with a particular color that "blends" into a darkened area. These tactics won't work as both genders and all armor pieces have the same hit box. Also, the lighting system on the Spartans will highlight players in the same way regardless of which base colors you choose. The player can earn new armor pieces by ranking up in the various Specializations, mastering Commendations and completing goals on Waypoint.

AIR ASSAULT | AVIATOR | C.I.O. | COMMANDO | DEADEYE HELMET | DEFENDER | ENFORCER | E.O.D.

E.V.A. | GUNGNIR | HAZOP | INFILTRATOR | LOCUS HELMET | MARK VI | OCEANIC | ORBITAL

PROTECTOR | RAIDER | RANGER | RECON | RECRUIT | SCANNER HELMET | SCOUT | SOLDIER

STRIDER HELMET | VANGUARD | VENATOR | WAR MASTER | WARRIOR

SPECIALIZATIONS

ENGINEER | OPERATOR | PATHFINDER | PIONEER | ROGUE | STALKER | TRACKER | WETWORK

INTRODUCTION

BASIC TRAINING

INTEL

CAMPAIGN

INFINITY

APPENDIX

Develop a specific way to hold your controller to aid in enemy takedowns.

Shooting: Middle or Index Finger? Some players prefer to shoot with their middle finger rather than their index finger because they have better aim with weapons and feel more comfortable when holding the controller. Switch up how you hold your controller and go back and forth with either finger until you find the one that's most natural to you. This will improve your game immensely: Just make sure you practice if you change how you hold the controller.

Shooting—the Claw: Some players use the "claw" technique: Position your hands so you never take your right thumb off the right joystick, thus enabling you to constantly aim your weapon while allowing you to press any of the A, B, X, and Y buttons with your index finger. You fire your weapon using your middle finger.

Learning how to press A, B, X, or Y with your index finger is the second part of the technique that requires some practice. It can take a few weeks to fully master the technique, but it can give you a very big advantage to players who do not "claw." Clawing can help improve every aspect of your game—aiming, melees, grenades, jumping, and even just movement in general.

WEAPONS DETAIL

This section presents—in alphabetical order—every piece of UNSC, Forerunner, and other weapon available in *Halo 4*. Any major advantages and disadvantages of each armament are discussed in general gameplay terms. This is all designed to improve your tactical weapons knowledge.

WEAPON NAME	TYPE	RANGE	MAGAZINE CAPACITY	HEADSHOTS?	INITIAL ROUNDS	ZOOM
UNSC INFANTRY WEAPONS						
Assault Rifle	Fully-Automatic	Short-Mid	32		160	
Battle Rifle	Semi-Automatic 3-round burst	Mid-Long	36	*	108	2x
DMR	Semi-Automatic	Mid-Long	14	*	42	3x
Frag Grenade	Grenade	N/A	N/A			
Machine Gun	Fully-Automatic	Short-Mid	255 (detached)			
Magnum	Semi-Automatic	Short-Long	8		24	2x
Railgun	Charged, Single Shot Explosive	Short-Mid	1		4	
Rocket Launcher	Explosive	Mid-Long	2		4	1.8x
SAW	Fully-Automatic	Short-Mid	72		216	
Shotgun	Semi-Automatic	Short	6		18	
Sniper Rifle	Semi-Automatic	Long	4	*	12	4x, 9x
Spartan Laser	Charged, Single Shot Explosive	Mid-Long	1 (energy based)		4	2.5x
Sticky Detonator	Latched Explosive	Short-Mid	1		4	
UNSC VEHICLE WEAPONS						
Scorpion, Main Cannon	Explosive	Long	N/A			
Scorpion, Machine Gun	Fully-Automatic	Short-Mid	N/A			
Warthog, Gauss Cannon	Semi-Automatic	Mid-Long	N/A			
Warthog, Machine Gun	Fully-Automatic	Short-Mid	N/A			
Warthog, Rocket Launcher	Explosive 5-rocket volley	Mid-Long	N/A			
Mantis, Machine Gun	Fully-Automatic	Short-Mid	N/A			
Mantis, Missile Launcher	Semi-Automatic	Mid	5			
Mantis, Foot Stomp	Melee w/Cooldown	Short	N/A			
COVENANT WEAPONS						
Beam Rifle	Semi-Automatic w/Overheat	Long	Overheat	*	10	3.5x, 9.5x
Concussion Rifle	Semi-Automatic	Short-Mid	6		18	
Covenant Carbine	Semi-Automatic	Mid-Long	18	*	72	2x
Energy Sword	Melee	Short	N/A			
Fuel Rod Cannon	Explosive	Mid	5		15	2x
Gravity Hammer	Melee w/AoE	Short	N/A			
Needler	Fully-Automatic	Short-Mid	22		44	
Needler (Supercombine)	Explosive	Short-Mid	N/A			
Plasma Cannon	Fully-Automatic	Short-Mid	255 (detached)			
Plasma Grenade	Grenade	N/A	N/A			
Plasma Pistol	Semi-Automatic	Short-Mid	Overheat		50	
Plasma Pistol (charged shot)	Charged EMP	Short-Mid			5	
Storm Rifle	Fully-Automatic	Short-Mid	Overheat		166	
COVENANT VEHICLE WEAPONS						
Banshee, Fuel Rod Cannon	Explosive	Mid-Long	N/A			
Banshee, Plasma Cannon	Fully-Automatic	Mid-Long	N/A			
Ghost, Plasma Cannon	Fully-Automatic	Short-Mid	N/A			
Wraith, Plasma Cannon	Fully-Automatic	Short-Mid	N/A			
Wraith, Plasma Mortar	Explosive	Mid-Long	N/A			
FORERUNNER WEAPONS						
Binary Rifle	Semi-Automatic	Long	2	*	6	4x, 10x
Boltshot	Semi-Automatic	Short-Mid	10	*	30	
Boltshot (Charged shot)	Charged Energy Blast	Short	2		6	
Incineration Cannon	Explosive w/submunitions	Mid	1		4	1.8x
LightRifle (Hip-fired)	Semi-Automatic (3-round burst)	Mid-Long	36	*	108	3x
LightRifle (Scoped)	Semi-Automatic	Mid-Long	12	*	36	3x
Pulse Grenade	Grenade	N/A	N/A			
Scattershot	Semi-Automatic	Short	5		15	
Suppressor	Fully-Automatic	Short	48		192	

ASSAULT RIFLE

Standard fully automatic firearm of all UNSC branches, effective at both close-range and mid-range combat.

BATTLE RIFLE

Utilizes precise, three-round burst functionality, making it a formidable mid-range, semi-automatic weapon.

Magazine Capacity: 32 rounds

Description: The Assault Rifle is an exceptionally resilient gas-operated, magazine-fed, automatic rifle designed to execute close-quarters combat with lethal efficiency, regardless of hostile counter-op environmental conditions or duration of use in the field.

Tactical Notes

〉 The amount of ammunition in a clip is 32 bullets.

〉 In FFA game types, players with mid-range weapons may finish your kills if you choose to roll with this weapon.

〉 When you hold the right trigger, the crosshair will bloom (expand slightly), so if you're far away from a fight or battle, it's wise to pace your shot, thus increasing your chance of killing an enemy by tapping the trigger.

〉 This is an exceptionally good weapon to use in close melee fights. You can inflict two melees in under just two seconds, making it a better weapon overall to use during some mid-range fights and just about all close-range-combat opportunities.

〉 The reload time isn't bad if you're going from one takedown to the next. Just like any other UNSC weapon, it's smarter to reload before you run out of all your ammo in a clip, because you'll perform the reload more quickly.

Magazine Capacity: 36 rounds

Description: The Battle Rifle is a gas-operated, magazine-fed, semi-automatic rifle optimized for three-round burst firing and proven to be an extraordinarily versatile weapon at a wide variety of ranges in the hands of a capable marksman.

Tactical Notes

〉 The amount of ammo in a clip is 36, which equates to 12 shots due to the three-round burst firing.

〉 The Battle Rifle is a semi-automatic weapon, that fires in three round bursts.

〉 This weapon is arguably one of the best weapons that can be employed at long, mid-, or close-range.

〉 Accuracy is key with this weapon: The three-shot burst affects when you take down an enemy, as missing with any of the three bullets can prolong a foe's life. Therefore, it is imperative that each burst entirely strikes a foe for quicker takedowns. Aiming for the head is the most effective way to eliminate enemies with this weapon.

〉 The Battle Rifle reload time varies if you use up all of the ammo in a clip prior to reloading, but it reloads relatively fast between multiple battles.

〉 The Battle Rifle's zoom feature makes it even more effective in helping you aim and place shots more accurately; this gives you an even easier time to complete objectives that you or your team are requesting.

〉 Melee strikes can be relatively fast after shooting, so use this at close-range as a backup takedown technique in case you're not hitting with all the shots you fire. Even if an enemy is up a shot—that is, has taken less damage—as you both enter closer combat, the high damage of this weapon's melee can allow you to win a fight.

》 DEVELOPER COMMENTARY

I'm not sure exactly what it is, but I definitely feel like I have more control over my bullet spread when pulsing my AR starts than in past games. No doubt about it, the Assault Rifle is definitely still at its best in close quarters.

– David Ellis (Mission Designer)

Relative to other Halos, this feels to me like a slightly more powerful *Halo 3* AR. Some people might have some prejudice against the weapon because it's not the newest, flashiest weapon on the block and there are a lot of other things that will catch your eye first. That being said, this is one of the best looking weapons in the game IMO. Gameplay-wise, we've tried to extend the range on the AR a bit from what it's traditionally been and made it a tad more accurate. This is one of my favorite weapons in *Halo 4* and I'm particularly fond of pairing it with a long-range rifle in MP using the Firepower Armor Abilities.

– Chris King (Lead MP Level Designer)

》 DEVELOPER COMMENTARY

Like a well-oiled baseball glove, pick up the Battle Rifle in *Halo 4* and you'll feel right at home. With the Battle Rifle being hitscan (projectiles register hits immediately upon trigger pull), it is definitely a force to be reckoned with at mid- to long-range. Roll into battle with a teammate or two at your side, and enemies will turn and run at the mere threat of your group shots. There's just something inherently satisfying about that triple thud unleashed with each trigger pull.

– David Ellis (Mission Designer)

DMR

Premiere marksman rifle of the UNSC, offering impressive single-fire accuracy at reasonably long distances.

Magazine Capacity: 14 rounds

Description: The DMR is a gas-operated magazine-fed marksman rifle that maintains a smart-linked, telescopic, rail-mounted sight for scout personnel. This rifle favors mid-range to long-range combat and offers impressive stopping power.

Tactical Notes

> The DMR has 14 shots per clip, and a max reserve capacity of 42 shots to expend before reload.

> This rifle has the advantage of being effective at any range and can remove a threat quickly. This rifle competes with the Battle Rifle in close and mid-range combat, but it is better at long-range takedowns.

> Further advantages include only a slight bloom when the weapon is fired, meaning this is recommended for those players relying on accuracy. The rifle's zoom feature optimizes this rifle still further.

> Due to the single-shot fire, you need to work on when to time your shot for maximum damage and impact. In close-combat situations, line up your reticle as best you can.

> The reloading speed is quick, but always reload between bouts of violence, when you're in relative safety, and prior to emptying your clip, as a clip reload takes slightly longer—a disadvantage that can get you killed.

> This is an extremely well-balanced weapon and is arguably the best choice of all UNSC weaponry.

» DEVELOPER COMMENTARY

This thing is absolutely ridiculous long-range. While it does feature a slight amount of bloom to balance it at extreme distances, for the majority of mid to long-range encounters it doesn't really come into play. The combination of the accuracy, headshot functionality and the improvements we have made to the aim assist system make this one of the best feeling guns in any Halo game IMO. One other thing worth mentioning on this one... I can't get over how awesome this weapon sounds – it has an insanely meaty punch to each shot and gives me an adrenaline rush just firing it!

– Chris King (Lead MP Level Designer)

This might surprise some people, but based solely on pure lethality, I'd have to give the ever-so-slight edge to the DMR right now. It's incredibly precise and simplified with lower rate of fire than in *Halo: Reach*. Now the only info you need to juggle in your head when going toe-to-toe is the middle of the reticle as you line it up to dome your unfortunate foe. For my money, Battle Rifle with group shot is greater than DMR, but if you're lone wolfing, DMR is the way to go.

– David Ellis (Mission Designer)

MACHINE GUN

Fixed weapon emplacement which can be removed and brought into combat with limited ammo and mobility.

Magazine Capacity: 255 rounds (detached)

Description: The Heavy Machine Gun is an air-cooled, gas-operated, drum-fed automatic weapon that is primarily used from a full-range, tripod-mounted position, although it can be removed from its mount and hefted into battle if the operator is physically capable.

Tactical Notes

> The Machine Gun lays some heavy damage on enemies very quickly; simply point, shoot, and rake the foe with massive bullet expenditure!

> When mounted, you have infinite ammunition.

> You can hold the right trigger and simply unload on foes, but the weapon does have an overheat point if held for too long. The recover time forces you to wait a few seconds before starting to fire again.

> The Machine Gun can be detached at any time to become a mobile weapon to help out teammates at any time (following them into an enemy base ether killing or weakening foes).

> When detached, the Machine Gun can run out of ammo. However, carrying a Machine Gun allows you to maneuver however you wish, jumping or strafing in any direction, which is usually better for enemy takedowns than standing at a fixed point.

> Machine Guns have about a 180-degree arc to aim around you. Never let enemies get behind you. If this happens, detach or flee from the turret.

> Choosing Gunner as your Support Upgrade will significantly improve your turret abilities. You'll be able to shoot longer when attached without overheating, and you'll get more ammo and move significantly faster when detached, turning the Machine Gun from a situational weapon to a deadly force.

INTRODUCTION

BASIC TRAINING

INTEL

CAMPAIGN

INFINITY

APPENDIX

MAGNUM

UNSC's personal sidearm of choice due to its excellence at close-range to mid-range engagements.

Magazine Capacity: 8 rounds

Description: The Magnum is a semi-automatic, recoil-operated, magazine-fed handgun and the standard personal sidearm of all branches of the UNSC post-2555. This weapon is surprisingly effective at reasonably long distances, proving its universal value in the field.

Tactical Notes

> The Magnum has eight shots per clip.

> Those with previous *Halo* experience may instinctively overlook the Magnum. This is unwise, as the weapon packs a considerable punch, even keeping up with most long- and mid-ranged weapons! Although mostly used as a last resort, its excellent damage and accuracy means it's well worth considering, even at the expense of a primary weapon.

> Pace your shots to secure an accurate kill on an enemy. Employ this plan, as you only have eight shots to either kill or weaken a foe before reloading (which leaves you vulnerable).

> The Magnum is a single-shot weapon, so precision is the key to using it properly, if you're expecting to win any fights.

> The Magnum has a useful zoom feature that can aid you in battle; use it to gain that additional accuracy you may need.

> This is a recommended secondary weapon, but expert players should find themselves switching between the Magnum and their primary weapon as the situation calls for it, rather than keeping it holstered.

> The Magnum has an average melee speed, with only a brief time to recover, making it reasonable to employ in these type of strikes.

›› DEVELOPER COMMENTARY

The Magnum in *Halo 4* is designated as a secondary weapon and as such it should be a just a little weaker than your primary options. With a faster rate of fire, it's more deadly than the DMR close-range, but a twitchy trigger finger will limit its effectiveness at longer ranges.

– David Ellis (Mission Designer)

The *Halo 4* Magnum isn't meant to compete with the big boys (DMR, Battle Rifle, Covenant Carbine, LightRifle) so its role is a bit different than in the past. It definitely won't compete with the *Halo: Combat Evolved* Magnum (although, what weapon will?) It's still lethal but best used as a backup (switch to a Magnum to finish someone vs. waiting for a long reload on your primary weapon) or to pair with a fully auto primary weapon like the AR or Storm Rifle (drop an enemy's shields and then finish them with a single headshot). In the hands of a skilled player though, this thing can still be a beast as it's one of the fastest firing guns in the game. The other big change I think players will notice is that we have drastically sped up animation times when using a pistol. So you will be able to switch to it quicker, pull off melees and grenade throws faster, etc. than you will with primary weapons.

– Chris King (Lead MP Level Designer)

RAILGUN

Powerful linear accelerator that fires explosive rounds at tremendous speed to efficiently eliminate targets.

Magazine Capacity: 1 HE Round

Description: The Railgun is a compact-channel linear accelerator that fires a high-explosive round at incredible speed, delivering kinetic and explosive force to both hard and soft targets alike. The brutal combination of accuracy, speed, and Firepower make the Railgun extremely capable at eliminating large, well-armored enemy personnel.

Tactical Notes

> The Railgun has only one bullet per clip, but it has a one-hit kill if the bullet directly connects with a foe.

> You can hold down the trigger and wait until the Railgun fires on its own, or you can shoot it as soon as the charge up bar fills. You have a 1- to 2-second window to decide when to fire the bullet (usually as soon as the foe's head is lined up in your sights).

> For advanced players, you should try to use the charge bar on the reticle to your advantage and become more accurate, instead of always waiting for the gun to fire on its own. When the gun is charged fully, there is a small delay before it is actually fired. Simply release the trigger after the bar fills up to control the release of the weapon. This ensures you'll be aiming at your target when it goes off at your control, rather than attempting to time the release.

> If the Railgun is shot on the ground adjacent to an enemy, the bullet causes some splash damage, removing the enemy's shields. If this occurs, immediately pull out another weapon (such as the Battle Rifle) to finish the job.

> Charging up the Railgun and using it to "peek and shoot" around a wall is a great way to surprise the enemy with a quick charge-up and release.

›› DEVELOPER COMMENTARY

First described to me as a junior Spartan Laser, the Railgun is anything but. The quicker charge times allow me to be a little more fast and free in engaging in 1v1 showdowns. I also find it more useful against vehicles in situations where, say, a Banshee gets a drop on me in the open. The lack of a zoom means you have to be careful at what range you're attempting to engage others, but when you do, the feeling of satisfaction is fantastic.

– David Ellis (Mission Designer)

I like the Railgun since it's basically a Sniper Rifle, Rocket Launcher, and Spartan Laser all wrapped into one. You charge it up to shoot a direct damage shot that explodes on impact. WIN!

– Kynan Pearson (Lead MP Level Designer)

ROCKET LAUNCHER

Devastating from close-range to mid-range and capable of tracking airborne vehicles.

Magazine Capacity: 2 rockets

Description: The Rocket Launcher is a portable, twin-tube, shoulder-fired rocket launcher capable of firing two 102-mm rockets with excellent destructive potency. It is easily one of the most pervasive explosive weapons within the UNSC's arsenal.

Tactical Notes

⟩ This weapon carries up to two rockets at a time, and it has a 2x scope.

⟩ The only time it heat-seeks its target is when fired on any flying vehicle. Aim your reticle at the Banshee and your rocket tracks the foe's movements and follows them. This is obviously advantageous.

⟩ The Rocket Launcher's payload causes massive splash damage and is extremely adept at taking down enemies at close and mid-ranges. It causes major damage against vehicles as well.

⟩ This powerful weapon becomes vital to control any locations where rockets spawn on a map during any game type. It's easy to use and is one of the most powerful weapons available.

⟩ However, it has a fairly long reloading time. Reload both rockets at once; this is more efficient than simply shooting one and reloading immediately afterward.

⟩⟩ DEVELOPER COMMENTARY

If you know anything about me, you'll know that I love any advantage I can use, and the Rocket Launcher is the ultimate advantage for me. It's big, it fires rockets. What's not to love?

– David Ellis (Mission Designer)

Functionally, it's similar to past versions. The big differences from past versions are that the projectile speed has been upped a hair to help compensate for the overall faster pace of our game and the splash damage is a bit larger.

– Chris King (Lead MP Level Designer)

SAW

Squad automatic weapon used during protracted engagements where sustained fire is required.

Magazine Capacity: 72 rounds

Description: The SAW (Squad Automatic Weapon), is a gas-operated, drum-fed, fully automatic machine gun that provides incredible sustained fire in the field and is capable of suppressing even the most heavily armored of infantry targets.

Tactical Notes

⟩ The SAW is a light machine gun with 72 bullets per clip.

⟩ It is extremely effective at close-range; you can drop a foe with around 15 to 18 bullets.

⟩ This can be devastating if you're expecting close combat and charge into an enemy territory to rake your foes with fire instead of resorting to one or two shots from your usual Battle Rifle or DMG.

⟩ This is easily one of the best close- and mid-range weapons available.

⟩ When holding down the trigger, the reticle's bloom expands, so if you employ it at shorter mid-range, try tapping the trigger to control the bloom; this makes the SAW more accurate.

⟩ The SAW has a fairly long reload time. This is problematic, as you're usually 'fully used up' at the wrong time and in the wrong place. We recommend that you wait until you're safe before reloading

⟩ This is a formidable weapon at close-range combat. Beware of foes using it for this purpose.

⟩⟩ DEVELOPER COMMENTARY

This is my favorite weapon. It's like the AR's mean older brother, or a more mobile turret emplacement.

– Chris Howard (SDE)

The SAW is, without a doubt, the most psychologically intimidating GUN in the game. It looks unlike any gun you've seen before in a Halo game, and packs a world champion-class punch when spraying molten projectiles at everything in your way. The SAW is also incredibly useful as a force modifier when encountering a vehicle on foot. A skilled SAW user will use every tool at his disposal to clear space while shredding surrounding vehicles. The comparison to the AR is apt, but whereas a skilled AR user (yes, they do exist) will use finesse to drop a foe, the SAW almost demands of you to unleash its fury by burning down enemies with overwhelming force. You do want to keep an eye out for the ammo count as before you know it you'll be hearing that familiar "click, click, click" of impending death.

– David Ellis (Mission Designer)

SHOTGUN

Dominant close-quarters weapon specializing in boarding actions, breach maneuvers, and urban operations.

Magazine Capacity: 6 shells

Description: The Shotgun is a pump-action weapon that fires 8-gauge cartridges with ruthless proficiency, making it the UNSC's most effective and useful close-quarters arm, particularly during urban engagements and boarding actions.

Tactical Notes

〉 This Shotgun has six shells in the chamber and a maximum capacity of 24.

〉 This is one of the most powerful weapons that the UNSC uses. Although seen by many as overpowered, the Shotgun has several disadvantages that can leave you without proper self defense on the battleground.

〉 Slow reloading and a vicious kickback are the two biggest downsides to this otherwise monstrous weapon. In addition, this has only six shots, so ensure you're as close as possible when firing on foes. In between shots, expect to lose your aiming precision due to the kickback. As this can cause you to spend too long reaiming and cost you a fight, timing your firing is important (fire when you have a clean shot and when you can survive after a missed shot).

〉 Firepower certainly isn't lacking here, so simply line up your target and fire. One or two shots take out just about any foe easily. Never use this gun for anything other than close-combat takedowns.

〉 Increase your chances of success by staying close to walls or in enclosed areas, and fully utilize this gun when the foes appear nearby.

》 DEVELOPER COMMENTARY

I've always been the kind of guy who loves to jump in the middle of a squad of enemies to see how many I can take out in my blaze of glory. As such, the Shotgun, if I might borrow a phrase, scratches that particular itch for me. With the aesthetic redesign, the Shotgun feels like a future bangstick designed with one purpose: to blow heads clean off their shoulders. I actually find this shotgun to be easier to use than the one in *Halo: Reach*, but when getting the jump on enemies, you better make that first shot count. Otherwise, you'll be left wondering what could have been while waiting to respawn.

– David Ellis (Mission Designer)

The new Shotgun model is SICK and definitely reads as a bit more futuristic than the previous versions. It actually has a lot longer range now, less damage falloff, and is quite a bit more powerful than say the *Halo: Reach* version overall, but some of that dialed up power is countered by the other changes in the game like Sprint by default, mobility-based armor abilities, and generally faster movement speeds. This is definitely one of my favorite ordnance weapons. I especially love finding one when I have the Speed Boost in MP.

– Chris King (Lead MP Level Designer)

SNIPER RIFLE

Considered the UNSC's best long-range rifle, boasting formidable stopping power and unparalleled accuracy.

Magazine Capacity: 4 rounds

Description: The Sniper Rifle is a gas-operated, magazine-fed, semi-automatic sniper rifle with exceptional accuracy and the ability to simultaneously breach both energy-shielding and high-density armor, making swift kills nearly effortless when this weapon is properly utilized.

Tactical Notes

〉 The UNSC Sniper Rifle holds four shots per clip before reloading.

〉 This is best at long-range, especially as the weapon has a 4x and 9x zoom scope. However, it can also be effective at middle-short ranges if you use "no-scoping" (firing without a scope) or "quick-scoping" (firing with very fast scoped line-up shots between firings).

〉 At melee range, striking with a "no-scoped" shot to the body and then connecting with a melee strike directly afterward is an effective way to utilize the Sniper Rifle in close combat.

〉 Scoring headshots with the Sniper Rifle is excellent for obtaining your own kills (instead of assisting in them), but if you're playing a team game, it's sometimes better to strike with body shots, as they're much easier to succeed in. Then give your teammates the opportunities to pick up the kill on the wounded foe.

〉 In a mid-range fight, hitting the body of a foe and then pulling out a Battle Rifle, DMR, or Covenant Carbine is a great way to finish off a foe instead of trying to hit with another sniper rifle shot.

〉 Ammunition conservation is key here; don't feel like you need to rush to fire off all of your bullets. Taking your time is key to obtaining some accurate shots into your opponents.

〉 This is also a great antivehicle weapon. For example, it takes only five shots to demolish a Banshee. To defeat a Scorpion tank, shoot the entry door twice to expose the opponent driver's head, and defeat him with a headshot. Try taking down an enemy Wraith driver if you're on higher ground; shoot the entry door once to expose the opponent's head, and drop him with a headshot. For Ghost and Warthog takedowns, simply fire at the enemy, as they're already exposed.

》 DEVELOPER COMMENTARY

The UNSC Sniper Rifle feels really, REALLY powerful this time around. I went back and tried the *Halo 3* and *Halo: Reach* Sniper rifles a few weeks back and was surprised how much more visceral ours felt. I think the big changes causing this are the new sound FX and the firing recoil (resets back to center after each shot). The recoil makes it a bit harder to line up again between shots but we have adjusted the accuracy and aim assist to help compensate. Overall, I find that I can be more successful with our Sniper Rifle than I could with the *Halo 3* or *Halo: Reach* ones so it's probably a tad bit easier to use.

– Chris King (Lead MP Level Designer)

SPARTAN LASER

Formidable nonlinear rifle that is highly proficient at destroying vehicles over long distances.

Magazine Capacity: 1 (energy based), 4 shots

Description: The Spartan Laser is a shoulder-fired, smart-linked nonlinear rifle that projects a superheated beam of energy that is incredibly effective at destroying both enemy personnel and vehicles. Design for this weapon occurred in parallel with the GUNGNIR-class of Mjolnir GEN1 armor, resulting in the informal name "Spartan Laser."

Tactical Notes

> The Spartan Laser's ammunition works differently from other weapons; it reduces in percentage terms (100 percent would be a fully loaded Spartan Laser). This weapon becomes empty when you reach 0 percent, negating the need to worry about reloading.

> This is mainly used to take out moving vehicles and other objects. The advantage of using this on a vehicle is the resulting explosion kills every enemy riding the vehicle too.

> This isn't recommended for firing unless you're zoomed in to take advantage of the increased accuracy and to avoid the lengthy time it takes to charge each shot. One exceptional feature of this weapon is that the scope has a bar that allows you to see how close you are to firing off the shot.

> This weapon is best utilized when fired from long-range, but a mid-range shot is also possible, depending on the wielder's accuracy. You can actually melee using this, too, but it isn't something to actively engage in!

> Try charging the Spartan Laser as you move, releasing the charge prior to firing if you haven't found an enemy to hit. Repeat this tactic, staying on the move and charging until you've removed the enemy threat.

» DEVELOPER COMMENTARY

Currently, I'd put the Laser just below *Halo 3*'s "red dot of death" and slightly above the *Halo: Reach* variant. It seems to have slightly less aim assist than *Halo 3*, but still packs a mean punch when you connect. In matchmaking, you will primarily see this as an occasional ordnance drop on maps and modes designed for BTB.

– David Ellis (Mission Designer)

Those are pretty accurate assessments. Still tears apart vehicles and still can be lethal against guys on foot when in the hands of a skilled player.

– Chris King (Lead MP Level Designer)

STICKY DETONATOR

Single-hand, short-range explosives launcher which can detonate remotely and at the operator's discretion.

Magazine Capacity: 1 grenade

Description: The Sticky Detonator is a low-profile single-shot weapon that launches a magnetically latched explosive, which the operator can remotely detonate when at a safe distance. Although previously manufactured in low quantities, this weapon's size and ease of transportability has made it ubiquitous in the years that followed the Covenant War.

Tactical Notes

> The Sticky Detonator can hold 4 explosive charges.

> This charge can be stuck to your opponent, a flag, a wall, a vehicle, or even the ball, and can be detonated at your leisure by pulling the trigger.

> Failure to pull the trigger results in the charge exploding after 30 seconds.

> This weapon has a built-in Motion Sensor system, which is a good way to check whether opponents are by your placed charge. If your enemy is in any part of the white circle when you detonate the charge, then they die in the ensuing explosion. However, your opponent can also crouch-walk next to the charge, as this doesn't show up on your Motion Sensor. Beware of these sneaky tactics, or try them yourself!

> This can be fired approximately 60 meters before exploding on its own (in midair) if it hasn't found a surface to stick to. Finding situations where you can fire a charge all the way across a map so it explodes in midair and hits enemies below is an effective way to take down their shields.

> When facing foes at mid-range, fire the charge onto the floor or a wall close to the enemy, and then detonate it immediately afterward. This usually results in a kill or, at the very least, shield depletion.

> Remember that if opponents spot a sticky charge waiting for them, they can shoot it once and blow it up on their own, retreating to avoid the explosion.

> Try firing charges so they stick onto enemies, and track them as they dash across a map; hopefully into a stronghold or a cluster of foes. Then detonate and try to take down multiple foes in the blast!

» DEVELOPER COMMENTARY

I totally agree with everything Frank and David have mentioned here. This is a really satisfying gun to use! The other thing I love about it is that it really lends itself to creativity on the part of players. I have seen members of the team employ some hilariously awesome tactics with this thing like hiding the sticky detonator projectile inside of empty vehicles, in clever locations on a map like behind grenade pickups, sticking it to a vehicle and then driving said vehicle at enemies and hopping out and detonating it, etc.

– Chris King (Lead MP Level Designer)

I love the Sticky Detonator because it's fun to stick a few grenades on a Warthog and drive it around like a parade float with festive streamers trailing behind.

– Bill Clark (Software Development Engineer)

FRAG GRENADE

The Fragmentation Grenade, which has existed relatively unchanged for centuries, is used to efficiently clear any dug-in enemies.

Description: The Frag Grenade is a standard, high-explosive, dual-purpose grenade that is extremely effective against personnel, particularly those who are dug in or fixed behind cover, due to its ability to ricochet around corners.

Tactical Notes

> The Frag Grenade is the most basic but arguably the most beneficial of all the grenade types.

> This grenade is useful prior to you or your team attempting a push forward: It cripples the enemy's shields, making them much more straightforward to clean up and kill with your mid-ranged weapons, such as the Battle Rifle, DMR, or Covenant Carbine.

> One excellent trick to try is instead of throwing the grenade at your opponent, lob it so it bounces where your foe is moving to, so they have no time to evade the explosion.

> Every map has a number of "grenade points," places around the map where you can throw a grenade at a wall or piece of scenery and watch the grenade bounce to where your opponent is standing. Use these ricochet points to surprise your enemy. Then finish them off as their shields are removed.

> COVENANT WEAPONS

BEAM RIFLE

Extreme-range sniper rifle, charging ionized hydrogen gas into a lethal beam of accelerated particles.

Magazine Capacity: 10 shots

Description: The Particle Beam Rifle is now the Covenant's primary long-range special application weapon, used almost exclusively by scouting personnel and designated marksmen. Through the ionization of hydrogen gas and the use of a linear accelerator, a powerful beam is emitted at hypervelocity speeds, lethally striking enemy targets.

Tactical Notes

> Choose this weapon if you intend to take out enemy snipers, as it has a couple of key advantages over the Sniper Rifle.

> As is the case with all energy weapons, this gun does not need to be reloaded. However, if you fire off too many shots at a rapid pace, the gun is liable to overheat, forcing a delay in additional shots.

> Overcome this by pausing between bursts of shots. In fact, just like the Sniper Rifle, two shots to the body or a single headshot is usually enough to defeat most foes.

> The advantage this weapon has over other "sniping" weaponry is that you're able to get two shots off more rapidly than the Sniper Rifle, allowing you to defeat rival enemy snipers much more quickly. The Beam Rifle is also slightly less cumbersome.

> Aiming for the head isn't always necessary with this weapon because of how quickly you can get off two body shots. When the situation calls for it, don't be afraid to go for the safer body shot.

》 DEVELOPER COMMENTARY

First off, I love that the Covenant sniper weapon is back for *Halo 4*. It's been sorely missed. Secondly, the new HUD elements on the Beam Rifle when zoomed in really help to sell this as a piece of alien technology. As before, the meta-game of managing the heat of your rifle and firing on enemies means that every shot counts. Get too hasty and you'll be looking down at your dead body in the flash of venting gas.

– David Ellis (Mission Designer)

The Beam Rifle is sick. What's not to like about being able to clear out an enemy team with a single weapon that when used correctly doesn't require a reload... and the sound is so satisfying.

– Kynan Pearson (Lead MP Level Designer)

CONCUSSION RIFLE

Heavy rifle which launches explosive bolts of plasma similar to Covenant mortar weapons.

Magazine Capacity: 6 shots

Description: The Concussion Rifle is a short-range antimateriel weapon that launches bursts of explosively charged plasma much like other mortar weapons. Upon impact, the plasma explodes concussively, threatening opposing infantry, equipment, and even light-armored vehicles.

Tactical Notes

》 Firing into groups usually results in a kill, its reliable at knocking players off ledges or into grenade blasts (when used in tandem), and it can easily overturn some vehicles if used right.

》 It takes three direct shots to kill an enemy at close quarters (the only time it makes sense to use this over other weaponry), but if your foe jumps during one of your shots and are struck, they're likely to go flying in the air, making it extremely difficult to hit with the remaining shots.

》 It can be entertaining to shoot this weapon down at the ground and give yourself a boost up into the air (although using this to climb structures is far less preferable than employing a more useful weapon and moving normally).

》 This weapon's main use is to stop a Mongoose or Warthog in their tracks.

》 DEVELOPER COMMENTARY

The Concussion Rifle and Brute shot have always been somewhat controversial in that players either love them or hate them – there doesn't seem to be an in-between. The biggest change to the *Halo 4* Concussion Rifle are the stronger physics impulses from the explosions along with faster projectile speed, which makes it work better in more open spaces and from a longer distance. That being said, I wouldn't recommend trying to use this in a duel with a DMR from across the map. I love the firing rate on this weapon but IMO, the best part about it is the emergent sandbox moments you can get from the strong physics impulses on the explosion. Try drilling a speeding enemy Warthog from the side, and watch as hilarity ensues!

– Chris King (Lead MP Level Designer)

I am impressed with the precision the AI can wield the Concussion Rifle with in Spartan Ops. They are really good at juggling my lifeless body after they obliterate me.

– Chris Howard (SDE)

COVENANT CARBINE

Notable semi-automatic mid-range accuracy, firing ballistic rounds unlike most other Covenant weapons.

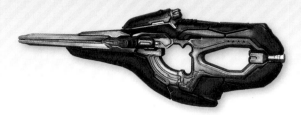

Magazine Capacity: 18 rounds

Description: The Covenant Carbine is a recoil-operated, semi-automatic, charger-fed marksman rifle capable of firing ballistic rounds at significant range. It is somewhat unique among Covenant weapons in that it is not dependent on superheated plasma or other energy-based material, but rather fires radioactively charged ballistic projectiles.

Tactical Notes

》 This weapon usually takes eight shots to kill an opponent. This compares to the DMR and Battle Rifle, both of which use up five shots to take down a foe.

》 Although this appears to be less powerful than either the DMR or Battle Rifle, the Covenant Carbine's rate of fire makes up for its low damage.

》 If you're a marksman with extremely adept accuracy, consider choosing the Covenant Carbine, as it can take down foes more quickly than the DMR or Battle Rifle.

》 This weapon is also extremely accurate, and unlike the DMR, the Covenant Carbine's target reticle does not "bloom"; where you aim is where the bullets will impact.

》 The Covenant Carbine is a great support weapon, allowing you to put a lot of damage on opponents from across the map without having to focus on finishing them with headshots.

》 DEVELOPER COMMENTARY

I can't decide if it's the size of the bolts you fire or some other intangible, but the Covenant Carbine feels (to me) like the most accurate weapon in the game. I find it especially useful for when I'm waiting to launch an ambush. Against inexperienced foes, the barrage of rapid fire shots can cause enemies to panic and make mistakes... to their doom. As Chris mentions below, it's great as a finishing weapon. I would recommend pairing it with a Plasma Pistol or Storm Rifle.

– David Ellis (Mission Designer)

Mathematically, this is the most lethal long-range rifle in the game in a one-on-one encounter. It fires extremely fast – double the rate of the other rifles, but it doesn't have the range of the DMR or LightRifle, and each individual shot is relatively weak. A player that can land the bulk of their shots and manage their ammo well can be extremely successful with it, though. Because of its headshot capability, it is also a great weapon for playing cleanup with teammates (have them drop opponent shields and then score the headshot). I love using this weapon but I can only use it in short bursts. The firing rate is so fast, it makes my fingers tired after a while!

- Chris King (Lead MP Level Designer)

INTRODUCTION

BASIC TRAINING

INTEL

CAMPAIGN

INFINITY

APPENDIX

ENERGY SWORD

Composed of superheated plasma, this sword remains the preferred close-quarters weapon of Elites.

Description: The Energy Sword, exclusively wielded by Sangheili, is a close-engagement weapon intended to express its owner's personal skill, clerical honor, and combat viability. The blade is composed of superheated plasma and folded against magnetic lines extending from its hilt, effectively creating a razor-sharp martial weapon with lethal functionality.

Tactical Notes

〉 This is a close-quarter weapon only. You're obviously at an extreme disadvantage at any range except melee.

〉 This Energy Sword differs from the one in *Halo: Reach*, where you could deflect a sword lunge with a regular weapon melee counter; it kills enemies in one strike.

〉 This is a great secondary weapon to stow and retrieve when you're fighting in close quarters to gain the edge on a foe.

〉 When facing an enemy who is holding the Gravity Hammer, attempt to "juke" them by backing up and darting forward until the foe swings their hammer and misses, giving you a short opening to take them down.

〉 This sword is excellent to employ with the Speed Boost and Overshield Ordnance Drops.

〉 If you see an enemy with an Energy Sword, immediately slam backward on your movement thumbstick and try to keep your distance. If you have the Hardlight Shield, you can attempt to block one of their attacks if they're already in range.

FUEL ROD CANNON

Typically used against heavy armor by launching charged fuel rods which violently detonate upon impact.

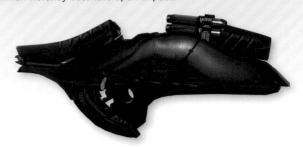

Magazine Capacity: 5 fuel rods

Description: The Fuel Rod Cannon is a shoulder-mounted ballistic weapon that launches extremely volatile 38 mm fuel rods at enemy targets, detonating on contact. The result is extraordinarily effective against armor, though it can be used rather viciously against infantry and other soft targets.

Tactical Notes

〉 This is a powerful weapon but not as damaging as a Rocket Launcher against vehicles.

〉 The Fuel Rod Cannon kills an opponent if you hit them directly.

〉 If you are moving backward or from left to right, there is a short distance in which you can aim to bounce the shots off the ground; this can lead to some epic kills!

〉 Although you can hit enemy infantry with this, adept foes are likely to dodge the attacks from all but the longest ranges.

〉 Be wary of the splash damage—you don't want to end up killing yourself or your teammates with an ill-placed blast.

GRAVITY HAMMER

Crude yet formidable close-range Brute weapon, substantially improved by way of a powerful gravity drive.

Description: The Gravity Hammer, though rarely encountered in recent years, is a powerful close-range weapon hailing from the totemistic traditions of the previous Covenant species known as the Jiralhanae. This hammer maintains a shock-field-generating gravity drive that increases damage on impact and can manipulate localized energy fields.

Tactical Notes

〉 This powerful weapon excels at close-range damage and little else.

〉 This is the weapon to use during Grifball matches.

〉 Simply rush your target, strike them down, and move on. The impact crushes foes and takes them out with a single strike.

〉 If you encounter a foe with an Energy Sword, expect to trade blows with them unless you're able to strike first. Timing your swing is imperative to avoid being dodged and countered.

〉 The Gravity Hammer is excellent to employ with the Speed Boost and Overshield Ordnance Drops.

〉 If you see an enemy with a Gravity Hammer, immediately slam backward on your movement thumbstick and try to keep your distance.

》 DEVELOPER COMMENTARY

The saying "If it ain't broke, don't fix it" applies here. This is one of my all-time favorite Halo weapons. There aren't a ton of changes that we made to it – more like nuanced tweaks. The animation speeds are a tad quicker, the area of effect has been expanded, the damage tuning tweaked but overall, it's pretty similar to past incarnations. Probably the biggest change comes in the form of the physics impulses – they are much more powerful now to compensate for the beefier vehicles in the game. This has the awesome side effect of making the Gravity Hammer ragdoll players and objects much more than it has in the past. In short, you should expect the hammer to function similar to past versions, but with more showboating flair!

– *Chris King (Lead MP Level Designer)*

NEEDLER

Exotic guided-munitions weapon, firing crystalline shards that home in, impale, and detonate on soft targets.

Magazine Capacity: 22 needles

Description: The Needler is a compact, fully automatic guided-munitions launcher that breaks off shards of chemically charged crystalline. When fired, the shards home in on sighted targets with specific heat signatures, impaling the targets just prior to simultaneously and violently detonating.

Tactical Notes

〉 Attempt to pick up this weapon at all times. Why? Because it's an incredibly powerful mid-range weapon that can turn the tide against foes armed with a Battle Rifle, DMR, or Covenant Carbine.

〉 Even against experienced players in short-range battles, they need to hit you with all of their shots, while you unload with a stream of pink needles and (usually) emerge victorious!

〉 If you surprise your enemy from behind and get the first shot off, then you're almost assured a takedown.

〉 The best defense is cover or dodging this weapon if you're at sufficient range, so if you're intending on using the Needler, it is vital to get in close or launch the attack first.

〉 If you hear this weapon being fired in your vicinity, it's time to dip, duck, and dodge your way to safety.

》 DEVELOPER COMMENTARY

The *Halo 4* Needler is probably the most powerful version of the gun to date. I love the new, more mechanical firing sounds of the gun as it feels more visceral. One of the big changes this time around is that the needles stick to shields again (in *Halo: Reach*, the needles only supercombined when shields were down). This makes it deadly for sure. However, its effectiveness is tempered by the overall faster pace of the game, which gives players a better chance of avoiding the needles. If you catch an opponent off-guard, they are in for a world of hurt.

– *Chris King (Lead MP Level Designer)*

The Needler is so bad-ass, some of us call it the "noobler". It feels like the *Halo 2* Needler to me. It will wreck your -Yoink!

– *Josh Lindquist (Sr. Software Development Engineer)*

PLASMA CANNON

Fully automatic energy turret, capable of being hefted into combat with limited mobility and operation.

Magazine Capacity: 255 shots (detached)

Description: The Plasma Cannon is a fully automatic directed-energy weapon, typically mounted on a gravity-synched fulcrum tripod with the capacity for a full range of fire. A capable operator can even decouple the cannon from the mount and carry it into combat.

Tactical Notes

〉 This hulking great weapon is mostly used for obtaining kills at short range, just like the Machine Gun.

〉 Short-range takedowns are preferred, as this weapon is very inaccurate at mid- and long-ranges.

〉 It doesn't overheat when detached and eventually overheats when mounted, so you may want to detach just before the Cannon gets too hot to shoot.

〉 The Plasma Cannon has about a 180-degree arc to aim around you. Never let enemies get behind you. If this happens, detach or flee from the turret.

〉 Choosing Gunner as your Support Upgrade will significantly improve your turret abilities. You'll be able to shoot longer when attached without overheating, and you'll get more ammo and move significantly faster when detached, turning the Plasma Cannon from a situational weapon to a deadly force.

PLASMA GRENADE

The Plasma Grenade, when triggered, is engulfed in latent plasma, allowing it to cling to targets before detonating.

Description: The Plasma Grenade is the Covenant's primary explosive, which, when triggered, becomes engulfed in latent plasma, allowing it to cling to specific heat signatures before violently exploding on a timed fuse. This grenade is particularly useful against vehicles, as targets with larger silhouettes are more susceptible to the explosive's adhesive properties.

Tactical Notes

〉 A Plasma Grenade packs a lot of power but is easily dodged by opponents.

〉 Therefore, this grenade is most effective when you're trying to stick it onto an enemy.

〉 This is also useful when trying to stop or slow an enemy as they try to escape along a route well trafficked by your foes. For example, if you're winning a 1v1 battle, throw one of these grenades behind the enemy so they won't attempt to run away; instead they have to commit to combat with you, even though they are weakened.

〉 This is also an excellent grenade to lob onto vehicles, since you can stick them to the surface, and the ensuing explosion slows or destroys the vehicle.

PLASMA PISTOL

Semi-automatic energy weapon capable of a scaled-burst effect which disables electronics.

Magazine Capacity: 50 shots, 5 charged shots

Description: The Plasma Pistol is the standard sidearm for most Covenant infantry. Typically used as a semi-automatic, directed-energy pistol, this weapon's scaled burst functionality allows it to fire an overcharged collection of plasma, temporarily incapacitating the power systems on both armor and vehicles.

Tactical Notes

〉 The Plasma Pistol is a powerful weapon to combine with a mid- or long-range primary weapon.

〉 Charge the weapon by holding down your shooting trigger, wait for a lock-on symbol around your target reticle, and then release the trigger to shoot a charged bolt that depletes the enemy's shields. This allows you to shoot them (ideally in the head) with your primary weapon, such as the Battle Rifle, DMR, or Covenant Carbine.

〉 It's often advantageous to dash around with this weapon charged, priming it in case you run into an enemy. However, this drains your energy quickly, and the key to using this weapon successfully is learning when to time your charge (usually when you see a foe or know you're able to engage one) and when to hold off (when no threats present themselves or when employing a different weapon).

〉 Don't become fixated on the charged shot; it's also an excellent idea to rapidly fire the Plasma Pistol at foes in close quarters and drain their shields using this technique as well.

〉 The Plasma Pistol is useful in Big Team Battle variants, as you're able to use the EMP (Electromagnetic Pulse) on vehicles, stopping them quickly if you don't have a heavy-duty weapon for the job.

〉〉 DEVELOPER COMMENTARY

Don't be deceived by the toy-ish looks. This is a powerful gun! To be effective with the normal shot, you will need to use it at close-ranges because the projectiles are extremely slow relative to other weapons. And since players spawn with it from the get-go as a secondary weapon, we've had to retune the number of charge shots down from the past (when charging, the energy drains pretty quickly in War Games compared to the past). It's still a great choice, though, especially on vehicle maps. If you are a fan of the Noob Combo, I'd recommend trying to scavenge a Magnum as a backup. The *Halo 4* pistols all have faster animation timings than in the past, allowing you to switch to them faster than any other weapon in the game. Charged Plasma Shot + Magnum headshot = WIN!

– *Chris King (Lead MP Level Designer)*

STORM RIFLE

Fully automatic energy weapon widely considered the successor to the traditional Plasma Rifle.

Magazine Capacity: 166 shots

Description: The Storm Rifle is the evolution of the standard Plasma Rifle and served various infantry during the violent Sangheili civil conflicts that followed the Covenant War. The weapon now includes a modular coil set, a high-mounted cooling shroud, and an extended barrel, all contributing to greater overall performance in the field.

Tactical Notes

〉 The Storm Rifle is a powerful weapon for short- and mid-range firing.

〉 Its main purpose is to knock down the shields of an opponent very rapidly.

〉 For best results, carry this with a Battle Rifle, DMR, Covenant Carbine, LightRifle, or Magnum, and then switch to one of those weapons to finish the foe off, once their shields are whittled down.

〉 You can also pair this weapon with a nice melee to your opponent's face, resulting in some phenomenally quick kills.

〉 Like the assault rifle, if you choose to rock this as your primary weapon in FFA games, you may see your kills picked off by opponents wielding headshot-capable weapons.

〉〉 DEVELOPER COMMENTARY

The Storm Rifle fills a role similar to that of the UNSC Assault Rifle, but somehow the Storm Rifle is just plain more frightening to come up against. Early in development, there weren't a lot of people using this weapon, despite how effective it was at close-range. That changed overnight when the weapons effects and sounds started to come online.

– *David Ellis (Mission Designer)*

This is a fantastic close-range weapon, once you figure out the rhythm on the overheat. I especially love using this weapon on smaller maps or in tight areas as it's incredibly lethal. It doesn't have the range or accuracy of the AR but if you manage the heat well, you can continue firing for quite a while and it will give you a significant advantage over other weapons that require longer reloads. It takes some getting used to, though. If you just hold the trigger down and let the gun reach its overheat state, you are faced with a long cool down penalty.

– *Chris King (Lead MP Level Designer)*

BINARY RIFLE

Extreme-range sniper rifle, designed to take down heavily armored infantry.

Magazine Capacity: 2 shots

Description: The Binary Rifle leverages the power of twin, core-mounted particle accelerators, offering the ability to neutralize enemies with a single shot, even those of considerable mass. The Binary Rifle was specifically designed to deal with the threat of the Flood, allowing infantry to snipe at extreme ranges with unparalleled accuracy and stopping power.

Tactical Notes

〉 This weapon is thoroughly recommended by MLG, which they refer to as "the Boss" and with good reason—it's unstoppable!

〉 This weapon is a one-hit kill no matter where you shoot your enemy. Have you hit your foe with this? Then they won't be getting up again. Line up more foes one behind another for multihit kills!

〉 However, the Binary Rifle has only two bullets per clip (although this is compensated for by the power each blast inflicts).

〉 This weapon also has a disadvantage when zoomed in; it emits three red lasers from your sights to the location where you're aiming, therefore giving the enemy notice prior to their execution.

〉 The laser sight could also be seen as an advantage, intimidating an opponent and startling them off their combat plans as they realize this extremely powerful rifle has targeted them.

〉 Combine this with the Promethean Vision for extremely satisfying enemy takedowns.

》 DEVELOPER COMMENTARY

Poo-inducing. That's how I describe the gut-clenching terror shuddering through my body every time I see the telltale laser sight of the Binary Rifle projecting across the map. Unlike other sniper rifles, this beastly harbinger of death is a one-hit kill rifle. ONE HIT. It's a pretty rare ordnance drop and in Matchmaking, it doesn't carry much ammo. But if you see the HUD marker announcing its arrival on the battlefield, RUN. Either towards the Binary Rifle in a mad scramble or away as fast as possible in the hopes that person wielding this weapon has difficulties tracking targets over extreme distances.

– David Ellis (Mission Designer)

The Binary Rifle is my favorite Halo power weapon ever. It's like Christmas every time you pick it up. A one-hit kill no matter where you hit an enemy. It's sooo good when you just barely clip someone's foot and then watch as they fragment into thousands of angry burning embers. I also love that even though it's incredibly powerful, when someone is zoomed in and looking to take a shot, you can see a laser leading to everything they are looking at. Points you right to where they are.

– Kynan Pearson (Lead MP Level Designer)

BOLTSHOT

Forerunner particle dilator used for both its precision at mid-range and its burst functionality when up close.

Magazine Capacity: 10 shots, 2 charged shots

Description: The Boltshot is a close-range particle dilator designed for precision-based infantry combat against organic material. The Forerunners began using weapons like these toward the end of the first century of their prodigious conflict with the Flood, and continued to do so till its conclusion 200 years later.

Tactical Notes

〉 Use this weapon for it's single fire accuracy, solid rate of fire, or charged shot.

〉 This weapon is primarily used to extract you out of a problematic situation when enemies are closing in on your location and other (or preferred) weapons are not available.

〉 Although you can utilize the Boltshot as a typical "pistol" by pulling the trigger, try holding the trigger to release a powerful charged shot that can kill even a fully shielded enemy.

〉 Practice holding and releasing the charged shot, and then employ it to really infuriate your foes! Play "possum" by staying by a wall or in cover, and bait your foe, beckoning them in close before giving them the business end of a charged Boltshot.

〉 Do not underestimate this weapon—charging a weak player with a Boltshot is a surefire way to end up on the wrong side of a tea bag.

》 DEVELOPER COMMENTARY

The Boltshot has become my go-to sidearm in MP because of the double functionality of the charge blast. Nailing someone coming around the corner with a one-shot kill is always satisfying.

– Paul Featherstone (Assistant Director of Photography)

I love the Boltshot because of its secondary fire mode. It's the ultimate risk/reward trade-off: you have to start charging at exactly the right time or the blast will fire before your enemy is at point-blank range. Get your timing right, though, and this handy little Forerunner pistol will send your opponents straight to Death Cam with a single shot. Unleashing the Boltshot on an unsuspecting player coming around a corner is immensely satisfying. It's also a great weapon to pair with weapons that are more effective at longer ranges, like the Battle Rifle, DMR, and LightRifle. Charging opponents wielding short-range weapons got you down? Don't worry, a couple of encounters with your trusty Boltshot will make them think twice about coming near you, making it that much easier to pick them off with a series of well-aimed headshots from your rifle of choice.

– Sam Wolpert (SDE)

INCINERATION CANNON

Extremely powerful shoulder-mounted particle weapon with an explosive after effect.

Magazine Capacity: 1 shot

Description: The Incineration Cannon is a shoulder-mounted munitions launcher that fires a high concentration of explosive particles along multiple streams, typically generating obliterative results. Such a weapon is equally effective against single enemy combatants and vehicles.

Tactical Notes

> Think of the Incineration Cannon as a rocket launcher on steroids. It should be given a wide berth, but use one against foes for a quick death.

> After the initial explosion, several additional detonations shoot out from the impact point, causing massive damage.

> Naturally, this takes down your enemies in a single shot, and all vehicles as well (as long as the secondary explosions connect).

> This weapon is to be feared.

> Use this weapon with precaution when around teammates, as the explosion radius doesn't care whether you're friend or foe.

» DEVELOPER COMMENTARY

This is another Forerunner weapon that has the ability to incinerate opponents. This can lead to especially impressive multi-kills given the large area-of-effect/submunitions. Not too long ago, I was able to kill four enemies with one shot, and watching them all dissolve in front of me was about as satisfying as it gets. Another cool moment I witnessed with this one involved a teammate firing it near a speeding Warthog with three enemy passengers, all of which were killed and starting dissolving while seated in the 'Hog. Rad! Worth noting here, this weapon has an especially long reload time; you have to reload between every shot, and the projectile itself is fairly slow. This means you really need to connect with your shot, or you will be at a disadvantage to your opponents.

– Chris King (Lead MP Level Designer)

This thing is a beast. If you see it pop up on your HUD, get ready with your grenades as you close distance because there's going to be another few Spartans making a beeline for it. Once you have this beauty in your hands, aim carefully because you have to reload after each shot. But it's so very, very worth it: the gentle pull of the trigger sends out a number of projectiles weaving towards your foe. Upon impact, these projectiles then blossom out from the initial detonation into a cascade of secondary explosions. Nothing feels better than slamming a fresh round into the cannon while watching three or four of your enemies disintegrate into electronic dust.

– Tom Mathews (SDE II)

LIGHTRIFLE

Precision weapon that fires beams of hard light for mid-range to long-range combat.

Magazine Capacity: 36 shots, 12 (scoped)

Description: The LightRifle was originally designed to achieve precision-based sniping with light-mass componential particle acceleration. The overall effect of the weapon is impressive, accurately firing a collection of hard light particles toward a target at incredible speed.

Tactical Notes

> It takes five shots to kill a foe using this weapon. However, if you zoom in with the LightRifle, you can drop a foe in four shots.

> When looking through the scope, if you strike a foe with every shot, you can remove three enemies using a single clip, making this a more impressive piece of equipment to use for those with excellent accuracy to their shots.

> This is a weapon that a talented player can use supremely well.

> If you see an enemy using this weapon, be sure to get in their face to counteract the increased damage dealt when zoomed. If they're foolish enough to try and zoom in a close-range battle, you'll find them easy prey.

» DEVELOPER COMMENTARY

Best of both worlds, master of subtlety, these are terms that I just wrote to describe the LightRifle. Neither quite captures the complexity of this piece of kit. I find both firing modes are a tiny bit less forgiving than the DMR and Battle Rifle, but definitely put in the time to master the subtle idiosyncrasies of the LR. Your efforts will be rewarded.

– David Ellis (Mission Designer)

The LightRifle is a long-range semi-auto precision rifle. It features a 3x zoom, hitscan projectiles that do headshots, but, most importantly, it features two firing modes. The best way to think of it is a hybrid of the Battle Rifle and DMR. When firing from the hip, it fires in three-round bursts, similar to a Battle Rifle. Once the player zooms however, the gun switches over to a more powerful firing mode and combines the normal three projectiles into a singular shot. When zoomed, the LightRifle can kill a Spartan in four shots (w/headshot). That being said, there are still tradeoffs here that make it balanced in line with the other semi-auto weapons. It fires slightly slower when zoomed, and it's just a smidge less viable from the hip versus the other stuff. Overall, this is a formidable weapon and has developed a cult following internally at 343.

– Chris King (Lead MP Level Designer)

SUPPRESSOR

Fully automatic Forerunner infantry weapon, firing bolts of hard light in rapidly accelerating succession.

Magazine Capacity: 48 bolts

Description: The Suppressor leverages a classic coil set architecture, accelerating charged bolts of hard light energy at high speeds toward enemy personnel. This weapon eventually proved to be an integral part of the Forerunner's arsenal when battling the Flood but remains incredibly useful against any and all organic material.

Tactical Notes

》 This weapon is extremely effective at short ranges. However, move away from closer combat and you'll find this much more problematic at taking down foes.

》 It is definitely wise to get the jump on enemies and shoot first, as you can quickly remove them as a threat if they're within range.

》 This is another weapon that can take down an enemy quickly when paired with a melee.

》 This weapon has an SMG quality to it, so if you've familiarized yourself with that weapon in previous *Halo* games, you'll feel comfortable with the Suppressor right away.

》 Contrary to its name, this weapon isn't silent—you'll still show up on Motion Sensor when firing it, and your weapon emanates enough noise to draw nearby enemies to your location.

》 DEVELOPER COMMENTARY

If you like close-quarters combat in tight spaces, this is the gun for you! Individual shots are relatively weak, but it more than makes up for it with sheer brute force. It features an enormous clip (48 bullets) and the fastest firing rate of any of the fully-auto primary weapons (roughly 150% faster firing than the AR or Storm Rifle). The projectiles slow down over time so to be effective, you really need to use it like an SMG, although you can still psychologically overwhelm enemies at range with a barrage of projectiles. I find myself always rolling with the Suppressor on Adrift as the tight hallways really favor the strengths of the gun. It's oh-so-satisfying to have someone come around a corner and be able to unload half a clip into them before they even realize what hit them.

- Chris King (Lead MP Level Designer)

At very close-range, the Suppressor lays down the smack far more quickly than either the AR or Storm Rifle. It's a great weapon in maps such as Adrift where you have plenty of cover and corners. If you play the ambush game or use cover to quickly close distance, you can be devastating with it. The Suppressor's effective range drops off quickly, so you don't want to get caught in the open or a long hallway with it. Pair that sucker with some form of precision weaponry - a Magnum or use the Firepower Tactical Package to get a second precision primary.

- Brad Welch (Lead Designer)

SCATTERSHOT

Close-combat weapon with a deadly blast at short-range and a versatile ricochet effect against hard surfaces.

Magazine Capacity: 5 shots

Description: The Scattershot is a prominent Forerunner channel weapon that was used for close-range defense toward the end of their war with the Flood. While practically unstoppable up close, the most remarkable attribute of the Scattershot is its schismatic dispersal effect, allowing its particles to strategically ricochet off hard surfaces.

Tactical Notes

》 This is an excellent (and new) alternative to the Shotgun.

》 It has a longer range than the Shotgun and can inflict damage at almost twice the speed.

》 However, the impact damage is weaker. Still, the range and speed make up for this deficit.

》 If you kill your enemy and every spread of the Scattershot's bullet blast connects, expect to witness an impressive death!

》 Do you have an enemy behind you but don't think you'll have time to turn around and blast them? Then aim at a wall in front of you and avoid the ricochet. Use this "bullet bounce" plan to shoot around corners at hiding or incoming enemies too.

》 DEVELOPER COMMENTARY

I love the Scattershot because it's so much freaking fun to use. I can't compare it to any other weapon. You can aim for your target like most weapons, which is no doubt how you will fire it for the first time like I did, but once I understood the projectiles and how they ricochet off hard surfaces (the non-meat-made surfaces), I started using it more strategically – aiming at floors, walls and ceilings. I've been able to bounce shots off corners and nail players, taking out shields then going in for the death blow. (It's true, I have been known to shriek wildly when I get one of these in a game).

– Vic DeLeon (Lead Mission Artist)

By now, I'm sure most people are pretty familiar with this one. It's a Forerunner shotgun, with ricocheting bullets that allow for really interesting tactics in tight spaces. Oh, and if you blast a guy up close, you get that totally sweet Forerunner incineration effect. This gun is definitely in my top three favorite power weapons. The FX, the animations, and it's just so satisfying to fire. If you use it correctly, you can go on an absolute terror. One pro-tip – I see some people try to use this from longer distances than they should. Don't be fooled by the projectiles; this weapon is lethal up close but you won't have much luck starting a dual against a DMR player 100' away.

– Chris King (Lead MP Level Designer)

PULSE GRENADE

The Pulse Grenade forcefully detonates and forms a hazardous ionization sphere which eventually collapses, destroying any nearby targets.

Description: The Pulse Grenade is a field-generating attenuation device used to damage any targets which fall within its ionization radius, eventually collapsing in a violent and deadly pulse of energy. This device appears to have been used to clear locations where the Flood had sufficient room to gather, organize, and grow, such as the vast redoubts formed during the parasite's Coordinated Stage.

Tactical Notes

⟩ When you throw this grenade, the impact point becomes the center of a radius that charges up and drains enemy shields if they pass through, and then the grenade detonates.

⟩ This is very effective if your foes are trying to push through in close-quarter combat and are attempting to reach you. Instead, they must step through a shield-removing grenade radius, becoming considerably weaker in the process.

⟩ These grenades don't stick onto opponents, so you're likely to use them to force foes to move in a different direction. Try blocking your foe's preferred paths with these grenades, then "herd" them to a hot spot where your teammates have an ambush ready.

⟩ This works very well against vehicles, as it drains your foe's shields even when they drive through the grenade's radius.

○ Note

When detonated it releases a pulse blast, damaging players in its spherical radius. The sphere of energy eventually collapses on itself, disintegrating anything in radius.

INTRODUCTION

BASIC TRAINING

INTEL

CAMPAIGN

INFINITY

APPENDIX

ARMOR ABILITIES

Armor abilities are additional hardware components that provide a specific combat ability. When using armor abilities properly and in certain situations, you can gain a huge advantage over your enemies. You can pick one armor ability in your loadout. Each one has a certain amount of time in which it can be used, as well as the time it takes to recharge. Enemies can't pick up your armor abilities when you die, so don't worry about them stealing these.

The following reveals the list of armor abilities that you can use, as well as tactics on how to utilize them to your advantage. You'll unlock the ability to add an armor ability to your loadout at Spartan Rank 3.

ABILITY NAME	RANK UNLOCKED
Promethean Vision	SR-3
Thruster Pack	SR-3
Hologram	SR-6
Jet Pack	SR-6
Active Camouflage	SR-10
Hardlight Shield	SR-10
Autosentry	SR-16
Regeneration Field	SR-16

> **Note**
>
> With vibration turned on, your controller vibrates slightly to indicate that your armor ability is fully charged. This can help you in situations where you aren't able to pay attention to the armor ability meter. Note that you can use your armor abilities before they are fully charged, but they will not last as long as they would with a full charge.

ACTIVE CAMOUFLAGE

Unlocked for purchase at Spartan Rank 10.

Basic Description: This allows users to generate a visual effect that is astonishingly close to invisibility. You can only stay fully camouflaged if you're standing still or crouch-walking. When Active Camouflage is in use, motion sensors will display a cluster of dots in the general vicinity of the user, alerting all players that a Spartan is hidden nearby. If you shoot, melee, or throw a grenade, your camouflage will go out for a short period of time.

When to Use: This is excellent to employ in Team Snipers and Free For All. It is also beneficial when sneaking into an enemy base to pull a flag. Active Camouflage is best used for ambushes. Even if the enemy can use their motion sensors to pinpoint a general location, so long as you only move slowly or sit still, they will have a difficult time finding you so long as the ability is active. You should equip Active Camouflage if you're planning on playing tactically and sneakily.

This guy doesn't know it, but he's already dead.

Counter Strategies: You can easily be seen when you're moving, so the enemy can spot you the majority of the time unless you're crouch-walking or standing still. If you want to stay camouflaged, you can't move around the map at all, which usually isn't helpful to you, your score, or your team. Pay attention to your Motion Sensor. If you see a mass of blue dots, Active Camouflage is being used. With experience you can get a feel for where the player is in relation to the dots. Check the corners and darkened areas inside the dot cloud.

AUTOSENTRY

Unlocked for purchase at Spartan Rank 16.

Basic Description: This is an automated turret that can be deployed to defend its user or command a key battlefield choke point. The Autosentry can be easily destroyed, but it also damages enemies.

When to Use: The Autosentry is useful when deployed near chokepoints, or when an important location needs to be locked down. It can also turn the tide in a competitive rifle battle, as getting up as little as one shot over your opponent (with your Autosentry damaging them in addition to your shots) can lead to a victory.

If you can get an opponent to round a corner and receive a shot or two from the Autosentry, you're likely to find yourself ahead in fights. Even the briefest distraction is great for your game.

The Autosentry can also serve as a notification that a foe may be approaching from an area that is currently unwatched. Set up your Autosentry to watch your back, and you'll have advance notice that an enemy is approaching when you hear it fire or get destroyed.

Counter Strategies: The Autosentry is extremely easy to destroy. Any weapon can take it out with haste. Pop a few shots in it (ideally from a weapon with the most expendable ammunition so you can keep the best bullets for enemy combat) and you'll be free to slay once more.

HARDLIGHT SHIELD

Unlocked for purchase at Spartan Rank 10.

Basic Description: This allows users to generate a protective barrier of hard light that stops most small-arms fire and some explosives. Hardlight Shields block and deflect a huge amount of damage from weapons and vehicles. This is helpful when you're leading a charge into an area and need to buy time for teammates to come help you. You also can jump once while using the shield: quickly let go of your armor ability button and press Jump before the shield disappears; then hold the armor ability button down again if you need to make a jump while using it.

When to Use: Employ the Hardlight Shield when initiating a charge so you can take the incoming enemy damage for your team. You can also use it to buy a lot of time if your teammates are attempting to come and help you. It is also very beneficial to use in 1v1 matches to deflect Plasma Pistol charges and block grenade explosions.

Cheat death for a few seconds longer.

The Hardlight Shield also serves as a good distraction. Walk into your opponent's base with the shield active, and your hardened shell may buy enough time for a teammate to sneak behind the unsuspecting or preoccupied foes.

Another great plan is to use it to check rooms without much danger to yourself. If you fear the enemy team may be occupying an area, walk in with your Hardlight Shield active and find out for sure—without risking your life.

Counter Strategies: When someone is using the Hardlight Shield, their normal shields do not recharge, so you can eventually take your enemy out with enough damage and time. Your enemy can't shoot either and they move a lot slower, so you can easily sprint up to inflict a melee strike, or toss grenades behind them to take them out. A well-placed grenade is the best counter to a Hardlight Shield user.

HOLOGRAM

Unlocked for purchase at Spartan Rank 6.

Basic Description: This allows users to generate a nearly identical holographic decoy of themselves to deceive enemies during combat. The Hologram does show up on Motion Sensor, and you can hide inside it. If you drop the Hologram at your feet, you can crouch or just walk inside it to conceal yourself for the short time the Hologram is out.

When to Use: This is very good to use in Team Slayer and it can sometimes help you escape situations in Free For All. It's also great for baiting ammo out of power weapons or checking areas you might not want to risk entering blind. Send your hologram running into a mystery room and listen for gunfire to see if anyone waits within. If you're lucky, your Hologram will take the last rocket to the face, allowing you to storm in and pick up the kill.

Unfortunately, your Hologram does not come equipped with a brain.

Counter Strategies: The downside to using the Hologram is experienced players will usually know when you're a Hologram because it just runs in a straight line, and most players know that running in a straight line is strategically terrible.

JET PACK

Unlocked for purchase at Spartan Rank 6.

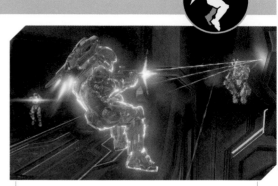

It's a bird...it's a plane...it's actually a sitting duck.

Basic Description: The Jet Pack allows users limited flight through a vertical lift-propulsion system similar to that of EVA reentry packs. You can use the Jet Pack for about three seconds to reach higher platforms or impossible-to-reach places. You can also use it to throw off your enemy's shot by Jet Packing right before they try to inflict a last headshot on you. Hammering the Crouch button will make it that much more difficult for your opponent to finish you off with a headshot.

When to Use: When you're in a 1v1 fight and want to force your foes to aim upward, use this ability. It's also useful when you want to scoot over buildings or walls in order to quickly move around the map. The Jet Pack is excellent for creating unexpected pathways (or exits if you're spotted or are using it to attract the enemy's attention!). It also allows you to maneuver around the map much faster, especially on more vertical maps (Adrift, Abandon, etc.).

When moving off a lift or man cannon, turn on your Jet Pack to try some unique movement and routes. You'll fly off the lifts (especially the man cannons on Adrift), and you might be able to get a jump on an unsuspecting opponent.

The Jet Pack is also great for avoiding power weapons that use splash damage. It's nearly impossible to kill a Jet Pack user with a Rocket or Incineration Cannon, so if you see this weapon in your enemy's hands, take to the sky.

Counter Strategies: Take care, as when you use the Jet Pack, you're opening yourself up to several new angles from which your foes can fire at you, since you're wide open in the air. It's also fairly difficult to shoot while operating a Jet Pack. Only activate this armor ability with a purpose in mind, whether it's to move to a specific place or get a better angle on a fleeing foe. If you see a Jet Packing enemy moving around the map, simply drop them quickly; just keep in mind the foe might be a decoy in team matches.

PROMETHEAN VISION

Unlocked for purchase at Spartan Rank 3.

Good luck hiding now, enemy scum....

Basic Description: This allows users to detect enemy signatures through walls and other hard surfaces. When using Promethean Vision, you can see your enemies and across most maps, as the range is extremely long. You can also see grenades being thrown, turrets, and vehicles when using this vision.

When to Use: Promethean Vision is very useful in practically any situation. Use it to see where your opponent is hiding or from which direction grenades are being thrown at you. Knowing your enemy's exact location can often be half the battle, and it will help eliminate nasty surprises. You can even become the "spotter" for your teammates if the others don't have this ability equipped, identifying campers and people attempting to ambush you while holding a shotgun or Energy Sword..

Counter Strategies: The only counter to Promethean Vision is the Support Upgrade Stealth, which makes it very hard for your enemy to see you when you're using this ability. The enemy can also see on their Motion Sensor if you're using Promethean Vision, so they will probably know you are scanning them. Your opponent's controller also makes a small vibration when you turn on Promethean Vision, which makes them aware someone used it and is scanning the map. When activated, this armor ability makes a distinct sound to alert others in the area. Additionally, it creates a pulse on motion sensors and keeps the user constantly on the sensors until they shut the ability off. Promethean Vision also has a very long recharge time.

HALO 4

REGENERATION FIELD

Unlocked for purchase at Spartan Rank 16.

Basic Description: The Regeneration Field allows users to release a short-range energy field that heals any nearby Spartans. Your shields will not regenerate if you are getting shot, so you are still vulnerable while in the regeneration zone.

When to Use: This is very effective when used behind cover or as cover itself; hide behind it and let your shields recharge before poking back out to fight. Use this when you have teammates next to you to help them regain their shields as well. Also try staging a Regeneration Field outside of a room prior to a breach. This will allow you and your teammates to retreat if needed and quickly be ready for another engagement.

Did someone call for a medic?

Counter Strategies: If your opponent uses the Regeneration Field in the open with no cover, you can keep putting shots in them to constantly remove their shields and eventually kill them. Their shields won't recharge if shots are hitting them. If they're behind cover, you can focus on banking grenades into their Regen Field or simply wait it out—it won't last forever, and they can't hurt you from behind cover.

THRUSTER PACK

Unlocked for purchase at Spartan Rank 3.

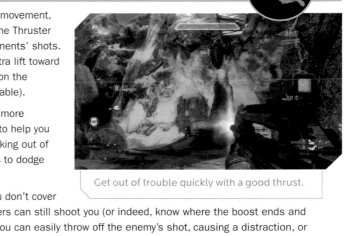

Basic Description: The Thruster Pack enables a powerful burst of movement, allowing you to evade or quickly close the gap. The advantage of the Thruster Pack is that you can use it in midair and really throw off your opponents' shots. Make sure you jump and mash the Crouch button to get a little extra lift toward your intended direction. If you simply use the Thruster Pack while on the ground to boost your speed, you won't go as far (but it's still advisable).

When to Use: Use the Thruster Pack to maneuver around corners more quickly, to grab a flag or ball with more speed than your foes, and to help you immensely during 1v1 battles. This ability is also excellent for backing out of fights that you might be losing. It is best used moving to the sides to dodge precision weapons and support weapons.

Get out of trouble quickly with a good thrust.

Counter Strategies: The downside to the Thruster Pack is that you don't cover a very long distance when you boost forward, so experienced players can still shoot you (or indeed, know where the boost ends and coincide their shots). However, when used properly with jumping, you can easily throw off the enemy's shot, causing a distraction, or get the small advantage over them that you need.

INTRODUCTION

BASIC TRAINING

INTEL

CAMPAIGN

INFINITY

APPENDIX

SUPPORT UPGRADES

Some of these upgrades will not be available via the standard unlock system, but rather via the Specialist system that was previously detailed. You can equip Support Upgrades in your loadouts beginning at Rank 12.

AMMO

Unlocked for purchase at Rank 12.

The Ammo upgrade gives you double the bullets to reload with for starting weapons and ordnance drops. For example, if you start with the DMR, instead of having 28 bullets to reload with, you have 56. For ordnance weapons, it will depend on which weapon you pick, but the weapon is still likely to have double (or close to double) the normal number of ammunition it usually drops with.

This is great to use if you plan on playing more of a support role and need the extra ammo for sitting back and helping your teammates; then you won't run out of ammo so quickly. Even power weapon retrieved from ordnance drops will start with more ammo. If you prefer to sit back and shoot a lot, this is a great upgrade to take with you.

AWARENESS

Unlocked for purchase at Rank 20.

This keeps your Motion Sensor on your screen when looking into a scope. Naturally, this is very useful in Free For All games, or if you plan on being a sniper for your team. If you're playing the role of the sniper and want to see your Motion Sensor while being scoped in the majority of the game, then take this Support Upgrade.

DEXTERITY

Unlocked for purchase at Rank 12.

This is one of the best Support Upgrades to have. It can be useful in any game type or map. It really speeds up your reload times and weapon swapping, cutting down on the seconds of downtime you have during the game.

Using Dexterity along with the Battle Rifle/Plasma Pistol combo is very effective since you can switch weapons so much faster. This allows for very fast reloads on all power weapons, which can really be devastating to the enemy when you are sniping, firing rockets, or utilizing any other power weapon that usually has a longer reload time. You will have very little downtime before shooting your next clip.

Having the ability to switch weapons quickly can also be very useful when using melee weapons like the sword so you can quickly pull it out to lunge at your enemy with amazing speed.

UPGRADE NAME	RANK UNLOCKED
Ammo	SR-12
Dexterity	SR-12
Awareness	SR-20
Sensor	SR-20
Explosives	SR-26
Ordnance Priority	SR-26
Drop Recon	Complete the Engineer Specialization
Nemesis	Complete the Stalker Specialization
Gunner	Complete the Pathfinder Specialization
Stealth	Complete the Wetwork Specialization
Stability	Complete the Rogue Specialization

DROP RECON

Unlocked after completing the Engineer Specialization.

Predict an ordnance drop before it happens.

Drop Recon allows the player to see the Waypoint at which a random ordnance drop will occur about 5 seconds before it actually drops into the map. Having a player on your team with Drop Recon enabled is important because it allows your team to know where to set up for the power weapons and gives you about 5 seconds to reach the location. Drop Recon increases your navpoint display range by 20%. Use on game types with random ordnance drops.

EXPLOSIVES

Unlocked for purchase at Rank 26.

This increases your grenade damage, and you receive a little less damage from enemy grenade detonations. Tournament-level players may wish to ignore this upgrade, since it offers only a very small difference in the offense damage a grenade inflicts and the damage you take, compared to normal. Grenades are devastating enough!

If you don't like dying by grenades, then this upgrade could be for you. However, grenades cause only a small percentage of the damage you take throughout a game, and it is not a big enough difference in damage to be very effective. However, this could be useful when paired with the Hardlight Shield or in game types where you'll likely be a sitting duck, such as Oddball or King of the Hill.

GUNNER

Unlocked after completing the Pathfinder Specialization.

Gunner: Turning the turret into a formidable weapon since the UNSC *Infinity* started simulations.

Gunner allows you to fire the Machine Gun and the Plasma Cannon without overheating, so long as they are mounted to their tripods. If you detach a turret from its mount, you suffer no penalty to your walking speed, you just can't sprint. This is recommended during Big Team Battle game types where there are more turrets to locate and detach. It's obviously useless for maps that lack turrets.

Your running speed is actually increased quite a bit. This helps you maneuver without being slow and easily dodged or cut down by foes. It also allows you to inflict major damage to the enemy if you run up on them with a detached turret (with the Gunner activated).

You're also able to dodge grenades much more competently due to your quicker movement, and you can stay alive longer to utilize the turret more effectively.

NEMESIS

Unlocked after completing the Stalker Specialization.

A righteous infliction of retribution manifested by an appropriate agent.

This places a mark on the person who killed you last for the next 4.5 seconds from the moment you respawn.

Having this in a close game or a "standoff" can be really useful, so you can pinpoint exactly where one of the players is on the opposing team. Then you can plan what you want to attempt with your team with a lot more forethought. If you are playing a 1v1, pick this upgrade.

ORDNANCE PRIORITY

Unlocked for purchase at Rank 26.

This upgrade adds a 40% bonus to the points earned towards an ordnance drop. This is useful only in Infinity Slayer or any other game type with actual ordnance drops.

In a large team game, it's good to have a few guys running with this upgrade in order to earn more drops for your team.

SENSOR

Unlocked for purchase at Rank 20.

This increases your Motion Sensor's range by about 20 meters. It is very useful in Free For All game types. If you're playing a game type that has the Motion Sensor on, this upgrade will usually give you the jump on your opponent.

You can also use this upgrade to avoid conflict, as you'll have a much clearer picture of the map as you choose how to navigate it. You can ensure you won't walk into areas where multiple enemies are waiting.

STABILITY

Unlocked after completing the Rogue Specialization.

Normally, when bullets strike you while you are scoped-in on a target, your aim is thrown off. Stability reduces this to a significant degree, making this an option for snipers having trouble with incoming fire. However, you still receive a reasonably hefty big whip upward when you are scoped in and being shot by a sniper rifle; however, it does help a little bit when you are out of scope and being shot at—the reticle only moves a little bit to the right.

This might be worth using if you are having trouble recovering from being shot at, but highly skilled players typically won't need this, as they can already readjust their aim to compensate for bullet fire.

STEALTH

Unlocked after completing the Wetwork Specialization.

Stealth is another Support Upgrade that you can use on any map or game type. It enhances you in three ways: It dampens your footsteps, it makes it a lot harder for your enemy to see you when they are scanning with Promethean Vision, and it increases you assassination speed.

A lot of players use headphones to hear player footsteps. Having this upgrade on can make you a lot sneakier when running around maps. This upgrade is the precise counter to Promethean Vision. When you have Stealth as your Support Upgrade, any enemies that have Promethean Vision won't be able to see where you are as easily, rendering their armor ability nearly useless! A lot of players are going to choose Promethean Vision, so this upgrade counters this well.

Having the faster assassination speed is a small bonus, as it only gives you a small amount of speed and is hardly even noticeable. Completing assassinations gives you more points, but you put yourself in a vulnerable position by going into the animation of the assassination. In fact, you could end up becoming the subsequent victim if another opponent sees you're prone during your kill!

TACTICAL PACKAGES

Tactical Packages can be added to your loadouts after Rank 7.

AA EFFICIENCY

Unlocked for purchase at Rank 14.

With this equipped, you can recharge your armor abilities more quickly so you can use them again if needed. If you tend to use your armor ability more frequently than normal, then this Tactical Package is ideal.

For best results, combine this type of package with armor abilities you use constantly, such as Promethean Vision, Hardlight Shield, and Regeneration Field. If you're playing a vertically oriented map, you may want to pair this with Jet Pack.

FAST TRACK

Unlocked after completing the Pioneer Specialization.

Do you want to level up your Spartan faster? This package will advance you in level more quickly, thus giving you access to more of the weapons, armor, armor abilities, and other accoutrements such as Emblems! You get this Tactical Package fairly late into the rank progression, which makes this more useful when trying to complete the various Specializations.

If all you do is win matches, then you're likely to rank up in no time, thus beating your teammates and rivals to all the fanciest upgrades!

FIREPOWER

Unlocked for purchase at Rank 24.

Pack heat with two primary weapons!

Firepower allows you to use a second primary weapon in your secondary weapon slot. For example, you can place a DMR as your primary weapon and a Battle Rifle as your secondary weapon.

This is a great package! As you're essentially getting two primary weapons, you receive a large amount of ammo for mid- to long-range shooting. This works especially well with big maps when you're constantly attempting long-range takedowns.

Also, if you're playing an objective game type, you can pick the Assault Rifle and Storm Rifle before trying to camp back at your base to kill opponents who go for your flag or objective.

UPGRADE NAME	RANK UNLOCKED
Mobility	SR-7
Shielding	SR-7
AA Efficiency	SR-14
Resupply	SR-14
Firepower	SR-24
Grenadier	SR-24
Fast Track	Complete the Pioneer Specialization
Requisition	Complete the Tracker Specialization
Wheelman	Complete the Operator Specialzation

GRENADIER

Unlocked for purchase at Rank 24.

This increases the amount of grenades you can hold by one. Grenadier also increases the number of grenades you spawn with. Although this might not seem like much, this is a huge advantage: It allows you to keep your enemy pushed back so they can't charge.

You can surprise a foe (who might have been counting the number of grenades you've thrown) with the extra grenade by popping their shields. Having this extra grenade may also become hugely advantageous for your team when making a push.

MOBILITY

Unlocked for purchase at Rank 7.

All my life...I've run so far away.

This is ideal for the offensive player who goes "heavy" and enjoys barging into enemy bases, as it grants you an unlimited sprint! Sprinting in all battles is obviously a key technique, mostly because it enables you to more quickly travel to and from bases or wherever your destination, and it works in any game type.

Are you the type of player who enjoys getting right back into the fight after losing a frantic battle, or do you just need to race to a location (such as to a flag or ball)? Then this is the Tactical Package for you.

All players begin with a sprint, but only Mobility allows you to continue your fast pushing toward completing an objective or reaching an area of ground that needs to be claimed. This may not be the optimal choice for some Slayer variants, as it can encourage you to become a little more reckless and enter into more battles (with a greater chance of deaths).

REQUISITION

Unlocked after completing the Tracker Specialization.

Requisition allows you to request a new ordnance drop when you have been granted one. This helps because sometimes you receive weapons or power-ups that the situation doesn't particularly call for. Instead, request a new drop; you receive three new choices to pick from. This also grants you a better chance to receive a power weapon.

Having this additional drop and choice of reward becomes very useful, as the power-ups granting you strength, speed, or shielding can help immensely later into a battle. By using Requisition, you're essentially doubling your chances of getting a power weapon that might turn the tide of the game.

RESUPPLY
Unlocked for purchase at Rank 14.

Just tell them you were looting their body, not victory crouching them.

In *Halo 4*, you can no longer pick up grenades from enemies to use for yourself, unless you have this package. With Resupply, you simply gather grenades from the dead bodies of foes and add them to your supply, up to your carrying maximum.

If you see bodies lying around, walk over to them and collect the grenades, if only to prevent others from using them. If you like to trash-talk with your enemies, you can mention you've killed your rival with his or her own grenades. That usually riles them up into making further mistakes!

SHIELDING

Unlocked for purchase at Rank 7.

This simply allows your shields to recharge at a faster rate than normal once they start recharging. If you prefer to be engaged in battle at all times, this will let you get back into the fight quickly.

An example of using this in battle would be when fighting an enemy, you may wish to stay alive and find cover. If a teammate shows up to help, you can return to the fray that much faster once your shields recharge at a more rapid rate.

Combine this with other defensive abilities, such as the Hardlight Shield. Shielding does not allow your shield to recharge while using the Hardlight Shield or while being shot while in a Regeneration Field. It also doesn't lower the time it takes for the shields to start, just the time it takes for them to recharge.

Use this to buy those few extra seconds so you can escape any battle you might be losing. When your shield starts recharging and shoots up faster than normal, return to combat if you can.

WHEELMAN

Unlocked after completing the Operator Specialization.

Get in: I'm driving.

Wheelman increases the long-term durability of your vehicle, by recharging health more quickly as well as how it reacts to EMP charges.

EMP charges will affect your vehicle for a shorter time when you get hit, thus making it easier to recover from it. Use this in a Big Team Battle where vehicles are utilized; otherwise there's little point in choosing this!

Wheelman is best used to gain that extra protection when you have the enemy flag, and you're riding in a vehicle (such as a Warthog or Mongoose), and there are other passengers protecting you.

275

VEHICLES

On the larger maps and more vehicle-focused game types, expect to drive or pilot any number of vehicles, both recognizable and new. The following data details the merits of each vehicle and how to employ them in the combat zone.

BANSHEE

The Banshee is a swift and agile airborne Covenant craft with twin plasma cannons and a formidable fuel rod cannon.

Don't forget to flip and barrel roll when making a quick escape.

Crew Capacity: 1 operator

Description: The Banshee continues to be the Covenant's primary aerial-engagement vehicle providing efficient ground support from above via its twin-linked plasma cannons and heavy fuel rod weapon. Despite its slight frame, the aircraft is surprisingly resilient in combat, largely due to its incredible maneuverability in atmosphere.

Tactical Notes

〉 Pilot a Banshee to claim air superiority across a map. The Banshee has a boost function and evasive-maneuver features (such as the barrel roll); employ any or all of these if you start to take heavy damage, and flee the immediate firefight quickly if the craft is becoming damaged.

〉 The Banshee is perfect for raking the enemy in covering fire while the rest of your team attempts to attack an enemy base or infiltrate a flag.

〉 The Banshee has two different firing weapons to toggle between (use the button that switches between your regular guns): a Plasma Cannon and Fuel Rod Cannon. The former is useful for spraying the battlefield and causing distracted foes to attack you. The latter is excellent for taking enemies out in a single explosion, if you can line up your bomb drop with accuracy.

〉 If combat takes a turn for the worse, you can also try flying in low and ramming into foes, splattering ground forces if the opportunity presents itself.

GHOST

The Ghost is the Covenant's dominant scouting vehicle: fast, mobile, and fully capable of engaging in direct combat with its twin-linked plasma cannons.

A nasty weapon with a crushing boost and a highly exposed driver. Ghost riding is dangerous but productive.

Crew Capacity: 1 operator

Description: The Ghost is the Covenant's dominant, single-manned scouting vehicle used for everything from deep reconnaissance and remote patrol to assault runs and convoy escort. A testament to its field effectiveness, the T-32 has remained largely unchanged for centuries, utilizing a single-mount rear-positioned seat, twin-linked plasma cannons, and excellent mobility, regardless of the terrain it finds itself deployed in.

Tactical Notes

〉 The Ghost is a very effective vehicle if you're trying to move to disparate locations on a map, as it can maneuver there quickly thanks to its boost feature. Besides being swift and adept at complex maneuvers, it can also be used to put pressure on the other team if used primarily as an offensive vehicle.

〉 The Ghost's weapon inflicts heavy damage on ground units and can tear through them very quickly. Try to force the enemy to jump when you're facing them down in a Ghost; next, hit your boost so you can slam into them as they drop down, and then mow them over.

〉 However, there's always the ever-present danger of being hijacked from an enemy ground unit you're stalking or one that you miss running over or gunning down.

〉 The only real downside to the Ghost is that you're highly exposed; the enemy can take the driver out from a distance, usually with mid- or long-range weapons. This can be done without damaging the vehicle itself, so the Ghost can be commandeered by enemy troops afterward.

MANTIS

The Mantis is a highly classified armor defense system with incredible Firepower and dexterity, despite its impressive size.

Mantis ground stomp.

Crew Capacity: 1 operator

Description: The Mantis is the result of half a century's worth of development and iteration, eventually culminating in an incredibly powerful armor system without equal. Utilizing an ultra-heavy four-barrel machine gun on one arm and a viciously potent multilaunch, high-explosive munitions launcher on the other, the Mark IX is an extremely competent arsenal and is currently employed only by the UNSC *Infinity* and several highly classified ONI teams.

Tactical Notes

〉 This impressive mech is mainly used to dominate a map: It brings formidable offensive capabilities, including missiles, a turret, and a stomping ability. You're able to charge up to five missiles with the left trigger and continuously use the turret with the right trigger for around five seconds until the turret overheats.

〉 Boarding a Mantis takes around four to five seconds before you can control the vehicle. This lengthy mounting time can lead to a large window of opportunity for enemies to fire at you, killing you before you can even take control. Be sure you have covering fire or no nearby foes before entering this vehicle.

〉 Enemies can hijack you from the rear. Fortunately, once inside the Mantis's cockpit, you're completely covered, so you don't need to worry about being picked off by snipers.

〉 The Mantis can crouch, allowing for some amusing (and possibly offensive) postures. If an enemy moves close to the Mantis your piloting's feet, use the stomping ability to take them out instantly.

〉 Aside from the Mantis's eventual explosive destruction, your only threat is the Firepower from Scorpion Tanks and Incineration Cannons; these can destroy a Mantis very quickly.

MONGOOSE

The Mongoose is a light all-terrain vehicle used to carry personnel and equipment swiftly through wildly varied terrain.

The Mongoose is great for quick getaways and exceptional jumps.

Crew Capacity: 1 driver + 1 passenger

Description: The Mongoose is a light all-terrain vehicle used almost exclusively for the transportation of personnel and materiel. However, when rear-positioned passengers are well armed, this vehicle can become particularly formidable in combat, balancing the ATV's speed and maneuverability with the passenger's Firepower.

Tactical Notes

〉 The Mongoose is mainly used to reach locations and transport teammates quickly around a map. To turn corners with greater precision, use the left trigger to stop the movement of your back wheels and drift. Also remember to press your Right Bumper to hit your brake and stop on a dime.

〉 One great way to utilize a Mongoose is to pick up your flag carrier for a swift route back to your own base to score.

〉 The Mongoose has a horn; use it by pressing the right trigger (default controls), and employ it so your teammates know when to mount the vehicle you're driving.

〉 You're very vulnerable in this vehicle because you're exposed at all angles from the driver's seat. It's also easy for your foes to hijack the Mongoose, pushing you out of the vehicle.

〉 Are you transporting a teammate without a flag? Then be sure your friend is attacking from the rear of the vehicle instead of resting!

INTRODUCTION

BASIC TRAINING

INTEL

CAMPAIGN

INFINITY

APPENDIX

SCORPION

The Scorpion is an impressive main battle tank that hefts a 90 mm primary cannon and an anti-infantry heavy machine gun.

Out of explosive weapons? Snipe off the hatch and pick off the driver to stop this menacing tank.

Crew Capacity: 1 operator, 1 gunner, 4 passengers

Description: The M808 Scorpion is easily the UNSC's most prominent main battle tank, offering impressive Firepower and effective anti-infantry suppression as well as substantial resiliency and maneuverability in the field. The Scorpion is usually deployed during asymmetric ground assaults, within escort convoys, or in any circumstance that requires heavy and mobile armor.

Tactical Notes

〉 The Scorpion is mainly used for dominating the map, mopping up enemies and obtaining quick takedowns with use of its primary cannon and anti-infantry machine gun.

〉 The driver can fire off a rocket with a cool down period of around two and a half seconds between firings.

〉 Be sure a teammate has hopped onto the Machine Gun turret to increase the vehicle's Firepower capabilities. This gun turret has a reticle bloom when shot, so watch your aiming. However, it can be fired for a while before it overheats. The only real drawback is that the turret gunner is extremely exposed.

〉 When facing down a Scorpion, if you haven't obtained a Spartan Laser, Rocket Launcher, or an Incineration Cannon, shoot the cockpit hatch off, exposing the driver's head and then execute him with a headshot. Try having a sniper remove the door with two Sniper Rifle shots, and then eliminate the driver with the third shot.

〉 Both the back of the tank and the driver's door can be hijacked.

WARTHOG (GAUSS, ROCKET, MACHINE GUN)

The Warthog is the UNSC's standard ground transport and is capable of mounting both anti-air and anti-armor weapon systems.

Board the Warthog and be ready to dominate!

Crew Capacity: 1 driver, 1 passenger, 1 gunner

Description: The Warthog is the UNSC's primary ground transportation vehicle, offering several variants typically differentiated by their bed-mounted weapon systems. Although some Warthogs are designed solely for transportation, most offer extremely versatile anti-aircraft or anti-armor options, which optimize the vehicles' light armor and deft mobility.

Tactical Notes

〉 This vehicle is mainly used to transport teammates, inflict damage, and rack up kills with the turret-mounted weapon.

〉 The Warthog comes in three variants: with a Machine Gun, Gauss Cannon, or Rocket Launcher.

〉 The "Rocket Hog" has a launcher on the back turret that shoots six rockets, with only a couple of seconds' cooldown between the shots. This is excellent for taking down vehicles or lone enemies.

〉 The "Gauss Hog" has a cannon that's primarily used to take out vehicles but can kill lone enemies as well; each gauss strike requires around a two-second cooldown between shots.

〉 Just like the Mongoose, the Warthog has the same ability to drift, has a horn, and has similar brake functionality, so employ similar tactics when using them.

〉 The Warthog is slower than the Mongoose, leading to some dangerous situations: Although you have more cover in a Warthog (in comparison to a Mongoose), enemies armed with Spartan Lasers or Incineration Cannons have an easy time picking off this target.

〉 It's time to exit a Warthog when the engine catches fire and the interior begins to flash red; this indicates that the Warthog is dangerous low on health. If a Warthog is abandoned in this state, it will explode around seven to eight seconds later.

〉 You're able to hijack all three seats—the driver, side seat, and gunner—and all lead to confusion if the enemy tries this plan! For some amusing moments, hijack a Warthog's gun while an opposing team's driver is in control.

WRAITH

The Wraith is the Covenant's primary armor, a highly mobile mortar tank with a separately manned anti-infantry cannon.

The Wraith is adept at lobbing shots in from a distance and keeping a team contained on large maps.

Crew Capacity: 1 operator, 1 gunner

Description: The Wraith is a large, heavily armored Covenant mortar tank designed to assault enemy fortifications with unrelenting brutality while maintaining relative safety due to its anti-infantry plasma cannon. Powered by a boosted gravity drive, the vehicle is capable of charging forward in impressive bursts of speed. The Wraith's primary weapon is its heavy plasma mortar, which lobs highly explosive, concentrated plasma in a parabolic arc, resolving most human battle tanks' problematic line of sight requirement.

Tactical Notes

> This slick battle tank is more mobile than the Scorpion but fires at a slower rate.

> The Wraith's main cannon offers strong Firepower and is very useful for bombarding the enemy from a long distance.

> It is advisable to have a teammate jump into the front turret, helping to stop ground units from reaching you as you career across a map.

> Without someone inside the turret, try the vehicle's boost function; it becomes handy, as you can run foes over at high speed and slay them.

> The biggest concern for a Wraith driver are ground units sneaking around and hijacking the vehicle from the sides or rear; otherwise the vehicle is almost indestructible unless it's facing a battle with a Scorpion, Mantis, or Banshee.

WAR GAMES

WELCOME TO WAR GAMES

Whether you've mastered the Campaign on Legendary difficulty and are craving some Spartan vs. Spartan combat or you're anxious to begin your multiplayer experience immediately, in War Games you can expect a plethora of new features, game types, and maps to continuously hone your battle tactics aboard the UNSC *Infinity*.

The following information is presented to ensure you receive the maximum tactical advantage in the combat zone. After reading the overview and the advice regarding your career path and weapon loadouts, choose a controller setting. Every weapon is covered as well as every armor ability, tactical package, and support upgrade. We provide copious details on every game type and offer a full debriefing on all of the War Games maps.

> **◐ Note**
>
> The following advice is an collection of information, gathered from months of on-site matches. We offer strategy gathered from top MLG players and experts from 343 Industries. The result is unmatched strategy designed to give you every advantage.

TIPS AND STRATEGIES – STRAIGHT FROM THE MLG PROS

The War Games portion of this guide was produced in collaboration with Major League Gaming (MLG), the world's largest eSports organization. MLG sent four of the most talented Halo players in MLG history to 343 Industries to deliver in-depth tips and strategies on every map and game type. By following the advice in this guide, direct from MLG and the world's best players, you'll be a hometown hero in no time.

> MORE ABOUT THE MLG PROS

The four players who provided the information for this guide don't just play Halo – they live Halo. Between them, they've spent more than 20 years competing in professional Halo tournaments, winning thousands of dollars in prize money along the way. If you want to know exactly how to dominate the competition, these guys have got you covered. Before you dive into the wealth of strategies contained in this guide, get to know the guys who wrote them:

STRONGSIDE

Name: Michael "StrongSide" Cavanaugh

Age: 24
From: Kentucky
Professional Player since: 2006
Favorite Game Type: Team Oddball
Favorite Map: Haven
Favorite Starting Weapon: DMR
Favorite Power Weapon: Binary Rifle

FAVORITE LOADOUT:
Primary Weapon: DMR
Secondary Weapon: Battle Rifle
Grenade: Frag Grenade
Armor Ability: Promethean Vision
Tactical Package: Firepower
Support Upgrade: Stability/AA efficiency

CONTROLLER SETTINGS:
Buttons: Bumper Jumper
Sticks: Regular
Inversion: Not Inverted
Sensitivity: 3
Crouch: Hold to crouch
Vibration: On
Claw or Not: Not

NOTABLE GAMING ACCOMPLISHMENTS:

> 1st place MLG 2007 National Championship(Halo2). Team did not lose a single game in the tournament.
> 1st place BIC Pro FFA MLG 2011
> 29 top 4 finishes at MLG tournaments
> 8 First Place finishes at MLG Championships
> 14 First Place finishes at major tournaments around the world
> Invented the "StrongSide" move

BIO:

Michael "StrongSide" Cavanaugh has been a professional Major League Gaming Halo player since July 2005. He has won 8 MLG tournaments including a National Championship where his team (Final Boss) did not lose a single game. Cavanaugh was the 13th player to be signed to a $250,000 contract by MLG. He has won countless other gaming events over the years throughout the US, Canada, Mexico, and the United Kingdom. StrongSide has had an extremely successful professional gaming career. He is a fan favorite and has emerged as one of the most dominant players in Major League Gaming and the Halo series. Cavanaugh made a name for himself in the Free For All (FFA) and 1v1 competitions. Within his first year of making an appearance in the Major League Gaming community he took first place in FFA and 1v1 at MLG Chicago 2005. He had a move named after him because he is so good at getting away and staying alive.

FLAMESWORD

Name: Michael (Mike) "Flamesword" Chaves

Age: 22
From: New Jersey
Professional Player since: 2009
Favorite Game Type: Team Regicide
Favorite Map: Haven
Favorite Starting Weapon: Battle Rifle
Favorite Power Weapon: Railgun

FAVORITE LOADOUT
Primary Weapon: Battle Rifle
Secondary Weapon: DMR
Grenade: Frag Grenade
Armor Ability: Jet Pack
Tactical Package: Firepower
Support Upgrade: Ammo

CONTROLLER SETTINGS
Buttons: Recon
Sticks: Default
Inversion: Default
Sensitivity: 4
Crouch: Hold to crouch
Vibration: No vibration
Claw or Not: Claw

NOTABLE GAMING ACCOMPLISHMENTS
> 2nd Place at 2010 MLG Dallas National Championships (*Halo 3*)
> 1st Place at 2011 MLG Dallas Championships (*Halo: Reach*)
> 1st Place at 2012 MLG Columbus Winter Championships (*Halo: Reach*)
> 1st Place at 2012 Arena Gaming Chicago (*Halo: Reach*)
> Voted 2010 Strides Pros' Choice Award for Best Leader
> Voted 2011 Strides Pros' Choice Award for Best Strategist

BIO:

After more than three years of working his way up the pro ranks, Mike Chaves is one of Major League Gaming's hottest players. A natural leader, after founding the Status Quo team in 2008, the player known as "Flamesword" steadily honed his own skills and put together a roster of teammates that gelled to capture *Halo 3* runner-up honors at the 2010 MLG Nationals. Then SQ elevated that momentum – and showed their versatility – by winning the first tournament of the 2011 season, which was also MLG's first-ever *Halo: Reach* event and the first tournament of the 2012 season with the new implementation of Zero Bloom to *Halo: Reach*.

Mike's story proves that a nice guy really can finish first –he believes in hard work and pursues excellence in everything he does. Winner of the 2010 Stride Pro Choice Best Team Leader Award, he's in the sport for the long haul and hopes that someday his name and reputation will be almost synonymous with Major League Gaming itself. Status Quo's organizer, top communicator, and all-around "big brother," Mike/Flamesword is taking a lead role not only for his team, but for the popularity of this fast-growing professional sport. In the meantime, Flamesword and "the Quo" have a hunger to win, and to prove that their initial successes are only a harbinger of greatness to come.

ELUMNITE

Name: Marcus "Elumnite" Lovejoy

Age: 24
From: Atlanta, GA
Professional Player since: 2008
Favorite Game Type: FFA Regicide
Favorite Map: Haven
Favorite Starting Weapon: Battle Rifle
Favorite Power Weapon: Sniper Rifle

FAVORITE LOADOUT:
Primary Weapon: Battle Rifle
Secondary Weapon: Plasma Pistol
Grenade: Frag Grenade
Armor Ability: Thruster Pack
Tactical Package: Mobility
Support Upgrade: Dexterity

CONTROLLER SETTINGS
Buttons: Bumper Jumper
Sticks: Default
Inversion: Not Inverted
Sensitivity: 4 Sens
Crouch: Hold to Crouch
Vibration: No Vibe
Claw or Not: Claw

NOTABLE GAMING ACCOMPLISHMENTS:
> Held MLG Pro Status for 4 years
> Only pro player from Atlanta for two years. (*Halo 3*)
> 22nd Place at MLG Orlando 2007 Pro FFA (*Halo 2*)
> Won the MLG Boost Mobile 1v1 *Halo 2* Sponsorship to go to Las Vegas
> Placed top 16 in 2007 MLG Vegas Nationals 4v4 (*Halo 2*)
> Multi top 16, and top 12 placings at MLG tournaments.(*Halo 3*)
> Back to Back top 8 placings at MLG tournaments *Halo: Reach*

BIO:

Marcus started gaming back when Sega Genesis was first released in 1989 and has been hooked ever since. Marcus realized that his individual playing skills were superior in comparison to friends and family.

Marcus found his love of first-person shooters when GoldenEye 007 was released in 1997. As the years passed, Marcus took his gaming skills to a more competitive level. He had to be better than people he played against and it wasn't limited to first person shooters, it was in fighting games too! Like Mortal Kombat, SoulCalibur, Marvel vs Capcom, just to name a few. His favorite of all the arcade games was Soul Calibur and his dad would have to drag him out of the arcade!

NADED

Name: Brett "Naded" Leonard

Age: 22
From: Bay Area of California
Professional Player since: 2005
Favorite Game Type: Team Oddball
Favorite Map: Abandon
Favorite Starting Weapon: Battle Rifle
Favorite Power Weapon: Sniper Rifle

FAVORITE LOADOUT:
Primary Weapon: Battle Rifle
Secondary Weapon: Boltshot
Grenade: Frag Grenade
Armor Ability: Promethean Vision
Tactical Package: Mobility
Support Upgrade: Drop Recon

CONTROLLER SETTINGS:
Buttons: Recon
Sticks: Default
Inversion: Not Inverted
Sensitivity: 3-4 sensitivity
Crouch: Hold to Crouch
Vibration: No Vibration
Claw or Not: Claw

NOTABLE HALO ACCOMPLISHMENTS:

> 9 top 3 4v4 placings in MLG tournaments for all Halo games
> 23 top 8 4v4 placings in MLG tournaments for all Halo games
> Top FFA/1v1 *Halo 2* player
> Stride Gum 2009 Player of the Year

BIO:

Brett "Naded" Leonard broke into the Halo scene in 2005 competing at his first MLG tournament for *Halo 2*. Ever since then he has competed in over 40 events placing in the top 3 numerous times in 4v4, free for all, and 1v1 tournaments in *Halo 2*, *Halo 3*, and *Halo: Reach*. Naded has been one of the top matchmaking players, having a level 50 in 2 playlists in *Halo 2* and a level 50 in every playlist in *Halo 3* while racking up countless hours of playtime. Naded is regarded as one of the most passionate Halo players of all time, playing with extreme intensity and emotion, especially during tournament play. He is known for his incredible slaying ability with all weapons, top of the line communication, as well as great leadership and teamwork skills.

More About MLG

Major League Gaming (MLG) (www.majorleaguegaming.com) is the world's largest eSports organization with millions of LIVE viewers, fans and competitors around the globe. MLG enables gamers to compete, improve their skills, and socialize through Gamebattles.com (www.gamebattles.com), the largest online destination for competitive console and PC gaming featuring more than 8 million registered gamers, and the annual MLG Pro Circuit featuring LIVE, in-person tournaments in cities nationwide. MLG broadcasts competitive play, analysis and more via online streaming to hundreds of thousands of fans in an average of more than 170 countries. The 2012 MLG Pro Circuit Spring Championship shattered records reaching more than 4.7 million unique online viewers over the weekend and 2.2 million unique viewers on Championship Sunday with more male 18-24 year old viewers than the 2012 Rose Bowl.

The first Halo game, *Halo: Combat Evolved*, was the inspiration for the league and the Halo franchise has been featured on the MLG Pro Circuit since the first tournaments in 2003. More than 1500 Halo players competed at the MLG Winter Championship in March 2012. Throughout the history of the league, pro players and amateurs alike have competed playing Halo games at MLG events for more than $4.2 Million in prize money.

Looking to take your game to the next level?

MLG's GameBattles.com is the ultimate place to play competitive Halo. Set up a team with your friends and compete in meaningful matches against opponents from all over the country from the comfort of your living room. There are ladders, tournaments, and more! As you get better as a player, you'll take on better and better competition in official MLG game types, allowing you to steadily improve as a player.

MATCHMAKING AND CUSTOM GAMES

The entirety of the *Halo 4* War Games experience is basically divided into two types of matches: Matchmaking and Custom Games. We guide you through them both.

> MATCHMAKING

Locate your fellow Spartans and join (or fight against) them as part of the Matchmaking system.

For those with previous *Halo* experience, the Matchmaking system follows the same concept (it functions very similarly to how it did in *Halo: Reach*). However, it is important to note several distinct changes.

The basic idea of Matchmaking is to partner players up into games using skill and network quality information to try and provide consistently entertaining and challenging game matches.

Halo 4 does away with the idea of splitting Matchmaking between ranked and social playlists. All play in Matchmaking contributes behind-the-scenes to your skill rating, and all gameplay contributes to ranking up your Spartan and unlocking new weapons, abilities, and more.

One key difference between *Halo 4* and previous games is that playlists are now much more focused on individual game types and less packed with poorly understood variants. Voting centers around map choices only. A few playlists still contain multiple game types for variety, but the majority are composed of single gameplay experiences across many maps.

Voting has been changed slightly, in that player votes now lock in. You cannot change your vote after you cast it. This reduces the amount of "gaming the vote" that takes place in the lobbies of previous games, as people quickly switch votes at the last minute.

"Join in Progress" is arguably the biggest Matchmaking update. You can now get matched into games that are already under way and that have open slots. You can also directly join friends and jump right into their game without waiting, if there's an open slot.

There are many different playlists, which are being constantly updated after the game's launch. Consult your Matchmaking menu in-game to see what the latest available options are.

For more information on upcoming playlists and other Matchmaking adjustments, go to halowaypoint.com.

> CUSTOM GAMES

Creating custom matches is a key part of War Games, and it works in precisely the same way as it did in previous *Halo* games. Play custom games with your friends, and make your own rules! There are loads of options, all listed below. Gained experience is reduced in Custom Games to keep players from trying to gain experience to the detriment of skill.

Custom Game Settings: A Brief Synopsis

All game types include the score to win the game, a time limit, lives per round, number of rounds, and if teams are on/off.

Depending on which game type you are editing, there are special options for that specific game type.

General settings include friendly fire, betrayal booting, team changing, map loadouts, loadout usage, vehicle set, and indestructible vehicles.

Respawn settings allow you to change the respawn time, suicide penalty, betrayal penalty, and death camp and allow you to synchronize with the team.

Ordnance settings let you change the initial ordnance, random ordnance, ordnance substitutions, personal ordnance, point requirement, point increase multiplier, and objective ordnance.

Last are the traits of the base player, respawn, and leader. Here you have so many more options; you can customize shields and health, weapons and damage, equipment, movement, and appearance of all players.

Be sure to play around with all the settings, creating your own amazing game type variants to put in your file share!

WAR GAMES: A TACTICAL PRIMER

You may be eager to show your prowess among your fellow Spartan-IVs and rank up as swiftly as possible. You may have only limited knowledge of *Halo* and feel intimidated about facing off against others in a cruel and fast-paced training simulation. Whatever your level of skill, you'll find this overview of general tactics to be invaluable in improving your abilities.

> INTRODUCTION: LEXICON

Throughout this guide, you'll likely run into some terms you may not be familiar with. Here's a quick rundown of some of these phrases and how to accomplish the maneuvers listed.

Peek Shooting

This technique is when a player uses a wall to peek in and out while shooting and timing those shots. It makes it difficult for an opponent to get solid hits on you. Timing the movement and shooting at the right time is the key; don't make the timing easy for the person shooting you.

Pushing

This is the action of moving forward to secure a map position or an objective, usually as a team. Do this only when a member of the other team is down/dead and you are trying to get power positions or set up around a map. You normally want to push with a teammate to ensure control of an area.

Juking

A juke is a movement that surprises the opponent, whether it's getting behind them, popping out where they don't expect you, or getting away by using a tricky route. This happens when one player loses the other in a 1v1 battle. The player with the weaker shield outsmarts the other player to buy himself time to recover shield and then kill his opponent, or he has a teammate come help him. During the juking, he ether kills his opponent or stays alive. Juking can also refer to a sudden side-to-side movement similar to strafing that is used to trick your opponent and give you a moment to recuperate from an attack.

INTRODUCTION   BASIC TRAINING   INTEL   CAMPAIGN   INFINITY   APPENDIX

Flanking

A flank occurs when a player moves in on a preoccupied enemy from the side or the rear, while his teammates engage from the front. One player from a team gets behind the team that has control of his base: He then comes around from the base of the other team, just as his own team is spawning, and cleans up weakened players who are fighting against his teammates.

Getting the Jump

Getting the jump is anything that gives you an advantage in a fight. This is typically done by getting the first shot on your opponent or approaching from an advantageous position.

Baiting

Think of this maneuver like fishing. You want to tempt the opponent with a lure, whether it's a seemingly free kill, a weapon, or even a vehicle. Once the opponent takes the bait, you (and hopefully other members of your team) swoop in for the kill.

Execute a bait when two or more team members don't know exactly where enemies are in an area. Instead of the whole team pushing in the same area, one player engages the enemy first while the others stay back but not too far away. The second player follows the first, staying just close enough to pop out and help at any time. When executed correctly, this can be extremely helpful, as both players tend to stay alive and know where the enemy is.

Hot Spots

Hot spots, also known as choke points, are locations on maps where there's a lot of traffic from players and enemies. Players around these areas need to remain in control, both of the physical location and of any weapons in the area. Setting up different angles of fire to cover hot spots is also recommended. The Maps section of this guide details every hot spot to help you understand how a map breaks down. Each hot spot has a nickname as well, so experienced teams can call out hot spots out and quickly know what's going on across an entire map without even looking.

Power Positions

These refer to high ground or otherwise advantageous positions where, once you have control, it becomes extremely difficult for the other team to regain. These locations are usually great places for a sniper because of the excellent vantage points. Use power positions to pick off enemies when they're spawning at their base. Knowing how to guard a power position and take one back from the enemy is one of the most important keys to improving as a *Halo* player.

Nading

Short for "grenading," this technique involves lobbing a grenade and can be used offensively or defensively. You can nade a spawn point to ensure that the opposition does not spawn in that particular area. You can also nade to keep a player from pushing up from their base or buy some time for your shields to recover.

Wall Shooting

This is the technique of using cover to protect as much of your body while shooting as possible. Use the wall to increase the accuracy of your shots and make it hard for the other player to get a good angle on you. This is advantageous for sniping; visualize a mental "box" of the area where you should be aiming, making it easier to get a hit on your foe, preferably a headshot.

Turtling Up

When teams get an early lead they may try to focus entirely on defense, 'turtling up' in their base or fortified location in an effort to minimize losses (like a turtle recoiling into its shell for protection). This can happen in Slayer game types, but it is most common in objective-based game types like Capture the Flag or Oddball, where teams get points based on maintaining an objective. Turtling up is extremely effective when done properly.

> PART 1: TEAMWORK

Teamwork is essential in *Halo*. Of course, there are Free For All game types such as Regicide and Rumble Pit, but even these game types are designed to increase your individual skills to help you prepare for team games: These are at the core of *Halo*, the famous rivalry between Red vs. Blue. Teamwork isn't that hard to put into practice and synchronize with your teammates; you just have to follow certain plans, and in no time you'll be competing with the best.

Now that we've established that your game improves when your teamwork is more proficient, it's time to learn two of the most important team skills to possess: the ability to communicate properly and the ability to roam the map with one or more teammates.

Proper Communication: Cut the Chatter!

Yelling anything except quick and precise information lessens the impact of your teamwork.

Arguably the most important aspect of teamwork is communicating with one another. Just because you talk a lot while you play doesn't make you a great communicator; in fact, you actually might be causing a lot of sound clutter. Being a good team communicator means knowing how to be precise with everything you say and knowing the callouts (or "hot spots" or "choke points") of the maps. When playing team games, you always want to remind your teammates to stay alive by literally saying "stay alive." This may seem obvious, but reminding your friends to give you or your other teammates a chance to help them keeps your team intact and stronger for longer.

Callouts in a competetive environment should be as terse as possible, while communicating important information such as, "No shields, on my X!"

Two other key phrases to use in team games are "I got your help" and "you got no help." Just like when you tell your teammate to "stay alive," these phrases give them a better understanding of their situations. If you tell your teammate that "he has no help," he should then avoid getting into a dangerous battle and should concentrate on using his surroundings to distract foes until the team comes to help him.

Saying "you got help" lets your teammate know he can try an aggressive move, because you or another teammate will cover his back. Utilizing these (or similar) phrases helps you communicate correctly. In short, try to have a friendly (but minimal) conversation with the people you are playing with once the match starts.

Roaming the Map: The Buddy System

Running around with a teammate is the quickest way to improve your kill/death ratio.

Once you have your communication down, you must be able to proficiently and effectively roam around every map with a teammate or two. Many pro gamers call this the "buddy system." Communication is important in the buddy system, because in a lot of team games, you want to approach many situations with a teammate. Communication plays a big part in the buddy system, as the player at the back of the pack informs the players at the front to stay alive, tells them if they have help or not, and plans "bait-and-switch" plays.

Bait-and-switch plays or moves usually occur when the player at the front of the group engages the enemy in battle and then attempts to traverse an escape route. The lead player's job is to distract the enemies into shooting and chasing them down. As this occurs, your teammate(s) either jump the enemy chasers from behind or leap from a location along the escape route (sometimes before the lead player reaches his location). Jumping in from where the lead player is escaping to is a great way to confuse the enemy, as they aren't usually expecting opposing teammates (or the lead player) to attack them when running away. Naturally, the lead player's teammate(s) are waiting along the escape route and have planned this ambush!

The buddy system doesn't only involve moving side by side with a teammate: Working together at opposite ends of a map is beneficial to your team games, too. If one of your teammates has a long-range (sniping) weapon, you (as lead player) need to sync up with him and enable your sniper to focus on watching your back. The lead player's job in this case is to prepare for the enemy to jump out into the open and possibly damage you as you engage them, coaxing your foe(s) into an open area where your sniper can take a clean (or easier) shot on a foe you're already weakening. Expect to take damage as you wait for your sniper to finish the job.

Being selfless is the key to successful teamwork. Don't worry if you die: This is the norm, especially if you're the lead player, out in the open, preparing to sacrifice yourself in a worst-case scenario so that (hopefully) your team can earn multiple kills in exchange for your life, which ends up benefiting the team rather than simply yourself. Even if you're taken down, it's worth it if your death results in an objective achieved for your team.

To perfect your communications and roaming, you want to know the callouts of the different parts of each map so you can use precise communication with your team. Additionally, when you are communicating with your team, try to speak naturally, like you're having a normal and friendly conversation. Once you learn the map and general callouts and communication, slowly apply it to the buddy system as you roam the map with your teammates.

In short, everyone on your team needs to know where everyone else is (both friends and foes), with minimum chatter.

> **Note**

We've provided names for all of the 'hot spots' for every map and they are shown later in this guide. Simply use the names chosen or make up your own for each location within a map.

> PART 2: MOVEMENT

It may seem obvious, but movement is defined as how you maneuver around a map. The way you move leads you to win more games if you're in the right places at the right times. This section focuses on how to reach these locations, and when.

Offensive and Defensive Moves

If you're trained in strafing, crouching, and jumping, your movement becomes more elusive and cunning.

Movement can be used as an offensive or a defensive tactic. Types of movement, such as strafing, crouching, and jumping, are offensive maneuvers or tactics, as they all help you win 1v1 battles. Combining these movements causes your foe to miss shots and lets you get kills. Types of movement such as looking downward while running away, making difficult jumps, and sprinting are more defensive in nature, as they help you flee from foes shooting you in the back; this takes away kills from your enemy and helps you stay alive.

Movement in *Halo 4* is much different than it was in *Halo: Reach*. The movement in *Halo 4* is geared toward *Halo 2* and *3* style maneuvering, such as higher and "floatier" jumping. However, added elements like sprint and the upgrades detailed in this guide also change how you move around a map too. This results in an excellent blend of balanced gameplay with an updated feel.

Movement and Firing

Can you move and aim properly with your controller thumbsticks? Then stay away from play!

Movement helps you improve your aim, which in turn leads to more kills. Aiming your shots with your left and right thumbstick makes it easier to hit, rather than just using your right thumbstick. By moving with your opponent, you can keep your shot lined up horizontally, enabling you to fine-tune your aim with your right thumbstick.

Making adept movements while you shoot is key to connecting on every shot you can. Bad movement can lead to uncomfortable situations and allow you to take much harder shots than necessary. The more you play, the more you will understand how important movement is: It is the key to connecting with as many shots as you can with any of the weapons.

Aiming

When aiming at your opponent, target his chest/body and work your way to his head to finish him off with a headshot. However, every Spartan in *Halo 4* has a hit box (an invisible box that inflicts damage when struck by a projectile) set up slightly differently than in past *Halo* games. The hit box for a Spartan's head/helmet is bigger and goes above and around the helmet, so even if your aim is just a bit above the helmet, it usually still counts as a headshot. This changes the way you can aim/shoot at your enemy: You have a bigger hit box to shoot your opponent in the head. Once you get a feel for this "invisible box" and how much extra area you have to aim at, shooting your enemy in the head and sniping becomes much easier.

Strafing

Strafing is an important basic skill to learn. Strafing can be as simple as moving to the side while keeping your weapon trained on the enemy. More advanced techniques involve jumping, or repeatedly crouching and standing while you strafe. This affects your movement speed and your overall target profile, which can help you survive a firefight that might otherwise end poorly for you. Strafing is a technique that requires practice: The more you attempt to strafe, the more you'll understand which directions you need to move so your opponent misses shots. Being really unpredictable is the most effective strategy, so using all the options you have (i.e., jumping, crouching, moving) makes it more difficult for your opponent to kill you. This is the entire reason for strafing.

> ◯ Note
>
> For more information on what happens when mashing the Crouch button, consult the Crouching section.

Jumping

Jump to reach vantage points and make yourself more difficult to hit.

Completing difficult jumps allows for some impressive escapes and enables you to travel around a map more quickly. Start up a custom game on your own and locate all of the routes and jumps on every map: This tremendously improves your map movement and general dexterity. Every map usually has a few key jumps and secret spots you can hide in; knowing them all allows you more options or routes to take, enabling faster travel around the area. You can reach teammates faster to assist them or use jumps to get away from danger once you've mastered where and when to jump.

Crouching

Crouch walking—the technique of moving while crouching—is imperative when you're playing game types that have Motion Sensor, as you don't appear while in this position. This increases the frequency at which you fire first on your enemy. You can also use crouching to try and make opponents miss shots. For example, if you are fighting a sniper and you're predicting he is about to try for a headshot on you, hitting the Crouch button sometimes makes him miss the shot. In another example, you can mash the Crouch button while jumping into the air; this causes your Spartan to make more of a "bobbing" motion rather than a smooth jump. Try this and your foe sometimes misses shots.

As previously mentioned, strafing and crouching at the same time allows for some unorthodox movements: Strafe left and right while simultaneously mashing Crouch. Your Spartan bobs his head up and down while moving quickly left and right. This can really throw off your foe's aim if you use it at the right time! Also use crouch to duck behind low cover that normally exposes you if you were standing up, and you can use it to peek up and down behind walls (while taking down foes); this is a great way to surprise opponents.

Sprinting

Sprinting has seen some changes in *Halo 4* that are important to recognize. For starters, every player starts with the ability to sprint. Previously in *Halo: Reach*, you needed to equip a specific item to be able to sprint. Another change is that being shot while sprinting causes you to slow down, while previously you were able to sprint through incoming fire without missing a step. Naturally, these changes may take some getting used to!

Sprinting remains a good way to evade enemy fire, or help extend jump distances to take shortcuts to help attack from unexpected positions, or escape enemy pursuers through routes they are unwilling to take. You are able to sprint for five seconds before needing to take a three second break to catch your breath.

INTRODUCTION BASIC TRAINING INTEL CAMPAIGN INFINITY APPENDIX

Movement-Related Upgrades

The Tactical Package "Mobility" and the Support Upgrade "Gunner" are the two perks that affect player movement. Mobility allows you to sprint forever, and Gunner allows you to move quicker when holding a detached turret. Mobility is definitely a recommended perk to try because you never have to worry about running out of sprint.

Running Away

There is true artistry in running from combat and actually making a successful escape. Using this defensive tactic makes it harder for your foes to kill you. Assuming you know the layout of a map while escaping, look straight down while running (not sprinting). This allows you to duck your head if you're getting shot in the back, making it more difficult for your enemy to inflict the final headshot; it can mean the difference between getting around a corner and into cover or dying before you reach the corner. While walking with your head down, moving in a left to right motion while walking forward also makes it more difficult for your enemy to successfully hit you. Your head comes back up when you sprint, so make sure you're running if you are trying to dodge that last incoming headshot.

It's important to know when to run away, and this was one of those times.

One more getaway plan is to sprint and execute difficult jumps into areas your opponent won't be able to target you. As previously noted, most maps have a few jumps that benefit you while you're trying to flee from your enemy, and these can keep you from dying if you know where and when to jump! Instead of using the usual routes, run around the maps and find the potential jumps and where they lead to. This cuts down on your route times and allows faster movement around a map.

> PART 3: CHOOSING YOUR ENGAGEMENTS

Picking the correct time to fight is one of the most important decisions you make. When you choose when to engage, make sure you have the upper hand. It isn't about winning every fight you're involved in. It's about staying alive when you know you're going to lose a fight and putting yourself in a power position using objects, structures, rocks or other scenery to your advantage. It's also extremely important to work properly with your teammates when playing team games.Even a less-skilled player who gives themselves these advantages prior to an engagement can beat players who have more raw talent.

Gaining the Advantage

When choosing which fights to be involved in, you want to know that you have the advantage. For example, in a 1v1 match, an advantage would be having already hit your enemy twice with two shots without your foe having struck you once. At this point, push at them knowing you can still miss a shot and win the fight. Conversely, if your foe has hit you more times than you've hit him, retreat from combat, backing down to wait for your shields to replenish. Every life and death counts! Another way to score an advantage is using grenades. This is a big part in your decision-making when gauging a time to engage in a fight. Use grenades to remove your opponent's shields and then finish with a headshot.

Starting combat against a distracted or badly wounded foe can tilt the odds in your favor.

Getting Greedy

You may have completed an excellent shot with your weapon, but sometimes you need to back down and wait for a better time to battle instead of going in "hot" and trying to mow down everyone. At some point, you're going to encounter someone at your skill level or better, and they'll be able to shoot just as well as you. When this happens, combat becomes all about playing it smart, figuring out the correct time and place to fight, and backing down when necessary. There are times when you have to leave a one-shot kill and let a teammate pick off your foe in team matches, or give up the kill and move on in Free For All matches.

Gaining the High Ground

Raining death on a foe down below is better than battling an enemy who is located at a high vantage point.

Scrambling to higher ground is a great way to gain the advantage on your opponents. For example, from the top of a building or tower, you have a bird's-eye view over more of the map than your foes. You can put shots into your opponent while keeping your own body hidden. This is the power position that is perfect for sniping.

Great Teamwork

It is rewarding—and imperative—that you work well with a teammate and move around together on a map team-shooting everyone in your path. Be sure you find the enemies on the other team who are running around by themselves (the "lone wolves") and take them out in a 2v1 confrontation, with you and a teammate emerging victorious. These fights are a gift; it is easy to pick these foes off before moving on to more tricky enemies. Great teamwork isn't only about being an offensive powerhouse with backup. If you're in a situation where you have a comfortable lead, turtling up in a safe spot with your allies is a better move than just running around on your own.

Weapons and Power-ups

When you grab a power weapon to make sure your opponent doesn't get control of it upon your death, you want to stay as safe as possible. Don't rush your actions when you have the weapon advantage, and don't be afraid to "waste" ammo.

Checklist of Advantages

Look out for the following advantages during your matches:

〉 Cover opportunities, such as walls, structures, and natural scenery, are particularly useful because they let you choose when to fight and when to back down and let your shields recharge.

〉 Stay alive and let your shields recharge; this gives you another chance to restart a fight or wait for a teammate to help you in a team game.

〉 Find a structure or piece of scenery (such as a rock) that covers your body and exposes only a section of your Spartan's form. This makes it more difficult for your foe to hit you, as they have just your head to shoot at, whereas you have their entire body to aim for. If you find the right scenery in the best place, firing from this location can be deadly for your enemies. Consult the Maps section of this guide for many examples of such locations.

〉 It isn't wise to place yourself in an open area, as you're obviously more vulnerable to being shot at from multiple angles. Furthermore, you're unable to see a foe's entire body when you're looking up, trying to find where the shots are coming from. The lower ground is a death trap!

〉 If you can master the technique of "peeking and shooting," timing your shots and movement correctly, you can peer out, fire at your foe, and drop back into cover before the enemy can return fire.

Exercising Patience

Patience is a large part of your success. You have a lot to learn about this game, and it won't happen in one day. Aside from reading this guide from cover to cover and learning every location on every map, it takes many gaming sessions to become a great player. Waiting for your foe to come to you instead of simply running out into the open is a better bet in almost every situation. As indicated earlier, patience can be executed in actions such as retreat or simply avoiding a conflict where you're certainly outgunned. In team games, turtling up is the most clear-cut form of patience, forcing the enemy to come to your defended position which ultimately puts them at a disadvantage.

Free-For-All Fighting

Knowing when to let a kill go and when to charge and pick up a few one-shot kills is very important. Try stepping into fights that are already going on so you can easily pick off a kill or two (or three) while not becoming the main target. Initiating battles most of the time simply hinders your ability to get kills; you usually whittle a foe down to a weakened spot, and then someone else picks them off with a headshot. Work smarter, not harder!

Grenades are incredibly valuable in a Free For All. One well placed toss can strip the shields off multiple enemies. Any time you can restock on grenades, do so.

Pay attention to ordnance drops! During some rule sets, random ordnance continues to fall onto the battlefield throughout the match. You can use this to your advantage. Rather than running over the power weapon to be the first one to it, you could always hang back and let other players exhaust eachother before you step in to finish them off. They can't take a power weapon or a grenade restock if they're all dead!

Weapon Proficiency

If you're exceptionally gifted with your weapon, you can play more freely throughout the maps, as you'll be confident that you'll likely emerge victorious in any battle. However, there are times when even the most impressive crack-shot might not have a target locked; this forces you to play with more intelligence and use the map to your advantage, going for the high ground and knowing the areas that are very effective when picking foes off or surprising them with a fight.

Opponent Prediction

If you already know how your opponent plays, it makes it easier for you to decide where the battle will be and when to catch your enemy off guard or in a weak state. When you begin a game, it should take around five minutes to ascertain what the opposing players are likely to attempt (and their bad habits you can prey on). Learn where your foes like to travel to and how aggressive or passive they are. After you figure this out, you can predict their movements and drop them with a greater degree of certainty.

Plan "B" It's fine for you to engage in combat where you might not have the advantage or you're fighting at a disadvantage, as long as you know you have an "out." This means retreating from the fight when the battle turns against you. Your escape plan could be as simple as retreating to a section of cover or as complex as knowing that a teammate is on his way with a timely flanking maneuver.

Target Priority

Having an idea as to who or what is a priority target during battle may take some experience before you finally get it down, but it is important to understand. If you're behind on points during a Slayer match, team up with allies to guarantee kills, or pick off weaker players more often. If you see multiple enemies, perhaps you should take out the one with the power weapon first. Look for hostile Spartans with their shields down, and put them away with a headshot.

WAR GAMES: TACTICAL ADVICE

With the basics down, it's time to learn a host of tips to further improve your game. Use these additional tactics when you can. There tips are from all four MLG Spartans and include the best loadouts to begin your games with, the best weapons to use, and other advice to increase your gaming prowess!

> TIPS FOR IMPROVING YOUR PLAY

No help when you've got the flag? Don't be afraid to defend yourself.

1. Jumping: This is very important when you're entering fights or disengaging from them. Use rocks, crates, and other scenery to reach higher ground. This can help in all types of objective games to cut off routes, complete shortcuts, or run in a flag faster so you can score.

2. Capturing the Flag: If you're holding power weapons and you're by the enemy flag, then it is better to provide supporting fire, guard the flag, and let a teammate without such a great weapon run with the flag. You can't drop the flag once you walk over it, so having rockets or a sniper rifle is useless. Instead, it's simply smarter to slay and chaperone a teammate once they take the flag.

3. Oddball: If you're in trouble during Oddball matches, and you know you're about to be taken down while holding the ball, look out for any teammates near your position and throw them the ball. It is much better to keep it out of the other team's hands.

4. King of the Hill: It is wise to sometimes simply skip a hill if it will be changing soon and set up for the next one, or you may risk rushing aimlessly to a hill that's too well defended and dying over and over again.

Try to control a point that's close to where the next hill moves to, and set up there. Now when the hill moves, you're in the location already and your opposition is likely to be farther away at the previous hill's position and also in a weakened state. This allows you to accrue time easily and relatively safely.

When playing properly on a team, there should be only one player in the hill so the remaining teammates can cover the other angles to help keep the hill dweller alive. The only time two teammates should be on a hill is toward the end of a game when you need to keep the hill at all costs for the points. So, if one teammate dies in the hill, there's a second to keep the time continuous.

5. Rushing: Never try to randomly run flags or rush an objective by charging in without help from your teammates.

6. Ordnance Discretion: When calling in Ordnance Drops it's important to remember a few things. First, don't always call in a drop as soon as you get one. Instead, wait for your current provisions to run dry, especially if they're doing the trick (which they likely are, as you just got an option for a drop!) Second, call in drops inside enclosed areas. If you do it in the open, the drop will be deployed from above the map and will be loud and noticeable. Instead, head to an interior or a location with an overhang and the ordnance will discretely materialize instead of dropping. And finally, don't always select a power weapon which is often a player's first reaction. If you've got a sweet weapon, selecting a power-up can sometimes make it even sweeter. There's nothing quite like using a SAW to cut down a handful of enemies only to be rewarded by an Overshield, allowing you to cut down the same enemies all over again almost immediately after.

> SPARTANS OF MLG: TIPS FROM ELUMNITE

Drop in an Overshield when you're going in for a kill. Effective use of ordnance is key.

1. Ability Combinations: Learn to combine the right type of armor abilities to help enhance yourself in the battle. Once you've chosen a couple of abilities, you'll probably stay with that setup. The abilities you choose influence the role you need to play on your team in future games, depending on the playlist.

2. Ability Weaknesses: Find out what armor abilities are weak against one another. Discovering these can be key to victory in games. Before a game begins, talk to your teammates about the abilities they are using, and make sure your entire team has a combined mixture of different weapons, Tactical Upgrades, and Support Packages.

3. Ordnance-Wrangling: Be smart about when and where you use your ordnance. Don't fill up your meter and call for a drop as soon as you can, especially if you're in danger of being killed before you can claim the drop. Usually, if the enemy teams see this, they're likely to pounce on you and attempt to secure the ordnance for themselves. The correct way to play is to ensure you have a clear area to drop your ordnance in the most proficient and safest manner possible. Expert players may even drop ordnance close to a group of enemies because they figure they'll be finding these foes anyway and can get a jump on them in the confusion. For example, drop an Overshield into the battle area just as you're about to fight, and employ it immediately.

4. Small Talking: Good communication in team games is the easiest way to win the game. Work on not just calling out where enemies are and how weak they are, but focus more on "small talking" to each other. Without constantly chattering (which is a bad plan), be more succinct in your verbal callouts, using phrases like "I have your help" or "I don't have your help," "stay alive" (if you can't immediately provide help), and "push here with me" (if you need to take an objective). These phrases let your teammates know what you need them to do if they're alone and determine whether it's wise for them to fight battles or simply wait until another teammate arrives.

5. Accuracy Above All: Work on strengthening the accuracy of both your shots and your map knowledge! Hone your talents on every weapon you normally use in loadouts. Playing on your own won't help you with your weapon techniques, but you can focus on learning routes throughout every map and finding the angles from which to overpower your enemy. Knowing what's around every corner at all times can affect a fight, and realizing you need to jump or escape ahead of time keeps your movements smooth.

6. Just a Heads-Up: Do you think of yourself as a master sniper? Well, there are occasions when you don't always need to automatically try for a headshot: for example, if you can hit the body and assist a teammate in finishing the job, especially if your friend was being attacked by the foe in question. Ultimately, preventing a teammate's death and giving them the kill is better than going for a pointless headshot at the expense of your teammate's life.

INTRODUCTION

BASIC TRAINING

INTEL

CAMPAIGN

INFINITY

APPENDIX

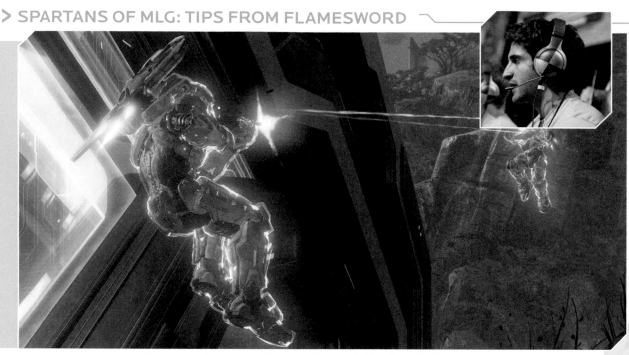

Fly over structures and make yourself harder to hit with the Jet Pack.

1. Hot Spots and Choke Points: Get a good grasp of the overview layouts of every map. It doesn't matter what game type you're playing; you must know the topography and the locations on a map where all the action occurs. Knowing every hot spot helps you in any game type, and knowing the callouts of the maps helps in every team-oriented game type.

2. Packing a Punch: Figure out what armor abilities work best for you and the subtleties of each. For example, the Jet Pack is a great armor ability, as it allows you to travel the greatest distances and you can fly over structures with ease. It also helps you in 1v1 matches because you can launch the Jet Pack just before you die, making it harder for your enemy to land a headshot on you.

3. Getting Skilled in the Kill: Individual skill is important, and there are many ways to increase it with playlists such as Rumble Pit, Regicide, and Team Snipers. Be sure to play these so you understand how to handle situations where you might be fighting more than one enemy at a time.

4. Passive or Aggressive? Find out what kind of player you are. If you are a passive player, you might want to use Firepower (check the Tactical Package) so you can have mid- to long-range weapons with which to provide as much support fire as possible. If you are an aggressive player, go for the Assault Rifle, Storm Rifle, or Suppressor so when you rush the enemy in close quarters, you can execute them quickly.

5. Exercise More Than Your Thumbs: Outside of *Halo 4*, be sure to stay physically active. A lot of my success in the pro gaming scene is due to my active and healthy lifestyle. Because of everything I do outside of the game, I am always calm and relaxed when it's time to game. Being calm helps you understand the scenarios you go through when playing and allows you to think more clearly on how to come out on top from them.

6. Jumping: Practice jumping! Jumping is effective in every *Halo* title, and in *Halo 4* your Spartan movement is the best to date, so you can really use some of the enhanced jumps to your advantage. This guide covers jumping techniques, so be sure to practice them over and over until you perfect them.

> SPARTANS OF MLG: TIPS FROM NADED

The team that controls a power weapon controls the game.

1. Don't Lose Focus: When playing online, it is very easy to lose focus when bad things happen. Complaining to your team instead of calling out enemy locations is doing nothing but losing you the game more quickly. If you train yourself to control your less desirable emotions, you'll not only improve individually, but also win more team games.

2. Preplanning: Starting custom games with your team and going over strategies for what everyone wants to do for specific maps/game types will allow your team to be more on the same page. Talking about the goals for each map/game type and then making minor adjustments as you practice will help your team get better every day.

3. Chatterbox: Using small talk while playing is a different form of communication. Calling out enemy locations is one way to communicate to your team, but when you want to be more personal with your callouts, talk to a teammate directly and plan on shooting the same area together. Talking with teammates is very important in helping them stay alive and being aware of the current situation. Working together with one member of your team at all times will help you improve your small talk, because then you will know who exactly you are working with and can directly communicate to them throughout the game. Always try to connect with the teammate closest to you.

4. Matchmaking: Playing Matchmaking is one way to improve your individual skills with weapons. The more games you play in any playlist, the more familiar you will be with properly hitting shots with each weapon. With enough practice and play time, you should reach a point where you have a good shot with all weapons and understand which weapons are better for each situation.

5. Power and Glory: Controlling power weapons will win you games. Always try to put a team effort into controlling weapons like the Sniper Rifle and Rocket Launcher. Typically, the team that better controls the power weapons throughout the game will win if they use them well enough.

6. Patience Is a Virtue: Being patient and calm while playing can help you realize that the game might not be as chaotic as you think. If you are getting too intense, take deep breaths while playing to calm down. Also, staying positive while playing and encouraging teammates in-game will go a long way toward getting more victories under your belt.

Know exactly where you are on every map? Then you're already halfway to victory.

1. Mapping It Out: Practice on the maps until you are familiar with them and learn all the callouts. This will allow you to get—and give—help. Find the best routes to run the flag, the best spots to snipe from, the preferred positions to hold and/or move the oddball, the best spots to lock and area down, the power positions, and the areas where you can be sneaky. You can also find some very useful jumps that will get you around the map more efficiently and that are incredibly sneaky and will have your opponent completely confused.

2. Bringing the Firepower: Become familiar with all the armor abilities, Tactical Packages, and Support Upgrades. Make multiple loadouts and practice with all of the armor abilities to become competent with them. Find the counters and combinations that have good synergy. Firepower is my favorite, so I can carry two mid-range weapons: the Battle Rifle and DMR.

3. Weapons Detail: Practice with all the weapons. Go into a custom game and play against your friends, using only one weapon to increase your proficiency with it. Set up a custom game with Overshields and a bottomless clip to practice aiming and shooting with the weapons at different angles and situations. The only way to get better with a weapon is to use it! Practice and become adept with every weapon. You want to win most of your individual fights. This makes you a great player who has the flexibility to play different roles.

4. Know When and Where to Nade: Learn and test out grenade points to get a surprise nade on your opponent. Grenade points are places on the map where you can bounce a grenade to a hot spot (where your opponent is) and weaken your opponent. There are many walls, windows, staircases, rocks, and structures you can use to make your grenade hit a spot you normally wouldn't be able to throw a grenade to.

5. A Night at the Theater: Save some of the gameplay footage of you losing and winning and watch them in-theater later on. Find out what you were doing correctly and what you were doing wrong.

With the game you lost, see what mistakes you made and what you could have done differently. With the games you won, see what you were specifically doing to win. Also watch what your enemy or enemy team is doing during a game you lost, and see what you could have done to stop them. You can always find many tips, tricks, jumps, grenade points, and strategies by watching gameplay in-theater. You also learn to predict your opponents' moves throughout the game, seeing where they are more prone to go and learning the particular routes they take. Mimic what other players are doing if it is working well; you can even make it better and make it your own.

6. Stay Unpredictable: Switch it up sometimes. You don't want to become predictable. You can run different routes and be more aggressive or passive in certain situations. Leave your opponent guessing at your every move. Sometimes doing something your opponent may think is stupid is the best way to get a jump on them. For example, doubling back to a fight when you normally would let your shields recharge will throw your enemies off, especially if they're in the middle of throwing a grenade or reloading.

7. Patience and Practice: You should be benefiting from your gaming session. Always try to learn something new every time. Back down and wait for your shields to recharge. Your patience may make your opponent restless and more aggressive, putting him in a bad position. If you want to be the best, you have to put the time in and practice! And always remember to have fun: It doesn't hurt to kick back and relax and play some Flood or other entertaining modes that aren't "serious."

8. Embrace the Outside: Stay healthy outside of gaming. Take a break sometimes and step outside! Do something other than gaming. Your mind will be fresh when you come back. Also, be active and exercise: Your reactions will improve and you'll make your snap decisions more competently if you keep your body and mind in good health.

> TOP 5 LOADOUT PACKAGES

Learning the loadouts that are right for your particular game type is very important, as is having predetermined loadouts so you can quickly get into the action. After hundreds of hours of testing, the following loadouts are some of the best specific packages we could come up with. The name of the loadout gives you an idea of the play style that goes with each one.

1. SPEED

Primary Weapon:	Secondary Weapon:	Grenade	Armor Ability	Tactical Package	Support Upgrade
Battle Rifle	Plasma Pistol	Frag Grenade	Thruster Pack	Mobility	Dexterity

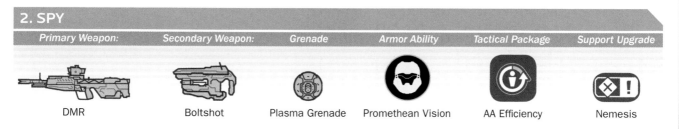

2. SPY

Primary Weapon:	Secondary Weapon:	Grenade	Armor Ability	Tactical Package	Support Upgrade
DMR	Boltshot	Plasma Grenade	Promethean Vision	AA Efficiency	Nemesis

3. AIR STRIKE

Primary Weapon:	Secondary Weapon:	Grenade	Armor Ability	Tactical Package	Support Upgrade
Covenant Carbine	Plasma Pulse	Plasma Grenade	Jet Pack	AA Efficiency	Stability

4. IRON WALL

Primary Weapon:	Secondary Weapon:	Grenade	Armor Ability	Tactical Package	Support Upgrade
Battle Rifle	Magnum	Frag Grenade	Hardlight Shield	AA Efficiency	Explosives

5. FIRST AID

Primary Weapon:	Secondary Weapon:	Grenade	Armor Ability	Tactical Package	Support Upgrade
DMR	Magnum	Frag Grenade	Regeneration Field	Shielding	Sensor

The Flood is back and more infectious than ever.

1. Limited Grenades: Unlike the previous *Halo* games, *Halo 4* doesn't allow grenade pick-ups unless you have the Tactical Package Resupply equipped. This changes the game, because you can't "waste" grenades like you used to; it now isn't wise to throw out your grenades as quickly as you want to. Each grenade is important now, so make each throw count.

2. Loadouts: Loadouts are a new feature to the *Halo* series. Tactical Packages and Support Upgrades are perks that make your Spartan much more proficient, and you're allowed one of each per loadout. Along with the perks, armor abilities makes a return with a few new abilities as well. Be sure to test all the combinations to find what suits you best.

3. Flag Waving: Flag tossing—which has been the most effective way to run flags in previous *Halo* games—has been removed. However, when you pick up the flag, you receive a pistol with unlimited ammo to defend yourself. This makes grabbing flags more appealing because you have one melee strike with the flag and the pistol in your right hand for ranged attacks. This combination of pole and pistol can lead to numerous epic kills!

4. Oddball Overhaul: The game of Oddball has been revamped! Pressing the Grenade Throw button, usually your left trigger, now lobs the Oddball like a football. This changes the way you play Oddball, because if you are about to die, you can throw the ball in the direction of your teammates or off the map to prevent the enemy from gaining the ball.

5. New Game Types: The new game types are Dominion, Extraction, Flood, and Regicide. Flood is similar to the zombie playlists you loved in *Halo 3* and *Halo: Reach*, but now when you're killed you take the form of the shambling Flood itself! Dominion and Extraction are modes that play like Territories from previous *Halo* games but have their own new fun flavor. Regicide is a new game type that puts a bounty over the king, who is usually the player in the lead.

6. Guns! Be sure to inspect the new arsenal of weapons, including the mighty and powerful Forerunner guns! These weapons pretty much stop everything in their path; this is Firepower you should never pass up. Each weapon has its own unique style; become comfortable with these weapons, as you can turn the tide of the game if you get the chance to grab them.

7. Ordnance Drops: This is a new feature of *Halo 4*. Certain game types give you the option of your own personal ordnance drop, which you get by accumulating points through kills, assists, EMP charges, multi-kills, and so on. Your own drop gives you the option of three items. These can be weapons, grenades, or even power-ups. Also, if you're (extremely) lucky, you can kill your opponent with your drop if you land it directly on their head!

> TOP 7: WEAPONS

These seven weapons are the ones you don't want to pass up if you come across them on the battlefield. Pick these up at all costs, even if just to keep them out of your enemy's hands. Just remember to do your best to properly pair it with your existing weapons. Don't end up with two snipers or two shotguns, severing your ability to compete in specific combat scenarios unless you properly weigh the risks.

1. BINARY RIFLE

This weapon is referred to as "the Boss" by the MLG players. Everyone who loved sniping in the past *Halo* games is going to love this new one-shot killing machine. There's never been a weapon like this in any previous *Halo* game, so you can only imagine how surprised your opponents will be when you're killing them with this weapon. Prepare for your foes to flee when they spot the three red lasers the gun emits when you're zoomed in. This weapon is mostly for mid- to long-range fights but can still be deadly at close range if you master the no-scope.

You have only two shots per clip, so make them count. You don't get zoomed out when you're struck by an enemy's shot either, so line up your reticle and fire away! In addition, you receive a total of six bullets: These should be six guaranteed kills. If this weapon appears in an ordnance drop, it is your number-one priority to make sure you or your team retrieves it first. The only counter to this weapon is the Hardlight Shield. You do not want this in your opponent's hands!

2. INCINERATION CANNON

Think of this weapon as a Rocket Launcher on steroids! Its splash damage covers a larger area than a normal rocket, making it exceptional for short- or mid-range fights. The weapon is pretty much unstoppable when it comes to taking down all vehicles with one direct shot. This is the optimal piece of killing equipment to have on a vehicle-friendly map.

3. ROCKET LAUNCHER

This is another weapon that excels on vehicle-friendly (and smaller) maps, as you're able to take down and inflict massive damage on vehicles. It also excels at taking down numbers of foes with its splash damage, as long as your foes are clustered near one another. It has an advantage over the Incineration Cannon too: You can fire off two rockets before needing to reload (compared to one with the Cannon); if you shoot a "Puckett" rocket (named after MLG commentator "Chris Puckett," who's known for his inability to net kills with the Rocket Launcher) at your enemy on your first attempt, you still have another chance to take down your opponent.

4. SNIPER RIFLE

This has always been a firm favorite; those playing previous *Halo* games know sniping is always entertaining! You have four shots in the rifle's clip, and these can take down an entire team with headshots before you need to reload! By placing yourself behind the rest of your team, you can pick enemies off while your team draws attention away from your position. This weapon is supremely adept at dropping foes and is exceptional at mid- or long-range battles. Even at close range, when you master the no-scope firing, it is lethal.

5. SCATTERSHOT

Think of this as the evolution of the UNSC Shotgun. It fires almost twice as quickly and has almost double the range. This is an extremely important weapon to carry on every one of the small enclosed maps or in tight or restrictive areas. You can take down multiple enemies with a single clip. Try sneaking up on your foes brandishing this gun, and they won't know what hit them! If you need to take control in a close-range battle, bring this out; it is unbelievably powerful in 1v1 close-range fights!

6. SAW

The SAW is an exceptional weapon. It is spectacular in short-range fights and works very well at mid-range as well. Compared to other short- to mid-range weapons, this one has more than the edge, simply because it partners extreme power with fast killing potential. Just aim at your adversary and spray away!

7. BEAM RIFLE

The Beam Rifle is one of the best sniping weapons available. It may not have the same power as a Binary Rifle, but it certainly stands up to the Sniper Rifle for sheer killing power and accuracy. It retains its accuracy even while fired from the hip, which allows for some amazing snapshots. What makes the Beam Rifle unique is that unlike the other two sniping weapons, it does not need to reload after two, four or even six shots. A fresh Beam Rifle comes with ten shots in the battery, and the only thing that will slow it down is if it overheats. You will not have to break visual contact with a potential victim just to reload, so you can stay scoped in on a target for follow-up shots.

Of course, the potential for overheating a Beam Rifle means that you will have to control your trigger finger and not fire the weapon too rapidly. However, even with this restriction, you can still put more shots on a target faster than the other two sniping weapons.

❯ BIG TEAM BATTLE: GENERAL TACTICS

The large-scale and bewildering Big Team Battles require a different mind-set. Here's the information to pour into your brain.

When the maps are large and the vehicles are rolling, you need a specific set of tactical plans to emerge victorious. If you want to survive and thrive at Big Team Battle games, be sure to familiarize yourself with the following loadouts and tactical knowledge.

Big Team Battles (BTBs) are predominantly played on *Halo 4*'s large maps:

COMPLEX	EXILE	LONGBOW	MELTDOWN	RAGNAROK	VORTEX

BTB Loadout Planning

Make sure that you have a good balance of loadouts throughout your team of eight so you can take advantage of as many armor abilities, Tactical Packages, Support Upgrades, and weapons as you need.

Primary Weapons

Choose primary weapons that are the most dangerous at long range, such as the DMR and the LightRifle. And you can never go wrong with picking the Battle Rifle. If you have "Firepower" on, then definitely pick at least one of the long-range weapons (DMR or LightRifle).

Secondary Weapons

The best option is definitely the Plasma Pistol, simply because you can stall vehicles with EMP and therefore take them down much more easily. You can also never go wrong with the Boltshot, which makes your close-range combat untouchable (when charging the weapon up) if the situation presents itself.

Grenades

Any of the three grenade types are a good option: Frag Grenades are the most basic grenade to choose for obvious reasons; they can get you some kills, but Plasma Grenades could be a better option, as you can stick them to vehicles (like the Banshee or Ghost) and inflict some serious and crippling damage.

armor abilities

Promethean Vision, Jet Pack, Hardlight Shield, and the Regeneration Field are the best choices. Promethean vision is good for every game type, but make sure that some teammates choose a different ability: Have two or three players with Promethean Vision and have the other players use a combination of the other Abilities previously mentioned. The Regeneration Field is very useful if you have multiple teammates next to you; drop it down to heal them all if the situation presents itself.

Tactical Packages

You can never go wrong picking Mobility, Shielding, AA Efficiency, or Firepower, but the Tactical Package to really consider is Wheelman. This increases the long-term durability of your vehicle and reduces the downtime if your vehicle gets hit with an EMP. Having this is incredibly important in BTB, because vehicles are such a large factor in controlling and dominating large maps: Having your designated driver or pilot players opting for Wheelman makes it a lot more difficult for the opposing team to take down your vehicles.

Support Upgrades

Ammo, Dexterity, Sensor, Stability, Stealth, or Nemesis are all great choices, but having a couple players on your team with Gunner and Drop Recon is very important. When playing BTB, there is a lot of turret usage (mounted or detached) throughout the game from Warthogs and Scorpions. Having teammates with Gunner allows them to dominate more with the Warthog (or any other vehicles with turrets that overheat), since the overheating time is greatly increased, which in turn leads to nonstop shooting.

Detaching turrets is a lot more powerful, since you can run a lot faster and catch other players off guard by taking them down very quickly with this strong weapon. Turrets are a critical part of BTB gameplay. Having a player with Drop Recon as well allows them to call out what and where the weapons are dropping 10 seconds before they appear on the map. This is crucial for controlling the power weapons (such as rockets or the Spartan Laser), and these power weapons are your best bet for taking down enemy vehicles.

Vehicle Command and Control

Before starting a BTB game, be sure you've already planned who is controlling each of the vehicles (including who is running to each particular vehicle). Those players should be equipped with Wheelman or Gunner in their loadouts; their mission is to begin controlling the map with vehicles from the very start. Having vehicles under your team's control and using them properly are the main keys to victory. Knowing where each vehicle spawns at the start makes it easier to plan which of your team is going for vehicles, so no vehicle is left behind. Treating vehicles like power weapons, and controlling both the vehicles and power weapons, allows your team to dictate the pace of play.

Every Big Team Battle player's worst nightmare.

Employ vehicles like the Warthog, Mongoose, and Ghost to charge an enemy base or objective. Attempting an impressive team push with the Warthog or Mongoose allows your team to (for example) pick up the enemy's flag and immediately mount a vehicle to make an escape back to your own base and score. Using the Ghost to quickly boost across the map is an excellent way to head behind enemy lines and start to outflank them.

Employ vehicles like the Scorpion, Wraith, Mantis, or Banshee to rack up the kills. In particular, the Ghost can potentially be one of the most dominant vehicles on the field. Combining speed and accurate Plasma Cannons, a good Ghost driver can be a nightmare to deal with. Staying alive and playing a little more passively allows you to keep control of these vehicles for longer periods of time. You don't want the enemy to hijack or EMP your vehicles due to your team being too aggressive with their driving or piloting. Keeping these vehicles for as long as possible is critical to winning. The Ghost can potentially be one of the most dominant vehicles on the field. Combining speed and accurate Plasma Cannons, a good Ghost driver can be a nightmare to deal with.

Sniping

Utilizing the Sniper Rifle, Beam Rifle, or Binary Rifle and being extremely passive (or defensive) with these weapons enables you to go on some impressive killing sprees. The enemy team won't be able to charge to your base freely if you're raining down high-caliber shots from the edge of a cliff, behind your own base. You have up to eight players who can snipe the opposition, so taking your time and waiting for your foes to close in on your base helps you land some easier headshots and even some clutch flag stops.

Ignore the cries of anguish and rude words emanating from your victims: Sniping is critical to your team's success!

Resource Control

Expanding on Vehicle Command and Control, you generally want to control all the resources on a map as best as you can. If you're playing with ordnance drops, know where they tend to spawn, and be ready to win the battles for power weapons. On vehicle heavy maps, do everything in your power to deny the enemy vehicles of their own, either by stealing them for your team, or just destroying them before the enemy can use them. Controlling resources and controlling spawns will all but help guarantee victory!

Objectives

The best way to capture a flag, or just an objective in general, is to begin a team push with vehicles like the Warthog and Mongoose, along with any ground forces that can come along for the ride. Immediately get your flag carrier in the backseat of a Mongoose or the side seat of a Warthog, as this is the most efficient way to capture the enemy flag.

Additionally, if your team has full control of a map, waiting for the right time to pull the flag is important, but don't be afraid to get sneaky when running the flag. There is such a large amount of combat carnage blowing up around both teams that you can sometimes get away with running the flag back to your base by yourself, or at least getting it far enough for one of your teammates to finish the run for you.

Completing an objective needs more than dogged determination: Try vehicular supremacy too.

Don't forget, waypoints point to everything that needs to be dealt with during objective based game types. Even flag carriers and newly crowned kings will show up on the HUDs of enemies across the whole map, with the word KILL flashing brightly next to their icons. Because objectives will always have an indicator pointing towards them, it's important to remember the "team" part of a Big Team Battle. Work together to accomplish your objectives.

Ordnance Drops

When playing a game type that has personal ordnance drops, you want to rack up as many points as you can in order to fill your Ordnance meter to finally call in the ordnance. When your Ordnance meter fills up, you're rewarded with three options from which to choose. One of these choices is sent down next to you (using the directional pad) and then picked up. There are some Tactical Packages and Support Upgrades to use with ordnance game types, such as Requisition, Ordnance Priority, and Drop Recon.

Don't be near the ordnance drop impact point because it can hurt you, and even kill you if it lands directly on top of your head. Obtaining multiple kills (like a Double Kill or Triple Kill) rewards you with more points that fill your Ordnance meter at a quicker pace

The sky is falling, and it's raining power weapons.

compared to normal kills. You can save your personal ordnance drop (even after you die), so keeping it for the right opportunity is a smart idea. When obtaining personal ordnance, the weapons and power-ups that you choose from are random and weighted to be balanced (for example, you don't get power weapons every time).

GAME TYPES: AN OVERVIEW

The term "game types" refers to the many different rule settings that are available in *Halo 4*. Many of these game types will be familiar to veteran players, but some of them don't exhibit the same gameplay as they did in past *Halo* games (such as Flood or King of the Hill). There are also a few new game types as well, such as Dominion, Extraction, and Regicide. Playing as many game types as you can helps you figure out all of the most pertinent strategies for them. These include all-new tactics such as throwing the Oddball or using the Magnum while running a flag.

This section reveals as much tactical knowledge as possible about every game type (listed here). For more general tactics, consult earlier in this Training section.

> Capture the Flag
> Dominion

> Extraction
> King of the Hill

> Oddball
> Infinity Slayer

> SWAT
> Slayer Pro

> Regicide
> Grifball

> Flood

> GAME TYPES: TACTICAL KNOWLEDGE

Capture the Flag (CTF)

The goal is to infiltrate the other team's base, grab their flag, and deliver it back to your own base.

General Tactics

> Always know where your flag is at all times.

> When going for a flag, remove it at the enemy's base. You almost never want to grab it while holding or attempting to find a power weapon; this is because you can't drop the flag once you've picked it up (unless you score or die).

> Follow the teammates who are running the flag back to your base to ensure a successful flag capture.

> The flag carrier is not completely defenseless—you're able to utilize a Magnum and hold on to the flag itself—so when running a flag, team up with someone to help you take down enemies and protect you.

> The flag is also a one-hit kill when using it as a bludgeoning device, so go ahead and give anyone who gets in your way a good thwack.

> Although the weapon you're carrying is a Magnum and has the same benefits and problems, it's more difficult to wield it as effectively with a flag on your arm. It's better to avoid all battles unless it's a last resort; your overriding goal is getting that flag home!

Team Tactics

> Coordinate with the rest of your team when preparing for a flag run: Attempt a "push" into the enemy base when the opposition has players down—that is, just defeated or in a disadvantageous position compared to your side.

> Never attempt to run with a flag without your team knowing or in a direction they aren't preparing to help defend; that simply makes it more difficult for your team if you're taken down during the run.

> Utilize vehicles whenever possible to attempt a swift run into the other team's base. However, be sure that any Warthogs have a gunner positioned on the turret, or you're simply wasting your own time and resources!

> Prepare for moments when you have to give up the flag to the opposition: Do this when you know you're going to be overstretched; it is better to return with a competent team later into the match.

> If your team is repeatedly succumbing to the enemy as they try to stop the opposing side from capturing your flag, pause and rethink: Instead of this stalemate, regain control of your own base and regroup. This ensures that the other team doesn't end up obtaining a second flag capture. If you continue to throw yourself hopelessly at defending a capture that's already long gone, you may end up giving up more than just that one point.

> It is always better to give up on a flag that you're trying to capture so you don't end up overextending yourself and relinquishing an important position to the enemy. Instead, bait the flag (with a grenade or Sticky Detonator), then hide nearby and try to ambush one or two foes.

> Similarly, when a team dies with a flag and you're nearby, there are likely to be enemies guarding the immediate area. The flag carrier's death should catch them off guard or confuse them; pounce on this killing opportunity.

Dominion

Capture bases and hold them for a set period of time, building them up to defend them against the other team, who are also attempting to seize control of the same base. Turrets, Shield Walls, and other defensive equipment can be added. Multiple bases can be seized at once.

General Tactics

> The most important point to remember is to always hold one base no matter what else is happening. Default to this tactic at all times!

> It takes up to 15 seconds to capture a base and 30 seconds to fortify it. Embed this knowledge into your brain!

> Whenever the Auto-Terminal is down, rebuild as much as possible, as these systems are extremely efficient against vehicles.

> Utilize the Shield Barrier to your advantage when enemies are charging your base—this will cut off the number of routes into your base and allow you to focus defenses.

Team Tactics

> Construct a plan at the beginning of the game regarding which base you're going to capture, and head there from the start. Claim a base as early as you can.

> Don't ignore any vehicles that may be parked on a particular map; these can mean the difference between holding down an area or giving it up. Pick players especially skilled in piloting or driving to obtain particular vehicles as early as possible.

> Make certain to defend your base for 45 seconds in order to score the points. Also, never leave the base when it's close to resupplying: Communication with your team to protect a base at this point is critical to your victory, as there's no way you can hold down a base by yourself!

Extraction

Two locations that must be taken over appear on the map at any one time. By securing a location for a period of time, you earn a point and a subsequent location on the map appears and becomes accessible. Secure the most points to win.

General Tactics

> Think of this game type as Dominion (and utilize the tactics detailed for that game type) but at a faster pace. Be warned: If you're not working together, the opposition will extract a control point with relative haste.

> Try to run the maps mostly in pairs of two (or more) to extract a control point more effectively. Strength in numbers is the key here.

> The armor ability Hardlight Shield is highly recommended for Extraction games.

King of the Hill (KOTH)

Maneuver to the indicated area (a "hill"), which one or more of your team must stay within in order to earn time and eventually win the game. The time a hill is accessible varies, depending on the settings. Earn points by controlling the hill and keeping the enemy away at the same time. More than one hill may be active at once.

General Tactics

> When you're "in the hill," you cannot use armor abilities or Sprint. Instead, try to keep your fighting down to a minimum unless you have help from a teammate. Huddle or snipe behind cover and let the points build up.

> If you can make it to the hill when an opposing player is already in there, contest it as soon as possible; halt the time they are accruing as quickly as possible.

> If you're close to capturing time in a hill, inform your other teammates to set up for the next hill rush; there should be an indicator when the rush is going to happen, too.

> If your team knows it is becoming pointless to keep rushing a hill that is too well protected, then ignore it and instead set up for a rush on the next hill.

Team Tactics

> Quickly set your team up around the hill to protect it, ideally from multiple angles. Learn all the choke points from which the enemy will attack.

> Cover all angles: Look for where the enemy tends to push up from in order to slay the player in the hill, and focus your defenses there.

> There shouldn't be a need for more than one team member to be inside the hill unless you have only two players working together to accrue time or your team requires only a few seconds to win the game. The reason is simple: you need the fewest teammates without armor abilities and Sprint as possible.

> When possible, switch out players in the hill who are weak with fresh teammates. This makes it much more difficult for the enemy team to finish hill dwellers and keeps a constant flow of "hill time" for your team.

Oddball

Locate and hold on to the ball for as long as you can without letting the other team take and hold it. Simply keep the ball away from the other team to win.

General Tactics

> Always move with the team. Never roam by yourself with the ball.

> While holding the ball, utilize the throwing feature when you're close to being killed; throw the ball to a teammate to keep it out of your opponents' hands.

> Learn from your King of the Hill matches, and have your team set up defenses around the ball holder: Protect the carrier at all costs, and position him in a location that your foes will have a hard time reaching.

> Are you close to the edge of a map and about to die? Then a cunning tactic is to throw the ball off the map and out of play, if possible. The ball respawns somewhere else on the map, allowing your teammates more of an opportunity to respawn themselves and fight for control.

> Typically, there are several places were a ball spawns on each map. Therefore, you want to react quickly when a "play ball" occurs.

> One of the best new tactics in Oddball involves passing the ball to your opponent as they try and take you down. By throwing them the ball, they'll be forced to pick it up. If they don't react quickly, you'll have time to take them down before they can drop the ball to kill you.

Infinity Slayer

Earn points to call in ordnance from overhead. These ordnance drops consist of three randomly generated weapons or power-ups, the latter of which can alter a Spartan's speed, shielding or ability to issue damage.

General Tactics

> This game type rewards players who control the power weapons and inflict kills with them: This is the best way to fill your ordnance or multikills and to complete sprees of any sort.

> When you finally pick up the available ordnance, choose the weapon or power-up based on your situational awareness: For example, if there are several enemies around a wall or behind you, and you have a power-up such as Overshield available to drop, then that is an optimal pick to make. Another example: The Damage Boost is best for situations when you're trying to tear through opponents and pick up as many points as you can.

> Are you in a highly dangerous area (where you're most likely to be killed), but you've just received an ordnance drop? Then it's actually smarter not to use it. Wait until you've been killed: There's little use in dropping ordnance just to have it stolen by the other team.

INTRODUCTION

BASIC TRAINING

INTEL

CAMPAIGN

INFINITY

APPENDIX

SWAT

Your Spartan's armor has no shields. This means you can be killed with a single headshot.

General Tactics

> Accuracy kills in this game type: Always aim for the head and attempt one-shot kills at every opportunity.

> Use height and cover: Stay in high positions and away from the middle of maps!

> The use of long-range weapons, such as the Battle Rifle, DMR, LightRifle, Magnum, and Covenant Carbine, is not only encouraged but is also imperative!

> Try to stay in an enclosed area (for example, inside a building) without exposing your head.

> Keep a lookout for shieldless players and freshly spawning players in order to pick off some easy kills.

> Stay close to your teammates, but don't make the mistake of clustering around one another; this simply creates multiple opportunities for your foes.

> Verbal communication in the form of callouts is even more important than normal here, as having the element of surprise and the knowledge of your enemy's position is key.

Slayer Pro

This has the same rules as Team Slayer but without any ordnance drops, and you spawn with a few predetermined loadout choices.

General Tactics

> Begin your match by ensuring you have appropriate loadouts: Choose two players to arm with Battle Rifles and the other two with DMRs. The variety of ranges these weapons offer best helps your team as they patrol the battlefield.

> Scan the combat zone for the drop weapons as soon as the match begins, and control these as often as you can to gain the upper hand.

> The combat taking place in this game type almost always occurs at mid- to long range, so it becomes imperative to stay alive whenever you're in a weakened state; take the time to recover your shield. Without a full shield, you're liable to be easily picked off from across the map.

> Scoop up grenades when you're around a drop area as often as you can.

Regicide

The objective of this game type is to slay the person in the lead, known colloquially as the "King." If you're playing Team Regicide, protecting the King (if he's on your side, of course) becomes imperative.

General Tactics When You Are NOT the King

> When the match begins, immediately search for the nearest enemy to slay, and execute them with haste. Even if this means being a little more reckless, you need to go for the first kill each time.

> To become the King, you must have the first kill of the game. As the game progresses, expect some back-and-forth fighting with another player for the King title. Instead of simply rushing a kill to get back at a King, take your time once a King has been initially "crowned."

> Deaths and time as King don't matter when it's all said and done—just focus on having the highest score at the end of the game.

- In a Free For All Regicide match, you still want to slay the King, but don't do so at the expense of your shields or ammunition supplies. Remember that every other player is likely to be stalking the King as well, so wait for the battles to begin, and steal kills to rack up points more safely (and sneakily!).

- Does the King have a power-up? Unless you have one as well, it isn't wise to fight a King at this time. Instead, run away and stay alive until the King becomes damaged or less powerful.

- Search for weapons around the map that better help you take the King down from long range; the safest method of Regicide is picking the King off while he's engaged in battle with another foe.

- Try to save power weapon ammunition, such as Rockets. Then employ them when confronting a King.

- Have you yet to be crowned? Don't panic! Even if you're never the King throughout most of the game, it's more important to become King during the final minutes of the match, where a clutch kill of the King (and the bonus that comes from doing so) can catapult you into first place just as the score to win is reached or the time expires.

General Tactics When You ARE the King

- If you're King for 30 seconds, you gain an Overshield. If you're King for 90 continuous seconds, you gain a Damage Boost. The power-up durations for each of these vary. For example, the Overshield power-up will last 120 seconds or until depleted from damage. The Damage Boost power-up will last 30 seconds and the Speed power-up will last 45 seconds.

- There's little time to wave at your subjects when you become King, especially as there's an indicator over your head that lets all the other players know where you are on the map!

- If you haven't armed yourself properly already, your first order of business is to look for a mid- to long-range weapon and a close-range one as backup.

- Remember that the enemy usually comes to you, so weapons like the Scattershot are useful for battles around corners. This is a great choice of weapon, as are any of the other power weapons if you're planning on decimating those who challenge you in close-quarter combat.

- You need to remain the King for as long as possible; therefore, it's less important to patrol the map looking for foes to slay. Instead, stalk a particularly defensible area of the map and let the enemies come to you. The longer you're King, the better your chances are for victory.

- Of course, the more kills you accrue, the greater the bounty on your head. When a foe finally takes you down, they receive a large number of points. So pay attention to whoever is in second place, and *never* fight them to the death if you can help it. Make a "tactical withdrawal" (that is, run away) from this foe, lest they overtake you in points.

- Resist the temptation to run around looking for kills. Letting your enemies come to you is a better plan, and be sure to have a weapon designed for close combat to deal with them. Remember, every time you die, you reward your foes with extra points.

Grifball

The addition of being able to throw the ball adds a whole new dimension to this game type.

General Tactics

Practice using the Gravity Hammer and Energy Sword until you learn the precise range of each.

Use the ball-throwing technique (see the Oddball section for additional tactics) to your advantage. Work on passing to open teammates or throwing the ball before a sure death to force your opponent to spend more time trying to set up for a score.

Remember that the Gravity Hammer isn't only a weapon, but it also works as a tool to pass the ball.

As someone famous once said, "A good Grifball defense is the best offense." Waiting for the other team to come to you can be the secret to scoring some points of your own.

Focus on working as a team and positioning your team to maximize the chances of keeping the ball away from the opposition.

Never lose sight of the ball!

Scoring occurs only when you walk into the "score point" with the ball. Throwing the ball there doesn't grant your team any points.

Flood

They're coming for your braaaaaaains!

Players infected with the Flood are forced to destroy uninfected Spartans, converting them into Flood combat form allies. The goal for uninfected Spartans is to survive the never-ending Flood onslaught, staving off transformation into the parasite.

General Tactics

- Wipe the impending sense of panic and doom from your mind, and work together with your teammates at all times, even when you've "changed sides" and you're working with your Flood brethren.

- Barricading is a good plan. Set yourself up in a room where there's only one way in and out.

- Bring out your Magnum for easier headshots until you're out of ammunition or you're overwhelmed.

READYING FOR WAR GAMES: FINAL THOUGHTS

> HUD OVERVIEW

Although you may be familiar with all of the icons and information displayed on the inside of your visor, it is worth remembering what everything means.

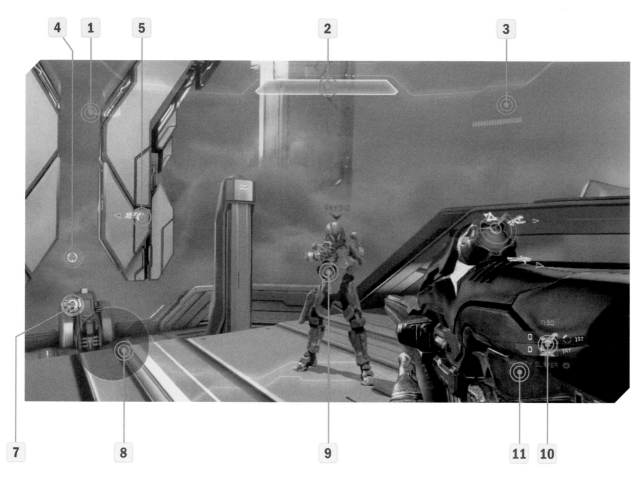

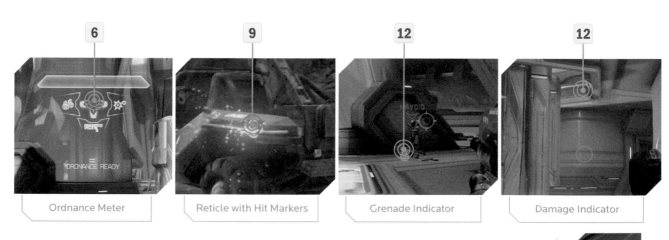

6 Ordnance Meter	**9** Reticle with Hit Markers	**12** Grenade Indicator	**12** Damage Indicator

13 Spartan ID

1 **Grenade supply:** In the top left of your HUD is the amount of each type of grenade (Frag, Plasma, Pulse) you have.

2 **Shield:** In the top center of your HUD is the amount of shields you have. This will indicate how close you are to dying. When your shields are depleted, this part of your HUD will flash red.

3 **Weapon and Ammunition:** In the top right of your HUD is the weapon you are currently using along with how many bullets you have in the clip. The number indicates how much ammunition you have left with which to reload.

4 **Ordnance:** If you earn enough points to receive personal ordnance, the Ordnance menu will appear right below your shield. In this menu, you can use the D-pad to choose which weapon or power-up you wish to drop next to you.

5 **Waypoints:** When a weapon from an ordnance is on the map, a waypoint and the item's exact location (in meters) will appear on your screen.

6 **Ordnance meter:** On the left side of your HUD in Ordnance game types is a small circle with the ordnance logo in the center. When you earn points, the circle starts to fill up. This is how you know how close you are to getting a personal ordnance.

7 **Armor ability meter:** Just above your motion sensor is your armor ability meter, which shows you how much time you have left to use your armor ability. When your armor ability is running out, it starts to flash red and shows an exclamation point.

8 **Motion sensor:** On the bottom left of your HUD is your motion sensor. This reveals a variety of information: The edge of the motion sensor has arrows indicating where weapons and enemies are if they can't be shown directly on the motion sensor, so you are more aware of where everything is on the map. The motion sensor also shows if weapons/enemies are above or below you. If there is an up arrow above a red dot of a weapon/enemy, then you know the weapon/enemy is above you on the map. If there is a down arrow below a red dot of a weapon/enemy, then you know the weapon/enemy is below you on the map. If there is no arrow at all, then they are on the same level of ground as you.

9 **Reticle:** In your screen's center is the weapon reticle. This is how you aim your weapon to connect with shots. Every weapon has a different reticle, so familiarizing yourself with them all and learning where to aim the reticles improves your shot.

10 **Score/time limit:** The bottom right of your HUD shows the players/teams, what place the players/teams are in, and the amount of points the top players/teams have. Above the score is the amount of time left in the game. Being aware of both the time and score will allow you to make better decisions in-game. Knowing if you are in a tie game or if the time limit is running out will allow you to make smarter plays in a lot of situations.

11 **Game type:** Below the score is what game type you are currently playing.

12 **Shot/Grenade/Damage markers:** When you connect with shots, indicators appear around your reticle. When grenades are near you, an indicator appears around your reticle showing you which direction the grenade is moving so you can move away. If you take damage, a red arrow points in the direction of the damage (and this damage marker also appears around your reticle).

13 **Spartan IDs:** Finding your teammate's Spartan IDs in-game is the optimal method of locating a buddy with whom to team-shoot. Look out for those IDs that appear right above your teammate with an arrow pointing down showing where they are located.

INTRODUCTION BASIC TRAINING INTEL CAMPAIGN INFINITY APPENDIX

Settings and Files

Controls: Finding the right control settings for yourself is a good way to change your game for the better; overlook this at your peril! Becoming comfortable with the way you hold your controller and what settings you play on is key to having confidence while playing. Don't be afraid to try new settings for a couple of games to see if you prefer something new: While you're trying these adjustments, it's important to give yourself a few games instead of giving up immediately.

Changing the way you use the controller takes time, but sometimes switching to a new controller setting can make a world of difference in your play. Ultimately, it's all about being comfortable—there is no setting that is universally better than any other, so figure out what works for you!

Button Layouts

There are many different button layouts to pick from. Here is a brief breakdown of each of them.

Default: This default layout for *Halo 4* moves away from past *Halo* games by having the Sprint ability on the left joystick button and having crouch now on the B button. Melee is your right bumper and Action/Reload is on the X button. New players will have no problem with this layout, but players with past *Halo* experience might have an issue with the relocation of crouch.

Southpaw: Southpaw is made for left-handed players, and compared to the Default setting, it simply switches the Fire Weapon and melee to the left side and the Throw Grenade and Use armor ability to the right side. If you're a leftie, you owe it to yourself to try this set up.

Boxer: This is the layout for players who want to concentrate and hone their melee combat talents. Melee is now your left trigger while Throw Grenade is your right bumper. Sprint is now your B button while Crouch is the left joystick button. This can improve some players' melees by switching to this layout since you can quickly pull the left trigger and aim melees a little more quickly and accurately.

Green Thumb: This switches the zoom to your right bumper and melee to your right joystick button. This is a very unorthodox button layout, with the intention of making it a little easier to scope in and shoot and allowing you to more easily use your melees. Having the Melee button on your right joystick button allows you to aim your melee and lunge without moving your thumb.

Bumper Jumper: This was an extremely popular layout in both *Halo 3* and *Halo: Reach*: The layout enables some players to jump and melee a little more easily. Jump is your left bumper, while melee is your right bumper. This allows you to have more of a "clawlike" style of play, making it easier to jump and aim. Your armor ability is now the X button and sprint is the A button. Previous bumper jumper users are likely to gravitate to this setup.

Recon: Recon was introduced in *Halo: Reach* to mimic the default button layout of *Halo 3*. Recon in *Halo 4* is almost identical to the layout in *Halo: Reach* as well, but with the new addition of the X button being Sprint. Players who used the Recon configuration in *Halo: Reach* should be just as proficient using this during *Halo 4*.

Fishstick: This is the newest addition to the *Halo* button layouts. If you prefer to zoom with your left trigger and melee with your right thumbstick, give this control setup a try, although pressing in thumbsticks isn't usually as accurate as button or trigger presses.

Stick Layouts

Inverted or Default (Not Inverted)

Inverted or Default is a choice between how you want your reticle to react to your thumbstick while aiming. It does not affect your movement in any way.

The default layout is not inverted. Move your right thumbstick up and your reticule will go up; move it down and your reticule will go down. This is the most basic setup and easiest to use if you haven't played a first-person shooter before.

For some players, inverted settings feel more natural. Often nicknamed *flight controls*, this setup reverses your aiming, meaning that moving the thumbstick down will move your reticule up and vice versa. There isn't an advantage to using either; it is personal preference and what you play best with.

Southpaw or Default

The default thumbstick setup in *Halo 4* means that you control your character's movement with the left thumbstick and your reticule with the right thumbstick. With Southpaw, the left thumbstick becomes your aim control and the right thumbstick handles player movement. This can be great for a left-handed person getting into FPS games. In addition to the Default and Southpaw stick layouts, there are the Legacy and Legacy Southpaw layouts.

Again, there isn't an advantage to using either; it is personal preference and what you play best with.

Sensitivity (1–10)

Being comfortable with your sensitivity speed is important. Each sensitivity mark between 1 and 10 is going to make you play differently during a game. Having a faster sensitivity (5 to 10) allows you to react more quickly, helping yourself and your teammates and allowing you to check your flanks (left and right sides) for enemies with greater haste.

Conversely, having a lower sensitivity (1–4) can allow for a more accurate shot (with any weapon) compared to higher sensitivities, but at the expense of turning quickly (to deal with a threat from your flanks or from any other direction where swift movement is necessary).

Most players choose a sensitivity range between 3 and 5, but figuring out which is optimal for you is vital, as it gives you more confidence in your shot placement and accuracy. Practicing on the same sensitivity for a long period of time will allow you to develop consistency in your shot.

> POSTGAME STATS COVERAGE

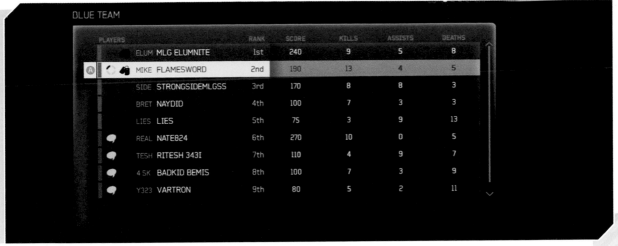

PLAYERS		RANK	SCORE	KILLS	ASSISTS	DEATHS
ELUM	MLG ELUMNITE	1st	240	9	5	8
MIKE	FLAMESWORD	2nd	190	13	4	5
SIDE	STRONGSIDEMLGSS	3rd	170	8	8	3
BRET	NAYDID	4th	100	7	3	3
LIES	LIES	5th	75	3	9	13
REAL	NATE824	6th	270	10	0	5
TESH	RITESH 343I	7th	110	4	9	7
4 SK	BADKID BEMIS	8th	100	7	3	9
Y323	VARTRON	9th	80	5	2	11

Looking for bragging rights? Even the player with the worst game can usually find something to crow about here.

In reality, stats don't mean anything when playing a team game, because you always want to make the right play for your team instead of playing for a K/D (kill/death) ratio. However, looking at the stats can be an entertaining way to break down what happened during a game.

On the first page of the aptly named Carnage Report, you can view your total score, total kills, total assists, and total deaths.

On the second page is your average life span, K/D spread, longest kill spree, and total medals. On the third page is your total weapon kills, total grenade kills, total melee kills, and total "other" kills.

When you click on a player's name, you bring up another page, allowing you to browse through every player's medals and tool of destruction. You'll also see who you killed the most, who killed you the most, and top medals.

> GUIDE TO A GOOD PLAYING ENVIRONMENT

It's difficult to win if you are distracted, or otherwise are suffering from less than ideal conditions. If you improve your game-playing environment, your kill/death ration is sure to improve.

Having complete focus is vital when you play. Having people trying to talk to you, a sibling listening to loud music, the TV blaring, or even your parents or significant other screaming on the other side of the door threatening to unplug the Internet leads to distraction. Distraction leads to failure.

Remove as many distractions as possible to focus on your gameplay. Some gamers like to sit on a sofa, a computer chair, or even lie down on a bed or recliner. Find the position you're most comfortable in, and attempt to play that way every time you game.

If you're going to be gaming for a while, make sure you're comfortable but keep a good posture; hunching your back or leaning to one side isn't good for your body. Poor posture can lead to back or arm pain at the end of a gaming session.

If you notice you're getting tired and starting to slouch, your game is probably suffering too. Take a break (ideally every hour) and raid the fridge or take a power nap. Then return refreshed and invigorated.

Keep the temperature of your room comfortable. Some enjoy air-conditioning, while others prefer the heat. Also be sure to play in comfortable clothing.

Everyone can get sick, and during those times you might still feel like playing some *Halo 4*. However don't be surprised if your performance suffers. Being sick can affect your mental state, which can lead to some questionable judgement calls. Your reactions might be slower, which can also be quite frustrating. Simply put, if you're not feeling well, get the rest, food, and medicine you need so you can recover. If that means you need to take some time off from the game, it might be for the best that you do so.

Being competitive can help you get better at anything you do in life, and *Halo 4* is no exception. However, being competitive doesn't mean you can't show some common courtesy, either over Xbox LIVE or when you're playing in the same room with a group of friends. Being a generally chill and agreeable person can make any match or event you participate in a more enjoyable time.

INTRODUCTION

BASIC TRAINING

INTEL

CAMPAIGN

INFINITY

APPENDIX

Learn where your foes will be and how long they take to reach there, and drop them as they arrive.

1. Enemy Movement: Pay attention to where your enemies tend to move to, camp, or snipe from. If you memorize the "hot spots" of each map (detailed in this guide), you'll have the edge on your opponent with an early nade or first shot on them in the battle.

> Know where your enemies like to snipe from: It decreases the kills they inflict on you when you're running around looking for them. You can then find a safe route to take them out.

> Know the hot spots or routes that your opponents like to frequent. This also gives you a head start as you prepare to fight them. If you can predict your enemies, you'll be one step closer to becoming a better player.

> You always need to be thinking where your opponent is or where your opponent is spawning.

2. Shots and Strafing: Focus on your shots and your strafing. You need to be sure you're hitting with all of your shots, as missing with even *one* shot allows your foe the upper hand in battle. Bring the pitch and yaw sensitivity down if you're having trouble aiming. Playing on a fast sensitivity is excellent if you want to turn around quickly, but it takes both time and practice to control the speed and accuracy of your aim.

> Take notice of your surroundings by using a wall or rock to peek and shoot at your opponent. This makes you infuriatingly difficult to hit, and your foe usually gets angry and makes a mistake.

> Pay attention to how you move when you're shooting: Are you moving forward in a straight line, standing still, or moving left to right? Moving in a straight line or standing still is the easiest way to aim and shoot your opponent...but it's easy for them to strike you as well.

> Left to right strafing works the best in most situations, as your opponent has the additional effort of using his right thumbstick to keep his reticle trained on you.

✪ Tip

Advanced Tip: Jumping and crouching is also good to use toward the end of a fight or if you are weak. These evasive moves make it increasingly difficult for your opponent to finish you off with a headshot.

> However, jumping and crouching also make it harder for you to shoot your opponent, although this problem is negated after lengthy practice sessions.

3. Backing Down: It doesn't make you any less of a Spartan killing machine to back down from a fight. In fact, it takes extra intelligence and cunning to realize when it's beneficial to break off from a fracas, rest, and then return to take down a troublesome foe.

> If you're down in shots during a protracted battle, retreat to stay alive, regain your shields, and return again. If possible, call for your teammates to help keep you alive. It isn't worth fighting to your death and giving your enemies another kill. This is just pride messing with you: Forget pride.

4. Power Weapons Knowledge: It's incredibly important to study and learn all the locations within a map, especially where the power weapons are placed. When a game begins, sprint to the power weapons on the map (splitting up your team to secure more than one, if necessary). Once you obtain the power weapon, you have the advantage.

> Familiarity with the maps, and where these weapons spawn, is key here.

✪ Tip

Advanced Tip: Sometimes it is worth baiting the power weapons. When your opponent is going directly for a power weapon, ambushing them or training your weapons at the power weapon's location allows you to score an easy kill and claim the power weapon afterward.

5. Learn the loadouts: Knowing how all of the different loadouts affect your gameplay is critical to your continued well-being.

› There are counters to every armor ability.

› Make multiple loadouts so you can swap them throughout a game if your foes are controlling the game due to their armor abilities. This keeps your game from becoming stale or predictable.

› It is advisable to have at least three of your favorite loadouts to choose from.

6. Sometimes Slaughtering. Sometimes Sneaky: It isn't necessary to plan every attack run around a tanklike, violent, running-and-gunning style of game. In fact, it's the quickest way to earning yourself a reputation for being predictable. Mimicking the style of a suicide Grunt is usually frowned upon in professional team circles.

› Instead, if you're behind multiple enemies, wait for the right moment to attack them. Don't simply start shooting and have them turn around and cut you down. Instead, bide your time, cut them down with quick, brief blasts from a location they don't predict, and stay stealthy.

› Or, attempt a subtle and quiet run up to your foe at the perfect moment, and initiate the battle with a well-timed assassination!

7. Wait. Did You Hear Anything? You're likely to hear the battle going on and your teammates radioing to each other. But there's a world of difference between hearing and actually listening. And then responding with intelligence:

› Listen to where shots are coming from and you'll have an idea of your opponent's location.

› Listen to what your teammates are calling out, and respond when needed. Keep your chatter to a minimum and help when you can.

› Utilize headphones. Play in a quiet environment. Invest in a surround-sound audio setup. Gain every advantage you can; if you can hear precisely where in the 360-degree sound field that sounds are coming from, you can react more quickly and instinctively.

> THEATER: IMPROVING AS A PLAYER

If you just got your posterior handed to you, consult the theater for the reasons why. This film doesn't lie.

For those with previous knowledge of the theater in *Halo: Reach*, expect a similar setup in *Halo 4*. Consult the instruction manual and onscreen menu for the basics of using this mode. The following section details how to use this mode to improve as a player:

› You can improve as a player simply by studying the gameplay footage you've stored on your console: Save some matches that you both win and lose throughout an extended gaming session, and then watch them in Theater mode later. Study them to figure out what you did correctly and incorrectly:

› With every game you lost, pinpoint the mistakes you made, and understand what you could have done differently to minimize that from occurring in the future.

› With every game you won, notice what you were doing to achieve victory. What locations were you successfully holding? What angles were you shooting from? Note that for future matches.

› Pour over footage of your enemies and enemy teams during games that you lost. See what you could have done to clinch the game for you or your team. You can always find several tips, tricks, jumps, grenade-impact points, and strategies by watching these replays.

› Watching replays allows you to predict your opponents throughout future games—seeing their patrol routes, the locations they favor, their preferred weapons, and the angles they shoot from.

› Did your opponent or opposing team implement a particularly impressive tactic or takedown? Then mimic what they did if it worked well for them, or add some of your own strategic planning and refine the tactic, making it your own.

› Viewing your gameplay helps minimize the mistakes you consistently make and allows you to advance both confidently and competently at a much faster rate than normal.

INTRODUCTION

BASIC TRAINING

INTEL

CAMPAIGN

INFINITY

APPENDIX

FORGE

Returning to *Halo 4* in grand style is the Forge. This special editing tool allows players to take existing maps and modify them with the Forge tool set. Introduced in *Halo 3,* Forge has resulted in changed levels and new Game Types created by the Halo community, soaring well above the expectations of the developers behind the games.

Forge has allowed dedicated fans to create enduring modifications of existing levels that have gained their own dedicated following. Over time, perhaps you will be able to create a new map variation, or a new battleground on one of the three Forge maps that thousands around the world will enjoy!

> UPDATES TO FORGE

Players familiar with Forge will recognize old features from previous iterations, but there are many key improvements to the toolset that 343 Industries has brought to the table, all of whom will help map-makers create more ambitious levels than ever before.

- ❭ Highlight Selection – No longer will players be confused as to which object they have selected for editing.
- ❭ Magnets – Objects can now be properly aligned without spending long minutes or hours ensuring that everything is connected just right.
- ❭ Duping Assets – You're now able to copy assets easily, which can help speed up the creation of more complex structures.
- ❭ Locking – No more accidentally ruining a whole section of a map because you moved something out of place. If you're satisfied with something, lock it into place.

Additionally, Forge mode has seen improvements to its visuals.

- ❭ Overall Lighting System - Single Probe Spherical Harmonic lighting (no really, that is what its called) ensures objects match the lighting of the map much more closely. A nice aesthetic improvement that can help make user maps look closer to what the proffessionals create.
- ❭ Object Integration – Cast shadows help integrate the forge objects into the map they are placed in, as well as helping place them spatially as a player.
- ❭ Visual Overhaul of Forge Objects – Updated geometry, materials and textures for increased visual fidelity and better integration with static map objects.

Forge users now have the ability to modify the properties of different sections of their creations, as opposed to making map-wide changes. Have low gravity environments outside of normal gravity zones!

- ❭ Player Movement – Forgers can create zones where player movement speed and jump height are greatly altered
- ❭ Shield power – Zones can be created to dramatically increase/ decrease shield power
- ❭ Player visibility – Zones can be created to affect player visibility
- ❭ Physics – Zones can be created to affect the physics/gravity of players and objects
- ❭ Damage – Zones can be created to affect players' Damage resistance / invulnerability

> FORGE MAPS

Forge allows for modifications to the 10 existing maps that come with *Halo 4*, with some limitations to the tools that can be used on these pre-fabricated locations. However, there are three specific Forge maps available for players to use that will allow them complete access to the entire Forge tool set.

IMPACT

LOCATION: Impact site with peculiar qualities.

This observation outpost was established to examine the site of a spectacularly violent meteor collision recorded by an ONI patrol drone in 2547. When researchers first arrived, they were startled to find a non-native fragment of the impacting agent had actually survived and was of unknown alien origin. More recently, interest in the site has grown as the fragment has proven to have originated from long before the earliest of known Forerunner artifacts.

EROSION

LOCATION: Underground on Eudemon X49-05, potential future UNSC colony world.

DESCRIPTION: With hundreds of human colonies now razed in the wake of the Covenant War, the UNSC has dispatched large numbers of advanced pioneer groups to survey potential new worlds. The discovery of Eudemon X49-05 was considered lucky, but concerns remain about the moon's structural integrity.

RAVINE

LOCATION: A ravine on Requiem.

DESCRIPTION: When ONI dispatched its first expeditionary group to this sector, it was believed that these impressive citadels were individual constructs strategically organized to protect this portion of Requiem. Teams on the ground now believe that they are actually the ramparts and battlements of an impossibly large structure below the surface of the sea.

MAPS

There are a total of 13 maps to choose from in your Matchmaking playlists. It is imperative that you use this guide to learn the layouts of each one and how you (or your team) can control them during games. There are three Forge maps (Erosion, Impact, and Ravine) and three default variations of them (Ascent, Relay, and Settler); six larger maps (Complex, Exile, Longbow, Meltdown, Ragnarok, and Vortex); and four small to medium maps (Abandon, Adrift, Haven, and Solace).

For each map, we provide a cartographical overview, which we further overlay with weapon drops and other helpful data. The map overview is also sectioned into different areas known as "hot spots," which have a name and tactical note; use this name to inform your teammates that you're moving or fighting in a particular hot spot. We also cover what to expect or do when you head into one of these areas. Finally, we provide additional strategic notes, usually regarding the usual game types played on the map in question.

> HOT SPOTS: WHAT'S IN A NAME?

Every map has been divided up into several hot spots. Each one has its own name (such as "Blue Base" or "Broken Bridge"), and most are named due to their features. Others (such as "Mohawk") are named because the hot spot is shaped like a particular object. And others (such as "Blue Cave" and "Top Jerk") have evolved through gameplay and easy associations. For example, "Top Jerk" refers to a rooftop location and the type of person who's camping out and sniping from the roof. Use these words when telling your teammates where you are or where to push or defend. The hot spots were named so they're easily remembered and heard during matches, but feel free to call any area anything you wish.

> HOT SPOTS: WHAT'S IN AN ICON?

Many of the hot spots across a map have an icon after their name. There are four types, and all refer to the type of activity you should expect (and sometimes avoid) at each area:

Choke hot spot: Expect high traffic, numerous enemies, and a well-used thoroughfare. Combat usually occurs here, and the location may be watched by enemy snipers.

Danger hot spot: This is an area of ground that is difficult to defend, has poor visibility for shooting angles, is sunken or low to the ground, or is in the open. Expect to be shot at if you're here. Avoid if possible.

Mirrored hot spot: This location features an identical (or mostly identical) facsimile, almost always on the opposite side of the map. Expect tactical advice to be the same for both locations. Usually these are "blue" and "red" variants of a hot spot.

Sniper hot spot: This location is excellent for sniping, as it has numerous angles and views across much of the map. Expect long-range fire from these areas.

> ### ▶ Note
>
> Just because a hot spot features this flag doesn't necessarily mean other hot spots aren't suited for sniping or other situations. These icons simply refer to the main locations for such activities.

ABANDON

Initial surveys of Erebus VII were promising and hopeful, but the events which followed tell a far darker story.

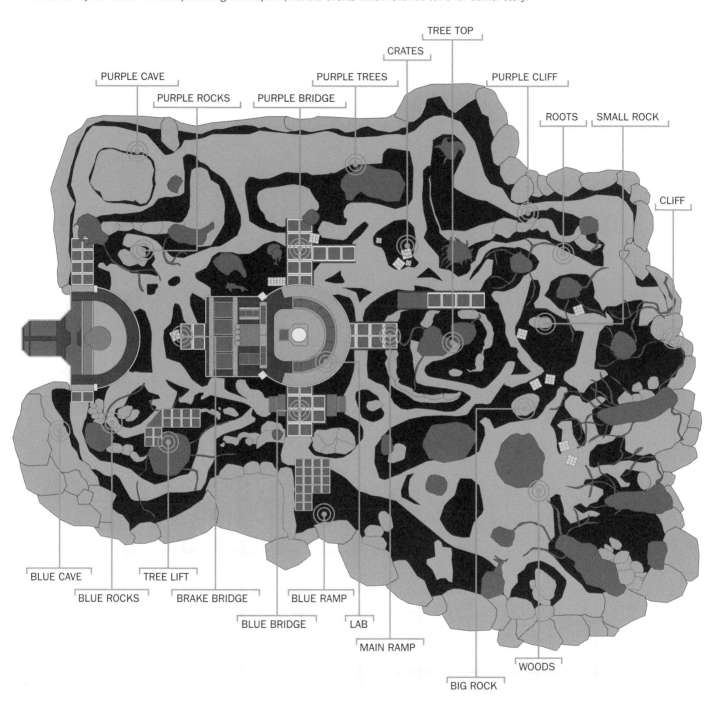

PURPLE CAVE

PURPLE ROCKS

PURPLE BRIDGE

PURPLE TREES

CRATES

TREE TOP

PURPLE CLIFF

ROOTS   SMALL ROCK

CLIFF

BLUE CAVE

BLUE ROCKS

TREE LIFT

BRAKE BRIDGE

BLUE BRIDGE

BLUE RAMP

LAB

MAIN RAMP

BIG ROCK

WOODS

Choke hot spot: Expect high traffic, numerous enemies, and a well-used thoroughfare. Combat usually occurs here, and the location may be watched by enemy snipers.

Danger hot spot: This is an area of ground that is difficult to defend, has poor visibility for shooting angles, is sunken or low to the ground, or is in the open. Expect to be shot at if you're here. Avoid if possible.

Mirrored hot spot: This location features an identical (or mostly identical) facsimile, almost always on the opposite side of the map. Expect tactical advice to be the same for both locations. Usually these are "blue" and "red" variants of a hot spot.

Sniper hot spot: This location is excellent for sniping, as it has numerous angles and views across much of the map. Expect long-range fire from these areas.

HALO 4

> HOT SPOTS

1. Blue Ramp

This is great to hold when you're carrying the ball in the Woods (20). You can keep opponents pinned down at the Lab (9) and spray bullets down when the other team tries to sneak into the Woods. This location is also great to head to during Rumble Pit and Regicide games. Move from the Blue Ramp (1) to the Blue Bridge (3) and back. When heading to the Blue Bridge, try to clean up, killing foes around the Lab and Tower (16). When you return to the Blue Ramp, watch for (and get easy kills on) players spawning in the Woods.

2. Big Rock

This natural protuberance is a good spot to take cover no matter the angle from which you are taking fire. Use the Big Rock, in conjunction with a Jet Pack, to juke your opponent right out of their boots.

3. Blue Bridge ◉

Hold this location, as it's the perfect support-fire spot. You can shoot toward the Cliff (7) or Tower (16) and retreat to the opposite side if you start taking fire from your opponent.

4. Blue Cave

Use this area when retreating behind a corner. You can use it to watch the lab tunnel (near 9) if holding a setup that revolves around the tower side of the map.

5. Blue Rocks

There's no reason to wait around here for too long; this area is mainly used if you want to wall-shoot (get shots off while a majority of your Spartan is behind cover), assuming you're in trouble, before running to Tower 1 (16).

6. Broken Bridge

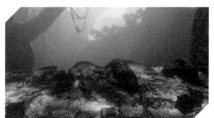

During Oddball, this is a great place to be, as you can drop down into Lab 1 (9A) and run away if necessary. You can also jump and cut off your opponent at Tower 2 (17).

7. Cliff ⚠

It's unwise to remain here; you're wide open to attack from almost every angle on the map.

8. Crates

The Crates give you enough room to wall-shoot instead of getting involved in a 1v1 fight in the wide open. Try to bait your enemy out so they have no cover, while you use the crates to dodge incoming fire.

9A. Lab 1 (L1)

The lower Lab level is an excellent place to which to bait the enemy team if you have Lab 3 (9C) under your control, as you can easily lift up to run away.

9B. Lab 2 (L2)

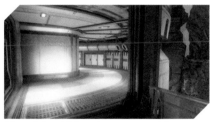

The midlevel laboratory area enables you to move from the Blue Bridge (3), Purple Bridge (21), and Lab 3 (9C) quickly. This is helpful for support players, as they can pick which bridge to shoot from depending where the enemy is located.

9C. Lab 3 (L3)

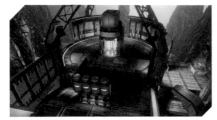

This is the "power position" to be in for all the game types. Stalking foes from this location is preferable, as you have a clear line of sight for the entire map. During Team Slayer variants, hold this along with either the Blue or Purple side of the map. If you can do this, you can force your foes to spawn only on the side you don't control most of the time, meaning you have less of the map to check for incoming foes.

In addition, you can hold the ball in here. Start by holding the ball in Lab 1 (9A), and when the ball carrier faces danger, he should throw the ball up the grav-lift to Lab 3 (9C). When holding the ball here, an endangered ball carrier can drop down to the Broken Bridge (6) or Main Ramp (10) (whichever route is safer), and return to Lab 1 to start the maneuver again.

10. Main Ramp

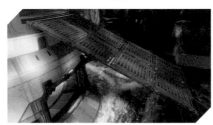

Utilize the Main Ramp when you're trying to bounce grenades into the Lab (9). This is a common choke point and features in numerous battles. Move off of this ramp quickly, or you'll be open to shots and lack cover.

11. Purple Cliff

This hot spot is great to hold on to when you're playing Rumble Pit or Regicide. You have a good line of sight toward Treetop (18) and Lab 3 (9C), enabling you to clean up with kills before looking toward the Woods (20), Cliff (7), and Roots (14). View foes at these points and catch them

spawning and off guard. This is also a great place to be during Team Slayer variants if you have Lab (9) control, so you can spot if the other team spawns around the Cliff and Woods.

12. Purple Rocks !

This is another spot you don't want to stand around in for too long, as the enemy can easily grenade you. However, it is effective to wall-shoot and run to Tower 1 (16) from here. You can maneuver on top of the Purple Rocks and jump toward the Purple Cliff (11) from here as well.

13. Purple Trees

There are a few trees to hide behind here, allowing you to catch all who come in unprepared with a sneaky assassination!

14. Roots

Use this area for cover when you're slowing pushing out of the Purple Cliff (11) spawning areas.

15. Small Rock

This is another rock that's used mainly for cover so you can regain shields while at the map's edge. You can push to Treetop (18) when your shields are up.

16. Tower 1 (T1)

There are no shooting angles from down here, but if timed perfectly in team games, you can lift up to Tower 2 (17) and take down any weak enemies.

17. Tower 2 (T2)

This is a good spot for Slayer variants when you're the lead, as it forces the other team to come to you.

18. Treetop

A commendable place for aggressive players to use when wall-shooting, if the opponent is spawning at the Cliff (7). This is also a great spot to be in to check the Purple Trees (13).

19. Tree Lift

This is your number-one escape route when you're milling around the Blue Cave (4) or Blue Rocks (5). You'll primarily use the lift to ascend into the Blue Cave, but if you're running away, you can use Flamesword's Pro Jump (detailed below) and drop to the bottom from Blue Cave for a quick getaway.

20. Woods

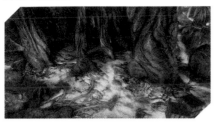

Hide here with the ball if your teammates have control of the Blue Cave (1). This forces the other team to engage you from the wide open, which allows for your team to easily pick them off. Try wall-shooting or peek-shooting (when you strafe in and out of cover while tagging your opponent with shots) from here.

21. Purple Bridge

If Blue Bridge (3) isn't suiting your needs, then switch over to this bridge! This is a great area to be when laying down support fire toward Cliff (7) or Tower (16) or when keeping foes contained in Purple Trees (13). This hot spot is very useful, because if you get in trouble, you can enter the Lab (9) and pick your escape route—either to the top (because you have teammates covering) or, if you are playing an individual game types, across Lab 2 (9B), to the bottom on the other side, near Blue Bridge's (3) entrance.

> TACTICS: TEAM GAMES

Be careful about roaming solo on this map, there's plenty of hiding places for crafty players.

To control the labs is to control the map.

Controlling the Top Lab (L3)

Make sure your team heads here; this position has a bird's-eye view over almost the entire map. The Lab's top floor also allows you to provide covering fire and clean up many kills your fellow teammates didn't manage to finish.

Don't step away from this location; it's almost always a good idea to keep at least one teammate patrolling here.

If the opposing force tries to charge the top Lab (L3), you have numerous escape options: you can drop to L2 or L1 and wait for your team to help; then use the Lift or ascend back to L3 and retake it.

If you've lost control of the Lab, attack it from disparate points (rather than clustered in the same place) with your teammates and reclaim that power position!

Packing a Punch

The Jet Pack is an excellent choice on this map, as you can fly up and land on top of the Lab, shooting down at foes inside. This gunfire is usually unexpected, heightening the chances of confusing your foes and eventually routing them.

On the Prowl

Watch the Lifts! Don't get too sidetracked with dropping foes from across the map; you never know when your opponent might be sneaking up on you. Snipers need spotters!

Another option is to stay low on the outskirts of the map; it's a great way to move around unnoticed. You might be able to sneak up to an opponent by limiting your fire and ducking behind a tree, rock, or other scenery.

INTRODUCTION · BASIC TRAINING · INTEL · CAMPAIGN · INFINITY · APPENDIX

In a situation like this, throw the ball at your enemy to force the guns out of their hands.

On the Ball: Position 1

Hang out with the Oddball by the Tower 2 and Purple Cave areas for maximum security from enemy fire. You should be able to rely on your team and the scenery to provide you with the protection you need.

Run back and forth from the Purple Cave and Blue Cave when the opposition is pushing at you from either flank.

Your teammates without the ball should employ Promethean Vision and Sensor; this gives your team the first jump on your foes, making it even more difficult for them to reach the ball.

Dropping the Ball

Remember you can always drop the ball and help take down enemies with your teams; this buys even more ball time. Although holding the ball and not helping gains you points, the long-term disadvantages outweigh the small score additions: Refusing to drop the ball makes it easier for the opposition to control the map. Instead of a 4v5 battle, drop the ball and even the odds to 5v5.

On the Ball: Position 2

Holding the ball down by the Cliff, Big Rock, or Woods and setting up a defensive barrier of teammates around you is another good setup when you're trying to keep the ball. You have numerous cover opportunities, and can bait the other team into charging you. If your team is losing control of this part of the map, you can throw the ball off the map's edge and make it respawn, decreasing the chances of the opposition gaining points.

On the Ball: Position 3

The Lift in the Lab is another great spot for holding the ball; it's also an excellent way to eliminate a potential attack point (the Lift itself). If the enemy assaults the Lift, give them a good smack with the skull, and send them to a long respawn. Be sure to watch for incoming grenades, though!

> SPARTANS OF MLG: EXPERT JUMPS

The following expert jumps are possible on this map. Practice, and look at the step-by-step picture guidance to perfect them, as they can considerably aid you in your maneuvering.

ELUMNITE

First-person perspective: Lab tunnel jump.

Third-person perspective: Lab tunnel jump. Find the crack in the wall allowing you a second jump onto the box.

FLAMESWORD

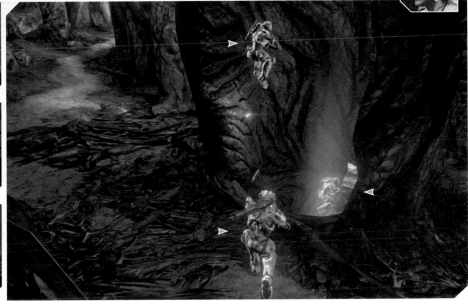

First-person perspective: Tree Lift dive.

Third-person perspective: Tree Lift dive. You must jump into the side of the wall to make this jump down through the lift.

INTRODUCTION

BASIC TRAINING

INTEL

CAMPAIGN

INFINITY

APPENDIX

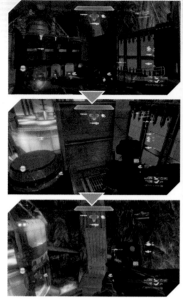

First-person perspective: jump on top of the Lab for a sneaky spot.

Third-person perspective: jump on top of the Lab for a sneaky spot. Timing is the key here. You must get to the very edge of the first box before making the long jump to the top.

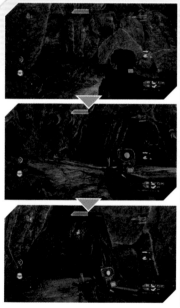

First-person perspective: Purple Cave jump.

Third-person perspective: Purple Cave jump. There's a sneaky little crack in the rock wall you can land on.

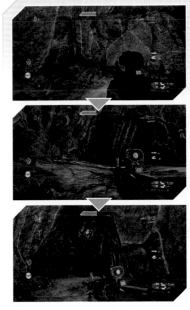

First-person perspective: Tree Jump to Top Lab (L3).

Third-person perspective: Tree Jump to Top Lab (L3). This is another timing jump. Practice makes perfect.

INTRODUCTION

BASIC TRAINING

INTEL

CAMPAIGN

INFINITY

APPENDIX

ADRIFT

Now fully dedicated to supporting the war effort, this mining vessel once served the UNSC's colonization efforts.

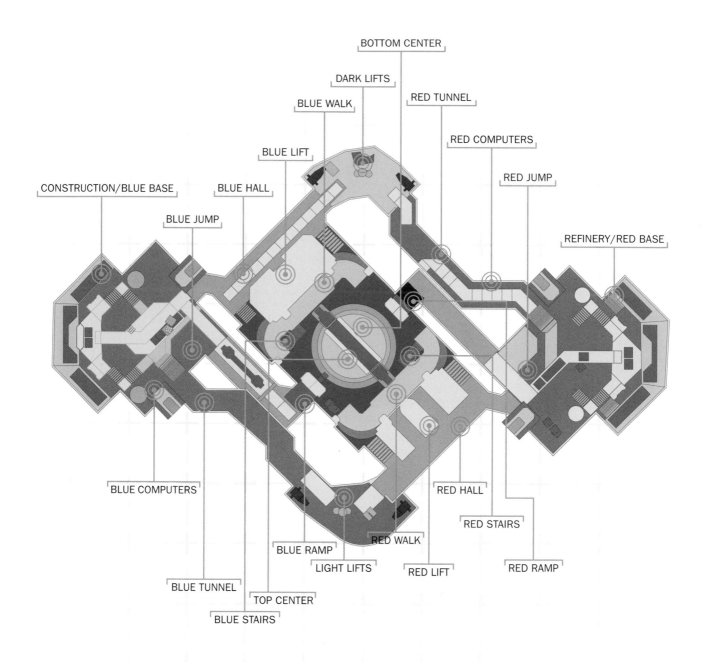

Choke hot spot: Expect high traffic, numerous enemies, and a well-used thoroughfare. Combat usually occurs here, and the location may be watched by enemy snipers.

Danger hot spot: This is an area of ground that is difficult to defend, has poor visibility for shooting angles, is sunken or low to the ground, or is in the open. Expect to be shot at if you're here. Avoid if possible.

Mirrored hot spot: This location features an identical (or mostly identical) facsimile, almost always on the opposite side of the map. Expect tactical advice to be the same for both locations. Usually these are "blue" and "red" variants of a hot spot.

Sniper hot spot: This location is excellent for sniping, as it has numerous angles and views across much of the map. Expect long-range fire from these areas.

> HOT SPOTS

Aside from a central area, this map is mirrored. Half of the map is labeled "red" and the other half "blue" (although they don't directly relate to the color of the team spawning there). Tactical advice applies to both locations unless otherwise stated.

1A. Blue Computers

1B. Red Computers

This is an excellent location to start your push toward the Top Center Room (8) or to the top of one of the two bases. If you spot incoming grenades, retreat from this location, as you're an easy target here, and the enemy knows you've taken damage.

2A. Blue Hall

2B. Red Hall

Push toward this location and then into the Top Center Room (8) when you have teammates also pushing from the Blue/Red Computers (1); this allows for two points of attack. This is also a sneaky route you can take to try and outflank or get behind the opposing team.

3A. Blue Lift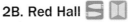

3B. Red Lift

Keep this area in mind when you're in the Top Center Room (8) and looking for an escape route. When you need a break from the action, retreat to this area and recharge your shields.

4A. Blue Ramp

4B. Red Ramp

Drop down and flee to this area if necessary. You don't want to hang around here for too long, though, as you don't have a great line of sight on anyone inside the Top Center Room (8).

5A. Blue Stairs

5B. Red Stairs

Utilize this area as cover, especially if you're caught at the lower level of the Top Center Room (8B); wait here to recharge your shields or make a run to the Blue/Red Lift (3) or Blue/Red Ramp (4).

INTRODUCTION BASIC TRAINING INTEL CAMPAIGN INFINITY APPENDIX

6A. Blue Tunnel

6B. Red Tunnel

Take this route if you're running the flag and an escort is helping you. This is also a sneaky route to take when trying to outflank or get behind your enemies.

7A. Blue Walk

7B. Red Walk

This is a reasonably safe spot to stay if your team has control of the Top Center Room (8). You can watch the opposite walkway and hall, and your teammates can check your back and tackle foes (with your help) attempting to attack you from behind. If the Mech Room isn't in your team's hands, stay out of this location, as there's no cover.

8A. Top Center Room

8B. Bottom Center Room

The upper room is the hub of violent activity on this map. If you stay here for too long, expect to receive enemy fire from every entrance into this section. Although there's a cubbyhole to hide in (briefly), don't expect to last here unless you've got a teammate backing you up.

The lower chamber isn't a safe place to stay either; although you have angles from which you can shoot foes above you, you're easily susceptible to grenades. Only head down here if you're attempting to flee.

9A. Construction Site: Blue Base

9B. Refinery: Red Base

It is strongly recommended that you hold this base in Team Regicide to protect your king. Position teammates at the top of the base, and target enemies who are lifting; you have great cover from this vantage point.

10A. Dark Blue

10B. Light Blue

Lift up here when you have teammates pushing into the Base (9) for a different point of attack. Go here to retreat from your opponents and get close to your teammates for backup.

HALO 4

11A. Dark Lifts

11B. Light Lifts

Head here when you want to lift to either base (9) and have the jump on your enemies. You can also use either Lift when retreating. Use the box at the lift for cover if an enemy is charging you.

12A. Dark Red

12B. Light Red

Lift here when you have teammates pushing into the base for a different point of attack. Go here to retreat from your opponents and get close to your teammates for backup.

> TACTICS: TEAM GAMES AND KING OF THE HILL

Corridors like these can be death traps with little useful cover.

"Mech" is the all important central hub of this map.

Go Ahead, Mech My Day

Controlling the Top Center Room in the middle of this map is of paramount importance, as it stops the opposition from swarming and enables you to spot foes much more easily. In order to help secure the Top Center Room, you also need to control the computers; this gives you the higher ground and a view over most of the map's center (the Top Center Room).

Hilltop Tips

When you're trying to lock down the hills on this map, control the doors and entrances with two or three of your teammates on the hill. Having more than one teammate at or near the hill is extremely advantageous.

If you're playing King of the Hill on this map, maneuver around almost continuously. The hill moves every 30 seconds, and sometimes you need to give up 5 to 10 seconds on a previous hill just to set up at the hill's new location.

Base Lockdowns

With the hills on the Red and Blue Bases, you need to lock the base down with your entire team, watching every entrance point. If you're attempting to take over the base, attack from several angles: from computers, lifts, hallways, and tunnels.

Don't Get Caught Short

This map has several long hallways, so don't get attached to using short-range weapons. They may be helpful when you round a corner and stumble into a foe, but if you're caught with a short-range weapon while running down a hallway, you're severely disadvantaged against a foe firing from long range.

INTRODUCTION · BASIC TRAINING · INTEL · CAMPAIGN · INFINITY · APPENDIX

Flying High

Try to gain the height advantage inside the Top Center Room: With so many entrances, it's important to hold Top Center as often as possible. Try not to drop down to pursue weakened foes unless it's absolutely necessary.

Equipping the Jet Pack on this map allows you to quickly move from place to place and take advantage of a very vertical map.

> TACTICS: CAPTURE THE FLAG

Route Markers

You have three excellent routes to take—Computer, Hallway, or Tunnel—but be sure you or your team escorts the flag carrier back to your base instead of leaving him to fend for himself. How your team plays will determine your favored route, but it's always better to vary your routes to keep your foes on their toes.

Be careful when traversing the exteriors of this map, there are always plenty of access points the enemy can use.

> TACTICS: TEAM SLAYER

Always watch elevated ramps and ledges to catch potential ambushers off guard.

Strength in Numbers

Running with at least one teammate is advisable, due to the sheer number of hallways. When the opposition steps around a corner and there are two (or more) of you ready to retaliate, you can light your foe up for an easy kill!

There are many escape routes if you're losing a 1v1 battle; turn and spring away toward your teammates for reinforcements.

Swordplay and Patience

Be patient when you've armed yourself with the Energy Sword. Bait your enemy to close in on you, and then time a sliced lunge to carve them up.

COMPLEX

Galileo's compartmentalized layout benefits protracted defensive stands in the unlikely event of an attack.

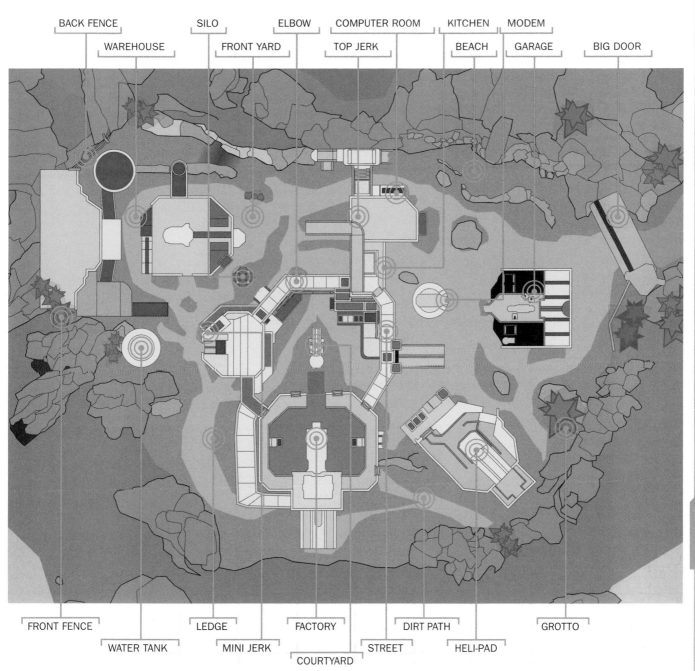

INTRODUCTION

BASIC TRAINING

INTEL

CAMPAIGN

INFINITY

APPENDIX

Choke hot spot: Expect high traffic, numerous enemies, and a well-used thoroughfare. Combat usually occurs here, and the location may be watched by enemy snipers.

Danger hot spot: This is an area of ground that is difficult to defend, has poor visibility for shooting angles, is sunken or low to the ground, or is in the open. Expect to be shot at if you're here. Avoid if possible.

Mirrored hot spot: This location features an identical (or mostly identical) facsimile, almost always on the opposite side of the map. Expect tactical advice to be the same for both locations. Usually these are "blue" and "red" variants of a hot spot.

Sniper hot spot: This location is excellent for sniping, as it has numerous angles and views across much of the map. Expect long-range fire from these areas.

1. Beach

Scout this area for some rocks that provide reasonable cover; this area is useful for sneaking up to Top Jerk (19).

2. Big Door !

The open area by this scenic point is dangerous; don't stand around here for too long! During team matches, if you see an enemy here, keep them alive for a few seconds so more of their team members spawn there—then take them all down!

3. Computer Room

This area provides a great hiding place when you need to retreat and recharge your shields.

4. Courtyard !

Another dangerous area that you needn't spend much time in. If you do hang out here, expect to come off second best in combat, as it is difficult to spot enemies above you from this position.

5. Dirt Path

This is the optimal location when firing on foes moving about on Top Jerk (19). You have excellent cover for peek-and-shooting opportunities and a reasonably safe escape route into the Factory (7).

6. Elbow

An open area if you're moving to and from the Kitchen (12) to the Mini Jerk (13). This has a view over the Front Yard (8), Silo (17), and Courtyard (4).

7A. Factory (Inside)

Seek out the Factory's interior; there's a lot of cover opportunities and your team can hold this area, cutting off all entry points to protect a king in Regicide matches.

7B. Factory (Outside) !

If you venture outside, prepare to be severely compromised. You have zero cover and very few good angles for taking shots at foes. Spend as little time as you can out here.

8. Front Yard !

This position is extremely open and can be seen from many areas: Don't run through here without cover. Avoid this location unless you have no other choice.

9. Garage !

This area has similar properties to the Big Door (2), an open area that you don't want to hang around at for too long. During team matches, if you spot a foe here, leave them alive for an extra few seconds so more of their team members spawn there—then kill them all!

10. Grotto

Utilize this as cover when you're heading around to the Helipad (11) or when you're tagging foes holed up on Top Jerk (19). The cover provided allows for peek-and-shooting opportunities.

11. Helipad !

The Sniper Rifle spawns here, but don't get caught waiting for it to appear; staying here for too long leaves you open to attacks from others. The opposing team is certainly going to be watching this spot too. Grab the Sniper Rifle and flee!

12. Kitchen

This is an advantageous position with excellent cover if you're trying to tackle foes milling about at the Garage (9), Helipad (11), Front Yard (8), and Warehouse (21).

13. Mini Jerk ⦿

This is the smaller of the two structures whose roofs you can climb onto. These are known as "Jerks" due to the type of player who enjoys camping up on these rooftops. This is an excellent power position if your team is also holding the Top Jerk (19). Stay alive up here and become a severe nuisance to the opposition with long-range takedowns.

14. Modem ⦿

Use this structure to hide yourself from foes on the Top Jerk (19). You're able to make your way underneath the Top Jerk from here before sneaking up behind your enemies on the Top Jerk and removing them as a threat.

15. Rock

This rock provides great cover and grants you a height advantage over foes at the Warehouse (21). This is a recommended position if you're trying to keep enemies pushed back, inside the Warehouse.

16. Front Fence

Grab the Sniper Rifle from this location and move toward the rear of the Warehouse (21) or the Back Fence (20), where you can set up a camping spot from which to snipe. Don't stay in this area for long; you're too exposed.

17. Silo

Utilize this scenery when you're trying to jump from the Warehouse (21) to the Elbow (6) or back again. It is much more efficient to use this maneuver instead of taking the long route along the ground.

18. Street

The Street offers excellent positioning for shooting foes who are spawning at the Big Door (2), and it has great cover opportunities.

19. Top Jerk ⦿

This is the optimal location on this map. (The term "Jerk" describes the type of player who enjoys prowling on these rooftops.) This is an extreme power position; you have a commanding view over the entire map and can pick off a huge number of enemies from here. Your main task is to stay alive up here; you don't want the opposing team controlling this area. With a massive height (and cover) advantage, there's no reason for you to be killed by someone down on the ground.

20. Back Fence ◎

This is a commendable position from which to stop and tag enemies who are on the Top Jerk (19) and at the Rock (15).

21. Warehouse !

This is the worst location to be caught by enemy fire; if this happens, try moving toward the base of the Mini Jerk (13) and escape to the Factory (7).

22. Water Tank

This is a reasonably good place to hide near. Also think about using the Water Tank to protect yourself from foes at the back of the Warehouse (21) when you're at the Rock (15).

⟩ TACTICS: TEAM GAMES, INFINITY PRO SLAYER, INDIVIDUAL GAMES

The wide open exteriors leave most players vulnerable to rooftop snipers.

Controlling Top Jerk

Scramble to the roof of Top Jerk, and begin to rattle off covering fire for your teammates. Weaken as many of your foes as possible while remaining alive; let the teammates in other locations finish your foes off.

Use the ramps around the Top Jerk as cover opportunities.

Don't be afraid to enter the Kitchen; you have additional cover and you can fire through the Kitchen's open windows.

Banish thoughts of greed from your mind; don't hog the kills and leave Top Jerk to chase down a wounded foe; it is much more important to control this power position at all times.

The roof of Top Jerk is extremely advantageous if you're trying to pick off foes who are running in the open.

There's no place like Top Jerk if you want to control this map.

Controlling Mini Jerk

This is another vital power position; try to combine control of this and Top Jerk to completely thwart the opposition! Mini Jerk gives you more angles from which to cover your teammates and pick off kills. The preferred plan is to hold Mini Jerk while trapping opponents back at the Warehouse.

Warehouse Warning

Avoid remaining back at the Warehouse or in the Factory; this leads to your team becoming trapped.

If you become stuck at the Warehouse, ascend to the top of this location, or move to the Back Fence to obtain a better position and better angles; then start with covering fire on your foes at Top Jerk or Rock to back them off their perches. This helps the rest of your team sneak out and try to flank the opposition.

Work for the Jerk

Is the enemy set up on both Jerks? Then your team needs to work cohesively to take over both Jerk positions by focusing on one Jerk at a time, removing the threat, setting up a sniper up there, and then concentrating on the second Jerk.

If your team is controlling one or both Jerks, the remaining teammates (who aren't sitting on the rooftop) need to maneuver around to the Elbow and Walkway to gain an even better tactical advantage.

With both teams focusing on the Jerks, you also want to make sure you've plotted out a safe route around the map (depending on the foes atop the Jerks and where they're focusing their fire). Always have an escape route, interspersed with scenic objects you can hide behind.

> RIFLES, ORDNANCE, AND LONG-RANGE RAMPAGING

It's easy to catch players out in the open on Complex.

Teams tend to focus a great deal of their time on long-range combat, so you need to stay away from the Assault Rifles and Storm Rifles when choosing your loadout or picking up weapons. Grab a trusty DMR, Battle Rifle, or Covenant Carbine if you want to rack up those kills.

There are several ordnance spawns on this map, but they're exposed to many lines of sight. Don't be intimidated; simply bait an ordnance drop and pick off foes who are drawn to the Navpoint (the indicator displayed when ordnance is on the map) in the hopes of obtaining a power weapon.

Staying in the open leads to a quick death on this map: Avoid being exposed for too long; always make sure you have a corner to head around, in case a foe begins pinging you with gunfire from across the map.

If it's late in the game and you have the lead, don't get reckless; it's better to sit in one of the many buildings on the map and force the enemy to come to you, or die trying!

Focus on securing the lines of sight with your team. By working together, you're able to gain a field of vision on nearly every long-range sightline on the map. Think of this as an advance warning system, reacting first as the other team looks to push you out of your power positions.

First-person perspective: Top Jerk sneaky jumps #1.

Third-person perspective: Top Jump sneaky jumps #1. This leap of faith is worth it after a little practice.

EXILE

Stranded on a remote world, a handful of survivors managed to use their ship's debris to thrive long after the crash.

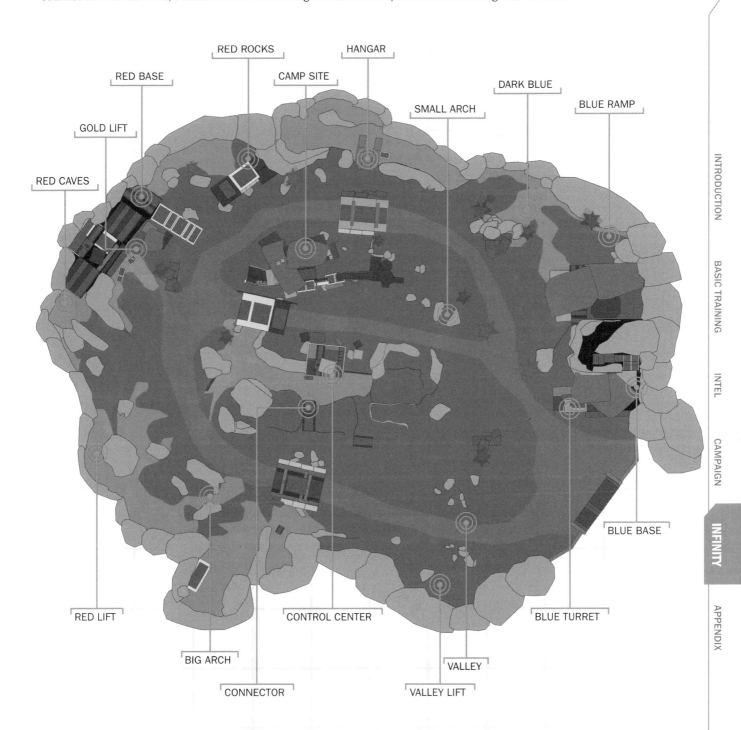

RED ROCKS
HANGAR
RED BASE
CAMP SITE
DARK BLUE
BLUE RAMP
GOLD LIFT
SMALL ARCH
RED CAVES
RED LIFT
CONTROL CENTER
BLUE BASE
BIG ARCH
BLUE TURRET
CONNECTOR
VALLEY
VALLEY LIFT

Choke hot spot: Expect high traffic, numerous enemies, and a well-used thoroughfare. Combat usually occurs here, and the location may be watched by enemy snipers.

Danger hot spot: This is an area of ground that is difficult to defend, has poor visibility for shooting angles, is sunken or low to the ground, or is in the open. Expect to be shot at if you're here. Avoid if possible.

Mirrored hot spot: This location features an identical (or mostly identical) facsimile, almost always on the opposite side of the map. Expect tactical advice to be the same for both locations. Usually these are "blue" and "red" variants of a hot spot.

Sniper hot spot: This location is excellent for sniping, as it has numerous angles and views across much of the map. Expect long-range fire from these areas.

1. Big Arch !

You're exposed to the enemy unless you stay by the arch's pillars that lead toward the Red Lift (15) and Control Center (9). This is also a good place to run to if you're receiving fire from a flying Banshee. Stay away from here during Capture the Flag matches if you're on the blue team, as it forces the red team to run toward the Valley (19), which is exposed to the turret atop the blue base, giving the blue team a leg up in controlling this area.

2. Big Bridge

Utilize the sides of the bridge for cover, and the tiny path underneath as a route if you're heading to the Hangar (12) or Camp Site (7), assuming you're trying to evade the enemy.

3. Big Door !

You don't want to be caught here by the enemy at any time: If you spot an opponent spawning here, don't push in toward them. Instead, sit back and shoot them for as long as you're able. This is a great spawn trap... as long as you're not the one spawning!

4. Blue Base

This is where the blue team usually spawns during team games. Use the vehicles parked here to immediately charge the enemy, or sit back and use the stationary turret on top of the base, depending on the situation.

5. Blue Ramp

If the opposition becomes trapped at the Blue Base (4), this is a useful route to take, as it allows you to reach the top of the base and gain the necessary height advantage to rain death down from above.

6. Blue Turret

This is a powerful weapon, but it's wide open to incoming fire. However, it's useful if you're trying to stop or slow an enemy charge from the Valley (19).

7. Campsite

This small camping area has numerous exits to use if you need to flee. You can also use all the cover if you're attempting to fire down on your opponents.

8. Connector

This is the quickest route if you want to head from the Valley (19) to the Campsite (7). This is a commendable escape route, as no matter which side you appear from, you have either ramps or jumps to reach the Control Center (9).

9. Control Center

The Control Center is one of the finest power positions: You're free to shoot pretty much everything on the map and secure flag routes.

10. Dark Blue ⦿

This is a good sniping spot toward the Red Base (13) and Control Center (9). If you utilize this hot spot correctly, you can catch your opponents off guard as they leave the Hangar (12), heading toward the blue areas.

11. Gold Lift

Hide here when you're around the red hot spots; the Lift is useful when ascending to the upper red levels.

12. Hangar

Like the Control Center (9), this is another power position. This places you in a higher location, allowing you to fire down toward the Blue Base (4), Campsite (7), Control Center (9), Big Arch (1), and the Red Lift (15).

13. Red Base

This is the initial spawn point of the red team. There's a stationary turret on the second level that allows a teammate to rake the map with heavy covering fire in many directions.

14. Red Cave !

This is where you land after using the Red Lift (15). Don't hang around here, as this offers enemies an easy opportunity to grenade you. You should land and immediately make a push for control of Red Base (13).

15. Red Lift

If you need to reach the Red Rocks (16) quickly, utilize this Lift. If you have a sniping weapon, try to get an MLG Top 10 Clip as you soar across the map!

16. Red Rocks

This is a small area with rocks to use as cover. There's a passage that leads to the Hangar (12) as well. The bigger rock can be used as part of a jump into the Red Base (13).

17. Short Arch

The Short Arch is an excellent place to head for, as there are several rock pillars that grant you cover. This enables you to head up the Control Center (9) ramp without too much difficulty and allows access to the Connector (8).

18. Small Bridge

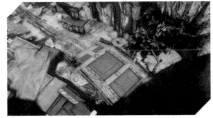

The Small Bridge is more compact than the Big Bridge (2), so don't confuse the two, but they both serve the same purpose. Take cover by heading underneath the bridge, then use the path to reach the Campsite (7) or Control Center (9).

19. Valley !

You should steer clear of this area, as it leaves you out in the open and susceptible to enemy fire. You should rush toward the Valley Lift (21) or Valley Bridge (20) as quickly as possible.

20. Valley Bridge

If you're caught in the open, use this bridge for cover. Try wall-shooting as you wait for your shields to recharge and then make your escape.

21. Valley Lift

This is the fastest way out of the Valley (19) if you're on the side with this Lift. You're propelled up to the Control Center (9) and placed back into the action.

INTRODUCTION   BASIC TRAINING   INTEL   CAMPAIGN   INFINITY   APPENDIX

The consequences for trying to run the flag through the open fields can be severe.

Sniper Rifles and Rocket Launchers

As soon as the match begins, you always want to send one of your team to your Sniper Rifle pickup. In addition, a couple other teammates must reach the Rockets and the Control Center. If you're on the red team, you spawn farther away from the Rockets, so don't attempt to reach them. Instead, use them for bait and slay the enemies when they try to reach them.

Avoiding the Valley

When you're pushing toward your opponent's base, you must head through the Hangar section of the map and through the Campsite and Command Center. The Valley is an unwise option; it's so open, you won't be able to make it across without the other team spotting you. However, you can try the Valley route if you're feeling sneaky; just don't do it too often!

Vehicular Victory

During Capture the Flag games, the preferred vehicle is the Warthog. Use it to drive to the enemy base, and when the moment arrives (after you've killed a few enemies and the immediate area is relatively quiet), hop out and pick up the flag, return, and make a clean getaway.

In order to control this map, be certain one or more of your team is commandeering the Scorpion. You can take complete control of the game and escort the flag back to your base. The vehicle spawns under the Big Arch. This is an excellent map to use the Wheelman armor ability and then drive or pilot the Scorpion, Warthog, or Banshee.

Key Strongholds

The most intense hot spot on this map is the Command Center. It is accessible from every side of the map. The Center offers an excellent view of the Campsite, and you can watch for flanking foes heading toward you through the Valley, under the Big Arch, and even as you reach the Center. Try to keep two of your team here to commandeer the Control Center; it's the heart of the map and everyone maneuvers through it at some point: unless you're here to stop them!

The other main location to reach and hold is the Hangar. You have a commanding view over the empire Campsite side of the map. This is a premium spot for sniping and sneaking around to infiltrate your opponent's base. You're able to offer covering fire and really attempt a large distraction to benefit your teammates.

HAVEN

Hidden deep within the clouds, harmonic resonance platforms are believed to sustain the existence of artificial stars.

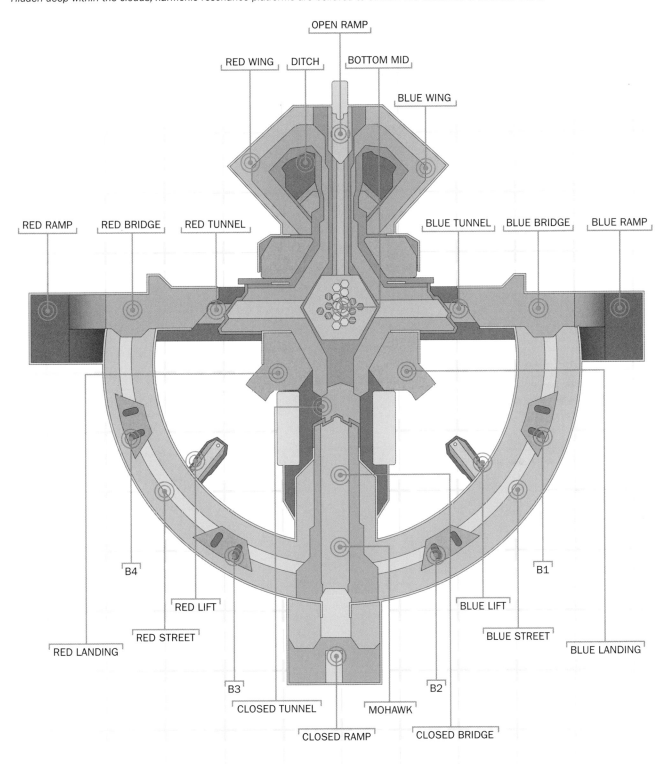

Choke hot spot: Expect high traffic, numerous enemies, and a well-used thoroughfare. Combat usually occurs here, and the location may be watched by enemy snipers.

Danger hot spot: This is an area of ground that is difficult to defend, has poor visibility for shooting angles, is sunken or low to the ground, or is in the open. Expect to be shot at if you're here. Avoid if possible.

Mirrored hot spot: This location features an identical (or mostly identical) facsimile, almost always on the opposite side of the map. Expect tactical advice to be the same for both locations. Usually these are "blue" and "red" variants of a hot spot.

Sniper hot spot: This location is excellent for sniping, as it has numerous angles and views across much of the map. Expect long-range fire from these areas.

1A. Block 1 (B1)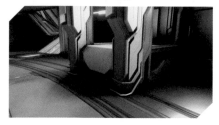

1B. Block 2 (B2)

1C. Block 3 (B3)

1D. Block 4 (B4)

Any of these four block outcrops are excellent for using as cover and for peek-and-shooting. Use them to hide and crouch in a corner if your opponent is running by, and tag them with an easy assassination before you're spotted.

2A. Blue Bridge

2B. Red Bridge

This is the main thoroughfare to Top Middle (14A). If you see an enemy heading this way, attempt to plant a grenade under their feet once they've committed to the jump needed to reach Top Middle.

3A. Blue Dropdown

3B. Red Dropdown

Both Dropdowns are excellent to as escape routes—just drop down and sprint away. This area is also good to traverse with a Jet Pack, so you can lift up behind an opponent.

4A. Blue Landing

4B. Red Landing

This is an excellent spot to take cover in; peek and shoot from any of the walls.

5A. Blue Lift

5B. Red Lift

Either Lift is another rapid pathway to Top Middle (14A); include the Lifts in a coordinated push. You can also jump past this Lift from Top Middle, making for a great escape route. Throwing grenades in the Lift is a recommended way of weakening foes at Top Middle. Either Lift takes you to Landing (4).

6A. Blue Loop

6B. Red Loop

When you're not moving through this area, constantly check it when you're holding down Blue or Red Ramp (8), and look for foes trying to flank you from underneath.

7A. Blue Plat

7B. Red Plat

Either of the Plats (platforms) offer excellent line-of-sight opportunities across to Mohawk (18) and both bridges: This is a good place to watch foes and react accordingly.

8A. Blue Ramp

8B. Red Ramp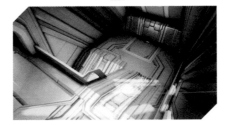

This is an important area to control; it's a power position because you have the luxury of many escape routes and a view of a large portion of this map, so you can spot or predict the locations of foes.

9A. Blue Sneaky

9B. Red Sneaky

As the name suggests, this is the preferred way to sneak up on the enemy when they're at Top Middle (14A) or on the Landings (4).

10A. Blue Street

10B. Red Street

Try either of the Streets; they're great routes to take when you're maneuvering your way over to the Blue or Red Ramp (8) and offer a lot of cover along the way.

11A. Blue Tunnel

11B. Red Tunnel

This is attached to the Bottom Middle (14B) area, and the enemy loves to try and outflank you by moving through here. Watch for them!

INTRODUCTION

BASIC TRAINING

INTEL

CAMPAIGN

INFINITY

APPENDIX

12A. Blue Window 📖

12B. Red Window 📖

Either of the windows are power positions, because you can block off a number of routes, such as the Mohawk (18) and Blue/Red Bridges (2), by hiding and firing from here.

13A. Blue Wing 📖

13B. Red Wing 📖

The Wings offer a way for you to sneak up on your opponents located at Top Middle (14A) by taking the lower route. Use the Blue/Red Wing pillar to peek and shoot, causing a distraction as your foes turn their attention to you: Meanwhile, your team should make a push into Top Middle from above.

14A. Top Middle

14B. Bottom Middle ❗

Top Middle is a very important power position, as you can see everything from the top of the map and pick off numerous foes with one-shot kills. Bottom Middle is more dangerous; you don't want to be caught down here at any time. There isn't much action, and you suffer from being too low down compared to your enemies when aiming and fighting.

15. Closed Ramp

This is another power position if you're holding the ball or holding this down in Slayer. There are many escape routes, and you can pick off kills from almost anywhere on the top of the map.

16. Closed Tunnel

Head in here when you're planning to sneak up through the nearby Sneaky (9) hot spots.

17. Ditch

Stand here only as a last resort, such as if you're weak and don't want to expose yourself to further punishment. However, maneuvering and ambushing from here can win you the battle.

18. Mohawk

Utilize this area when you're trying to push into Top Middle (14A); it has great cover opportunities.

19. Open Ramp ❗

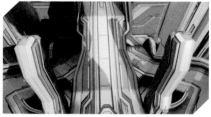

This area is risky to move about in, as it's easily naded, and there's little cover to use.

20A. Pillar 1 (P1) 📖

20B. Pillar 2 (P2) 📖

Each of the four pillars around this map are excellent to use for peek-and-shooting or for sneaking up on an opponent.

20C. Pillar 3 (P3) 📖

20D. Pillar 4 (P4) 📖

INTRODUCTION

BASIC TRAINING

INTEL

CAMPAIGN

INFINITY

APPENDIX

> GENERAL TACTICS

Haven is a fast paced arena. At any moment you could suddenly find yourself outflanked and out gunned.

The Strongest Survive

Stalk the weaker players first; it is always better to pick up a kill from a shieldless or damaged foe than engaging in a 1v1 duel.

Tip for the Top Middle

Although tempting, it's almost never a good idea to rush Top Middle for kills unless you spawn at the Open Ramp. Top Middle is where incompetent players leap around, waiting to be shot. However, charging Top Middle from Open Ramp allows you to pick up a kill or two by stealing them from weakened players already fighting one another. This is quicker than heading to Bottom Middle and taking a longer route looking for kills.

Sneaky Ledge Clambering

Use the Sneaky ledges to your advantage as much as possible when engaging and disengaging the enemy. The two ledges in question allow you to reach Top Middle at two different locations: the Blue/Red Landing or the lower Tunnels on both sides.

Where to Nade

Employ grenades at the Ramps whenever possible. You can pick up easy kills by throwing Frag Grenades into these areas (where players are spawning or fighting). Top Middle is a heavily trafficked area where constant fighting occurs; this is another option for easy nade kills with Frag Grenades.

Hide and Sneak

You don't need to fully expose yourself to the entire field of battle by jumping out to finish off kills. There are windows on the Blue/Red Streets, and these gaps allow you to see the Top Middle and bottom Tunnels; search for foes here and pick up some safe kills. You stay healthy with these takedowns, instead of being weakened through pointless fights. So, sit at one of the Street windows, popping off foes. When one enters the Street near your position, engage them in a 1v1 duel with a full shield and with a rack of kills already completed!

Fortune favors superior numbers and superior firepower.

Setting up for the Win

When playing with teammates, holding the Closed Ramp is important, as the side of the map with Mohawk gives you more cover opportunities. While holding the Closed Ramp, control either the Blue or Red Street: This enables you to shoot through Window to Top Middle, damaging the enemy as they jump across the Bridges.

With the Streets claimed, your teammates can jump to Top Middle and finish off any kills before retreating back to your team's starting positions and holding the Closed Ramp and Streets once more.

Players positioned at Window should always check the Bottom Middle for foes trying to flank. Just because it appears most of the action is happening up at Top Middle doesn't mean you can forget about the sneakier foes heading along the Bottom Middle of this map.

Similarly, the player positioned on the Closed Ramp needs to head up and down the stairs to help bring down foes at Top Middle while checking for flankers at Bottom Middle.

Carnage at Top Middle

As you might have guessed, Top Middle is usually a death trap. There's always fighting and foes milling about here. But the previous strategy yields better results than leaping about in the open: If the opposition is set up as described, heading into Top Middle usually leads to you becoming trapped and flanked by the enemy.

If you're at Top Middle, don't stay here for long, as you'll be picked off: You want to storm one side of this map with all your teammates in a massive push to overwhelm and claim the side for yourself.

Landings are great to hold when you're at Top Middle and pushing toward the Closed side, if the other team is set up. From Landing, you have cover from Closed and can put shots into foes at Windows, enabling the push to occur.

Open Ramp Advice

Avoid the Open Ramp; it is usually a one-sided battle against foes with a better line of sight than you. If the other team is keeping you back on this ramp, drop and push toward one of the tunnels to infiltrate either the Red or Blue side of the map.

> TACTICS: INFINITY/PRO SLAYER

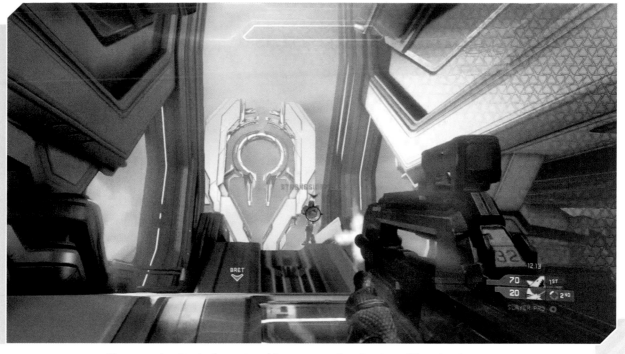

The ramps leading to the center of the map are often the sites of fierce battles.

Trapped in the Middle

Choose a couple of your team to control Top Middle, putting fire into your opponents and keeping them pushed back into the Closed Ramps (Red and Blue). Meanwhile, your other teammates should be flanking from other directions or sneaking under the map through the Tunnels. Trap foes in the middle of this map, with nowhere to run!

Spawn Slaughtering

Figure out where the opposition is spawning; it takes some time on this map. Once you kill a foe, you'll have an idea of where they're going to appear: Now take time to set up and throw primed grenades that explode as your foe spawns or catches them (or the opposing team) off guard.

Knowing When to Nade

Grenades play a vital role to your Slayer strategy: You want to lob nades at the right time and not just waste them. Lob them at a location where you know your opponents are or before you make a push; this "pops" your opponent's shields before you pick them off with a headshot. Don't get into the bad habit of mindlessly throwing all your grenades across the map as soon as you spawn!

> TACTICS: ODDBALL

Five Steps to Victory

Step 1: Hold the ball on the Red or Blue Ramps while watching for enemy attacks from the Top Middle and Bottom Middle.

Step 2: Have two teammates at the Window or Street hot spots and watch the closed bridge and Red/Blue Bridge. One of the players can move toward the Red/Blue Bridge to cause enemies to split their fire.

Step 3: Position one teammate on the Closed Ramp: They should be constantly checking the Closed Bridge and Closed Tunnel areas for infiltrators. They always need to be giving the ball carrier covering fire to funnel the enemies into the Red/Blue Bridge, as there's no cover on those bridges once they've jumped over.

Look who's got the ball.

Step 4: One teammate must move from the ball to the Loop. Head toward Blocks 2 or 3 to ensure the enemy isn't coming from the opposite Loop. If this player has a confrontation, you need to put shots into your foe and drop them as you back up to your own Loop; do this until your teammate on the Closed Ramps radios that he's coming in to help. Then double-team the enemy. The player on the Loop also checks the Ball Tunnel to see if anyone is sneaking underneath.

Step 5: Continue with this plan until enemy dominance is complete!

LONGBOW

Powerful channel-based mass drivers like these were once used to launch monitoring relays deep into space.

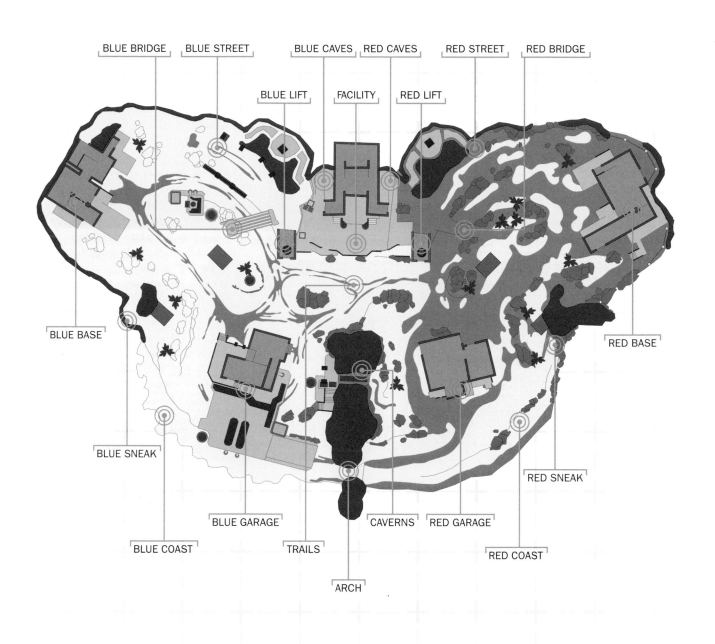

BLUE BRIDGE BLUE STREET BLUE CAVES RED CAVES RED STREET RED BRIDGE

BLUE LIFT FACILITY RED LIFT

BLUE BASE

RED BASE

BLUE SNEAK

RED SNEAK

BLUE GARAGE CAVERNS RED GARAGE

BLUE COAST TRAILS RED COAST

ARCH

Choke hot spot: Expect high traffic, numerous enemies, and a well-used thoroughfare. Combat usually occurs here, and the location may be watched by enemy snipers.

Danger hot spot: This is an area of ground that is difficult to defend, has poor visibility for shooting angles, is sunken or low to the ground, or is in the open. Expect to be shot at if you're here. Avoid if possible.

Mirrored hot spot: This location features an identical (or mostly identical) facsimile, almost always on the opposite side of the map. Expect tactical advice to be the same for both locations. Usually these are "blue" and "red" variants of a hot spot.

Sniper hot spot: This location is excellent for sniping, as it has numerous angles and views across much of the map. Expect long-range fire from these areas.

> HOT SPOTS

1. Arch ◉

This enclosed area provides an overhead pathway on the map's coast side. A lot of fighting happens around the Facility (11), so you can employ stealth play and drive vehicles through this back route to reach the garage on either side of the map. This makes an ideal spot to hide your vehicle if you need your shields to recharge. It's also a solid location from which to snipe and keep the opponent back at their coast and cave.

2A. Blue Base 📖   2B. Red Base 📖

These are the spawning points for both the red and blue teams. There are numerous locations inside each base, so if you're playing Team Slayer and have the lead, be sure to act like the king of these castles and force the opponent to come inside! Stay aggressive at your opponents' base, as you gain the best line of sight for support fire.

3A. Blue Bridge 📖   3B. Red Bridge 📖

This long bridge connects to the Red or Blue Base (2); cross it to easily access your base, but you mainly want to use it to drive over or run by rapidly. However, this places you in an open area with no cover, and if there are enemies in the area, your only escape is by winning the fight or dropping underneath this locale.

4A. Blue Cave 📖   4B. Red Cave 📖

Use the Cave to sneak across from your base without being spotted or shot at as you try to gain control over the Facility (11). Head to this location when carrying the flag, as it gives you perfect cover: Just make sure your team has control of the Facility or you might be walking into a massacre you won't survive.

5A. Blue Coast 📖   5B. Red Coast 📖

An area behind the garages by the sea, the Coast is very vehicle-friendly. However, don't ever walk out here unless you're heading to the Caves (4) and making a sneaky push into the opponents' base.

6A. Blue Garage

6B. Red Garage

This is basically a secondary base for red and blue. These garages usually have a vehicle for you to operate. The roof of these garages are just as helpful as the roof of the main bases (and even better if you have both), as you can lay cross fire on spawners.

7A. Blue Lift

7B. Red Lift

These are little rooms on both sides of the map that allow you to lift to one of the sides of the Facility (11). They are good to use when you're near them and an adversary is shooting you from afar. The lift brings you right to cover, unless an insanely brutal firefight is under way for dominance of the Facility.

8A. Blue Sneaky

8B. Red Sneaky

This is a pleasant place to hide. If you find yourself in a battle you can't win, try escaping to here. It's also a recommended position to run the flag to. Have a teammate with a vehicle waiting for you, as you can easily drive down the Coast (5), watching the sunset before capturing your flag.

9A. Blue Street

9B. Red Street

This is covered by a wall with excellent protection (there are only two angles from which to receive fire). The ramp leads to the Facility (11) or the Blue and Red Bases (2), depending on which way you're headed. This is the preferred path to the Facility, compared to the Blue and Red Bridge (3), as you actually have cover and can sprint into the Blue or Red Cave (4) as you make your escape.

10. Cavern

A hideout with massive protection that's great for hiding a king in Team Regicide.

11. Facility

This compound is in the middle of the map, a separate base between the Blue and Red Bases (2). It is a shortcut and a power position to have when pushing to the other team's base. Having control of it allows you to force the opponents to go around the outskirts of the map, unless they want to keep attempting to break your team's dug-in positions.

12. Trails

These are the roads that cross in front of the Facility (11) and run from one base to the other. When you're trying to capture the flag, these roads are a quick way to run the flag in a Warthog. There are various rocks and hillocks to put support fire where necessary.

> GENERAL TACTICS

Take advantage of the long paths between the two halves of Longbow, and pack long-ranged firepower at all times.

Power Weapon Planning

There are Sniper Rifles that spawn at both of the bases. The top of the Facility is a great place from which to snipe, as you have a commanding view over both sides of the map. Another sniping spot is the Blue/Red Sneaky, mainly because no one expects you to be there! You can also pick off spawning foes, assault their base, and enter it from the Sneaky hot spots.

Rockets spawn at both the Blue and Red Bases. These are great for taking out any vehicles causing your team trouble or storming into a base full of enemies. Try not to waste them shooting at enemies across the map, but keep a hold of them until you reach areas of clustered enemies.

The Facility Choke Point

Facility is the main hive of activity on this map; your team should attempt to reach this hot spot and control it. You will have views over most of the map. During CTF, keeping Facility makes it very straightforward to run the flag back to your base. Move it to the Blue/Red Street, and then head to the Blue/Red Caves that are attached to the Facility.

Two Spartans Are Better Than One

Work with a teammate when you're moving to and from the hot spots on the map. This is a large map, and you're likely to be shot at from many different angles. However, you can also pick off many kills if the enemy team makes the mistake of having players running solo.

Sneaking Around the Coast

It isn't wise to move about the Coast locations, unless you're trying to sneak around to your opponent's base. If this is your plan, be sure to head through Blue/Red Sneaky to ease your access.

Base Assaults

Try to reach the top of your opponent's base and kill or wound every foe who is spawning. This gives the rest of your team time to push up and catch your foes in a cross fire. This plan also pulls the enemies back into their base. Try your best to stay alive while attempting this sandwiching maneuver, or your foes only need to worry about one place to focus their fire on.

If you're part of the blue team, try to control the red team's spawning areas by ascending to the top of their base. There's great cover here—fall back to the top of the ace and crouch, and your opponent won't see you. Let your shields recharge, and then pop back out and weaken or kill your foes.

If you're part of the red team, stay away from the top of the blue base and instead make your way to their Sneaky; you have great cover and you can get numerous shots on foes who are spawning or running up to their Street hot spot.

Third-person perspective: Jet Pack jump.

First-person perspective:
Jet Pack jump.

HALO 4

MELTDOWN

The catastrophic effects of this reactor's systemic breakdown will eventually rend this icy moon into pieces.

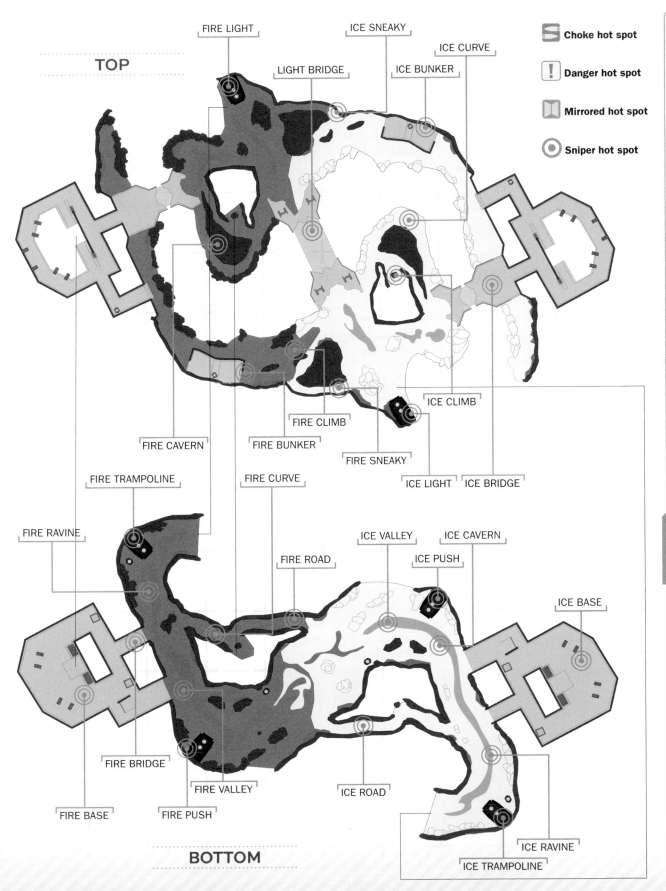

TOP

FIRE LIGHT

ICE SNEAKY

ICE CURVE

LIGHT BRIDGE

ICE BUNKER

Choke hot spot

Danger hot spot

Mirrored hot spot

Sniper hot spot

ICE CLIMB

FIRE CLIMB

FIRE CAVERN

FIRE BUNKER

FIRE SNEAKY

ICE LIGHT

ICE BRIDGE

FIRE TRAMPOLINE

FIRE CURVE

FIRE RAVINE

ICE VALLEY

ICE CAVERN

FIRE ROAD

ICE PUSH

ICE BASE

FIRE BRIDGE

FIRE VALLEY

ICE ROAD

FIRE BASE

FIRE PUSH

ICE RAVINE

ICE TRAMPOLINE

BOTTOM

INTRODUCTION

BASIC TRAINING

INTEL

CAMPAIGN

INFINITY

APPENDIX

1A. Fire Base

1B. Ice Base

This is the starting point for the red/blue team. Each base has an arsenal of vehicles that you want your team to discuss before the game so you know who is doing what. You only want teammates in here if they are defending the objective or forcing opponents to come in (if you're playing Slayer game types).

2A. Fire Bridge !

2B. Ice Bridge !

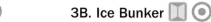

This connects the Base (1) to the road in front of each base, respectively. Only use these bridges to reach Light Bridge (12) or Curves (5). There's no point in holding, as you are wide open and away from cover. Walk out here only if you are escorting your team's flag carrier out of the enemy's base or into your own.

3A. Fire Bunker

3B. Ice Bunker

Use this to take a breather if you're running a flag. This is also a good stopping point if you need to recover your shields or you're waiting for other teammates to respawn and help you finish a flag capture or a push. This is a good place to control, as the Bunker has a little window that you can shoot out of, granting you good weapon-aiming angles.

4A. Fire Cavern

4B. Ice Cavern

These caverns are used primarily for escape routes, as you can lose your opponents around all the little corners. Use this area to switch positions from Roads (9) and Curves (5); trick your opponent by holding them back in their base. There are times an objective may be inside, so be prepared to enter and melee everything in your path.

5A. Fire Curve

5B. Ice Curve

This hot spot wraps around the central part of the map and is mainly used for getaways, as it's right above the Fire/Ice Cavern (4). Use your Curve for getaways and to keep your opponents stuck in their base. For easy kills, wait for them to cross their Bridges (2) and then unload on them while they have no cover.

6A. Fire Light

6B. Ice Light

These lights lift you in the direction of the Light Bridge (12). Push this side of your base if you are trying to reach the center of the map as quickly as possible.

7A. Fire Push

7B. Ice Push

This is the lift right outside of the Bunkers (3) that sends you to Ice or Fire Curve (5). Use this to quickly make your way to the top middle part of the map and surprise your opponent.

8A. Fire Ravine

8B. Ice Ravine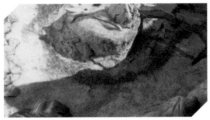

This is directly below the Fire/Ice Bridges (2) that connect to the Fire/Ice Caverns (4) and the Base (1). Each has access to a Ghost and a Warthog, enabling vehicular dominance. You can use either Ravine as your starting spot for your drive-by with the Warthog all the way through your opponent's Valley (11) or vice versa.

9A. Fire Road

9B. Ice Road

This section of the map is the main thoroughfare when you run the flag in a vehicle. Crossing the Fire/Ice Bridge (2) is dangerous, but if you can reach the Road and Fire/Ice Sneaky (10), it might just be the fastest path to score the flag.

10A. Fire Sneaky

10B. Ice Sneaky

Both these locations have a few rocks protruding up from the ground and are mainly used to hide from enemies while you're planning a push or recovering your shields after a fight.

11A. Fire Valley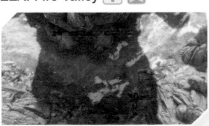

11B. Ice Valley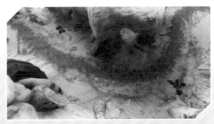

Both Valleys are open areas with little cover, but they are excellent if you're using vehicles such as the Ghost or Warthogs and you need to cover the ground quickly.

INTRODUCTION

BASIC TRAINING

INTEL

CAMPAIGN

INFINITY

APPENDIX

12. Light Bridge

This bridge is the center of the map. It's an advantageous place to be, as the bridge has two little barricades on each side that can lead to good cover as you stay up top at this power position. No matter what side you are on, you have the Caverns (4), Roads (9), Curves (5), and Sneaky (10) hot spots nearby; pick the one you think will give you the best chance of escape.

> GENERAL TACTICS

Expect the zones just outside of the bases to always be fiercely contested in team-based game types.

Power Positioning in the Center

Taking control of the central part of this map is most important. You want to be near the Light Bridge and either the Fire or Ice Sneaky hot spots. Holding the center area affords you many lines of sight, and with the barricades on the Light Bridge, you have the cover and the Sneaky areas close by to flee to if the area becomes too dangerous to continue defending.

The Bunkers are useful, as they afford you a lot of cover. With correct teamwork and proper patrolling of the middle of the map, you can assist extremely well from here.

During CTF games, being on your opponents' Curve is hugely important, as you have both cover and the ability to lay down a vast amount of oppressing fire to keep your foes stuck at their base. If you get into trouble, you can enter the Fire or Ice Cavern (depending on where you are), and change locations while still maintaining a threat to the enemy base with your continuous supporting fire.

Vehicular Vengeance

This is another large map, meaning that once again, vehicle control is the key to your success. Place a Warthog around the enemy to keep your adversaries from escaping their base. Have the Warthog driver work with a teammate around the door entrance area, so the vehicle baits a foe out to attack the vehicle before the teammate at the door ambushes and unloads on them.

When playing CTF games, keep a Mongoose outside the enemy bunker; a driver can hold down the bunker, locking that side of the map down while a second team member goes in for the flag and moves to the portal in the base to reach their Bunker. Then simply hop onto the Mongoose, drive through Sneaky, and retrieve the flag for the win.

During CTF play, if your team is winning and the game is close to finishing, place a Warthog or a Ghost inside your own base above or behind your flag, with a few teammates close by. This makes it almost impossible for your foes to kill you all and take your flag. Welcome to the wonderful world of base camping!

Demolition Advice

If you're playing Demolition, overload the Caverns with a few teammates to keep control of the arming spot. Make it difficult for your foes to take all of you out before they have a chance to defuse.

Other Advice

Use the Caves and Caverns to sneak behind the enemy as you try to outflank your foes and fire on them from another (disparate) angle. Take a teammate with you to shoot opponents; this map is so large, there's likely to be numerous long-range battles, and two of you taking down foes is an incredible threat to your enemy and an advantage to your team.

RAGNAROK

Now integrated into the War Games simulation, this curiously hidden gorge was once the site of a Spartan deployment.

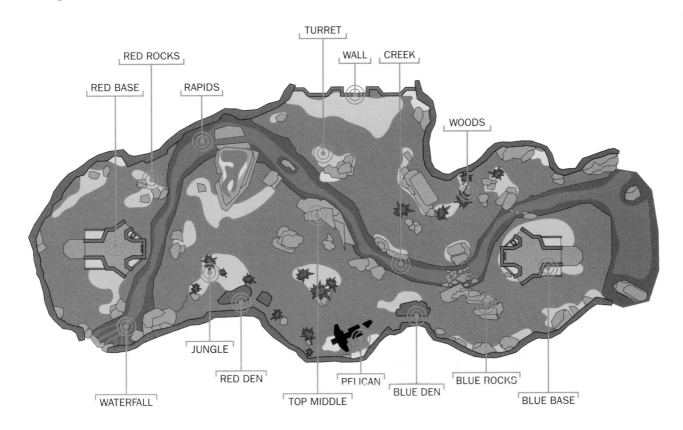

Choke hot spot: Expect high traffic, numerous enemies, and a well-used thoroughfare. Combat usually occurs here, and the location may be watched by enemy snipers.

Danger hot spot: This is an area of ground that is difficult to defend, has poor visibility for shooting angles, is sunken or low to the ground, or is in the open. Expect to be shot at if you're here. Avoid if possible.

Mirrored hot spot: This location features an identical (or mostly identical) facsimile, almost always on the opposite side of the map. Expect tactical advice to be the same for both locations. Usually these are "blue" and "red" variants of a hot spot.

Sniper hot spot: This location is excellent for sniping, as it has numerous angles and views across much of the map. Expect long-range fire from these areas.

> HOT SPOTS

1. Blue Base

This is where you retrieve your vehicles, but try not to remain here for long periods of time; you run the risk of becoming spawn-trapped by a cunning enemy.

2. Blue Den

This is a sneaky way to maneuver toward the downed Pelican (6).

3. Blue Rocks

This rocky outcrop has good cover opportunities and should be a stop during a push out of your Base (1). If you're on the red team, you can also set up here to attempt to spawn-camp the blue team.

4. Creek

This Creek is a sneaky pocket or indent through which to drive your Mongoose or Warthog when you're attempting to maneuver out from your Base (1).

5. Jungle

Utilize the lift from your Base (1) to reach this area, and maneuver to the map's top for viewing and sniping opportunities.

6. Pelican

This is a preferred location to hold down and keep the red team pushed back into the Red Den (9). You have exceptional cover, and firing from here can be a huge annoyance for the opposition.

7. Rapids

Lift to here from the Red Base (8), and sneak your way around to Top Middle (11).

8. Red Base

This is where you retrieve your vehicles, but try not to remain here for long periods of time; you run the risk of becoming spawn-trapped by a cunning enemy.

9. Red Den ⚠

This is an extremely enclosed area and is problematic if you're here for too long, as it's easy for your foes to kill you while you're milling about in here.

10. Red Rocks

Race to this position and use it to aim at the red team as they spawn at their Base (8).

11. Top Middle ◎

Be sure you have one or more of your team attempting to claim this area: It allows you to give great covering fire and provides a commanding view over both bases. This is a sniper's paradise.

12. Turret

The Sniper Rifle spawns here, so you only need to head to this location when it appears. After grabbing the Rifle, move to a different location, such as Top Middle (11).

13. Wall ⚠

Unfortunately, there's no cover at all; you don't want to be caught out here by yourself, so this area is best avoided.

14. Waterfall

Although the water is clear and fresh, there's no need to do any paddling around here; there's rarely any action in this location (and it doesn't have Top Middle's [11] line-of-sight opportunities for a sniper). Not an important location.

15. Woods

Lift from the Red Base (8) to reach here, and use this on your way toward a battle for control of Top Middle (11).

> GENERAL TACTICS

A well-piloted Mantis can dominate the skies and and the ground across all of Ragnarok.

Top Middle Ground Control

Controlling the top of the hill (Top Middle) is imperative: You can see every location on the map. This is the most important power position on the map. Avoid moving to the Wall if the opposition is atop the Top Middle hill; you have no cover to utilize once you're spotted and they start shooting.

Vehicles Rule

Make sure vehicle drivers and pilots come equipped with Wheelman: This is important for both the Mantis and the Banshee. The Banshee needs to give the Mantis cover from the air so you can control both the ground and air game.

Drive a Mongoose or Warthog near the top of the Top Middle hill; use either vehicle to move the flag back to your base after lifting from the enemy's base to Top Middle.

The team that controls the vehicles wins the game, so vehicle command is imperative. Destroy or steal your enemy's vehicles when they spawn (your team should be driving or piloting the Banshee, Mantis, Warthog with a driver and gunner, and Ghost). Have one or two teammates on foot, depending on how many vehicles you have; their role is to cause distractions.

Need a plan for completely destroying your enemy? Control all the vehicles and power weapons. Once you've reached this goal, it becomes nearly impossible for your adversaries to drive the vehicles out from their base when they have only their starting weapons.

Other Advice

Antivehicle Plasma Pistols are a wise choice when choosing a secondary weapon. When playing Slayer variants, avoid pushing into the opposition's base. You want to keep them trapped at their base for as long as the game lasts while your team holds the Top Middle. Control the Pelican area; the cover afforded is excellent and you can really annoy the enemy from here.

SOLACE

A testament to the Forerunners' technological prowess, this installation was designed to suspend the death of a star.

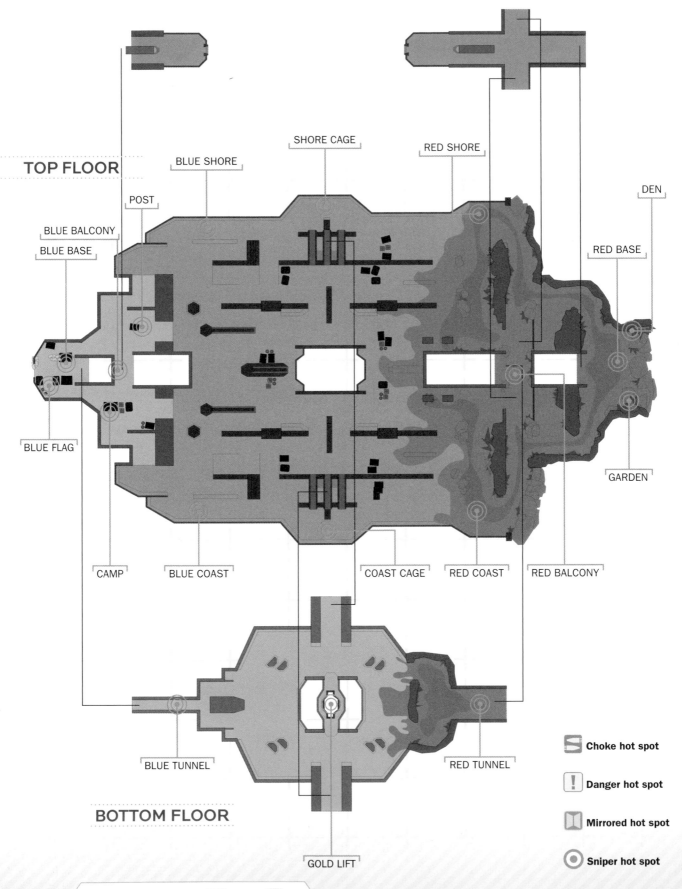

TOP FLOOR

SHORE CAGE

BLUE SHORE

RED SHORE

DEN

POST

BLUE BALCONY

BLUE BASE

RED BASE

BLUE FLAG

GARDEN

CAMP

BLUE COAST

COAST CAGE

RED COAST

RED BALCONY

BLUE TUNNEL

RED TUNNEL

BOTTOM FLOOR

GOLD LIFT

Choke hot spot

Danger hot spot

Mirrored hot spot

Sniper hot spot

HALO 4

> HOT SPOTS

1A. Blue Balcony !▯◉

1B. Red Balcony !▯◉

The Balconies are strong positions to hold, as you can place shots all over the top side of the map. You can also spawn-trap foes at the opposing Flag (3) location. This is a preferred location to prowl, in every game type.

2A. Blue Coast ▯

2B. Red Coast ▯

On either of the Coast sides of the map, there's a divider you can utilize to take cover. From here, you can aim at foes on the opposite Balcony (1) and Coast (2).

3A. Blue Flag ▯

3B. Red Flag ▯

The rear of the base area is where the flag spawns during flag-based game types.

Blue Flag: This has crates in the back of the base; if you're sneaky, you can hide back here and wait to catch opponents off guard.

Red Flag: This is a lot more open than the Blue Flag, so you don't want to mill about in this area unless you're watching the Garden (10) or Den (9) for your team as they hold down the Balcony (1).

4A. Blue Shore ▯

4B. Red Shore ▯

On each of the Shore sides of the map, there's a divider that you can use as cover. From here, you can fire on opponents on the opposite Balcony (1) and Shore (4).

INTRODUCTION

BASIC TRAINING

INTEL

CAMPAIGN

INFINITY

APPENDIX

5A. Blue Tunnel

5B. Red Tunnel

This is an underground passage that enables access to and from the Blue Base or Red Base to the lower side of the map. Try to avoid the Red Tunnel in particular, as there's a ledge above it that gives the enemy the upper hand if they're around the Red Base.

6. Camp

7. Post !

Both of these hot spots are in a section of the Blue Base that you don't want to be caught in: They are easy areas to grenade. Try to catch your opponents in either area but don't get caught here yourself! Camp and Post are good spots for Regicides, though, as you can patrol the entire base and move into this location to clean up any kills, just like the Den (9) and Garden (10).

8A. Coast Cage

8B. Shore Cage

This is an area on the Coast (2), with a similar area on the Shore (4) that allows you access toward the bottom middle of this map. You can jump on top of this location and shoot foes on either Balcony (1) if needed. If a flag is being run along the bottom middle and you're taking fire, don't think twice about getting back to the top side of the map by walking through either cage.

9. Den

10. Garden !

These are two sections of the Red Base you don't want to be caught in; both areas are adjacent to the Red Tunnel (5B), and your opponents can be waiting above you on top to drop down and rake you with fire. However, this is a good place for Regicide matches, as you can patrol the entire base and move into the spot to clean up kills, just like the Camp (6) and Post (7).

11. Gold Lift

The Gold Lift in the map's center allows you to ascend to the top middle and bottom middle areas of this map: Use this area only if you're running away to drop down to Bottom Middle, or if you need to reach Top Middle immediately.

Tactics: Free For All and Regicide

Bringing an Energy Sword to a gun fight.

HALO 4

Subterranean Strategy

Holding the tunnels and bases on either side of the map and having a power weapon to back you up makes it simple to pick off the enemies who are spawning. If you're patrolling the Tunnels, the Scattershot is the weapon to carry.

> GENERAL TACTICS

The tight corridors inside each base can be deathtraps for both attacker and defender.

Running the Flag Top and Bottom

If you're running the flag along the Bottom Middle of the map and you're taking fire, scramble back up to the top side of the map to avoid further punishment; head through the Cage to get there.

There are several different routes to take with the flag on this map; figure out the ones that work well for you and your team. For example, have someone set up at your Balcony, and use the routes up top. Conversely, if top control isn't happening, run the flag low and try to catch the other team by surprise; even if they react accordingly and try to thwart you down below, they'll still leave their power positions up top, which your team can benefit from by moving to and holding them instead.

Backup from the Balcony

Another key is having a teammate to support you from the Balcony. They can place shots on foes across the map, ensuring you never need to start a fight on your own. Back everyone up!

Order a few teammates to the top of your Balcony to keep the opposition from reaching their Sniper Rifle. Meanwhile, seize control of your Sniper Rifle and cover your opponent's Sniper Rifle position until you have a teammate who can infiltrate and grab theirs as well. This is easier if they have a Jet Pack to reach it. Snipers are very important on this elongated map.

Spawning Plans

Have another teammate on the Balcony to offer covering fire and watch the enemy spawn behind your team as they invade the other base. Keep the enemy spawning inside their base; position your team at Top Middle and on your Balcony, and watch both side exits to lock in the other team.

Side Control

Work in unison to control one base and one complete side of this map. You don't want your team to be too spread out, as the map's layout doesn't allow for much help from your teammates if you're on the left or right sides simultaneously. Instead, lock down territory you can keep.

Other Advice

Think about employing the Jet Pack as an armor ability; it's very useful on this map. When the game starts, it's also important to have a couple teammates moving toward Bottom Middle to grab the Incineration Cannon.

Although this may seem suicidal, a coordinated assault through Bottom Middle is an excellent plan. If you're getting dominated up top, move the battle underground and rely on your close-range game instead.

FLAMESWORD

First-person perspective: Sneaky Jump to Top Red Balcony.

VORTEX

ONI personnel remain convinced that these ancient structures somehow harness the planet's torrential wind for power.

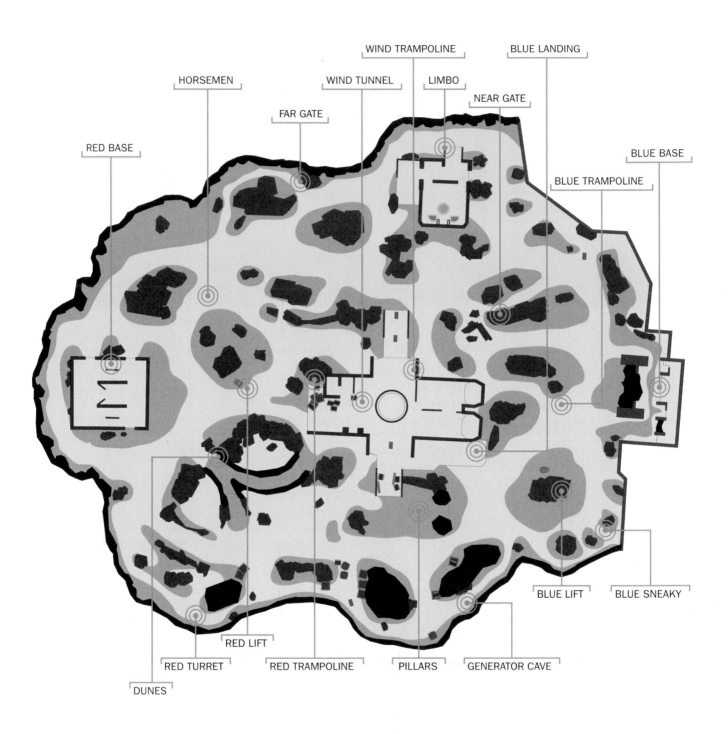

Choke hot spot: Expect high traffic, numerous enemies, and a well-used thoroughfare. Combat usually occurs here, and the location may be watched by enemy snipers.

Danger hot spot: This is an area of ground that is difficult to defend, has poor visibility for shooting angles, is sunken or low to the ground, or is in the open. Expect to be shot at if you're here. Avoid if possible.

Mirrored hot spot: This location features an identical (or mostly identical) facsimile, almost always on the opposite side of the map. Expect tactical advice to be the same for both locations. Usually these are "blue" and "red" variants of a hot spot.

Sniper hot spot: This location is excellent for sniping, as it has numerous angles and views across much of the map. Expect long-range fire from these areas.

> HOT SPOTS

1. Blue Base

This is good to hold if you're retreating from a battle. Draw your opponents in and use the cover inside to your advantage. Use grenades at the entrances to weaken foes trying to storm your position.

2. Blue Landing ◉

This is an exceptional place to hold if you're on the red team and have the blue team trapped at their base. Take proper cover while aiming at foes around the Blue Lift (3) and Blue Sneaky (4). You always have the option to run into the Wind Tunnel (18) to recover if you're low on shields.

3. Blue Lift

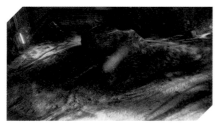

Take this route if you want to reach the high ground from the blue side of the map. Lift takes you to Blue Landing (2), allowing you to reach the Wind Tunnel (18) and lock down the center of the map.

4. Blue Sneaky

As the name implies, this is a sneaky route to take if you're leaving or entering the blue side of the map. It's also a good area to bring a flag to, as you're able to use the rocks for cover and move on when you have cover fire. Take Blue Lift (3) to push the flag toward the map's center.

5. Blue Trampoline

This lift in front of the Blue Base (1) underneath the Wind Tunnel (18) brings you into the Tunnel itself. Cover is sparse, so if you're being pursued, run to the Trampoline and pretend you lifted, evading the enemy by faking them out.

6. Dunes ◉

This upper cliff area is great for camping, allowing you to shoot down on the Red Base (12). There's a cave here you can use as an escape or simply to change your position as you continue to plug foes at the Red Base with bullets.

7. Generator Cave

This cave is filled with various lights and generators. You can bring the flag to this area, as you've got a lot of cover in here. However, don't hang out here for too long unless there's an objective here or you're trying to flank the enemy. There's no real reason to linger here any longer than you need to, and you'll be out of the action, serving no help to your team.

8. Far Gate

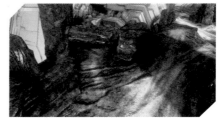

This passage leads to Limbo (11). It's a great route to traverse with vehicles, so you can avoid all the fighting occurring in the middle of the map.

9. Near Gate

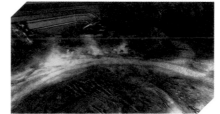

Try holding down this location during objective-based games. There's a turret lodged in the wall here, enabling you to lay down some heavy fire on the Blue Base (1). You can also hide behind the rocks here if you're waiting for your shields to recharge.

10. Horseman

There are a few rocks you can use as cover here, on your way to Red Base (12). Stay close to the rocks, or you'll be exposed in the wide open, completely giving away your position.

13. Red Lift

This is the fastest method of heading from the red side of the map to the Wind Tunnel (18). This Lift propels you to the backside of the Wind Tunnel, allowing your team to gain control of the center of this map.

16. Pillars

This is an open area leading to Window Tunnel (18) with a few rocks for cover. You should use the rocks to wall-shoot and keep enemies stuck at the Blue Lift (3) and Blue Sneaky (4). Pillars is also used to hold the enemy team back to the Generator Cave (7); toss in grenades from here to flush them out.

11. Limbo

This structure looks like a base, but there's little to do here unless you're attempting to flee from the Blue Base (1). Lingering here for too long may force your teammates to spawn here as well, causing some trouble for your team. This is an advantageous place for vehicles to hide if they're low on shields, before they return to the battlefield.

14. Red Trampoline

This is the lift in front of the Red Base (12), underneath the Wind Tunnel (18), that allows access into the Tunnel. There are few cover opportunities, so if you're being pursued, race to the Trampoline and pretend you lifted, evading the enemy via trickery.

17. Wind Trampoline

This is the lift directly underneath the center of the Wind Tunnel (18) that allows access into the Tunnel. Like the other "Trampolines," you can use the small area of cover at the base to hide from your foes as you pretend to Lift.

12. Red Base

There's little need to enter the Red Base unless you're in need of cover. It's easy to trap yourself in here, as there are only a couple of exits. Make this location a priority to reach only if there's an objective.

15. Red Turret

This small cliff has a stationary turret and a great view over the Dunes (6). This is a spot to try and ambush vehicles from, as they try to enter or escape Red Base (12).

18. Wind Tunnel

The Wind Tunnel is the power position on this map. You can easily move into the Tunnel to get an angle and shoot anywhere on the map. Try to bolster your ranks and keep a few teammates (during team games) in the Tunnel to help each other if the opposition tries to sneak in. Deal with foes together, then return to place supporting fire across the map.

> GENERAL TACTICS

I've got you covered.

Driving Advice

If you're controlling the Wraith and keeping teammates in the Wind Tunnel watching all of the lifts, you're set up for map dominance. If you're playing a game type with objectives, you must take control of the vehicles. This map has several vehicle escape routes; learn them quickly so you can flee the battlefield as fast as possible—the objectives make this imperative.

On the side of the map with Limbo, there's a back path with a lot of cover from Limbo; always be prepared to drive toward Far Gate or Near Gate to reach cover.

You can drive around Blue Sneaky to take cover near the rocks before stepping on the gas and heading behind the dunes. On the drive, you're also able to use the cover from Stonehenge.

Setting up Camp

There are many camping positions on this map to take advantage of and control the pace of the game. Utilize all of the closed-off bases for this purpose.

On Maneuvers

Bring a few teammates to sneak around the sides of the map; this can lead to some major flanking plays. Keep a sniper at the farthest rock or ledge you can reach; you can devastate the enemy team, pinning them down.

The best way to run this map is in teams of two when you're controlling the Wind Tunnel. Due to this map's vast size, you don't want to lose control of the middle (the Wind Tunnel). With partners, your team can inflict kills more quickly, back each other up, and shoot across the map more effectively.

Controlling Limbo is another fine plan, as it halts your foes from flanking from that side. Now you can predict your enemy's movements: If you don't see them on your side, you know they're pushing down the center of the map where you can lay down support fire or have your teammates check if they're trying flanking maneuvers via the Generator Cave.

FORGE MAP VARIANTS

The final three maps are the named variants of the Forge maps you can mold and create your own versions of. The variant name is first, followed by the original Forge map name in parentheses.

> ASCENT (EROSION)

Sites like this allow researchers the ability to closely observe a world's inner workings prior to colonization.

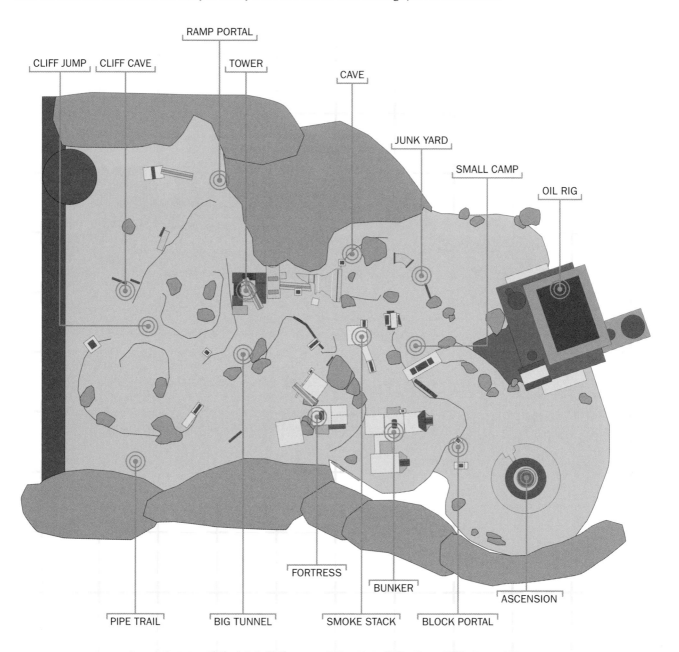

Choke hot spot: Expect high traffic, numerous enemies, and a well-used thoroughfare. Combat usually occurs here, and the location may be watched by enemy snipers.

Danger hot spot: This is an area of ground that is difficult to defend, has poor visibility for shooting angles, is sunken or low to the ground, or is in the open. Expect to be shot at if you're here. Avoid if possible.

Mirrored hot spot: This location features an identical (or mostly identical) facsimile, almost always on the opposite side of the map. Expect tactical advice to be the same for both locations. Usually these are "blue" and "red" variants of a hot spot.

Sniper hot spot: This location is excellent for sniping, as it has numerous angles and views across much of the map. Expect long-range fire from these areas.

> HOT SPOTS

1. Ascension

This area consists of three pillars that rise to meet each other; the top can be used for hiding or jumping purposes, if you want a better chance at catching a foe off guard.

2. Big Tunnel

This is an excellent exit to escape down if you're engaged in a close-range fight and taking damage. Flee and cut off your foe's aiming angles.

3. Box Portal

Utilize this to teleport to the Ramp Portal (12) on the map's other side. Use it to cover a large area quickly, reach a teammate there more easily, or complete an objective with more haste.

4. Bunker ◉

Attempt to hide yourself here and snipe at foes, picking up some easy kills. This is also an excellent place to hold the ball, due to the cover dotted around this hot spot.

5. Cave

This enclosed area has cover potential if you find yourself engaged in a battle against two or more adversaries. This is a commendable place to hold, as it connects to two other power positions: Smoke Stack (14) and Tower (15). Escape to either of them or use the shortcut to reach higher ground.

6. Cliff Cave ◉

A great place to snipe from while utilizing the excellent vantage point. This is another key position to hold, as you're able to see (and shoot at) anyone on the entire map.

7. Cliff Jump

From here, you can jump up to the Cliff Cave (6) and connect to other areas of the map very easily.

8. Fortress ◉

This two-level structure provides a lot of protection with some great lines of sight here from both floors. Fight from either of them. This is a power position.

9. Junkyard [!]

The array of objects and scenery in this section can be used to your advantage, either as cover during battles or as protection when you're attempting to escape.

10. Oil Rig

This massive, scenic hot spot is mainly used as cover, or you can climb it when fighting battles.

11. Pipe Trail

A lengthy pathway that you can use to run the flag; there's little exposure to the enemy once you're using the Trail.

12. Ramp Portal

The second of the two portals on this map allows you to teleport to the map's opposite side and the Box Portal (3). These are useful during flag runs; utilize them as often as you can.

13. Small Ramp

This ramp connects to the Ramp Portal (12), allowing easier access to the Portal itself.

14. Smoke Stack [!]

A scenic protrusion that has little strategic value to utilize, although you can spot players very easily in this area.

15. Tower ◎

Arguably one of the most important power positions on this map; you must hold this at all costs. From this Tower, you can see across the entire map and fire across it too!

> GENERAL TACTICS

Feeling Your Wraith

The large scale of this map means you must establish vehicle dominance immediately to stand any hope of winning. Controlling the Wraith is the key to victory, as you can rip through enemies when you're close or repeatedly fire deadly shots across the map toward your enemy locations and trap them, ideally while the rest of your team keeps you safe from hijacks and finishes off the dug-in foes.

Optimal Vantage Points

Try sniping in the Tower; this location gives you angles of fire across most of the map. Both the Tower and the Fortress are optimal places to control, as you have protection and a large number of shooting angles from which to aim at the opposition. There's great cover potential at either locale too.

Stay in the Caves

The few caves are yours to control and are especially important to take if you don't have a vehicle. Use any cave to leap out at a passing vehicle while you EMP them with your Plasma Pistol. Caves also allow you to take a sneaky route to reach the Tower.

Dodge the Debris

Avoid the Junkyard if you hope to make a lasting impression with your team on this map; the only benefit to this area is the scattered debris to use for cover. Aside from that, this is simply an open field waiting for Spartan corpses to be added to the detritus.

Portal Ambush

The Portals are important to keep watching and are vital if you have the Wraith on the Cliff side so that enemies don't sneak up behind you. This is the easiest and safest way for your foes to reach you, so stay one step ahead of them and deliver damage as they appear.

> RELAY (IMPACT)

Collision craters rarely elicit the need for embedded teams, but the contents of this particular site demanded it.

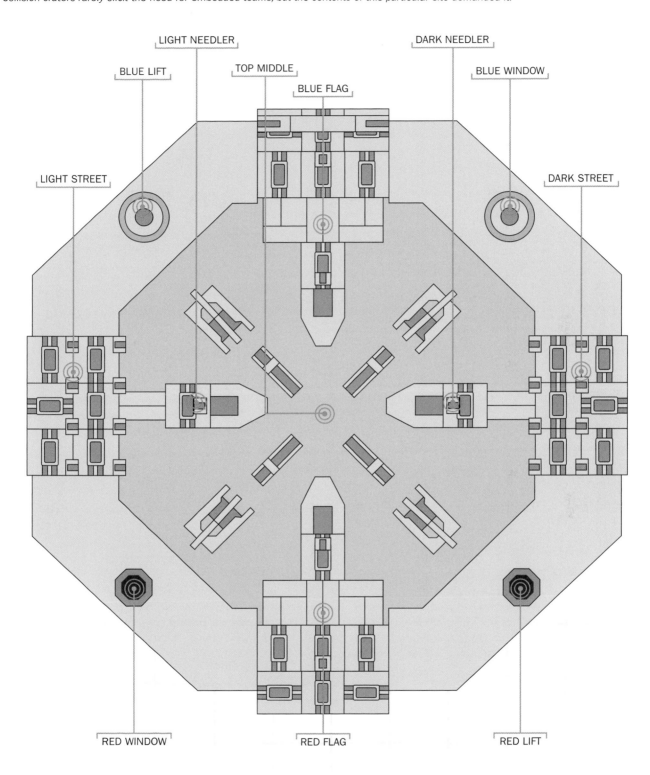

LIGHT NEEDLER
DARK NEEDLER
BLUE LIFT
TOP MIDDLE
BLUE WINDOW
BLUE FLAG
LIGHT STREET
DARK STREET
RED WINDOW
RED FLAG
RED LIFT

Choke hot spot: Expect high traffic, numerous enemies, and a well-used thoroughfare. Combat usually occurs here, and the location may be watched by enemy snipers.

Danger hot spot: This is an area of ground that is difficult to defend, has poor visibility for shooting angles, is sunken or low to the ground, or is in the open. Expect to be shot at if you're here. Avoid if possible.

Mirrored hot spot: This location features an identical (or mostly identical) facsimile, almost always on the opposite side of the map. Expect tactical advice to be the same for both locations. Usually these are "blue" and "red" variants of a hot spot.

Sniper hot spot: This location is excellent for sniping, as it has numerous angles and views across much of the map. Expect long-range fire from these areas.

1A. Blue Flag

1B. Red Flag

It's okay to remain for a while at the location of your team's flag. However, it isn't wise to spend the entire match here. Aid your teammates as they push out by remaining here and locating incoming foes on your friends' routes and attacking the enemy. Then push out yourself. When pushing into the other team's flag area, feel free to remain on the prowl at this enemy location, quickly picking off enemies as they spawn before running an objective or looking to move elsewhere.

2A. Blue Lift [!]

2B. Red Lift [!]

These Lifts shoot you through the central part of the map. If you use them, prepare to be peppered like a clay pigeon. In Free For All games, this can be a great way to pick off a few weak players from above as you sail through the air from the Lift launch.

3A. Blue Window

3B. Red Window

Controlling these Windows allows you to impose your will on anyone trying to move to a new location on the map.

4A. Dark Needler [!]

4B. Light Needler [!]

Avoid pushing out too far at these Needler locations, unless you're confident you (or your team) have the advantage. This is a wide-open platform; you don't want to be caught down on shots because you're wandering out here, exposing your location and unaware of where you're being struck from!

5A. Dark Street

5B. Light Street

This is a narrow path with plenty of cover. Use this location instead of Dark/Light Needler (4); you get in just as many shots while avoiding incoming fire. Use this path to flank around your opponent if your team is pushing hard up the middle or the other side of the map.

6. Top Middle

Top Middle is a great spot to hold if you have teammates at both Windows (3). If you're at Top Middle, try rapidly firing shots at opponents, but make sure you can quickly back down when necessary. This is a very powerful position to hold, but without a lot of cover, you're liable to be taken down quickly.

7. Bottom Middle

This has a good amount of cover due to the map's structure, but it isn't an optimal spot to be in, unless (in individual games) your enemies are running around here, fleeing from others; this allows you to get some easy cleanup kills. Your enemies will most likely be shooting down on you, so avoid being down here and at a height disadvantage, unless you're trying for a sneaky play and attempting to flank behind your opponent.

> GENERAL TACTICS

Low-Down Tactics

Try to use the lowest parts of the map to sneak around; this is the key to outflanking your enemy. Be sure you're watching both Dark Street and Light Street throughout the entire game so foes don't simply run straight into your base.

Dangerous Lifts

Don't use the Lifts too often, with the following exceptions: Fly across and stay alive without getting either team hot. Try running the flag to obtain better coverage from teammates, or try moving the flag more quickly.

When playing team games, make sure you're controlling the enemy team's Lift as often as possible. This is important when playing objective-based game types, as you can fire a lot of rounds from the Lift. If you need to reach the other side quickly, you can simply use the Lift and respond to any of your teammates' radio chatter.

It is worth considering the paths underneath the Lifts if you need cover or an escape route.

Window Watching

Controlling the Windows and the ramps in front of the Windows to reach higher ground enables you to strike with hard-hitting shots the enemies dotted everywhere on this map.

Relay is a completely symmetrical map, so controlling the high ground and using the slanted pillars in front of the Windows to obtain better shots on your enemy is the optimal position for your team to hold, especially if you're trying to cover a flag runner.

Free For All Planning

In Free For All games, stay patient and move to the corners around the Lifts, Windows, and Streets. When the other players die, and with the new instant spawn, you can drop a great deal of your opponents in a spawn-killing frenzy. If you're in one of the corners, you're blocking the spawn area itself, and this usually leads to an opponent spawning across from you: easy pickings!

Tip for the Top

Controlling Top Middle is an effective method of distracting enemies. However, be careful when you're stepping into open areas on this map, as there are numerous angles your foes (or you) can use to shoot opponents off the higher grounds of Top Middle and the slanted pillars.

INTRODUCTION

BASIC TRAINING

INTEL

CAMPAIGN

INFINITY

APPENDIX

Seismic scans indicate that these looming citadels only hint at the enormous structure which lies beneath.

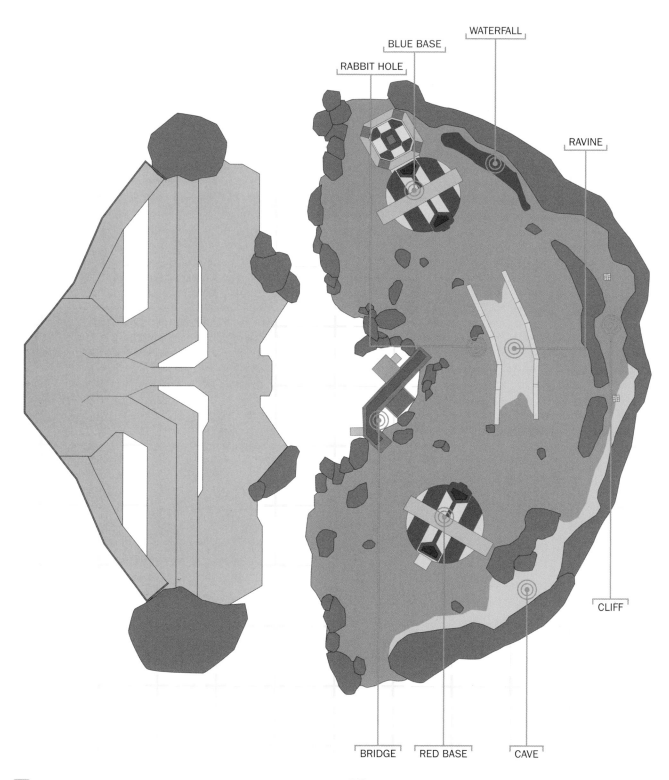

RABBIT HOLE

BLUE BASE

WATERFALL

RAVINE

CLIFF

BRIDGE   RED BASE   CAVE

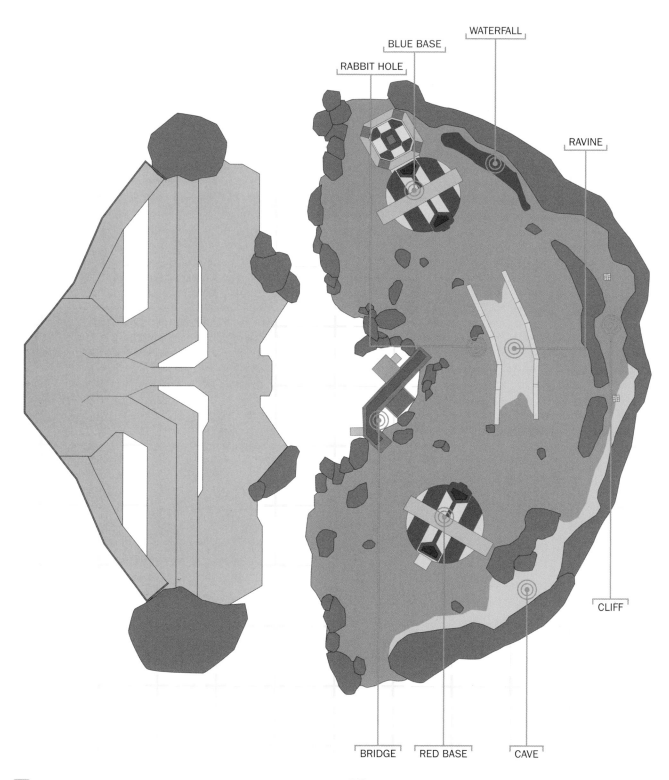 **Choke hot spot:** Expect high traffic, numerous enemies, and a well-used thoroughfare. Combat usually occurs here, and the location may be watched by enemy snipers.

Danger hot spot: This is an area of ground that is difficult to defend, has poor visibility for shooting angles, is sunken or low to the ground, or is in the open. Expect to be shot at if you're here. Avoid if possible.

Mirrored hot spot: This location features an identical (or mostly identical) facsimile, almost always on the opposite side of the map. Expect tactical advice to be the same for both locations. Usually these are "blue" and "red" variants of a hot spot.

Sniper hot spot: This location is excellent for sniping, as it has numerous angles and views across much of the map. Expect long-range fire from these areas.

> HOT SPOTS

1A. Blue Base

1B. Red Base

These are the locations where the blue and red teams spawn. Both provide extremely helpful cover opportunities if you're holed up within.

2. Bridge ◉

The bridge and immediate vicinity are located around the middle of the map. This is a power position: It is imperative that you control this locale, as you can start an exact reconnoiter of where the enemy team is located before moving out as a team and cutting off your foes.

3. Cave ◉

The Cave is arguably the most important power position and place to hold on this map. You're afforded exceptional cover and numerous angles to view and fire on both bases.

4. Rabbit Hole

This is mainly used as an escape thoroughfare. It's easy to escape here, due to its location on the map. Use this as an escape route when you're in trouble and need to reach safety.

5. Ravine

The Ravine is located underneath the central area of the map. Use it to flank over to the Bridge (2).

6. Cliff ◉ [!]

Use the Cliff to gain a height advantage over your opponent and scope out a majority of the map. If you've got a sniper, you can do some serious damage from here. Otherwise, don't linger for too long, as you're liable to be focused on and cut down quickly.

INTRODUCTION

BASIC TRAINING

INTEL

CAMPAIGN

INFINITY

APPENDIX

Cliff Control

After wandering around Settler for a few minutes, it becomes clear that this is a rather diminutive and basic setting, with only two bases. Therefore, expect the action to be frenetic and often confusing at times.

Utilize the cliff, as it's the tallest place on this map. Controlling it gives your team a substantial advantage, especially if you have a sniper camping up here.

With a cliff sniper, flag runs are extremely straightforward, as your sniper is able to cover the rest of the team easily.

The Ravine, Rabbit Hole, and Bridge are all thoroughfares to try and sneak by when your team lacks cliff control. Vary the times you move into these locations so your team becomes less predictable.

The Ravine offers you a lot of cover opportunities. The Bridge has a large glass panel to hide behind: Making sure your team controls the Cliff as much as possible while watching the Ravine and Bridge is the key to consistently winning this map.

SPARTAN OPS

INTRODUCTION

BASIC TRAINING

INTEL

CAMPAIGN

INFINITY

APPENDIX

The Spartan Program began under dubious circumstances. Children were selected and kidnapped from their families and replaced with terminally ill flash clones. Their parents would assume that their child merely died of disease. The training of the Spartans was brutal, and sometimes fatal.

Spartans were originally a means to quell human insurrection in outlying colonies, and the Covenant were initially not a factor driving the research. After the disastrous first contact at the human colony world of Harvest, Spartans were directed at the new alien threat. They became the most successful soldiers on the ground.

Spartans could never be listed as "Killed In Action." The UNSC knew that even the presence of a single Spartan at any desperate battle was enough to steady beleaguered ground troops. Propaganda built up the Spartans as perfect soldiers, unkillable machines of war, therefore the loss of any Spartan could only be reported as "Missing In Action." Over the three decades of war with the Covenant, many Spartans went MIA, and none was more famous, more feared by the enemy, than the Master Chief Petty Officer John-117.

In the aftermath of the Human-Covenant war, the feats of Spartans had passed into legend, and their numbers severely depleted. In a post-war galaxy, the UNSC knew that it needed the Spartans. The Spartan-IV project was intended to fill that gap, to create an entire branch of the UNSC that would continue that legend against foreign and domestic threats. The new Spartans are all volunteers, the best and brightest humanity has to offer all led by veteran survivors of the war.

Welcome to the Spartans. Welcome to Spartan Ops.

As a new member of the Spartan corps' Fireteam Crimson aboard the UNSC *Infinity*, you will undertake missions on the shield-world of Requiem, where the war against the resurgent Covenant rages on. Taking place in the aftermath of *Halo 4*, players are able to experience an entirely new story line with their own Spartan-IV, and earn experience points after every battle to unlock new weapons, armor types, armor abilities, Tactical Packages, and Support Upgrades. The best thing about Spartan Ops is that anything you unlock through these missions actually applies to the War Games multiplayer. If you feel like you're struggling against the competition's arsenal, you can always accomplish a few Spartan Ops to reach those needed upgrades.

Spartan Ops are found by choosing the *Infinity* option on the main menu. If it's your first time doing so, you'll see a cinematic that primes you for the action to come. Then you're taken to the main Infinity menu, where you can access everything to do with multiplayer.

SO YOU THINK YOU'RE THE MASTER CHIEF OR SOMETHING?

If you've played the Campaign on Heroic or Legendary, you probably have a few ideas about what you'll be able to do against the Covenant and their Promethean allies.

❭ The Enemy Is Tougher: You might try firing up a Spartan Ops mission on Heroic, thinking that you're hot stuff, only to find yourself getting killed again and again. Some Spartan Ops on Heroic are at least as hard, if not harder, than the toughest sections of the Campaign on Legendary, and it only gets harder. You will see higher ranking enemies appear earlier into your Spartan Ops, and they are all generally tougher to kill. Every enemy will try much harder to avoid taking damage, which makes weapons like grenades or rockets less effective, as the enemy is more likely to dodge away from them.

❭ The Odds Are Worse: You can expect overwhelming enemy numbers from the very beginning of your Spartan Ops. There's a reason why these missions are not being handed off to regular grunts. Even a squad of four Spartans will be hard-pressed to achieve victory. We can guarantee this: you will never fight so hard just to get close to a switch that needs to be pushed.

❭ Lone Wolves Are Dead Wolves: While it is entirely possible to slog your way through each chapter by yourself, if you're trying to avoid getting killed repeatedly, you'll be moving with your group. Your chances greatly improve if you bring friends along for the ride, focus your fire, and in general, stick close to your allies to support each other. A maximum of four players can participate in a Spartan Ops mission.

❭ No Rush: Because the odds are so stacked against you, rushing headfirst into any battle is not the best call to make. If you are overly aggressive and try to take the fight to shorter ranges, you'll most likely be dying more often and have to make your way back to the fight each time. This ties back to the lone wolves advice. If you're going to rush at an enemy position, have some backup to cover your flanks.

❭ Your Starting Arsenal Is Limited: If you haven't participated in War Games, you might be surprised that your Spartan-IV's available loadout is fairly limited in the beginning. The Assault Rifle isn't exactly a threatening weapon on higher difficulty Spartan Ops, and a Magnum is at its best when the enemies are unshielded and there is plenty of spare ammo nearby. Your starting grenade type is the Frag Grenade. Any other weapons or explosives will have to be found in the field. On top of all that, you lack any Armor Abilities, Tactical Packages, and Support Upgrades. It's totally possible to succeed despite these disadvantages, but you'll want to look into getting new weapons and equipment as soon as possible.

❭ Use the Best Tools: Headshots are the quickest way to bring down most of the enemies you face, so you always want to bring weapons like the Magnum, Battle Rifle, Covenant Carbine, DMR, or LightRifle within your loadouts.

❭ Ammo Crates, Best Crates: Many Spartan Ops missions have UNSC ammo crates strewn throughout the maps. These locations allow you to stay fully stocked for your UNSC firearms. These locations can make excellent points to make a stand against encroaching waves of enemies, as you can really cut loose with your firepower and not be pressured too much by limited ammo. Ammo crates never disappear during a mission, so you can always fall back if necessary to rearm and catch your breath. In general, always know where these crates are, so you can guarantee that you will have firepower when you need it most.

❭ **ON THE NEXT, EXCITING EPISODE OF ...**

Spartan Ops tell a story distinct from the Campaign. How it's delivered is actually quite unique. At launch, the first episode, consisting of 5 missions, will be made available. Periodic updates from 343 Industries will add a new episode to the story free of charge, each including a new set of five missions, until the season is finished. Every mission can be played on all four difficulty levels available to the main Campaign, which will affect your total reward at the end of the mission. All of the Spartan Ops detailed in this guide will be from Season One, Episode One. All missions were completed on Heroic difficulty, while playing co-operatively with another Spartan.

SEASON ONE: EPISODE ONE

> CHAPTER ONE: LAND GRAB

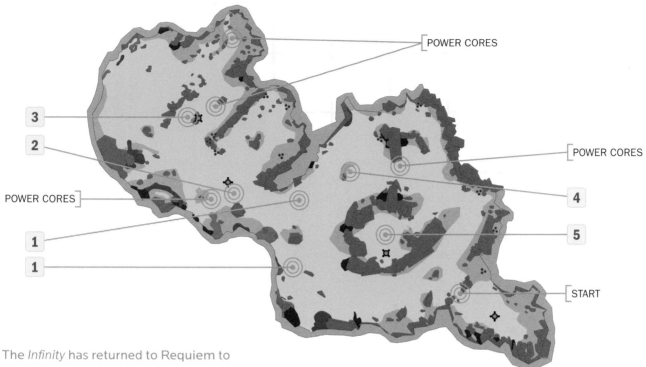

- POWER CORES
- POWER CORES
- **3**
- **2**
- POWER CORES
- **4**
- **1**
- **5**
- **1**
- START

The *Infinity* has returned to Requiem to contest ownership of its potential wealth with the rapidly expanding Covenant presence. Army, Navy, Marine, and Spartan assets are being deployed all over the shield-world to begin a systematic campaign to dislodge the enemy from wherever they are, while providing protection to UNSC non-combat assets there to study the Forerunner installation. Spartan Miller is on hand to provide Fireteam Crimson with tactical and strategic support over the radio.

⌃ MISSION BRIEFING

Your first operation on Requiem as a member of Fireteam Crimson is going to set the tone for all Spartan Ops going forward. Expect extensive foot and armored presence throughout the sector. The Covenant have had some time to set up before the *Infinity* arrived. Your primary targets are a set of wireless distribution power cores scattered throughout the area. With the cores down, you're to clear the area of all Covenant, as well as any reinforcements that may show up in response to your assault.

Map Location: Quarry

> RECOMMENDED LOADOUT

If you're just starting out, the basic kit every Spartan-IV starts with is not a terrible liability. However, not having a vehicle is. This map has a lot of ground to cover, and trying to do so on foot is neither fun nor fast. The Pelican drops you off at a makeshift UNSC depot where there are plenty of Warthogs to choose from, along with a score of Marines ready to man their guns. You can also find Ghosts parked close to the Warthogs. It's highly recommended that players upgrade to Wraiths as soon as possible to leverage their plasma mortars against the enemy.

Objective One: Destroy the Power Cores

The starting zone has plenty of good vehicles to open up with. If you're playing with additional players, It's not a bad idea for one player to choose the Gauss Warthog. If you don't have a full squad, you can use the nearby Marines to man the guns on any of the Warthogs.

You're quickly given your orders to destroy a series of power cores that are currently at the heart of local Covenant communications. Their locations are indicated by HUD navigation markers. Before you rush off into combat, look for Wraiths parked throughout the valley. A good "all-around" set up for a four-player game would have at least two Wraiths, a Gauss Warthog, and a Machine Gun or Rocket Warthog. The gunner positions on the Warthogs would be manned by the Marines. This provides a good, balanced setup that lets the Warthogs protect the heavier Wraiths from troops that get a little too brave. Another good set up is for the four players to each take a Wraith of their own, and rain plasma mortars from afar.

» KEY COMBAT TIP

We really recommend sticking to long range vehicle-based combat tactics for this mission. Trying to do this on foot is totally possible, but can also be very time consuming. On that note, be careful with your vehicles, particularly the Wraiths! There are only a finite number of rides available to take on this mission. Losing your Wraiths due to carelessness can put a serious damper on your ability to complete the mission.

You can expect extensive resistance from the Covenant, and this mission will provide a taste of things to come. You face larger than average resistance, and depending on your difficulty setting, you will be seeing tougher enemy variants than you would see on equivalent Campaign difficulties.

2 Two guard platforms and a hostile Wraith protect this position next to one of the power cores. It's the natural chokepoint that leads into the valley section where other power cores are located. Another is found outside the smaller enclosed valley. If you're playing on a team, you can split your attention between objectives to destroy them quicker.

Expect Phantoms to start arriving regularly throughout the fighting once you start destroying power cores. They typically bring Ghosts and Wraiths to the fight, as well as high-ranking Elites and Grunts. After the first core

goes down, you can expect that the surviving cores will see regular reinforcements until they too are destroyed. This isn't a problem if you've got a Wraith or two on your side. You can easily destroy reinforcements and cores from a safe distance. Just don't get careless and let an enemy Wraith blast you with its mortars.

Objective Two: Neutralize the Incoming Covenant

As soon as the power cores are destroyed, Phantom Dropships begin arriving in the smaller valley **3** . There's nothing fancy here: This is simply a battle for survival that ends only when every last Covenant scum is dead. With four players, this next section can become a rout. You might have so much firepower available that a targeted Phantom may not even have the chance to deploy any troops.

More troops begin arriving throughout the valley by Drop Pods **4** . At this point, all hostiles should be marked with a red marker on your HUD, which makes finding them a lot easier. Generally, the enemy presence here is guiding you to your ultimate destination.

5 A Phantom drops a large contingent of Covenant on top of this hill, with more hostiles gathering at the bottom of the hill, including a hostile Wraith. Be careful on your advance up this hill, as Hunters are among the Covenant deployed. Avoid charging up the hill unless absolutely necessary. If possible, rain plasma mortars from your Wraiths onto the hilltop. Some groups of players may elect to send up a spotter to ensure the mortars are hitting the right targets. When the enemy's numbers fall below a certain threshold, they receive new markers on your HUD to help emphasize their locations. Once the quarry has been pacified of all threats, your Pelican will arrive at the top of the hill for extraction.

> CHAPTER TWO: SNIPER ALLEY

Having proven your worth to Commander Sarah Palmer, Fireteam Crimson is specifically selected for a new mission. A Forerunner facility has been occupied by the Covenant forces, and the Marines have been unable to to dislodge the enemy from their positions. Palmer wants your Fireteam to drop directly behind their defenses and eliminate the hostiles, layer by layer, until the facility is open to the UNSC.

⌃ MISSION BRIEFING

This mission is named Sniper Alley for a reason. After breaking your way through a series of defense lines enhanced by barrier fields, you're exposed to Jackal Snipers firing from a multitude of positions, and there are no convenient Wraiths or Warthogs to help you clear out the enemy. After breaking through the defenses, you're to call in artillery to destroy a shield generator located in the canyons outside of the facility.

Map Location: Sniper Alley

> RECOMMENDED LOADOUT

Take any precision headshot weapon you can get your hands on. The starter Magnum is fine, and you can take a Plasma Pistol from the enemy to enable headshots on Elites. Depending on your chosen difficulty, you might expect the Grunts to be packing Fuel Rod Cannons, which can be a good weapon to take for yourself. They make great crowd-clearing weapons, though the enemy is more keen to avoid being hit directly by this weapon. Close to your starting position, you can find ammo crates, one of which contains a Battle Rifle. Near the first shield barrier, you can also find a DMR. It's even possible to get your hands on a Beam Rifle or a Covenant Carbine from your dead enemies. The UNSC weapons are preferred, as the ammo crates in the area can replenish them to full ammunition.

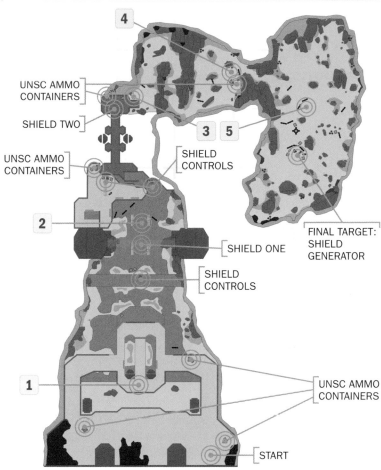

UNSC AMMO CONTAINERS, SHIELD TWO, UNSC AMMO CONTAINERS, SHIELD CONTROLS, SHIELD ONE, SHIELD CONTROLS, FINAL TARGET: SHIELD GENERATOR, UNSC AMMO CONTAINERS, START

Objective One: Secure the Area

1 You start near the facility entrance atop a walkway, with connecting ramps leading down to a lower area. Grunts initially make up the resistance found on the walkway itself, with more Grunts led by Elites positioned on the lower level. An energy shield blocks the way beyond these enemies, with Shade Turrets flanking the barrier and providing fire support for their allies. This can be a brutal start for newer players, specifically because the ranges are short enough that on higher difficulties, the Grunts with Fuel Rod Cannons can be suffering incarnate.

Be careful about advancing down the ramps from the upper walkways. Jackals have positioned themselves to have overlapping fields of fire on the ramps. You can use the walkway to safely engage them from above. In general, the starting walkway is a very good place to engage the enemy from. There are two ammo crates near where the mission begins which will help people armed with weapons like the Battle Rifle, Magnum, or DMR stay topped off for ammunition.

Once the enemy is cleared out of the sector, a waypoint marking the controls to the energy barrier will appear on your HUD. Interact with the controls to lower the barrier and press on.

2 More Grunts and Elites greet you on the other side of the barrier, and you can clearly see another barrier in the distance that prevents you from

continuing beyond the bridge leading to the canyons outside of the base. This time, two control panels are marked on your HUD.

Now that you're out in more open space, you can expect to start taking fire from Jackal Snipers with Beam Rifles on the same platform where one of the switches is located. If you're with a team, try to have at least one player counter-snipe the Jackals while any other teammates focus on bringing down the enemies near the controls, or enemies rushing towads the team on the ground level. When its safe, use the two control panels to lower the next shield.

3 With the way across the bridge now opened, a Phantom drops in to try to deny your crossing. Simultaneously, Jackals on the other

end of the bridge, with Jackal Snipers farther into the canyon, attempt to coordinate a defense against your assault. Drop Pods land on the other side of the bridge to deploy more troops once the Phantom retreats.You have a significant positional advantage if you use the walkways and ledges near both control panels, with clean lines of sight directly over the bridge.

4 With this latest wave of hostiles defeated, cross the bridge into the winding canyon path beyond. Elites rush up the path toward the bridge, while

another Phantom and some Drop Pods deploy reinforcements farther downhill. Expect a significant number of Jackal Snipers to be among the enemies in this section. Try not to peek over the hill recklessly. It's almost better if you force the Covenant to advance uphill toward you. The Elites are much easier to handle when they have to walk into a hail of your fire.

As you clear out groups of enemies, slowly advance down the hill, watching for Drop Pods or Phantoms to bring in reinforcements. Elites will almost always charge uphill after you, so when you see reinforcements arrive, you and any team members you have should position yourselves in such a way that keeps you safe from sniper fire and also ready to mow down Elites if they come at you in numbers.

Objective Two: Clear the Area

5 At the bottom of the hill, a Shade Turret and multiple Jackal Snipers are positioned throughout the lower valley with a sizeable contingent

of Covenant troops. Do not recklessly charge out into the open. Make sure you deal with Shade Turret gunner and Jackal Snipers first. Fortunately, you get an ordnance drop that may contain some extremely helpful weapons to deal with the coming storm. Phantoms and Drop Pods bearing more Covenant troops begin making deployments throughout the valley.

Expect heavy Elite presence. The enemy tends to be deployed near a guard platform a little ways away from the foot of the hill. The ordnance drops should include weapons like a Rocket Launcher or Railgun. With a single rocket you can take the guard platform out of the game, while a Railgun is excellent for bringing down Elites quickly.

If things are looking too grim in the valley itself and the enemy is pushing you back, you can fall back up the canyon towards the bridge. Doing so will funnel the enemies through a more confined space, and you can leverage a height advantage against them. This may be a good time to pick up a Plasma Pistol to set up headshots on Elites.

Your objective in this area is to paint a shield generator so that it can be destroyed by friendly artillery, and once the area is clear of hostiles, it is designated on your HUD. Once it is destroyed, Commander Palmer orders your team to a Pelican for extraction.

> CHAPTER THREE: THE CHALLENGE

Fireteam Crimson and Fireteam Majestic are being deployed to a pair of identical Forerunner constructs north of the Spartans' primary operations in order to clear out Promethean resistance at either structure. Commander Palmer decides to make a bit of a contest out of the mission: Whichever team clears out their respective combat area first will be awarded the respect of their peers.

⌃ MISSION BRIEFING

Don't let the early banter fool you, this is a serious operation. Early waves of Promethean Crawlers and Watchers arrive with numbers that even the Chief didn't face on his own. Communications interruptions will require you to destroy local jamming equipment, then power down the Forerunner structures in the area. Expect significant Promethean resistance to build up as soon as you begin disabling their equipment. After your objectives are complete, clear the evac zone of hostiles so the Pelican doesn't get shot down.

Map Location: Fortress

> RECOMMENDED LOADOUT

You need a headshot-capable weapon nearly at all times to keep the Crawler hordes culled to manageable levels, and for this we recommend weapons like the DMR or Battle Rifle. If you're stuck with a Magnum, you're still effective against them, though you may want to try and locate a LightRifle from weapons caches hidden throughout the area. In a pinch, the Boltshots recovered from the Crawlers make good backup weapons against all threats. A good secondary weapon to upgrade to is the Binary Rifle, found in the remains of Crawler Snipes. One Binary Rifle shot will kill a Watcher, a quick way to prevent them from supporting the Crawlers.

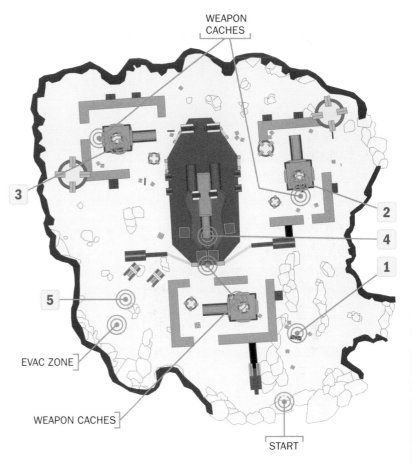

WEAPON CACHES

3

2

4

1

5

EVAC ZONE

WEAPON CACHES

START

Objective One: Investigate the Area

Things start off relatively peaceful. The Crawler and Watcher presence is minimal, so work on clearing them out. Communications between Majestic and Crimson are being disrupted by a jamming device, but you can't do anything about it until you destroy the first wave of hostiles. There aren't many, but be mindful about charging ahead recklessly. Even a small number of Crawlers can ruin your day if they surround you. Keep them outside of melee range and concentrate on headshots.

Objective Two: Destroy the Jammer

1 The jammer is marked on your HUD, and by now should be undefended. Destroy it by interacting with the control console. A pleased Commander Palmer announces that the competition between the Fireteams can begin.

Objective Three: Turn Off the Jamming Arrays

2 **3** Two more jamming arrays are marked on your HUD, and a sizeable force of Crawlers warps into the area. As you approach the arrays, small slipspace portals open over the targets, disgorging Watchers. If you've brought precision weapons like the Magnum, DMR, or Battle Rifle, you can easily wipe them out with headshots. Try to avoid staying out in the open, as getting surrounded by Crawlers can lead to a swift death.

All varieties of Crawler will arrive in defense of the jamming arrays, with the most lethal of them being the Crawler Snipe. Find cover! Even on Heroic difficulty in Spartan Ops, the Crawler Snipe can one-shot a fully shielded Spartan-IV.

Regardless of whichever jamming array you deactivate first, expect more Watchers to arrive to reinforce from a portal above the array. Don't forget that Watchers can reconstruct the fallen remains of Crawlers, so if you see them beginning the reconstruction process, kill them before they can finish. Listen for Palmer to call out that more Watchers are arriving, and prioritize them.

›› KEY COMBAT TIP

Watchers left unattended for long enough will start to construct beam turrets throughout the area, which can make your traveling between locations difficult.

Once you have deactivated the jamming arrays, a considerable Crawler and Watcher force shows up to try to exact revenge, usually near the array you took down last. Be somewhere other than near the array itself, somewhere defensible and relatively safe, before they swarm you.

Objective Four: Turn Off the Main Power

4 The central tower is marked with your next objective once the jamming arrays are down. By now, the Promethean presence is starting to reach dangerous levels. You'll want to hoof it to the central structure as quickly as possible so you can have somewhere safe from which bring down the enemy numbers.

❱❱ KEY COMBAT TIP

There is a weapons cache on the side of the tower opposite its ramp entrance and it contains an Incineration Cannon. This can be effective at clearing dense concentrations of Crawlers in a pinch.

Climbing the tower, you meet even more Crawlers and Watchers at nearly every step of the way.

More Crawlers and Watchers greet you at the top of the tower, near the main power controls. Deal with them, and then use the console to complete the objective.

Objective Five: Move to the Evac Zone

5 Much to Fireteam Majestic's annoyance, you have finished your mission well before they have, and Commander Palmer wants you to move to an evac zone for pickup. More Crawlers assault the tower in an effort to stop you. Clear them out and get to the evac zone!

Objective Six: Clear the Evac Zone

You're not done yet. Crawlers and Watchers begin swarming the evac zone, and you're ordered to clear the area of hostiles before the Pelican arrives to pick you up. Actually defending the zone from within it can be brutal due to the sheer number of enemies and lack of good cover. Consider looking for cover at the small structure where one of the jamming arrays once stood. You can make use of the walls there for protection.

As the fight around the evac zone wears on, ordnance drops are regularly delivered to help you even the odds, but these are at the evac zone itself. If you're playing in a four-Spartan team, you can have one or two members break off from the group and cover the evac zone from the central tower. This can cause the enemy to split their attention between two sets of threats, which can make this last attack more manageable.

Other teams of players might just retreat as a squad directly to the tower as soon as "Clear the Evac Zone" flashes onto their HUDs. This isn't a bad call either. The central tower can provide good protection from the swarm of Crawlers and Watchers. Whatever you choose to do, once you eliminate the enemies and reinforcements stop arriving, the mission is complete.

Commander Palmer decides to lean on Fireteam Crimson more, after embarrassing Fireteam Majestic during the previous mission. The *Infinity's* science division has identified a Forerunner structure within Requiem's jungles that they would like to investigate, but it must first be cleared of the hostile presence.

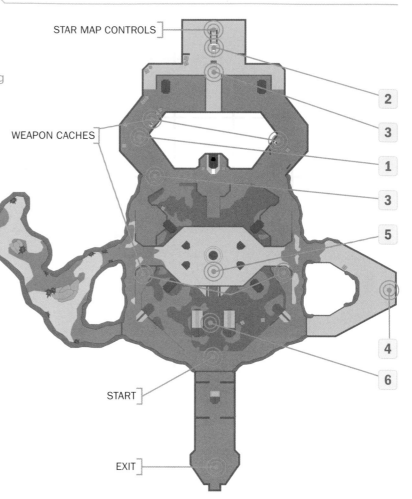

STAR MAP CONTROLS

WEAPON CACHES

2

3

1

3

5

4

6

START

EXIT

⩙ MISSION BRIEFING

If you're being sent somewhere, it's almost always for a good reason, and there is definitely a good reason for it today. The Forerunner facility appears dormant at first, but the mission quickly devolves into your fight for survival against a determined Promethean defense force. The Prometheans clearly control the facility, and may attempt to lock it down to deny you a chance to retreat. This will be Fireteam Crimson's first encounter with the Promethean Knights, so prepare your gear accordingly.

Map Location: The Refuge

> RECOMMENDED LOADOUT

Crawlers, Watchers and Knights mean that weapons like the DMR, Battle Rifle, LightRifle, and the Magnum are essential. We would normally recommend the Plasma Pistol earnestly, but in this mission the only way you'd get replacements for it is if you died and respawned with one, or if an ally died and you picked up theirs. A Scattershot is also a great anti-Knight weapon, if you're quick on the draw and the Knight isn't armed with one of its own. There are a number of weapons caches positioned throughout the facility that grant you access to fully loaded Promethean weapons.

Armor abilities can be a major deciding factor in your survival. The Hologram can turn Knights backs to you for quick assassination, and having a Hardlight Shield is good for falling back while trying to buy time for your shields to recharge. Another good armor ability is the Jet Pack. There are a number a raised ledges and walkways you can quickly reach to gain positional advantage on enemies like the Knights.

Objective One: Investigate the Area

It's all quiet as you arrive at the facility, but power fluctuations have been detected farther in. You're given a waypoint marker to head toward, so get walking. Be sure to check out the main chamber you start in thoroughly. Weapon caches filled with LightRifles can be found on the lower level. This will be an incredibly dominant and useful weapon in the fighting to come.

1 Just around the corner is an ambush led by Crawlers. It's officially "go time." Put down the Crawlers and investigate the new waypoint. You locate the source of the power fluctuations: a star map. To recover the star map, you need to access a separate control panel located only a few meters away from the map itself. **2** When you hit this switch, things get really interesting.

Objective Two: Regroup at the Exit

3 Spartans, we are leaving! Crawlers begin to flood into the room the star map was in. After the first wave is toast, a new waypoint is brought up. As you advance down the hall you entered the star map room from, more Crawlers and a pair of Promethean Knights teleport into the area to stop you. The larger chamber you started in becomes filled with more Crawlers and Knights after this first group is dealt with. If you feel that the ground level of the large chamber is becoming too hot, you can take to the upper ledges and ramps. If you're playing in a team, you can split your people between the upper and lower levels to set up some pretty nasty killzones.

As you continue fighting, the exit to the facility is suddenly cut off.

Objective Three: Find Door Controls

4 You're not out of luck yet, though. Spartan Miller marks the location of a set of controls that will reopen the facility and allow the Fireteam to escape. Now it's just a matter of cutting through the hordes of Crawlers, Knights, and their Watcher guardians to reach the controls.

Don't forget: the multiple ramps and walkways you use to funnel hostiles into advantageous positions can also be used against you, if you're the one climbing up the ramps. Be vigilant and keep your eyes at the top of each ramp as you advance to avoid unpleasant surprises.

Objective Four: Eliminate Hostiles

5 The way out is clear, but your mission isn't finished until you make it safe for the UNSC scientists to enter the facility. Annihilate the remaining Prometheans, all of which are conveniently marked on your HUD. Crawler Snipes start making appearances during this last wave, so make sure you're ready to quickly eliminate them.

When Miller calls out a warning that Watchers are on station, this also marks the arrival of a squad of Knights at the main facility chamber. Palmer correctly orders you to wipe out the Watchers first. Doing so prevents any resurrection of fallen Knights.

6 With that wave beaten, two Knight Battlewagons and another group of Crawlers, with Watcher back-up, appear back at the facility exit. Once you've destroyed this last bit of resistance, the only presence remaining in the facility is that of Fireteam Crimson. The mission is complete!

INTRODUCTION

BASIC TRAINING

INTEL

CAMPAIGN

INFINITY

APPENDIX

Finding the map at the Forerunner facility has provided an unexpected windfall of valuable intelligence about Covenant movements across Requiem. An archeological dig being spearheaded by Covenant forces is close to a potential breakthrough, and Fireteam Crimson has been deployed to interrupt this operation and steal any information or artifacts that may have been recovered by the enemy. For all intents and purposes this sounds like a simple smash-and-grab operation, but if it really were simple, the Spartans wouldn't have been deployed.

⌃ MISSION BRIEFING

The Covenant are defending this site with the largest force you've seen to date. Expect multiple defensive lines standing between you and your objectives throughout the Forerunner facility, and multiple high-ranking Elites to be in charge of much of the defenses. In addition to the Covenant obstacles, the Prometheans also appear to be making a stand around a structure the where the Covenant were focusing their archeological efforts. The Prometheans will also need to be eliminated for the UNSC to uncover whatever it is that they are trying to protect.

Map Location: The Cauldron

We're back to having the Covenant as opponents again, and by now you might be able to purchase the Plasma Pistol with your Spartan Points. Pack it and any headshot-capable weapon at your disposal to start with. This mission has plenty of long sightlines that allow players to snipe enemies in relative safety, so always try to have at least one weapon that takes advantage of this. There are plenty of Plasma Pistols and Needlers to snatch from dead Covenant, which make dealing with the Elites and Knights easier.

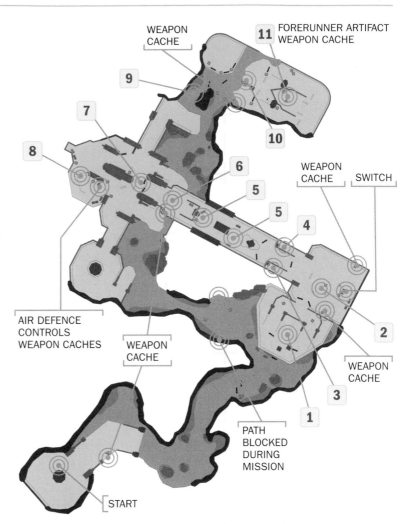

Objective One: Clear the Area

1 You start out in a cavern, but quickly climb out of it and into the maw of a massive Covenant guard force of Grunts, Jackals, and Elites. A Grunt on a Plasma Cannon provides overwatch from a raised walkway, while a Drop Pod descends from above and deploys even more troops. Phantoms fly overhead, providing additional fire support with their Concussion Cannons. This should set the tone for the mission!

2 Behind the Plasma Cannon gunner, more Covenant troops may potentially be lying in wait, if they didn't charge down the ramps to the lower level. The ramps themselves are an excellent spot to split up a team of players, so that both ramps are occupied by Spartans. Each group provides overlapping fields of fire on the enemy.

» KEY COMBAT TIP

The Plasma Cannon is a risky weapon to use on higher difficulty settings of Spartan Ops. The enemy is extremely accurate with one-shot kill weapons like the Fuel Rod Cannon, and the Plasma Cannon makes you too slow to reliably evade their fuel rods. They do make good support weapons if you have other allies to help draw enemy fire, while you take the Plasma Cannon to a safe spot.

Whatever they are guarding behind the locked doors on the upper walkways must be extremely vital. When the enemy is defeated, a switch is marked on your HUD. Once it is depressed, two more switches 3 4 are marked on your HUD, and they require you to advance up a set of ramps where Elites have been delivered via Phantom. Hit the two switches to open the sealed doors 5 and proceed with the mission.

Objective Two: Clear the Base

5 More Covenant arrive on the other side of the wall from a Drop Pod, Elites use Jet Packs to fly over the wall to greet you, while another force rushes through the doors. Be careful about engaging them from the walkways where the switches were located. A careless jump can land you in the lava far below.

Past the doors, twin ramps lead up to where the Drop Pod deployed its troops, though by the time you finish dealing with the first group, the second is likely to be on their way down the ramps already. Expect at least four to six Elites between these two groups.

At the top of those ramps 6 , you find a weapons cache filled with Covenant Carbines, Storm Rifles, and Plasma Pistols. This platform has another  ramp that takes you down into the base, where another team of Covenant awaits 7 . Stick to the high ground while engaging them if at all possible, but beware of another Phantom strafing run.

INTRODUCTION

BASIC TRAINING

INTEL

CAMPAIGN

INFINITY

APPENDIX

Objective Three: Deactivate the Shields

8 Local defenses make extraction impossible. You must deactivate the shields to open an air corridor for the Pelican. As soon as you disable the  shields, Prometheans Crawlers swarm into the area **7** where the last group of Covenant tried to make their stand. More stream in from a side entrance to the base **9** , complete with Watcher support. Beware of Crawler Snipes among this assault!

10 When you've secured the area around the first switch, you can advance toward the next waypoint and handle the Watchers and Crawlers  camped near it. As you crest the hill, be wary of the Knight presence, especially any Knight Lancers armed with Binary Rifles. If you've recovered a Binary Rifle from a fallen Crawler Snipe, you can try to pick off the Knight Lancers in two quick headshots, but don't ignore the other Knights advancing toward you at the same time. Make no mistake, this can be a long cat-and-mouse battle until those Lancers are out of the picture. Fortunately, you have a good amount of cover to take advantage of. If you're playing with allies, you set up overlapping fields of fire. The enemy is less fearsome when they can't concentrate their wrath on one spot alone.

The structure that the Prometheans are protecting can be the source of additional frustration. Knights sometimes like to teleport up to the top of the building, using it for cover while they regenerate. Try to avoid rushing the building unless you are confident that you can survive the dash across open ground to close the gap with the enemy.

When you manage to defeat the Prometheans, a switch is marked for you atop the structure the Prometheans were protecting. Once you activate it, a Forerunner artifact is uncovered.

Objective Four: Defend the Area

Fireteam Castle has yet to take care of their side of things with regard to the air defenses, which leaves your team stranded next to the artifact while an angry mob of Crawlers and a pair of Knights begin their assault in an attempt to retrieve it. Deal with them quickly, as Covenant craft are inbound as well. After you pacify the area surrounding the artifact, the Pelican arrives. Grab the artifact for extraction, and the mission is complete!

FUTURE EPISODES

This first episode should set the tone for all upcoming Spartan Ops content. For more coverage on Spartan Ops in the future, visit the Prima website at http://www.primagames.com/. As the saga of the Spartan Ops continues, we will provide additional walkthrough content on the website, matching the weekly updates from 343 Industries. We'll see you on the field, Spartans.

THE APPENDIX

The Appendix chapter includes charts that you may already be familiar with from previous chapters, but also includes additional information to improve your Spartan Rank, and a complete list of *Halo 4* Achievments.

> MEDALS

Medals are awarded for scoring points in any number of ways. You can get medals for kills, kill streaks, or kills made in specific ways. Some medal types are awarded specifically for accomplishing game type specific tasks, like capturing a flag, or contesting a designated territory. Medals not only represent point values, but they also add to your Ordnance meter in War Games. The greater the ordnance point value, the more the meter fills, and the sooner you will be able to call down Ordnance.

ICON	NAME	EVENT	MEDAL POINTS	ORDNANCE POINTS
	KILL MEDALS			
	Kill	Generic Kill	10	10
	Grenade Kill	Kill an opponent with a grenade explosion	10	10
	Plasma Kill	Kill an opponent with a Plasma Grenade.	10	10
	Headshot	Kill an opponent with a headshot	10	10
	Melee	Hit and kill an opponent with a melee attack	10	10
	Beat Down	Hit and kill an opponent with a melee attack from behind	10	10
	Splatter	Hit and kill an opponent with your vehicle	10	10
	Assasination	Kill an opponent by performing an assassination	15	20
	Airsassination	Kill an opponent by performing a mid-air assassination	25	25
	Supercombine	Kill an opponent with a needle supercombination	10	10
	Sword Kill	Kill an opponent with an Energy Sword	10	10
	Hammer Kill	Kill an opponent with a Gravity Hammer	10	10
	Vehicle Kill	Kill an opponent using a vehicle weapon	10	10
	Rocket Kill	Kill an opponent with a Rocket Launcher	10	10
	Fuel Rod Cannon Kill	Kill an opponent with a Fuel Rod Cannon	10	10
	Sniper Rifle Kill	Kill an opponent with a Sniper Rifle	10	10
	Binary Rifle Kill	Kill an opponent with a Binary Rifle	10	10
	Beam Rifle Kill	Kill an opponent with a Beam Rifle	10	10
	Railgun Kill	Kill an opponent with a Railgun	10	10
	Splaser Kill	Kill an opponent with a Spartan Laser	10	10
	BONUS/STYLE MEDALS			
	Protector	Save a teammate by killing his attacker	5	5
	Killjoy	End an opponents killing spree	5	5
	Hijack	Board a land-based vehicle by forcibly removing the opponent in it	5	5
	Revenge	Kill the opponent responsible for your last death	5	5
	Kill from the Grave	Kill an opponent after you die	5	5

ICON	NAME	EVENT	MEDAL POINTS	ORDNANCE POINTS
	Ordnance Earned	Earn personal ordnance rewarded from the Infinity	5	5
	Close Call	Kill an opponent while your health is low and survive	5	5
	Avenger	Kill an opponent who recently killed your teammate	5	5
	Reload This	Kill an opponent who is reloading	5	5
	First Strike	Earn the first kill of the match	5	5
	Last Strike	Earn the final Kill Cam	5	5
	Headcase	Kill a sprinting opponent with a headshot	5	5
	Retribution	Assassinate the opponent responsible for your last death	10	5
	Hail Mary	Get a long-range grenade kill	10	5
	Snapshot	Kill an opponent with a sniper rifle while not zoomed in	10	5
	Vehicle Destroyed	Destroy an opponents vehicle, killing the driver	10	10
	Skyjack	Board an aircraft by forcibly removing the opponent in it	10	10
	Vengeance	Kill an opponent that stole your ordnance	15	15
	Showstopper	Stop an assassination by killing the assassinating opponent	15	15
	Busted	Kill an opponent attempting to hijack or skyjack a vehicle	15	15
	Bulltrue	Kill an opponent who is lunging with a Sword	15	15
	ASSIST/SUPPORT MEDALS			
	Assist	Assist a player in achieving a kill	5	5
	Vehicle Destroy Assist	Assist a player in destroying a vehicle	5	5
	Bodyguard	Get a spree of 3 Savior, Protector, or Guardian Angel Medals	5	5
	Wheelman	Drive a vehicle and have a passenger kill an opponent	5	5
	Guardian Angel	Save a teammate's life from a long distance	5	5
	Road Trip	Load up a Warthog or Mongoose with teammates and splatter an enemy player	5	5
	Flyin' High	Achieve a massive jump with a passenger in the Mongoose or Warthog	5	5
	Wingman	Get a spree of any 5 assist types	5	5
	EMP Assist	EMP someone and have a teammate kill them	5	5

MEDALS CONT.

ICON	NAME	EVENT	MEDAL POINTS	ORDNANCE POINTS
	Distraction	Distract an opponent who is then killed	5	5
SPREE MEDALS				
	Comeback Kill	Achieve a kill after dying 3 times in a row	5	5
	Double Kill	Kill 2 opponents within 4 5 seconds of one another	5	5
	Triple Kill	Kill 3 opponents within 4 5 seconds of one another	5	5
	Overkill	Kill 4 opponents within 4 5 seconds of one another	10	5
	Killtacular	Kill 5 opponents within 4 5 seconds of one another	10	5
	Killtrocity	Kill 6 opponents within 4 5 seconds of one another	10	5
	Killamanjaro	Kill 7 opponents within 4 5 seconds of one another	15	5
	Killtastrophe	Kill 8 opponents within 4 5 seconds of one another	15	5
	Killpocalypse	Kill 9 opponents within 4 5 seconds of one another	25	5
	Killionaire	Kill 10 opponents within 4 5 seconds of one another	50	5
	Killing Spree	Kill 5 opponents without dying	5	5
	Killing Frenzy	Kill 10 opponents without dying	10	5
	Running Riot	Kill 15 opponents without dying	10	5
	Rampage	Kill 20 opponents without dying	15	5
	Untouchable	Kill 25 opponents without dying	15	5
	Invincible	Kill 30 opponents without dying	25	5
	Inconceivable	Kill 35 opponents without dying	25	5
	Unfriggenbelievable	Kill 40 opponents without dying	50	5
	Extermination	Wipe out an enemy team with at least an Overkill	50	25
MODE SPECIFIC MEDALS				
CAPTURE THE FLAG				
	Flag Capture	Deliver the opponents flag to your base	100	100
	Flag Carrier Kill	Kill an opponent who is carrying a flag	5	5
	Flag Kill	Kill an opponent while holding a flag	5	5
	Flag Defense	Kill an opponent close to your flag, or help return it	5	5
	Flag Runner	Capture 2 flags in one game	15	15
	Flag Champion	Capture 3 flags in one game	25	25
	Flag Assist	Help a teammate score a flag	10	10
	Flag Driver	Drive a Flag Carrier close to your capture point	5	5
	Flag Joust	Kill a flag carrier while holding a flag	15	25
	Flagsassination	Perform an assassination while holding a flag	15	15

ICON	NAME	EVENT	MEDAL POINTS	ORDNANCE POINTS
REGICIDE				
	King Spree	Get 5 kills in a row as King	15	10
	Kingtacular	Survive for 30s as King	25	25
	Reign of Terror	Survive for 90s as King	50	50
	Regicide	Kill the King	Varies	Varies
	Execution	Assasinate the King	15	15
	Kingslayer	Kill the King 3 times in a row	15	10
	King Assist	Assist a player in killing the King	5	5
	Savior	Kill an opponent shooting at your King	5	5
	King Kill	Kill an opponent as the king in regicide	5	5
	King Joust	Kill a King as the King in Regicide	10	10
DOMINION				
	Base Capture Initiated	Initiate a base capture	5	5
	Capture initiation Assist	Be within a base when a teammate initiates the capture	5	5
	Base Captured	Initiate a successful base capture	10	10
	Base Conqueror	Initiate 5 successful base captures	15	15
	Capture Assist	Be within a base when it is captured	5	5
	Base Saved	Reclaim a contested base your team owns	5	5
	Base Assist	Be within a contested base when your teammate reclams it	5	5
	Fortification Assist	Be within a base your team controls when it fortifies	5	5
	Resupply Assist	Be within a base your team controls when it resupplies	5	5
	Security Chief	Reclaim 5 contested bases your team owns	10	10
	Base Offense	Kill an enemy player inside an enemy controlled base	5	5
	Base Defense	Kill an enemy player inside a base your team controls	5	5
	Turret Destroyed	Destroy an enemy auto-turret	10	10
	Demolition Expert	Destroy 10 enemy auto-turrets	15	15
	Turret Constructed	Build an auto-turret	10	10
	Chief Engineer	Build 10 auto-turrets	15	15
	Gotcha!	Kill an enemy player while they are constructing an auto-turret	15	15
	Shield Door Destroyed	Destroy 5 enemy team shields	5	5
	Breach	Destroy 10 enemy team shields	10	10
	Sapper	Destroy 15 enemy team shields	15	15
	Hero!	Instigate a successful capture that saves the team from Last Stand	25	25

ICON	NAME	EVENT	MEDAL POINTS	ORDNANCE POINTS
	Kill Shot!	Get the Final Kill in Last Stand Mode	25	25
	Survivor	Survive Last Stand without dying	15	15
EXTRACTION				
	Site Extracted	Successfully extract a site	25	25
	Extraction Assist	Provide support nearby when a beacon is extracted	5	5
	Beacon Armed	Successfully plant a beacon	10	10
	Arm Assist	Provide support nearby when a beacon is armed	5	5
	Arm Stopped	Kill an enemy planting the beacon	5	5
	Site Defense	Kill an attacker in the supply site	5	5
	Site Offense	Kill a defender in the supply site	5	5
	Stay Back	Kill an enemy while planting or defusing the beacon	15	15
	Site Saviour	Convert 3 beacons without dying	15	15
	Expert Extraction	Extract 3 beacons without dying	25	25
	Beacon Converted	Successfully convert a beacon	10	10
	Convert Assist	Provide support nearby when a beacon is converted	5	5
	Convert Stopped	Kill an enemy converting the beacon	5	5
KING OF THE HILL				
	Hill +5	Hold and survive in the hill for 5 seconds	10	10
	Hill +10	Hold and survive in the hill for 15 seconds	15	15
	Hill +15	Hold and survive in the hill for 30 seconds	25	25
	Hill Dominance	Hold and survive in the hill for its entire duration	25	25
	Vehicle Hill +5	Hold and survive in the hill for 5 seconds using a vehicle	10	10
	Vehicle Hill +10	Hold and survive in the hill for 15 seconds using a vehicle	15	15
	Vehicle Hill +15	Hold and survive in the hill for 30 seconds using a vehicle	25	25
	Vehicle Dominance	Hold and survive in the hill for its entire duration using a vehicle	25	25
	Hill Defense	Kill an enemy while holding a hill	5	5
	Hill Assist	Assist killing an enemy taking a hill	5	5
	Hill Offense	Kill an enemy holding a hill	5	5
	Assault Assist	Assist killing an enemy defending a hill	5	5
	Hail to the King	Kill 5 enemies while controlling the hill	25	25
	First Point	Be the first player to earn a point from a hill	5	5
	Regime Change	Overtake a controlled hill (10 seconds) and hold it for 10 seconds	10	10
ODDBALL				
	Carrier Kill	Kill an enemy carrying the oddball	5	5
	Carrier Kill Assist	Assist killing an enemy carrying the oddball	5	5

ICON	NAME	EVENT	MEDAL POINTS	ORDNANCE POINTS
	Ball Kill	Kill an enemy with a melee Ball attack	5	5
	Smooth Moves	Get a Triple Kill with the oddball	15	15
	First Touch	Be the first player to pick up the ball	5	5
	Long Bomb	Throw the ball to a player at least 15m away	15	15
	Nice Catch!	Catch a ball thrown farther than 15m from you	15	15
	Interception	Catch a ball thrown by an enemy player	10	10
	Catch	Catch a ball thrown by a teammate	5	5
	Ball Holder	Hold onto the ball for 5 seconds	5	5
	Ball Keeper	Hold onto the ball for 15 seconds	10	10
	Ball Master	Hold onto the ball for 30 seconds	15	15
	Ball Hog	Hold onto the ball for 45 seconds	25	25
	Magic Hands	Hold onto the ball for 1 minute	50	50
	Balsassination	Assasinate a player using the oddball	15	15
FLOOD				
	Flood Conversion	Convert a Spartan to the Flood	5	5
	Alpha Conversion	Convert a Spartan to the Flood as an Alpha	5	5
	Infector	Kill 2 Spartans in a row as a Flood without dying	10	10
	Carrier	Kill 3 Spartans in a row as a Flood without dying	15	15
	Juggernaut	Kill 4 Spartans in a row as a Flood without dying	25	25
	Gravemind	Kill ALL Spartans in a row as a Flood without dying	50	50
	Flood Kill	Kill a Flood	5	5
	Flood Kill Assist	Assist killing a flood	5	5
	Flood Hunter	Kill 4 Flood in a row as a Spartan without dying	15	15
	Flood Surivor	Kill 6 Flood in a row as a Spartan without dying	25	25
	Flood Exterminator	Kill 10 Flood in a row as a Spartan without dying	50	50
	Last Man Standing	Be the last surviving Spartan	15	15
	Final Conversion	Kill the last remaining Spartan	10	10
	Flood Victory	Contribute to the Flood total conversion of all Spartans	Varies	Varies
	The Ancient One	Survive the entire round as a Flood and convert at least one Spartan	50	50
	Clever	Survive the entire round as a Spartan	50	50
GRIFBALL				
	SCORE!	Score the Grifball	10	10

Halo 4 allows player to gain ranks and earn points to unlock new pieces of equipment for their weapon loadouts, or reveal new armor abilities to customize the look of their Spartan.

COMMENDATION NAME	DESC.	REQ.	LV1 XP	REQ.	LV2 XP	REQ.	LV3 XP	REQ.	LV4 XP	REQ.	LV5 XP	REQ.	LV6 XP	REQ.	LV7 XP	MASTERY REWARD
WEAPONS																
Assault Rifle	Kill an enemy Spartan with the Assault Rifle	10	250	25	500	50	750	100	1000	250	2500	500	5000	1000	10000	
Magnum	Kill an enemy Spartan with the Pistol	5	250	10	500	25	750	50	1000	100	2500	250	5000	500	7500	
Battle Rifle	Kill an enemy Spartan with the Battle Rifle	10	250	25	500	50	750	100	1000	250	2500	500	5000	1000	10000	
DMR	Kill an enemy Spartan with the DMR	10	250	25	500	50	750	100	1000	250	2500	500	5000	1000	10000	
Sniper Rifle	Kill an enemy Spartan with the Sniper Rifle	5	250	10	500	25	750	75	1000	250	2000					
SAW	Kill an enemy Spartan with the SAW	5	250	10	500	25	750	75	1000	250	2000					
Shotgun	Kill an enemy Spartan with the Shotgun	5	250	10	500	25	750	75	1000	250	2000					
Railgun	Kill an enemy Spartan with the Rail Gun	5	250	10	500	25	750	75	1000	250	2000					
Sticky Detonator	Kill an enemy Spartan with the Sticky Detonator	5	250	10	500	25	750	75	1000	250	2000					
Rocket Launcher	Kill an enemy Spartan with the Rocket Launcher	5	250	10	500	25	750	75	1000	250	2000					
Spartan Laser	Kill an enemy Spartan with the Spartan Laser	5	250	10	500	25	750	75	1000	250	2000					
UNSC Loudout Weapon Mastery	Master all UNSC Loadout weapons	1	12500													Stance (Breach)
UNSC Ordnance Weapon Mastery	Master all UNSC Ordnance weapons	1	12500													Stance (Standoff)
Energy Sword	Kill an enemy Spartan with the Energy Sword	5	250	10	500	25	750	75	1000	250	2000					
Gravity Hammer	Kill an enemy Spartan with the Gravity Hammer	5	250	10	500	25	750	75	1000	250	2000					
Needler	Kill an enemy Spartan with the Needler	5	250	10	500	25	750	75	1000	250	2000					
Storm Rifle	Kill an enemy Spartan with the Storm Rifle	10	250	25	500	50	750	100	1000	250	2500	500	5000	1000	10000	
Covenant Carbine	Kill an enemy Spartan with the Covenant Carbine	10	250	25	500	50	750	100	1000	250	2500	500	5000	1000	10000	
Plasma Pistol	Kill an enemy Spartan with the Plasma Pistol	5	250	10	500	25	750	50	1000	100	2500	250	5000	500	7500	
Fuel Rod Cannon	Kill an enemy Spartan with the Fuel Rod	5	250	10	500	25	750	75	1000	250	2000					
Beam Rifle	Kill an enemy Spartan with the Beam Rifle	5	250	10	500	25	750	75	1000	250	2000					
Concussion Rifle	Kill an enemy Spartan with the Concussion Rifle	5	250	10	500	25	750	75	1000	250	2000					
Covenant Loadout Weapon Mastery	Master all Covenant Loadout weapons	1	10000													Emblem - Energy Armor Skin - Recon Surge SURG
Covenant Ordnance Weapon Mastery	Master all Covenant Ordnance weapons	1	10000													Stance - Standoff
Boltshot	Kill an enemy Spartan with the Boltshot	5	250	10	500	25	750	50	1000	100	2500	250	5000	500	7500	
Scattershot	Kill an enemy Spartan with the Scattershot	5	250	10	500	25	750	75	1000	250	2000					
Suppressor	Kill an enemy Spartan with the Suppressor	10	250	25	500	50	750	100	1000	250	2500	500	5000	1000	10000	
LightRifle	Kill an enemy Spartan with the LightRifle	10	250	25	500	50	750	100	1000	250	2500	500	5000	1000	10000	
Binary Rifle	Kill an enemy Spartan with the Binary Rifle	5	250	10	500	25	750	75	1000	250	2000					
Incineration Cannon	Kill an enemy Spartan with the Incineration Cannon	5	250	10	500	25	750	75	1000	250	2000					
Forerunner Loadout Weapon Mastery	Master all Forerunner Loadout weapons	1	7500													Emblem (Hardlight), Armor Skin (Warrior MTRX)

COMMENDATIONS CONT.

COMMENDATION NAME	DESC.	REQ.	LV1 XP	REQ.	LV2 XP	REQ.	LV3 XP	REQ.	LV4 XP	REQ.	LV5 XP	REQ.	LV6 XP	REQ.	LV7 XP	MASTERY REWARD
Forerunner Ordnance Weapon Mastery	Master all Forerunner Ordnance weapons	1	7500													Stance (Believe)
Turret	Kill an enemy Spartan with any turret	5	250	10	500	25	750	75	1000	250	2500					Armor Skin (Enforcer TRBL)
Frag Grenade	Kill an enemy Spartan with the Frag Grenade	5	250	10	500	25	750	75	1000	250	2500					
Plasma Grenade	Kill an enemy Spartan with the Plasma Grenade	5	250	10	500	25	750	75	1000	250	2500					
Pulse Grenade	Kill an enemy Spartan with the Pulse Grenade	5	250	10	500	25	750	75	1000	250	2500					
Weapon Mastery	Master all weapon commendations	1	15000													Armor Skin (Protector DRFT)

ENEMIES

COMMENDATION NAME	DESC.	REQ.	LV1 XP	REQ.	LV2 XP	REQ.	LV3 XP	REQ.	LV4 XP	REQ.	LV5 XP	REQ.	LV6 XP	REQ.	LV7 XP	MASTERY REWARD
Grunt Slayer	Kill Grunt Infantry	125	250	250	500	500	750	750	1000	1000	2500	2500	5000			
Grunt Imperial Slayer	Kill Grunt Imperials and Space Grunts	75	250	150	500	300	750	450	1000	600	2500	900	5000			
Grunt Ultra Slayer	Kill Grunt Ultras	25	250	50	500	100	750	150	1000	250	2500	350	5000			
Jackal Slayer	Kill Jackal Infantry	75	250	150	500	300	750	450	1000	600	2500	900	5000			
Jackal Major Slayer	Kill Jackal Majors	25	250	50	500	75	750	125	1000	250	2500	500	5000			
Jackal Ranger Slayer	Kill Jackal Rangers	10	250	25	500	50	750	75	1000	150	2500	300	5000			
Elite Slayer	Kill Elite Infantry	25	250	50	500	75	750	125	1000	250	2500	500	5000			
Elite Zealot Slayer	Kill Elite Zealots and Rangers	10	250	25	500	50	750	75	1000	150	2500	300	5000			
Elite Officer Slayer	Kill Elite Officers	5	250	15	500	30	750	60	1000	90	2500	180	5000			
Elite Hero Slayer	Kill Elite Generals	3	250	7	500	21	750	42	1000	63	2500	84	5000			
Hunter Slayer	Kill Hunters	5	250	10	500	25	750	50	1000	100	2500	250	5000			
Covenant Destroyer	Master all Covenant Kill commendations	1	10000													Emblem (Covenant), Armor Skin (Orbital AEON)
Crawler Slayer	Kill Crawler Infantry	125	250	250	500	500	750	750	1000	1000	2500	2500	5000			
Crawler Specialist Slayer	Kill Crawler Snipers	75	250	150	500	300	750	450	1000	600	2500	900	5000			
Crawler Leader Slayer	Kill Crawler Primes	25	250	50	500	75	750	125	1000	250	2500	500	5000			
Knight Slayer	Kill Knights	25	250	50	500	75	750	125	1000	250	2500	500	5000			
Knight Battlewagon Slayer	Kill Knight Battlewagons and Rangers	10	250	25	500	50	750	75	1000	150	2500	300	5000			
Knight Hero Slayer	Kill Knight Commanders	5	250	15	500	30	750	60	1000	90	2500	180	5000			
Watcher Slayer	Kill Watchers	75	250	150	500	300	750	450	1000	600	2500	900	5000			
Forerunner Destroyer	Master all Forerunner kill commendations	1	10000													Emblem (Promethean), Armor (Vanguard)

VEHICLE

COMMENDATION NAME	DESC.	REQ.	LV1 XP	REQ.	LV2 XP	REQ.	LV3 XP	REQ.	LV4 XP	REQ.	LV5 XP	REQ.	LV6 XP	REQ.	LV7 XP	MASTERY REWARD
Splatter	Splatter an enemy Spartan with a vehicle	5	250	10	500	25	750	50	1000	75	2000					Emblem (Splatter), Visor (Verdant)
Mongoose Destroyer	Destroy enemy occupied Mongooses	5	250	10	500	25	750	50	1000	75	2000					
Warthog Destroyer	Destroy enemy occupied Warthogs	5	250	10	500	25	750	50	1000	75	2000					
Mantis Destroyer	Destroy enemy occupied Mantises	3	250	6	500	9	750	27	1000	75	2000					
Scorpion Desrtroyer	Destroy enemy occupied Scorpions	3	250	6	500	9	750	27	1000	75	2000					
Ghost Destroyer	Destroy enemy occupied Ghosts	10	250	20	500	40	750	80	1000	160	2000					
Banshee Destroyer	Destroy enemy occupied Banshees	5	250	10	500	25	750	50	1000	75	2000					
Destroy Wraith	Destroy enemy occupied Wraiths	5	250	10	500	25	750	50	1000	75	2000					
Wheelman	Earn Vehicle Skill medals	10	250	25	500	50	750	250	1250	250	2500					Armor Skin (Aviator BOND)
Vehicle Mastery	Master all Vehicle commendations	1	10000													Emblem (Vehicular), Armor Skin (Air Assault VERG)

INTRODUCTION
BASIC TRAINING
INTEL
CAMPAIGN
INFINITY
APPENDIX

COMMENDATIONS CONT.

Commendation Name	Desc.	REQ.	LV1 XP	REQ.	LV2 XP	REQ.	LV3 XP	REQ.	LV4 XP	REQ.	LV5 XP	REQ.	LV6 XP	REQ.	LV7 XP	Mastery Reward
PLAYER																
Hail of Death	Call in Personal Ordnance	5	250	10	500	20	750	40	1000	60	2000					Emblem (Ordnance), Armor Skin (EVA BRCH)
Dawn	Complete Campaign Mission 1 on Legendary difficulty	1	0													
Requiem	Complete Campaign Mission 2 on Legendary difficulty	1	0													
Forerunner	Complete Campaign Mission 3 on Legendary difficulty	1	0													
Infinity	Complete Campaign Mission 4 on Legendary difficulty	1	0													
Reclaimer	Complete Campaign Mission 5 on Legendary difficulty	1	0													
Shutdown	Complete Campaign Mission 6 on Legendary difficulty	1	0													
Composer	Complete Campaign Mission 7 on Legendary difficulty	1	0													
Midnight	Complete Campaign Mission 8 on Legendary difficulty	1	0													
Legend	Complete all Campaign Missions on Legendary difficulty	1	0													Emblem (117), Armor (Mark VI), Arms (Mark VI), Legs (Mark VI), Visor (Legendary)
Spartan Slayer	Take out enemy Spartans	25	250	50	500	150	750	300	1000	600	2500	1200	5000	2400	10000	Armor (C.I.O.), Emblem (Extracted)
Bullet in the Brain	Take out enemy Spartans with headshots	15	250	50	500	100	750	200	1000	400	2500	800	5000	1600	10000	Armor Skin (Defender CTRL)
First Strike	Get the first kill in a match	5	250	10	500	25	750	50	1000	50	2000					Stance (Assault)
Multikill	Quickly kill multiple enemy Spartans	5	250	10	500	25	750	50	1000	100	2500	250	5000	500	10000	Armor Skin (Infiltrator TRAC)
Backstab	Assassinate Covenant and Forerunner enemies	10	250	25	500	50	750	100	1000	100	2000					Armor Skin (Venator RPTR)
Assassin	Assassinate enemy Spartans	5	250	10	500	25	750	50	1000	50	2000					Armor (Venator)
Spartan Spree	Kill multiple enemy Spartans without dying	5	250	10	500	25	750	50	1000	100	2500	200	5000	400	10000	Armor Skin (Soldier ZNTH)
Assistant	Earn any Assist medal	25	250	50	500	250	750	500	1000	1000	2500					Visor (Sunspot)
Close Quarters	Earn any CQC medal	25	250	50	500	250	750	500	1000	1000	2500					Arms Skin (Twin-plated AEON)
Combat Opportunity	Earn any Combat Skill medal	10	250	25	500	50	750	250	1000	500	2500					Armor (Ranger)
Payback	Kill the enemy Spartan that just killed you	25	250	50	500	250	750	500	1000	500	2000					Legs Skin (Contoured CHVR)
Protector	Protect a teammate	10	250	25	500	50	750	100	1000	250	2000					Armor Skin (Ranger STRK)
Avenger	Kill an enemy Spartan that just killed a teammate	15	250	30	500	90	750	180	1000	360	2000					Visor (Blindside)
From the Brink	Kill an enemy Spartan while close to death	15	250	30	500	60	750	90	1000	180	2000					Visor (Cyan)
Perfection	Complete a match without dying and get at least 15 kills	1	1000	2	2000	3	3000	4	4000	5	5000					Arms Skin (Contoured CHVR)
Exterminator	Killed every enemy Spartan that finished the match	3	1000	5	2000	7	3000	9	4000	18	5000					Legs Skin (Recruit TIGR)

COMMENDATIONS CONT.

COMMENDATION NAME	DESC.	REQ.	LV1 XP	REQ.	LV2 XP	REQ.	LV3 XP	REQ.	LV4 XP	REQ.	LV5 XP	REQ.	LV6 XP	REQ.	LV7 XP	MASTERY REWARD
GAME TYPES																	
Slayer Victory	Win a match in any Slayer gametype in matchmaking	10	250	25	500	50	750	150	1000	300	2500					Armor (Gungnir)
Slayer High Score	Finish in the Top 3 Players in any Slayer gametype in matchmaking	3	250	5	500	15	750	30	1000	50	2000					
Slayer Mastery	Master all Slayer commendations	1	7500													Emblem (The Slayer)
Hail to the King	Win a match in any Regicide gametype in matchmaking	5	250	10	500	25	750	50	1000	150	2500					Armor Skin (EOD SHDW)
Kingslayer	Kill the King in any Regicide gametype in matchmaking	10	250	20	500	40	750	60	1000	80	2000					
Executioner	Assassinate the King in any Regicide gametype in matchmaking	2	250	5	500	15	750	50	1000	50	2000					
Regicide Mastery	Master all Regicide commendations	1	7500													Emblem (Kingslayer)
Flag Victory	Win a match in any Capture the Flag gametype in matchmaking	5	250	10	500	25	750	50	1000	150	2500					Armor Skin (Vanguard CNVG)
Deadly Flag	Kill enemy Spartans while carrying the Flag in any Capture the Flag gametype in matchmaking	3	250	5	500	7	750	15	1000	30	2000					
Carrier Takedown	Kill an enemy flag carrier in any Capture the Flag gametype in matchmaking	10	250	25	500	50	750	75	1000	100	2000					
Defender of the Flag	Protect your team's flag in any Capture the Flag gametype in matchmaking	10	250	25	500	50	750	100	1000	250	2000					
Flag Mastery	Master all Capture the Flag commendations	1	7500													Emblem (Flag)
Dominion Victory	Win a match in any Dominion gametype in matchmaking	5	250	10	500	25	750	50	1000	150	2500					Armor (Commando)
Captured	Initiate a base capture in any Dominion gametype in matchmaking	5	250	10	500	20	750	40	1000	60	2000					
Base Defense	Earn Dominion defense medals in any Dominion gametype in matchmaking	10	250	25	500	50	750	75	1000	150	2000					
Dominion Mastery	Master all Dominion commendations	1	7500													Emblem (Dominated)
Hill Victory	Win a match in any King of the Hill gametype in matchmaking	5	250	10	500	25	750	50	1000	150	2500					Armor (War Master)
Top of the Hill	Earn hill hold medals in any King of the Hill gametype in matchmaking	5	250	10	500	25	750	50	1000	75	2000					
Hill Defense	Earn hill defense medals in any King of the Hill gametype in matchmaking	10	250	25	500	50	750	75	1000	150	2000					
Hill Mastery	Master all King of the Hill commendations	1	7500													Emblem (The Hill)
Oddball Victory	Win a match in any Oddball gametype in matchmaking	5	250	10	500	25	750	50	1000	150	2500					Armor Skin (Scout APEX)
Carry the Oddball	Earn Oddball carry medals in any Oddball gametype in matchmaking	5	250	10	500	25	750	50	1000	75	2000					
Oddball Beatdown	Kill an enemy Spartan with the Oddball in any Oddball gametype in matchmaking	5	250	10	500	25	750	50	1000	100	2000					
Drop that Ball!	Kill an enemy Spartan who is carrying the Oddball in any Oddball gametype in matchmaking	10	250	25	500	50	750	100	1000	100	2000					
Oddball Mastery	Earn Max Level in all Oddball Commendations	1	7500													Emblem (Baller)
Flood Victory	Win a match in any Flood gametype	5	250	10	500	25	750	50	1000	150	2500					Armor Skin (Commando FRCT)
The Parasite	Earn Flood medals in any Flood gametype in matchmaking	10	250	25	500	50	750	75	1000	150	2000					
Gravemind	Master all Flood commendations	1	7500													Emblem (Infected)

INTRODUCTION

BASIC TRAINING

INTEL

CAMPAIGN

INFINITY

APPENDIX

SPECIALIZATION 0 : SPARTAN-IV

RANK	RANK NAME	SPARTAN POINTS	LOADOUT ITEMS AWARDED	LOADOUT ITEMS UNLOCKED FOR PURCHASE	UNLOCKED APPEARANCE ITEMS
1	SR-1	0	Loadout 1: Weapon - Assault Rifle, Plasma Pistol / Grenade - Frag Grenade / Armor Ability - None / Support Upgrades - None / Tactical Packages - None		Armor (Recruit), Arms (Recruit), Legs (Recruit), Emblem (Recruit), Visor (Recruit), Stance (Recruit)
2	SR-2	1		Weapons: Battle Rifle / DMR	
3	SR-3	1	Armor ability slot in all Loadouts	Armor ability: Thruster Pack / Promethean Vision	
4	SR-4	1			Foreground Emblems (Set 1)
5	SR-5	1		Weapons: Storm Rifle / Covenant Carbine	
6	SR-6	1	Loadout 2	Armor ability: Jet Pack / Hologram	
7	SR-7	1		Tactical Pkgs: Mobility / Shielding	
8	SR-8	1		Weapons: Plasma Grenade / Plasma Pistol	Armor - Warrior
9	SR-9	1			Arms - Twin-Plated
10	SR-10	1		Armor ability: Hardlight Shield / Active Camo	Legs - RG-63 Counter
11	SR-11	1			Armor - Air Assault
12	SR-12	1		Support Upgrades: Dexterity / Ammo	armor ability - Jet Pack
13	SR-13	1			Stance - Heroic
14	SR-14	1	Loadout 3	Tactical Pkgs: Resupply / AA Efficiency	
15	SR-15	1			Armor - Soldier
16	SR-16	1		Armor ability: Autosentry / Regen. Field	
17	SR-17	1			Armor - Aviator
18	SR-18	1		Weapons: Pulse Grenade / Boltshot	
19	SR-19	1			Foreground Emblems (Set 2)
20	SR-20	1		Support Upgrades: Awareness / Sensor	Visor - Solar
21	SR-21	1			Background Emblems (Set 1)
22	SR-22	1		Weapons: LightRifle / Suppressor	Arms - GC-09 Locking
23	SR-23	1			Legs - LG-50 Bulk
24	SR-24	1		Tactical Pkgs: Grenadier / Firepower	Armor - Utility
25	SR-25	1			
26	SR-26	1	Loadout 4	Support Upgrades: Explosives / Ordnance Priority	Armor - Recon
27	SR-27	1			Armor - EVA
28	SR-28	1			Foreground Emblems (Set 3)
29	SR-29	1			Visor - Frost
30	SR-30	2			Arms - Inner-Plated
31	SR-31	1			Legs - Outer-Plated
32	SR-32	1			Stance - Assassin
33	SR-33	1			Background Emblems (Set 2)
34	SR-34	1			Arms - Outer-plated
35	SR-35	1			Legs - XG-89 Narrow
36	SR-36	1			Foreground Emblems (Set 4)
37	SR-37	1			Armor - War Master
38	SR-38	1			Armor - Scout
39	SR-39	1			Arms - Contoured
40	SR-40	2			Legs - Contoured
41	SR-41	1	Loadout 5		Armor - Orbital
42	SR-42	1			Armor - Infiltrator
43	SR-43	1			Armor - Hazop
44	SR-44	1			Background Emblems (Set 3)
45	SR-45	1			Armor - EOD
46	SR-46	1			Visor - Midnight
47	SR-47	1			Armor - Oceanic
48	SR-48	1			Arms - XV-27 Shifting
49	SR-49	1			Legs - Overlocking
50	SR-50	2			Stance (Last Stand), Armor (Enforcer), Foreground Emblem (Rank Up) & Background Emblem (Moving Up)

SPECIALIZATION 1 : WETWORK

Rank	RANK NAME	LOADOUT ITEMS FREEBIES	UNLOCKED APPEARANCE ITEMS
1	WK-1		Foreground Emblems (Wetwork 1-4)
2	WK-2		Chest - Wetwork
3	WK-3		Shoulders - Wetwork
4	WK-4		Helmet - Wetwork
5	WK-5	DMR skin - Noble NBL	Background Emblem (Doused)
6	WK-6		Wetwork Visor
7	WK-7		Chest - Wetwork Skin - Shard - SHRD
8	WK-8		Shoulders - Wetwork Skin - Shard - SHRD
9	WK-9		Helmet - Wetwork Skin - Shard - SHRD
10	WK-10	Mod - Stealth	

SPECIALIZATION 2 : OPERATOR

Rank	RANK NAME	LOADOUT ITEMS FREEBIES	UNLOCKED APPEARANCE ITEMS
1	OP-1		Foreground Emblems (Operator 1-4)
2	OP-2		Chest - Operator
3	OP-3		Shoulders - Operator
4	OP-4		Helmet - Operator
5	OP-5	Magnum skin - Static STC	Background Emblem (Operated)
6	OP-6		Operator Visor
7	OP-7		Chest - Operator Skin - Surface - SRFC
8	OP-8		Shoulders - Operator Skin - Surface - SRFC
9	OP-9		Helmet - Operator Skin - Surface - SRFC
10	OP-10	Mod - Wheelman	

SPECIALIZATION 3 : PIONEER

Rank	RANK NAME	LOADOUT ITEMS FREEBIES	UNLOCKED APPEARANCE ITEMS
1	PR-1		Foreground Emblems (Pioneer 1-4)
2	PR-2		Chest - Pioneer
3	PR-3		Shoulders - Pioneer
4	PR-4		Helmet - Pioneer
5	PR-5	Plasma Pistol skin - Fracture FCT	Background Emblem (Pie Is Near)
6	PR-6		Pioneer Visor
7	PR-7		Chest - Pioneer Skin - Adept - ADPT
8	PR-8		Shoulders - Pioneer Skin - Adept - ADPT
9	PR-9		Helmet - Pioneer Skin - Adept - ADPT
10	PR-10	Mod - Fast Track	

SPECIALIZATION 4 : PATHFINDER

Rank	RANK NAME	LOADOUT ITEMS FREEBIES	UNLOCKED APPEARANCE ITEMS
1	PT-1		Foreground Emblems (Pathfinder 1-4)
2	PT-2		Chest - Pathfinder
3	PT-3		Shoulders - Pathfinder
4	PT-4		Helmet - Pathfinder
5	PT-5	Assault Rifle skin - Predator - PRD	Background Emblem (A*)
6	PT-6		Pathfinder Visor
7	PT-7		Chest - Pathfinder Skin - Core - CORE
8	PT-8		Shoulders - Pathfinder Skin - Core - CORE
9	PT-9		Helmet - Pathfinder Skin - Core - CORE
10	PT-10	Mod - Gunner	

SPECIALIZATION 5 : ENGINEER

Rank	RANK NAME	LOADOUT ITEMS FREEBIES	UNLOCKED APPEARANCE ITEMS
1	EN-1		Foreground Emblems (Engineer 1-4)
2	EN-2		Chest - Engineer
3	EN-3		Shoulders - Engineer
4	EN-4		Helmet - Engineer
5	EN-5	Suppressor skin - Shatter - SHA	Background Emblem (Stalking You)
6	EN-6		Engineer Visor
7	EN-7		Chest - Engineer Skin - Edge - EDGE
8	EN-8		Shoulders - Engineer Skin - Edge - EDGE
9	EN-9		Helmet - Engineer Skin - Edge - EDGE
10	EN-10	Mod - Drop Recon	

SPECIALIZATION 6 : STALKER

Rank	RANK NAME	LOADOUT ITEMS FREEBIES	UNLOCKED APPEARANCE ITEMS
1	SK-1		Foreground Emblems (Stalker 1-4)
2	SK-2		Chest - Stalker
3	SK-3		Shoulders - Stalker
4	SK-4		Helmet - Stalker
5	SK-5	Battle Rifle skin - Dunes - DNE	Emblem 5 - BG
6	SK-6		Stalker Visor
7	SK-7		Chest - Stalker Skin - Crush - CRSH
8	SK-8		Shoulders - Stalker Skin - Crush - CRSH
9	SK-9		Helmet - Stalker Skin - Crush - CRSH
10	SK-10	Mod - Nemesis	

SPECIALIZATION 7 : ROGUE

Rank	RANK NAME	LOADOUT ITEMS FREEBIES	UNLOCKED APPEARANCE ITEMS
1	RG-1		Foreground Emblems (Rogue 1-4)
2	RG-2		Chest - Rogue
3	RG-3		Shoulders - Rogue
4	RG-4		Helmet - Rogue
5	RG-5	Covenant Carbine skin - Reign - RGN	Background Emblem (Going Rogue)
6	RG-6		Rogue Visor
7	RG-7		Chest - Rogue Skin - Focus - FCUS
8	RG-8		Shoulders - Rogue Skin - Focus - FCUS
9	RG-9		Helmet - Rogue Skin - Focus - FCUS
10	RG-10	Mod - Stability	

SPECIALIZATION 8 : TRACKER

Rank	RANK NAME	LOADOUT ITEMS FREEBIES	UNLOCKED APPEARANCE ITEMS
1	TK-1		Foreground Emblems (Tracker 1-4)
2	TK-2		Chest - Tracker
3	TK-3		Shoulders - Tracker
4	TK-4		Helmet - Tracker
5	TK-5	Boltshot skin - Piston - PST	Background Emblem (Found You)
6	TK-6		Tracker Visor
7	TK-7		Chest - Tracker Skin - Adroit - ADRT
8	TK-8		Shoulders - Tracker Skin - Adroit - ADRT
9	TK-9		Helmet - Tracker Skin - Adroit - ADRT
10	TK-10	Mod - Requisition	

INTRODUCTION

BASIC TRAINING

INTEL

CAMPAIGN

INFINITY

APPENDIX

Personnel identity in the field is a key component of communication during combat. *Infinity*'s Spartans can personally customize their identity's emblem, selecting from both longstanding and new options. Through increasing one's rank as well as completing Commendations and Challenges conducted by Waypoint, Spartans can gain access to an even wider variety of exclusive emblems.

EMBLEM ICONS FOREGROUND

ICON	NAME	UNLOCKED BY
	Recruit	SR-1
	Tomcat	SR-4
	Triad	SR-4
	Bear Claw	SR-4
	Wasp	SR-4
	Campfire	SR-4
	Cup of Death	SR-4
	Active Rooster	SR-4
	Bulltrue	SR-4
	Leo	SR-4
	Drone	SR-4
	Atomic	SR-19
	Grunt	SR-19
	Dog Tags	SR-19
	Yin Yang	SR-19
	No Camping	SR-19
	Radioactive	SR-19
	Crosshairs	SR-19
	Anchor	SR-19
	Runes	SR-19
	Cone'd	SR-19
	Flaming Ninja	SR-28
	Stuck	SR-28
	Halt	SR-28
	Black Widow	SR-28
	Flaming Horns	SR-28

ICON	NAME	UNLOCKED BY
	Wolf	SR-28
	Valkyrie	SR-28
	Spartan Helmet	SR-28
	Pirate	SR-28
	Snake	SR-28
	Headshot	SR-36
	Skull King	SR-36
	Spartan Swords	SR-36
	Horse	SR-36
	Crossed Swords	SR-36
	Helmet	SR-36
	Jolly Roger	SR-36
	Spartan League	SR-36
	Rank Up	SR-50
	Wetworks	WK-1
	Stealth	WK-1
	Arrow On Target	WK-1
	Killer Bee	WK-1
	Operator	OP-1
	Winged	OP-1
	Anchored	OP-1
	Hog Tire	OP-1
	Pioneer	PR-1
	Arrowhead	PR-1
	Compass	PR-1

ICON	NAME	UNLOCKED BY
	Missile	PR-1
	Pathfinder	PT-1
	Lens	PT-1
	Grid	PT-1
	Recon Bot	PT-1
	Engineer	EN-1
	Screw	EN-1
	Wrench	EN-1
	Network	EN-1
	Rogue	RG-1
	Muzzled	RG-1
	Patch	RG-1
	Avian	RG-1
	Stalker	SK-1
	Foxed	SK-1
	Evil Stare	SK-1
	The Eye	SK-1
	Tracker	TK-1
	Planetary	TK-1
	The Trail	TK-1
	Celestial	TK-1
	Mastery	SR-130 - Base + all Specializations
	Projectile	Commendation : UNSC Loadout Weapon Mastery
	Energy	Commendation : Covenant Loadout Weapon Mastery

ICON	NAME	UNLOCKED BY
	Hardlight	Commendation : Forerunner Loadout Weapon Mastery
	Splatter	Commendation : Splatter
	Covenant	Commendation : Covenant Destroyer
	Promethean	Commendation : Forerunner Destroyer
	Vehicular	Commendation : Vehicle Mastery
	117	Commendation : Legend
	Ordnance	Commendation : Hail of Death
	The Slayer	Commendation :Slayer Mastery
	Kingslayer	Commendation : Regicide Mastery
	Flag	Commendation : Flag Mastery
	Extracted	Commendation : Spartan Slayer
	The Hill	Commendation : Hill Mastery
	Baller	Commendation : Oddball Mastery
	Infected	Commendation : Gravemind
	Dominated	Commendation : Dominion Mastery
	On Your Shield	Waypoint
	Raider	Waypoint
	Raider Distort	Waypoint
	Wiseguy	Waypoint
	1k Club	Waypoint
	LASO	Waypoint
	Circle	SR-21
	Diamond	SR-21

EMBLEM ICONS BACKGROUND

ICON	NAME	UNLOCKED BY
	Plus	SR-21
	Square	SR-21
	Triangle	SR-21
	Vertical Stripe	SR-21
	Horizontal Stripe	SR-21
	Cleft	SR-21
	Criss Cross	SR-21
	Buzz Saw	SR-21
	Star	SR-33
	Cowboy Hat	SR-33

ICON	NAME	UNLOCKED BY
	4 Diamonds	SR-33
	Sun	SR-33
	Hexagon	SR-33
	Chalice	SR-33
	Cog	SR-33
	Octagon	SR-33
	Crown	SR-33
	Cancel	SR-33
	Horizontal Stripes	SR-44
	Gradient	SR-44

ICON	NAME	UNLOCKED BY
	Horizontal Gradient	SR-44
	Oval	SR-44
	Vertical Oval	SR-44
	Blunt Diamond	SR-44
	Blunt Diamond 2	SR-44
	Asterisk	SR-44
	Shield	SR-44
	Ball o' Fire	SR-44
	Moving Up	SR-50

ICON	NAME	UNLOCKED BY
	Doused	WK-5
	Operated	OP-5
	Pie is Near	PR-5
	A*	PT-5
	Engineered	EN-5
	Going Rogue	RG-5
	Found You	TK-5
	Stalking You	SK-5
	Maximum	SR-130 - Base + all Specializations

HALO 4

All achievements available in *Halo 4* at launch, as well as how to earn them, are listed here.

ACHIEVEMENTS

ICON	ACHIEVEMENT NAME	DESCRIPTION	GAMERSCORE
	Knight in White Assassination	Assassinate a Knight in any Spartan Ops mission.	20
	Badge	Change your Emblem in the Spartan ID card.	5
	PWND	Change your Service Tag in the Spartan ID card.	5
	Armorer	Change your Spartan's armor in the Spartan Armor card.	5
	What a Poser!	Change your Spartan's pose in the Spartan ID card.	5
	The Challenger	Complete 25 Challenges.	15
	The Challenged	Complete a Challenge.	5
	Crimson Alone	Complete a Spartan Ops chapter solo on Legendary.	20
	Operation Completion	Complete a Spartan Ops Mission on any difficulty.	15
	A Legendary Episode	Complete all chapters in Spartan Ops Episode 1 on Legendary difficulty.	40
	Dedicated to Crimson	Complete all chapters in the first 5 episodes of Spartan Ops on any difficulty.	80
	Bropocalypse	Complete any Campaign mission co-operatively on Heroic or harder.	10
	Skullduggery	Complete any Campaign Mission with 3 or more Skulls on Heroic or harder.	15
	What Power Outage?	Complete Chapter 4, Episode 5 of Spartan Ops without losing a generator on Heroic or harder.	20
	Dawn	Complete Mission 1 on any difficulty.	10
	Requiem	Complete Mission 2 on any difficulty.	10
	Forerunner	Complete Mission 3 on any difficulty.	10
	Infinity	Complete Mission 4 on any difficulty.	10
	Reclaimer	Complete Mission 5 on any difficulty.	10
	Shutdown	Complete Mission 6 on any difficulty.	10
	Composer	Complete Mission 7 on any difficulty.	10
	Midnight	Complete Mission 8 on any difficulty.	10
	Bromageddon	Complete the Campaign co-operatively on Heroic or harder.	40
	I Need a Hero	Complete the Campaign on Heroic or harder.	40
	The Legend of 117	Complete the Campaign on Legendary difficulty.	70

ICON	ACHIEVEMENT NAME	DESCRIPTION	GAMERSCORE
	Wake up John	Complete the Campaign on Normal or harder.	20
	Lone Wolf Legend	Complete the Campaign solo on Legendary difficulty.	90
	Game Changer	Create and save a Custom Game type in War Games.	5
	The Cartographer	Create and save a Custom Map in Forge.	5
	Contact the Domain	Find a Terminal in the Campaign.	10
	Terminus	Find all of the Terminals in the Campaign.	50
	Roses vs Violets	Find one of the RvB Easter Eggs in Spartan Ops.	20
	This is my Rifle, this is my Gun	In Mission 3, carry a UNSC weapon all the way through on Heroic or harder.	20
	No Easy Way Out	In Ch 1, Ep 5 of Spartan Ops survive all enemy waves during the defense on Normal or harder.	20
	Digging up the Past	In Mission 1, find and access Chief's record.	20
	Midnight Launch	In Mission 2. get significant air in the Warthog at midnight.	20
	Pop, Lock and Rocket	In Mission 5, guide the missile to the Gravity Beam without colliding with any debris.	20
	Mortardom	In Mission 5, hijack a Wraith and use it to kill at least four enemy Wraiths on Heroic or harder.	20
	Explore the Floor	In Mission 6, trick or force a Hunter to fall to his demise.	20
	Give Him the Stick	In Mission 7, take out both Hunters using only the Sticky Detonator.	20
	Whack a Mole	In mission 9, kill 5 Crawlers in one hit with the Gravity Hammer.	20
	Bros to the Close	Make it through mission 4 without one preventable Marine death on Heroic or harder.	20
	Movin' on Up	Rank up your Spartan-IV to SR-20.	25
	Not Some Recruit Anymore	Rank up your Spartan-IV to SR-5.	10
	The Director	Save a Film Clip from the Theater.	5
	Snapshot!	Save a Screenshot from the Theater.	5
	Rescue Ranger	Save at least one Marine in Chapter 3 of Episode 2 of Spartan Ops on Heroic or harder.	20
	Sharing is Caring	Upload a File to your File Share.	5
	The Dongblainer	Win 20 War Games matchmaking matches.	30
	I <3 Red vs Blue	Win 5 War Games matchmaking matches.	10

> TERMINAL LOCATIONS

All Domain Terminals found in the main Campaign of *Halo 4* are listed here, including page numbers to allow users of the guide to quickly flip to the relevant pages for maps and more detailed location information.

DOMAIN TERMINALS LOCATION	DESCRIPTION	WALKTHROUGH PAGE
Mission Two: Requiem	Located just before the elevator after the last Major Firefight of the mission. Very easy to miss if you are in hurry! Check under the ramp leading up to the elevator platform.	Page 80-81 (map and detailed location)
Mission Three: Forerunner	Just before exititing the area where Major Firefight: The Split Canyon takes place, check underneath the balcony platform where the exit to the next area is located.	Page 88 (map), Page 90 (detailed location)
Mission Four: Infinity	Right after you exit the cutscene where you meet Spartan Palmer and Commander Lasky, turn around as soon as you regain control of the Chief to find the Waypoint Terminal.	Page 112-113 (map and detailed location)
Mission Five: Reclaimer	After reuniting with Cortana inside the Forerunner facility and fighting your way past the Promethean ambush, check the corridors afterwards carefully to avoid missing this Terminal.	Page 138-139 (map and detailed location)
Mission Six: Shutdown	On the first section of the third tower you must infiltrate, you can find this Terminal hidden behind a central pillar, on one of the platforms on the edge of the map.	Page 152-153 (map and detailed location)
Mission Seven: Composer	During your first visit to the chamber that holds the Composer, check the natural cave formations in the area to find the Terminal.	Page 169-170 (map and detailed location)
Mission Eight: Midnight	The final Terminal can be found hidden at the center of the third corridor. t-junction you come across just after the ground battle begins.	Page 184, 186 (map and detailed location)

INTRODUCTION

BASIC TRAINING

INTEL

CAMPAIGN

INFINITY

APPENDIX

> WEAPONS

Weapon damage does not change across multiple difficulties, but enemy health and shielding does. You can use this chart to see the overall damage potential of all the weapons available in the game. Weapons that are headshot-capable are marked accordingly.

WEAPON NAME	TYPE	RANGE	MAGAZINE CAPACITY	HEADSHOTS?	INITIAL ROUNDS	ZOOM
UNSC INFANTRY WEAPONS						
Assault Rifle	Fully-Automatic	Short-Mid	32		160	
Battle Rifle	Semi-Automatic 3-round burst	Mid-Long	36	*	108	2x
DMR	Semi-Automatic	Mid-Long	14	*	42	3x
Frag Grenade	Grenade	N/A	N/A			
Machine Gun	Fully-Automatic	Short-Mid	255 (detached)			
Magnum	Semi-Automatic	Short-Long	8		24	2x
Railgun	Charged, Single Shot Explosive	Short-Mid	1		4	
Rocket Launcher	Explosive	Mid-Long	2		4	1.8x
SAW	Fully-Automatic	Short-Mid	72		216	
Shotgun	Semi-Automatic	Short	6		18	
Sniper Rifle	Semi-Automatic	Long	4	*	12	4x, 9x
Spartan Laser	Charged, Single Shot Explosive	Mid-Long	1 (energy based)		4	2.5x
Sticky Detonator	Latched Explosive	Short-Mid	1		4	
UNSC VEHICLE WEAPONS						
Scorpion, Main Cannon	Explosive	Long	N/A			
Scorpion, Machine Gun	Fully-Automatic	Short-Mid	N/A			
Warthog, Gauss Cannon	Semi-Automatic	Mid-Long	N/A			
Warthog, Machine Gun	Fully-Automatic	Short-Mid	N/A			
Warthog, Rocket Launcher	Explosive 5-rocket volley	Mid-Long	N/A			
Mantis, Machine Gun	Fully-Automatic	Short-Mid	N/A			
Mantis, Missile Launcher	Semi-Automatic	Mid	5			
Mantis, Foot Stomp	Melee w/Cooldown	Short	N/A			
COVENANT WEAPONS						
Beam Rifle	Semi-Automatic w/Overheat	Long	Overheat	*	10	3.5x, 9.5x
Concussion Rifle	Semi-Automatic	Short-Mid	6		18	
Covenant Carbine	Semi-Automatic	Mid-Long	18	*	72	2x
Energy Sword	Melee	Short	N/A			
Fuel Rod Cannon	Explosive	Mid	5		15	2x
Gravity Hammer	Melee w/AoE	Short	N/A			
Needler	Fully-Automatic	Short-Mid	22		44	
Needler (Supercombine)	Explosive	Short-Mid	N/A			
Plasma Cannon	Fully-Automatic	Short-Mid	255 (detached)			
Plasma Grenade	Grenade	N/A	N/A			
Plasma Pistol	Semi-Automatic	Short-Mid	Overheat		50	
Plasma Pistol (charged shot)	Charged EMP	Short-Mid			5	
Storm Rifle	Fully-Automatic	Short-Mid	Overheat		166	
COVENANT VEHICLE WEAPONS						
Banshee, Fuel Rod Cannon	Explosive	Mid-Long	N/A			
Banshee, Plasma Cannon	Fully-Automatic	Mid-Long	N/A			
Ghost, Plasma Cannon	Fully-Automatic	Short-Mid	N/A			
Wraith, Plasma Cannon	Fully-Automatic	Short-Mid	N/A			
Wraith, Plasma Mortar	Explosive	Mid-Long	N/A			
FORERUNNER WEAPONS						
Binary Rifle	Semi-Automatic	Long	2	*	6	4x, 10x
Boltshot	Semi-Automatic	Short-Mid	10	*	30	
Boltshot (Charged shot)	Charged Energy Blast	Short	2		6	
Incineration Cannon	Explosive w/submunitions	Mid	1		4	1.8x
LightRifle (Hip-fired)	Semi-Automatic (3-round burst)	Mid-Long	36	*	108	3x
LightRifle (Scoped)	Semi-Automatic	Mid-Long	12	*	36	3x
Pulse Grenade	Grenade	N/A	N/A			
Scattershot	Semi-Automatic	Short	5		15	
Suppressor	Fully-Automatic	Short	48		192	

> SKULLS

This is a listing of all the Skull modifiers that affect the Campaign. Tweak the challenge in the ways you see fit, for more points, or for repeated deaths to Plasma Grenades, if that's your thing.

SKULL	PRIORITY	DESCRIPTION
Famine	Primary	Weapons drop with 50% less ammo
Tilt	Primary	Damage tables are modified
Mythic	Primary	Double enemy health
Catch	Primary	Enemies are grenade happy - twice as often, twice as fast
Black Eye	Primary	Shields don't recharge except from melee attacking enemies
Tough Luck	Primary	Enemies always make every saving throw, always berserk, always dive, never flee...
Iron	Primary	Co-op reverts to previous checkpoint on player death. 1P restarts mission.
Thunderstorm	Primary	Major upgrade to all enemies
Cloud	Primary	Motion sensor is disabled with this setting
Cowbell	Secondary	Acceleration Scale from Explosions is 3x
Iwhbyd	Secondary	Common combat dialog becomes less common and vice versa
Blind	Secondary	HUD, arms and weapons are hidden
Grunt Birthday Party	Secondary	Grunts explode as if they were plasma grenades when killed with a headshot

HALO 4
FORWARD UNTO DAWN

THE STORY OF HALO 4 BEGINS AT DAWN

OWN IT ON BLU-RAY™ AND DVD DECEMBER 4

HALO.XBOX.COM

 Microsoft Studios

 343 INDUSTRIES™

 DVD VIDEO

 Blu-ray Disc

 TV 14

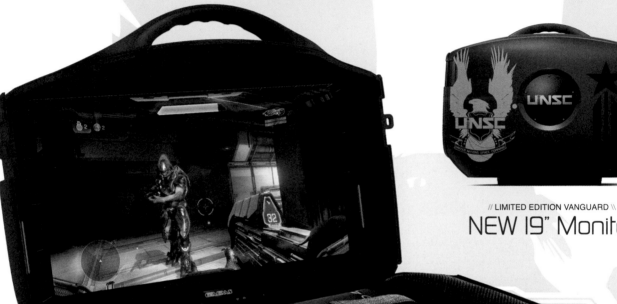

MEGA BLOKS · **HALO**

UNSC MANTIS

HALO.MEGABLOKS.COM
JOIN THE BLOKS BRIGADE

NEW COLLECTION COMING SOON

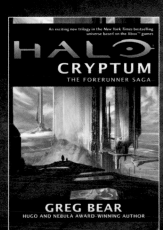
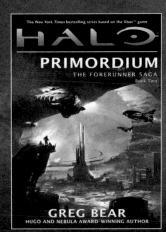
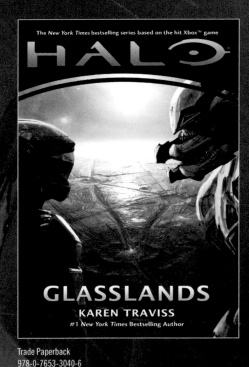

HALO

WAYPOINT

Your official connection to Halo 4 and the Halo Universe. Dig deep into your Halo 4 career, including your Infinity stats, game history, and campaign progress. Connect and share content with your Xbox LIVE friends and the Halo community.

AVAILABLE ON XBOX 360, WEB, TABLET & PHONE

CHECK STATS

COMPARE WITH FRIENDS

UNLOCK ARMOR AND MORE!

HaloWaypoint.com

SPECIAL THANKS FROM 343 INDUSTRIES

We would like to thank Prima Games for their tireless effort on this project, especially including the following people: Aaron Lockhart & Debra Kempker for orchestrating this partnership. To Paul Giacomotto for managing such a massive project and generally taking care of everything we needed along the way; you've been great. To Alex Musa for bringing his unique voice to the strategy guide and for helping out with so many other things. To David S. J. Hodgson for bringing your extensive experience to this project, we're glad to have you back for this guide. To Sonja Morris for making all of the many maps in *Halo 4*. Major League Gaming (MLG) for providing such talented gamers to work on this project, including: Marcus "Elumnite" Lovejoy, Michael "Strongside" Cavanaugh, Michael "Flamesword" Chaves, Brett "Naded" Leonard and also Kyle Magee and John Nelson for coordinating the work. To Raphael van Lierop for your help on the interviews. And finally, everyone who worked on *Halo 4*, this guide wouldn't exist without your hard work, dedication and passion.

The following people from 343 Industries made significant contributions to the content in this guide:

Bonnie Ross, Frank O'Connor, Kiki Wolfkill, Chris Lee, Josh Holmes, Kevin Grace, Che Chou, Matt J. McCloskey, Christine Finch, Matt Skelton, Carlo Woo, Kristofer Hall, Ryan Davison (Yoh Services LLC), Kenneth Scott, Scott Warner, Kevin Franklin, Christopher Schlerf, Chris Haluke, Bryce Cochrane, Jeremy Patenaude, Corrinne Robinson, Tyler Jeffers, Brian Reed, Carlos Naranjo, Rick Achberger (Yoh Services LLC), Tiffany O'Brien (iFusionIT LLC), Nicholas Gallagher (Yoh Services LLC), Michelle Ballantine (Yoh Services LLC), Christy Cowan (Hanson Consulting Group), Brad Welch, Chris King, Matt Aldridge, Neill Harrison, Gavin Carter, Jaemus Wurzbach, Can Tuncer, Sean Binder, Kyle Hefley, Kolby Jukes, Nicole Makila, Kynan Pearson, Derrick Hammond, David Ellis, Chris Shaules, Adrien Cho, CJ Saretto, Justin Harrison, Humberto Castaneda, Jessica Shea, Desmond Murray, Kyle Dolan, Alex Cutting, Adrian Brown, Joel Gifford, Jeff Guy, Joe Whitman, Rob Sempsey, Jennifer Yi, Bryan Koski, Nicolas "Sparth" Bouvier, David Bolton (Populus Group LLC), Jihoon Kim, John Wallin Liberto, Thom Scholes, Linda Hayashikawa (Pitney Bowes), Chad Pfarr, Caleb Metheny (Apex Systems, Inc), Steve Lang, Primo Pulanco, Justin Ireland (CompuCom Systems Inc), Sam Tian (Aditi), Patrick Daly (Aditi), Steve Markham (Volt), Nick Elgin (Volt), Kelsey Fukuhara (Volt), James Harper (Volt), Sam Anderson (CompuCom Systems Inc), Chris Youngs (Volt), Zak Kalles (CompuCom Systems Inc), Jose Gamboa (Volt), Karl Hohnstein (CompuCom Systems Inc), Madeline Rick (Aditi), Greg Willet (Volt), Hunter Schneider, Devon Smith (Experis), Jacob Grandstaff (Experis), Lesean Johnson (Experis), Michael Arvat (Experis), Sean Manley (Experis), Tim Toulouse (Experis), Annie Dennisdóttir Wright (Aquent LLC), Christopher Buckley (Aquent LLC), Bill Clark, Chris Howard, Josh Lindquist, Paul Featherstone, Sam Wolpert, Tom Mathews, Vic DeLeon, John Wallin Liberto, Tiana Los (Yoh Services LLC), Bryan Lane (Unisys), Darren Little (Insight Global), Cade Myers (Wimmer Solutions Corporation), Rachelle Bilbruck, Kathy Gehrig, Logan Jacobson, and everyone else who helped with this project, we couldn't have done it without you.

A complete list of credits for *Halo 4* can be found at: http://www.microsoft.com/games/mgsgamecatalog/halo4credits.aspx

PRIMA OFFICIAL GAME GUIDE

HALO 4

WRITTEN BY ALEXANDER MUSA, DAVID S.J. HODGSON, RAPHAEL VAN LIEROP, AND MAJOR LEAGUE GAMING (MLG).

(MLG Strategy Experts- Michael "StrongSide" Cavanaugh, Michael "Flamesword" Chaves, Brett "Naded" Leonard, Marcus "Elumnite" Lovejoy, Kyle Magee, and John Nelson)

Licensing Manager: Aaron Lockhart

Product Manager (Prima Games): Paul Giacomotto

Product Manager (343 Industries): Ryan Davison (Yoh Services LLC)

Executive Author: David S.J. Hodgson

Design & Layout: In Color Design

Map Illustration: 99 Lives

Copyeditor: Carrie Andrews and Sara Wilson

Components- Jamie Knight, Melissa Smith, Rick Wong

Production- Erika Pepe

Australian warranty statement:

This product comes with guarantees that cannot be excluded under the Australian Consumer Law. You are entitled to a replacement or refund for a major failure and for compensation for any other reasonably foreseeable loss or damage. You are also entitled to have the goods repaired or replaced if the goods fail to be of acceptable quality and the failure does not amount to a major failure.

This product comes with a 1 year warranty from date of purchase. Defects in the product must have appeared within 1-year, from date of purchase in order to claim the warranty.

All warranty claims must be facilitated back through the retailer of purchase, in accordance with the retailer's returns policies and procedures. Any cost incurred, as a result of returning the product to the retailer of purchase - are the full responsibility of the consumer.

AU wholesale distributor: Bluemouth Interactive Pty Ltd, Suite 1502, 9 Yarra Street, South Yarra, Victoria, 3141. (+613 9646 4011)

Email: support@bluemouth.com.au

Prima Games
An Imprint of Random House, Inc.
3000 Lava Ridge Court, St. 100
Roseville, CA 95661

www.primagames.com

SPECIAL THANKS

Special thanks from Alexander Musa- Where to begin? What can I say? It isn't every day you get to work with an amazing team and the amazing support we received over the course of putting this guide together. I could fill up a whole page just to list everyone who helped out in some way on this book. To 343: Thank you Ryan, for putting up with our presence in the offices while also managing our requests and questions quickly. We're in debt to you and your multi-tasking skills. More thanks is due for the testers who came together for our multiplayer sessions and the ridiculously swift co-op run of the whole campaign to show off some new tricks I didn't think were possible. To anyone and everyone who had even the slightest to do with this book at 343, you're all awesome. Thanks for letting me in on the new start of something huge. To MLG: Thanks for taking the time to send four of the best players in the league to work on this thing we call *Halo 4*. Extra special thanks to Kyle McGee for keeping our rambunctious rascals in line while they taught me new trash talk phrases that I can't wait to not get to use because I'll never be quite as good as them.

To the Pros: Marcus (OH. MY. GOD.) "Elumnite" Lovejoy, Michael (LEEEEEEETS GOOOOO) "Strongside" Cavanaugh, Michael (ElumKrypto) "Flamesword" Chaves, and Brett (DUUUUUUUUUUUUDE) "Naded" Leonard, thank you all for showing me how to be a graceful loser in *Halo 4*...mostly by completely and utterly destroying me when I so much as looked at you funny from some place across the map. You guys were an inspiration to watch. Best of luck in your future endeavors, and hopefully we'll work together again. To Mark, Targa, Sara and Sonja: Without you guys, we wouldn't have a book like this. I apologize for all late content and emails from the past, present, and hopefully the future, because you're the best around. To PrimaGames: We did it, Paul, who kept me sane and on task. We did it, David, who taught me all about the various bits and bobs I could put into a guide. We freakin' did it. Look at this thing! Lookit! To everyone else at the Prima offices, thanks for the kindness and support you've all shown over the last year or so. I'm livin' the dream because of you guys. To my friends, my parents, and the rest of my extended family, thank you for understanding when I disappear in my cave for weeks or months at a time to go to work, thank you for just being. Alright, what's next?!

Special thanks from David S.J. Hodgson- To my wife Melanie; Mum, Dad, Ian; Liz, John, and Cameron; Ron & Fez; Eastside Dave; all at 343 Industries for their exceptional help and patience; Alex, Raphael, Strongside, Flamesword, Elumnite, Naded, Jason, Kyle (and all at MLG) for their diligent work and splendiferous pwnage; and Paul, Carrie, Sonja, Mark and Targa for helping craft this artisan-quality tome.

Special thanks from Raphael van Lierop- To Hill, Esme, and Rem for your uncompromising love and support.

Special thanks from Paul Giacomotto- To Debra Kempker, Andy Rolleri, Mark Hughes, Aaron Lockhart for the confidence to take on an amazing franchise title like *Halo 4*. To the authors- Alex, Hoagie, Raph, and Kyle for tremendous amounts of work and dedication. To MLG pro's- "StrongSide", "Flamesword", "Elumnite", and "Naded" for staying calm in your excitement and pro's when it counted most. To Mark and Targa for being absolute professionals at your craft and brilliant to work with. To Carrie and Sara for digging through the mounds of text. To Sonja and 99 Lives for giving their all and coming through. To our in-house designers- Jamie, Melissa, and Rick for speed and care. To Erika for incredibly long email chains and keeping it all straight. To amazing friends and contributors- Donato Tica, Jeff Barton, Fernando Bueno, Jesse Anderson, J.J. Zingale, Todd Manning, Josef Frech, Dominic Ricci, and Paul Bernardo. And last but not least, to my loving family- Babe, Brandon, Gianna, Brett, and Cooper.

Special thanks from Prima Games- We had the opportunity to work with some amazing people at Microsoft Game Studios and 343 Industries. A warm hearted "Thank You" to- Christine Finch for opportunity to be part of something very special and providing tremendous support. Bonnie Ross, Kiki Wolfkill, Josh Holmes, Frank O'Connor, Kenneth Scott, Chris Haluke, Christopher Schlerf, Kevin Franklin, Scott Warner, and Bryce Cochrane for the time and shared experiences during a busy time. Kris "with a K" Hall for providing backup and helping the process move forward. Last but not least...Ryan Davison. Ryan, you wore many hats during this project. You proved to be a patient babysitter, guru with Excel, technical wizard at updating builds, screenshot editor, gatherer of information, facilitator of progress, and most importatnly one of the key ingredients for a high-quality published strategy guide. I'm not sure we can thank you enough, but know there's probably another box of snacks and gummy candy headed your direction. Thanks to everyone at 343 Industries for your support and making a fantastic and entertaining video game.

To Major League Gaming- You proved to be great partners on this project and added a level of expertise that's unmatched. Thanks!

The following people made significant contributions to the content in this guide-

343 INDUSTRIES-

CHRISTINE FINCH

RYAN DAVISON

KRISTOFER HALL

BONNIE ROSS

BRYCE COCHRANE

CHRIS HALUKE

CHRIS KING

CHRISTOPHER SCHLERF

FRANK O'CONNOR

JESSICA SHEA

KENNETH SCOTT

KEVIN FRANKLIN

KIKI WOLFKILL

SCOTT WARNER

TYLER JEFFERS

MAJOR LEAGUE GAMING (MLG)-

KYLE MAGEE - MULTIPLAYER PROJECT MANAGER, AUTHOR

JOHN NELSON - MULTIPLAYER PROJECT MANAGER

MICHAEL "STRONGSIDE" CAVANAUGH - MULTIPLAYER STRATEGY EXPERT

MICHAEL "FLAMESWORD" CHAVES - MULTIPLAYER STRATEGY EXPERT

BRETT "NADED" LEONARD - MULTIPLAYER STRATEGY EXPERT

MARCUS "ELUMNITE" LOVEJOY - MULTIPLAYER STRATEGY EXPERT

JASON MUNO – COORDINATOR, PLAYER RELATIONS

KASEY KRAMER - SENIOR DIRECTOR, PRODUCT MARKETING

GERALD WANG - SVP, BUSINESS AFFAIRS AND GENERAL COUNSEL

SUNDANCE DIGIOVANNI – CHIEF EXECUTIVE OFFICER

ISBN: 978-0-307-89569-1   ISBN: 978-0-307-89570-7   ISBN: 978-0-307-89694-0   ISBN: 978-0-307-89695-7

Printed in the United States of America